C000261666

PHOTOSHOP 6 KNOW YOU CO

DAVID D. BUSCH

ISBN: 0-7821-2918-8
288 pp; 7 1/2" x 9"
$24.99

▶ Discover the amazing new capabilities of Photoshop 6 with this book.

▶ Perfect for graphic designers and Web design professionals who want to learn all the tips and tricks of the newest version of this incredible graphics tool.

▶ Features easy-to-follow techniques and helpful examples to spark the imagination and creativity, for those who just need to know how to do *this one thing*!

▶ Includes sections on combining images, retouching images, correcting color, and working on the Web.

PHOTOSHOP, PAINTER, & ILLUSTRATOR SIDE-BY-SIDE, 2ND EDITION

WENDY CRUMPLER

ISBN: 0-7821-2923-4
380 pp; 8" x 10"
$49.99 US

▶ The second edition of this incredible full-color book gives side-by-side comparisons between the three most popular graphics software packages: Photoshop, Illustrator, and Painter. The perfect resource for every graphic artist!

▶ Graphic artist and author Wendy Crumpler shows you how to use the best features of all three programs to achieve the effects you're looking for.

▶ Features a gallery of art illustrating the effects discussed, and includes access to an exclusive companion web site containing updated charts and information upon the release of updated software.

PHOTOSHOP® 6
COMPLETE

SYBEX® SAN FRANCISCO ▸ PARIS ▸ DÜSSELDORF ▸ SOEST ▸ LONDON

Associate Publisher: Dan Brodnitz

Acquisitions and Developmental Editor: Bonnie Bills

Compilation Editor: David D. Busch

Editor: Colleen Wheeler Strand

Production Editor: Teresa Trego

Technical Editor: Scott Onstott

Book Designer: Maureen Forys, Happenstance Type-O-Rama

Electronic Publishing Specialist: Maureen Forys, Happenstance Type-O-Rama

Proofreaders: Dave Nash, Laurie O'Connell, Yariv Rabinovitch, Nancy Riddiough

Indexer: Nancy Guenther

Cover Designer: Design Site

Cover Illustrator: Stephen Romaniello

ACKNOWLEDGMENTS

This book is the work of many, both inside and outside Sybex including publishing team members Dan Brodnitz and Bonnie Bills, and the editorial/production team of Teresa Trego, Colleen Strand, Scott Onstott, Maureen Forys, Nancy Guenther, Dave Nash, Laurie O'Connell, Yariv Rabinovitch and Nancy Riddiough.

David Busch deserves particular thanks for making sure all of the material in this book was up-to-date, organized, and flowed together in a cohesive manner, as well as for being one of the valued contributors of source material.

And of course, thanks go to our other contributors who have allowed their work to be excerpted in *Photoshop 6 Complete*: Molly Holzschlag, Steve Romaniello, Richard Schrand, Matt Straznitskas, Wendy Crumpler, Erica Sadun, Deborah Ray, Eric Ray, and Mark Minasi. Without their work, this book could not be made.

CONTENTS AT A GLANCE

CONTENTS

Part II ▶ Photoshop in Depth

Chapter 10　▫　**Altered States: History**　　**245**

Part III ► Fun With Photoshop 6

Part IV ▸ Photoshop 6 and the Web

Chapter 19 □ More On Web Graphic Formats   509

Chapter 27 □ **Troubleshooting Ink-Jet Printers**   **735**

INTRODUCTION

Photoshop 6 Complete is a one-of-a-kind computer book—valuable both for the breadth of its content and for its low price. This thousand-page compilation of information from some of Sybex's very best books provides comprehensive coverage of the most recent version of Photoshop. This book, unique in the computer book world, was created with several goals in mind:

- ▶ To offer a thorough guide covering all the important user-level features of Photoshop at an affordable price

- ▶ To acquaint you with some of our best authors, their writing styles and teaching skills, and the level of expertise they bring to their books—so that you can easily find a match for your interests and needs as you delve deeper into Photoshop

Photoshop 6 Complete is designed to provide you with all the essential information you'll need to get the most from Photoshop and your computer images. At the same time, Photoshop 6 Complete will invite you to explore the even greater depths and wider coverage of material in the original books.

If you have read other computer "how-to" books, you have seen that there are many possible approaches to effectively using the technology. The books from which this one was compiled represent a range of teaching approaches used by Sybex and Sybex authors. From the quick, concise Photoshop 6 Visual JumpStart to the wide-ranging, thoroughly detailed Mastering Photoshop 6 style, you will be able to choose which approach and which level of expertise works best for you. You will also see what these books have in common: a commitment to clarity, accuracy, and practicality.

In these pages, you will find ample evidence of the high quality of Sybex's authors. Unlike publishers who produce "books by committee," Sybex authors are encouraged to write in their individual voices, voices which reflect their own experience with the software at hand and with the evolution of today's personal computers. When our authors speak to you of their personal techniques in the first person, you know you are getting the benefit of their direct experience. Nearly every book represented here is the work of a single writer or a pair of close collaborators. Similarly, all of the chapters here are based on the individual experience of the authors, their first-hand testing of pre-release software and their subsequent expertise with the final product.

In adapting the various source materials for inclusion in *Photoshop 6 Complete*, the compilation editor preserved these individual voices and perspectives. Chapters were edited to minimize duplication, omit coverage of non-essential information, update technological issues, and cross-reference material so you can easily follow a topic across chapters. Some sections may have been edited for length in order to include as much updated, relevant and important information as possible.

WHO CAN BENEFIT FROM THIS BOOK?

Photoshop 6 Complete is designed to meet the needs of a wide range of computer users working with the newest version of Adobe's flagship image editor. Photoshop is an extraordinarily rich editing package, with some elements that everyone uses, as well as features that may be essential to some users but of no interest to others. Therefore, while you could read this book from beginning to end—from upgrade decisions, to installation, through the features, and on to expert tinkering—all of you may not need to read every chapter. The contents and the index will guide you to the subjects you're looking for.

Beginners Even if you have only a little familiarity with computers and their basic terminology, this book will start you working with Photoshop. You'll find step-by-step instructions for all the operations involved in running the program, along with clear explanations of essential concepts. You'll want to start at the very beginning of this book, Part I, which covers the basics.

Intermediate Users Chances are you already know how to do routine image editing tasks in Photoshop. You know your way around most of the menus, the majority of the tools, and perhaps a few more advanced features. You also know that there is always more to learn about working more effectively, and you want to get up to speed on as many of Photoshop's capabilities as you can. Throughout this book, you'll find instructions for just about anything you want to do. Nearly every chapter has nuggets of knowledge from which you can benefit.

Power Users   Maybe you're a hardcore graphics professional looking to take advantage of Photoshop's expanded capabilities, or the unofficial guru of your office, or an Internaut ready to try Web publishing using Photoshop graphics. There's plenty for you here, too, particularly in the chapters from the Mastering book and *Photoshop, Painter & Illustrator Side-by-Side.*

This book is for people using Photoshop in any environment. You may be a SOHO (small-office/home-office) user, working with a stand-alone computer or a simple peer-to-peer network with no administrators or technical staff to rely on. Or, you may be working with Photoshop in a professional setting and simply want to become more skilled with your most important graphics tool.

How This Book Is Organized

Here's a look at what's covered in each part of this book.

Part I: An Introduction to Photoshop 6   Here you'll find the information you need to get started with Photoshop, including detailed descriptions of all its key tools and basic image editing features.

Part II: Photoshop 6 In-depth   Once you've mastered the basics, this part will let you dig deep into Photoshop's capabilities and perform sophisticated tasks that will transform your images.

Part III: Fun with Photoshop 6   If you find doing new and sometimes mind-boggling things with images enjoyable, you'll love the creative techniques for text effects, 3D, and more, revealed in this part.

Part IV: Photoshop 6 and the Web   Photoshop and its companion program ImageReady have all the tools you need to create graphics that are an attraction, rather than a distraction, on your Web pages. Learn some of the secrets of Web masters in this part.

Part V: Printing Your Images   When it's time for your images to leap off the screen and onto the printed page, you'll want to use this part of the book as a handy reference and constant companion.

Complete Photoshop Reference   From the rich lexicon on this reference section's glossary to detailed descriptions of Photoshop's key special effects filters, everything you need to know—now—is available at your fingertips.

A Few Typographic Conventions

When a Photoshop operation requires a series of choices from menus or dialog boxes, the ➣ symbol is used to guide you through the instructions, like this: "Select Image ➣ Adjust ➣ Levels." The items the ➣ symbol separates may be menu names, toolbar icons, check boxes, or other elements of the Photoshop interface—anyplace you can make a selection.

This typeface is used to identify Internet URLs and HTML code, and **boldface type** is used whenever you need to type something into a text box.

You'll find these types of special notes throughout the book:

TIP
You'll see a lot of these Tips—quicker and smarter ways to accomplish a task, which the authors have based on many hours, spent testing and using Photoshop.

NOTE
You'll see Notes, too. They usually represent alternate ways of accomplishing a task or some additional information that needs to be highlighted.

WARNING
In a few places, you'll see a Warning like this one. There are not too many because, thanks to Photoshop's multiple levels of Undo and versatile History feature, it's hard to do irrevocable things in Photoshop unless you work at it. But when you see a warning, do pay attention to it.

YOU'LL ALSO SEE SIDEBAR BOXES LIKE THIS

These sections provide added explanations of special topics that are referred to in the surrounding discussions, but that you may want to explore separately in greater detail.

FOR MORE INFORMATION

See the Sybex Web site, www.sybex.com, to learn more about all the books contributed to *Photoshop 6 Complete*. On the site's Catalog page, you'll find links to any book you're interested in. You'll also find links to places where you can download some of the example Photoshop files mentioned in the book.

We hope you enjoy this book and find it useful. Happy image editing!

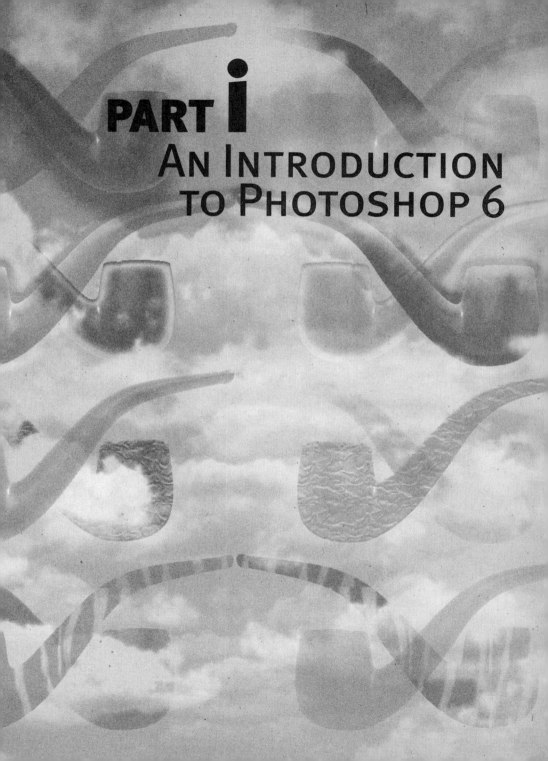

PART i
AN INTRODUCTION
TO PHOTOSHOP 6

Chapter 1

INTRODUCING GRAPHICS

Just as word-processing software has changed the mechanics of writing, so graphics software has changed the nature of drawing and design. Effects that were previously extremely labor-intensive and costly to produce are now quite easily performed by anyone with rudimentary design skills, a vivid imagination, and tools like Adobe Photoshop.

Today, Photoshop has become an essential tool in many industries. In the print shop, Photoshop is part of the complex process of making color separations. In the photography studio, it is the primary color-correction and photo-retouching tool in use. In the design studio, it is essential for producing illustrations. Engineers, architects, urban planners, video technicians, cinematographers, multimedia publishers, medical illustrators, and Web designers all benefit from Photoshop's power and versatility.

Adapted from *Mastering Adobe GoLive 4* by Molly E. Holzschlag and Stephen Romaniello

ISBN 0-7821-2604-9   640 pages $34.99

GRAPHICS PAST AND PRESENT

Look at an old *LIFE* magazine from the 1930s or 1940s; the photographs are almost all black and white and often lack the slick precision of today's magazine photos. You'll see watercolors and pen-and-ink illustrations. This handmade look is not at all like the in-your-face hyperreality of today's illustrations. Layouts of old were also less dynamic and more predictable. If a space alien saw an old copy of *LIFE* and assumed that it was representative our culture, it could draw the conclusion that we humans are color-blind! Of course, before Kodachrome and other color films became widely used, black-and-white images were the norm because that was all we had to use.

Although older publications have an undeniable charm and beauty that is distinctive to their era, their esthetic appearance is a result of the available technology of the day. Magazine publishers of the 30s and 40s did all of their "imaging" manually with airbrush, paint, pen and ink, or optically with a camera.

Special effects, known back then as "trick photography," were performed by the photographer in the camera, using special setups or double exposures. Or they were produced in the darkroom with enlarger tricks, special development techniques, and cleverly manipulated stacks of film. More recently, we have experienced a revolution in image technology, in which the evolution of an image does not stop with the camera, darkroom, or retoucher's brush. Tools like Photoshop can move the Eiffel Tower to Times Square, or provide a tabloid newspaper with photos of a long-dead rock star pumping gas at a convenience store. Because images can be transformed so easily today, we have not only changed the way we perform our imaging tasks but also altered the way we *perceive* images. We no longer believe something is real or true simply because we are shown a picture of it.

Images can also be given much wider distribution than they were 60 years ago. The Web is the one of the primary sources of images today, reaching places that even *LIFE* magazine could not. Images are more easily published and accessed than ever before. In fact, we could say that this is an era of self-publication. With universal access to this powerful medium, any individual can put their message into cyberspace—and reach millions by doing so.

IMAGING TECHNIQUE AND TECHNOLOGY

There is very little expertise required to publish a basic Web page, and the results can be either charming or problematic. The Web has affected the quality of how we present ourselves to the world. Without the tools and techniques necessary to create, edit, and optimize graphics, many individuals publish—despite the best of intentions—Web sites that are neither technologically optimized nor visually efficient. Anyone who wants to create good-looking sites has to learn professional graphic techniques.

The integration of illustration and imaging software into Web technologies will expand the capabilities of the designer and publisher. Images and graphics are fundamental to the success of communicating the message. If a Web designer or publisher has the ability to control the content of the images on the Web, how they appear, and how quickly they load, this will greatly enhance the credibility of their page.

VECTOR VERSUS RASTER ART

There are two types of static art (as opposed to animations and motion pictures) that can be created on a computer: *vector*, or line art and *raster*, or pixel-based art. Each art type has a distinctive look, feel, and working procedure. Web designers who have expanded their capabilities to include a basic hands-on knowledge of the different software that produce this kind of art have an arsenal of tools that can produce almost any graphic element imaginable.

Vector Art

Vector graphics consist solely of lines and curves that are created mathematically such that each plotted point in the illustration relates to quantity and direction at the same time. If you create a vector graphic and save it for future editing in vector format (the native format of a vector program, such as Adobe Illustrator), you can re-open and modify that file in terms of quantity and direction. Within the vector application, you can make a vector graphic larger and smaller without losing quality because you are simply altering the math involved. Photoshop creates vector graphics in limited ways when you use the Pen tool to create a path, the Type tool to create text, the Line tool to create straight lines, or the Shape tool to create closed shapes. These vector objects are converted to pixels when you are done working on a Photoshop image.

Vector art is composed of Bézier curves, which define shapes or objects. Bézier curves were first introduced to the European automobile industry in the 1960s for the purpose of maintaining the integrity of drawings during the design process. Eventually, computer-aided drafting and design (CAD or CADD) software, running on workstations that could cost a million dollars or more, brought the ability to produce drawings that could be electronically edited and scaled to engineers and designers who had been tediously working with manual drawings, overlays, and pin registration systems.

The mainstream drawing programs for computers were pixel-based. These programs produced results with stair-stepped pixelated lines and shapes, a phenomenon known as the *jaggies*. Adobe Illustrator, which was released in 1988, was the first computer illustration program to become available to the general public. Its effect on the drawing process for published art work was revolutionary. It empowered the artist to draw hard-edged graphics on a computer. When printed, these graphics were composed of clean, sharp lines and edges.

This was particularly valuable for illustrators but also for typographers because type fonts can be rendered using the same technology. At this point in history, the personal computer's status graduated from being merely an amusing and expensive sketch pad to a full-fledged, production-oriented design tool.

Vector-based illustration software (such as Adobe Illustrator, Macromedia Freehand, Corel Draw, or page layout programs that can generate Bézier curves) are sometimes referred to as *object-oriented* software. When you draw Bézier curves with these programs, you are creating *vector objects* that define lines, space, shape, and color by creating Postscript code. Figure 1.1 shows the Postscript code used to create the stapler illustration. These programs are a good complement to programs like Photoshop, which work with pixels and have only limited vector-oriented features. Indeed, many graphics professionals use a combination of the two types of programs to achieve the looks they want. You'll find a more complete comparison between Photoshop and programs like Illustrator in Chapter 12.

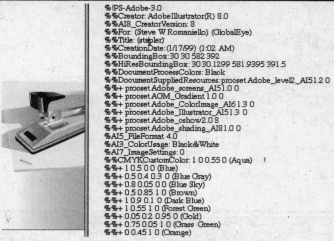

```
%!PS-Adobe-3.0
%%Creator: AdobeIllustrator(R) 8.0
%%AI8_CreatorVersion: 8
%%For: (Steve W Romaniello) (GlobalEye)
%%Title: (stapler)
%%CreationDate: (1/17/99) (1:02 AM)
%%BoundingBox: 30 30 582 392
%%HiResBoundingBox: 30 30.1299 581.9395 391.5
%%DocumentProcessColors: Black
%%DocumentSuppliedResources: procset Adobe_level2_AI51.2 0
%%+ procset Adobe_screens_AI51.0 0
%%+ procset AGM_Gradient 1.0 0
%%+ procset Adobe_ColorImage_AI6 1.3 0
%%+ procset Adobe_Illustrator_AI51.3 0
%%+ procset Adobe_cshow 2.0 8
%%+ procset Adobe_shading_AI8 1.0 0
%AI5_FileFormat 4.0
%AI3_ColorUsage: Black&White
%AI7_ImageSettings: 0
%%CMYKCustomColor: 1 0 0.55 0 (Aqua)
%%+ 1 0.5 0 0 (Blue)
%%+ 0.5 0.4 0.3 0 (Blue Gray)
%%+ 0.8 0.05 0 0 (Blue Sky)
%%+ 0.5 0.85 1 0 (Brown)
%%+ 1 0.9 0.1 0 (Dark Blue)
%%+ 1 0.55 1 0 (Forest Green)
%%+ 0.05 0.2 0.95 0 (Gold)
%%+ 0.75 0.05 1 0 (Grass Green)
%%+ 0 0.45 1 0 (Orange)
```

FIGURE 1.1: Postscript code for the stapler illustration

Inside the Postscript-compatible printer is a device called a *Raster Image Processor* (RIP). The RIP interprets the code into a bitmap, which the printer's marking engine uses as a guide to print the image.

NOTE

The advantage of a vector image over a raster image is that vector art is entirely resolution independent. Vector art can be made larger or smaller with no degradation to the integrity of the design. An image can also be printed at any size at the maximum resolution of the printer without becoming pixelated.

A Bézier curve (see Figure 1.2) is composed of several elements, including two anchor points, one segment, two direction lines, and two direction handles. Continuous paths may share an anchor point. Direction lines define the direction of a curve; therefore, straight paths or sharp corners do not have them.

Object-oriented software extends your capability to produce high-impact color graphics that are appropriate for many Web sites. Vector software is especially good for the creation of logos, charts, maps, cartoons (see Figure 1.3), highly detailed technical illustrations, and images that require hard-edges, smooth blends, and dazzling colors. Vector software is also perfect for the creation of some kinds of special text effects and graph art.

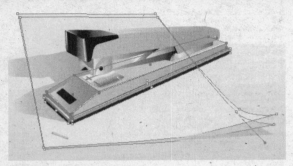

FIGURE 1.2: A Bézier curve

FIGURE 1.3: Max Cannon's Red Meat cartoon is created in a vector program.

Actually, vector art never appears on the Web in its original form. With the exception of Adobe Acrobat Portable Document Files (PDF) and images displayed on the Web using helper applications like Macromedia Flash, all images that appear on the Web are pixel-based raster images, like those produced in Photoshop. For a vector graphic to appear on the

Web, it must first be converted by saving or exporting it to a Web-compatible format, such as JPEG or GIF (see Chapter 18).

An image that is created in Illustrator can be exported as a GIF or saved as a JPEG format directly. It can also be saved as an Illustrator EPS file and opened in Photoshop for image enhancement and the addition of special effects. The image will automatically be *rasterized* (see Figure 1.4). This means its vector information will be converted into pixels once the file leaves the vector environment.

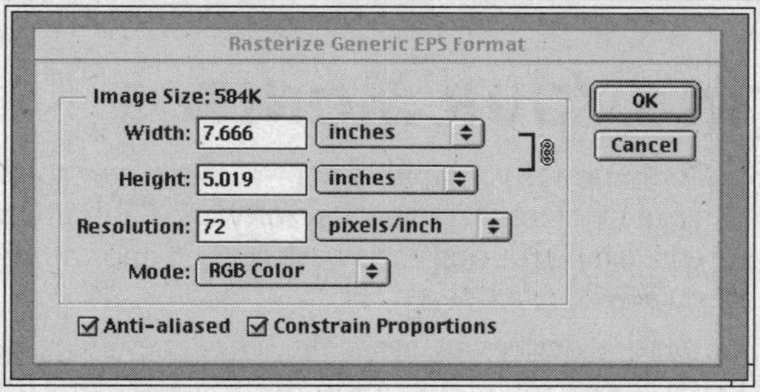

FIGURE 1.4: A Raster window

Raster Art

Raster graphics are *bitmapped* files. You're probably familiar with these. They include TIFs, BMPs, GIFs, and JPEGs.

You can compare raster art to a grid. A grid is like a map of bits. Color and other information is placed in each of the little squares within the grid, fixing it in a specific place. In the same way, the information in raster graphics is fixed in quantity and direction. For that reason, raster graphics are larger and harder to modify than vector art, which uses complex mathematical statements to store its information. Because of its grid-like structure, you can make raster graphics smaller without losing too much quality; but when you make them larger, you force each bit to stretch out, resulting in blurry, blotchy graphics.

Raster programs use bitmaps, which are simply a mosaic of pixels. *Pixels* are the basic physical unit of a digital image. They are individual tiles of colored light that are set up on a grid and create an image, as shown here. The pixels are so small that when the eye sees them, it blends them together and creates a photographic image. The pixels can be selected and edited with a variety of tools and operations in Adobe Photoshop.

CALIBRATING YOUR MONITOR

A calibrated monitor improves your ability to produce images appropriate for all color settings in imaging or illustration software. Calibration will ultimately assure consistency during each work session and will ensure more predictable on-screen results.

Mechanical calibration devices are available. While they are more accurate, they are also fairly cost prohibitive for most people, ranging from $600–$1,200. Adobe bundles Gamma software with Photoshop. Gamma is a measurement of the midtone contrast of a monitor, and Adobe Gamma will help you calibrate your monitor to achieve smooth results.

Adobe Gamma software is automatically loaded into the Control Panel on Macintosh and Windows systems when Photoshop is installed. Before calibrating the monitor, you should let it warm up for at least 30 minutes. Set the ambient light in the room to the level that you use under normal working conditions. Change the background color on your screen to neutral gray for best results.

The Gamma Wizard walks you through calibration step by step. It explains how to control brightness, contrast, gamma, white point, and black point. To start calibrating your monitor, follow these steps:

1. Start the Gamma Wizard (see Figure 1.5).

2. Click the Step By Step Wizard radio button, and then click Next.

3. Click the Load button.

4. In Open Monitor Profile, select Adobe Monitor.

5. Select Next and follow the wizard's instructions to adjust the brightness and contrast of your monitor.

6. At the final window, you can compare results. Once you are satisfied, save the profile.

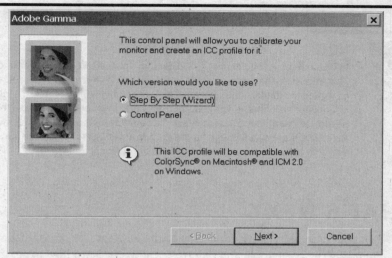

FIGURE 1.5: The Adobe Gamma Wizard

Choosing the Right Color Space

The next step in calibration is to choose an RGB space in which to edit images. Photoshop 6 lets you work in RGB spaces other than those defined by your monitor. You need to choose the one that best simulates the environment in which you intend to use your image. For the Web, for instance this will be the sRGB option. To choose an RGB space, follow these steps:

1. In Photoshop 6, Choose File ➢ Color Settings ➢ RGB Setup. The RGB Setup dialog appears.

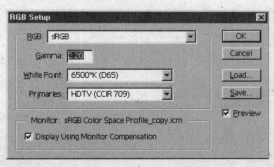

2. In the Working Spaces area, make sure that the sRGB choice is selected from the drop-down list.

3. Click OK.

NOTE

In Photoshop, Adobe made the sRGB color space its RGB color space default. This attests to the popularity of the Photoshop as a Web-design tool. sRGB is designed to simulate the display of an inexpensive VGA monitor in a Microsoft Windows environment. The assumption is that most people who use the Internet are not graphics professionals and do not use high-end computer monitors. When you work on an image for the Web, you should see it as Web surfers will see it so you can make color corrections accordingly.

What's Next

The next chapter will introduce you to the key features of Photoshop 6, including the basic tools and palettes. You'll also learn how to set up your preferences so Photoshop works exactly the way you want it to.

Chapter 2

INTRODUCING
PHOTOSHOP 6 FEATURES

Using Photoshop 6 and mastering its myriad controls and functions can be a lifelong endeavor, or at least seem like it. Power users—those people who have learned the intricacies of the program over the years and who push the program to its limits—are still finding new and intriguing ways to create eye-catching and award-winning images using the program. But, before you can win your own awards with your Photoshop images, you need to start with the basics, and that's what will happen in this chapter.

You'll get acquainted with some of Photoshop's basic controls and tools, and you'll experiment with some of the new tools that come with Photoshop 6, such as the Preferences settings, Photoshop's redesigned toolbox and palettes, the Notes tool, and old favorites like the Background Eraser, Magic Eraser, and Magnetic Lasso.

Adapted from *Photoshop 6 Visual JumpStart* by Richard Schrand
ISBN 0-7821-2866-1   288 pages $19.99

SETTING UP PHOTOSHOP

Before you begin working with Photoshop, you may want to choose
options to control certain ways that Photoshop behaves and the appearance of some Photoshop elements. If you have extra plug-ins or more than
one hard drive, you also can set up Photoshop to use these resources.

Setting Preferences

You can set up Photoshop so that the workspace is the most comfortable
for you. This is accomplished via the Preferences dialog box.

1. Start up Photoshop 6. From the menu bar, select Edit ➤ Pref-
    erences ➤ General. The menu selection looks like this under
    Mac OS; (If you're using Windows, the Image Cache entry
    will read Memory & Image Cache.)

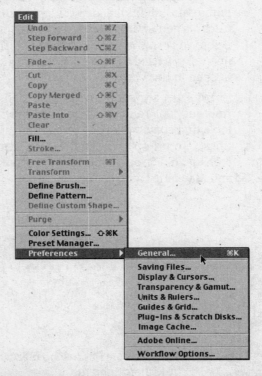

2. Select the options you want for the general layout of the pro-
    gram. For example, the Show Tool Tips option will help you

with tool selection. You should keep this option active until you are familiar with the Photoshop tools and their position in the toolbox. Click the Next button located on the right side of the Preferences dialog box.

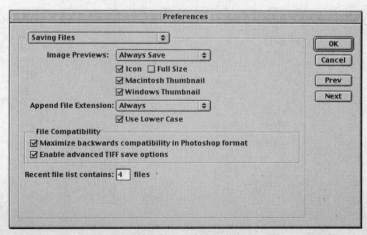

3. The Saving Files options relate to how your image files will be saved. For example, for ease of file identification, you should select Always Save for Image Previews. This way, you have a small visual representation of your file. The setup you see here (with some changes to the defaults) is a good starting point. The Icon/Full Size and Macintosh/Windows Thumbnail choices are available only under Mac OS. After you've chosen your preferred options, click Next.

4. The Display & Cursors options let you choose how your image will appear, as well as which cursor icon will be displayed when you choose various paint tools. For example, choosing Precise for both the painting and other cursors makes the pointer appear as cross-hairs, which is helpful for working with your images. Click Next after you've set these options.

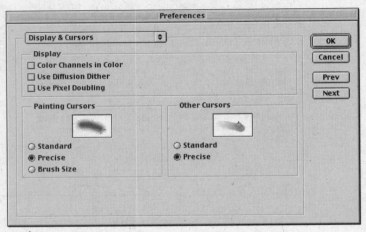

5. The Transparency & Gamut options let you determine how transparent (or invisible) areas of your image's background will be displayed, as well as how colors that are *out of gamut* (or out of the range that can be worked with using a particular color model) will be shown. Use the pop-up menus to change the settings to suit your preferences. Click Next when you're finished.

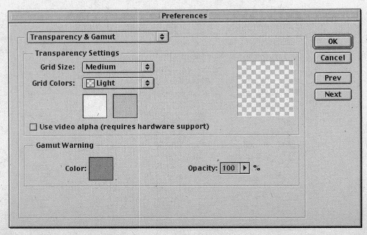

6. The Units & Rulers options let you select how your image is measured, how the ruler option will be displayed, how columns and gutter widths are measured, and how text size will be displayed. Unless you're working on a file that will be sent to a professional printer, it's best to change the Unit setting for Rulers to Inches, since this is the most common form of measurement in the U.S. Click Next after choosing your desired options.

7. The Guides & Grid options allow you to select colors and styles for the nonprinting guides and grids that Photoshop displays to help with exact placement of elements. You can also choose the spacing of the grid. For now, leave the default settings. Click Next to move on to the Image Cache settings (for the Macintosh) or Memory & Image Cache settings (for Windows).

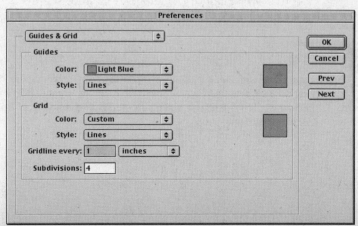

8. Both Macs and Windows have the Image Cache options, which are used for cache levels and histograms. Image caching helps to speed up screen redrawing when you make changes to images. You can choose to use the cache for histograms, which are graphs of the brightness values of images. For now, leave these options at their default settings. This is the Macintosh Image Cache dialog box.

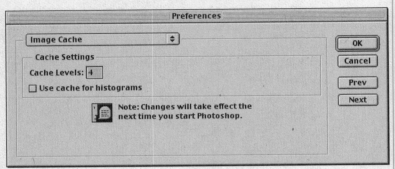

9. The Windows Memory & Image Cache dialog box has an additional section, Physical Memory Usage, which determines how much of your computer's RAM will be allocated to Photoshop. If you're using Photoshop 6.01, you can set this value to any amount you like, making sure you leave enough for other applications you may want to have open at the same time as Photoshop. If you have Photoshop 6.0 (which lacks a Version 6.01 bug fix), you should set the value no higher than 30 percent, to avoid a conflict with Photoshop's memory management and Windows' Internet capabilities.

TIP

Mac users can allocate memory to Photoshop by selecting the Photoshop application icon, pressing Command+I and choosing Memory from the Get Info drop-down list. Then set the preferred size to the amount of RAM you want to dedicate to Photoshop.

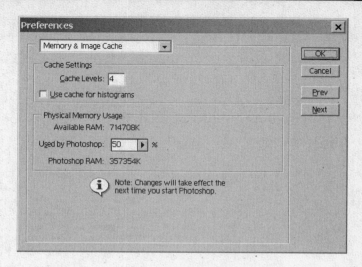

10. Click OK to close the Preferences dialog box.

The Preferences dialog box also includes Plug-ins & Scratch Disks options, which you'll set in the next sections.

Adding Plug-ins

Plug-ins extend the creative options of Photoshop. There are numerous companies and individuals who have created plug-ins for the program. Photoshop automatically recognizes the plug-ins in its main plug-ins folder, but if you have extra Photoshop-compatible plug-ins stored with other programs (such as Adobe Illustrator), you need to set up Photoshop to recognize them.

1. Select Edit ➤ Preferences ➤ Plug-Ins & Scratch Disks.

2. Click the Additional Plug-Ins Folder check box and click the Choose button.

3. An Additional Plug-Ins Folder dialog box appears. Navigate to the additional plug-ins folder you want to use, and then click the OK button. The Macintosh file navigation dialog box is shown here; the Windows dialog box does the same thing using a Windows Explorer–style configuration.

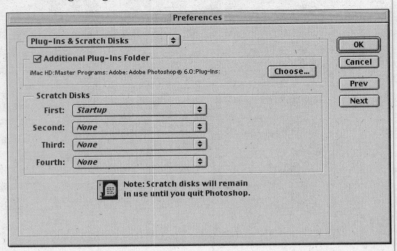

NOTE

If the plug-ins folder you selected does not have Photoshop-compatible plug-ins, they will not show up in the Filters menu.

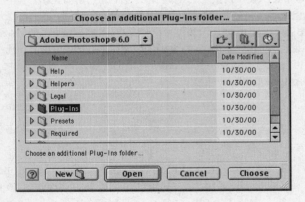

4. Click OK to save your settings and close the dialog box.

After you select an additional plug-ins folder, you will need to restart Photoshop in order for any of the plug-ins in that folder to appear in the Filter menu on the menu bar.

Using Your Hard Disk As Memory

Photoshop likes to have as much memory as is possible to do its job efficiently. To figure out memory requirements for the program, use a three-
to-one ratio; in other words, the amount of RAM available should be
triple the size of the image file you're working on. For example, if you
have a file that is 50MB, you should have 150MB of RAM. For a 100MB
file (which is not unusual when dealing with high-resolution images), you
should have 300MB of RAM installed on your system.

Unfortunately, it's not always possible (financially or otherwise) to buy
the maximum amount of RAM for your computer. But if you have a large
hard drive or, even better, more than one hard drive on your system, you
have some options for managing Photoshop's memory requirements: You
can set up free space on your main hard drive, through *scratch disks*, or
you can assign space from your second hard drive to handle the extra
memory requirements.

1. Select Edit ➤ Preferences ➤ Plug-Ins & Scratch Disks.

2. In the Scratch Disks section of the dialog box, Startup should
    already be selected in the First box. If you have a second hard
    disk, select that disk from the First pop-up menu.

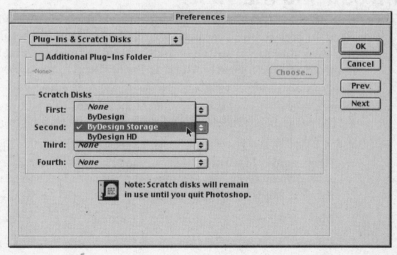

NOTE

With *scratch disks* assigned, Photoshop will use open space on your hard
drive(s) and use that open space as extra memory when necessary.

3. In the Second, Third, and Fourth boxes, select other disks if you have more drives attached to your system.

4. Click OK to save your settings and close the dialog box.

TIP
You'll learn about additional Preferences settings (for grids and guides) in Chapter 5.

GETTING TO KNOW THE PHOTOSHOP TOOLS

After you've set up Photoshop, you can start to spend some time learning where the various tools are and what they are used for. All of the tools are located in the toolbox on the left side of your screen. The toolbox also offers other controls for working with your images and getting online.

Introducing the Tools

The toolbox holds the Photoshop tools you will use to create and modify images. In many cases, the space occupied by an icon you see actually holds several tools. To switch to another tool in the same area, press and hold down the mouse button over the tool icon in the toolbox to see the other tools, and then click to select the tool you want to use.

Here's an overview of the main tools that are shown when you first start the program, starting with the top-left tool and moving from left to right, row to row:

Rectangular Marquee   Allows you to select a rectangular portion of an image so you can move it to another location or modify what is inside the selected area.

Move   Allows you to move image elements.

Lasso   Allows you to draw around a particular element in your image to select it.

Magic Wand   Gives you the ability to select specific colors.

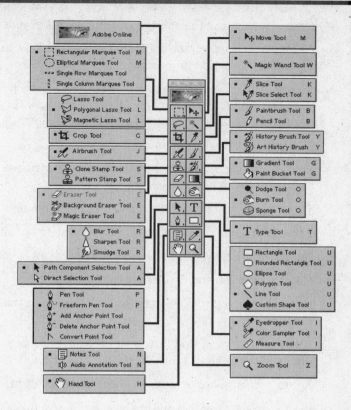

Crop   Allows you to select an area of an image and crop the image to that specified area.

Slice   Lets you cut the image into sections, which is handy for creating Web graphics.

Airbrush   Just like its real-world counterpart, gives you the ability to paint onto the image with an airbrush effect.

Paintbrush   Again, like its real-world counterpart, lets you paint onto the image with a painting effect.

Clone Stamp   Lets you copy a portion of an image and recreate it in another area of the image.

History Brush   Allows you to paint a copy of an image (in this case, called a state or snapshot) onto the current version of the image.

Eraser   Gives you the ability to erase portions of your image.

Gradient   Gives you the ability to assign a gradient to a background or a selection in your image.

Smudge   Lets you smudge areas of the image, much like when you color with a crayon or chalk and then rub your finger over colors next to each other, smudging them together.

Dodge   Lets you lighten image areas.

Path Component Selection   Lets you work with and modify paths you create in your files.

Type   Gives you the ability to add text to your image.

Pen   Allows you to create a path by laying down points.

Rectangle   Lets you create a rectangular element in your image.

Notes   Lets you add textual notes to the image.

Eyedropper   Lets you select a specific color in an image for use in another part of your image.

Hand   Gives you the ability to pan across your image on the screen.

Zoom   Enlarges or reduces an image on your screen.

When you select a tool, the information in Photoshop's Options bar changes to reflect that tool's settings. You can modify how the tool reacts to an image by changing the settings in the Options bar.

TIP

When you first start Photoshop, the Options bar appears at the top of the screen, but you can move it anywhere in the workspace. To move the Options bar, drag it by its left edge.

Using Other Toolbox Controls

At the bottom of the toolbox, you'll find a set of controls that provide easy access to common Photoshop functions.

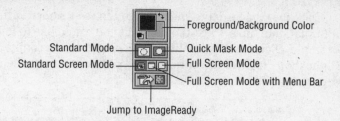

Foreground/Background Color

Standard Mode
Standard Screen Mode

Quick Mask Mode
Full Screen Mode
Full Screen Mode with Menu Bar

Jump to ImageReady

These seven controls work as follows:

Foreground/Background Color   Opens the Color Picker so you can choose a color, or swaps the foreground and background colors (when you click the arrow on the upper-right side of the control).

Standard Mode   Switches to Standard mode, which is the mode most often used to build images.

Quick Mask Mode   Switches to Quick Mask mode, which is the mode used to add or create a mask (which helps you delineate between the areas that will be affected by an operation and those that won't).

Standard Screen Mode   Shows all of the controls and your workspace in the default window setup.

Full Screen Mode with Menu Bar   Displays a full-screen window with a menu bar and all open palettes and windows.

Full Screen Mode   Displays a full-screen window without a menu bar and all open palettes and windows.

Jump to ImageReady   Opens ImageReady, the companion program to Photoshop.

Getting Online

The Go to Adobe Online button (the one with the picture icon) is located at the very top of the toolbox. Clicking it takes you to Adobe's Photoshop Web site, which can be valuable to even the most experienced Photoshop users.

Click the Go to Adobe Online button to see a screen with numerous informational links. Click the link that you would like to follow. For example, click the Support link if you need to access online support for Photoshop. You will be connected to the Internet and taken to area you selected.

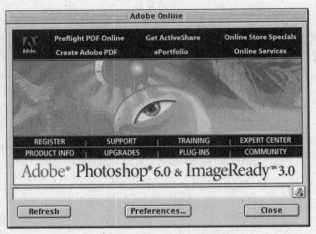

WORKING WITH PALETTES

Photoshop 6 makes it easy for you to create a work area that contains the program elements that you use most often in a way that is most conducive to your work habits.

Accessing and Arranging Palettes

You can show and hide Photoshop elements and change the way that they are grouped. For instance, you can arrange different windows into groups to help you save screen real estate if you're working on a smaller monitor.

1. Click Window in the menu bar to open the Window menu. This menu list choices for hiding and showing the various windows, called *palettes* in Photoshop. This list is divided into groups, so when you choose one in the group, the others will also appear in the set.

2. Select Show Character. You will see the Character palette. Notice that this palette has a Paragraph tab, which you can click to access the Paragraph palette.

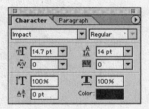

3. If the Layers palette isn't already displayed, select Window ➤ Show Layers. Notice that the Layers palette has Channels and Paths tabs. Each of the tabbed palettes can be "torn away" from the group. Click the Layers tab, hold down the mouse button, and drag the palette to another location on the screen, away from its group.

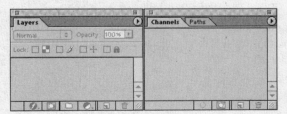

4. Select Window ➤ Reset Palette Locations to return the palettes to their original arrangement.

Grouping Palettes

In addition to separating palettes, you can group them, as follows:

▶ Group different palettes together by dragging the appropriate tab onto another tab in a different palette, creating a new group that will remain together until you rearrange the palettes again.

▶ Create multiple groups in one palette by dragging a tab from one palette onto another palette.

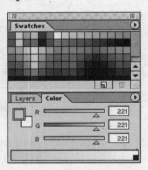

▶ Collapse a section of multiple palettes or an entire palette (so all that appears are the tabs and their names), by double-clicking a tab in the section or the palette group. Double-clicking a tab again opens the section or palette.

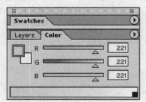

▶ Group your palettes in Photoshop 6's new Palette Well. Only the tabs of the palettes will be visible until you click on them.

Then, the palette will become visible until you click back in your image area.

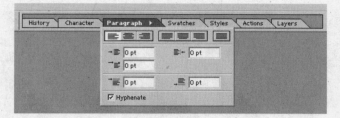

When you become more familiar with Photoshop, you can set up the palettes as you like.

Choosing Palette Options

Notice the circular button with an arrow inside it to the right of the tabs in any of the Photoshop palettes. Clicking this button displays a pop-up menu with more choices for that palette. Let's work with the Swatches palette as an example.

1. If the Color palette is on your screen, click the Swatches tab. Otherwise, select Window ➢ Show Swatches. Click the arrow button to see the palette's options menu.

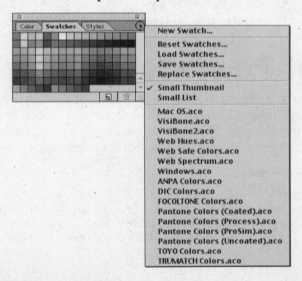

2. Select Pantone Colors (Process).aco. Then resize the window to show more of the color swatches that are available to you.

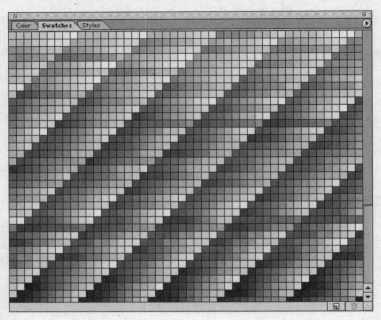

3. To return to the default color set, click the Palette Options menu button and choose Reset Swatches.

Using Power Tools

There are some wonderful tools included in Photoshop that can make your life a lot easier, especially when modifying photographs. To experiment with them, download the MugShot.jpg image from the Sybex Web site or use a photographic image of your own that has a lot of elements.

NOTE

To download the sample files provided for this book, go to www.sybex.com and enter **2991** (this book's ISBN) into the Search box. Click the title of this book and then the Downloads link, then select the desired file.

Getting Rid of the Background with the Background Eraser

It's not unusual to have a picture in which the background is too distracting or full of unwanted elements. For example, suppose that in the MugShot.jpg example, all you really want is that guy, without any of the things behind him. This is when you want to use the Background Eraser tool, which erases similar colors.

1. To open an image file, select File ➤ Open. In the Open dialog box, navigate to the file you want to use. If you downloaded the MugShot.jpg image from this book's Web site, open the folder where you stored the image, select MugShot.jpg, and click Open to open the file.

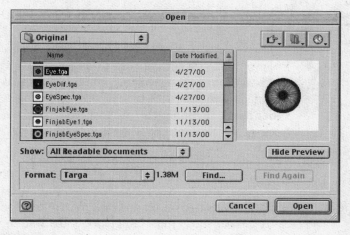

NOTE

Click the Show Preview button on the Open dialog box to see a preview of the selected image. Click Hide Preview to turn off the preview display.

2. Click the Eraser tool in the toolbox and hold down the mouse button. This reveals the expanded list of tools. Click Background Eraser Tool to select it.

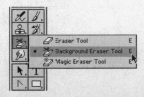

3. You should now see the Background Eraser's options bar at the top of the screen. In the options bar, click Brush and choose the Hard Round, 19 *pixels* brush.

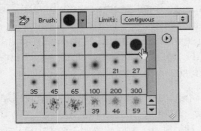

TIP

By double-clicking a brush icon, you can open a dialog box that lets you rename the brush.

4. In the options bar, click the button adjacent to the Tolerance text box. This opens a slider bar. Use this slider to change the Tolerance setting to 50% by dragging the triangle along the slider bar. The higher the number, the more accurate the Background Eraser tool will be in erasing similar colors.

5. Choose a section of the photo that you want to erase and click it. In the MugShot.jpg example, click the wall in the background. While holding down the mouse button, drag the cursor over the wall. Notice how it erases anything with a similar color.

6. As you drag the cursor along the image, take a look at the Foreground/Background Colors indicator in the toolbox. Notice how the colors change.

7. Place the cursor on the back wall next to the guy's hair and drag down, making sure not to move into the hair at all. If you do that, the color parameter set by the brush will change and erase the hair, too.

8. Because this is just a quick introduction to the Background Eraser tool, select File ➢ Revert to go back to the original image before moving on. If you continued using the Background Eraser tool, you could erase the entire background, while leaving the subject alone.

Erasing Similar Colors with the Magic Eraser

Like the Background Eraser tool, the Magic Eraser tool shares the Eraser tool location in the toolbox. The Magic Eraser tool works differently from the Background Eraser tool, in that it will erase all colors in a picture that are similar (based on the Tolerance setting) to the one you select. With your practice image still on the screen, let's see how this tool works.

1. Click the Eraser tool in the toolbox and hold down the mouse button. In the expanded list of tools, click Magic Eraser Tool to select it.

2. In the Magic Eraser tool's option bar, change the Tolerance setting to 25% by typing **25** in the text field, and deselect the Contiguous check box. Make sure Anti-aliased is checked. (You'll learn more about how these options work in Chapter 3.)

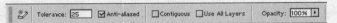

3. Click the wall behind that guy in the picture. All similar colors in the image will be erased.

4. Choose Edit ➢ Undo Magic Eraser to undo what you just did.

5. In the Options bar, select the Contiguous check box.

6. Click the same spot as you just did in Step 3. Notice that the Magic Eraser tool now only erases the color that is within a boundary set by the image colors. Once a color change is recognized, erasing is stopped.

7. Select File ➢ Revert to go back to the original image before continuing.

Selecting Similar Color Areas with the Magnetic Lasso

The Magnetic Lasso tool is one of the great discoveries of the twenty-first century. Okay, I'm overplaying it, but it really can be a massive lifesaver if you have an image with some difficult elements you want to select. The Magic Eraser tool works by sampling colors based on where the selector is. As you drag around the edge of the image element, it keeps the border of the selection even with that sampled color. Continuing with your practice image, see how the Magnetic Lasso works.

1. Click the Lasso tool in the toolbox and hold down the mouse button to display the pop-up list.

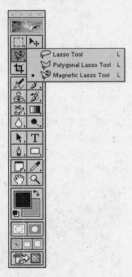

2. In the Tool list, click Magnetic Lasso Tool to select it.

3. In the Options bar, change the Feather setting to 5 pixels and the Width setting to 1 pixel.

4. Click the edge of the shirt, and then begin dragging the mouse around it. Notice how the Magnetic Lasso tool follows the edge. Once you've worked your way back to the starting

point, click the mouse button to connect the starting and ending points. The shirt will be outlined and selected.

5. The outline indicates that that particular area is selected and can be modified. However, in this example, you want to get rid of everything except the shirt. To do that, choose Select ➢ Inverse. This reverses the selection, so that the selected area is everything in the picture *except* the shirt.

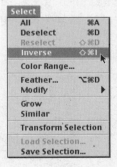

6. Choose the Eraser tool (not the Magic Eraser or Background Eraser tool). In the Options bar, click Brush and set the Soft Round, 300 pixels brush.

7. Now erase everything, and don't worry about erasing over the shirt, because it won't be affected.

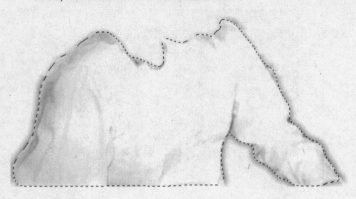

Creating Notes

The Notes tool is extremely handy item that you definitely want to get used to using. If you have created a great effect, keeping notes about how you did it will help jog your memory when you want to recreate that effect. And, if you plan to send the image to someone else to show how you created the effect, the recipient can read the notes as well.

Photoshop provides tools for creating text notes as well as audio notes. You can add as many notes as you like to highlight particular areas of your work in a file.

Let's add some notes to an image. You can either continue with the practice image you used in the previous sections or open another image file.

1. Select the Notes tool.

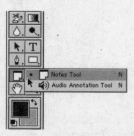

2. Click a spot on your image. A note window appears. Type your message in the window.

3. When you're finished, collapse the note by clicking the small box in the upper-left corner of the note window. All that is left is a small icon indicating a note is attached.

4. If you have a microphone attached to your computer, you can attach an audio note using the Audio Annotation tool. Click the Notes tool in the toolbox and hold down the mouse button. In the tool list, click Audio Annotation Tool to select it.

5. Click the image. A recording dialog box appears (the Macintosh dialog box is shown; the Windows dialog has only Start

and Stop buttons, and lacks the controls of the Mac version). Record your message.

6. When you have finished your recording, click Save.

7. A speaker icon appears on the image to alert the recipient or yourself that an audio note has been attached. Double-clicking this icon plays back your recorded note.

Using File Features

Photoshop includes features for setting up your files for viewing or storage. To access these features, select File ➤ Automate.

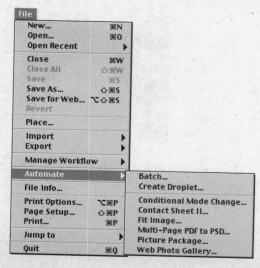

Contact Sheet

Contact Sheet II lets you create a contact sheet from a series of photographs or images stored in a common folder.

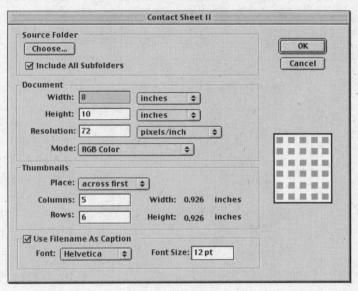

Picture Package

Picture Package lets you create a page with a photograph at various sizes. This is exactly like the photo sheets you get from a school photography package.

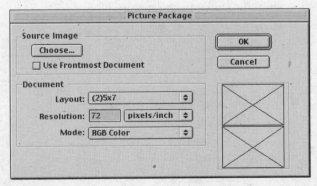

Web Photo Gallery

Web Photo Gallery allows you to set up a page for viewing on the Web. The small images (or thumbnails that are created) act as links to view the larger image.

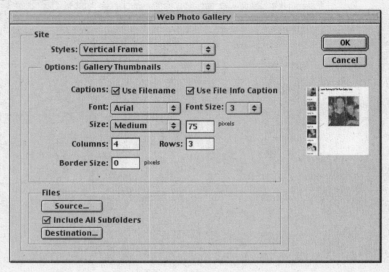

Convert Multi-Page PDF to PSD

Convert Multi-Page PDF to PSD is a very handy tool when you have a *PDF (Portable Document Format)* form you want to use in a Photoshop document. This automatically turns each page of the PDF document into a Photoshop file that you can manipulate.

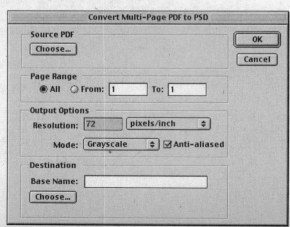

WHAT'S NEXT

This chapter gave you a head start in some Photoshop basics. In the next chapter, you're going to learn specifically how to work with the selection tools and basic painting tools.

Chapter 3
USING THE EDITING TOOLS IN PHOTOSHOP 6

There are some basic Photoshop tools that you will use over and over again. These tools are literally the power behind the concept of Photoshop, so learning to work with them will be paramount to your success with the program. Photoshop 6 has added a number of powerful updates to the toolset. Here, you'll learn how to use some of the editing tools that let you change your images, including the Lasso tools, for isolating parts of your images; the Magic Wand tool, for selecting image areas by color, the Clone Stamp and Pattern Stamp tools, for replacing parts of your image; and the Paintbrush tool and filters, for coloring and adding effects to your images.

Adapted from *Photoshop 6 Visual JumpStart* by Richard Schrand

ISBN 0-7821-2866-1   288 pages $19.99

Selecting Areas with the Lasso Tools

The Lasso tools are some of the most useful tools in Photoshop. With them, you can select areas of a picture simply by drawing around those areas. In Chapter 2, you experimented with the Magnetic Lasso tool, which surrounds an element of an image based on the first pixel color assigned to it. Here, we will look at the Lasso and Polygonal Lasso tools.

TIP

I highly recommend purchasing a graphics tablet for use with Photoshop. Graphic or drawing tablets act like pencil and paper, allowing you to literally draw around an image. The leading vendor of graphics tablets is Wacom (www.wacom.com), but many other companies produce them.

Selecting Free-Form Shapes

Of the three choices you have in the Lasso tools area, the Lasso tool is the main one. It is a free-form tool, meaning that it is not limited to straight lines. To get a feel for working with the Lasso tool and selections, do the following:

1. Open an image file and select the main Lasso tool from the toolbox.

TIP

If you don't like the way the cursor appears on the screen, you can change it through the Display & Cursors page of the Preferences dialog box (select Edit ➢ Preferences ➢ Display & Cursors). See Chapter 2 for more information about Preferences settings.

2. Zoom in on your subject by pressing the Ctrl/Command+plus key combination, so you can be more precise when tracing an image.

NOTE

Throughout this book, key combinations are shown for both Windows and Macintosh systems, in the format *Windows keystrokes/Mac keystrokes*. Ctrl/Command means to press the Control key with Windows, and the Command key with a Macintosh. Alt/Option means to use the Alt key in Windows, and the Option key with a Mac.

3. Begin drawing around the area you want to select, keeping as close as you possibly can to the subject. Notice how a line appears as you are tracing the edge of the subject.

TIP

If you are using a mouse rather than a drawing tablet, don't worry about tracing around an entire subject. In the Options bar, click the Add To or Subtract From icons to extend the selected area or deselect portions of a selected area, respectively.

4. When you're finished, you will see your subject surrounded by a moving dotted line (called *marching ants*).

5. To delete the selected image, press the Delete key. To cut the selection to the Clipboard, select Edit ➤ Cut (notice the shortcut is Ctrl/Command+X).

6. To *invert* your selection, so that everything except what you traced is deleted, choose Select ➢ Inverse (notice the shortcut is Shift+Ctrl/Command+I), and then delete the selected portion.

Selecting Straight Edges

Unlike the main Lasso tool, the Polygonal Lasso tool creates straight lines in horizontal, vertical, or angled planes. You can use this tool in conjunction with the other selection tools to select complex image elements. Here's how:

1. Open an image file that contains elements with straight edges.

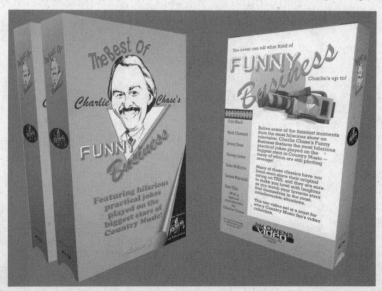

2. Press and hold down the mouse button over the Lasso tool icon in the toolbox to reveal the other sections, and then choose the Polygonal Lasso tool.

3. Click to set the first point. Move the mouse to the next point in the image and click again. Repeat this process until the portion of the image you want to select is completely surrounded.

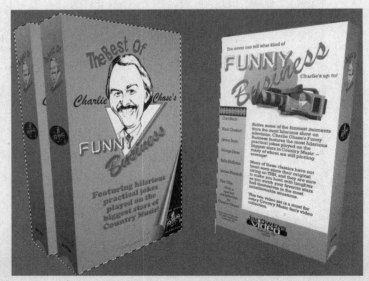

Modifying the Lasso Tool Settings

The settings for the Lasso tools make them more or less sensitive. The controls for the Lasso tools are located in the Lasso tool's Options bar.

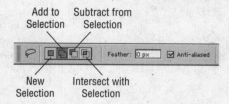

From left to right, these tool-modification controls work as follows:

New Selection option   allows you to create a new selected area with the tool. If you have already traced around a portion of the image and want to keep that as a selection, hold down the Shift key while tracing around the new area.

Add to Selection option   works the same as holding down the Shift key when New Selection is active.

Subtract from Selection option   allows you to trace around a portion of a selected area, deselecting that portion of the image.

Intersect with Selection option   removes all of the selected areas except for those included in your new selection.

Feather setting   determines whether the edges of the selected area are sharp or blurred. *Feathering* is set in pixel increments.

Anti-aliased option   determines whether the edge of the selected area is smooth or jagged. *Anti-aliasing* adds a small border around edges to blend into the surrounding area.

Let's see how some of the modification tools work.

1. Using the Lasso tool (the main one), select a portion of your image.

2. Click the Add to Selection button. Draw around another area of the picture. Both areas are now selected.

3. Select Subtract from Selection. Use the Lasso tool inside one of the selected areas. That area is no longer a part of your selection.

4. Select Intersect with Selection and draw an area between your two selections. The areas within your selection are the only portions left selected.

TIP

To be more precise when outlining objects with many of Photoshop's tools, zoom in as close as you can without losing sense of what you are looking at. You can zoom in up to 1600 percent of the image size.

SELECTING COLORS WITH THE MAGIC WAND

The Magic Wand is an indispensable tool you will use often. With it, you can choose specific colors or shades of gray for modification within your image.

The Magic Wand's option bar contains settings that let you control how the tool selects colors. The New Selection, Add to Selection, Subtract from Selection, Intersect with Selection, and Anti-aliased options work the same as they do with the Lasso tools, as described in the previous section. The Magic Wand also offers the following modifiers:

Tolerance setting   controls the sensitivity of the Magic Wand; the higher the number, the more variations of the color you are selecting are included.

Contiguous option   selects only the colors that are touching the area you click. When this is deselected, all instances of the selected color in the entire image are chosen.

Use All Layers option   chooses all instances of the selected color simultaneously in all open layers (when you have more than one layer with image information).

Let's see how the Magic Wand and some of its controls work.

1. Open an image file and select the Magic Wand.

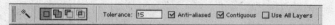

2. Place the Magic Wand cursor over a color in your image. In the options bar, change the Tolerance to **15** and make sure that the Contiguous and Anti-aliased check boxes are checked.

3. Click the color you want to select. It becomes outlined with the marching ants.

4. Press Ctrl/Command+D to deselect the selection. Change the Tolerance to **50**. Now click in the same area as before. Notice how much more of the color is selected this time.

5. Deselect the selected color. Change the Tolerance back to **15** and turn off Contiguous. Click the color you want to select. Notice how all similar colors are outlined by the marching ants.

CLONING WITH THE STAMP TOOLS

Two other tools that will become part of your most-used toolset are the Clone Stamp and Pattern Stamp tools. The Clone Stamp tool is particularly useful. You will find that it is invaluable for fixing blemishes in photographs, changing the look of an image, and creating and applying new patterns to your images.

Working with the Clone Stamp Tool

Now you will get a feel for what can be accomplished by using the Clone Stamp tool.

1. Open an image file. (I choose a picture of two of my children, so that I can play mad scientist and clone my son's face onto my daughter's head.)

2. Select the Clone Stamp tool. You'll see that the Clone Stamp's Option bar has several interesting settings. We'll examine these more closely later, after we've experimented with the Stamp tools. For now, just make sure that the following settings are selected:

   Brush: 21 Soft-edged

   Mode: Normal

   Opacity: 100%

   Aligned: Selected

3. Place the cursor over the part of the image you want to clone and, while holding down the Alt key (Option key), click the area.

4. Place the Clone Stamp brush over the area you want replaced. Hold down the mouse button, and the cloning process begins. (Oh, the things you could do to photos of your boss; that is, unless you're the boss.)

5. Move the Clone Stamp tool over another part of the image. Notice that, with the Aligned option turned on, the clone area remains constant with the placement of the brush.

6. Select File ➢ Revert to return your image to its original state.

7. Turn Aligned off. Repeat steps 3 and 4.

8. Move the cursor to another area. Hold down the mouse button and clone the image into this new area. Notice that with Aligned off, you clone the original selection again.

Cloning Patterns with the Pattern Stamp Tool

The Pattern Stamp tool has one major difference from the Clone Stamp tool: a Pattern option that allows you to clone using a pattern. Let's try it out.

1. Select an area of your image by encircling it with the Lasso tool (the main one). This provides you with an area where the change will take place and, even if you go out of the lines, the other parts of the picture won't be affected.

2. Select the Pattern Stamp tool. Notice that the modifiers now include a Pattern option. Photoshop comes with a number of preset patterns that you can use.

3. For this example, choose the brick pattern. Move the Pattern Stamp tool into the selected area and paint in the new pattern.

Notice that all of the detail in the selected area has been lost. This is because you are simply replacing the one image with your new one. You can modify how the Pattern Stamp and the Clone Stamp tools blend images by adjusting the settings on the options bar, which are discussed next.

Modifying the Stamp Tool Settings

The Options bar for the Clone Stamp tool contains settings for painting cloned areas. The Use All Layers option works similarly to how it does with the Magic Wand tool, giving you the ability to sample an area to be cloned from one layer and painted onto another layer. The other options are described in the following sections.

Brush Options

The Brush setting gives you access to various styles and sizes of brushes that paint the cloned information onto other parts of the image. The predefined brushes range in size and edge softness, as well as include some fancy brush styles for more artistic use. Click the down arrow to the right of the current brush setting to see the Brush menu.

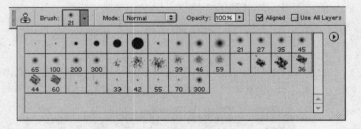

For more control over the Brush setting, click the right-pointing arrow at the top-right side of the Brushes menu. This opens a pop-up menu that offers options for modifying the brushes, opening other stored brush sets, and changing how the brush icons appear on the screen.

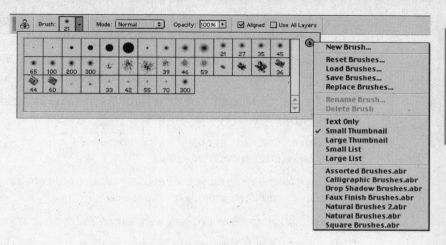

Mode Options

The Mode setting controls the blending mode, or the way that a brush paints the cloned area over the new area. (Photoshop also uses these blending modes when it merges layers, as you'll learn in Chapter 6.) Click the Mode drop-down arrow to see the available blending modes. If you want to experiment with these modes, undo the pattern change (Edit ➢ Undo Pattern Stamp) from the last exercise, and then use the Clone Pattern Stamp tool over a small region of the selected area. You can undo each change before working with the next effect.

Dissolve gives the edges of the image a rough, uneven edge that makes it appear to look like it's dissolving the further out it goes.

Multiply blends the upper and lower layers, multiplying the brightness values, and darkening anything in the lower layer.

Screen adds brightness to the area by blending the top and bottom images. Technically, this and the other modes work on a pixel-by-pixel basis.

Overlay blends the light and dark areas of the top layer with the light and dark areas of the bottom layer, effectively increasing the contrast and color intensity.

Soft Light   gives a nice, subtle look to the mixture of the original image and the cloned area or pattern.

Hard Light   is harsher version of Soft Light, which makes the lighter areas of the cloned area or pattern stand out more.

Color Dodge   acts much like Hard Light, but actually lightens the underlying cloned area or pattern.

Color Burn   uses the lighter areas of the cloned area or pattern to darken the underlying image's color.

Darken   looks for the darker areas of an image in the top and bottom layer and then uses the darkest area.

Lighten   is the same as Darken, only it uses the lightest areas.

Difference   blends the upper and lower layer, showing the difference between the two (easier seen than explained).

Exclusion   combines the colors together in a more muted way than Differences does. This is accomplished through inverting the light areas. Black (or dark) areas are not affected.

Hue   replaces the colors of the cloned area or pattern to affect the *hue* of the underlying color(s).

Saturation   replaces the *saturation* of the bottom image with that of the top image.

Color   combines the hue and saturation of the top and bottom pixels.

Luminosity   changes the brightness of the image on the lower layer.

If you experiment, you will see that a lot of different effects can be generated simply by changing the Mode setting for the Clone Stamp and Pattern Stamp tools.

Opacity Setting

The Opacity percentage determines the transparency of the painted image. The range is 0%, which is totally transparent (and thus, useless for the purpose of the cloning), to 100%, which is completely opaque (does not allow any of the underlying image to show through).

Aligned Setting

As you saw in the exercise using the Clone Stamp tool, the Aligned option keeps the area that is being cloned constant. Using Aligned, when you select an area to act as the source, release the mouse button, and move to another area of the image, the sample area will be relative to the location of the new point. When the Aligned option is not active, no matter where you place the Clone brush on the document, that selected area will be used.

PAINTING WITH THE PAINTBRUSH TOOL

Just as its name suggests, the Paintbrush tool gives you the ability to paint on your image, whether it's to create a background or to change the color of a portion of your image.

As with the other tools, you can change the tool options to create some interesting effects.

In the Paintbrush tool's Options bar, the Brush, Mode, and Opacity settings work similarly to how they do with the Clone Stamp and Pattern Stamp tools, the Wet Edges option gives the effect of watercolor on the edge of the paint. The Brush Dynamics settings change the way that the brush applies "paint" to the workspace.

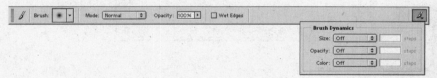

Setting Brush Dynamics

The Brush Dynamics settings can help you create some interesting looks when painting. For example, you can make your brush stroke fade or taper off at a designated distance. Let's experiment with some of the Brush Dynamic effects.

1. Select File ➤ New to create a new document. (Its size and resolution are not important for this example.)

2. Select the Paintbrush tool.

3. Leave the default settings for the other options and click the Brush Dynamics button (on the far right of the toolbar) to display the Brush Dynamics settings.

4. Click the Size pop-up menu and choose Fade. In the adjacent Steps text box, type **15**. Then click in the document window and drag with the Paintbrush tool to create a brush stroke. Notice how the stroke tapers off into nothingness.

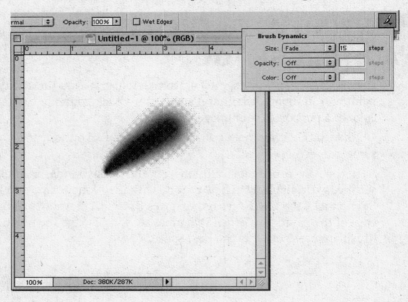

NOTE

The Stylus option will be available only if you have a drawing tablet (such as a Wacom tablet) attached to your computer. Stylus refers to the pen used to draw on a drawing tablet.

5. Press Ctrl/Command+Z to undo the brush stroke.

6. Select Fade from the Brush Setting's Opacity pop-up menu. In the Steps text box next to Opacity, type **15**. Draw a second brush stroke. Notice how the stroke not only tapers off, but also fades out.

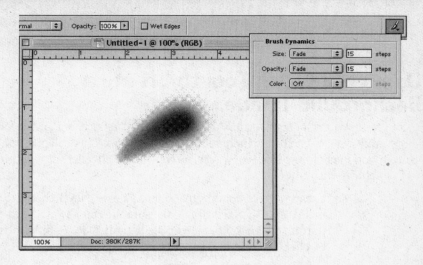

7. Press Ctrl/Command+Z to undo the brush stroke.

8. Select Fade from the Brush Setting's Color pop-up menu. In its Steps text box, type **7**. Color Fade tells the program to fade from the foreground color to the background color over a certain amount of time.

9. Click the background color swatch in the toolbar and select a different background color. Then create another brush stroke on your document.

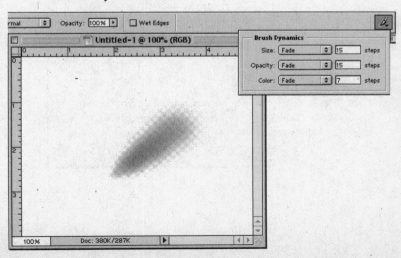

10. Turn off all of the Brush Dynamic settings and close the document.

Using the Brush Tool to Create a Background Image

Next, you will create a galaxy-like background using the Paintbrush tool and some of the filters included with Photoshop. This will give you a good idea of how this tool works, as well as the effects that you can achieve with filters.

1. Create a new document (select File ➢ New) that is 5×5 inches and 72 pixels dpi. Make sure the color swatches at the bottom of the toolbar are at the default Black/White setting by clicking the small squares.

2. Choose Edit ➢ Fill and fill the document with the foreground color.

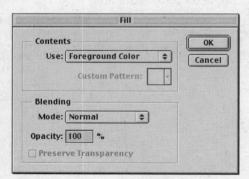

3. Select the Paintbrush tool.

4. If the Color palette isn't open, select Window ➤ Show Color to open it. Choose a nice shade of yellow.

5. Change the Brush setting to Soft Round, 65 pixels. Make sure all of the Brush Settings are set to Off.

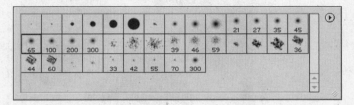

6. Create a diamond-like pattern on the workspace. Do this by painting on the workspace with the Paintbrush tool, overlapping the lines you create.

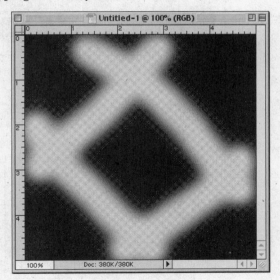

7. Change the Brush setting to Soft Round, 35 pixels and select a greenish color. Use the Paintbrush tool to create a checkerboard pattern over the pattern you just created.

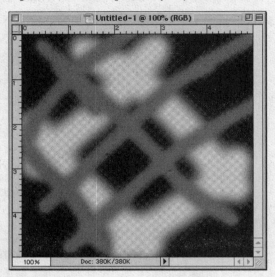

8. Select Filter ➢ Distort ➢ Twirl.

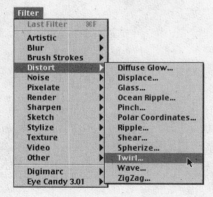

9. In the Twirl dialog box, set the Angle to its maximum level of 999 by either typing it into the text box or moving the slider all the way to the right.

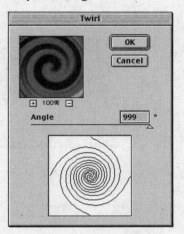

10. Select Filter ➢ Blur ➢ Gaussian Blur.

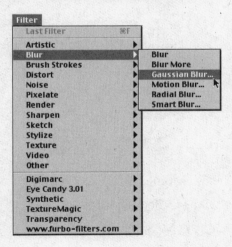

11. In the Gaussian Blur dialog box, set the Radius to **5** pixels. To see the effect before you click OK, select the Preview check box.

12. Choose Filter ➢ Render ➢ Lighting Effects.

13. In the Lighting Effects dialog box, set the following parameters:

Style: 2 O'Clock Spotlight

Light Type: Spotlight

Intensity: 17

Focus: 91

Gloss: −67

Material: −58

Exposure: 0

Ambience: 20

Texture Channel: Red

White Is High: Selected

Height: 96

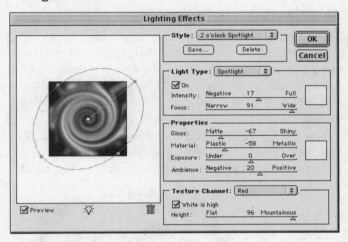

You now have a pattern that looks like a green-and-yellow galaxy.

OTHER TOOLS TO LEARN

Once you've mastered these tools, you'll find that Photoshop has other tools that do similar things but with added capabilities. You already know a lot of what you need to use these tools.

The Airbrush

The Airbrush tool simulates an artist's paint sprayer. Unlike the Paint Brush, with the Airbrush, paint builds up when you continue hold it in one place and press the mouse button—it "puddles" just as a real airbrush would. The Airbrush has brush size and blending mode options, just like the regular brush, but it also has a Pressure slider. Increasing pressure increases the darkness of the stroke.

Use the Airbrush for soft retouching effects, especially when colorizing grayscale drawings and photographs. The airbrush paints a soft spray of color that is unequaled for hazy glows and overlays of hue.

The Pencil

The Pencil is considered a Painting tool—even though it paints a hard-edged line that is visibly not anti-aliased. Use the Pencil whenever you want a coarser drawing-tool look. All the brush sizes, blending modes, and opacity options apply, just as they did with the Paintbrush and Airbrush.

Auto Erase is a feature exclusive to the Pencil tool. To try it out, follow these steps:

1. Select a 9-pixel pencil (fourth from the left on the Brushes palette) and set your foreground color to solid black. Screen color should be white.

2. In the Options bar, click on the box marked Auto Erase.

3. Draw a black line against a white background. Release the mouse button. Press the mouse button again as you draw over the black line you just created. No mystery here: Photoshop uses the background color to "erase" the line drawn in the foreground color.

The Paint Bucket Tool

You can use the Paint Bucket tool to fill selection or to fill a solid-colored area where no pixels are selected. Just choose the tool, and click the "drip" area of the bucket inside the area you want to fill with color.

By default, the Paint Bucket fills with the foreground color, but you can select a pattern instead in the Options bar. You may also choose a blending mode, use anti-aliasing, set Opacity, and direct Photoshop to fill only areas that are connected, or contiguous.

The Paint Bucket has a Tolerance setting, just like the Magic Wand and includes a check box in the Options bar that lets you fill all layers of an image with a color. This is useful if you've expanded the canvas size of an image and find your new image is surrounded on all sides with a transparent band. If you like, you can fill this area of all the layers at once.

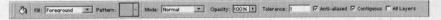

The Gradient Tool

The Gradient tool is used to create a smooth transitional fill between the foreground and background color within a given area. If there is a selection, the gradient will be applied to the selection. If there is no selection, the gradient is applied to the entire image. Gradients can begin with the foreground color and end with the background color or use a combination of colors. You can select the type of transition from a drop down-list in the Options bar.

You can also choose from five gradient types: linear, radial, angle, reflected gradient, and diamond gradient. Gradients are useful for creating soft sunset and dawn effects, adding three-dimensional shading to objects, generating backgrounds for graphics, or applying a gradient to a layer mask to allow blending a layer with another.

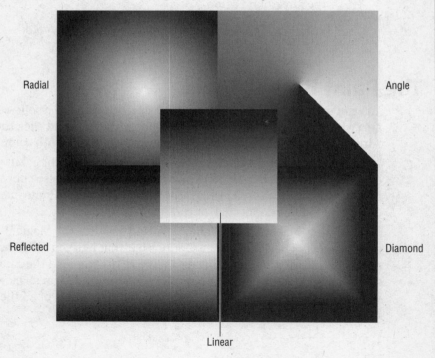

Radial

Angle

Reflected

Diamond

Linear

WHAT'S NEXT

We'll further our investigation of Photoshop's editing tools in the next chapter, in which you'll learn to use the Eraser, History and Art History Brushes, and tools to blur, smudge, and sharpen your images.

Chapter 4

USING IMAGE-MODIFICATION TOOLS IN PHOTOSHOP 6

You've already experimented with some modification tools (back in Chapter 3). Now it's time to work with some of the more advanced ones. The tools that you'll learn about in this chapter deal with erasing areas from an image, forms of cloning, and emulating a photographer's darkroom techniques.

Here, you'll learn how to use some of the more sophisticated image-editing tools, including the Eraser tools, for removing parts of your images; the History Brush and Art History Brush tools, for painting layers over layers; the Blur, Sharpen, and Smudge tools, for changing an image's focus; the Dodge and Burn tools, for lightening and darkening image areas.

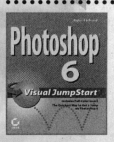

Adapted from *Photoshop 6 Visual JumpStart*
by Richard Schrand
ISBN 0-7821-2866-1   288 pages $19.99

ERASING WITH THE ERASER TOOLS

As you would expect, the Eraser tools allow you to erase portions of your image. Photoshop provides three separate tools for erasing: Eraser, Background Eraser, and Magic Eraser. As their names imply, these tools have specific functions to help you manipulate your images. To select a specific eraser, move your cursor over the Eraser tool in the toolbar and press and hold down the mouse button to make the pop-up menu appear.

Straightforward Erasing with the Eraser Tool

The Eraser tool simply erases anything it comes in contact with, which allows you to create some interesting layered effects. You will first try it with its default settings, and then see the effects of changing some tool options.

1. Open an image to practice on and select the Eraser tool in the toolbar by clicking it.

2. Move the cursor over the portion of the image you want to erase and, while holding down the mouse button, drag the Eraser tool over the area you want to remove.

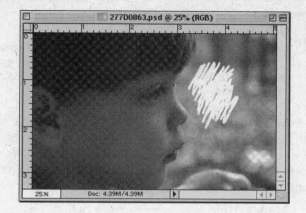

3. Select Edit ➢ Undo Eraser to return the image to its original state.

4. In the Options bar, change the brush size to Soft Round, 100 pixels and select the Wet Edges check box.

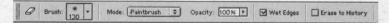

5. Erase the same area of your image. This time, as you continue holding down the mouse button, the erased area expands as if something wet were spreading across the image.

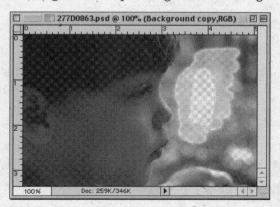

NOTE

The Wet Edges feature doesn't erase a selected area completely, because it is simulating erasing with water. To fully erase an area, go over it a few times. Make sure to release the mouse button and then press it down again before continuing to erase.

As you've seen, the Brush setting works in a similar way to how it does with the tools you've experimented with in previous chapters. The Wet Edge option gives a "wet brush" effect, where the edges of the erased area fade back to 100 percent opacity. The other settings on the Eraser tool's Options bar work as follows:

Mode setting   determines the way that the Eraser tool interacts with the image, giving you more control over the look of the erased area. Access the different modes by clicking the pop-up menu button.

Opacity setting   lets you determine the strength of the eraser effect: 0% has no effect on your image, and 100% completely erases the selected area. You can either type in a percentage or use the pop-up control.

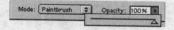

Erase to History setting   determines how the Eraser tool is affected by the History parameters you have assigned (see the "Painting with the History and Art History Brushes" section later in this chapter).

Getting More Control with the Background Eraser

You played with the Background Eraser tool a bit in Chapter 2, where you saw that it can be used to erase the background elements in an image, creating a transparency in the affected area. In the toolbar, the Background Eraser is represented by a pair of scissors over the eraser.

The Background Eraser's Options bar includes several settings that give you more control over the area that is to be erased.

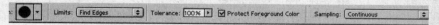

Brush setting works the same as it does with the main Eraser tool.

Limits setting specifies how the eraser will interact with the area. You have three choices:

Discontiguous erases a sampled color no matter where it appears in the image.

Contiguous erases only the area where the eraser is, removing the pixels surrounding that particular spot.

Find Edges preserves the sharpness of the nonselected areas near the area you want to erase.

Tolerance setting controls the color range for erasing. A low tolerance (down to 0%) erases a small range of colors; a higher tolerance (up to 100%) erases a wider area of colors.

Protect Foreground Color option protects areas of the picture that match the foreground color.

Sampling setting controls how colors are erased. There are three choices:

Continuous erases colors continuously as you drag the eraser across the image.

Once erases only the color you first click, which is handy for erasing single colored areas.

Background Swatch erases only the color specified in the background swatch in the toolbox.

TIP

The best use of the Background Eraser tool is to quickly create a "safe area" around a subject so you can erase the rest of the unwanted parts of your image more easily.

Let's try using the Background Eraser tool with some color controls.

1. Open an image that has a subject that can be separated from the background.

2. Select the Eyedropper tool in the toolbox.

3. Select a color in the subject.

4. Select the Background Eraser tool in the toolbox.

5. In the Background Eraser tool's Option bar, set the following options:

    Brush: Hard Round, 13 pixels

    Limits: Contiguous

    Tolerance: 50%

    Protect Foreground Color: Selected

    Sampling: Continuous

6. Begin erasing the area next to the color you just selected in your subject.

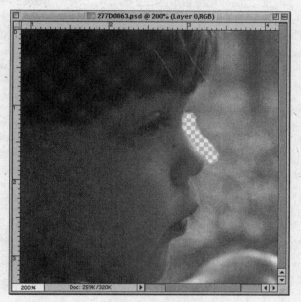

7. When you move into a new area of the picture where the subject color has changed, resample the color with the Eyedropper tool.

8. Select the Background Eraser and erase some more of the background.

9. Repeat steps 7 and 8 until you've outlined your subject.

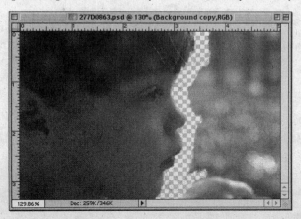

Color Erasing with the Magic Eraser Tool

The Magic Eraser tool is another tool you were introduced to in Chapter 2. As you saw in the example in that chapter, the Magic Eraser tool erases the specific color you select. The Magic Eraser tool's Options bar lets you control how colors will be erased.

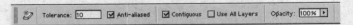

These options work as follows:

Tolerance setting   determines how many variations of a color the tool will affect. The lower the number, the fewer color variations it will recognize; the higher the number, the more variations it will affect.

Anti-aliased option   smoothes the edges of the erased area.

Contiguous option   erases colors only in the area you choose. If this option is not selected, all instances of the selected color throughout the picture are erased.

Use All Layers option   allows you to choose colors to be erased from any layer that might be in your document.

Opacity setting   controls how strong the erasure effect is. Its range is 0% (no affect) to 100% (the chosen color will be completely erased).

PAINTING WITH THE HISTORY AND ART HISTORY BRUSHES

The History Brush and Art History Brush are two fascinating tools that can help you create some fantastic effects. To work with these tools, you will need to have the History palette open, because they use a previous version of your image.

Painting Layers with the History Brush

In a nutshell, the History Brush tool allows you to paint areas of one layer onto another. It can be used to create sophisticated *montages* or to build other effects that would otherwise take a lot more time to create.

As an example, you will add some light effects to an image using the History Brush tool.

1. Open an image that could use some light effects.

2. Select Window ➤ Show History to open the History palette.

Part i

NOTE

Photoshop's History palette keeps track of all of the changes you've made to an image during the current working session, as a series of states. You can revert to a previous state simply by clicking it in the History palette. You can also save *snapshots* of an image at any stage it in its development and quickly retrieve the snapshot version from the History palette.

3. Click the circular button with the right-pointing arrow in the upper-right corner of the History palette and select New Snapshot from the palette's Options menu.

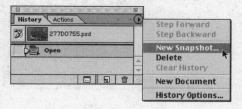

4. The New Snapshot dialog box will open. You can give the snapshot a name and tell Photoshop where the snapshot information will come from. In this case, leave the defaults and click OK.

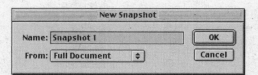

5. A new element named Snapshot 1 has been added to the History palette. Click this element to activate it.

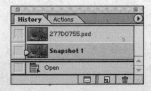

6. Open the Layers palette if it isn't already displayed (select Window ➤ Show Layers) and click the Create New Layer button. Click the eye icon for the Background to make it invisible. (This way, you will be able to see the History Brush effect.)

7. With this new layer selected, click the check box next to Snapshot 1 in the History palette. A paintbrush icon will appear.

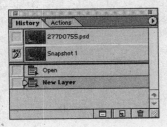

8. Select the History Brush in the toolbox.

9. In this example, you want to create streaks of light across the image. Set the following options in the History Brush's Options bar:

Brush: Soft Round, 65 pixels

Mode: Dissolve

Opacity: 100%

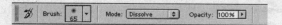

10. With the History Brush, paint a few streaks across the layer. As you do, you'll see the image you used as your snapshot appear.

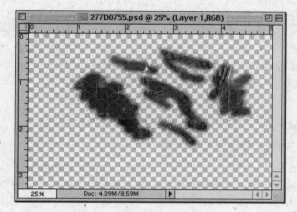

11. Change the Mode setting to Screen and paint over the streaks you already created. Notice how the image becomes much lighter.

12. Make the Background visible (click to display its eye icon in the Layers palette) to see how your streaks of light look.

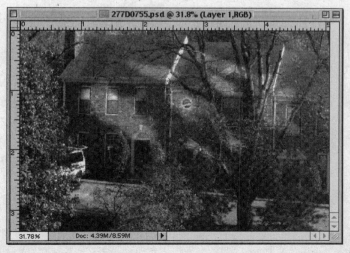

TIP

By using the History Brush with Mode set to Screen again, you can continue to lighten the areas for a stronger effect.

As you saw in this example, the Brush setting for the History Brush determines the size of the brush you will "paint" with. The Mode selections are the same as those in the Layers palette, but here they affect the brush strokes only. (You can also combine layer Mode effects with the History Brush.). As with the other tools, the Opacity setting determines how clear or opaque the brush strokes will be.

Making Masterpieces with the Art History Brush

With the Art History Brush tool, you can turn your image into a Picasso or van Gogh, or even an original masterpiece that looks like a painting. The keys to creating art effects with this tool are its Option bar settings. Along with the same Brush, Mode, and Opacity settings as the History Brush, the Art History Brush offers these options:

Style setting   determines how the "paint" is laid onto the layer. Access the different styles by clicking the pop-up menu button.

Fidelity setting   determines how true to the original the colors are. The lower the fidelity, the more variance there is from the original.

Area setting   specifies how large an area is covered by the paint strokes.

Spacing setting   determines how far apart the paint strokes are when they are laid onto the layer.

To create a painterly masterpiece, continue working with the practice document you've been using for the previous exercises or open another image, and then do the following:

1. Open the History palette's Options Menu, select New Snapshot, and click OK in the New Snapshot dialog box to accept the defaults.

2. In the Layers palette, select the snapshot you just created. Then click the Create New Layer button to add a new layer. (Keep the Background visible.)

3. With this new layer selected, click the check box next to Snapshot 2 in the History palette.

4. Select the Art History Brush from the toolbox.

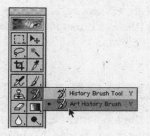

5. In the Art History Brush's Options bar, set the following options:

   Brush: Chalk, 23 pixels

   Mode: Normal

   Opacity: 100%

   Style: Dab

   Fidelity: 61%

   Area: 5 px

   Spacing: 48%

6. With the Art History Brush, paint onto Layer 1.

7. Select File ➤ Save and save this file as a layered Photoshop (.psd) file. We'll use it later in the book when discussing lighting effects.

Using Photographer's Tools

Now let's look at the tools included in Photoshop that emulate techniques photographers use to modify photos: the Blur, Sharpen, Smudge, Dodge, and Burn tools.

Softening Areas with the Blur Tool

Sometimes, a photograph needs a little help to make it really stand out. In many cases, you can improve a picture by separating the subject from the background. This is where the Blur tool can come in handy. (The Blur tool is the one that looks like a big raindrop in the toolbox.)

Let's see how the Blur tool works.

1. Open a photograph that has a subject that needs to stand out from the background.

2. Select the Blur tool in the toolbox.

3. In the Blur tool's Option bar, select a large brush and change the Pressure setting to 95%. Leave the other settings at their defaults.

4. Click and drag the Blur tool over the image background. You can do this as many times as you like (make sure to release the mouse button and then depress it again before going over an area you've already worked on).

TIP

To protect your foreground or your subject, use the Lasso tool and outline the subject, then choose Select ➤ Inverse to reverse the outlined and selected area.

Gaining Clarity with the Sharpen Tool

If there are areas in your photograph that you would like to make clearer, you can try using the Sharpen tool. You can continue working with the photo you used the Blur tool on to see how the Sharpen tool works.

1. Click and hold down the mouse button on the Blur tool icon, and then select the Sharpen tool from the pop-up list.

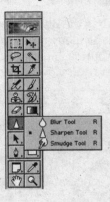

2. In the Sharpen tool's Option bar, set the brush size to Soft Round, 100 pixels and the Pressure setting to 100%. Leave the other settings at their defaults.

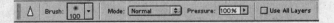

WARNING

You can oversharpen an image very quickly, making the sharpened area look strange to the viewer. Make sure you go over an area only once with the Sharpen tool.

3. Click and drag the Sharpen tool over the area of the image that you want to sharpen.

Smearing Areas with the Smudge Tool

You can use the Smudge tool to do quick repairs on a damaged photograph, to make edges blend better, or to get rid of unwanted blemishes or dark rings under the eyes. The tool works by literally smearing the pixel information. Because it functions this way, you should be careful to work with small strokes as you use this tool.

TIP

With careful use of the Smudge tool, you can make your friends look ten years younger. So if you do this type of work on a photograph, expect high praise for your amazing photographic prowess.

The Smudge tool is in the same toolbox spot as the Blur and Sharpen tools. To select it, click and hold down the mouse button on the Blur tool icon, and then select the Smudge tool from the pop-up list.

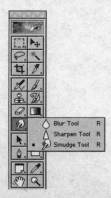

As an example, notice the circles under this poor author's eyes. Using the Smudge tool with a brush size of Soft Round, 21 pixels and a Pressure setting of 25%, I can make those bags quickly disappear.

You blend from your starting point to your ending point. So to make this work, I start from beneath the lower eyelid and move upward slightly, until the bags are gone.

The Smudge tool's Finger Painting option lets you add color while smudging. When you select this option, the Smudge tool smudges using the selected foreground color at the beginning of each dragged stroke.

Lightening Shadows with the Dodge Tool

Some of your photos may have unwanted shadows. You will want to lessen their effect on the overall image by lightening them, call *dodging* in photographic jargon. This is what the Dodge tool can do. You can, through the tool's Range setting, lighten the shadows, *midtones*, and highlights of the image to give it a whole new look.

TIP

Make sure to keep the Exposure control set fairly low. Much like the Opacity control, Exposure determines how drastically a modification affects the image. By keeping it low, you can incrementally make changes until you have the image just the way you want it.

Try using the Dodge tool on a photo with dark areas, such as the example shown here.

1. Choose the Dodge tool (which looks like a straight pin with an oversized ball on top) from the toolbox.

2. In the Dodge tool's Options bar, set the following options:

   Brush: Soft Round (any size you like)

   Range: Midtones

   Exposure: 11%

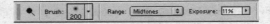

3. Click and drag with the Dodge tool to lighten areas of the photo. Use small strokes as you work with the Dodge tool, focusing on specific areas first, and then the surrounding areas afterward. This will allow for a nicer blending effect.

4. Switch between Midtones and Highlights until you have lightened the features, such as the eyes in this example, as you want them.

NOTE

In this example, if I had used the Shadow selection for the Range, I would have lightened the eyelashes too much, because this tool works on the darkest pixels first.

Darkening Areas with the Burn Tool

Burning, in the photographic sense, means to darken an area. That's just what the Burn tool does—it darkens areas that might be overexposed. To see how this affects your photograph, do the following:

1. Select the Burn tool from the Dodge tool toolbox position's pop-up list. (It's the one that looks like a hand.)

2. In the Burn tool's option bar, set the following options:

    Brush: Soft Round (any size you like)

    Range: Highlights

    Exposure: 10%

3. Click and drag the Burn tool over the brightest area of your picture. For example, in the photo used in the previous exercise, spots on the shirt are too bright. Dragging the Burn tool over them tones down the bright areas.

3. Switch between Highlights and Midtones until you're satisfied with the look of your image.

WHAT'S NEXT

Unless you're an artist, you probably won't create many Photoshop
images from scratch. In most cases, you'll be working with a photographic image or other artwork that you've scanned in or grabbed with
your digital camera. The next chapter will show you how these devices
complement Photoshop.

Chapter 5
GETTING IMAGES INTO PHOTOSHOP

I f you want to put photographs into your Web pages, presentations, newsletters, and other applications, you'll need to get that information into a computer. Today, designers have a whole range of ways to do this—from flatbed scanners to digital cameras. There are even companies that will digitize images for you.

This chapter is dedicated to all of this exciting technology, as well as the more down-to-earth issue of positioning, cropping, and scaling digitized images after they are captured so you can begin working on them in Photoshop.

Adapted from *Photoshop 5.5 for the Web*
by Matt Straznitskas
ISBN 0-7821-2605-7   670 pages $39.99

What Is Digitizing?

Digitizing is the process of turning real-world, analog information into a format that can be used by computers. The converted information is called *digital* because it is made up of strings of ones and zeroes (digits).

Visual information can be digitized in a number of ways. Scanners capture a hard-copy photograph so that it can be edited in Photoshop. Digital cameras skip the scanning process altogether and directly digitize real-world objects like people, places, and things.

Scanning

Flatbed scanners (the most common type) look and operate something like a photocopier. You lift the lid, place the original face down on the scanner's glass, and either push a button or activate a software interface within Photoshop. Then a moving light bar reflects light off your original into a sensor. Electronics within the scanner convert the analog image into digital format and direct it on to your computer and Photoshop. Many scanners have built-in image manipulation capabilities. They can sharpen, scale, and adjust brightness or contrast even before Photoshop gets ahold of the pixels. However, most of the time you'll be doing the bulk of your image manipulation within Photoshop. The tricky part is getting the image into your favorite pixel editor in the first place.

Every scanner comes with its own software interface, but, fortunately, all of them fit right into Photoshop's File ➤ Import menu. When I need to scan an image, I fire up my AGFA Arcus II color scanner and launch Photoshop. The scanner has special scanning software, called FotoLook, that is accessed via Photoshop's File ➤ Import command. Figure 5.1 presents the FotoLook interface.

While every scanner/software combination is somewhat different, the process of scanning is essentially the same. Rather than do the entire scan first, it's best to test it using the Preview option. Preview does a very quick scan to show you if everything is OK. As you can see in Figure 5.2, I managed to scan in a picture of my truck upside-down.

WARNING

It is important to clean any dust off the scanner's glass surface before scanning. Otherwise, your image will be marred by little white specks.

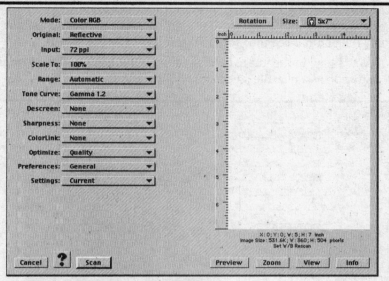

FIGURE 5.1: The FotoLook interface

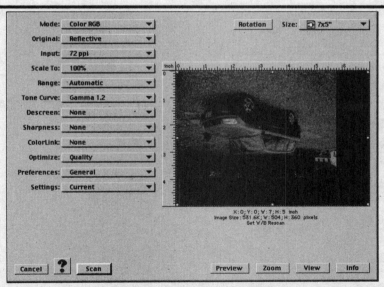

FIGURE 5.2: Oops, the Preview shows that I put the image in the scanner upside down.

After a quick manual flip, I preview the image again. This time, I see a lot of space around the image. I use the software's selection tools so that only the photo is scanned (see Figure 5.3).

Now I scan in the image for real, and it is automatically dumped into Photoshop as a new file (see Figure 5.4).

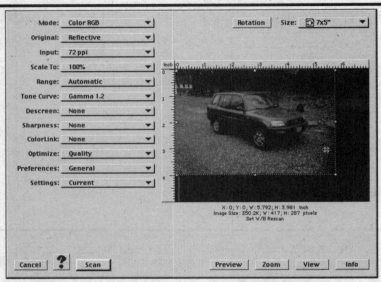

FIGURE 5.3: Using the selection tools so that only the photo is scanned, not the area around the photo

FIGURE 5.4: The software automatically dumps the scan into Photoshop as a new file.

Sometimes you'll either forget to preview an image or intentionally do so because you think everything is set up properly. Often, the result is an image scanned upside-down or at a 90-degree angle. To reorient the file, just choose Edit ➤ Transform ➤ and whichever rotation command you need.

NOTE

Most scanned images are somewhat blurry and often benefit from having the Unsharp Mask filter applied.

Your best bet for learning how to use your scanner's software is to play with it, trying to scan different kinds of images and learning the basic controls. While Photoshop can cure multiple ills, it's best to get the best possible image in the first place.

Digital Cameras

Due to their popularity, lots of digital cameras are on the market, and it's easy to see why—they provide a quick, immediate way to capture images. No running to the pharmacy to get your pictures developed; just link your camera and computer with a USB or serial cable, or, perhaps, pop a CompactFlash or SmartMedia card into a card reader. Within a few seconds, your images have been transferred to your computer and are ready to work on.

I use an Epson digital camera, which I purchased because I was used to traditional cameras and liked the Epson's familiar zoom, built-in flash, and aperture settings.

Once you take your photos, you need to physically get them into your computer. While some cameras store images on removable floppy disks, the Epson ships with a special software/cable combination to download your pics into either a Mac or Windows computer. Figure 5.5 displays the software interface and a series of photos taken with the camera.

The software provides an Export Photos option that can export the images to a Photoshop-friendly format. I use the PICT format because it retains the maximum amount of image data, unlike the JPEG format that throws out information for the sake of file size. Figure 5.6 shows the result of opening an exported image in Photoshop.

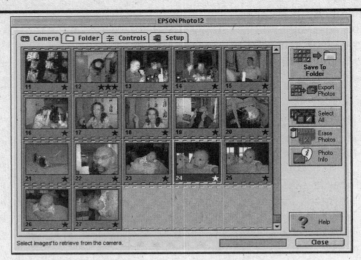

FIGURE 5.5: A selection of pictures taken with a digital camera, displayed in the Epson software

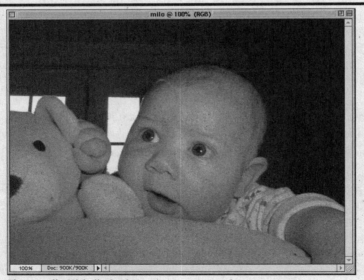

Photo credit: Michelle Carrier

FIGURE 5.6: An image exported with the Epson software and opened in Photoshop.

Digital cameras are an exciting tool, and one that will probably become a basic part of your repertoire. Prices are dropping, resolution is increasing, and the features available in the latest digital cameras are jaw-dropping.

Predigitized Images

Stock photo houses, like Photodisc and Digital Stock, provide a vast array of images that can be purchased and delivered to you either online or as a CD-ROM. Also, Kodak's PhotoCD service puts pictures taken with a traditional camera directly on a CD-ROM. There are now Web-based equivalents of this service, providing Internet delivery of your images. All of these services eliminate the need for purchasing a scanner, and they can be a good alternative to purchasing digitizing equipment if you prefer traditional cameras or don't plan on capturing images on a regular basis.

NOTE

One of the nice things about some Photodisc images, particularly the object collections, is that they come with paths that are already created. This makes selecting an object from the background very easy.

Positioning

Photoshop provides three ways to help position digitized images and other graphic elements, and they all work together. Rulers provide indicators that sit around the left and top edges of the graphic. Guides are horizontal and vertical rules that you can place around an image area. The Grid feature places a regular structure over an image and makes lining up image elements a snap.

Rulers

To make rulers visible, select View ➤ Show Rulers (or press Ctrl+R). As Figure 5.8 shows, rulers are placed along the left and top sides of the image.

FIGURE 5.7: Rulers visible along the left and top sides of the image

Set the zero point by clicking and dragging from the graphic's upper-left corner. When you release, a new zero point is established. To make the zero point return to its original position, double-click in the square in the upper-left corner.

TIP

Photoshop provides the Measure tool to measure non-90-degree angles. To use the tool, simply select it from the Toolbar and click from one point to another. Measurements are reflected in the Info palette.

Guides

Guides are accessed by selecting View ➤ Show Rulers and then clicking and dragging from the horizontal and vertical ruler area. Figure 5.9 shows four guides dragged onto the image.

To adjust the positioning of a guide, select the Move tool from the Toolbar and place it on the guide you'd like to move. The cursor changes to a different icon, indicating that it's close enough to move the guide.

Guides don't print, but more importantly, they aren't visible when an image is converted to a GIF or JPEG (common Web file formats) and viewed in a Web browser. Figure 5.8 shows and image with four guides.

FIGURE 5.8: An image with four guides

The View menu provides three other guides-related options:

Snap to Guides forces any element that you move to automatically snap to a nearby guide.

Lock Guides locks all guides into place so you don't mistakenly move them during image editing. Reselect View ➤ Lock Guides to move a guide.

Clear Guides allows you to start fresh, which is a convenient housecleaning feature.

TIP

To change the color or style of the guides, select Edit ➤ Preferences ➤ Guides & Grid.

Grid

The Grid feature is a very helpful option for creating Web layouts with a rigid, modern structure. To activate the Grid feature, select View ➤ Show Grid (or press Ctrl+'). A grid of lines is placed over the current image (see Figure 5.9).

By selecting View ➤ Snap to Grid, any elements that you move will automatically position along the structure. You can adjust the spacing of the Gridlines and Subdivision options by selecting Edit ➤ Preferences ➤ Guides & Grid.

FIGURE 5.9: An image with the Grid feature turned on

CROPPING

Designers spend a good deal of their time cropping images so that they precisely mortise together when placed on a Web page *and* create the smallest file size possible. Photoshop provides two commands (Canvas Size and Crop) and one tool (Crop) to slice away parts of an image.

The Canvas Size Command

The quickest but least precise way to crop a graphic is with the Image ➢ Canvas Size command. From the Canvas Size dialog box (shown next), you can adjust the Width and Height values. The Anchor option provides 9 locations from where new canvas space will be added or subtracted.

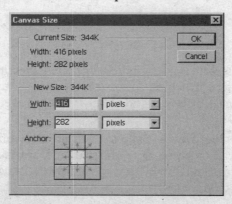

If you input a Width and/or Height amount that is less than the current value, you will be warned that your image is about to be clipped.

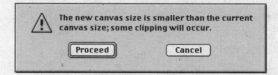

Figure 5.10 shows my earlier scan with a new canvas height value of 100 pixels.

FIGURE 5.10: A graphic clipped via the Canvas Size command

NOTE

The Canvas Size command is more commonly used to add space around an image.

The Crop Command

The Crop command works in conjunction with the selection tools and is particularly effective when used with the Guides/Snap to Guides feature.

As you may recall, the scan of my truck has a lot of "dead" area. To clip this away, set up four guides around the image and then, with the Snap to Guides feature on, draw a rectangular selection around it (see Figure 5.11).

To clip the image, select Image ➤ Crop. As Figure 5.12 shows, the graphic is now more appropriately framed.

FIGURE 5.11: The scanned image with guides and an active rectangular selection marquee

FIGURE 5.12: The cropped image

TIP

Prior to Version 6.0, Photoshop's Crop command could only crop a rectangular selection at right angles to the image borders. You can now use any selection to crop an image. Photoshop uses the highest, lowest, leftmost, and rightmost points of the selection as the boundaries for the crop, as shown in Figure 5.13.

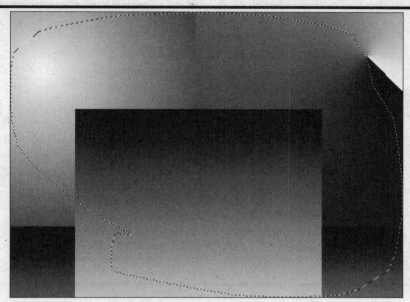

FIGURE 5.13: Cropping an irregular selection

The Crop Tool

The main advantage of using the Crop tool is the ability to quickly adjust a selection area and to crop an image without using a menu command—it's the "hands-on" way to crop.

To use the tool, select it from the Toolbar and click and drag within an image to define the area to crop. As you can see in Figure 5.14, the result is a selection marquee with handles.

You can use the Crop tool to adjust the dimensions of the selection area, but the tool's real power is its ability to rotate an area and then crop it with the Image ➢ Crop command. Figure 5.15 shows a rotated selection and the results of using the Crop command.

TIP

Double-click the Crop tool to access the Cropping Tool Options palette and create fixed-size crop selections.

FIGURE 5.14: Using the Crop tool results in a selection with adjustment handles.

FIGURE 5.15: Rotating a selection area and using the Image ➢ Crop command to crop and reorient the image

Scaling

When you adjust the size of an image, all of the action happens in the Image Size dialog box.

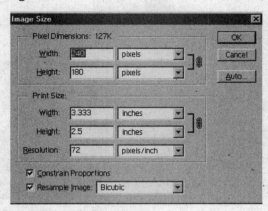

The dialog box is broken up into two distinct areas: Pixel Dimensions and Print Size. If you deactivate the Resample Image option, the Pixel Dimensions feature is unavailable. Since the print size of the graphic is irrelevant to Web designers, it is important to keep the Resample Image option activated.

The Resample Image feature is an algorithm that tries to figure out what an image should look like if it were shrunk or enlarged. Because Photoshop images are made up of little colored squares, the program guesses what color the remaining or additional squares should be.

In Figure 5.16, at top I have taken the captured frame from a cow video and reduced it from 240 pixels wide by 180 pixels high to 100 pixels wide by 75 pixels high. It looks quite good at that size—Photoshop has done an excellent job of figuring out which pixels to remove.

In the middle image, however, I took the 100 × 75 image and scaled it up to 300 × 225. As you can see, the image has lost much of its sharpness. Zooming in on the face of one of the cows shows how much detail has been lost in the bottom image. (Clearly, making an image larger is a major no-no in Photoshop. The Scaling feature does a good job figuring out what information to discard, but it can't guess at missing detail. Always scale down, not up. If you need an image to be bigger, scan it at a higher resolution.

FIGURE 5.16: Reducing the image to 100 × 75

TIP

Scaling an image down will tend to soften it. Apply the Unsharp Mask filter (select Filter ➤ Sharpen ➤ Unsharp Mask) if it becomes too blurry.

WHAT'S NEXT

This concludes Part I and our discussion of Photoshop's most basic features. Next, we'll look at Photoshop's more advanced features in some depth, including Layers, Channels, Paths, and color correction.

PART ii
PHOTOSHOP IN DEPTH

Chapter 6

LAYERING YOUR IMAGE

All digital images are completely flat; even the most three-dimensional-looking images only *look* as if they have depth. Photoshop images appear on flat screens, but they can look three-dimensional in part because of the power of layers to help create the illusion.

Layers are critical to working dynamically in Photoshop. Images on individual layers can be edited separately and moved independently of each other. The stacking order of layers can help determine the position of visual elements within the picture plane. In short, working with layers gives you tremendous control over the image during the process of creating it.

This chapter will help you learn how to create and blend layers, use layer styles, consolidate layers, and work with Type layers.

Adapted from *Mastering Photoshop 6*
by Steve Romaniello
ISBN 0-7821-2841-6   896 pages $49.99

THE ILLUSION OF DEPTH

The illusion of three-dimensionality is really quite remarkable, but because we see it so often, we take it for granted. The visual effect of depth on a flat surface is created by the use of techniques that mimic what we see in the world with the stereoscopic vision provided by our two eyes.

One technique, called one-point perspective, achieves the effect by the use of converging lines that intersect at a vanishing point. An object whose contours align with the perspective lines will appear to recede in space.

Another method of producing the effect of depth is to adjust the relative scale of visual elements in an image. Larger objects appear closer to the viewer than smaller ones. Because this visual phenomenon is a naturally occurring characteristic of sight in the 3D world, when we see it in a picture we subconsciously draw the conclusion that the objects exist in space when, in fact, the picture is two-dimensional.

The position of an object in an image also contributes to the illusion of depth. If one element blocks out a portion of another element, the obstructing element will appear to be in front of the obstructed one. Another common device, atmospheric perspective, uses tonality to simulate distance. As objects recede in space, they appear lighter and less distinct due to the presence of dust and haze in the air.

The fact remains, however, that no matter how many devices are used to produce three-dimensionality, and no matter how deep the image appears, unless its surface is textured, it is as flat as a pancake.

Photoshop images are close to being an exception to the flat-as-a-pancake rule. They appear on screen as flat images of colored light, and they have a specific height and width. They can also have depth in the form of *layers*. A Photoshop layer is like a piece of clear glass (see Figure 6.1). Parts of the image can be pasted to the glass. If you have different parts of the image separated onto multiple layers, you can shuffle their position in the stack, allowing one part of the image to appear in front of another. Because the layers isolate each part of the image, you have the added advantage of being to able to individually control the contents of each layer separately.

FIGURE 6.1: Layers in a Photoshop document

When a part of the image is isolated on an individual layer, it can be singled out and manipulated at any time. A layer can be moved horizontally or vertically, or repositioned anywhere in the stack, to help produce the illusion of depth. The color relations of pixels on superimposed layers can be modified, and their level of opacity can be adjusted. Special layer styles can be applied to produce realistic shadows, embosses, textures, patterns, and glowing effects.

Part ii

LOOKING AT THE LAYERS PALETTE

At the heart of all this power is the Layers palette (shown in Figure 6.2). It is the control center from which most layer operations are performed. By default, the Layers palette is clustered with the Channels and the Paths palettes, (unless you've moved it to the Palette Well or dropped it into a different grouping). If the Layers palette is not displayed, you can access it by choosing Window ➢ Show Layers or by pressing the F7 key on an extended keyboard.

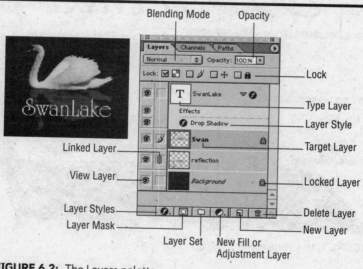

FIGURE 6.2: The Layers palette

Each layer in the palette is separated from the one directly below or above it by a thin line. Each layer's row includes a thumbnail of the layer's contents, the layer's name, and any layer styles, masks, or locks applied to that layer. In the far left column is an eye icon which, when displayed, indicates that the contents of the layer are visible. Immediately to the right of this visibility indicator is another column that displays a brush icon if the layer is the target layer, a small chain icon if the layer is linked to another layer, or a mask icon if the layer is a Fill or Adjustment layer.

Above the layer stack are Lock check boxes, which enable you to lock the transparency (prevent any changes to be made to transparent portion of the layer), editing (block changes to all portions of the layer), and movement (prevent moving of layer contents). At the top-left of the Layers palette is a list of blending modes that can alter the color relations of layers in the stack. And to the right of the blending modes is the Opacity slider that controls the level of transparency of a targeted layer's contents.

Many layer actions can be accessed from the palette pull-down menu (shown in Figure 6.3). Clicking the small triangular icon on the top-right of the palette reveals these options.

FIGURE 6.3: The Layers palette pull-down menu

The Background Layer

When you scan or import an image from another program and open it in Photoshop, the Layers palette displays one thumbnail, labeled *Background*. You can think of the Background as an image mounted to a board. If you were to cut away a portion of the image with an X-ACTO knife, you would see the board underneath—in this case, the background color behind the Background contents. The contents of all of the layers float on top of the Background. Unlike a layer, the Background is opaque and cannot support transparency. If the document contains more than one layer, the Background is always at the bottom of the stack and cannot be moved and placed in a higher position. When new layers are added to the document, their content always appears in front of the Background.

By default, the Background is locked. If you want move its contents, adjust its opacity, or reposition it in the Layers stack, you need to convert it to a layer. Like many of Photoshop's operations, there is more than one way to perform this task. To convert the Background into a layer from the menu, choose Layer ➢ New ➢ Layer From Background. The quickest method is simply to convert the Background from the Layers palette, following these steps:

Macintosh   Option-click the Background's name or thumbnail to display the New Layer dialog box. Enter a name for the new layer in the Name field and click OK.

Windows   Alt-click the Background's *name* to automatically change it into a layer named Layer 0. Alternatively, Alt-click the Background's *thumbnail* to display the New Layer dialog box, then enter a name for the new layer in the Name field and click OK.

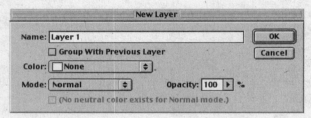

By default, Photoshop names the converted layer Layer 0, but I recommend that you give it a name that readily identifies it. The New Layer dialog box also lets you color-code your layer and adjust its opacity. You can also group it with other layers if, for example, you're using it to make a clipping group. See Chapter 7 for more on clipping.

TIP

If your image is composed entirely of layers, you can convert one of your layers into a Background. Target a layer and choose Layer ➤ New ➤ Background From Layer.

TIP

Naming your layers is essential to establishing an efficient workflow. The default numbers that Photoshop assigns to new layers become quite anonymous when their content is too small to be recognized on the thumbnail or if there are 30 or 40 of them in the document. In addition, as you move layers around in the Layers palette, you'll soon find that Layer 3 may be above Layer 9, or in some other non-logical order. Naming each layer with a descriptive title is a fast way to organize the components of your image for easy identification.

Naming Layers

To change the name of a layer, use one of these methods to bring up the Layer Properties dialog box:

- ▶ Option-click (Mac) or Alt-double-click (Win) the layer name in the Layers palette.

- ▶ Control-click (Mac) or right-click (Win) a layer and choose Layer Properties from the context-sensitive shortcut menu.

- ▶ From the Layers palette pop-up menu, choose Layer Properties.

In the dialog box, type a name in the Name field and click OK.

Viewing and Targeting Layers

The content of a layer can be concealed or revealed by clicking the eye icon in the first column of the Layers palette. To reveal or conceal the contents of more than one layer at a time, click the eye next to each of the desired layers. To conceal all but one layer, press the Option or Alt key while clicking its eye icon. With the same key held down, click the icon again to reveal all layers.

Choosing Your Thumbnail Size

The thumbnails that represent each layer display the content in miniature. You can choose from three different sizes of thumbnails, or you can choose to display no thumbnail at all. To specify a thumbnail display, pull down the palette menu and choose Palette Options. In the dialog box that opens (Figure 6.4), click the desired thumbnail size and then click OK.

FIGURE 6.4: Options for Layers palette thumbnails

Targeting a Layer

You can apply virtually any Photoshop operation to affect the contents of a layer, but first you must target the layer you want. A *targeted* layer is active and ready to be edited. To target a layer, click its name, which appears to the right of the thumbnail. You will see a colored highlight in the text field and a brush symbol in the second column to the left of the layer's thumbnail (as in Figure 6.5). Only one layer can be targeted at a time; a targeted layer must be visible to be affected. Certain effects can be applied to multiple layers simultaneously by linking them (see "Linking Layers" below) or grouping them.

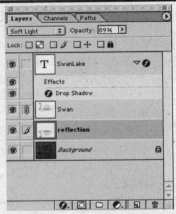

FIGURE 6.5: The swan's *reflection* is the targeted layer.

Understanding Transparency and Opacity

Since transparency is invisible, it's difficult to display. If a color like white represents transparency, how is the viewer to know what is transparent, what is translucent, and what is opaque? Photoshop solves this problem by displaying transparency using two colors in the form of a checkerboard.

If you see an area on a layer that is displayed as a gray checkerboard, then the area is totally transparent. This means that either it is devoid of pixels or the pixels are completely transparent. If it's displayed as a combination of image and checkerboard, then it is semitransparent; and if it's displayed totally as image, then it's opaque. Figure 6.6 illustrates the difference between opaque and semitransparent images.

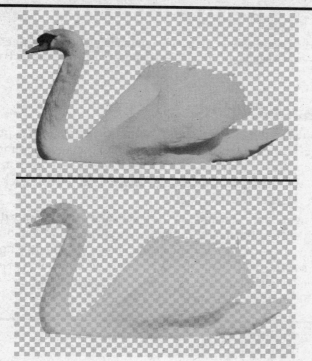

FIGURE 6.6: The swan at the top is displayed at 100% opacity; the swan at the bottom is displayed at 50% opacity.

If only one layer is displayed and its content is surrounded by areas of transparency, the image will appear against a gray checkerboard. If the color of the image is predominantly gray and the checkerboard becomes difficult to see, the color and size of the checkerboard can be changed in the Transparency & Gamut Preferences to better reveal the image.

Controlling Opacity

The Opacity slider enables you to adjust the level of transparency of all the pixels on a targeted layer, so that you can see through the image to the underlying layers in the stack. Click the arrow next to the Opacity field on the Layers palette; a slider pops up, which you can drag right to increase or left to decrease opacity. Or enter a value from 0 to 100 percent directly in the box.

Part ii

TIP

If any tool is active other than the painting and editing tools, you can press any number between 1 and 100 to change the Opacity value of the targeted layer.

Changing Layer Order

The stacking order in the Layers palette determines the plane of depth where the visual elements appear. The content of the topmost layer in the Layers palette appears in the front of the image. The further down in the stack a layer is, the farther back its content appears, all the way back to the bottommost layer or the Background.

You can change a layer's position in the stack, and consequently its visual plane of depth in the image. In the Layers palette, click and drag the thumbnail or name of the layer you wish to move. As you drag up or down, you will see the division line between layers become bold (as in Figure 6.7). The bold line indicates the new location where the layer will appear when the mouse is released.

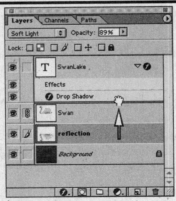

FIGURE 6.7: You can change a layer's position in the stacking order.

Another method of changing the position of the layer in the stack is to choose an option under Layer ➤ Arrange, or use the equivalent key command. In the Arrange submenu, you are presented with four options, as shown in Table 6.1.

TABLE 6.1:   Shortcuts for Positioning Layers

POSITION	MACINTOSH SHORTCUT	WINDOWS SHORTCUT	RESULT
Bring To Front	Shift+Cmd+]	Shift+Ctrl+]	Moves the layer to the top of the stack
Bring Forward	Cmd+]	Ctrl+]	Moves the layer on top of the layer immediately above it
Send Backward	Cmd+[	Ctrl+[	Moves the layer under the layer immediately below it
Send To Back	Shift+Cmd+[	Shift+Ctrl+[	Moves the layer to the bottom of the stack but in front of the Background

Linking Layers

Let's say you've positioned two elements of a logo on separate layers, and you are quite content with their visual relation to each other, except that they are a little too large and they need to be moved a half inch to the left. You can transform or move two layers simultaneously by *linking* them.

To link one or more layers, target one of the layers. Click in the column to the immediate left of the thumbnail on the layers that you want to include in the link. A chain icon appears, like the one next to the text layer in Figure 6.8, indicating that the layers are linked. You can then choose the Move tool or any transformation function (Edit ➢ Transform), and the layers will scale, rotate, distort, etc., all together.

WARNING

When you apply a transformation operation to linked layers, the transformation marquee will surround only the content of the targeted layer. If you proceed with the operation, all of the linked elements will transform.

Linked layers are used for the purpose of transforming and moving multiple layers simultaneously. To apply other effects to multiple layers, there are specific layer-based operations like the following.

Adjustment Layers   for color, brightness, and contrast adjustments and color mapping functions (see Chapter 9).

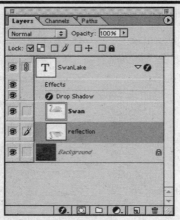

FIGURE 6.8: Linked layers are indicated with a chain icon. Here the reflection is linked to the Type layer.

Layer Masking to conceal and reveal portions of two sequential layers in the stack.

Blending Modes to apply a preprogrammed color formula to affect the relation between the pixels on a layer and the layer immediately below it in the stack.

Layer Sets for grouping, opacity control, positioning of multiple layers in the stack, and transforming or moving layers (see the following section).

Fill Layers to apply a solid color, gradient, or pattern to an independent layer. When the opacity is adjusted, the Fill layer affects the underlying layer. A Fill layer also contains a layer mask, so that the color, gradient, or pattern can be superimposed onto a specific area of the image.

Clipping Groups for using the content of one layer to clip portions of another.

Grouping Layers in Layer Sets

Earlier versions of Photoshop supported a mere 99 layers; Photoshop 6 now supports an unlimited number. The potential to produce enormous quantities of layers made a layer-management tool an absolute necessity. *Layer sets* have been introduced to let you consolidate contiguous layers into a folder on the Layers palette. By highlighting the folder, you can apply certain operations to the layers as a group. The layers in a layer set, like Swan and Reflection in Figure 6.9, can be can simultaneously revealed or concealed by clicking the eye icon for the set in the Layers palette; the whole set can be repositioned in the stack, moved, and—like linked layers—transformed using any of the transformation tools.

FIGURE 6.9: The Swan and Reflection layers make up a layer set.

NOTE

Although you can perform transformations and repositioning to both layer sets and linked layers, layer sets differ from linked layers in that they contain contiguous layers—that is, layers that are sequenced immediately above or below each other in the stack. Layers that are linked can be anywhere in the stack.

You can also determine which color channels will be affected. To reveal the layers within the set, click the triangle to the left of the folder so that it points down. To conceal the contents of the layer set to eliminate clutter, click the triangle so that it points to the right.

There are a few different ways to create a new layer set:

▶ From the Layer menu, choose Layer ➢ New ➢ Layer Set.

▶ From the Layers palette menu, choose New Layer Set.

▶ Click the Layer Set icon in the Layers palette. By default, the first layer set will be named Set 1.

With the first two commands, the Layer Set dialog box appears. You can name the layer set, color-code it, and specify the color channels of which the images will be composed.

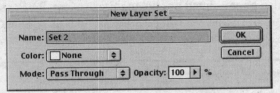

To add a layer to a set, drag the layer name to the layer set.

TIP

A fast way to create a layer set is to link the layers that you want in the set. Then choose Layer ➢ New ➢ Layer Set From Linked. All of the linked layers will be consolidated into one set.

WARNING

However, when you convert linked layers into a layer set, they will all become contiguous and their position in the stack may change.

Locking Layers

Photoshop 6 offers four controls in the Layers palette that prevent a layer from being modified. Each lock is represented by an icon at the top of the palette; to lock a layer, target the layer and check the box for the lock type you want.

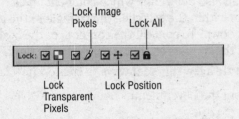

Lock Transparent Pixels   This function is comparable to Preserve Transparency in earlier versions of the software. It protects the areas of the targeted layer that don't contain pixels from being edited. If you attempt to paint on a transparent area, for example, the tool will not respond, so in a sense, Lock Transparency works like a mask. The areas that do contain pixels will still respond to any Photoshop operation. Locking transparency does not protect transparent areas from the effect of transformations like scaling, rotating, or moving.

Lock Image Pixels   The entire targeted layer is protected from editing functions like painting, color adjustments, or filters. You can, however, transform or move the content of a layer. Menu operations that you can't perform are grayed out. If you attempt to apply a tool function, you will be greeted with a circle with a line through it.

Lock Position   Checking this option prevents you from moving a targeted layer or applying Edit ➢ Free Transform or any of the Edit ➢ Transform operations such as Scale and Distort. When the Lock Position box is checked, these menu items are grayed out.

Lock All   You can protect a targeted layer from all editing functions by checking the Lock All box.

CREATING NEW LAYERS

It is often necessary to create a new layer, either to add new content to the image or to isolate an existing element. When a new layer is added, the file size of the document increases commensurate with the quantity of information on the new layer. Adding several new layers can significantly increase the amount of space the image consumes on your disk. This however, is a small inconvenience for the power that layers deliver. As part of your workflow, though, you'll no doubt want to consolidate layers during the imaging process to decrease the file size (see "Consolidating Layers" later in the chapter).

Creating a New Empty Layer

Here is an another example of redundant Photoshop operations. Two of these operations produce identical results, and one produces similar results with a slight variation. All three create a new layer; let's try them:

▶ From the Layers menu, choose Layer ➢ New ➢ Layer. The New Layer dialog box appears. Name the layer and click OK.

Part ii

▶ From the Layers palette pop-up menu, choose New Layer. The New Layer dialog box appears. Name the Layer and click OK.

▶ Click the New Layer icon (next to the trash icon at the bottom of the Layers palette). A new layer, named Layer 1, appears in the stack immediately above the targeted layer. To rename the new layer, Option-click or Alt-double-click its name, or Option/Alt-click the New Layer icon itself. The Layer Properties box appears; enter the name and click OK.

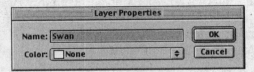

TIP

You can also access the Layer Properties dialog box from the Layer menu or from the Layers palette pull-down menu.

Creating a New Layer with Content

There are two potential sources for the content of new layers; elements cut or copied from another layer or Background, and elements dragged and dropped from another document. Whatever their source, the end result isolates the content onto a separate layer so that it can be moved, edited, or rotated in the stack.

Copying an Image to a New Layer

When you choose Layer ➤ New ➤ Layer Via Copy, the selected portion of the image is duplicated and moved to the same position on a new layer. By default, the first new layer you copy or cut is assigned a number that hasn't been used.

WARNING

The name that Photoshop assigns to a new layer depends on the technique you choose to create the new layer and the existing content of the Layers palette. It will appear as Layer 0, Layer 1, or some other number. To avoid the confusion of inconsistent labels, rename your new layer immediately upon creating it.

To copy the contents of a layer to a new layer:

1. Target the layer or Background that you intend to copy.

2. Make an accurate selection of the area on the layer or Background using one of the selection tools or techniques.

3. Choose Layer ➢ New ➢ Layer Via Copy, or press Ctrl/Command+J. The content within the selection marquee is copied to a new layer and is placed immediately above the layer from which it was copied. The new layer automatically becomes the target layer. In Figure 6.10, I selected just the swan on the Background and copied it to a new layer.

FIGURE 6.10: Layer ➢ New ➢ Layer Via Copy

4. Option-click (Mac) or Alt-double-click (Win) the name of the layer to display the Layer Properties dialog box, and rename the Layer.

5. Click OK.

Cutting an Image to a New Layer

When you cut a selected portion of an image to a new layer, the contents of the selection is either filled with the current background color (if it's on the Background) or replaced by transparency (if it's on a layer). It is transferred to the same position on a new layer.

1. Target the layer or Background with the element(s) that you intend to cut.

2. Make an accurate selection of the area using one of the selection tools or techniques.

3. Choose Layer ➢ New ➢ Layer Via Cut, or press Shift+Ctrl/Command+J. The content is cut to a new layer, leaving a transparent hole in the original layer or an area filled with

the background color (if it was cut from the Background). The new layer is placed immediately above the targeted layer. In Figure 6.11, I again selected the swan on the Background, but this time I *cut* it to a new layer.

FIGURE 6.11: Layer ➤ New ➤ Layer Via Cut

4. Option-click or Alt-double-click its name to display the Layer Properties dialog box.

5. Name the layer and click OK.

Dragging a Layer from Another Document

A layer from an open document (and all that layer's contents) can be copied to another open document simply by dragging and dropping it. The layer will appear immediately above the targeted layer in the stack.

TIP

The *source* document is the document you will get the layer from. The *destination* document is where you will put the layer.

1. Open the source document and the destination document so that they both appear on screen.

2. Target the layer or Background on the Layers palette of the source document.

3. Drag the layer name or thumbnail from the source to the destination document until you see an outline of the layer. Release your mouse.

4. Option-click or Alt-double-click the layer's name to display the Layer Properties dialog box to rename the layer.

5. Name the layer and click OK.

Dragging a Selection from Another Document

The contents of a selection can be copied from an open document and placed in another open document by dragging and dropping. When you drag and drop a selection, a new layer is automatically created in the destination document and will appear immediately above the targeted layer in the stack. Let's try it:

1. Open the source document and the destination document so that they both appear on screen.

2. Target the layer or Background on the Layers palette of the source document.

3. Make an accurate selection of the area to be moved.

4. Choose the Move tool. Drag the selection from the source to the destination document until you see a rectangular outline. Release your mouse when the outline appears where you want the selection to be placed.

5. Option-click or Alt-double-click the layer's name to display the Layer Properties dialog box to rename the Layer. Click OK.

Duplicating Layers

Two techniques produce identical results for creating an exact copy of a layer. The copy will be placed directly above the original layer; the name of the copy will be the name of the original plus the word *copy*. The new layer will have the same opacity, styles, and blending mode settings as the original. To duplicate a layer, do *one* of the following:

▶ Target the layer to be copied. Choose Duplicate Layer from the Layer menu or from the Layers palette pop-up menu.

▶ Drag the layer's name or thumbnail to the New Layer icon in the Layers palette. If you Option/Alt-drag, you'll be able to name the new layer from the Layer Properties dialog box that automatically appears.

Part ii

Removing Layers

Layers can be eliminated from the Layers palette (deleting the contents of that layer in the process). To discard a layer, do *one* of the following:

▶ Target the layer to be deleted. Choose Delete Layer from the Layer menu or from the Layers palette pop-up menu.

▶ Drag the layer's thumbnail or name to the trash icon in the Layers palette.

BLENDING LAYERS

Imagine having two color slides on a light table. Let's say you sandwich a red transparent gel between the two slides. The image you see would be a combination of the bottom slide and the top slide affected by the tint of the gel. But suppose instead of just the tinted image, you had the ability to slide in more complex, specific effects, such as color saturation, color inversion, or color bleaching.

That's how *blending modes* perform. They are preprogrammed effects that determine the color relations between aligned pixels on two consecutive layers in the stack. Figure 6.12 demonstrates many applications of blending.

FIGURE 6.12: Examples of blending modes applied to an image

A blending mode can be assigned to a layer a couple of different ways.

▶ Target the layer, then use the Mode pop-up list at the top of the Layers palette (directly under the palette title tab) to choose the desired blending option.

▶ Double-click the layer name or thumbnail to display the Layer Style dialog box. From the list on the left, choose Blending Options: Default. In the General Blending area, choose your blending mode and opacity level.

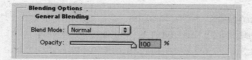

The options in the General Blending area are identical to the those at the top of the Layers palette: a pop-up menu for choosing a blending mode and an opacity control. But by using the General Blending area of the Layer Style dialog, you have the additional ability to save the settings as a style and apply them to a different layer. (See "Using Layer Styles" later in the chapter.) When you adjust opacity and apply a blending mode from within the dialog box, the mode and opacity setting in the Layers palette change to reflect the adjustment.

Advanced Blending

The Advanced Blending area (Figure 6.13) lets you control several different characteristics of the color relations between the targeted and the underlying layer.

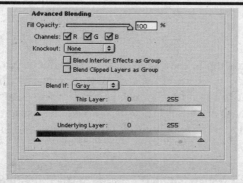

FIGURE 6.13: The Advanced Blending options

Part ii

Fill Opacity   This value controls the interior opacity of the pixels in the layer. However, if the image has a style applied to it, such as Drop Shadow, Fill Opacity does not affect the style. Move the slider to select a percentage between 0 and 100, or enter a value in the field.

Channels   You can choose which channel to blend. Choosing any one or two of the channels excludes the color information from the others; consequently, the pixels on the layer will change color depending on their color content.

Knockout   You can use this option to cut a hole through the content of the layer. Knockout works hand in hand with the Fill Opacity and Blend If sliders. As you move the sliders, Shallow knocks out the image to the layer underneath it; Deep punches a hole clear through all layers to the background.

Blend Interior Effects As A Group   If you check this box, the Fill Opacity and Blend If sliders affect any interior effects applied to the layer, like Inner Shadow or Inner Glow. If unchecked, the effects are excluded from blending.

Blend Clipped Layers As A Group   If you check this box, the Fill Opacity and Blend If sliders affect layers that are included in a clipping group.

Blend If   You choose the specific color components to be affected by the blend. Choose Blend If Gray to affect all of the colors, or pick a specific color channel to affect. The Blend If color sliders let you accurately adjust the highlight, midtone, and shadow areas to be blended.

LAYER STYLES

When introduced in Photoshop 5, they were called layer effects. Now they are referred to as *layer styles*, and they jazz up your images with dazzling realistic enhancements like drop shadows, neon glowing edges, and deep embossing. Layer styles are really efficient, canned effects that simplify operations that used to require tedious channel juggling and layer manipulation.

Layer styles apply their effects to the edges of the layer; they are translucent or soft-edged, through which the colors of the underlying layer can be seen, so the content on the target layer should be surrounded by transparency.

When a layer has been affected by a style, an italic *f* icon appears to the right of its name in the Layers palette (like the one next to Layer 1 in Figure 6.14). In Photoshop 6, the Layers palette can be expanded to reveal a list of the layer styles that have been applied, by clicking the small arrow to the left of the *f* icon. Clicking any one of these effects will display its controls so that you can modify it.

FIGURE 6.14:   Image with a Drop Shadow and a Bevel and Emboss effect

Using Layer Styles

If you want to create, define, or edit a layer style, access the Layer Style dialog box (Figure 6.15) by doing *one* of the following. If a layer is targeted when you open this dialog, the style you choose will be applied when you click OK.

- ▶ Choose Layer ➤ Layer Style.

- ▶ Double-click the layer's thumbnail or title.

- ▶ Double-click the Layer Style icon at the bottom-left of the Layers palette.

From the Layer Style dialog box, you can choose an effect. To display the extensive controls for each effect, click its name. Many of the controls have similarities, and experimentation with a live preview is the best way to see the result of your efforts. Under the Preview button is a swatch that demonstrates the effect on a square. This is very helpful to see the result of combination effects.

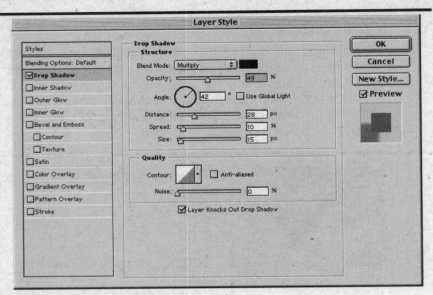

FIGURE 6.15: The Layer Style dialog window

Figure 6.16 demonstrates several samples of the layer styles effects. (This comparison is also available in the color section.)

Each layer style provides a unique and potentially complex set of options. Experimentation with the controls and with combinations of styles is the key to producing the best possible effect for your particular image.

Drop Shadow   Every object casts a shadow if placed in the path of a light source (except vampires). Drop shadows are a key element in creating, credible realistic images. The Drop Shadow will be the same shape as the pixels on the target layer. This is a fast way to give your image a realistic look. There are two sets of controls:

Structure   determines the opacity, size, and position of the shadow.

Quality   determines the contour of its edges and its texture.

Inner Shadow   As a drop shadow is cast outward, away from the layer content, an inner shadow is cast from the edge inward toward its center. Use this style to model your image or to create inner depth. The settings are similar to Drop Shadow for controlling the

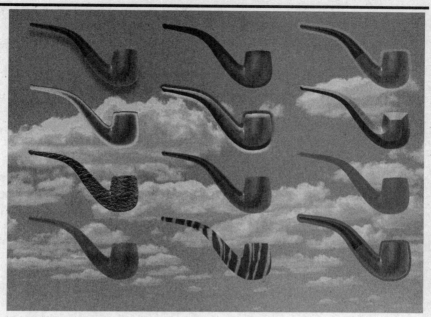

FIGURE 6.16: Layer styles demonstrated on pipes

Structure and Quality of the effect, except that Choke, a term used in the printing industry to indicate an inward expansion, replaces Spread, a term for outward expansion.

Outer Glow This style is perfect for a neon look. It creates a halo of a light color around the outside edge of the layer's content that can be as soft- or hard-edged as you like, depending on the settings you choose.

Inner Glow The best way to describe this effect is a soft-edged, light-colored stroke. Use Inner Glow to create a halo from the edge of the layer's content inward.

Bevel and Emboss The Bevel and Emboss style applies a highlight and a shadow to the layer content to create the illusion of three-dimensional relief. You can choose from five styles of embossing, each of which applies a different kind of sculptured surface. Twelve separate options let you minutely control structure and shading of the effect.

Contour   You can control the shape of the edge of your Bevel and Emboss effect by editing its contour. Double-click the name Contour on the Styles list. Choose a contour from the pop-up list. Adjust the range of the contour with the Range slider. A smaller percentage decreases the range of the contour relative to the bevel; a larger percentage increases the range.

To create a new contour, click the icon to display the Contour Editor (Figure 6.17). Click the New button and name the contour. A dotted line on the graph displays the profile of the current contour. Edit the position of the anchor points by dragging them, or click the dotted line to place new anchor points. Check the Corner box if you want a corner point, or uncheck it if you want a smooth point. Drag the anchor points to modify the curve to the profile of the edge you want. The Input value represents the percentage of the horizontal position of an anchor point; Output represents the percentage of the vertical position of an anchor point. Click OK when you're satisfied with your settings to save the new contour.

TIP

As you create a contour, a live preview in the image window will display the results on your image.

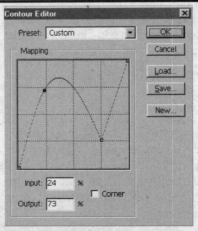

FIGURE 6.17: The Contour Editor

Texture   The Bevel and Emboss Texture option lets you map a textural surface to your layer's content. Display the texture controls by clicking the word Texture in the styles list. Choose a pattern from the pop-up list. The Texture controls use the Pattern presets as a source for textures . Essentially, it applies the colorless texture of the pattern to the content of the layer. You can move the sliders to adjust the scale and depth of the texture. Checking the Invert box changes the appearance of the texture from emboss to relief.

TIP

You can reposition the texture while in the Texture dialog box by clicking the texture in the image window and dragging.

Link the textural style to the layer by checking the Link With Layer box. If you move the layer, the texture moves along with it. If the box is unchecked, the texture will remain in place while the layer moves.

Satin   To produce the effect of light and shadow bouncing off a satiny surface, Photoshop applies a soft-edged shadow across the middle of the layer's content. Controls let you determine its size, position, opacity, and contour.

Color Overlay   This style is a no-brainer. It simply fills the layer's content with a color that you select by clicking the swatch. You can control its opacity.

Gradient Overlay   Similar to Color Overlay, Gradient Overlay applies a gradient to the pixels on the layer. You can choose a gradient from the current Gradient palette, or create one on the fly by clicking Gradient to display the Gradient Editor. From the menu, you can control the opacity, style, angle, and scale of the gradient.

Pattern Overlay   If you have one or more patterns stored in the current Patterns presets, you can overlay a pattern on the layer content as an effect. This is similar to the Bevel and Emboss Texture option. The difference is that Pattern overlay applies the colors as well as the texture of the pattern. You can control the opacity and scale of the pattern, and you can link the pattern to the layer so that it will accompany the layer if the layer is moved horizontally or vertically.

Part ii

Stroke   To apply an outline as an effect to the edge of the image, choose Stroke. You can determine the color and size of the stroke and whether it's placed on the inside, middle, or outside of the edge of the layer content. The best new feature of this effect is Fill Type, which applies a gradient or pattern to the stroke; this is excellent incentive to use the Stroke layer style instead of the similar Edit ➤ Stroke.

Applying Layer Styles

There are several ways to apply a layer style. If you have a style defined and wish to simply apply it, target the layer, then click the Layer Style icon at the bottom-left of the Layers palette and choose the style from the list that pops up.

The Layer Style dialog box can be used to apply a style, by following one of these methods:

▶ Target the layer, choose Layer ➤ Layer Style, select a style by checking its box from the Layer Style dialog box, and click OK.

▶ Double-click the layer's thumbnail or title; select a style and click OK.

▶ Target the layer, double-click the Layer Style icon at the bottom-left of the Layers palette, select a style, and click OK.

TIP

Checking the style's box in the Layer Styles dialog box applies the style to the layer. To view the controls of a particular layer style however, you must click the style's name.

Saving Layer Styles

If you've applied one or more styles or blending options to a layer, and you're satisfied with the result, you may want to save the style to later apply it to a separate layer. To save a style, click the New Style button in the Layer Style dialog window. You'll be prompted to name your new style.

WORKING WITH TYPE LAYERS

When you enter type in Photoshop using the Type tool, a new layer is automatically created. The layer is conveniently named with the text.

Type layers are pretty much like any other layer in that they can be edited, transformed, reordered in the stack, and modified by applying effects to them. The thumbnail of a Type layer is identified by a capital *T*. If you've entered type and want to edit it, double-click the thumbnail to automatically highlight it.

Several Photoshop operations cannot be applied to Type layers, including color adjustments or filters that only affect pixels. Before a text layer can be affected by these operations, it must first be *rasterized.* Rasterization converts the vector information of the type fonts into pixel-based information. Once you've rasterized the type, you can no longer edit it with the Type tool. To rasterize a type layer, target the layer and choose Layer ➤ Rasterize ➤ Type.

TIP

For the big picture on generating and editing type, read Chapter 13.

CONSOLIDATING LAYERS

At some point during the process of creating a brilliant digital image, you will have accumulated more layers than you can shake a mouse at. This can present problems, because with the addition of each new layer, the size of your file will increase depending on how much information the layer contains. Having too many layers also presents an organization problem. It can become quite time-consuming to have to scroll through dozens of layers in order to find one. For these reasons—I can't stress it enough—*name your layers*.

But even with a multitude of named layers, you may still have trouble locating the one you need. Therefore, in the interest of streamlining your workflow, you should, from time to time, *merge* your layers.

Merging layers combines the content of two or more layers into one. You can merge visible layers, linked layers, and you can merge down from a targeted layer. You can flatten the image so that all of the layers are consolidated into one Background.

WARNING

Before you flatten the image, be sure that you are done editing the layer's content and no longer need the layer operations. It is wise to flatten a duplicate version of the image instead of the original, because once the image has been saved and closed, it cannot be unflattened.

TIP

A fast way to merge layers without losing them is to hold down the Option/Alt key and select a Merge function from the Palette menu. This merges the layers into a new one, but doesn't delete the original layers. You can then check the merged layers before duplicating the image for flattening. To quickly flatten the duplicate image, conceal all layers from view except the merged layer. Then choose Layer ➤ Flatten Image ➤ Discard Hidden Layers.

Merge Visible Layers

This operation merges the content of all of the visible layers into one layer. You will probably use this method more than any of the others, because you can see in the image window exactly what the new merged layer will look like. Let's merge visible layers:

1. Only the layers you want to merge should be visible. In the Layers palette, click the eye icon next to any visible layer that you don't want to merge, to conceal it from view.

2. Target one of the visible layers.

3. From either the Layer menu or the Layers palette pop-up menu, choose Merge Visible.

The contents of the visible layers will be merged into the targeted layer. That layer will retain its previous name.

Merge Linked Layers

This operation merges the content of all of the linked layers into one layer.

1. In the Layers palette, click the second column to link the layers that you want to merge. Only the layers you want to merge should be linked.

2. Target one of the linked layers.

3. From either the Layer menu or the Layers palette pop-up menu, choose Merge Linked.

The images on the linked layers will be merged into the targeted layer, which keeps its previous name.

Merge Down

This operation merges the content of the targeted layer and the layer immediately below it into one layer.

1. In the Layers palette, target a layer.

2. From either the Layers menu or the Layers palette pop-up menu, choose Merge Down.

The layer retains the name of the bottommost layer.

Flatten Image

Flattening your image eliminates all layers and places all of the content onto one Background. Because most other programs aren't able to read Photoshop's native layers format, you must usually flatten the image when you are saving your image to a format such as EPS for use in a desktop publishing program or to GIF or JPEG for use on the Web.

WARNING

TIFF format now supports Photoshop layers. Even so, when saving your file as a TIFF to be imported to another program, remember that layered documents have much larger file sizes and will consequently take longer to print. It's a good idea to flatten a duplicate version of the document before saving it as a TIFF that will be imported elsewhere.

1. Be sure all of your layers are visible. Photoshop will discard layers that are not visible.

2. Choose Flatten Image from either the Layers Menu or the Layers palette pop-up menu.

WHAT'S NEXT

Layers are one of your bread-and-butter tools that you'll use in every Photoshop session. Paths, Photoshop's vector-oriented drawing and selection tool, are used much less often, because bending and manipulating Bézier curves is not an intuitive process. In the next chapter, you'll learn enough about Paths that you, too, can take advantage of this valuable tool more frequently.

Part ii

Chapter 7
DRAWING PATHS

Photoshop provides several methods for isolating areas on the image with selections, as you saw in Chapter 3. Still, making accurate selections can be difficult or time-consuming, because each image presents different problems. The Pen tools and the Paths palette add more capabilities to further enhance the accuracy and speed of making selections and defining the smooth edges. Once you've learned to draw with the Pen tool, you'll find it indispensable because it can be the easiest and fastest way to select images with long, smooth curves.

This chapter covers topics that include using the path tools and Paths palette, drawing and editing paths, using paths to apply color, working with paths and selections, and exporting paths. You'll also learn about the new Photoshop 6 Shape tool.

Adapted from *Mastering Photoshop 6*
by Steve Romaniello
ISBN 0-7821-2841-6   896 pages $49.99

THE PATH TOOLS

If you are familiar with vector illustration programs, the Paths function in Photoshop will be familiar to you. Paths are *vector objects* that mathematically define specific areas on an image by virtue of their shape and position. Vector objects are composed of anchor points and line segments known as *Bézier curves,* like the ones shown in Figure 7.1. (See Chapter 1 for more information on these terms.)

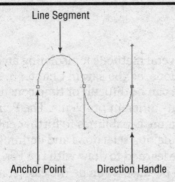

FIGURE 7.1: Components of Bézier curves

Paths enable you to create straight lines and curves with more precision than the selection tools. If the path is left open-ended, it can be stroked with a color to form a curved line. If its two end points are joined, it encloses a shape. The path can be filled with color, stroked with an outline, or stored in the Paths palette or the Shape library for later use. Most importantly, it can be converted into a selection where a Photoshop operation can be implemented.

The primary path maker is the Pen tool, which has three variations, located in the Tool palette. To pick a Pen tool, click its icon or type P. If you hold down the mouse button, you can expand the Tool palette to display all of the other Path tools (Shift+P cycles through these). Photoshop 6 has two tools for drawing paths and four tools for editing paths. There are also two tools designed specifically to move a path or a portion of a path.

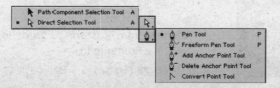

Path-Drawing Tools

Pen tool   draws paths by clicking and dragging.

Freeform Pen tool   draws a freeform line that converts itself to a path when the mouse is released.

Freeform Pen tool with the Magnetic option   (sometimes simply called the Magnetic Pen) intuitively defines edges based on contrasting colors.

Path-Editing Tools

Add Anchor Point tool   adds anchor points to existing paths.

Delete Anchor Point tool   removes anchor points from existing paths.

Convert Point tool   changes a corner point to a curve or a curve to a corner point.

Path Component Selection tool   selects and moves the path as a unit.

Direct Selection tool   selects and moves individual anchor points and segments.

DRAWING PATHS

Each of the path-drawing tools has a unique method of creating a path outline; choose the one that is most comfortable for your situation. Learning to draw accurately with the Pen tools can be challenging at first, because Bézier curves are unlike any other form of traditional drawing. With a little practice, however, as you become familiar with the process, your speed and accuracy will increase.

The Pen Tool

 The Pen tool enables you to draw straight lines and smooth curves with more control and precision. The basic techniques for drawing paths in Adobe Photoshop are similar to the techniques used in Adobe Illustrator. Usually, a path is drawn to follow the form of the area to be isolated, and then the path is edited and refined to a considerable degree of accuracy.

The Pen tool Options bar displays options that let you control its behavior. Before you draw the shape, specify in the Options bar (Figure 7.2) whether to make a new Shape layer or a new work path. This will affect how the shape can later be edited. If you choose the Shape Layer icon, Photoshop generates an independent Shape layer (see "Creating Lines and Shapes" at the end of this chapter). If you choose the Work Path icon, Photoshop draws an independent path on the current layer or Background. Check the Auto Add/Delete feature to automatically add anchor points when one of the Pen tools is placed on a segment or delete a point when a Pen tool is placed over an anchor point. If you check Rubber Band, you can preview the path as you draw.

TIP

Using the Zoom tool or the Navigator to view the image more closely greatly enhances your ability to draw with precision.

Creates a work path   Shows path before drawing

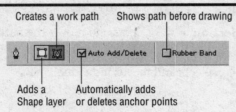

Adds a   Automatically adds
Shape layer   or deletes anchor points

FIGURE 7.2: The Pen tool Options bar

Straight Paths

A straight path consists of two anchor points joined by a straight line segment. You add additional segments to the straight path by moving the cursor and clicking the mouse. The segments can abruptly change direction as the corners zigzag their way across the document.

Drawing a Straight Path

1. Select the Pen tool and click the image where you want to begin the path. An anchor point appears; release the mouse button.

2. Click (and release) your mouse at the next point on the image. A line segment with another anchor point appears.

3. Continue to click and move your mouse to produce a series of straight line segments connected by corner anchor points.

Curved Paths

A curved path consists of two anchor points connected by a curved segment. Direction handles determine the position and shape of the line segment.

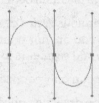

Drawing a Curved Path

1. Select the Pen tool and place the cursor on the image where you want to path to begin.

2. Click your mouse *and drag*. An anchor point with a direction handle appears. Without releasing the mouse button, drag the handle in the direction you want the curve to be placed.

3. Release the mouse and move the cursor to the next point on the image.

4. Click your mouse and drag. A curved segment with another anchor point and direction handle appears. Drag in the opposite direction of the curve.

5. With the mouse button still depressed, adjust the direction handle until the curved line segment is in the desired position and release the mouse.

Tips for Drawing Curved Paths

▸ Drag the first point in the direction of the peak of the curve and drag the second point in the opposite direction. Dragging the first and second point in the same direction produces an S curve, which is undesirable because its shape is difficult to control.

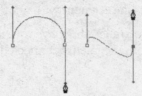

▸ Use as few anchor points as possible to assure a smooth path.

▸ Place the anchor points on the sides of the curve and not on the peaks or valleys, to maintain better control and smooth transitions.

▸ A path is a continuous series of segments connected by anchor points. You can add anchor points to the middle of a segment, but you can only add segments to the endpoints of an open path.

▸ An anchor point can only connect two segments.

▸ If you should stop drawing and want to add a new segment to a path, resume drawing by first clicking one of the end points with a Pen tool.

▸ If you are drawing an open path and want to begin a second path that is not connected to the first, click the Pen tool icon on the Tool palette before starting the new path.

Changing the Direction of a Curved Path

You can draw a scalloped path by changing the direction of the curve. When performing this operation, it helps to think of the Option or Alt key as a turn signal. In the following example, the segments will curve upward.

1. Select the Pen tool. Click the image where you want to begin the path and drag up. An anchor point with a direction handle appears. Without releasing the mouse button, drag to adjust the direction handle; then release.

2. Click where you want the next part of the curve. Click your mouse and drag down. A curved segment with another anchor point and direction line appears; release the mouse.

3. Place your cursor on the last anchor point and press Option or Alt (the turn signal!). Click and drag the direction handle up and release the mouse.

4. Move your cursor to the next location, click your mouse, and drag down. Adjust the segment so that the curve is the desired length and position.

5. Repeat Step 3.

6. Repeat Steps 2 through 4 until the desired number of curves are drawn.

Adding a Curved Path to a Straight Path

Usually, paths you draw are combinations of straight and curved paths. These techniques combine the two into one continuous path.

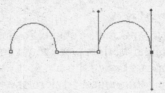

1. Select the Pen tool and click the image where you want to path to begin. An anchor point appears; release the mouse button.

2. Click the next point on the image. A straight segment with another anchor point appears.

3. To add a curved segment, place your cursor on the last anchor point, and press Option or Alt while holding down the mouse button and dragging up.

4. Release your mouse button and move your cursor to the next location.

5. Click your mouse and drag down to finish the curve. Release the mouse when the size and position of the curve is achieved.

Adding a Straight Path to a Curved Path

1. Select the Pen tool, click the image where you want to begin the path, and drag up. An anchor point with a direction handle appears. Without releasing the mouse button, drag the direction handle in the direction of the curve.

2. Release the mouse and move the cursor to the next point.

3. Click your mouse and drag down. A curved segment with another anchor point and direction line appears. Release the mouse.

4. Place your cursor on the last anchor point, press Option or Alt, and click your mouse once.

5. Move your cursor to the next location and click your mouse to complete the segment.

Closing a Path

By closing a path, you create a shape. To close a series of straight paths, draw at least two paths, then place your cursor on the first anchor point. A little circle appears beside the cursor to indicate that the path is ready to be closed. Click the mouse. To close one or more curved paths, draw at least *one* path and click the first anchor point.

The Freeform Pen Tool

 Drawing with the Freeform Pen tool is similar to drawing with the Lasso tool. If you place your cursor on the image, click, and drag your mouse, the Freeform Pen will be followed by a trail that, when the mouse is released, produces a path (see Figure 7.3). The Freeform Pen tool is a fast way to draw a curve but doesn't offer the same control as the Pen tool. You can't control the number or placement of anchor points. Paths created by the Freeform Pen usually require editing or removal of excess anchor points after the path has been completed.

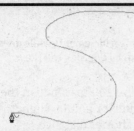

FIGURE 7.3: The Freeform Pen tool draws an unrestricted path.

When you select the Freeform Pen, the Options bar provides new settings: Curve Fit and Magnetic. You can specify the Curve Fit between 0.5 and 10.0 pixels to determine the sensitivity of the tool to the movement of your mouse. A lower tolerance produces a finer curve with more anchor points; a higher tolerance produces a simpler path with fewer anchor points.

The Magnetic Pen Option

The performance of the Freeform Pen tool with Magnetic checked (also called "the Magnetic Pen tool") is similar to the Magnetic Lasso (see Chapter 3). It intuitively snaps to defined areas of contrast within an image as you drag. Where the Magnetic Lasso converts to a selection, the Magnetic Pen converts to a path.

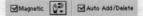

To access the Magnetic Pen, select the Freeform Pen tool (click and hold the cursor on the Pen tool in the Tool palette, and choose the Freeform Pen from the fly-out; or type Shift+P once or twice to select the tool) and check the Magnetic box in the Options bar. Then click the magnet icon to display the Magnetic Options:

Width   Enter a distance in pixels from the edge that the tool will be active. Higher values mean the tool is "attracted" at a greater distance.

Contrast   Enter a value between 1% and 100% to determine the tool's sensitivity in detecting contrasting borders. Higher values detect edges of greater contrast, while lower values increase the tool's sensitivity to low-contrast edges.

TIP
You can increase the detection width in one-pixel increments while drawing by pressing the [key. You can decrease the width by pressing the] key.

Frequency   Enter a value between 1 and 100 to establish the rate at which the Magnetic Pen places anchor points. Higher values place more anchor points over a shorter distance.

Stylus Pressure   If you are working with a stylus tablet, check Stylus Pressure. As you drag, the pressure of the stylus will correspond to the Width setting. An increase of pressure on the stylus will narrow the pen width.

Drawing with the Magnetic Pen

1.   Click the image to set the first point.

2.   Release the mouse button and drag. A path will follow along the most distinct edge within the Pen width. Periodically, the Pen places anchor points along the specified border, while the most recent segment remains active (see Figure 7.4).

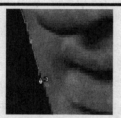

FIGURE 7.4: A path made with the Magnetic Pen "snaps" to a line of contrasting pixels.

3.   Press Return (Mac) or Enter (Win) to end an open path. You can resume drawing the open path by clicking the last anchor point and dragging.

4.   If you stop dragging and double-click, you create a segment that connects the last anchor point with the first one and closes the path. You can also close the path by hovering over the first anchor point. The little circle appears. Click once.

TIP

You can temporarily turn off the Magnetic option by holding down the Option (Mac) or Alt key (Win) with the mouse button depressed to draw a straight path, or with the mouse button released to draw a freeform path.

EDITING PATHS

Once a path has been drawn, all or part of it can be moved or reshaped. Anchor points can be added or omitted, and corners can be converted into curves or curves into corners.

   The path-editing tools include the Path Component Selection tool, the Direct Selection tool, the Add Anchor Point tool, the Delete Anchor Point tool, and the Convert Point tool.

The Path Component Selection Tool

   The black arrow, the Path Component Selection tool, selects all of the anchor points and segments of a path. The path can then be repositioned anywhere on the image by dragging with this tool.

TIP

Another method of selecting a path is to use the Path Component Selection tool to click and drag a marquee that touches any part of the path. All the anchor points will appear solid, indicating that the entire path is selected.

A path can be duplicated by dragging and dropping it with the Path Component Selection tool and the Option or Alt key depressed, as seen in Figure 7.5.

Aligning Paths

The Path Component Selection tool enables you to automatically align and distribute paths and vector objects such as lines and shapes. You cannot align or distribute shapes on separate layers. To align multiple paths, select two or more paths with the Path Component Selection tool by dragging a marquee that touches the objects, or by Shift-clicking the paths. From the Options bar, choose one of the alignment options shown in Figure 7.6.

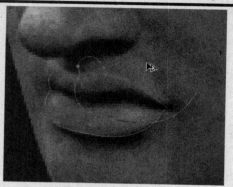

FIGURE 7.5: Option/Alt-drag to duplicate a path.

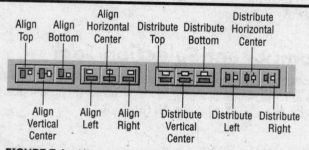

FIGURE 7.6: Alignment features of the Path Component Selection tool

The Align choices match up the edges or centers of paths and objects, as follows:

Top	Aligns the top edges of the path or vector object
Vertical Center	Aligns the vertical midpoints.
Bottom	Aligns the bottom edges.
Left	Aligns the left edges.
Horizontal Center	Aligns the horizontal midpoints.
Right	Aligns the right edges.

The Distribute choices position the edges or centers of paths and objects over equal distances, in these ways:

Top	Distributes the top edges of the path or vector object.
Vertical Center	Distributes the vertical midpoints.
Bottom	Distributes the bottom edges.
Left	Distributes the left edges.
Horizontal Center	Distributes the horizontal midpoints.
Right	Distributes the right edges.

The Direct Selection Tool

 The Direct Selection tool selects or modifies a segment or the position of an anchor point on a path. It is essential for reshaping the path once it has been drawn.

To select, move, or edit a segment or anchor point, choose the Direct Selection tool. Click a segment or anchor point to select it. Click and drag an anchor point to reposition it or a segment to reshape it. To deselect a path, click anywhere on the image.

TIP

You can toggle from any of the Pen tools or path-editing tools to the Direct Selection tool by pressing the Command (Mac) or Ctrl (Win) key.

Reshaping Paths

To alter the shape of a path once it has been drawn, follow these steps:

1. Choose the Direct Selection tool.

2. Click an anchor point to select it.

3. Click and drag one of the anchor point's *direction handles* until the desired shape of the curve is achieved (as in Figure 7.7).

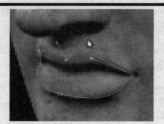

FIGURE 7.7: Reshaping a path

Editing Anchor Points

After you have drawn a path around an area on the image, you may need to refine it by adding or deleting anchor points. When you do, you increase your ability to edit the path.

WARNING

It might be tempting to add dozens of anchor points, to facilitate the drawing of a path. Extra points are not recommended, because they increase the path's complexity and compromise the smoothness of the shape.

Adding and Deleting Anchor Points

To add an anchor point, choose the Add Anchor Point tool and click the path. A new anchor point will appear. To delete an anchor point, choose the Delete Anchor Point tool. Click an anchor point, and the two segments connected by the point join into one.

Converting Anchor Points

There are two types of anchor points. Smooth points connect curved or straight lines that flow into each other. Corner points connect lines that change direction. An anchor point can be converted from corner to smooth or smooth to corner (see Figure 7.8) by clicking the point with the Convert Point tool. Click a smooth point and it converts to a corner point; to convert a corner point, click it and drag out the direction handles until the desired curve is achieved, and release the mouse.

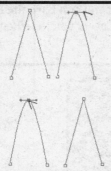

FIGURE 7.8: Converting (top) a corner to a smooth point and (bottom) a smooth to a corner point

Part ii

Transforming Paths

Like selection outlines and selection contents, paths can be modified with the Transformation tools. Once the path has been drawn, you must select it with one of the arrow tools. If you select it with the Path Component Selection tool, you can employ any of the transformation operations in the Edit menu, including Free Transform, Scale, Rotate, Skew, Distort, Perspective, or Flip, to edit the entire path. If you select one or more points or segments with the Direct Selection tool, you can apply any of the transformation operations to the selected part of the path.

Combining Paths

If you have drawn two or more paths that intersect, you can combine them into one path. Select both paths with the Path Component Selection tool by pressing your mouse button and dragging a marquee that touches both of them, or by clicking them in sequence while pressing the Shift key. On the Options bar, click the Combine button. The elements of both paths combine into one continuous path.

THE PATHS PALETTE

The Paths palette is the central control for all path operations. Like a layer or a channel, a path can be stored to a palette so it can later be edited or converted into a selection. The Paths palette (Figure 7.9) can be accessed by choosing Window ➤ Show Paths. (If you still have the Paths palette in the default cluster—grouped with the Layers palette—then pressing the F7 function key will also bring it up.)

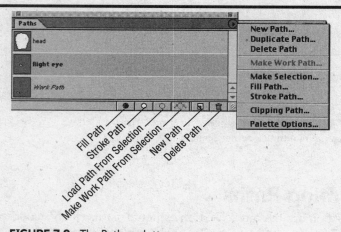

FIGURE 7.9: The Paths palette

Work Paths

When you begin drawing a path with the Pen tool, it appears as a thumbnail in the Paths palette, named Work Path. The work path is a temporary element that records changes as you draw new sections of the path. If you complete a path on an image, click the Pen tool, and draw another path. It will appear on the same Work Path thumbnail as the first path. If you wish to create separate additional paths, it is necessary to save the work path to the Paths palette.

TIP

You can increase or decrease the size of the Paths palette thumbnails, or turn them off, by choosing Palette Options from the palette pull-down menu and clicking the radio button next to the desired thumbnail size.

Saving Paths

Saving a path to the Paths palette has a distinct advantage over saving selections as alpha channels (which are described in Chapter 8): The file size of a document does not substantially increase with each saved path.

Once your path has been drawn and appears as a Work Path thumbnail, you can save it by choosing Save Path from the palette menu. A dialog box appears where you can name the path; if no name is entered, the path name defaults to Path 1. You can also save a path by dragging the Work Path to the New Path icon at the bottom of the palette.

The Paths palette lists saved paths from top to bottom in the order in which they were created. The paths can be reorganized within the list by clicking the path's name or thumbnail and dragging it to the desired location.

Displaying Paths

To display a path, click the path's name or thumbnail in the Paths palette. Photoshop allows only one path to be displayed at a time. When displayed, it will appear on the image. You can edit it, move it, add other paths to it, or delete portions of the path. To conceal a work path or saved path from view in the image window, click the empty portion of the Paths palette.

Deleting Paths from the Image Window

To delete a path from the image, do one of the following:

▶ Select an entire path with the Path Component Selection tool. Press the Delete or Backspace key. If it's a work path, the path and its icon are deleted. If it's a saved path, the path is deleted from the image window, but its empty thumbnail remains in the Paths palette.

▶ Select a part of the path with the Direct Selection tool. Press the Delete or Backspace key once to delete the selected part of the path or twice to delete the entire path.

Deleting Paths from the Palette

 You may want to discard a path from the Paths palette. To do so, target the path's name in the palette and perform one of the following operations:

▶ Drag the path thumbnail to the trash icon at the bottom of the palette.

- ► Choose Delete Path from the Paths palette pull-down menu.
- ► Click the trash icon in the Paths palette. In the dialog box that appears, click Yes.
- ► Target the path in the Paths palette. Press the Delete or Backspace key.

USING PATHS TO APPLY COLOR

You can apply color to an area of an image within a closed path or to the edge of a path.

Filling a Path

To fill the area within a path, draw an open or closed path or display an existing path from the Paths palette by clicking its thumbnail. Choose a foreground color. Choose Fill Path from the Paths palette pull-down menu.

The Fill Path dialog box appears (Figure 7.10), the top two fields of which are identical to the Fill dialog box in the Edit menu. In the additional Rendering field, you can enter a Feather Radius for the edges of the path and check the Anti-Aliased option. Click OK when you have the settings you want.

 You can fill a path with the current Fill Path dialog box settings by clicking the Fill Path icon at the bottom of the Paths palette.

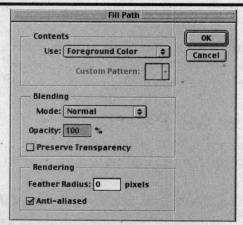

FIGURE 7.10: The Fill Path dialog box

Stroking a Path

A path can be stroked with a line of a specific color and width. This is an important operation in Photoshop because it is really the only way to precisely create smooth curved lines. Try drawing one with the Paintbrush or Pencil; it's quite difficult to achieve satisfactory results. Drawing an open path, editing it to your exact specifications, and then stroking it with a color produces perfect results every time.

To color the line of a path, draw a path or load one from the Paths palette. Choose a foreground color; then, from the Paths palette pull-down menu, choose Stroke Path. The Stroke Path (Figure 7.11) dialog box appears; pick a tool from the pop-up list. When you click OK, the stroke will be painted with the current characteristics of the chosen tool as defined in the Options bar.

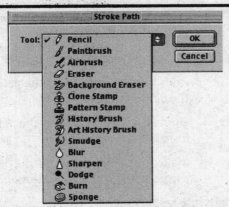

FIGURE 7.11: The Stroke Path dialog box

You can quickly stroke a path with the current tool characteristics set in the Stroke Path dialog box by clicking the Stroke Path icon at the bottom of the Paths palette.

CONVERTING PATHS

The primary reason to use paths is the ease and facility with which you can precisely define regions of an image. While some of the new selection tools offer unique selection techniques, there is nothing quite like the paths operations to quickly and precisely surround an area.

Paths are easy to edit and require less real estate on your disk to store. Eventually, though, you are going to need to convert your path into a selection to be able to apply a Photoshop operation to the area it surrounds.

Converting a Path to a Selection

You can determine the characteristics of a new selection and its relation to active selections on the image. Target the path in the Paths palette, and choose Make Selection from the Paths palette pull-down menu. A dialog box is displayed that enables you to choose the characteristics of the new selection (Figure 7.12).

Feather Radius	Sets distance in pixels for feathering of the selection outline.
Anti-Aliased	Determines whether the selection will possess an anti-aliased edge.
New Selection	Makes a selection from the path.
Add To Selection	Adds the area defined by the path to the active selection.
Subtract From Selection	Omits the area defined by the path from the active selection.
Intersect With Selection	Makes a selection from the overlap of the path and the active selection.

Click OK to convert the path into a selection.

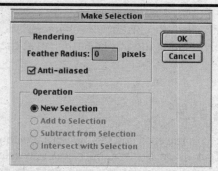

FIGURE 7.12: The Make Selection dialog

You can convert a path into a new selection by clicking the Load Path As Selection icon at the bottom of the Paths palette.

Converting a Selection into a Path

To convert a selection into a path, draw a marquee with one of the selection tools. Choose Make Work Path from the Paths palette menu. A dialog box is displayed that enables you to set the tolerance of the path in pixels. Tolerances with low values produce more complex paths with greater numbers of anchor points, while tolerances with higher values produce simpler paths. Click OK to convert the selection into a path.

 You can also convert a selection into a path by clicking the Make Work Path From Selection icon at the bottom of the Paths palette.

You might use the ability to make selections from paths to modify a typeface, as in Figure 7.13. To modify type, first create it with the Type Outline tool, then click the Make Work Path From Selection icon. Modify the path outlines as desired, then click the Load Path As Selection icon. The selection can be either filled, or an image can be pasted into it.

Part ii

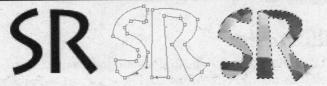

FIGURE 7.13: Modifying type by using paths

IMPORTING AND EXPORTING PATHS

Photoshop paths can be utilized by other programs, where they can be modified. You can transfer a path directly from Photoshop to popular vector-based drawing programs like Illustrator or FreeHand, or vice versa, to take advantage of either program's unique path-editing features.

Copy and Paste

If you're moving the path from Photoshop to a vector-based drawing program, select the entire path with the Path Component Selection tool and copy it to the clipboard (by choosing Edit ➤ Copy or pressing Ctrl/Command+C). Open a document in the other program and paste the path into it. The paths remain fully editable in either program.

When you paste a path into Photoshop, a dialog box appears that asks you to choose to place the path as a rasterized image (Pixels), a vector path, or a Shape layer.

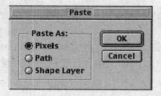

Drag and Drop

You can drag and drop a path from Photoshop to Illustrator. With both programs running, select the path with the Path Component Selection tool. Drag the path onto the Illustrator pasteboard. The new Illustrator path is fully editable.

Paths to Illustrator

If you can't run Photoshop and Illustrator simultaneously, you can export the file as an Illustrator EPS file using the File ➤ Export ➤ Paths to Illustrator command. In the dialog box that appears, for Write, choose Work Path. When you quit Photoshop, launch Illustrator, and open the document, the exported path will be fully editable in Illustrator.

NOTE

For more on working with Photoshop and Illustrator, see Chapter 12.

CLIPPING PATHS

When saving Photoshop documents into vector drawing applications or to desktop publishing programs, it is sometimes necessary to "knock out" portions of the image—that is, make them invisible. The Clipping Paths option in the Paths palette pull-down menu enables you to create a path that will knock out the area outside the path when it is opened in another program. The interior portion of the path will be displayed and the area outside the path will completely transparent.

To create a clipping path, follow these steps:

1. Draw a path around an area on the image (see Figure 7.14).

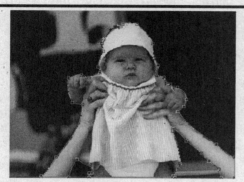

FIGURE 7.14: Selecting the area with the Pen tool

2. From the Paths palette pull-down menu, choose Save Path.

3. Choose Clipping Path from the palette menu.

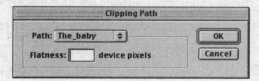

4. Select the name of the path from the pull-down submenu. Click OK.

5. For most paths, leave the Flatness setting blank. When you print the image, the printer's default flatness setting will be used to define the shape. However, if you experience printing problems, then save the path with new settings (see sidebar).

TIP

The path name is outlined (Mac) or boldfaced (Win) in the Paths palette, indicating that it is a clipping path.

TROUBLESHOOTING CLIPPING PATH POSTSCRIPT ERRORS

A *raster image processor (RIP)* is software on a computer or a device inside an imagesetter or PostScript printer that interprets a vector curve by connecting a series of straight line segments together. The *flatness* of a clipping path determines the fidelity of the lines to the curve. The lower the setting, the more lines are produced and so, the more accurate the curve.

If a clipping path is too complex for the printer's capabilities, it cannot print the path and will produce a limitcheck or PostScript error. Any printer can be jammed up with a complex clipping path, although you may find that a clipping path may print perfectly well on a low-resolution printer (300–600 dpi) because it uses a higher flatness value to define the curve. The same clipping path may not print on a high-resolution imagesetter (1200–2400 dpi). If you run into printing problems on an image with a clipping path, trouble-shoot them in the following ways.

▶ Increase the Flatness settings and resave the file. Flatness values range from 0.2 to 100. Enter a flatness setting from 1 to 3 for low-resolution printers and 8 to 10 for high-resolution printers.

▶ Reduce the number of anchor points in the curve by manually eliminating them with the Delete Anchor Point tool.

▶ Re-create the path with lower Tolerance settings:

1. Target the path in the Paths palette.

2. Click the Load Path As Selection icon at the bottom of the palette.

3. Click the trash icon to delete the path but leave the selection.

4. Choose Make Work Path from the palette's pull-down menu. In the dialog box, decrease the Tolerance to 5 pixels (a good place to start).

5. Name and save the new work path.

6. Choose Clipping Path from the palette pull-down menu.

7. Save the file in EPS format.

Images containing clipping paths must be saved in EPS format, and therefore can only be imported into programs that support EPS images. It's best to save a copy of the image so that the original image retains Photoshop's attributes.

To save a clipping path as an EPS:

1. Choose File ➢ Save As. Check the As A Copy option.

2. From the Format list, choose Photoshop EPS. A dialog box appears.

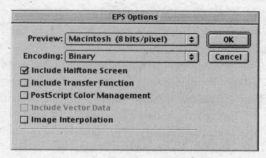

3. Choose a Preview option, depending on the type of computer and the platform you are using: Macintosh or Windows, 1 bit or 8 bit.

4. Choose Binary for the Encoding setting.

5. Click OK.

6. Open a document in a desktop publishing program or vector drawing program, and place the EPS image (see Figure 7.15).

FIGURE 7.15: The image clipped by the path

CREATING LINES AND SHAPES

Photoshop 6 handles lines and shapes quite differently than its predecessors did. In fact, it has an entirely new interface for creating and managing shapes that is more like Illustrator's. Like type, lines and shapes are vector objects. You draw a predefined shape using one of the Shape tools or a custom shape using the Pen tool. Once drawn, shapes can be edited by adjusting their anchor points with the path-editing tools. When you create a shape, it appears on an independent layer with a Layer Clipping Path thumbnail next to a Color Fill Layer thumbnail.

The shape also appears as a separate path in the Paths palette. To apply any filter to a shape, it must first be *rasterized* or turned into pixels. If you flatten the image, shapes are automatically converted to pixels.

Like paths, shapes are vector objects. The Shape tool can instantly create rectangles, rounded rectangles, ellipses, polygons, lines, and custom shapes that are editable using the path-editing tools. The Shape tool icon in the Tool palette, when clicked, expands to reveal all of the available tools. Once you've chosen a shape from this flyout, click in the image and drag to size the shape.

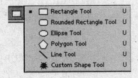

The Shape Tool Options Bar

As you choose a different shape from the Tool palette or from the Shape list in the Options bar, the Options bar changes to accommodate specific characteristics of the shape. Figure 7.16 illustrates the differences in the Options bar when the three different drawing options are selected.

Options Bar Feature	Function
Create New Shape Layer	Makes a shape and a path on a new layer.
Create New Work Path	Makes the path outline of the shape on an existing layer or Background.

Part ii

Options Bar Feature	Function
Create Filled Region	Fills an area with the foreground color in the form of the shape.
Shape List	Lets you choose a shape.
Shape Options Panel	Lets you enter specifications for the size and proportion of the shape.
Layer Style	Attaches a layer style to the shape layer (available with New Shape Layer).
Shape Characteristics	Assigns values for the characteristics of a particular shape, or choose a custom shape.
Mode	Lets you select a blending mode for the shape (available only with New Shape Layer or Filled Region).
Opacity	Opacity slider for the shape (available only with New Shape Layer or Filled Region).
Anti-Alias	Applies an anti-alias to the shape (available only with Filled Region).

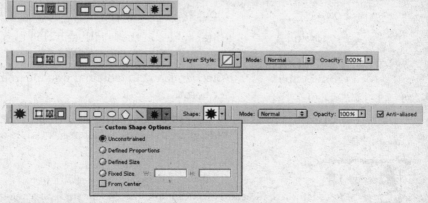

FIGURE 7.16: The Options bar of the Shape tools

Drawing Shapes

To draw a shape, first choose a foreground color. Click the Shape tool in the Tool palette and choose a tool type from the expanded palette or from the Options bar. Click in the image and drag to form the shape.

Since shapes are vector objects, you use the Path Component Selection tool, Direct Selection tool, or path-editing tools to move or edit a shape or add and delete anchor points.

Each shape performs slightly differently. The Options bar of each shape lets you adjust its individual characteristics. For example, you can enter a value for the radius of the corners on the Rounded Rectangle tool, or for the number of sides on the Polygon tool.

The Rectangles and Ellipse Tools

As with the selection Marquee tools, icons on the Shape tool Options bars let you add, subtract, intersect, or exclude areas from a shape as you draw. Clicking the arrow to the right of the Shape tool icons on the Options bar offers additional controls on a pop-up panel. When you choose the Rectangle, Rounded Rectangle, or Ellipse tool, the down-arrow on the Options bar offers you these choices:

Unconstrained	Checking this button sizes and proportions the shape as you draw.
Square (or Circle)	Checking this button constrains the shape.
Fixed Size	Input values for the shape's Width and Height.
Proportional	Enter values in the Width and Height fields to define the shape's proportion.
From Center	Check this box to radiate the shape from a center point.
Snap To Pixels	Aligns the shape to the on-screen pixels (Rectangle and Round-Cornered Rectangle only).

TIP

To constrain the Rectangle or Round-Cornered Rectangle to a square or the Ellipse to a circle, hold down the Shift key as you drag.

The Polygon Tool

When the Polygon tool is selected, a Size field in the Options bar allows you to set the number of the shape's sides. The Polygon Options panel choices differ from those of the other shapes. Figure 7.17 illustrates the wide variety of shapes you can create by adjusting these settings.

FIGURE 7.17: Polygon examples

Radius	Enter a corner radius for a round-cornered polygon.
Smooth Corners	Rounds the corners of the polygon.
Indent Sides By	Enter a percentage value to curve the sides inward.
Smooth Indents	Rounds the indents.

The Line Tool

When the Line tool is selected, you can enter a value in the Options bar for the Weight of the line in pixels. Choices in the Line Options panel determine what type of arrow will appear at either end of the line. Check the Start or End boxes, or both, to produce an arrowhead at the beginning and/or end of the line. Enter values in Width, Length, and Concavity for these characteristics of the arrowhead. (Figure 7.18 demonstrates the wide variety of possibilities in these settings.)

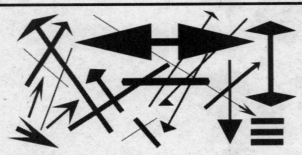

FIGURE 7.18: Examples of lines, with and without arrowheads

The Custom Shape Tool

You can generate custom shapes with the Shape tool. With the Custom Shape tool selected, the Options panel displays these options:

Unconstrained	Manually determines the proportion of the shape as you draw.
Defined Proportions	Drag to constrain the proportion of the shape.
Defined Size	Draws the shape at the size it was created.
Fixed Size	Enter values for the shape in the height and width fields.
From Center	Radiates the shape from a center point.

The Options bar Shape menu lets you choose from 14 predefined custom shapes. You can create additional shapes with the Pen tool and save them to this list.

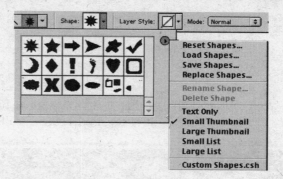

The pull-down submenu on the panel provides a list of commands that let you Save, Load, Reset, Delete, and Replace custom shapes, plus several palette-viewing options. The Custom Shapes.csh option at the bottom rung of the submenu replaces the default list with 63 additional shapes.

Drawing Custom Shapes   To practice applying custom shapes, open the file Empty_Face.psd from the Sybex Web site for this book.

NOTE

To find the practice files for this book, go to the www.sybex.com and enter 2991 in the search box. When you get to the page for this book, follow the links to the download area.

1. Choose a foreground color.

2. Make a new empty layer by clicking the New Layer icon in the Layers palette. Name the layer **Watch Shapes**.

3. Click the Shape tool in the Tool palette.

4. In the Options bar, click on the Custom Shape icon to display the Shape Options panel. Click the Unconstrained radio button.

5. In the Options bar, click the Shape menu arrow to display the default custom shapes. Click the arrow on the panel to display the list of commands in the pull-down submenu; choose Custom Shapes.csh to load the additional 63 shapes.

6. Click a shape in the Shape menu. Place your cursor on the watch face at the 12 o'clock mark, click, and drag until the shape is the size and proportion you want. To reposition the shape, press the spacebar while dragging. Then release the mouse.

7. Choose additional shapes from the Shape menu and repeat Step 6 for all of the hours on the clock, as in Figure 7.19.

FIGURE 7.19: The watch face adorned with custom shapes

Defining Custom Shapes   To create a custom shape, follow these steps:

1. Use one of the Pen tools and draw a shape outline.

2. Choose Edit ➤ Define Custom Shape.

3. Choose the Custom Shape tool. The new shape will appear in the Shape menu in the Shape tool Options bar.

What's Next

Channels and masks have some similarities with layers, which you learned about in this chapter. In the next chapter, you'll learn how to work with channels and use Photoshop's Quick Mask mode.

Part ii

Chapter 8

USING CHANNELS AND QUICK MASK

It's raining outside. You're dry and warm in front of your computer working on an assignment to colorize a black-and-white group photograph of 34 mariachis. You've spent the last hour and 15 minutes carefully selecting their pants, tunics, and sombreros, and you're about to apply the Hue and Saturation command to simultaneously color all of their costumes a brilliant turquoise. You hear thunder in the distance! The lights flicker! Your screen goes dead.

Fortunately, you've been regularly saving your work. Or have you? You restart your computer, launch Photoshop, and open the image. The 34 mariachis are there, but without the precious selection marquee over which you lovingly labored for so long.

If you haven't saved the selection (independently of saving the image file itself), more than an hour of work has just gone

Adapted from *Mastering Photoshop 6*
by Steve Romaniello
ISBN 0-7821-2841-6   896 pages $49.99

down the tubes. However, before you utter a stream of unprintable obscenities, remember, you've learned a valuable lesson: Save your selections using a Photoshop facility called *alpha channels*. In this chapter, you'll learn what channels are, how to work with the Channels palette, perform channel operations, and work with Photoshop's Quick Mask mode.

CHANNEL YOUR ENERGY

There are two types of channels in a Photoshop document. *Color channels* are graphic representations of color information. Having access to this information enables you to perform powerful modifications and corrections to the appearance and color values of the image. *Alpha channels* are selections that have been made with the selection tools and stored for later use.

Color channels are composed of information segregated by color. Each color channel is actually a separate grayscale image representing one of the primary colors of the color space you are working with (i.e., red, green, or blue in an RGB scheme, or cyan, magenta, yellow, or black in a CMYK). When you view the color channels superimposed upon each other in an image, you see the full-color composite image. An alpha channel is also a grayscale image. Like a color channel, it can support 256 shades of gray. Unlike a color channel, however, an alpha channel does not contain information that contributes to the image's appearance. Instead of the values of gray representing tonality or color, they represent the areas of opacity, semi-transparency, or transparency of a mask.

ALPHA CHANNELS AND FILE SIZE

Bear in mind that although alpha channels are stored selections and do not affect the way the image appears, they are perceived by Photoshop as part of the image and therefore increase the file size of the image proportionally each time you save a selection. Photoshop supports up to 24 total channels (except in bitmap images and 16-bit images, which don't support alpha channels) in a document. Images with alpha channels can become quite large and consume a great deal of disk space, so it is best to delete your alpha channels when you are absolutely sure you are done with them.

Photoshop provides many features that help you isolate parts of the image, so that you can perform edits and adjustments to them. It's helpful to think of an alpha channel as a tool that you create, store, and later use to isolate a region so that a tool or command can ultimately be applied to it.

LOOKING AT THE CHANNELS PALETTE

Channels are displayed in the Channels palette (Figure 8.1). (To access the Channels palette, choose Window ➢ Show Channels. Or you can press the F7 key to display the Layers/Channels/Paths cluster.)

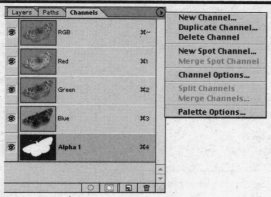

FIGURE 8.1: The Channels palette

The composite channel appears at the top of the palette. The individual color channels appear underneath, each labeled with the name of the color that they represent and a key command that displays them in the image window. As in the Layers and History palettes, the first column, to the left of the thumbnail, displays or conceals an eye icon that tells you what you can see—in this case, it indicates which channels are displayed. Clicking to turn off the eye next to the Red channel, for example, reveals the content of the Green and the Blue channels. Clicking the composite channel eye reveals or conceals the full-color image.

If you save a selection to an alpha channel, it is placed underneath the color channels in the stack in the order in which it was created.

Part ii

Saving Selections as Alpha Channels

Because making an intricate selection can sometimes be difficult or time-consuming, Photoshop enables you to store selections to the Channels palette so that they can be used when you need them. It is wise to save a selection as an alpha channel if the selection is complex, if you need to refine it, or if you going to use it more than once.

To save a selection, follow these steps:

1. Make a selection with one of the selection tools.

2. Choose Select ➤ Save Selection.

3. In the dialog that appears (Figure 8.2), designate the document where the selection will be saved.

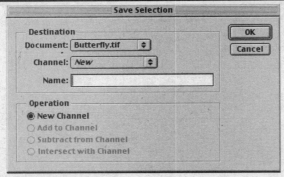

FIGURE 8.2: The Save Selection dialog box

Document   You can save a selection as an alpha channel to the document where the selection was made, or to any open document that is the exact same height, width, and resolution. Their names will appear in the Document pop-up list. Choosing New creates a new document with no color channels and one alpha channel in the Channels palette.

Channel   Choosing New here makes a new channel. You can name the new channel in the Name field. If you don't name it, the saved selection will appear on the Channels palette titled Alpha 1, 2, etc. Selecting a channel name in the Channel pop-up list writes over an existing channel.

Layer Mask You can save a selection as a layer mask from the Channels dialog box. The name of the layer mask defaults to Layer Mask 1. It appear in the Layers palette and the Channels palette.

4. If you have an active selection on the image and you choose a channel name to write over, the Operation area presents you with four options. To choose, click the radio button next to the operation.

Replace Selection discards the original mask channel and replaces it with an entirely new alpha channel.

Add to Selection has the effect of adding the new selected area to the alpha channel.

Subtract from Selection omits the new selected area from the alpha channel.

Intersect with Selection creates an alpha channel of the area where the original channel and the new selection overlap.

5. Click OK to save the selection.

 You can quickly save a selection as a new alpha channel by clicking the Save Selection As Channel icon at the bottom of the Channels palette.

Viewing Color Channels

It is often necessary to examine a color channel in black and white to better observe the brightness relationships of its pixels. By default, color channels are displayed in the Channels palette as black-and-white thumbnails and in the image window as grayscale images. You can display color channels as color overlays by choosing Edit ➤ Preferences ➤ Display & Cursors ➤ Color Channels in Color.

Viewing Alpha Channels

Once an alpha channel has been saved, you can display it or conceal it in the Channels palette. As with viewing color channels, you view or conceal alpha channels by clicking the eye icon to the left of the channel's thumbnail.

Once a selection has been saved as an alpha channel, it can be viewed in the image window: click the channel's name or thumbnail (see Figure 8.3). By default, black represents masked areas, and white represents selected areas. Areas represented by gray are semitransparent.

FIGURE 8.3: An alpha channel displayed in the image window

When color channels and alpha channels are both visible, you see the alpha channels as superimposed translucent color overlays. By default, the overlays are 50% red, which is designed to resemble *Rubylith*, a traditional red-tinted masking film used in the graphic arts industry.

The Channel Options

You may need to change the color of an alpha channel overlay if you are looking at more than one channel at a time, or if the content of the image closely resembles the color of the overlay. If you double-click the thumbnail of the alpha channel, the Channel Options dialog box appears (Figure 8.4). You can then set display options for that channel. The radio buttons in the Color Indicates area let you choose Masked Areas or Selected Areas to be displayed as color overlays, or if you are working with spot colors, you can designate a spot color channel.

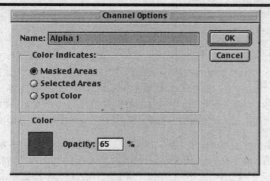

FIGURE 8.4: The Channel Options dialog box

WARNING

Always check the Channel Options dialog to see if Masked Areas or the Selected Area are represented by color. Look at the alpha channel in the image window by its thumbnail. When masked areas are represented by color, the masked area will appear black and the selected area will appear white. The reverse is true when color represents selected areas.

To change the color of a mask, proceed as follows:

1. Double-click the channel thumbnail to display the Channel Options dialog.

2. Click the swatch to bring up the Color Picker.

3. Choose a color and click OK.

You can specify the opacity of the mask from 0% to 100%, which affects only the way you see the mask and not its masking characteristics. Reducing the opacity helps you see the image more clearly through the mask.

Loading Selections

Once saved to the Channels palette, the alpha channel can be loaded as a selection. Loading a selection surrounds the area with a selection marquee just as if you outlined it with a selection tool.

Part ii

To load a selection, follow these steps:

1. Choose Select ➢ Load Selection.

2. In the Load Selection dialog box, the options are similar to the Save Selection dialog. From the Document pop-up list, choose the name of the document where the channel was made. This list will display all alpha channels from all open documents that are the same height, width, and resolution.

3. From the Channel pop-up list, choose the source channel to be loaded. This list displays all alpha channels and layer masks from the current document. The Invert box loads an inverse selection of the mask.

4. If you have an active selection on the image, the Operation area presents four options:

    New Selection   loads a new selection on the image, replacing any currently selected area, if there is one.

    Add To Selection   adds the loaded selection area to an active selection marquee.

    Subtract From Selection   omits the loaded selection area from an active selection marquee.

    Intersect With Selection   loads the area where the loaded selection and an active selection marquee intersect.

5. Click OK to load the selection.

 You can quickly load a selection by dragging its icon to the Load Channel As Selection icon at the bottom of the Channels palette.

EDITING CHANNELS

It is sometimes desirable to change portions of the channel using the painting or editing functions. If, for example, you missed a small part of the selection while using the Lasso tool, you can alter the contents of the mask channel with the Paintbrush to include the areas that were excluded from the original selection. Any painting or editing function that can be applied to a grayscale image can be applied to an alpha channel.

Fine-Tuning Alpha Channels by Painting

Suppose that after having saved a selection there are inaccuracies visible on the mask that weren't visible on selection marquee. You can fine-tune these and other flaws by painting directly on the alpha channel.

Here's a practice exercise on how to alter the contents of an alpha channel:

1. Open the file Alpha_Head.psd, available for download from the Sybex Web site (www.sybex.com).

FIGURE 8.5: The open document Alpha Head

2. View and target the alpha channel in the Channels palette by clicking its name or thumbnail. The channel will appear in the image window.

3. Notice that the foreground and background color swatches in the Tool palette have changed to black and white, and the Swatches palette only displays black, white, and gray. This is because a channel is a grayscale image and does not support color.

4. Choose the Paintbrush, Airbrush, Pencil, or any tool that deposits foreground color.

5. Choose a brush and paint out the eyes of the head with the foreground color (black) as in Figure 8.6. The resulting painting will, by default, alter the selection to mask the newly painted areas when the selection is loaded.

Part ii

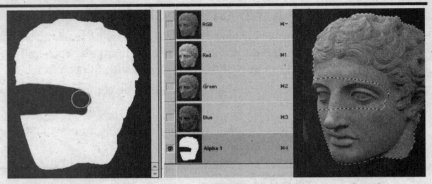

FIGURE 8.6: Painting on the mask overlay (left) alters the selection when the channel is loaded (right).

TIP

In order to produce a more precise selection, it is often necessary to see the image while you are altering the mask channel. You can view both the alpha channel and the composite channel by clicking the eye icons next to them in the Channels palette. Target the alpha channel and apply the paint.

6. Target the RGB channel to view the full-color image.

7. Use Select ➤ Load Selection and choose Alpha 1 from the Channel pop-up list, to see the result.

TIP

If you paint with white, you will erase the masked areas. Painting with a shade of gray will create a partially masked area, the degree of masking depending on how light or dark the paint is. The darker the shade of gray, the more an area will be masked; black will produce areas that are entirely protected.

PERFORMING CHANNEL OPERATIONS

You can perform several operations within the Channels palette that change the structure of the document. Some of these operations produce shifts in the color mode, and some disperse the channels into several documents.

WARNING

Because of the radical changes to the color information, it is always a good idea to make a copy of the document before implementing most of these channel operations. To duplicate the document, choose Image ➢ Duplicate.

Duplicating Channels

When you duplicate a targeted channel, you get an exact copy of it in the Channels palette. You should duplicate the channel if you want to experiment with modifying it by painting, applying a filter effect, or any other editing function. Also duplicate the channel if you want to convert a copy of the channel into a mask. Click the arrow in upper-right corner of the Channels palette and scroll down to the Duplicate Channel command (see Figure 8.1).

NOTE

The Duplicate Channel option will be dimmed if the composite channel is targeted, because you can only duplicate one channel at a time.

    A fast way to duplicate a channel is to drag it to the New Channel icon at the bottom of the Channels palette.

Deleting Channels

You can delete a targeted channel from the document by choosing Delete Channel from the palette pull-down menu. You can delete alpha channels and maintain the integrity of the image. If you delete color channels, however, the color mode of the image will change to Multichannel (see "Using Multichannel" in this chapter). If you delete the Red channel of an RGB image, for example, the remaining color channels will convert to Magenta and Yellow (Multichannel documents always default to CMYK descriptions). You cannot delete the composite channel.

    A fast way to delete a channel is to drag it to the Delete Current Channel icon (the trash icon) at the bottom of the Channels palette.

Splitting Channels

Photoshop can split a document's channels into independent grayscale documents. The title of each window is automatically appended to the

Part ii

channel's color name as a suffix in the image title bar at the top of the window. For example, a CMYK document named Box will be divided into four channels: Box Cyan, Box Magenta, Box Yellow, and Box Black. Alpha channels will be converted to separate grayscale documents. This option is useful as a first step in redistributing channels or for making a single document out of the channels information. This is not a process you'll use every day unless you're a printer who needs to isolate the color information to a single document, or if you have very specialized needs to analyze the channel information. The new documents are not automatically saved, so you should save them to your hard disk.

To split a channel, first flatten the image. Choose Split Channels from the Channels palette pull-down menu. When you perform this operation, the original document is automatically closed.

Merging Channels

Separate channels can be merged into a single Multichannel document by choosing Merge Channels from the Channels palette pull-down menu. The images must be open, grayscale, and the exact same height, width, and resolution. A dialog box appears that allows you to assign a color mode to the image based on the number of images open. Three open images will produce an RGB, Lab, or Multichannel image; four open images will produce a CMYK or Multichannel image. Click OK and another dialog enables you to determine the distribution of the color channels. You can create some rather surprising color distortions by switching color information between channels.

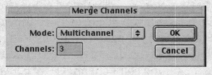 

Using Multichannel

An image's channels can be divided into an individual series of channels. When you choose Image ➤ Mode ➤ Multichannel, the new channels lose their color relationship to each other and appear as individual grayscale channels within a single document so there is no composite channel. This is useful if you want to separate the color information of a composite channel like a duotone, tritone, or quadtone and view the color information of each ink color separately. The Multichannel operation converts the Red, Green, and Blue channels on RGB images into separate Magenta, Cyan, and Yellow channels, within the same document.

Mixing Channels

Channel Mixer is a Photoshop feature that enables you to adjust the color information of each channel from one control window. You can establish color values on a specific channel as a mixture of any or all of the color channels' brightness values. The Channel Mixer can be used for a variety of purposes, including:

- Creating an optimal grayscale image from an RGB or CMYK file
- Making a high-quality sepia tone from a CMYK or RGB file
- Converting images into alternative color spaces
- Swapping color information from one channel to another
- Making creative color adjustments to images by altering the color information in a specific channel

About Spot Color Channels

The spot channel features in the Channels palette pull-down menu are used to create images that are output to film for printing on printing presses. Their most frequent application is used on grayscale images for two- and three-color print jobs. They are also used on four-color process (CMYK) images when additional areas of solid rich color, varnishes, and special inks are specified. Spot colors are usually printed with PANTONE or other custom color inks.

USING QUICK MASK MODE

As you become more proficient in Photoshop, the speed of performing tasks will become more crucial to your particular style of work. As you understand the relations of tool functions and begin to recognize the logic and similarity of the various windows, palettes, and toolbars, you'll want to explore shortcuts that accelerate your work. Selecting areas on a Photoshop image can be the most time-consuming part of the image-editing process; Quick Mask mode can accelerate the selection making and enhance the precision.

 You can toggle directly into Quick Mask mode on the Tool palette by pressing the letter Q or clicking the Quick Mask icon.

Quick Mask mode is an efficient method of making a temporary mask using the paint tools. Quick Masks can quickly be converted into selections or be stored as mask channels in the Channels palette for later use. By default, the Quick Mask interface is similar to the channels interface in that Photoshop displays a colored overlay to represent the masked areas.

TIP

Quick Mask is versatile way of making or editing selections using many of Photoshop's painting and editing tools. You can even use the selection tools to define areas of the Quick Mask to edit.

When you choose Quick Mask mode from the Tool palette, a temporary thumbnail labeled Quick Mask, in italics, appears in the Channels palette. The thumbnail will change appearance as you apply color to the Quick Mask (see Figure 8.7).

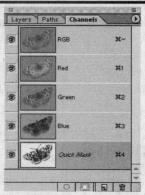

FIGURE 8.7: A Quick Mask thumbnail in the Channels palette

Quick Mask Options Window

The Quick Mask Options dialog is identical to the Channels Options dialog and can be accessed by double-clicking the Quick Mask icon. To practice creating a mask in Quick Mask mode, follow these steps:

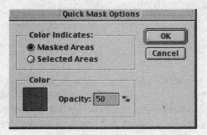

1. Open the file Guitar.psd, dowloadable from the Sybex Web site.

2. Click the Quick Mask icon in the Tool palette. Notice that the foreground and background swatch colors in the Tool palette become black and white.

3. Choose the Paintbrush from the Tool palette. Set Brush options in the Options bar.

NOTE

If you want to be sure that the area is completely masked, set the Opacity slider in the Paintbrush Options bar to 100%. Setting the opacity to 50%, for example, will paint with translucent color; the result is that the painted area will be only partially masked.

4. Choose a Brush from the Brush menu and paint over the guitar. Painting on a Quick Mask is similar to painting on an alpha channel with the composite channel visible. By default, as you paint, if the foreground color is black, the paint tool will deposit a red color. If the foreground color is white, the paint tool will erase the mask color.

5. When you have finished painting the guitar, click the Normal mode icon from the Tool palette. The masked area is outlined by a selection outline. By default, the areas that were painted

Part ii

are now excluded from the selection. You've selected the background. If you want to select the guitar, choose Select ➤ Invert to invert the selection.

6. After all that work, you should save the selection to an alpha channel. Click the Save Selection As Alpha Channel icon at the bottom of the Channels palette.

TIP

Once a Quick Mask has been made, I recommend that you carefully examine it for missed areas and pinholes. It is quite easy to make mistakes because it can be difficult to see omissions and errors on the image. The best way to examine the Quick Mask is to view it as a grayscale image. You can see the Quick Mask as a grayscale by turning off the eye icon on all the other channels in the Channels palette except for the one to the left of the Quick Mask. Examine it carefully to assure that the masked areas are solid and opaque. If necessary, apply more paint to deficient areas.

Quick Mask is ideal for cleaning up selections that you have made with one of the selection or marquee tools. You can paint a few pixels at a time with a small brush or the Pencil, greatly enhancing the precision of making selections.

WHAT'S NEXT

Everybody talks about whether they should do color correction to their images, and the next chapter will show you how to do something about it. You'll learn a half-dozen different ways to adjust the tonality and color of your images.

Chapter 9

ADJUSTING TONALITY AND COLOR

Adjusting and correcting color is the number one use of Photoshop among professional graphics workers, and most other serious Photoshop users also find this image editor's correction tools invaluable as well. Almost every photograph that finds its way onto your computer—whether it is scanned, copied from a Photo CD, transferred from a digital camera, or downloaded from the Web—will need some color adjustment, from minor tweaking to major surgery. Inferior photographic techniques, like bad lighting, poor focus, or under- and overexposure, are a major cause of color problems in images; however, other variables can significantly degrade color and tonality. The type and quality of the equipment that is used to digitize the image is a factor—an expensive film scanner with a high dynamic range can "see" many more variations of tone than an inexpensive digital camera.

Adapted from *Mastering Photoshop 6*
by Steve Romaniello
ISBN 0-7821-2841-6   896 pages $49.99

In the process of capturing an image, software interprets the information collected by the scanner or digital camera. The algorithms used to describe the subtle variations of color and assign values to the pixels can vary. Consequently, the color range, or *gamut* of each device often differs considerably.

Inevitably, you will use Photoshop's color adjustment features to enhance contrast and remove color casts—two basic operations that compensate for the multitude of variables that can occur during input. In this chapter, you'll learn how to measure tonality and color, make quick adjustments, work with Photoshop's Levels controls, adjust Curves, and balance color. You'll also explore using Adjustment Layers and see how the Unsharp Mask filter can improve your images.

MEASURING TONALITY AND COLOR

When you first open an image, you should scrutinize it carefully to determine what the colors on your monitor represent. Be aware that sometimes the on-screen image doesn't accurately represent the image's actual colors. Be sure to calibrate your monitor using Adobe Gamma or a hardware device to create a "ground zero" before performing any color adjustments (see Chapter 1 for more information on calibrating your monitor).

Look at the image's histogram to determine the distribution of tonal values within the image and whether the image has sufficient detail. To view the histogram, choose Image ➤ Histogram.

NOTE

To more accurately display the actual tonal values within an image, you should avoid using the Image Cache to generate the histogram. Choose Edit ➤ Preferences ➤ Image Cache (Mac) or Memory & Image Cache (Win). Uncheck the Use Cache For Histograms box, quit the program, and then relaunch it. (See Chapter 2 for more on setting memory preferences.)

Histograms

A *histogram* is a graph composed of lines that show the relative distribution of tonal values within an image. The more lines the graph has, the more tonal values are present in the image. The height of a line displays the relative quantity of pixels of a particular brightness. The taller the line, the more pixels of a particular tonal range the image contains (see the example in Figure 9.1). The histogram looks like a mountain range on some images, because there can be a total of 256 total values represented at one time and the lines are so close together that they create a shape. The dark pixels, or shadows, are represented on the left side of the graph; the light pixels, or highlights, are on the right. The midtonal range is in the center portion of the graph.

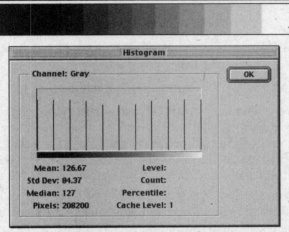

FIGURE 9.1: A histogram representing an 11-step grayscale. Notice that there are 11 lines of about the same length, because the amount of each value is equal in the image.

When you choose Image ➤ Histogram, the numbers below the graph to the left represent statistical data about the image's tonality. The numbers in the right column indicate values about a specific level or range. To view data about a specific level, place your cursor on the graph and click your mouse. To display data about a range of pixels, click the graph and drag to the left or right to define the range.

Value	Definition
Mean	Average brightness value of all the pixels in the image
Std Dev	(Standard deviation) How widely brightness values vary

Value	Definition
Median	The middle value in the range of brightness values
Pixels	Total number of pixels in the image or selected portion of the image
Level	The specific pixel value between 0 and 255 of the position of the cursor if you place it on the graph
Count	Total number of pixels in the Level
Percentile	Percentage of pixels equal to and darker than the Level
Cache Level	The current image cache setting

A histogram can tell us about tonal characteristics of an image. For example, a histogram where tall lines are clustered on the left side of the graph and short lines on the right indicates that the image is dark, or *low key*. A histogram where the tall lines cluster on the right side of the graph indicates that the image is light, or *high key*. Compare Figures 9.2 and 9.3.

Histograms can also indicate deficiencies in the image—for example, a histogram devoid of lines on the left and right ends of the graph indicates that most of the pixels are in the midtone range; therefore, the image lacks highlights and shadows and is of poor contrast. A histogram that has gaps in the graph could indicate that there is insufficient detail in the image (see Figure 9.4).

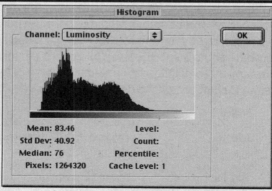

FIGURE 9.2: A histogram representing a dark, or low key, image

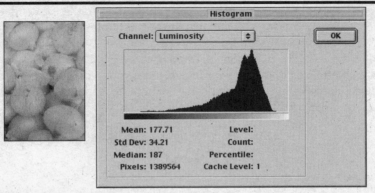

FIGURE 9.3: A histogram representing a light, or high key, image

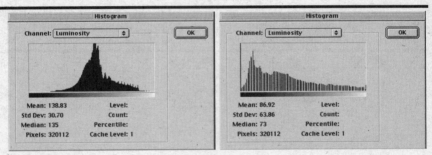

FIGURE 9.4: Histograms representing (left) an image with poor contrast and (right) an image with insufficient detail

The Info Palette

The Info palette enables you to accurately measure the color of a single pixel or determine the average color of a group of pixels. You can use these areas as markers when you make adjustments to the image. To access the Info palette, choose Window ➢ Show Info. The Info Palette has four panes. The two in the top row are called the First Color Readout and Second Color Readout. The bottom row shows the *x* and *y* coordinates of the position of the cursor, and the height and width of the selection.

The First Color Readout and Second Color Readouts can be set to display color information about the pixels at the cursor position, using your choice of nine different modes, listed in the table below. For example, Actual Color shows the color values using the current color mode of the image (typically RGB or CMYK.) You can set the First Color Readout for Actual Color, for example, and use the Second Color Readout for another type of color information (such as Web color, which shows the numeric color values in the hexadecimal units used by HTML code). To see the Info Palette's readouts for your image, place your cursor anywhere on the image. As you drag over the image, the numeric values for the pixel under the cursor are displayed.

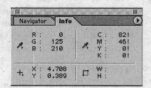

Choosing Palette Options from the Info palette pull-down menu lets you choose from other color spaces for each of the information fields (Figure 9.5). The modes in the Info Options pop-up described here:

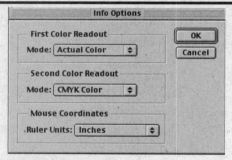

FIGURE 9.5: The Info Options dialog box

Setting	Explanation
Actual Color	Color values of the current mode of the image
Grayscale	Density of black ink that would be deposited if the image were printed in black and white
RGB	Color of the numeric brightness values, from 0 (black) to 255 (white) of each the red, green, and blue channels
Web Color	RGB hexadecimal equivalents of the sampled color

Setting	Explanation
HSB	Hue, saturation, and brightness values of the sampled color
CMYK	Percentages of cyan, magenta, yellow, and black that would be output to process color separations
Lab	Lightness (L), green–red (a), and blue–yellow (b) values of a CIE Lab color image
Total Ink	Cumulative percentage of ink densities of the combined CMYK separations in a four-color process print
Opacity	Cumulative level of opacity on all of the visible layers of an image

The Eyedropper Tool

 When using the Info palette, it is often more accurate to measure a group of pixels, rather than just one, in order to get a better idea of the general tonality of a specific area. When you configure the Eyedropper tool to sample an average, the readings in the Info palette, or any other operation that uses the Eyedropper to sample color, will reflect the new configuration.

In the Eyedropper Options bar, choose Point Sample to sample a single pixel. Choose 3 by 3 Average to sample the average color of a 9-pixel square, or a 5 by 5 Average to sample the average color of a 25-pixel square.

You will usually get the best results by averaging a 3 × 3 square; however, on high-resolution images greater than 400 pixels per inch, you may want to try the 5 × 5 option.

The Color Sampler Tool

 The Color Sampler tool is a way to mark areas of the image for before-and-after comparisons of color adjustments. Prepress professionals will find this tool useful to adjust areas to target CMYK values.

To place a color marker, expand the Eyedropper tool in the Tool palette and choose the Color Sampler. Place the cursor on the image and click your mouse. The cursor leaves a marker and the Info palette expands to display the data for that particular marker, as in Figure 9.6.

FIGURE 9.6: The image with Color Sampler markers and the expanded Info palette

You can sample up to four colors and record the information in the Info palette. To change the color space of a marker, click the arrow next to the Eyedropper icon in the Info palette and drag to the desired color space in the pull-down list shown in Figure 9.6.

To move a marker you've already placed, choose the Color Sampler tool and drag the marker to a new location.

Choose the Color Sampler tool and drag the marker off the image window to delete it. Or choose the Color Sampler tool, press the Option/Alt key, and click the marker.

While a color adjustment is being made to the image, the Info palette displays two numbers for each value, divided by a slash. The number on the left is the numeric value of the sampled color prior to the adjustment, and the number on the right represents the new values of the color after the adjustment. You can compare these values and, with a bit of experience reading these numeric color relations, determine the effect the adjustment will have on the targeted area.

MAKING QUICK ADJUSTMENTS

They say never sacrifice accuracy for speed. Sometimes, however, it's expedient to use one of Photoshop's semiautomatic operations to perform fast adjustments to correct simple problems. This group of commands can change tonal values in an image quickly but lacks the precision of the high-end adjustment features.

WARNING

Using the semiautomatic adjustment features hands over the control of how your image looks to the software. Photoshop is not necessarily the best judge of the aesthetic qualities of your image. So use caution when applying these commands. Occasionally, you'll luck out and they'll work just fine. But more often than not, they don't achieve the best possible results.

Part ii

Brightness/Contrast

Choose Image ➤ Adjust ➤ Brightness/Contrast to perform a global adjustment of brightness or contrast to a selected area or the entire image. The top slider controls how dark or light the image appears, by pushing the pixel values lower when you move the slider to the left, or higher when you move the slider to the right. The slider on the bottom increases or decreases the contrast, by changing the pixel values toward the midtone range when you move the slider to the left, or toward the highlight and shadow ranges when you move the slider to the right. Check the Preview box to see the results.

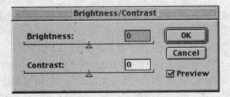

TIP

Be sure that the Preview box, found in all of the adjustment operations, is checked to see the changes to the image before OKing them.

Auto Levels

If you choose Image ≻ Adjust ≻ Auto Levels, Photoshop will make the lightest pixel in each color channel white and the darkest pixel black. It will then distribute all of the other pixels proportionately. By default, the Auto Levels command ignores the lightest and darkest 0.5% extremes when choosing the lightest and darkest colors, so as to choose more representative colors. If you use Auto Levels, watch the image carefully, because it can potentially introduce color casts that you will need to eliminate.

You can change the default 0.5% white-point and black-point percentage by choosing Image ≻ Adjust ≻ Levels or Curves. Press the Option/Alt key to display the Options button. Click the button and enter a value from 0% to 9.99% in the Black Clip or White Clip box. Adobe recommends a number between 0.5% and 1% for the least color distortion.

Auto Contrast

Choose Image ≻ Adjust ≻ Auto Contrast to adjust the overall contrast relations in an image. Like Auto Levels, Auto Contrast maps the lightest highlight to white and darkest shadow pixel to black and maintains the color balance. By default, the Auto Contrast command clips the lightest and darkest 0.5% of the light and dark extremes so as to choose more representative colors.

Variations

If you need a little help visualizing what a color adjustment might look like, choose Image ≻ Adjust ≻ Variations. The Variations command displays thumbnails of potential adjustments, like the ones in Figure 9.7, in the color saturation and value of the image, enabling you to visually choose the most appropriate alternative. The two thumbnails at the top of the window display the original image, labeled Original, and the current image with adjustments, labeled Current Pick. The circle of thumbnails below shows what the image will look like if you add more of a specific color. The Current Pick thumbnail, which is in the center of the circle, changes as you click any one of the color thumbnails. To undo the addition of a color, click the thumbnail opposite it to introduce its complementary color and neutralize the effect.

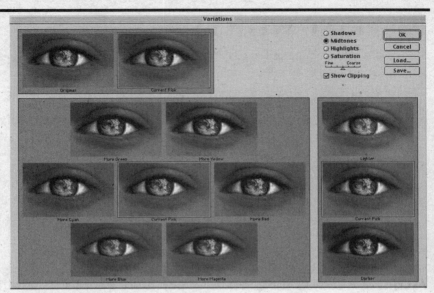

FIGURE 9.7: The Variations dialog box

You can increase and decrease the amount of color to be added, by moving the Fine/Coarse slider: Fine produces small adjustments, and Coarse produces large ones. You can choose to focus the adjustments on specific areas of tonality by clicking the Highlights, Midtones, or Shadows radio buttons.

Clicking the Saturation radio button transforms the color circle into three thumbnails. Click the left thumbnail to desaturate and the right thumbnail to saturate the image.

The field at the right controls the brightness of the image. Click the top thumbnail to lighten the image and the bottom to darken the image.

As you're using the Variations command, you may notice the proliferation of highly saturated color in the thumbnails. These are gamut warnings, and they're there to enlighten you to the fact that some of the colors may be outside of the range of the current color space, which could result in areas of flat or dithered color. To turn off the gamut warning, uncheck the Show Clipping box.

WORKING WITH LEVELS

The Levels command displays an image histogram, which you use as a visual guide to adjust the image's tonal range. Levels initially gives you three points of adjustment. The black slider on the left of the graph determines the darkest pixel in the shadow areas, which is called the *black point.* The white slider on the right determines the lightest pixel in the highlight area, called the *white point.* Move the black and white sliders to adjust the shadow and highlight extremes, respectively, of the image. The middle or gamma slider determines the median value between the black and white points. Move the slider to the right to decrease the median value, thereby making all values lower than the median darker, or to the left to increase it, making all values higher than the median lighter.

Where Input Levels increase contrast, Output Levels decrease contrast. Move the white slider to the left and the black slider to the right to reduce the range of contrast in an image. You can eliminate the extremes of the highlight and shadow in an image. Printers frequently do this to control ink coverage in preparing files for the press. For example, if the black arrow is moved from 0 to 12, values below 5% (equivalent to a 95% dot value) won't print.

When you perform a Levels adjustment, you are actually reassigning pixel values. For an example, suppose you have a low-contrast image like the prairie dogs in Figure 9.8. Here are the basic steps to increase the contrast in this picture:

1. Open the `prairie_dogs` image, dowloadable from the Sybex Web site.

NOTE

To download practice files mentioned in this book, navigate to the Sybex Web site (www.`sybex`.`com`) and enter **2991** into the search box. When you get to the page for *Photoshop 6 Complete*, follow the links to download the file.

2. Choose Image ➢ Adjust ➢ Levels. The histogram displays the deficiency in the highlight and shadow areas, where the absence or shortness of lines indicate there are few pixels.

FIGURE 9.8: These prairie dogs need more contrast.

3. Move the white slider toward the center until it is aligned with the lines on the right of the graph, or until the Input Level box on the right reads 180.

4. Move the black slider toward the center until it is aligned with the lines on the left of the graph, or until the Input Level value on the left reads 33.

5. Move the midtone slider to the right to darken the midtone range a little, until the middle Input Level value reads 0.95.

6 Click OK.

7. Choose Image ➢ Adjust ➢ Levels again. The range of pixel values in the histogram has been redistributed to encompass the length of the entire graph. The lines that had a value of 33 now have a value of 0 (black). The lines that had a value of 180 now have a value of 255 (white), and the median midtone has also changed.

Figure 9.9 shows the histogram before and after the correction. Look at the before and after (Figure 9.10) versions of the prairie dogs in the color section to see the difference this makes in your image.

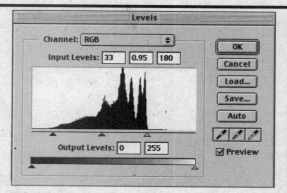 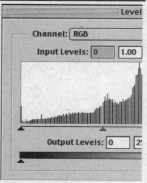

FIGURE 9.9: Sample Levels dialogs, before and after adjustment

FIGURE 9.10: The after Prairie Dog image

Adjusting Channels

If you perform a Levels adjustment on the composite channel, you have only three points of adjustment. If you adjust the Levels of each channel individually, you have nine points of adjustment in an RGB or Lab color image and 12 points of adjustment on a CMYK image. This triples or quadruples the power of the Levels command; it also can produce weird color combinations. To choose a specific channel in which to work, scroll down the Channel pop-up list in the Levels dialog box.

TIP

When adjusting the levels of individual channels, you may need to reset the Levels adjustment several times before producing the right combination of values. To do so, press the Option/Alt key. The Cancel button becomes the Reset button. Click it to begin again. Note that this cancels all of the operations that you have performed in the dialog box, not just the individual channels. To cancel only the last operation, press Ctrl/Command+Z.

Determining White and Black Points

You can use the Levels command in Threshold mode to locate the highlight and shadow areas of an image. You can then assign specific values to those points to redistribute all of the other pixel values between those values.

Finding the Highlight and Shadow Points

1. Be sure that the composite RGB channel is selected from the Channels palette.

2. Open the Levels dialog box (Image ➤ Adjust ➤ Levels) and check the Preview box.

3. Press the Option/Alt key and slowly drag the white Input Level slider to the left. A high-contrast preview appears. The visible areas of the image are the lightest part of the image.

4. Repeat the process with the black shadow slider, dragging it to the right to identify the darkest areas of the image.

You can assign specific values to the darkest shadow areas and the lightest highlight areas of an image and then redistribute the brightness information based on the light and dark extremes of the image. Prepress professionals frequently determine CMYK values for highlight and shadow areas based on the characteristics of their printing presses. When you determine the white point, you use the lightest printable area of the image that contains detail, not a specular white that when printed will contain no ink. The shadow areas will be the darkest area that contains detail and not an absolute black.

Setting the White Point

1. To set the target ink values, open the image `Dreamcar.psd` available for download from the Sybex Web site. (see Figure 9.11).

FIGURE 9.11: The Dreamcar before the Levels adjustment

2. In the Eyedropper Options bar, set the Eyedropper tool to 3 by 3 Average.

3. Choose Image ➢ Adjust ➢ Levels.

4. Double-click the white eyedropper. The Color Picker appears.

5. Enter values for the highlight. Enter these recommended values if you are printing on white paper: 5% cyan, 3% magenta, 3% yellow, and 0% black. The RGB values for this color are 239, 239, 240. The grayscale density is a 6% dot (you can determine the highlight density by the subtracting the Brightness value, B, in the Color Picker from 100).

6. Locate the lightest area on the image but not a specular white. In the case of the Dreamcar, it's the rear fender. Click the area to set the highlight.

Setting the Black Point

1. Double-click the black eyedropper. The Color Picker appears.

2. Enter values for the shadow. Enter these recommended values if you are printing on white paper: 74% cyan, 67% magenta, 66% yellow, and 86% black. If you are working in the Adobe RGB (1998) color space, the RGB values for this color are 13, 13, 13. The grayscale density is a 95% dot. (As with the highlight value, you can determine the shadow density by the subtracting the Brightness value, B, in the Color Picker from 100.)

WARNING

The total ink coverage of all the CMYK values should never exceed 300%. You can try other values of ink depending on the paper, printer, and press you are using. Another frequently used set of values for printing on white stock is 80, 70, 70, 70.

3. Locate the darkest area on the image that still contains detail. In this case, it's the left-front tire. Click your mouse there to set the shadow. Your Dreamcar should now look like Figure 9.12.

TIP

The process for determining the white point and black point is the same for both the Levels and Curves operations. I'll discuss Curves just a couple of pages on.

FIGURE 9.12: The Dreamcar after adjusting the Levels

Saving and Loading Levels Settings

Once you've made a correction to the image, you may want to apply it to another image with the same color problems. Let's say you shot a roll of film at the wrong ASA and consequently underexposed all of the images.

You can adjust one image and apply those settings to the entire group. By first saving and then loading the settings.

To save and load a setting, proceed as follows:

1. Choose Save from the options on the right side of the Levels dialog.

2. Choose a folder in which to save the settings, name them, and click OK. Click OK again to close the Levels dialog box. Now that you've saved them, you can reload them at any time.

3. To load the settings, choose Load from the options on the right side of the Levels dialog.

4. Locate the folder where the settings were saved and click Open to open the settings.

ADJUSTING CURVES

Curves are Photoshop's most powerful color adjustment tool. Where levels give you the ability to change three to nine points of adjustment, curves enable you to map many more. You can adjust an image's brightness curve to lighten or darken an image, improve its contrast, or even create wild solarization effects.

When you open Image ➤ Adjust Curves, Photoshop displays the Curves dialog box (Figure 9.13).

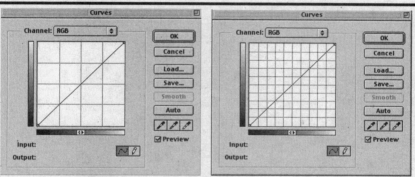

FIGURE 9.13: (left) The default Curves dialog box, showing the 16-cell graph. (right) Option/Alt-clicking the grid changes to a 100-cell graph.

The Graph

By default, the graph is divided into 16 squares each representing 16 brightness levels. Press your Option/Alt key and click the graph to refine the grid into 100 squares, each representing 256 brightness levels for finer adjustment. The horizontal axis of the graph represents the *input* levels, or the colors of the image before the adjustment. The vertical axis represents the *output* levels, or the color of the image after it has been adjusted. By default, for RGB images, dark colors are represented by the lower-left corner and light colors are represented by the upper-right corner of the graph. The diagonal line from bottom-left to top-right represents the brightness levels of the image. Adjustments are made to the image by changing the shape of this line.

Figure 9.14 provides an illustration of the power of curves. The basic photograph (a) is underexposed in the shadows. If you click the center of the diagonal line in the Curves dialog and drag it toward the upper left, you will lighten the image, as in (b). If you bend it toward the lower right, you will darken it (c). If you perform either of these operations, you are altering the position of the midtones.

A classic S curve, as shown in (d), will increase the contrast of the image by darkening the shadows and lightening the highlights. A roller-coaster curve (e) pushes the pixel values all over the graph and creates wild solarization effects.

FIGURE 9.14: Examples of curve adjustments; (a) is the unadjusted image.

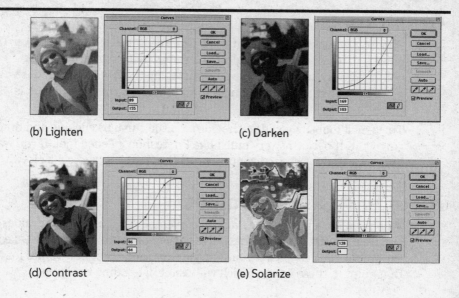

(b) Lighten

(c) Darken

(d) Contrast

(e) Solarize

Part ii

The Brightness Bar

The horizontal brightness bar below the graph represents the direction of the values of the graph. By default, for RGB images, the light values are on the right and the dark values are on the left, but they can be easily switched by clicking the center arrows. If you reverse the graph, the light values will switch to the bottom and left and the dark values to the top and right. If you are working on an RGB or Lab image and you switch the direction of the brightness bar, the numeric input and output values change from a measurement of channel information to ink coverage. This can be useful if you are planning to convert your image to CMYK.

TIP

The default Curves dialog box for a CMYK image is reversed from the RGB or Lab image. The brightness bars display dark values on the top and light values on the bottom. The input and output values are in percentage of ink coverage.

Graph Tools

 Choose a graph tool in the Curves dialog to edit the brightness curve. The point tool is selected by default. Click the curve to establish anchor points, which can then be moved by dragging them with your mouse. As you drag, you can see the changes to your image if the Preview box is checked.

 The pencil tool lets you draw freeform on the curve by clicking and dragging on it. It performs very much like Photoshop's Pencil tool. If you want to draw a straight line, click once, press the Shift key, and click elsewhere.

Input and Output Values

When you move the cursor over the curve, the input and output values change to reflect its position relative to the horizontal and vertical axes of the graph. You can click a point on the curve and enter new values for that point in these boxes, which will result in bending the curve.

Channels

If you perform a curves adjustment on the composite channel, you affect all of its channels simultaneously. As with levels, you can work with more precision by adjusting the channels individually. To choose a specific channel in which to work, scroll through the Channel pop-up list in the Curves dialog box.

TIP
You can also select a combination of channels by Shift-selecting them in the Channels palette before opening the Curves dialog box.

Lock-Down Curves

It helps to work with a *lock-down curve* so that other colors in the image are unaffected when you make the adjustment.

A lock-down curve stabilizes the curve and prevents it from bending. The brightness values that are affected when manipulating the curve can then be better controlled. To make a lock-down curve, follow these steps:

1. Choose Image ➢ Adjust ➢ Curves to open the Curves dialog box.

2. Press Option/Alt and click the grid to display the 100-cell grid.

3. Place your cursor on the diagonal line at the exact point of intersection of the horizontal and vertical grid lines. Click your mouse.

4. Click each intersection point along the diagonal line, as in Figure 9.15.

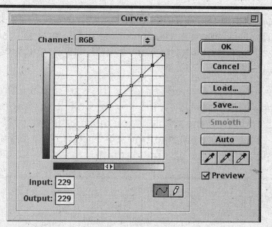

FIGURE 9.15: A lock-down curve

5. Choose Red from the Channel pop-up list. Repeat the process.

6. Repeat the process for the Green and Blue curves. This way, if you need to lock down a specific channel, the curve will be contained within the file.

7. Choose Save and designate a location for your curve. Name the curve **Lockdown_Curve.acv** and save the file. You can now load the curve on any RGB document in any channel at any time.

Determining the Position of a Color

You can pinpoint a color and determine its exact location on the curve. You can then place an anchor point and make a precise spot adjustment to that color only.

To determine the location of a color, follow these steps:

1. Open the file Watermelon.psd downloadable from the Sybex Web site.

2. Choose Image ➢ Adjust ➢ Curves to display the Curves dialog box.

3. Choose Channel ➢ Red.

4. Choose Load from the options on the right side of the dialog. Load the lock-down curve you made in the previous section, or load Red_Lockdown_Curve.acv, also available on the Web site.

5. Place your cursor on the red center of the watermelon. Press the Option (Mac) or Alt (Win) key and click the mouse. Observe the circle on the graph as you move your cursor (Figure 9.16). Press your Command (Mac) or Ctrl (Win) key and click the mouse to place an anchor point.

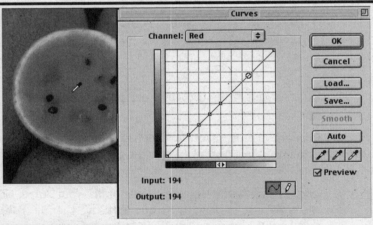

FIGURE 9.16: Determining the anchor point

6. Place your cursor on the anchor point, click your mouse, and drag straight upward until the Output reads 242, as in Figure 9.17. The targeted red in the watermelon intensifies because you've increased its brightness value. All the other colors in the image are left at their original values because you locked them down.

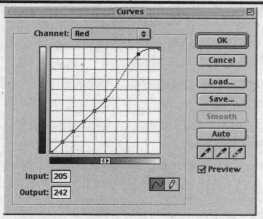

FIGURE 9.17: The watermelon with the Curves adjustment

Saving and Loading Curve Settings

As with levels, once you've made a curves adjustment to the image, you can save the settings and load them to another image:

1. Choose Save from the options on the right side of the Curves dialog box.

2. Choose a folder in which to save the setting, name them, and click OK.

3. To load the settings, choose Load from the options on the right side of the Curves dialog.

4. Locate the folder where the settings were saved and click Open to load the settings.

BALANCING COLOR

After the tonal values have been corrected, you may want to make further adjustments to eliminate the color casts or over- or undersaturation. Color in the image can be balanced using several different methods:

Color Balance   is used to change the overall color mix in an image.

Selective Color   adjusts the quantities of cyan, magenta, yellow, or black in specific color components.

Levels and Curves   enable you adjusts brightness values of individual channels. (See the previous sections in this chapter.)

Hue/Saturation   lets you change the basic color characteristics of the image.

Replace Color   lets you replace the hue, saturation, and brightness of specified areas.

Channel Mixer   is a method of blending colors from individual channels. (See the section on the Channel Mixer in this chapter.)

Color Balance

Color balance is used to adjust the overall mixture of colors in the image and especially to eliminate color casts. To use the Color Balance command, be sure that the composite channel is targeted in the Channels palette.

1. Choose Image ➢ Adjust ➢ Color Balance; the Color Balance dialog box is displayed. (You can also bring this up with the keyboard shortcut Ctrl/Command+B.)

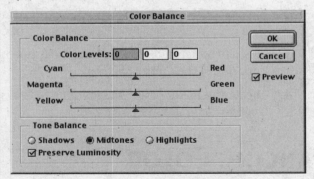

2. Click the Shadows, Midtones, or Highlights radio button to select the tonal range in which you would like to focus your adjustment.

3. Check Preserve Luminosity to maintain the tonal balance of the image and affect only the colors.

4. To increase the amount of a color in an image, drag a slider toward it. To decrease the amount of a color, drag the slider away from it.

TIP

Each color slider represents two color opposites. By *increasing* the amount of a specific color (by moving the slider toward its name), you, in effect, *decrease* its opposite.

Selective Color

The Selective Color command is designed to adjust CMYK images; however, you can use it on RGB and Lab images too. Selective color lets you determine the amount of cyan, magenta, yellow, and black that will be added to predefined color ranges. This is especially good for prepress professionals who need to control ink densities.

1. Target the composite channel in the Channels palette.

2. Choose Image ➤ Adjust ➤ Selective Color; the Selective Color dialog box appears.

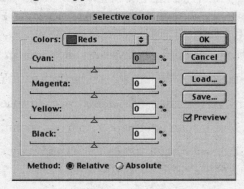

3. From the Colors pop-up list, choose the color range you want to affect. The list shows reds, yellow, greens, cyans, blues, magentas, whites, neutrals, and blacks. Adjust the CMYK

Part iii

sliders to determine how much of each process color the target color will contain. (Some colors may not contain any of the process color, so they will not be affected.)

4. Choose a method:

   Relative   changes the existing quantity of process color by a percentage of the total. For example, if you start with a pixel that is 80% cyan and add 10%, 8% is added to the pixel (10% of 80 = 8) for a total of 88% cyan. You cannot adjust specular white with this option, because it contains no color.

   Absolute   adds color in absolute values. If, for example, you start with 30% cyan in the pixel and add 10%, you end up with a pixel that is 40% cyan.

5. Drag the sliders to the right to increase the amount of the process color component in the selected color or to the left to decrease it.

The Channel Mixer

The Channel Mixer enables you to adjust the color information of each channel from one control window. You can establish color values on a specific channel as a mixture of any or all of the color channels' brightness values. The Channel Mixer can be used for a variety of purposes, including:

▶ Creating an optimal grayscale image from an RGB or CMYK file

▶ Making a high-quality sepia tone from a CMYK or RGB file

▶ Converting images into alternative color spaces

▶ Swapping color information from one channel to another

▶ Making color adjustments to images by altering the color information in a specific channel

▶ Creating weird-looking stuff

The Channel Mixer does not add or subtract colors per se; it combines values from each channel with those of the target channel. The effect is similar to copying the Red channel, for example, and pasting it on the Blue channel. The Channel Mixer, however, offers much greater control by allowing you to vary the degree of the effect.

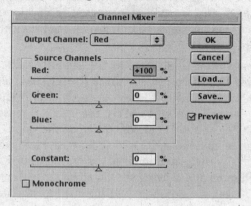

To use the Channel Mixer, follow these steps:

1. Target the composite channel in the Channels palette.

2. Access the window by choosing Image ➤ Adjust ➤ Channel Mixer.

3. Target the channel to be affected by choosing the Output Channel from the pop-up list.

4. Adjust the color sliders to modify the color relations between channels.

Swapping Colors within Channels

You can adjust color information globally on a particular channel or within a selection marquee, so that portions of the image can be quickly altered, corrected, or converted independently while previewing the results.

When you choose a channel by name from the Output Channel pop-up list, the value next to the corresponding Source Channels color slider reads 100%, which represents the total amount of that color in the image. The values can be increased to 200% or decreased to −200%.

The performance of the Channel Mixer depends on the color mode of the image. When working in CMYK, increasing the numeric value of the color cyan or dragging its slider to the right increases the amount of cyan in the Cyan channel. Decreasing the numeric value or dragging to the left subtracts cyan from the channel.

Part ii

Adjusting the color slider of any other color, such as magenta, while the Cyan channel is targeted, changes the amount of the cyan in the Cyan channel based on the relation between the brightness values of magenta and cyan.

When working in RGB mode, the Channel Mixer performs differently. Increasing the numeric value shifts the selected color toward the color of the selected channel, while decreasing the value shifts the color toward its complement. (As with CMYK, the limits of these changes are 200% and −200%.) You can therefore decrease the value of red if you target the Red channel and move the Red slider to the left, which shifts the color toward cyan—the compliment of red on the color wheel. Targeting the Green channel and moving the Green slider to the left shifts the color toward magenta. Targeting the Blue channel and move the Blue slider to the left shifts the color toward yellow.

The Constant slider is like having an independent black or white channel, with an opacity slider added to the targeted color channel to increase or decrease the channel's overall brightness values. Negative values act as a black channel, decreasing the brightness of the target channel. Positive values act as a white channel, increasing the overall brightness of a channel.

TIP

Increasing the brightness of a color channel does not necessarily mean that the image will become lighter. It actually adds more of the channel's color to the image. You can demonstrate this by targeting the Blue channel, for example. Move the Constant slider to the right, and any image will turn more blue. Drag it to the left, and it will turn more yellow (the complement of blue on the color wheel).

Making Optimal Grayscales

Converting a color image directly to a perfect grayscale has been a hit-or-miss process. With the Channel Mixer, you can easily make a perfect grayscale from an RGB or CMYK image, by manual correction and previewing.

When you convert an RGB image to a grayscale, Photoshop uses an algorithm to convert the brightness values from the 16 million colors in its three color channels into 256 shades of gray in the gray channel. By applying the Channel Mixer to the unconverted RGB file, you can control how the image looks prior to the conversion. By moving the sliders, you can emphasize brightness and contrast within the image.

1. Check the Monochrome box in the Channel Mixer.

2. Adjust each of the color sliders until optimal contrast is achieved.

3. Move the Constant slider to darken or lighten the image.

4. When you're satisfied with the results, click OK.

5. Choose Image ≻ Mode ≻ Grayscale to convert the image.

Using Adjustment Layers

When you apply an adjustment operation like Levels, Curves, Hue/Saturation, or the Channel Mixer to an image, you directly affect the information on a layer or on the Background. The only way to change these operations is to return to them in the History palette, which can have complicated and unexpected results if you've done a lot to the image since. Photoshop's Adjustment layers segregate the mathematical data of the adjustment to a separate layer that can be re-edited at any time during the imaging process. Adjustment layers are very handy indeed, and another element in Photoshop's arsenal that keeps the process dynamic.

Creating an Adjustment Layer

1. Choose Layer ≻ New Adjustment Layer and select the type of Adjustment layer you want from the submenu.

2. The New Layer dialog box appears. Name, color-code, and set the opacity and blending mode of the layer, if desired.

3. The Adjustment dialog appears. Make the adjustment and click OK. The new Adjustment layer appears on the Layers palette.

4. In Photoshop 6, the Adjustment layer has an attached layer mask (as in Figure 9.18), which lets you selectively conceal portions of the adjustment.

Part ii

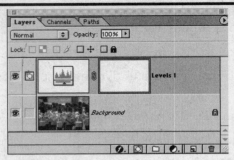

FIGURE 9.18: An Adjustment layer, with thumbnails for the adjustment and for a layer mask

By default, an Adjustment layer will affect all of the layers below it in the Layers stack. You can, however, designate an Adjustment layer to affect *only* the layer immediately below it in the stack. Option/Alt-click the line that separates the Adjustment layer and the layer just below it. The title of the grouped layer becomes underlined, indicating that the two layers are now grouped. You ungroup an Adjustment layer in the same way.

TIP
You can also group a layer by clicking the Group with Previous Layer check box in the New Layer dialog box.

Using an Adjustment Layer as a Mask

The ultimate power of Adjustment layers is the ability to selectively apply an adjustment to the image. An Adjustment layer can act as a mask so that you can conceal portions of the effect. To try out this process, display the Layers palette and follow these steps:

1. Open the document `Mr_Parrot.psd` (available from the Sybex Web site).

2. Choose Layer ➢ New Adjustment Layer➢ Hue/Saturation.

3. In the Hue/Saturation dialog box, drag the Hue slider to radically alter the color scheme of the image. Click OK.

4. In the Layers palette, target the Adjustment layer.

5. Choose black as a foreground color and white as a background color in the Tool palette by pressing the D key.

6. Choose the Paintbrush. Paint the head of the parrot until its feathers are restored to their original red color. If you make a mistake, paint the mistake out with white.

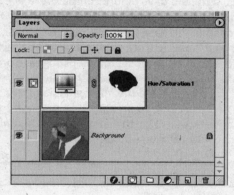

APPLYING THE UNSHARP MASK FILTER

You might ask what a filter description is doing here in the color adjustment chapter? The answer to the question is the Unsharp Mask (USM) filter is a contrast-adjustment tool that goes hand-in-hand with color correction, and if used properly, it can further enhance the color relations and contrast of the image and make it really "pop."

USM exaggerates the transition between areas of most contrast while leaving areas of minimum contrast unaffected. It can help increase the contrast of an image and fool the eye into thinking fuzzy areas of the image are in focus.

To apply the USM, choose Filter ➤ Sharpen ➤ Unsharp Mask (see Figure 9.19). The USM filter has a preview in which you see a thumbnail version of the image. You can reduce or enlarge the preview by clicking the – or + signs. This is helpful if you want to compare the affected preview to the original, unsharpened image. Check the Preview box to see the effect on the image itself.

IF IT'S A SHARPEN FILTER, WHY IS IT CALLED "UNSHARP" MASK?

Many of the operations performed in Photoshop today were derived from traditional optical techniques performed in a process camera. Back in the old days before computers, a special mask was cut to protect parts of images when they were being "bumped" or exposed to increase their contrast. This mask would leave important flesh tones and other critical areas unaffected while enhancing the contrast of the most prominent edges to produce the illusion of sharp focus. Since the area within the mask was being protected and the area outside the mask was being sharpened, the term for the process came to be known as an *unsharp mask*. Photoshop essentially performs the same operation, only digitally and with more control and less labor.

FIGURE 9.19: The Unsharp Mask interface

You'll have a chance to try Unsharp Masking the image at the end of the following Hands-On section for practice.

To apply the USM, move one of its three sliders:

Amount   By moving the slider, or entering a value from 1% to 500%, you determine how much sharpening will be applied. The higher the value, the more the image will be sharpened.

Applying only an Amount, however, will not sharpen the image. In order to see the effect, you must also specify a Radius.

Radius   By moving the Radius slider or entering a value, you control the thickness of the sharpened edge. Lower values produce thinner, sharper edges; higher values produce wider edges with more overall sharpening of the entire image.

Threshold   To control the numeric value of adjacent, contrasting pixels, move the Threshold slider. The slider determines how different the pixels must be from the surrounding area before they are considered edge pixels and sharpened. The slider restores smooth areas that acquire texture when the Amount and Radius are applied—the higher the value, the greater the restoration. Too much Threshold will reverse the effect of the USM.

The goal in sharpening an image is to apply as much USM as possible without blowing out areas, shifting colors, creating dark or light halos, or amplifying noise and unwanted detail. These flaws can make the image appear garish or artificial. You can avoid most problems by applying one or more of the methods discussed in the following sections.

Small-Dose Technique

USM works better in smaller doses. Apply USM several times with smaller settings, keeping the Amount and Radius lower and the Threshold higher. Sharpen gently several times with the same low settings. Press Ctrl/Command+F to reapply the filter with the same values, or reduce the values slightly each time. Keep a close watch on the image as you sharpen it. Sharpen the image until it appears a little too sharp. To see an overall comparison, toggle between the original thumbnail in the History palette (Window ➢ Show History) and the last line of the History list where sharpening was applied.

Flesh-Tone Technique

This technique works particularly well on flesh tones. The problem presented by flesh tones when applying any sharpening filter is the tendency to increase the texture of the skin so that it appears rough or porous. To

Part ii

avoid this problem, apply a larger Amount and smaller Radius. Keeping the Radius low affects only the edge pixels while reducing the sharpening of noise and unwanted detail. Adjust the Threshold to eliminate excess texture in the flesh tones and other areas of low contrast.

Lab-Mode Technique

This method is specially designed to avoid color shifts. In essence, you will be applying your sharpening to the brightness information only. Like RGB mode, Lab mode segregates the image data into three channels. In RGB, however, red, green, and blue channels each contain 256 brightness levels. In Lab mode, the information is divided into an *a* channel (red and green hues), a *b* channel (blue and yellow hues), and an *L* or lightness channel (the brightness information). The L channel is where the USM will be applied.

1. Choose Image ➤ Duplicate to make a copy of your image.

2. Choose Layer ➤ Flatten Image.

3. Use Image ➤ Mode ➤ Lab Color to convert to Lab mode. Don't worry, there is no appreciable loss of color information in this conversion as there is when you convert from RGB to CMYK.

4. Choose Window ➤ Show Channels. Target the Lightness channel by clicking its thumbnail.

5. Click the eye next to the composite Lab channel in the Channels palette so that the full-color image is visible in the image window.

6. Choose Filter ➤ Sharpen ➤ Unsharp Mask.

7. Move the Amount, Radius, and Threshold sliders to produce the desired effect.

What's Next

Nobody's perfect, so you'll find that you may want to reverse or undo what you've done to an image. You may not have made a mistake; it may be that you simply liked an older version better, or you need to restore some image area that was removed or modified. The next chapter will show you how to use Photoshop's very own time machine, the History palette.

Chapter 10

ALTERED STATES: HISTORY

P hotoshop's History capabilities let you change your mind, backtrack, or even delete a single step you may have carried out in the past. Why is that important? Because as we've seen, using layers and saving selections to alpha channels during the editing process keeps the image dynamic. As you continue to work, you can use the History feature to make changes to the image at any time. In other words, you *never have to make a commitment*—that is, until you finally settle down and publish your work.

Photoshop takes the concept of commitment-phobia to the max with the extreme flexibility of its History palette. The History palette is Photoshop's answer to the concept of multiple undos. Where some programs provide a system of undoing operations backward in sequence, Photoshop's interactive History palette features sequential and nonlinear editing. That is, you

Adapted from *Mastering Photoshop 6* by Steve Romaniello
ISBN 0-7821-2841-6   896 pages $49.99

don't need to step backward through all the intervening steps to eliminate one particular step. You can delete *only that step* from the history of modifications you have done.

This chapter explores Photoshop's undo and history features. In this chapter, you'll learn several ways to undo what you've done, including using the History palette and working with snapshots.

UNDOING WHAT YOU'VE DONE

It's difficult to make a (permanent) mistake in Photoshop, because Photoshop can instantly undo most errors. You don't have to ever compromise, because you can reverse any operation. With this in mind, you can feel confident to experiment freely with your images.

The Undo Commands

There are several techniques that reverse unwanted edits. Let's say you are carefully cloning out the blemishes on Uncle Herman's portrait. You've drunk too many double espressos, and your hand is a bit jittery. You slip, you drag a little too far, and you place a big wart on the tip of his nose.

An easily corrected mistake? Yes! The first course of action is to head straight to the top of the Edit menu and select Undo, which will instantly revert the image to the moment before you made the fateful clone stroke. When you order Undo, you get a new command on the Edit menu, Redo, which restores the undone action. You can toggle back and forth between the previous artwork (Undo) and the later look (Redo) by selecting the command again, or better yet, use the key commands in the list below.

Photoshop 6 takes the Undo command a step further than previous versions by adding two additional commands to the Undo operations:

Step Backward   This undoes the last command and then continues in a backward sequence through the operations you've performed, undoing them one at a time. As the operations are undone, you see them disappear one by one in the image window.

Step Forward   If you've applied the Step Backward command more than once, you can restore the undone operations by choosing Edit ➤ Step Forward. As the operations are redone, you see them appear one by one in the image window.

You'll use these operations so frequently that it's worth remembering their corresponding key commands:

Command	Windows	Macintosh
Undo	Ctrl+Z	Command+Z
Step Backward	Ctrl+Alt+Z	Command+Option+Z
Step Forward	Shift+Ctrl+Z	Shift+Command+Z

TIP

As you apply them, the Step Backward and Step Forward commands move one by one through the state list in the History palette. See "The History Palette" later in this chapter.

Begin Again

Another lifesaving operation reverts the image to the last time you saved it. Suppose you've been working on an image for 10 minutes since your last Save, and you decide that somewhere along the line you went astray and the image is not going in the direction you want it to. You have gone too far to make corrections, so you decide you want to begin again. Choose File Revert, and the image will be reopened to the last saved version.

PHOTOSHOP'S TIME MACHINE

The *history* of a Photoshop image is simply a record of work that has been performed on it. Photoshop automatically records every edit, operation, or technique that you apply to an image. As you work, each event, called a *state*—whether it's a paint stroke, filter, color correction, or any other operation—is listed in the History palette (Figure 10.1). You can target a specific state on the list and display its contents in the image window. Like riding in a H.G. Wells time machine, you can freely move through the history of the document, alter states, and in so doing affect the outcome of the final image.

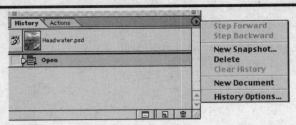

FIGURE 10.1: The opening History palette: nothing has been done yet.

The History states are not layers. They don't contain isolated parts of the image per se. Rather, each state is a record of how the image looked after a specific tool or operation was applied to it. The history is exclusively a record of the changes to the image during the current work session. Once the image is closed, the history is wiped clean, and when you reopen the document, the history begins again. The history cannot be saved or transferred to another image. Program changes to preferences, palettes, color settings, and Actions are not recorded.

The History Palette

The recorder for all of the states is the History palette, which you access by choosing Window ➤ Show History. By default, when the image is opened, the History palette displays a snapshot. The opening snapshot is a picture of the image as it appeared when it was last saved. It is from this point on where you will make changes to the image. Each time you perform an operation, the History palette produces a state with the name of the operation or tool that was used—for example, Paintbrush, Levels, Smudge Tool, etc. The most recent state is at the bottom of the History stack; note that in Figure 10.2, opening the document is at the top. The higher the state appears in the stack, the earlier in the process the state was made.

Changing History

They say you can't change history, but in fact, you can. If you want to move backward in time and see a previous state, click it in the History palette. The image window will display the image as it was during the targeted state. All states below it in the History palette are grayed out.

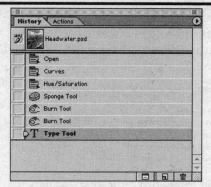

FIGURE 10.2: The History palette after a few operations

WARNING

Be careful! Viewing an earlier state is safe, but if you actually work on the image with a state targeted *earlier* than the most recent, all states below it will be deleted.

For example, if you paint a brush stroke with the Paintbrush on an early state, all states below it will be replaced by one state called Paintbrush. Later, I'll show you how to avoid this by using the Allow Non-Linear History option.

Increasing History States

What allows Photoshop to remember all of the History states is, of course, memory. Each state is stored in your computer's RAM or on the scratch disk. When you exceed the current limit on states, the oldest state is deleted to make room for the most recent state. The number of History states is limited to 20 by default. You can increase or decrease the default number of History states by selecting Edit ➢ Preferences ➢ General ➢ History States and entering a number from 1 to 100.

WARNING

Specifying an excessive number of History states earmarks memory for the History cache and takes the allocation away from Photoshop's other operations. This could compromise Photoshop's performance. Whenever possible, keep the number of states at the default.

Looking at History Options

You can change the behavior of the history by checking options in the History Options window. In the History palette pull-down menu, choose History Options to view or change these settings:

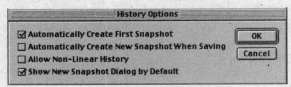

Automatically Create First Snapshot   preserves a snapshot of the original image upon opening it and places its thumbnail at the top of the History palette (see the next section, "Working with Snapshots").

Automatically Create New Snapshot When Saving   generates a snapshot of the current state when saving and adds its thumbnail to the top of the History palette.

Allow Non-Linear History   allows you to discard or edit a previous History state without deleting more recent states.

Show New Snapshot Dialog By Default   automatically displays the Snapshot dialog box when a new snapshot is created.

WORKING WITH SNAPSHOTS

At any point in time, you can save the current image to a snapshot (see Figure 10.3). By saving a snapshot, you can explicitly preserve various states of the image. Snapshots don't count toward the History state limit; they're saved, period, and you don't have to worry about that state being discarded when the limit is exceeded. But of course, they use up memory and, like the rest of the history, are discarded when the file is closed.

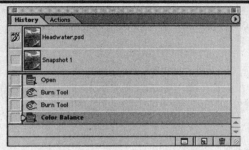

FIGURE 10.3: History palette with a snapshot

Saving Snapshots

Click the History palette pull-down menu and choose New Snapshot. The dialog box that appears allows you to name the snapshot and determine which combination of layers the snapshot will be made from.

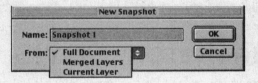

Full Document   makes a snapshot of all the visible layers and the Background.

Merged Layers   makes a snapshot of all the layers and merges them into one layer.

Current Layer   makes a snapshot of the currently targeted layer.

A fast way to make a snapshot is to target a history state and click the Create New Snapshot icon at the bottom of the History palette.

Saving a Snapshot as a New Document

If you want to work on multiple versions of the image or preserve it in a particular state, you can save a snapshot as a new document.

1. Save the History state as a snapshot.

2. Target the snapshot in the History palette and choose New Document from the pull-down menu.

3. Choose File ➤ Save As and save the document to a location on your disk.

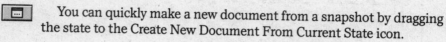 You can quickly make a new document from a snapshot by dragging the state to the Create New Document From Current State icon.

Deleting Snapshots

When you no longer need them, you can discard your snapshots. Here are several ways to do it:

▶ Drag the snapshot to the trash icon in the lower-right corner of the History palette.

▶ Click the snapshot and choose Delete from the History palette pull-down menu.

▶ Click the snapshot and then click the trash icon.

EDITING HISTORY STATES

The primary purpose of Photoshop's history is to keep the editing process dynamic. There are several ways to use the History palette to keep the workflow flexible so that you can experiment freely and confidently.

For all history operations, to target a state, click it in the History palette.

Deleting History States

Sometimes you'll want to delete a state. Try any of these commands:

▶ Drag the state to the trash icon at the bottom of the History palette.

▶ Target the state, then choose Delete from the palette pull-down menu or click the trash icon.

▶ Target a state. All states beneath it will be grayed out. Perform an edit to the state and the grayed-out states will be purged.

▶ Choose Clear History from the palette menu to clear all of the states. Clearing the history retains the snapshots.

▶ Choose Edit ➤ Purge ➤ Histories. All the states but the one at the bottom of the list will be deleted. The snapshots are retained.

Non-Linear History

If you do delete a state, then by default, you'll also eliminate all of the states underneath it. You can, however, change the default. From the History palette pull-down menu, choose History Options and check Allow Non-Linear History.

The Allow Non-Linear History option gives you the ability to eliminate or edit a state in the History palette and still preserve all of the states below it in the stack. For example, you can target a state, make changes to it, save the altered state as a snapshot, target the most recent state and continue working on the image. Experiment carefully with this option, because you can produce strange and unexpected results.

The History Brush

The History Brush tool, which we looked at briefly in Chapter 4, enables you to delete portions of a state. You use the History Brush to restore parts of the image back to a prior event. You can erase portions of a state even if you've edited them later on or painted over them. The Source column at the far left of the History palette tells Photoshop which state you want to return to.

For example, suppose you paint a brush stroke on an image. As you continue to work, each time you perform an operation, a new state is added. If you later decide that you only want to retain half of a brush stroke, here's how to do it:

1. Open the History palette.

2. Click the states from bottom to top in sequence, until you determine the state where you made the brush stroke. (As you click through the history, the brush stroke will suddenly appear within the image.)

3. Click the Source column to the left of the *previous* state, just above the state with the brush stroke. A History Brush icon appears in that column.

TIP

By choosing the previous state as the Source, you are telling the History palette that this is what you want the erased portions of the image to look like. You are actually painting with the previous state in order to eliminate the portion of the brush stroke.

4.   Choose the History Brush from the Tool palette and retarget the most recent state.

WARNING

If the Allow Non-Linear History option is not selected, you must target the last state in the history if you want to avoid losing the intervening states.

5.   Paint on the portion of the brush stroke you want to eliminate.

The Art History Brush

 It's called the Art History Brush because it's quite handy for creating instant Impressionist effects (Impressionism being an important move-ment in the history of art). And I mention it here only because it is in the History Brush flyout on the Tool palette. But it does *not* use the history to alter the image as the History Brush does, except, like any other tool or operation, its effects are recorded as a state each time you apply it. (See Chapter 4 for a description of the Art History Brush.)

Painting with a Snapshot

You can use a snapshot in a similar manner as using the History Brush. Suppose you take a snapshot of an edit you made with a filter. After undoing the filter or eliminating its state, you can selectively apply the snapshot to specific portions of the image. If you save the snapshot as the full document or a single layer, the History Brush will paint from one layer to the corresponding layer on the targeted state. (The color section of the book includes a demonstration of painting with the History Brush.)

To paint with a snapshot, follow these steps:

1. Apply a filter, brush stroke, color adjustment, or any other effect to the image.

2. Choose Make Snapshot from the History palette pull-down menu.

3. Choose Edit ➤ Undo to undo the effect.

4. Click the Source column next to the new snapshot.

5. Choose the History Brush from the Tool palette. Choose a brush size and specify opacity and other brush characteristics in the Options bar.

6. Paint on the areas of the image that you want to affect.

Other History-Editing Features

There are a couple of history-editing features scattered throughout the program that you should be aware of.

The Eraser Tool   With the Erase to History option selected, the Eraser tool erases to a designated History state. You must designate the History state by clicking the Source column in the History palette next to the state you wish to erase to.

Fill From History   Choose Edit ➤ Fill ➤ Use History to fill a selected area with a designated state. You must designate the History state by clicking the Source column in the History palette next to the state you wish to fill with.

What's Next

Why reinvent the wheel? Photoshop's Actions facility lets you record steps for almost any procedure and play them back with the click of the mouse. The next chapter shows you how to use this valuable time-saver.

Part ii

Chapter 11

USING ACTIONS

Many people go through daily rituals. For example, if you go to an office every morning, you probably turn on the computer, log in to a network, check your e-mail, look at your schedule, and visit one of your favorite Web sites for daily news. What if you could sit in front of your computer, turn it on, and have all those actions done automatically for you? That's the basic idea behind the Actions feature in Photoshop, applied to image-editing tasks instead of office routine.

This chapter covers everything you'll need to know about actions, including what they are, how they're created, and how to use them as special effects. When you're finished, you'll have a whole new perspective on how actions can be used to make your image processing more efficient and convenient. In this chapter you'll learn how to create, troubleshoot, and import Actions, and use them to build your own filters.

Adapted from *Mastering Photoshop 5.5 for the Web* by Matt Straznitskas

ISBN 0-7821-2605-7   672 pages $39.99

The Convenience of Actions

When you create a particular project, like a Web site for instance, you ultimately decide on a single "look and feel." Header graphics will use a certain font with a certain color, and your photographs may have a standard height and width, and a black or white border. Preparing all of these graphics can get very monotonous.

Actions take some of the drudgery out of creating such graphics by recording a sequence of commands so that you can repeat them automatically with the click of a single button. The amount of time you can save by creating an action to do the dirty work of processing these images into your desired format is amazing! All you have to do is open up your graphic, create a new action, start recording, and do what you'd normally do. Once you're finished with your process, you hit the Stop button and you're ready to use your action.

It is possible to automate all of the tools in the Toolbar, modify layer modes, and do pretty much everything else in the application. As you'll see, there's almost nothing that can't be included in an action.

Creating an Action

When working with actions, you can either start from scratch or open an existing image and enhance it. The key to creating and maintaining actions is through their palette. Select Window ➤ Show Actions from the Menu Bar to access the Actions palette.

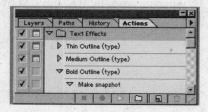

Using the Actions Palette

The Actions palette has several different parts: the list that displays the actions and their parts, the row of option buttons at the bottom, and the palette menu in the upper-right corner of the palette. When working with actions, you will use all three.

TIP

Before creating an action, think it through. It often helps to write down each step before you begin recording. This will prevent you from wasting a lot of time editing your actions after you record them.

Starting a New Action Set

Prior to making your first action, it's a good idea to start your own *action set*. This set is the folder where you store the actions you create. Photoshop comes with its own action set called Default Actions. To create your set, follow these steps:

1. If you make the Actions palette active and all you see are rows of buttons, the palette is currently in "button" mode. Click the flyout menu at the right side of the palette and deselect Button Mode.

2. Click the folder icon at the bottom of the Actions palette. This icon lets you create a new action set. As shown here, the New Set dialog box appears, asking you to name your new set.

3. Enter a name for your action set in the Name text box and click OK. In the example, I've chosen the name My Set.

4. Once your new set appears in the Actions palette list, you should save it. Click the arrow at the upper-right corner of the palette. A drop-down menu appears.

5. Choose Save Actions from the drop-down menu (see Figure 11.1). A dialog box appears, asking you to choose a filename for your set. Type a name and save it.

Part ii

New Action...
New Set...
Duplicate
Delete
Play

Start Recording
Record Again...
Insert Menu Item...
Insert Stop...
Insert Path

Action Options...
Playback Options...

Clear All Actions
Reset Actions
Load Actions...
Replace Actions...
Save Actions...

Button Mode

Actions.atn
Commands.atn
Frames.atn
Image Effects.atn
My Commands.atn
Production.atn
Text Effects.atn
Textures.atn

FIGURE 11.1: Save Actions selected on the Actions palette menu

Making a New Action

Once you've created your own set to store actions in, you're ready to create your first action. Before you start, make sure you are ready to record the action. Once you click the Record button in the New Action dialog box, recording begins. Follow these steps:

1. Click the New Action icon (the paper icon located between the Trash and New Set icons) on the Actions palette. The dialog box shown here appears, offering you several options.

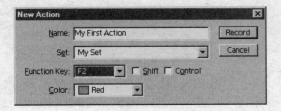

2. Type a name for your action in the Name text box. It's a good idea to make it as descriptive as possible. Vague action names often lead to mistakes when choosing an action to use on a particular set of images.

WARNING

Never test an action on original work. Always make a copy of the file you're working on or use something you're not too worried about messing up.

3. Once you've named your action, choose which action set to associate it with. By default, it should say the name entered earlier—My Set, in this example. If you didn't create a new action set, it will default to the Default Actions set.

4. Choose a keyboard shortcut for your action from the Function Key drop-down list. This is a great idea because you won't have to click Play every time you want to run your action—you can just use your keyboard shortcut. In the example, I've chosen F2.

NOTE

Adobe has tripled the amount of keyboard shortcut options by adding the use of the Ctrl/Command and Shift keys.

5. Choose a color from the Color drop-down list. When the list of actions is in Button mode (shown here), your actions are presented as one-click, color-coded buttons.

Part ii

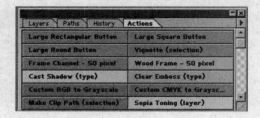

6. Click the Record button to begin recording your action. When you're finished recording (covered in the next set of steps), you'll click the Stop button (the black square on the Actions palette).

The next section takes you through a recording session exercise.

Recording an Action

This section shows you how to record an action that opens a new file, adds some text, applies a shadow, and rotates and crops the entire image. Prepare to record an action as described in the previous section, click the Record button, and follow these steps:

1. Choose File ≻ New and make a file that is 400 pixels wide by 100 pixels high, 72 dpi, in RGB color mode, and with a transparent background.

2. Click OK. You'll notice in the Actions palette that the list item Make appears under the name of your new action (see Figure 11.2).

3. Choose the Type tool and click anywhere in your image.

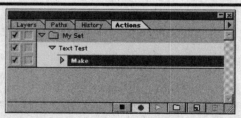

FIGURE 11.2: The Actions palette and an empty, new graphic

4. Choose your Type options from the Options bar.

5. Enter some text, then click the Commit checkbox on the Options palette. Notice that the list item Make Text Layer appears in the Actions palette (see Figure 11.3).

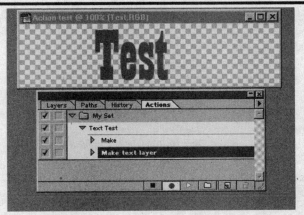

FIGURE 11.3: The Actions palette and a graphic with text

6. Now you're going to add a text effect to your text.

7. Select Layer ➤ Layer Style from the Menu Bar and choose Drop Shadow.

8. Play around with the Drop Shadow options until you're satisfied with how the graphic type looks, then click OK. As shown in Figure 11.4, a new action item that says "Set Layer Style of Current Layer" appears.

9. Select Image ➤ Rotate Canvas ➤ 90° CW from the Menu Bar Your current action item says "Rotate First Document" (see Figure 11.5).

10. Choose the Marquee tool and select your text, eliminating the excess canvas from the selection.

11. Select Image ➤ Crop from the Menu Bar.

12. Click the Stop button to end recording.

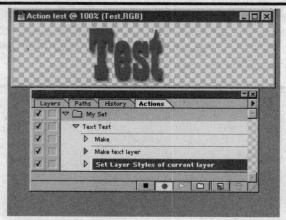

FIGURE 11.4: The new action item for a graphic with drop-shadowed text

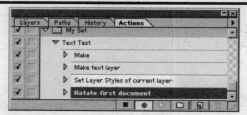

FIGURE 11.5: The rotated graphic and its action item

The above process may seem like a lot of steps, because it is. The point of the exercise is to show you just how many things you can automate using actions. Most of the time, your actions will involve far fewer steps.

Saving Actions

Once your action is complete, it's time to save it. Highlight My Set in the Actions palette and choose Save Actions from the palette's drop-down menu. Notice that Photoshop does not let you save individual actions—it saves them by set.

TIP

As you create more actions, it's a good idea to name your sets by the type of actions that they include. This will make it a lot easier to find what you're looking for.

Playing Back Actions

When you've finished creating your action, you'll want to view it. Follow these steps:

1. Once you've saved your new action, close the image you used to create your action. (You don't need to save it.)

2. Select your first action and click the Play button (the white triangle) on the Actions palette. Notice that it completely re-creates the last graphic you created, faster than the blink of an eye.

3. Go to the Actions palette menu and choose Playback Options. The Playback Options dialog box appears.

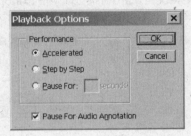

4. You have three playback options for your actions:

    Accelerated   This option is the default. This will cruise through your action so you can get on with other things.

    Step by Step   This option slows things down a little.

    Pause For   This lets you choose the number of seconds your action pauses between steps—very useful in seeing just where a potential action snafu may be occurring. (You can also click the check box to pause for an Audio Annotation.)

    Choose an option and click OK.

Editing Actions

When running the example action, you may notice that you never have the option to change the original text. This action isn't terribly useful if all it does is create a graphic with the exact same text over and over again. It would be best to modify your action so you or someone you're working with can create the same effect using different text. Since you want others to insert their own text, you can have a window appear that allows them to insert unique text. Here's how:

1. In the Actions palette, select the Make Text Layer option (within your action) and then go to the palette menu.

2. Look at the column to the left of the Actions list. You'll see what looks like a depressed button (shown here next to the Make entry). Click that space. A small icon has appeared on top of the depression, and other symbols have also been added to the previous parts of the action—it looks like a tiny dialog box with three dots in it. This represents modal control. Modal controls allow you to stop your action and let the user specify options for the text through a dialog box.

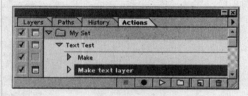

3. Go back to the name of your action, highlight it, and press the Play button again. When it gets to the Text icon, you can enter text.

4. This time through, change the options. Choose a different font, color, and size. Click the Commit button.

This continues the process of the action; and, although you have different text options, you have a similar effect on the text. You can use modal controls for any option that has a depression next to it.

Excluding Commands

There may be a point when you want to exclude a step or command in a particular action because it's not always appropriate. Deselecting the check mark in the far-left column of the Actions palette will deactivate the command, and the task will not be performed the next time you run the action. A red check mark will appear next to actions with excluded commands.

Explaining Steps

Suppose you created a new action for a friend who's not very experienced with Photoshop. You can record a message that will stop the action process and explain the next step to them. Follow these steps:

1. Highlight the appropriate step in the Actions palette (in the example, this would be Make Text Layer) and choose Insert Stop from the palette's flyout menu.

2. In the dialog box that appears, type in your message, as shown here.

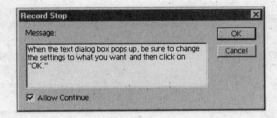

3. Click the Allow Continue checkbox if you want the action to automatically move on to the next step after the message.

4. Click OK.

You now have a mini-tutorial that explains how to use this action. This comes in very handy when you're creating complex actions that need explaining. There might also be some instances where you cannot automate a particular procedure. If so, you can explain what the user needs to do.

NOTE

Action messages are effective for letting users know what types of images the action will work on—some might just work on graphics, while others are effective strictly on photographs.

Deleting Actions

Sometimes an action won't work properly and will need to be discarded. As an example, close the graphic you have created with your action and run the action again. This time, choose a much larger font size. Notice that by the time the action finishes up, more than half of your image is chopped off (see Figure 11.6). What happened? When I chose the Marquee tool to select the layer and crop it, it was only set to select for the original font size—smaller than the font used the second time around.

How do you remedy the situation? There's not much you can do with modifying the selection process for now. Your best bet is to delete the selection and crop steps of the action. Perhaps you'll stumble across a solution later. Besides, you can always append that new step to your current action. To delete the selection and crop steps, select them with your mouse and drag them to the Trash icon, as shown here.

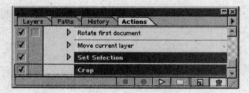

FIGURE 11.6: Chopped-off text graphic

TIP

To select more than one step at a time, hold down the Ctrl key (PC) or Command key (Mac) as you click all your desired selections.

Appending Extra Steps to Existing Actions

Even though in the previous example there wasn't a solution to the crop problem, suppose you still want to add more steps to your action. For example, you decide to give the image a more "plastic" look. Select the action and click Play. This will create an image to use as you add new steps. After it finishes running, click the Record button—the black circle at the bottom of the Actions palette.

To run any filters on the current type layer, you have to "render" it. That is, make it so it's no longer specifically a text layer. Select Layers ➤ Rasterize ➤ Type from the Menu Bar. Then select Filter ➤ Artistic and choose Plastic Wrap. Play around with the options until you're satisfied, then click OK.

Choose Stop on the Actions palette's list of recorded commands. Two new options appear in your menu: Rasterize Type Layer and Plastic Wrap. If you want to move these new options anywhere within the action, all you have to do is click and drag. If you try to move the Plastic Wrap option up above Set Layer Effects and run the action from scratch, you'll get an error.

TIP

There are some points during the creation of an action where certain menu items cannot be used. Make sure you test your actions after rearranging options.

Re-recording Actions

Sometimes you don't necessarily want to add a new step to your action, but you want to modify the settings of one of the existing steps. Rather than trashing and re-recording an entire action, you can simply delete just one step, append it, and move it into place.

The Record Again option takes care of this situation quite nicely. Select the action element you wish to re-record and choose Record Again from the Actions palette menu (see Figure 11.7). The dialog box for that option opens so you can modify your settings. After you click OK, the recording stops, and your fixed item works.

There might also be times when you're not so sure about an entire action. You might want to modify several steps, but you're not sure which ones. By selecting the entire action and choosing Record Again from the Actions palette menu, you will be walked step-by-step through each option until you're finished. You can choose to either modify an option or leave it as is.

When you're re-recording actions, it's a good idea to make a copy of the entire action. To do this, click an action and select Duplicate from the Actions palette menu. Use the copy to make any changes and, when you're sure it works, delete the original.

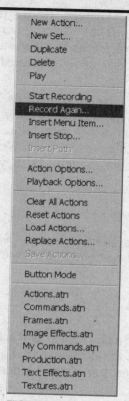

FIGURE 11.7: Selecting Record Again from the palette menu

TROUBLESHOOTING ACTIONS

There are times when an action will go wrong. Maybe it didn't work as you had planned or you were unsure of the steps involved. That's when troubleshooting kicks in. Also known as "debugging," *troubleshooting* is when you work out the kinks in a program or script—or in this case, an action.

The best way to troubleshoot an action is methodically, step by step. You may notice that each list item within an action has a little triangle pointing to the right. Click the triangle, and it displays all the specs for that action. If something's wrong with it, you'll probably be able to determine it there.

TIP

Don't forget you can re-record a list item within an action by double-clicking it or by choosing Record Again from the Actions palette menu.

THE LIMITATIONS OF ACTIONS

Since Photoshop 4, Adobe has greatly expanded the types of things that can be done in an action. However, there are a couple limitations. For instance, while you can record the selection of the painting, drawing, and toning tools, you cannot record any actual use of them. Tool options, Photoshop preferences, and any of the View menu options cannot be recorded.

The solution is to insert a menu item into your action. If you go to the Actions palette menu and choose Insert Menu Item, you can then choose something from any drop-down menu. These methods help deal with any limitations that actions might pose.

TIP

The title of each action list item is the equivalent of what you would type under the Insert Menu dialog box for that action.

IMPORTING EXISTING ACTIONS

Photoshop comes with an amazing amount of prerecorded actions. They are divided into seven categories:

Buttons   This set of actions creates some great 3D buttons for use on Web pages.

Commands   This is a set of fairly common menu commands to be inserted in various new actions.

Frames   This is a set of complex actions that create elaborate frames for use with pictures. They can be used for creating unique picture galleries.

Image Effects   These actions create cool image effects like blizzards, light rain, aged photos, and much more.

Production   These actions are primarily for preparing images for print production. Included is an action for creating a transparent GIF.

Text Effects   These effects can be great for the graphical text used on Web pages.

Texture   This makes some interesting textured swatches that can be applied in the creation of backgrounds.

To use these actions, go to the Actions palette menu and choose Load Actions. The Photoshop actions are located in the Goodies ➤ Actions directory.

NOTE

Be sure you read the directions to the actions. Some will have the word "selection" in parentheses. This means part of the graphic you want to modify needs to be selected. Others will specify whether the graphic needs to be grayscale or in color.

Actions as Filters

Avid Photoshop users know that there are dozens of commercial filter products available for sale as Photoshop plug-ins. However, several actions that now come with Photoshop can provide many of the same effects. This section takes an in-depth look at a few.

Photo Effects

Photo galleries are everywhere on the Web, especially on personal home pages. Photoshop's pre-prepared Frames and Image Effects action sets provide some realistic-looking effects for such graphics.

Frames

Here's how to experiment with a few Frame actions provided by Adobe:

1. Replace the current actions with the Frame action set using the Actions palette's flyout menu.

2. Open a photograph. Figure 11.8 displays a photo before any effect is applied.

FIGURE 11.8: A photograph before using the Photo Corners action

3. Choose the Photo Corners action.

4. Click the Play icon. Figure 11.9 displays the photo after the effect is applied.

You also have a few choices with selections in photographs:

1. Choose a photograph with a person or animal.

2. Using the Elliptical Marquee tool, select a portion of your photograph. Figure 11.10 displays a photo before any effect is applied.

FIGURE 11.9: The photograph with photo corners added

Part ii

FIGURE 11.10: A photograph before using the Vignette action

3. Select the Vignette action. The higher the feathering amount you select, the better the effect.

4. Click Play. Figure 11.11 displays the results.

FIGURE 11.11: The photograph after using Vignette

Effects like these usually take a lot of work, but with actions you can create them in just seconds.

Image Effects

The Image Effects action set is a great tool and offers everything from faux weather effects to aged photo effects. Here's how to use it:

1. Replace the current actions with the Image Effects action set by choosing Load Actions from the Actions palette drop-down menu.

2. Open up an outdoor photograph. Figure 11.12 displays a "before" photo.

3. Select the Blizzard action.

4. Click Play. Figure 11.13 displays the "after" version.

FIGURE 11.12: An outdoor picture with clear skies

FIGURE 11.13: The same picture with a blizzard

OK, so you're probably not going to use this effect all that often. Still, someday you may need to, and it's good to know that it's available. Here's another effect:

1. Open up any photograph (see Figure 11.14).

FIGURE 11.14: A landscape photo before taking action

2. Select the Oil Pastel action.

3. Click Play. See Figure 11.15 for the results.

If all goes well, you've given your photograph a more painterly look.

FIGURE 11.15: A landscape photo after taking action

Text Effects

Photoshop's Text Effects action set gives you ways to create dynamic text graphics. Here's how to implement the Brushed Metal action:

1. Replace current actions with the Text Effects action set using the palette menu.

2. Open a new image.

3. Using the Type tool, create some text in your new image and rasterize it (see Figure 11.16).

4. Select the Brushed Metal action.

5. Click Play and view the results (see Figure 11.17).

FIGURE 11.16: Text before adding effects

FIGURE 11.17: Text after adding the Brushed Metal effect

Cleansing the Palette

Once you discover the wonderful world of actions, you may get a little overzealous and load several sets into your Actions palette. This can get very messy. The best thing to do is to clear your palette after you're done with each set. If you don't want to choose Clear before you load a new set, choose the Replace Actions option from the Actions palette drop-down menu. This clears the palette before the new set loads,

TIP

You can use the Reset Actions command to restore the default actions settings that shipped with Photoshop.

Part ii

ACTIONS SUMMED UP

Actions provide a great way to automate most of the monotonous, repetitive tasks found in Photoshop and Web image creation. As long as you think logically and plan out an action ahead of time, you will be able to develop some very useful shortcuts. In time, you can drastically reduce the amount of time it takes to create a large number of graphics for a given project.

Actions also allow you to apply some cool special effects to text and images. Photoshop ships with lots of these effects, but there is also a growing list of Web sites dedicated to providing homemade actions. And if you're creative enough, you might be one of the people providing such actions to these sites.

WHAT'S NEXT

Although it's a favored tool, Photoshop is rarely the only weapon in a graphics professional's armory. Often, you'll find Adobe Photoshop, Corel Procreate Painter (formerly simply Corel Painter), and Adobe Illustrator installed on the same computer and working side-by-side. It helps that all three are available for and work identically on both Macintosh and Windows platforms. But the real reason for the widespread use of this trio is that each of these programs excels at different types of tasks. In the next chapter you'll find a comparison that will help you decide whether you can take advantage of these Photoshop "add-ons."

Chapter 12

MOVING ON: PHOTOSHOP, PAINTER AND ILLUSTRATOR

If your goal is to master Photoshop, do you really need to learn another pixel-based image editor like Corel's procreate Painter (formerly Corel Painter, MetaCreations Painter, and Fractal Design Painter)? Should you tackle a vector-based drawing program like Adobe Illustrator? Absolutely not. You don't even have to go digital at all. If your work is so fabulous and distinctive that clients are lined up waiting to pay whatever you ask, by all means keep doing what you're doing... and please, teach the rest of us!

Most of us these days need the computer. In a brief ten years or so, it has changed from being the cutting-edge tool in only a few well-to-do shops into the everyday processor of the work we do.

Adapted from *Photoshop, Painter, and Illustrator Side-By-Side* by Wendy Crumpler
ISBN 0-7821-2923-4   400 pages $49.99

If you use the computer, you don't have to necessarily know more than one application. You may find that your signature style fits nicely within the confines of one application, and that's great—you'll certainly save on upgrades. But there are reasons, good reasons, to use more than one application.

You probably work on the computer to save time and make your work easier to revise. But you may be slowing yourself down unnecessarily by trying to accomplish all types of work in one application. What if you could save 15 minutes a day using a different application? Doesn't sound worth it? But what if you project that into saving 5 hours a month or 60 hours a year? It starts to sound more reasonable to plunk down another 400 to 600 dollars. The truth is you'll be saving time, reducing aggravation (how much is that worth to you?), and having more fun using better tools.

Does this sound like I'm slamming Photoshop? No. I'm saying that Painter is built to do some tasks with amazing grace and beauty. Illustrator makes it much easier to build shapes because it's designed to be a shape-building and -manipulating tool. Photoshop has its strengths as well; It's a color corrector's dream. I wouldn't think for a moment of trying to adjust critical color in Painter. Its tools are basic and unusable for most delicate color adjustments.

Each of these applications is a powerhouse in its own right. But to harness that power, you do best to use the strengths of the given application. The beauty of using these three particular applications together is that the weakness of one is very often the strength of one of the others.

I'll start with Photoshop. You already know that it is a joy to work with. Most of the tools are intuitive and robust. In my opinion, its major strengths are its ability to manipulate color and its compositing power.

When it comes to color, no other application comes close to Photoshop. Half of the artists that I spoke to mentioned Photoshop's superior color capabilities as one of the reasons they rely on Photoshop. If you learn how to read color output from the Info palette and calibrate your monitor well, you can get accurate color from almost any output device, as you'll see in Chapter 26. I'm not telling you that the monitor you use will always display that color, but Photoshop will always give you an accurate readout of what the color is in numeric values. And if the color is not what you want it to be, you open Photoshop's color correction tools and fix it.

That may sound simple, and Adobe has done an enormous amount of work in the past few years to make the process as simple as possible. In truth, color correction is not as simple as an automatic adjustment. But if critical color is what you need, Photoshop has all the tools to achieve your goal. I know artists who manipulate color in Painter and are relatively happy with the results. I know artists who manipulate color in Photoshop and are ecstatic. In Painter, you can adjust the RGB curves of a file; in Photoshop, you can adjust the RGB or CMYK curves, and you can save your adjustment to an Adjustment layer or to a settings file, which can be loaded to process multiple images.

The Adjustment layer is another element of Photoshop's color superiority, and it's mentioned over and over again (along with Photoshop's better Layers palette) as a primary reason for using the application. You can have multiple adjustments to a single layer, and each adjustment can be masked so only portions of the image are affected by the adjustment. These adjustments never change the underlying color values of the file until you merge the adjustment layer or flatten your file. Unlike Painter, where most changes to the color alter the original values of the file, with Photoshop's adjustment layers you can change the value of the adjustment repeatedly and still get back to the original color at any time.

Did I mention that you can have a mask associated with an adjustment layer? And a mask associated with the layer itself? And alpha channels, which are masks that can be used with any layer? And clipping masks on a layer with or without a layer mask? Photoshop's superior masking ability and its friendlier user interface for layers is another reason it is both the color and compositing champion.

What is it particularly about the Layers interface that works for artists? Photoshop shows you its layers and their masks side-by-side on the same palette (see Figure 12.1). A heavy black border tells you whether you are editing the layer or the mask. Painter makes you open two separate, large palettes for layers and masks, so you have to look in two places to figure out what you're doing. I asked artists what their favorite feature is in Photoshop, and the most common answer is layers and layer masks.

The third most common answer for favorite feature is the History palette and multiple Undos.

There are additional important tools that Photoshop does better: Color Range, Gaussian Blur, and Unsharp Mask are among them. Though Painter has similar tools, its preview is usually too small, meaning you have to scroll around to get an idea of what the overall affect will be. And sometimes you only have a slider to work with, rather than a field for text entry. Not only do I want precision the first time I run a filter or effect, I want to be able to use that exact same value again and again, if necessary. Photoshop makes this easier and is therefore a better production tool.

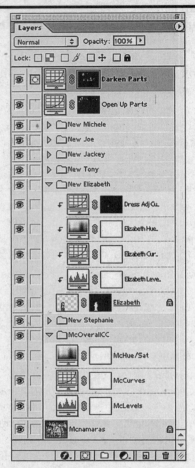

FIGURE 12.1: This needs a caption.

If Photoshop does all of these things better, why use Painter at all? The answer is simple: to paint. If you love the way oil colors combine for unexpected and delightful results, if you've ever marveled at the delicacy of watercolor spreading like fog across paper, if you've ever blended pastels until the color was seamless and perfect, you have to try Painter. If you are used to the Adobe interface, don't let all of those giant palettes intimidate you. In Painter you need to find and use the few indispensable tools. These will include Brushes (maybe a few, but maybe a whole arsenal), Paper, and Effects.

The pressure sensitivity of Painter's brushes is one aspect of its superior painting ability. These days, a graphics tablet with a pressure-sensitive stylus is nice to have in Photoshop, important in Illustrator, but an absolute necessity in Painter. Painter is about naturalistic artwork. You'd think it ludicrous to switch colored pencils from dark red to medium dark red in the middle of a stroke. You'd simply lighten the pressure of your stroke. Painter can do that with bells on as long as you have a pressure-sensitive tablet. And Wacom's Intuos tablet has 1,024 levels of sensitivity. In addition, there's an airbrush tool that you can add to your Intuos tablet that includes a wheel to control the spray and can recognize the tilt and bearing of the tool. It's pretty incredible. I've had several different tablets and, for the artist (especially if you are a traditional airbrusher), the Intuos airbrush and Painter together are mind-boggling. If you've been using only Photoshop's airbrush, just switching to Painter's airbrush is a big improvement. If you've been using the Painter airbrush with a regular stylus, try the Intuos tool and you won't want to do anything but airbrush for days. It's completely addictive and well worth the additional expense.

But wait, there's more. Painter's brushes can lay down multiple colors in one stroke. This doesn't mean a fade from one color to the other as in Photoshop. It means two or more colors for the entire length of the stroke if you like. You can use Color Variability to lay down multiple colors and Brush Loading to pick up multiple colors. So, if you are using an "oil" brush, you can pick up the underlying color on a bristle-by-bristle basis. This is incredible technology that produces beautiful artwork.

NOTE
Painter is also the only one of the three applications that can paint with depth, giving the digital equivalent of piling paint on the canvas.

I mentioned using a paper grain in Painter and how easy it is. That's because there is always a paper grain associated with your painting. You must use a brush with a Grainy method subcategory, such as Gritty Charcoal to paint with grain, or use an effect that allows you to access Paper (many do), but both are simple to do. If you are a pastels artist, you can set up a custom palette full of brushes that react to the paper surface. This includes blending brushes, such as Coarse Smear, that don't disturb the grain unless (just like real life) you press hard and push the color down into the paper. Painter is that good. Suppose you inadvertently use the wrong brush or have to delete a portion of your artwork, and you somehow lose the grain? Then you can use Effect ➤ Surface Control ➤ Apply Surface Texture to get it back. This is one of my favorite commands, and I'm not the only one. Of the artists that I queried who are using Painter, the most often cited reason was the natural media brushes. The second reason was Texture. For one artist, the ability to quickly apply texture was the main reason to use Painter.

NOTE

Photoshop does have a Texturizer filter, and it does a very nice job of creating texture on a file or areas of a file. But when you pick up your brush to paint again, you lose that texture. So think of it this way: If the work you do is primarily photographic, use Photoshop; if it's painterly, use Painter.

With two applications that do so much, why on earth use a third? What exactly does Illustrator have to add that couldn't be done elsewhere? In a word, precision. It's the only one that has the capacity to handle the complex lines and areas generated from computer data for mapmaking and other critical line-oriented applications.

The most-used feature of Illustrator? The Pen tool. Now, both Photoshop and Painter have Pen tools, so why does everyone who uses the Pen Tool use it in Illustrator? Precision and control in drawing. The Pen tool in Photoshop has come a long way and now actually builds shapes on their own layers, yet when we asked artists if this had changed their basic method of working, the overwhelming answer was "no." Illustrator gives you commands and options for more precision in how you build the shapes and how you combine them.

Illustrator lets you hide other shapes to get them out of the way when you are drawing. You can switch views to check only the outlines of your paths to make sure everything is accurate. You can view the outlines of some paths while viewing the artwork for others. You can create specialized views of areas of your artwork and switch between them with simple shortcut keys. You can make a guide out of any shape to help build curves or angles that are unusual or difficult. You can keep all your shapes on one layer or move them to separate layers, whichever works for the illustration. When you need to redraw a shape, you have a wide array of tools and commands to help you.

Another Illustrator feature, and second on its list of most often used tools, is the Pathfinder palette. If you are adept at drawing shapes with the Pen tool, you'll appreciate how quickly some shapes can be generated by uniting or dividing basic shapes. If you're not adept at the Pen tool, you'll like not having to struggle, because Illustrator can do so much of the work for you. Unite and Divide definitely get the most use, according to my survey, but Minus Front (or Back), Crop, Soft Mix, and Hard Mix were also mentioned. If you use Illustrator, but not the Pathfinder palette, you are definitely doing things the hard way.

Next on the list of important features of Illustrator was its type handling.

Though most of the artists said that the upgrades to Photoshop and Illustrator had not changed their basic work process, type is one area where Photoshop will be giving Illustrator a run for its money. Photoshop's type-handling abilities are very robust in version 6. If basic type is all you've been using Illustrator for, you can now accomplish your work completely in Photoshop. I know at least one illustrator and one production manager who have already done so.

NOTE

That said, I'll reiterate that if you need specialized type, like type on a curve or painted with multiple fills or strokes, Illustrator's still the place to be.

So here's what you need to know in a nutshell. For scanning, compositing, and color correction, use Photoshop; for building shapes, blocking in a basic illustration, or specialized type handling, use Illustrator; and for painting and texture, use Painter. Like all rules and dictums, you can choose to follow this or not.

There's no right way, there's only what works.

DIFFERENCES BETWEEN PHOTOSHOP, PAINTER, AND ILLUSTRATOR

One of the most difficult aspects of switching applications is navigating the interface differences. Some very strong applications have failed because they were close in function to another application with a larger market share, but too different in methodology for the public to make the transition. Over and over again, the artists that I've spoken with tell me that they love the breadth of using more than one application, but despise having to wrestle with function keys, shortcuts, and remembering where commands are in different programs. I'm going to give you some of the major areas that trip people up. Getting used to seeing the screen from different applications is rather like switching spoken languages. You may get confused about verb endings, but you get to the point that you can converse reasonably well and feel comfortable wherever you go.

Tools

In this section, we'll take a look at some of the differences between the tools that are available in each of the three programs.

Tool Options

Certainly the biggest news in interface differences is Photoshop's Options bar. This sleek little palette is open by default but can be closed by choosing Window ➢ Hide Options. Almost everything you need to know about every tool is accessible from the Options bar, and many functions that used to be contained in their own palettes are here as well. You no longer double-click a tool icon to get its options; you just check the top of the screen to see what's happening in the Options bar.

One of the best features of the Options bar is that it changes depending on what you are doing with a tool or command. Let's say you are drawing a shape for a Shape layer. When you click the shape tool, the Options bar has icons for whether the shape is to be a new Shape layer, a new path in the Paths palette, or a new filled area. It also shows you the different shapes you can choose.

If you click each shape icon, you'll notice that the Options bar changes to give you choices for that particular shape. Right beside the shape icons is a drop-down panel that will show you the current options for the chosen shape. If you click the Custom Shape icon, you get an additional drop-down arrow from which you can access the custom shapes presets. For all the shapes, there is a drop-down for layer style, another for blending mode, and an Opacity selector. After you draw one shape, the Options bar changes; you still have the shape icons, but layer style, blending mode, and opacity are gone. Instead, you have shape interaction icons, which let you decide how additional shapes will affect the first one.

Switch to the Path Component tool, and the Options bar changes to help you manipulate the shapes on screen. Select Edit ➢ Free Transform and the Options bar changes again, giving you input areas for any transformation you want to make. With things changing so quickly and with so many pop-ups and drop-downs, you might think you'd find the Options bar annoying. But the beauty of the thing is that it's so very quiet; it never interferes with your work—it's just there to help. And if you don't like where it sits, you can move it around the screen. It docks nicely at the top or bottom of the screen to save space. Every person I've spoken to since the introduction of Photoshop 6 thinks the Options bar is great, and I'm convinced that the best interface designers in the world clearly work at Adobe.

Illustrator did make some minor interface changes at version 9 but mostly in the Layers palette and the new capabilities of transparency, appearance, and effects. The tool options remain virtually unchanged from previous versions. Illustrator has some tools whose options or preferences are reached by double-clicking to bring up an options palette and others (such as gradients and type) with separate palettes that need to be opened to access the power of the tool. Painter tool options are always on the Controls palette, unless a separate palette (such as Brush Controls) or palette section (such as Art Materials: Nozzles) applies to the tool.

Tool Keyboard Shortcuts

This is certainly one place where it's easy to get confused. It's bad enough that each application can have different shortcut keys for virtually the same tool, but even worse is the fact that shortcut keys may change within an application from version to version. You used to type A for both the Selection and Direct Selection tools in Illustrator. Now, the Selection tool is called the Move tool and you type V to access it, just as in Photoshop. You used to cycle through the tools in a tool bay by using Shift plus the tool shortcut letter in both Photoshop and Illustrator. Now that doesn't work in Illustrator, and some of the Photoshop tool shortcuts have changed.

This is not done purposely to make artists crazy, but it certainly adds an unnecessary level of frustration. Luckily, Illustrator lets you adjust the keyboard shortcuts for all the tools. Use Edit ➤ Keyboard Shortcuts to set up shortcuts for both your tools and menu items. Find the key whose shortcut you want to create or edit, click in the Shortcut area, and type the key or keys (you can use the Shift key) you want to use. If the shortcut is currently used by another tool, an alert will tell you. You can also type in a symbol that you want to appear in the menu bar or tool tip.

Part ii

(See Figure 12.2.) Once you've set up the shortcuts, you can save them to a special set and can export your keyboard shortcuts as a text file that can be printed out for reference. (See Figure 12.3.) Illustrator ships with an Illustrator 6 set, if you still prefer those shortcuts.

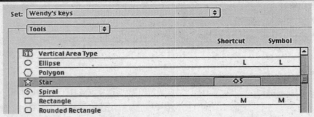

FIGURE 12.2: Input a letter or number to use as the shortcut. You can use Shift as well for tool shortcuts. For menu shortcuts, you must use Command as part of the shortcut.

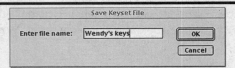

FIGURE 12.3: Once you customize your set, save it with your name, so you can reload it if someone else wants to use a different set.

Photoshop changed a couple of its tool shortcuts for version 6. The Pencil tool is now accessed by typing B, same as the Paintbrush (Shift+B toggles between them), and the Paint Bucket shortcut is now G as it is stored in the tool bay with the Gradient tool. Typing K now gives you the Slice tool. If you use the Pencil or the Paint Bucket a lot, you have to learn a new shortcut—sorry. If you want to completely disable the ability to cycle through tools using the Shift key, use Edit ➤ Preferences ➤ General and deselect Use Shift Key For Tool Switch.

Painter has about half as many Toolbox tools as the other applications and uses a different keyboard shortcut for every tool. Unfortunately most of the shortcut keys differ from the Adobe products, but the ones that are the same are some of the most important: B for Brush, P for Pen, C for Crop, and W for Magic Wand. Text (T) is also the same, but I don't consider it to be a primary tool for most types of work since Painter introduced Dynamic text. The Paint Bucket (K) is the same as Photoshop's old shortcut. I'd love to see both Photoshop and Painter give you the ability to customize your tool shortcuts.

Sampling Color When in Painting Tool

In Photoshop, you can bring up the Eyedropper to sample color in the middle of using a painting tool by holding down the Option key. You do the same thing in Painter by holding down the Command key. In Illustrator, if you hold down the Option key while using the Paintbrush, you get the Smooth tool. You have to actually switch to the Eyedropper tool (shortcut key I) to sample attributes.

Background or Paper Color

Paper color and Background color are not synonymous. When you open Photoshop and you choose a color for the Contents of a new document, you can choose to make the workspace white, transparent, or the "Background Color."

Choosing the Background or Paper Color

Now, how do I say this? In Photoshop, background color is temporary, a fleeting thing that will change as you work with brushes, or do masking, or one of a hundred other little chores. You'll change it without noticing. And then, you'll pick up the Eraser tool to make some changes and erase to a color you didn't even know existed. On the other hand, in Painter, you set the Paper Color when you open a new file, via the Color Picker. (See Figure 12.4.) This is more comparable to choosing a paper color in traditional media. Do you want a warm or cool paper? Remember that the color will show through when you use a grainy media such as chalk or pastels. And, when you erase in Painter, you erase to this paper color no matter what the current secondary color is set to.

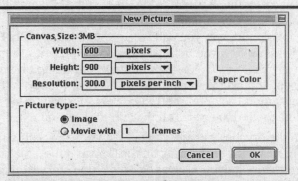

FIGURE 12.4: In Painter, choose a paper color that compliments your artwork. Click the color swatch to bring up the Color Picker.

Part ii

Illustrator doesn't need to ask you about the background color or paper color. Every new document opens with a white artboard. If you want a colored background for the artwork that you build in Illustrator, you can build a colored background to size in Illustrator, place your artwork on a colored background in your page layout program, or place a file from Photoshop or Painter in Illustrator to serve as the background. If you know you're going to print on colored stock, you have one further option and that is to set up your document to Simulate Colored Paper. To do this, use File ➢ Document Setup and go to the Transparency options. (See Figure 12.5.) Change the color on the Grid Size swatch to match your paper then turn on Simulate Colored Paper. When you exit the dialog, your artboard changes to the color you've chosen and you get a preview of how any artwork you've built will look when printed. If you have to print on some crazy paper color, you'll really appreciate this feature.

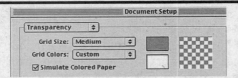

FIGURE 12.5: Illustrator's Simulate Colored Paper option is in the Document Setup dialog under Transparency.

Changing the Background or Paper Color

What if you want to change the color of your background? In Illustrator you'd click the object you've built to contain the color of the background and change its fill color, or change the color in the page layout program, or place a different raster file. If you're using the Simulate Colored Paper option, you'd just change the color of the grid. It really wouldn't be a big deal to change the color any way you had set up your document. In Photoshop, a lot depends on how you built your document. If you've kept a single layer with a background color, then built all your Image layers on top of that, you could quickly Command/Ctrl+Delete to change that layer to the current background color on the Toolbox or Color palette, or even Option/Alt+Delete to fill that layer with the current foreground color.

Depending on the brushes you are using in Painter (especially Grainy or Drip brushes), you might be painting on the Canvas quite a bit because you want the underlying Canvas color to either show through or mix with the color you are applying. Let's say you started with a nice

Chinese white canvas but later decided that an ivory or pale ochre would really be more appropriate to the piece. If all of your artwork is on independent layers, you're in luck. You can simply fill your Canvas layer with the color you want, then make sure you set the same color as your new paper color (Canvas ➤ Set Paper Color).

The real problem arises when you have created your artwork on the Canvas layer. If you set a new paper color, it doesn't mean that the color you originally chose as your paper will magically disappear and be replaced by the new color. Unfortunately, you have to erase, or select and delete, all of the old color to have the new color show through. (See Figure 12.6.) You might be able to do this reasonably well with Color Select or Magic Wand, or it could be impossible. Plan accordingly. In Painter 6.1 you can work on a layer with Pick Up Underlying Color enabled or not. The check box on the Objects: Layers palette, seen in Figure 12.7, tells brush types that use "brush loading" to pull color from all of the visible layers, including the Canvas.

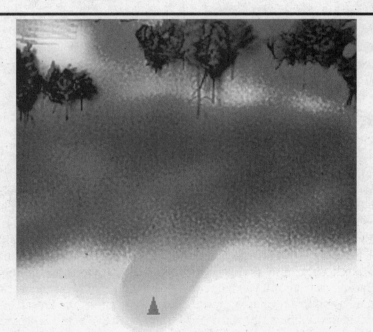

FIGURE 12.6: If you are working on the Canvas and change the paper color mid-drawing, the original color remains as if you had put it down with a layer of paint. You must erase the old color (white in this case) to see the new.

FIGURE 12.7: The Palette Knife brush pulls color from the background into the layer when Pick Up Underlying Color is checked.

Erasing to the Background, Transparency, Paper Color, or White

If you are using the default colors, you think of the "background" of a Photoshop file (or perhaps I should say, what you erase to) as being white, but it certainly doesn't have to be. If you set up a document that uses Background Color as the Contents of the new file, and that background color is green, you'll get a big green screen. Later, if you erase something when your background color is 50% gray (maybe you've been editing a mask), you'll erase gray streaks onto your green file. Probably not what you mean to do, so choose carefully. This is what happens when you are painting on the Background layer. If you paint on a floating layer or turn your Background layer into a regular layer, you need to be aware of the Preserve Transparency option at the top of the Layers palette. When it is off, you erase to transparency in a layer; when it is on, you erase to the current background color.

On Painter's layers, if Preserve Transparency is on, you erase to the current paper color. If Preserve Transparency is off, you erase to transparency. When you are on the Canvas level, you always erase to the current paper color. On both layers and Canvas, the exception is the Bleach variant of the Eraser brush—it always erases to white, regardless of the transparency setting. If you expect to erase to white in either application, make sure you have the layers and colors set up correctly, or use the Bleach Eraser in Painter.

Screen

What does your screen look like when you open a new or existing document? It can take more than a few moments to orient yourself if you have only worked in one of the applications; the window that opens looks different in each.

Document or Artboard Size

One of the first issues to deal with is the size of the document. Both of the raster applications, Photoshop and Painter, will open a new window that is exactly the size you specify in inches, pixels, or other unit of measure. (See Figure 12.8.) More than likely, you'll fill every pixel of the file with image before you place it in a layout program or print it.

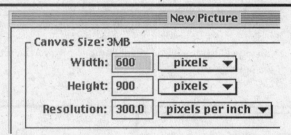

FIGURE 12.8: Both Photoshop and Painter give you a working document only as large as you specify.

Illustrator comes from a different direction altogether. It's oriented to traditional graphic arts, in which you have a page size that you use, but place that page on a drawing board where you can hold all the elements as you move them around, try different layouts, lay things down, peel things up. It's one of the more confusing aspects of setting up a document in Illustrator. It is not necessary to build the page the size of your final artwork. In fact, Illustrator doesn't even ask you what size document you want when you ask for a New document. It gives you whatever size is used in your Adobe Illustrator Startup file. Unless you've done some modification, that's going to be 8.5" × 11". No matter. When you save your file as an EPS, the file is only as large as the art it contains. Neat and efficient.

Part ii

If you want to change the size of the artboard to match the size of your artwork, use File ➤ Document Setup to enter the dimensions for your image, as shown in Figure 12.9. If you get margin lines that are disconcerting to you, use View ➤ Hide Page Tiling to hide them, or set up your page size in the Page Setup (Print Setup for Windows) to match the dimensions in your Document Setup. (See Figure 12.10.) This sometimes depends on what print driver you have chosen; some will not accept custom page sizes. As you often build artwork that is larger than the printer on which you proof your work (perhaps a laser printer or inkjet with maximum print size of 8.5" x 11"), you may need to tile the artwork for proofing.

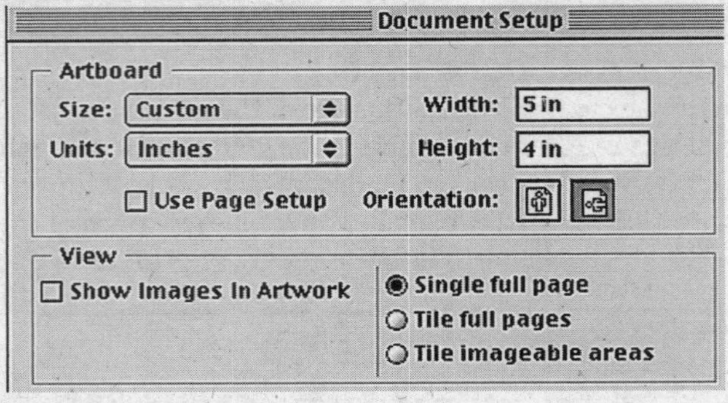

Document Setup

Artboard

Size: Custom ⬍   Width: 5 in

Units: Inches ⬍   Height: 4 in

☐ Use Page Setup   Orientation: [⬛] [⬛]

View

☐ Show Images In Artwork   ⦿ Single full page
                                ◯ Tile full pages
                                ◯ Tile imageable areas

FIGURE 12.9: You can change Illustrator's Document Setup to give you an artboard the exact size of the finished art.

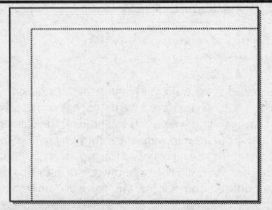

FIGURE 12.10: If you wonder why you have these strange margin lines, larger or smaller than your sheet, it's because your Document Setup and Page Setup are not the same dimensions.

If you are printing directly from Illustrator, it's usually a good idea to set up your artboard larger than your final printed piece to accommodate crop marks, trim marks, registration marks, and maybe bleeds. I generally use the Single Full Page or Tile Full Pages options because they show me the printable area of my page, then I use the Page tool to move around the artboard to print the area I want. (See Figure 12.11.) If you'd just like to print the entire piece without stopping to manually tile, choose Tile Imageable Areas. Most printers will not print to the edges of a page, and that limit is marked by the dotted line on the inside of the page boundary. Make sure you place all of the artwork you want to print inside those print boundaries. It's not particularly intuitive, is it?

FIGURE 12.11: Use the Page tool to reposition the printable page over the area of the artwork you want printed.]

Rotate Page or Constrain Angle

Painter does a lot to support artists who have been working traditionally, and being able to rotate the entire page to accommodate your drawing style is one aspect of that support. The Page Rotate tool is a pop-up of the Grabber hand. (See Figure 12.12)

FIGURE 12.12: The Page Rotate tool is a pop-up of the Grabber hand.

Click and drag the page with it and you get an arrow pointing to the direction of the new orientation. When you release the mouse or stylus, your page rotates. When you want to reorient to perpendicular, click once in the image with the Page Rotate tool (or double-click the Page Rotate tool). Figures 12.13 and 12.14 show an image before and after it has been rotated.

Part iii

FIGURE 12.13: Click and drag with the Page Rotate tool as if you were rotating any other element on the page.

FIGURE 12.14: The entire page now is at an angle that makes drawing more natural.

Illustrator doesn't go quite as far to make drawing easy for you, but it does have the Constrain Angle in the General Preferences, where you can enter the desired angle, as shown in Figure 12.15. This can aid you immensely when you are doing a drawing that requires something other than 90° for your X and Y axes. Then, when you hold down the Shift key, objects you draw are constrained to that new angle.

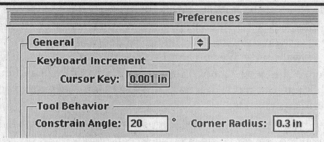

FIGURE 12.15: Though you don't rotate the page, you can constrain objects you draw to something other than 90°.

Fit in Window

There's no built-in keyboard shortcut for Fit in Window in Painter, and you'd be amazed how many times I hit the old Command/Ctrl+0 to fit the artwork in the window. Set up a function key, or double-click the Grabber hand to Zoom to Fit.

Outline Mode

It's not as important in Painter that you be able to see the outlines (line art) that comprise your illustration, but you might expect that you'd be able to if you are used to working with vector objects. The ease of switching between Preview and Outline mode is another reason that you might choose Illustrator to build shapes. In Painter you would have to select the shapes and remove stroke and fill to see the lines only. If you prefer to work in that mode, then under Edit ➢ Preferences ➢ Shapes set the Pen tool to draw with no stroke or fill. In Photoshop, though you see the lines of the paths, you usually view them against the image; unless your artwork is simple, the paths can be difficult to see. You can turn off the eye icons for all your layers and view paths against the transparency background, but that might not be too helpful either.

Screen Mode

In both Photoshop and Illustrator, to rotate among screen modes (Standard, Full Screen With Menu Bar, and Full Screen), type F or click the Screen Mode icons at the bottom of the Toolbox. The screen modes in the applications look a bit different from each other, however. Illustrator's modes show you the artboard and the pasteboard (all white), while Photoshop shows you the file surrounded by whatever color you have chosen as "edge" (gray by default, but you can change it) when in Full Screen With Menu Bar mode, but switches to a black background when you go to Full Screen mode.

In Painter, type Command/Ctrl+M or use Window ➤ Screen Mode to toggle between the regular mode and full-screen mode.

Palettes

There are minor and major differences between the applications and their use of palettes. In my opinion, Photoshop and Illustrator are easier to use because of the simplicity and elegance of their palette design. Still, Painter has much to offer, especially its custom palettes. I'll try to show you the major differences here, but the only way to truly understand how the palettes work is to use them and get a feel for them. You'll also find some specifics on palettes under the chapters that pertain to major palettes such as Layers, Brushes, and Color.

Tear-off Palettes

Only Illustrator has tear-off palettes. Any tool that has more than one option can be torn away from the Toolbox into its own little floating palette. (See Figure 12.16.) If you find in building your artwork that you switch a lot between the Star tool and the Spiral tool, just click and hold down the Oval tool until you see the tiny triangle on the far right. If you move the mouse or cursor over that triangle, the palette tears off. Clicking the Close box on the upper-left corner of a torn-off palette returns it to its home.

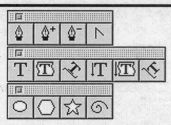

FIGURE 12.16: You can tear off any tool that has multiple options and move it around your artwork.

Grouping, Docking, and Collapsing Palettes

Here are the major differences in the operation of palettes, and I do mean major. Illustrator and Photoshop let you change the grouping of palettes to accommodate your workflow. There are default groupings such as the Layers, Channels, and Paths palettes in Photoshop, but if you never work with Paths, you could pull that palette by its title tab out of the group and close it. If you need to see both the Layers and Channels palettes at the same time (which is often the case), you can ungroup them or expand them in their bay. This way, you can keep only the palettes you really need open on your desktop. Within a group of palettes, you bring one to the front by clicking its tab.

Painter's palettes contain many sections that cannot be ungrouped from the parent. It's really too bad, because you may only need one or two of the sections at any time. It would be especially nice in Painter to be able to choose only the palettes you need and group those three or four together. Another feature of Painter palettes is they automatically expand to show you the entire palette section when you click its name or triangle. This can be great; it also can be annoying when you want to keep several palettes in view but you expand one that automatically covers the others. Avoid this by docking the palettes under each other. If you drag the title bar of a palette under the bottom of another palette, you'll feel the palette snap to the bottom. When you arrange the palettes this way, opening a palette section expands that section but does not increase the size of the palette itself. You can then use the scroll bar or Grabber hand to move to the portion of the palette that you need to see. Photoshop and Illustrator both dock their palettes also, but as they don't automatically expand it's not as vital to dock. In both those applications, you can also use the scroll bar to view other portions of the palette.

To keep the palettes handy but unobtrusive in Photoshop and Illustrator, use the icon on the top right of the palette to Minimize/Maximize (Windows) or Resize (Macintosh) the window, which collapses the palette but keeps visible all of the title tabs in the group. (See Figures 12.17a and 12.17b.) You can also double-click the palette tab, but if you double-click the title bar of a palette in Photoshop and Illustrator, it collapses too small to see the title tabs of the group. In Painter, you open and collapse palette sections by clicking the section name or arrow. Shift-click collapses all sections, but there is no way to completely collapse an entire palette.

FIGURE 12.17A: In Illustrator and Photoshop, you click the icon at the top right of the window...

FIGURE 12.17B: ...to collapse the palette but keep the title tabs of the group visible.

Palette Well and Docking to Screen

Another nifty idea from Photoshop is the palette well, a little storage area within the Options bar for you to place palettes you refer to occasionally. To dock a palette in the well, drag it from your screen into the open space at the right end of the Options bar. From the palette well, you can click the tab of a palette to display it, but when you go back to work in your document, the palette pops back into its place. If you want to keep the palette available, pull it out of the well and onto your work area or use View ➤ Show and choose the appropriate palette. The palette well is only available when you use a screen resolution greater than 800 × 600.

If you find you need to work with a palette more often than those in the well or you want to keep one open while you work sometimes, you might try docking that palette to the bottom of your screen. To do this, grab the palette tab and move it all the way to the bottom of the screen. If the palette is open, it will collapse and "snap" to the bottom of the screen. When you want to use the palette, double-click the tab and it will open, as shown in Figure 12.18. Double-click again to close and "snap" back, or you can use the Collapse button at the upper right of the palette dock to expand and collapse the palette. Convenient, and you don't have to learn any keyboard shortcuts to show and hide your palette.

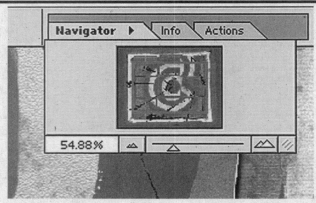

FIGURE 12.18: When you click the tab, the palette pops up. Go back to work and it disappears.

Drawers

Painter assumes that most users are visually oriented and therefore want icons to help them choose art materials to use. That may be, but they sure make for big palettes. If, however, you are a person who likes to see before you use, you're in luck. Painter has drawers on many of its palettes, which you can open for a look at all the materials within. Drawers appear on the Brushes, Gradients, Papers, Patterns, Weaves, Nozzles, Dynamic Layers, Scripts, Image Portfolio, and Selection Portfolio palette sections. Click the light blue "pushbar" to open the drawer and see icons for the other materials inside. When you click an icon in the drawer, it is brought to the front of the drawer (the row of icons that is visible even when you close the drawer). If you'd like to replace a specific icon on the drawer front, drag the new icon on top of the old one. The icon you replaced returns to the drawer. If you want to lock an icon on the drawer front so it is always available to you, click it and hold the mouse or stylus down until a green light appears under the icon. Unlock it the same way. You can lock all but one icon on a drawer front; one must remain replaceable with other items from the drawer.

Resizing Presets

Artists work differently, one from the other, and what suits you may be annoying to someone else. Palette size is a perfect example. Some people want their palettes as small as possible; others want to see all the options all the time. Photoshop allows you to change the size of the preset palette panels that pop up from the Options bar to accommodate your personal style. If you like to see all the options, you can lengthen or widen the palette (your choice). If you prefer to take up as little screen space as possible, you can narrow the palette and use a scroll bar to see all the options, as shown in Figure 12.19. When you reopen Photoshop, it remembers how you have your palettes set and will display them accordingly. (This only works when you resize the palette from the Options bar, not from the Presets Manager.)

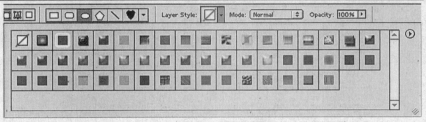

FIGURE 12.19: You can make your preset panels quite large if you want to display all the options.

Rearranging Palettes

In both Photoshop and Illustrator, you can dock palettes together in a palette bay. In addition, Photoshop 6 has a new way to rearrange palettes within the palette bay. You can grab a title bar and move it up or down (but not out of the bay), and the palette will expand but still be part of the bay. You can still move the palettes as a group, but you can have two or three palettes open in the bay at the same time, as shown in Figure 12.20.

Although Painter does not allow you to group and ungroup palettes, you can do a bit of rearranging to keep often-used sections at the top of a palette. Click in an open area of the title bar (not on the title or triangle) of the palette section you want to move and drag it to a new location in the palette.

Part ii

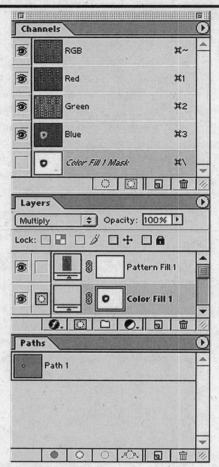

FIGURE 12.20: You can open one or all of the palettes in a bay, and they always travel together.

Opening and Closing Palette Sections

To open a Painter palette section, either click its name or the triangle to the left of its name. Clicking the section name closes other open sections; clicking the triangle leaves the others open. Close an open palette section with another click. You can also shift-click a section triangle to open or close all the sections in that palette at once.

Current Settings Shortcuts

When you see a Painter Art Materials palette section that has an icon on the right side of its title bar, that's a Current Settings shortcut. If you click directly on the icon, you get a pop-up menu of all the items currently available in that section, plus the Load Library command. If you can orient verbally rather than visually, using this pop-up means you won't need to open the palette section unless you want to change some of the options. The Art Materials: Color section is the exception; its Current Settings icon shows you the current primary color, but nothing happens when you click it.

Scrolling Open Palettes

All three applications give you a scroll bar on the right side when an open palette has more information than the current palette window can accommodate. Painter gives you an additional way to scroll an open palette. If you click in an empty space on an open palette, you get the Grabber hand and can move the palette up or down that way. If no empty space shows, you must use the scroll bar. If your palettes are not docked, opening another palette section will expand the palette window, usually eliminating the need to scroll.

Showing and Hiding Palettes

Here's one that will surely trip you up: How do you hide or display the palettes? If you answer Command/Ctrl+H, it's clear that you are a Painter user; in Photoshop or Illustrator, Command/Ctrl+H shows or hides the extras (Photoshop) or the edges (Illustrator). (This is a keyboard shortcut you use a lot, especially in Photoshop.) To hide the palettes in the Adobe applications, use the Tab key. Use Shift+Tab when you want to hide all palettes but the Toolbox. If you want to hide or show just one or two palettes in Painter, use the shortcuts: Command/Ctrl+1 for the Toolbox, Command/Ctrl+2 for Brushes, and so on. The shortcuts list can be viewed in the Window drop-down menu, as shown in Figure 12.21.

Saving Palette Layouts

Both Photoshop and Illustrator save the current location of your palettes when you quit the application. When you reopen the application, you should find the palettes right where you left them. In Photoshop, this is a preference item, so turn it on if you find your palettes always in the default layout when you open the program. Saving the last location of the palettes

Part ii

is great and Painter does it too, but Painter goes them one better. You can save specific layouts for certain types of tasks, such as working on masks. Creating custom palettes and saving layouts for specific images can save time on projects. Painter ships with a default docked palette layout which you can quickly switch to if your palettes have gotten out of hand.

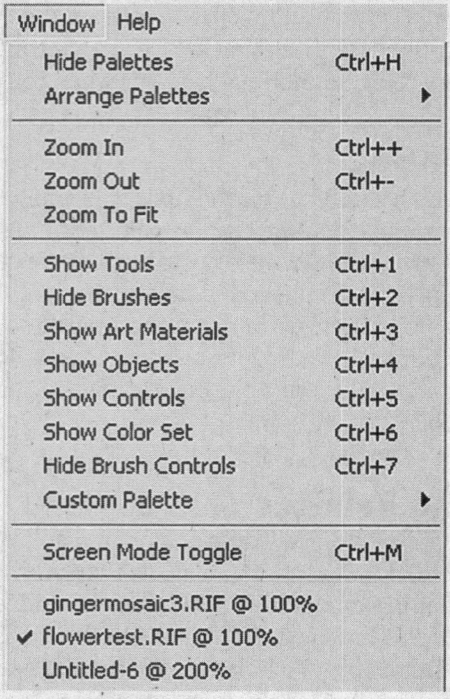

Window	Help	
Hide Palettes	Ctrl+H	
Arrange Palettes		▶
Zoom In	Ctrl++	
Zoom Out	Ctrl+-	
Zoom To Fit		
Show Tools	Ctrl+1	
Hide Brushes	Ctrl+2	
Show Art Materials	Ctrl+3	
Show Objects	Ctrl+4	
Show Controls	Ctrl+5	
Show Color Set	Ctrl+6	
Hide Brush Controls	Ctrl+7	
Custom Palette		▶
Screen Mode Toggle	Ctrl+M	
gingermosaic3.RIF @ 100%		
✔ flowertest.RIF @ 100%		
Untitled-6 @ 200%		

FIGURE 12.21: Here is the Window menu on Windows. Ctrl+H hides all palettes. You can also use keyboard shortcuts to hide or show individual palettes.

Info palette

Painter doesn't have an Info palette, though the Controls palette often has a lot of useful information. Illustrator's Info palette gives you the x-y coordinates, the size of a selected object, and the angle and size of transformations. Photoshop's Info palette gives you the x-y coordinates of the current cursor location, a color readout of that spot in two color spaces of your choice, the angle, the width and height of any selected areas, and color sampler readouts for up to four places in your file. It also gives you the coordinates of any transformation that you make.

Navigator

Painter does not have a Navigator palette, and if you have gotten used to using one, you'll really miss it. The Navigator in Photoshop and Illustrator work exactly the same, although they look very different. Illustrator's Navigator shows you the artboard size, with its margins as well as the pasteboard around it, as shown in Figure 12.22. Photoshop will never show you area outside the pixel information of the file. (See Figure 12.23.) Other than that, there's no difference. Both use the Grabber hand to reposition the viewing area. Click and drag the view rectangle to reposition it, or use the pointing finger and simply click where you'd like the view rectangle to be placed. Command-drag the zoom rectangle in the Navigator window to zoom the image correspondingly. You can type in a specific magnification, use the view buttons on either side of the slider, or use the slider itself to change the size of your view. The color of the viewing rectangle is Photoshop's only option; in Illustrator you can change that as well as whether you want the program to show dashed lines as solid in the Navigator window, and at what point size the type should be legible in the Navigator window. If you want to see items positioned off the Artboard, uncheck View Artboard Only from the palette pop-up.

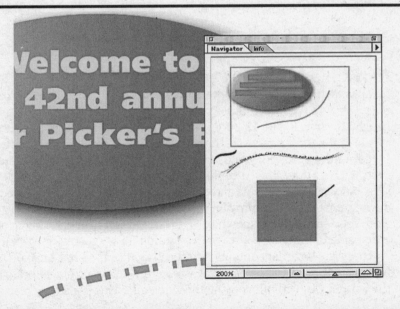

FIGURE 12.22: The Illustrator Navigator shows you the entire artboard and the portion that you are currently viewing. You can also choose to view items positioned off the artboard.

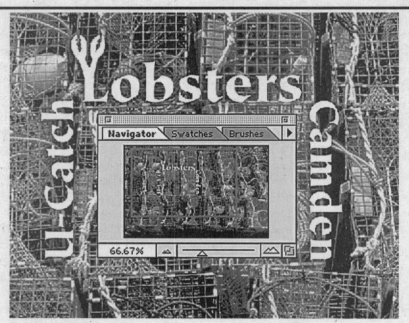

FIGURE 12.23: The Photoshop Navigator shows the whole file or a portion of it—no surrounding space.

Movers and the Preset Manager

I really like this feature of Painter. With a Mover you can organize your art materials into specific libraries that meet your needs; for example, see the Brush Mover in Figure 12.24. Although you can add swatches to documents in Illustrator and save those as libraries, it's not so easy if you want to move things around; you'd have to open all the appropriate documents first. With a Mover, the current library opens automatically on the left side, but you can close this and open another if you like. Then open the destination or source library on the right side or create a new library to store your materials, as shown in Figure 12.25. You can open and close either side to find new source or destination files. To move an item, click and drag the box that contains it to the other library. That's all you need to do, and it gives you an easy way to copy an element from a library on the Painter CD, without copying the whole file. This is also the place where you can delete elements from a library or rename your materials. Be careful: there is no Undo on Delete.

FIGURE 12.24: The Brush Mover is probably the most often used mover.

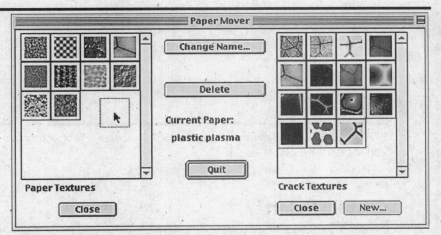

FIGURE 12.25: Drag the material from one library to the other and drop it to add it to the library.

Photoshop has added a Preset Manager in version 6—a welcome addition. Use Edit ➤ Preset Manager; from here you can load additional presets to the current ones, choosing to append or replace the current set. (See Figure 12.26.) Then you can delete unneeded items and save that group as a new set. You have preset palettes for Brushes, Swatches, Gradients, Styles, Patterns, Contours, and Custom Shapes. Activate the Save Set, Rename, and Delete buttons by clicking a swatch in the palette. By the way, the Rename button is to rename a swatch, not the preset palette itself.

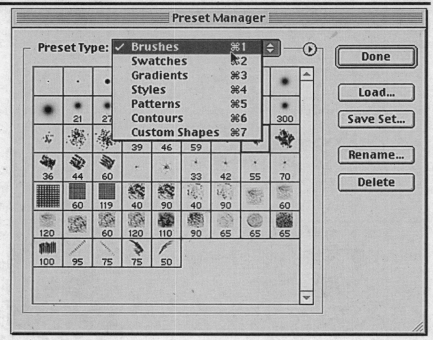

FIGURE 12.26: Materials for any of the "pop-up" palettes in Photoshop can be loaded from the Preset Manager.

Custom Palettes

Painter's custom palettes are much more than a place for special brushes. One custom palette can contain almost all of the materials and commands needed for a style of work. You can include brushes, gradients, papers, weaves, patterns, looks, nozzles, Dynamic layers, scripts, and commands. For everything except the commands, you simply drag the item off your regular palette onto the custom palette, as shown in Figure 12.27. You can also drag from custom palette to custom palette using the Control and Shift keys. For commands go to Window ➤ Custom Palette ➤ Add Command. You'll be prompted to choose the correct palette and command you want to place. Window ➤ Customize Palette ➤ Organizer is where to go to delete or rename custom palettes.

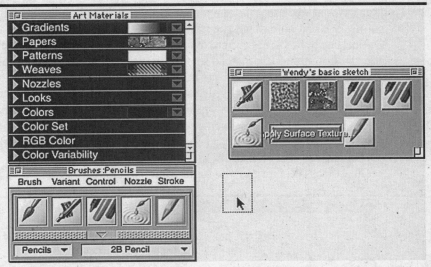

FIGURE 12.27: Drag brushes or art materials directly to the custom palette. Add commands via the Window menu.

Part iii

Border Icons

Painter has quite a few more border icons than either Photoshop or Illustrator. This could be helpful or annoying depending on how you work.

Drawing Mode or View Size

The first icon on the bottom left of the Painter window is the Drawing Modes icon. This position in Photoshop and Illustrator is occupied by the View Size indicator. This not only shows you the current magnification at which you are viewing the document, it also allows you to change the magnification by typing in a number. I'll describe the other icons in a bit more depth as we go along.

Info or Status Bar

All three applications have an Info or Status bar at the lower left of the window. In Painter this pop-up window (it has the i for information) gives you the print preview for your current page setup, the size in pixels and inches, and the resolution, as shown in Figure 12.28. Photoshop and

Illustrator ask you to choose which information is to be shown. In Photoshop, click and hold down the Info bar to get the print preview. Add the Option key to see the size in pixels, number of channels, and resolution; add the Command key instead to see the tile size and the number of tiles in the image. Illustrator's Status bar is also different. By default, it tells you which tool you are currently using. It can also show you the date and time, amount of free memory, number of Undos available, or current color profile. You choose which you want to see using the flyout, and your display stays that way until you change it again. By the way, you can option-click to get some additional information that's probably not too useful unless you plant by the lunar calendar. Oh, those wacky engineers!

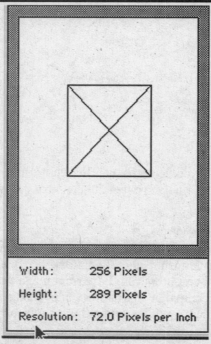

Width:	256 Pixels
Height:	289 Pixels
Resolution:	72.0 Pixels per Inch

FIGURE 12.28: Painter's Info bar gives you both the print preview and the size.

Tracing Paper or Dim Layout

The first icon above the vertical scroll bar on the Painter window is the Tracing Paper icon. This option is only available when the clone source and the current document are exactly the same size. Although Illustrator does not have a border icon, you can dim images in a layer by double-clicking the layer name in the Layers palette, selecting the option, and entering a value. You can dim placed images or items rasterized by Illustrator (this includes items rasterized using the Effects menu). Vector artwork on the layer will not be dimmed.

Show or Hide Grid

Painter is oriented to people who draw or paint, and one thing that many artists do to transfer a photo or sketch to canvas is make a grid and fill in areas based on the grid. Painter understands that it is helpful to be able to refer to the grid when necessary, but turn it off to paint. So, you have an icon right there on the window. What could be faster except maybe a shortcut key? (Don't forget, you can set up function keys if you are a big keyboard user.) On the menu bar, it's Canvas ≻ Grid ≻ Show Grid. This is also where you'll find the options for grid type and color.

In both Photoshop and Illustrator, the guides and grid are preference items (Edit ≻ Preferences ≻ Guides & Grid). Their dialog boxes are almost identical. In Illustrator, Command/Ctrl+; (semicolon) shows and hides the guides; Command/Ctrl+Shift+" for the grid. For Photoshop, Command/Ctrl+' shows or hides the guides; Command/Ctrl+Option/Alt+' toggles the grid.

Output Preview or Soft Proofing

I don't talk much about color management in this book, but it has quickly become an issue for all types of artists. Painter's Output Preview icon lets you preview your art with a click; unfortunately its color management abilities are minimal. The preview button does not work unless you have set options by using Canvas ≻ Output Preview. (See Figure 12.29a and 12.29b.) The first time you set this up using Kodak Color Correction, you are asked to set your profiles and whether you want to show a Gamut Warning for unprintable colors, as shown in Figure 12.30. To change your profile, choose Canvas ≻ Preview Options. Under Edit ≻ Preferences ≻ Functions Keys, you can set a keystroke to quickly go to the Kodak settings.

FIGURE 12.29A: When Output Preview is off, the monitor icon is dark.

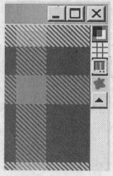

FIGURE 12.29B: With Output Preview on, the monitor icon is colored.

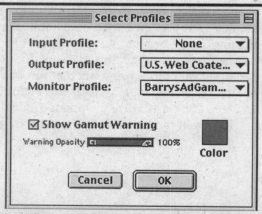

FIGURE 12.30: When you set or change the preview, you get this dialog box. .

Photoshop has a shortcut key (Command/Ctrl+Y) to soft-proof your document, and Photoshop 6 does something many of us have been waiting for: You can set up different scenarios for output, then switch between them using View ➤ Proof Setup. Working CMYK and standard Windows and Mac RGB setups are included in the submenu, but you can save settings for all your printers and have them available at your fingertips. (See Figure 12.31.) These previews affect the color display only; the pixel data remains unchanged. You can also use the Preview to take a look at the individual CMYK channels of your document.

In Illustrator, you also use View ➤ Proof Colors to soft-proof, but there's no shortcut key (but you can set one up using Keyboard Shortcuts). Just like Photoshop, you choose your settings from View ➤ Proof Setup, but unlike Photoshop you cannot save custom settings to choose from the submenu.

Because so much of our artwork now has to be repurposed for several uses, it would be nice if all three applications let you set up profiles that you could switch between easily—say, one for Web, one for ink-jet proofs, one for SWOP-coated. Photoshop has once again led the way. I expect we'll see more applications that have this capability soon. If you're interested in color management, see the "Producing Consistent Color" chapter of the Photoshop manual or the color management information in Photoshop 6 Artistry.

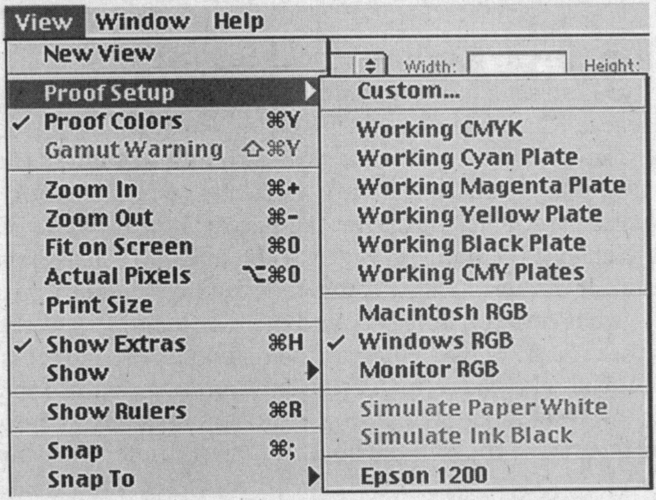

FIGURE 12.31: In Photoshop 6 you can quickly switch between different proofing conditions.

Preferences

No matter what application you are trying to work with or learn, it's a good idea to roam around the preferences and see what is there to make your life easier. Photoshop and Illustrator have very large preference sections—so big that both applications recently split the color settings out of the Preferences section and into an area specifically for color. One of the nicest things about the Preferences area of both applications is the ability to set preferences in multiple categories at the same time. In Painter, once you accept a preference, its dialog box closes; you have to pull down from the menu again to set preferences in a different area. In this section, I won't talk about every preference—many of them are covered in other chapters. Instead, I'll try to mention the things that may not be covered anywhere else in the book, or the settings that are particularly important.

Brush Tracking

This is a preference item that I wish could go further and be associated with particular brushes. As it stands now, you'll probably have to change this preference as you draw or paint if you switch media. You may draw with a much more deliberate stroke with a pencil or marker than you do with an oil brush. Make sure you know where this preference item is (Edit ➤ Preferences ➤ Brush Tracking) if you plan to use Painter; set a function key shortcut if you use it often.

Function Keys, Actions, and Scripts

In Painter you can set a function key for most menu commands, in the Preferences "Customize Keys" dialog box. You are limited to setting 24 different keys: the F keys on your keyboard, with or without the Shift key. If you want to do anything more complicated, record a Script. Also, the Customize Keys dialog box is not the easiest thing to work with. If you want to change the function key for a command, you have to go to the function key rather than the command (use the Summary button to quickly see what keys you have set), and there's no easy way to clear function keys that you don't use. Where Painter shines is its ability to record complex brushstrokes via scripts. You can record as you create your image at a low resolution, then playback the script at a higher resolution. Watch the pre-made scripts in the library to learn Painter tricks from the experts.

Photoshop and Illustrator both have very strong Actions palettes. They work exactly the same, allowing you to save simple actions (such as a single function key) or very complex scripts to perform production tasks. (For more about Photoshop Actions, see Chapter 11.) These scripts are highly editable and can save enormous amounts of time for certain production tasks. Illustrator also has a Keyboard Shortcuts dialog where you can change keystrokes to access tools and menu items. This allows you to make Illustrator 9 work more like a previous version of Illustrator or some other software that you use. Although you can set up menu items in Photoshop to work with function keys, you cannot set shortcuts for tools. However, under File ➢ Automate you can set up batch processing of your files and create droplets, which are little applets that can sit on your desktop to process files. It's how I processed all the screen shots for this book. Take a look at the Scripts and Actions that are included with the programs to start to understand how you can speed up your own work.

Undos and History

Painter and Illustrator let you set the number of Undos in their preferences. Use Edit ➢ Preferences ➢ Undo in Painter, which allows up to 32. Use File ➢ Preferences ➢ Units and Undo in Illustrator, where the number is limited only by the amount of available memory.

Photoshop no longer has multiple Undos. It has the History palette, discussed in Chapter 10, which I must say beats your basic Undo to pieces. The History palette shows you what you've done and allows you to click a particular state without having to Command/Ctrl+Z a bunch of times (you can use Command/Ctrl+Option/Alt+Z to step back to previous states). The maximum number of History states is 100. You can also use the History palette to take snapshots of your work at different stages, then click a snapshot to quickly return to that state. You can also use the History palette in conjunction with the History and Art History brushes (and also the Fill command) to paint from any past step. You can also choose to work in a nonlinear fashion, which is confusing but can allow you even more options.

Transparency & Gamut

Photoshop and Illustrator let you alter the look of the underlying transparency. In Photoshop, I don't think it's that useful an option; certainly, I've never found the need to change the size or color of the underlying grid. But this is also the area that has the Gamut Warning color and opacity that show up when you use the View ➤ Gamut Warning command, and that is useful. In Illustrator the controls for the Transparency grid are under File ➤ Document Setup. This is also where you Simulate Paper Color.

Smart Guides

Only Illustrator has Smart Guides. It's another way to help you accurately position objects on a page and in relation to one another. You choose these options under Edit ➤ Preferences ➤ Smart Guides. If you check all the display options, be prepared—it's like having a chatty aunt following you around the kitchen as you prepare an intricate dinner. If you are familiar with vector-based objects, you probably already know whether you are dragging to and from an anchor point or a center point, so you can probably go without the Text Label Hints. If you are building a file with specific angles needed, make sure you set those up in the Angles area. You can set custom angles like 18 and 43 degrees. Smart Guides can make moving objects along an angle a breeze. However, once you set everything up nicely in your preferences, you must turn Smart Guides on under the View menu to actually get the feedback as you work. And if you have Snap To Grid on, you won't be able to use the guides at all, so pick one or the other. It's nice that a shortcut key is set up for you already (Command/Ctrl+U), because Smart Guides are something you want to use only when you really need them. At other times you'll probably find them a hindrance.

Scale Strokes And Effects

If you want to always scale the stroke weight and applied effects of an item when you use the Scale tool or Transform palette, check this item in Illustrator's General Preferences. But it's not necessary if you want to choose on a case-by-case basis whether to scale. You can always choose this in the dialog box of the Scale tool or the pop-up menu of the Transform palette. If you turn this option on anywhere, your choice is reflected in all three places. That means that if you want this set as the global preference but then you scale an item without scaling its stroke and effects, make sure you turn the preference back on.

Use Preview Bounds

If the measurements of objects in your drawing must be exact, you'll probably want to turn this Illustrator general preference item on. Both the Transform and Info palettes are capable of reading the exact width and height of elements, including the portion of strokes or effects that are outside the path. Turning this preference on can also help you position objects exactly, as you are now given the X and Y coordinates of the edge of the stroke rather than the edge of the path.

WHAT'S NEXT

The next chapter will compare the type capabilities of these programs. Although Photoshop's text capabilities got much better with Photoshop 6, you'll see that other tools, such as Illustrator, can give you additional options.

Part ii

Chapter 13

WORKING WITH TYPE

I f you love type, you're in luck. Photoshop, Painter, and Illustrator each have powerful tools for creating nifty text effects. But, if you have to set a lot of scaleable type and need the ultimate in control, Illustrator may be the best Photoshop text "accessory" you have at your disposal.

Adapted from *Photoshop, Painter, and Illustrator Side-By-Side* by Wendy Crumpler
ISBN 0-7821-2923-4   400 pages $49.99

TYPE SIDE-BY-SIDE

Where you build your text will depend a lot on what sort of output you plan to do and what specific effect you need to accomplish. Some of you, who have been using only Illustrator to set type, will now find that you can accomplish most if not all of your work in Photoshop. The side-by-side comparison in Table 13.1 will update you on some of its new features.

TABLE 13.1:   Side-by-Side Comparison of Photoshop, Painter, and Illustrator

	PHOTOSHOP	PAINTER	ILLUSTRATOR
		TEXT BASICS	
Basic text operation	All type set with the Type tool is fully editable on screen (unless converted into outlines) and will print as vector outlines unless rasterized. Set horizontal or vertical. Type Mask option makes text-based selections on any layer.	Dynamic text is fully editable in the dialog window but prints as bitmaps. Vector text ("Shape text") can be set using the Text tool with every letter a separate Shape layer and prints as vectors.	All text includes the text itself, the type object, and an associated path or shape. Attributes of each can be changed independently. All text is fully editable until converted into outlines or rasterized. Set point text, area text, or path text, either horizontally or vertically.
Creating text	Type tool puts type on its own layer, on single lines (point text) or within a bounding box (paragraph text).	Objects: Dynamic Layers and choose Dynamic Text; puts type on its own layer, as point text or text on a path.	Type tool sets type as an object on any layer. Flyout has special tools for type on a path and area type, but all kinds of type can be set with basic tool.
Creating text shapes	No text shape tool, but any text can be converted to outlines.	Text tool in the Toolbox creates Shape text (vector-based objects). Each letter is on a separate Shape layer.	No text shape tool, but any text can be converted to outlines.

Continued on next page

TABLE 13.1:   Side-by-Side Comparison of Photoshop, Painter, and Illustrator

	PHOTOSHOP	PAINTER	ILLUSTRATOR
Creating vertical text	Click Vertical icon in Options bar; characters appear upright or rotated 90°. Before or after input, you can use Character ➤ Rotate Character to change the orientation.	You cannot set vertical text, but you can type each letter with a return and adjust to any rotation in Dynamic Text, or you can set Shape text and rotate each shape.	Three tools: Vertical Type, Vertical Area Type, and Vertical Path Type. Use Vertical Path Type tool to set the type at zero degrees. Use the regular Path Type tool to set type rotated by 90 degrees.

TYPE SPECIFICATIONS

	PHOTOSHOP	PAINTER	ILLUSTRATOR
Specification basics	Set basic attributes from Options bar; other specifications in Character palette. Can set all specifications before typing or after highlighting text. Keyboard shortcuts to change specifications operate on highlighted text.	Choose specifications for Dynamic text in Dynamic Text dialog, before or after entry. Set specifications for Text tool in Controls: Text palette before typing.	All specifications except color from Character palette or Type menu. Set specifications before typing or after highlighting for all or some of the text. Keyboard shortcuts to change specifications operate on highlighted text or selected type object
Font	Font family and font face lists in Options bar or Character palette	Font list in Dynamic Text dialog box or on Controls: Text palette	Font list on Character palette, or use Type ➤ Font
Size	Enter Size in Options bar or Character palette. Shift-drag corner handles of bounding box to resize without changing vertical or horizontal scale.	Adjust or choose Size in the Adjustment tab of the Dynamic Text dialog box, or drag the text on the image with the Size tool active. For Shape text, choose Size on Controls: Text palette before typing; after text has been entered, it can only be resized with Effect ➤ Orientation ➤ Scale.	Enter Size in Character palette. Choose type object with Selection tool to change size of all its text, or highlight specific letters with Type tool. Keyboard shortcuts change Size by amount set in Preferences. Shift-drag corner handles of bounding box to resize without changing vertical or horizontal scale.

Continued on next page

TABLE 13.1: Side-by-Side Comparison of Photoshop, Painter, and Illustrator

	PHOTOSHOP	PAINTER	ILLUSTRATOR
Leading	Enter value in Character palette. Can have different values for each line.	Set Leading value in the Adjustment tab of the Dynamic Text dialog box. Leading applies to all lines. Cannot set a Leading value for Shape text.	Enter value in Character palette. Can select area text with Selection tool and change leading for entire block of text, or highlight one line with the Type tool to lead that line differently.
Kerning and tracking	To change spacing between two letters, click with Type tool between them and set Kerning value in Character palette or use keyboard shortcuts. To change overall spacing, set Tracking in Character palette before typing, or after highlighting.	n.a. You cannot kern letter pairs, although with Shape text you can manually move letters closer or farther apart. Set Tracking value in Adjustment tab of Dynamic Text dialog box. For Shape text, set a Tracking value on the Controls: Text palette before you type, but you cannot change it later.	To change spacing between two letters, click the Type tool between them and set Kerning value in Characters palette or use keyboard shortcuts. To change overall spacing, set Tracking in Character palette. Can also use the Selection tool to highlight an entire block of text to track.
Color	Choose color before typing using the Color square on Options bar or Character palette. Clicking the square brings up the Color Picker. You can also apply a color overlay to the type affecting the entire layer.	Before, during, or after input of Dynamic text, choose text color from the Art Materials: Color or Color Set palettes. For Shape text, choose the color before input of each letter. After input, double-click a Shape layer to change attributes or select multiple Shape layers and use Shapes ➤ Set Shape Attributes.	Choose fill and stroke color before typing using the color squares on the Toolbox or Color palette. After type is input, use the Selection tool to select and change color of all text, or use Type tool to highlight selected text and choose new fill or stroke color with color squares. Color may also be affected by styling the type object.

Continued on next page

TABLE 13.1: Side-by-Side Comparison of Photoshop, Painter, and Illustrator

	PHOTOSHOP	PAINTER	ILLUSTRATOR
Horizontal and vertical scale	Set vertical and horizontal scale in Character palette. Can also drag handles of bounding box to resize and scale all text.	Two tools control relative ratio of horizontal and vertical text: drag in the image with the Stretch tool, or use the V/H Ratio slider in the Dynamic Text dialog box. Ratio applies to all the text on the layer. Cannot set a ratio for Shape text but can use Effects ➢ Orientation to change the look of text shapes.	Set vertical and horizontal scale in Character palette. Can also drag handles of bounding box to resize and scale all text.
Baseline shift	Enter value in Character palette, or use keyboard shortcuts to shift text.	n.a. There is no baseline shift in Painter. Move whole layers up or down with the Adjuster tool or arrow keys.	Enter a value in Character palette. Or after entering text, highlight all text with the Selection arrow or a portion of the text with the Type tool, and enter a Baseline Shift value or use keyboard shortcuts.
Anti-aliasing	Three kinds of anti-aliasing for type: Crisp makes type appear sharper, Strong makes it appear heavier, and Smooth makes it appear smoother.	n.a. Both Dynamic and Shape text are anti-aliased.	n.a. Although if you make outlines then rasterize the type, you are given an option to anti-alias.
Type styles	Faux Bold, Faux Italic, Caps, Small Caps, Superscript, Subscript, Underline, Strikethrough, Ligatures, and Fractional Widths available from Character palette pop-up.	In Font drop-down list, choose Other and select Regular, Italic, Bold, or Bold Italic. Can use Slant option in the Dynamic Text dialog box to apply a sort of faux italic; can set the vertical/horizontal ratio above 50 to fatten up the letters.	You cannot use applied styles in Illustrator. Use Type ➢ Change Case for all caps, all lowercase, or mixed case. Use Type ➢ Smart Punctuation for ligatures and special punctuation. Use Type ➢ MM Design to tweak multiple master fonts.

Part ii

Continued on next page

TABLE 13.1: Side-by-Side Comparison of Photoshop, Painter, and Illustrator

	PHOTOSHOP	PAINTER	ILLUSTRATOR
Copying type specifications	n.a.	n.a.	Use the Eyedropper and Paint Bucket to copy and paste type specs.
EDITING TEXT			
Selecting text	Click Type layer name in the Layers palette to change options on entire layer. Drag with Type tool to select any amount of text for editing. Or use keyboard shortcuts to select text.	Double-click Dynamic Text layer in the Layers palette. In the text-entry area, drag to highlight any amount of text or double-click to highlight a word.	Drag with a Type tool to highlight any amount of text in a text block. Select entire text block with Selection arrow. Shift-click with Selection arrow to select multiple blocks of text.
Advanced Illustrator features	n.a.	n.a.	Find and replace text or fonts, Import Text, Show Hidden Characters, Spell Check, and Smart Punctuation
PARAGRAPH SPECS			
Paragraph basics	Alignment icons for point text on the Options bar; icons for point text and paragraph text on the Paragraph palette. Left, right, and first-line indents, space before, and space after available on Paragraph palette.	Align all text on a Dynamic Text layer flush left, centered, or flush right using Align icons in main section of dialog. No margins or indents.	Align point text flush left, centered, or flush right on a line-by-line basis. Align area text the same by paragraph, plus justified by full lines or all lines. Left, right, and first-line indents, and space before available on Paragraph palette.
Hyphenation and justification	Paragraph ➢ Hyphenation to set hyphenation preferences. Paragraph ➢ Justification for word and letter spacing, glyph scaling, and auto leading setting.	n.a.	Paragraph ➢ Hyphenation to set hyphenation preferences. Paragraph ➢ Show Options to set word and letter spacing or to set auto hyphenation.

Continued on next page

TABLE 13.1: Side-by-Side Comparison of Photoshop, Painter, and Illustrator

	PHOTOSHOP	PAINTER	ILLUSTRATOR
Application-specific commands	Can use multiline composition to give paragraph text a more even color with fewer hyphens.	n.a.	Fit Headline, tabs, text wrap, columns, linking
TYPE ON A PATH			
Path type basics	Allows you to warp type. Target layer that has type you want to warp, then click the Warp Text icon on the Options bar or use Layer ➤ Type ➤ Warp Text. All type on layer is warped. Adjust Bend and Distortion sliders in the Warp Text dialog to edit curve.	Allows you to place type on a curve. Enter text in the Dynamic Text dialog box, then choose curve style in the Baseline tab: Straight, Vertical, Baseline, and Transform. All type on layer is set on curve. Drag points and handles to edit curve.	Allows you to place type on a curved path. Build the path first, then use either one of the Path Type tools or the regular Type tool to set the type on the path. Drag points and handles to edit curve.
Changing path shape	Though you don't actually change the shape of the path, you can change the amount of bend or distortion.	Use the path-editing tools in the Baseline tab of the Dynamic Text dialog box.	Use regular path-editing tools. You cannot split a type path with scissors, or delete a type path without deleting the type.
Moving type on a path	n.a., although with paragraph text you can change indents.	Use alignment icons in the Dynamic Text dialog box"", or use the ± entering slider in the Baseline tab.	Use either the Selection or Direct Selection arrow to click the text, then grab the I-beam at the beginning of the text and drag it.
Flipping type across the path	n.a., although you can flip a Type layer using Edit ➤ Transform ➤ Flip Horizontal or Vertical.	In Dynamic Text dialog, use the Angle slider (results vary with baseline style). Or use Effects ➤ Orientation to flip the layer horizontally or vertically; it ceases to be Dynamic and becomes an Image layer. For text shapes, use Effects ➤ Orientation to flip.	Use the Selection arrow and either double-click the I-beam or drag the I-beam across the path.

Continued on next page

TABLE 13.1:   Side-by-Side Comparison of Photoshop, Painter, and Illustrator

	PHOTOSHOP	PAINTER	ILLUSTRATOR
TEXT EFFECTS			
Text effect basics	Any layer effect can be added to a Type layer. You can also use text as a clipping mask to mask Fill, Adjustment, or Image layers. Change opacity at the layer level; change blending modes both at the layer level and for the individual effect. Use contours for more variety.	Dynamic Text allows you to add many effects, mostly from the Appearance tab. Change opacity for either text or shadow in the Appearance tab, or for both at the layer level.	Live effects and transparency can be added to the Type Object but not to the text itself. Strokes and fills can be on the text itself or the type object.
Filling text	Text itself can only be filled with color, but you can use overlays for patterns or gradients or use Fill layers above the text and make the Type layer a clipping layer.	Can use color, gradients, patterns, or weaves as fill for either the text itself or the shadow when you use a Dynamic Text layer.	Can fill or stroke type with color or a pattern. Using the Appearance palette with the type object, you can add multiple fills and strokes with opacities, blending modes, and effects.
Transforming text	Text can be rotated, scaled, skewed, or flipped with Edit ➢ Transform or Edit ➢ Free Transform.	Use the adjustment tools in Dynamic Text to maintain the layer's edibility. Text shapes and Dynamic text cannot be transformed using Effects ➢ Orientation without committing the layer.	Text can be transformed using any of the transformation tools in the Toolbox or Object ➢ Transform.
RENDERING TEXT			
Rasterizing text	Layer ➢ Rasterize ➢ Type or Layer ➢ Rasterize ➢ Layer turns the Type layer into a regular layer which can be painted or filtered.	Dynamic text is rasterized. Objects: Dynamic Layers ➢ Commit turns a Dynamic Text layer into an Image layer, which can be painted or have effects applied. Use Shapes ➢ Convert To Layer to change a text Shape layer to an Image layer.	Object ➢ Rasterize to turn text into bitmap information

Continued on next page

TABLE 13.1:   Side-by-Side Comparison of Photoshop, Painter, and Illustrator

	PHOTOSHOP	PAINTER	ILLUSTRATOR
Outlining text	Layer ➢ Type ➢ Convert To Shape to create a Shape layer from your text. Layer ➢ Type ➢ Create Work Path to create a path that can be used as a selection on any layer or as a clipping path for the file.	Shape text is already outlines. For Dynamic text, see workaround in "In Depth" section.	Type ➢ Create Outlines to convert text into shapes that can be edited with path-editing tools.
TRANSFERRING TYPE BETWEEN APPLICATIONS			
Transferring from Photoshop	n.a.	Painter does not read Photoshop Type layers. You can rasterize the layer if there are no effects applied, and it comes in as an Image layer.	Type layers rasterize when you open a Photoshop file into Illustrator. If you have applied effects, Type layers will flatten.
Transferring from Painter	When saved as a Photoshop file, Dynamic text comes in on its own layer but is rendered and no longer editable. Shape text is rasterized.	n.a.	When exported to Illustrator via File ➢ Export ➢ Adobe Illustrator File, Shape text comes in as paths, although not always accurately. You can save as Photoshop, TIFF, or EPS and open or place those files.
Transferring from Illustrator	Export your document into Photoshop format. If you want to be able to edit the text, make sure you click Editable Text in the Write Layers area. You need the 9.02 update for this.	Painter cannot read Illustrator 9 files. You must first Create Outlines from the type in Illustrator and save it as Illustrator 8. Then use File ➢ Acquire ➢ Adobe Illustrator File in Painter. You can also copy outlines from Illustrator and paste into Painter.	n.a.

TYPE IN DEPTH

If you need text handling that rivals a page layout program, use Illustrator. You can spell check, wrap text around a graphic, and link text blocks for copy flow. Painter 6 made a giant leap with the addition of Dynamic Text layers as well as retaining its vector-based Text tool. Painter 7 went a step further by combining both dynamic text and vector text into a single, new Text tool. (The Painter illustrations in this chapter are from the earlier Painter 6 release.) Not only is Dynamic text editable, you can apply pretty amazing effects from within the dialog box, not the least of which is being able to set type on a path. Photoshop 6 now works with vector type. You can set both point and paragraph text, and you have many of the same controls as Illustrator. In fact, if you've been using Illustrator to set your type, the Character and Paragraph palettes will make you feel right at home. They look exactly like Illustrator's, only with fewer options. You can also warp your text in Photoshop. Where you set type depends on your specific needs, but all three packages do a great job.

Text Basics

In this section, we'll cover some of the basic differences in text manipulation between the three applications.

Basic Text Operation

Both Photoshop and Illustrator set editable text directly in your image; this is vector-based and will print to the output resolution of your printer. Painter 6 sets editable text through the Dynamic Text dialog (click this option on the Objects: Dynamic Layers palette section), or in the image (but not editable) with the Text tool. (Painter 7 combines both these capabilities into the Text tool.) Dynamic text is rasterized and prints to the resolution of the file; the Text tool sets shapes, with one letter shape on each layer and all the attributes of any other Shape layer. In all three applications, if vector shapes are altered with things like transparency or compositing, they may not print as vector graphics but rather must be rasterized first.

Photoshop also has a Masked Type option, to create only a selection marquee in the shape of type, which can be used on any layer. I find it easier and more flexible to create regular type on a layer and Ctrl/Command-click that layer to get a selection marquee when I need it. Or use the Type layer to create a clipping group to mask other art. To create a type mask in Painter, set the letters as Shape text, then use Shape ➤ Convert To Selection. Or use Dynamic text, commit it to an Image layer, copy the layer mask, and load a selection from the new mask. And remember, you can always set type in Illustrator and bring it into either program to use as a mask.

Creating Text

The basic tool of typesetting in both Photoshop and Illustrator is the Type tool. In Photoshop, this sets type on its own layer, one layer for each time you use the tool. (The first 31 characters become the layer name.) Where you click in the document determines the insertion point. Some options, such as font or color, can be applied to one or more letters that are highlighted; you can change these directly from the Options bar. For other type options, you need to use the Character or Paragraph palettes. To enter point text, click with the tool and start typing. Input a carriage return when you want a new line to start. For paragraph text, click and drag with the tool to set the size of the bounding box (or Alt/Option-click or -drag to bring up a dialog for text box size); specifications set in the Paragraph palette apply and text wraps automatically.

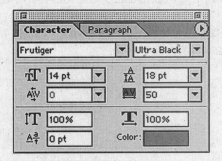

Once you enter your text, click the Commit button (the checkmark on the Options bar) to leave text mode and re-enable other tools' keyboard shortcuts. To resize the bounding box without scaling the type, make sure you are in the Text tool and that you have clicked in the text flow. If you resize the bounding box with the Move tool or Free Transform as shown here, you change the type as well. You can switch type between point text and paragraph text using Layer ➤ Type ➤ Convert To. Be careful with this command, though; it's easy to lose words going from paragraph to point text.

I love   the way
your voice enfolds me.
Holds me. Caresses my
cheek. Touches my hair.
I'm there. Whenever your
warm voice surrounds
me. Strong as your
arms. Gentle as your
fingers. It lingers.
Long after you
are gone.

The Type tool looks the same in Illustrator and functions similarly. Clicking in the document sets the insertion point, on whatever layer is currently active. Text attributes are set in the Character palette, either before typing or after highlighting the desired text. The main Type tool is also called the Point Type tool. It sets the type on a single line until you press Return, and type does not wrap by itself. Drag with the tool to set a text bounding box to hold area text; specifications set in the Paragraph palette will apply. In Illustrator, you can also select a pre-built shape with the Move tool then click inside the shape and type. Pay attention to the Type tool icon; you'll see it changes as you near a path or shape to allow you to set path type or area type.

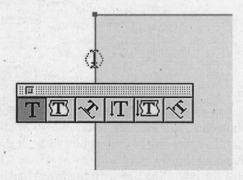

If the shape you selected was filled or stroked, that paint style will be lost, but you can use the Direct Selection Arrow to select the shape itself for repainting. If text overflows, resize your type inside the shape, edit the shape, or link that text box to another. I consider Painter's main text tool to be the Dynamic Text layer, created from the Objects: Dynamic Layers palette section. When you click the Apply button there, the Dynamic Text dialog box appears where you input the text and choose its characteristics. Dynamic text can be point text or text on a path. From within the dialog, you can set type specifications, alignment options, effects, and path shape.

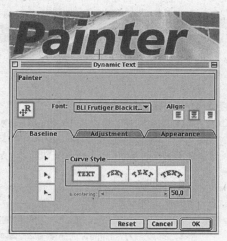

Creating Text Shapes

If you want to set vector-based type, or rotate, scale, or color letters separately in Painter, set Shape text using the Text tool from the Toolbox. This is the same tool as in previous versions of Painter, and it still sets each letter on its own Shape layer. You can group the layers to make moving the letters easier, but if you try to collapse them into one layer, they become an Image layer. Still, for certain effects, this is the way to go.

You might even find instances in Illustrator when you need each letter to be set separately, such as the ability to tilt all the letters while maintaining the baseline (tilting is different than skewing or shearing.)

Creating Vertical Text

In Photoshop, click the Vertical icon in the Options bar to set text vertically, or use Layer ➤ Type ➤ Vertical to change the orientation. This is the default orientation of type when you use the Vertical option of the Type tool:

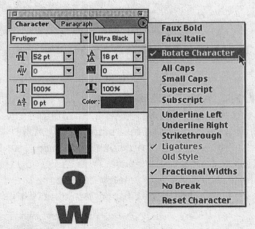

After input, highlight all the letters you want to rotate and turn off Rotate Character.

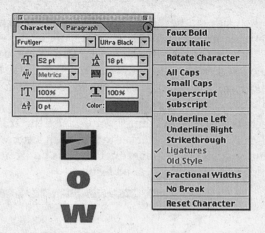

As with the Illustrator Vertical Type tool, if you have more than one line of type, it reads top to bottom and right to left. Illustrator also has Vertical Area Type and Vertical Path Type tools. Vertical Area Type sets type from right to left to support Asian characters, so you probably won't use this option too often. Here, the type on the left was set with the Vertical Type on a Path tool. The type on the right was set with the regular Path Type tool.

The Vertical Path Type tool allows you to set type that stacks vertically along a path. Illustrator also has an orientation command (Type ➤ Type Orientation) that can switch the type from vertical to horizontal or vice versa. In Photoshop you can rotate some or all of the text, so the letters are on their sides rather than straight up and down, by highlighting the text you want to change and unchecking Character ➤ Rotate Character. In Illustrator, when you use the regular Path Type tool, the letters follow the direction in which the path was drawn, so if you build a path from top to bottom, text will flow from top to bottom in a straight line rather than stacked letter by letter.

To set vertical type in Painter, you can use the Text tool and move the letters manually, but it's quicker to type each letter with a return in Dynamic Text and then adjust angle (90° is horizontal), leading, rotation, and slant to get the desired result.

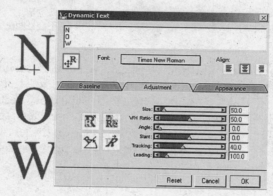

Type Specifications

Photoshop went a long way to make using type easy in version 6. It is easy, if you remember a few basics. You can change the specifications of all type on a layer by choosing that layer in the Layers palette and changing the settings on either the Options bar or Character palette when the Type tool is active. You must highlight characters with the Type tool to change them individually. And, when you edit text or specifications from within the text itself, make sure you check the commit button on the Options bar to be able to use keyboard shortcuts to access other tools. The primary type specifications are right there on the Options bar for you to choose when you first activate the Type tool. Here, on top is the Options bar before you set text; on bottom how the bar appears when you edit.

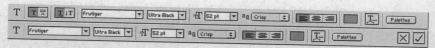

The specifications that you don't see there, such as Kerning and Baseline Shift, are on the Character palette, which can be accessed from the Palettes button on the Options bar or from Window ➤ Show Character. This is also the path to the Paragraph palette, where you can set further specifications. For Painter's Dynamic text, changes apply to all text on a layer and all the specifications that you set are within the dialog. You can choose the font, face, color, size, angle, slant, and other specifications and effects. You can change the specifications at any time until you commit to an Image layer. If you need vector artwork, use the Text tool to set individual letter shapes. These shapes have all the editing possibilities of any other Shape layer but are not editable as text. You choose the specifications for these shapes before you type in the Controls palette. Go to Type ➤ Character for Illustrator's Character palette; it's almost exactly the same as Photoshop's but you choose the type's color differently. Ctrl/Command-clicking the kerning, tracking, vertical scale, horizontal scale, or baseline shift symbol in the palette will return the input field to its default value.

Font

Painter has two distinct type tools to deal with. First, the Text tool. Choose a font from the Controls: Text palette before you type. Once you have entered a character, there is no way to change any of its type characteristics. It is now a shape and can be manipulated as such. With Dynamic text, you choose the font in the main section of the Dynamic Text dialog (go to Other Fonts if a font you want isn't on the short list), before or after input. The Font list only shows the last six typefaces that you have used. If you choose the Other Fonts menu item, you get the Choose Font dialog box, which shows you all installed fonts.

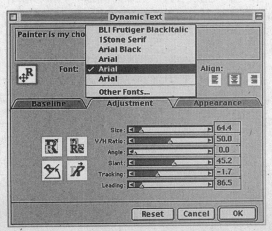

Part ii

It applies to all the text on the layer; you cannot change the font of individual letters or words. Create multiple Dynamic Text layers if you want more flexibility.

In Illustrator, the Font drop-down list is in the upper portion of the Character palette. You can type in the first few letters of a font name, and Illustrator will try to guess what you want. Choose the font before you enter the text, or if the text has already been entered you can highlight some or all of it to change. Photoshop has both font family and font face drop-down lists, available from the Options bar or the Character palette. Choose the font before entering text or, if text has already been input, highlight some or all of it and choose a new font, or type in the first few letters and Photoshop will fill in the rest. Note: It lists all the fonts in your system, even if there are no corresponding outline fonts.

Size

If you use the Painter Text tool for entering text, you must choose the size on the Controls: Text palette before typing. After entry, this text is a shape that can be scaled with Effects ➢ Orientation. In the Adjustment tab of the Dynamic Text dialog box are two ways of choosing type size: a Size slider, which allows you to interactively scale the type as you move the slider or input a number in points, and the Size tool on the top-left side, which lets you drag in the image itself to resize the type.

In Photoshop you can set the units to use for type size (and leading) points, pixels, or millimeters in your Units & Rulers preferences. Ctrl/Command+Shift+> increases (and Ctrl/Command+Shift+< decreases) the size of highlighted type by 2 points, 2 pixels, or 1 mm; adding the Alt/Option key changes size by increments of 10 pixels, 10 points, or 5 mm. When the red box borders this symbol, you can drag on the text in the image to resize it.

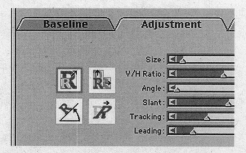

Illustrator's Size list has preset sizes for type, or you can input a value in the field before you begin typing. You can also highlight text (either with the Type tool or by selecting the type object) and use keyboard shortcuts to increase or decrease the size. Use Ctrl/Command+Shift+> to increase, or Ctrl/Command+Shift+< to decrease, size by the amount set in Preferences ➢ Type And Auto Tracing. Add the Alt/Option key to either shortcut to change the size by 10.

Leading

You cannot set leading (the height from one text baseline to the next) for Painter 6's Shape text; you must move the letters manually. For Dynamic text, set the leading in the Adjustment tab of the dialog box before or after you set the type. Leading pertains to the entire layer in Painter; you cannot set individual lines. Use the slider or input the value you want for leading.

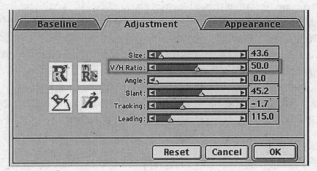

You can change leading line by line in Photoshop by highlighting a line and entering a value in the Leading field of the Character palette. You can start with one value before you input text and change it line-by-line as you type. Pressing the Alt/Option key plus the up or down arrow changes leading of highlighted text by 2 points, 2 pixels, or 1 mm, depending on your Units & Rulers preferences; adding the Ctrl/Command key multiplies the increment by 5. The keyboard shortcut must have at least one character highlighted to work, but it's better to highlight the entire line because otherwise Photoshop gets a bit confused about what the actual leading is.

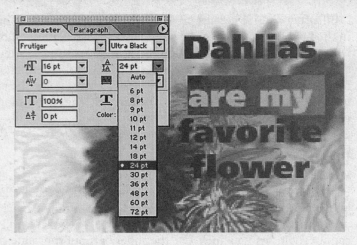

In Illustrator, you can set leading for point type and area type, but not path type because it is always a single line. Choose the leading value you want in the Character palette before you input the text; after input, you can choose all the text by clicking the baseline with the Selection arrow, or use the Text tool to highlight a single line to change. Same keyboard shortcuts as Photoshop, but the increment of change for Alt/Option+up or down arrow is set in the Type and Auto Trace preferences. As with Photoshop, you can use the keyboard shortcuts with a single highlighted letter, but it's better to highlight the entire line.

Kerning and Tracking

Tracking and kerning are not the same thing. Kerning applies to a pair of letters. Tracking adds an equal amount of space between all letters of a word or blocks of text. Photoshop and Illustrator let you kern letter pairs. Click with the Type tool between the two characters you want to adjust and enter a value in the Kerning field. You can type in a number (negative numbers decrease the space), or you can use Alt/Option+left or right arrow to tighten or loosen the kerning by 20. Adding the Ctrl/Command key kerns by 100. (To kern vertical type, use Alt/Option+up or down arrow as if you were changing the leading, but the value shows up in the Kerning area.) Use the Metrics setting in Photoshop to use the font's built-in kerning values; in Illustrator use Auto.

All three applications track type. Painter even lets you set a value for tracking Shape text, but only before you enter the text. In the Dynamic Text dialog box, set tracking for the entire layer by moving the Tracking slider or inputting a value in the entry area. You can set a tracking value before you input the Shape text, but cannot change it later.

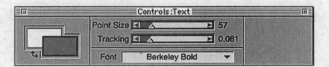

In Photoshop and Illustrator, you can use the same keyboard shortcuts for tracking that you use for kerning, but instead of having the cursor between two letters, you must have at least two letters highlighted (you usually track words lines or blocks). Highlight the word, line, or lines that you want to track.

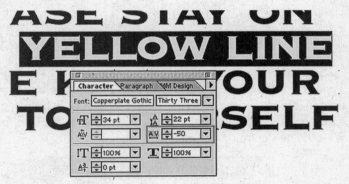

Color

In Painter's Dynamic Text, the color of the text is the color of the text. Period. You have to start a new Dynamic Text layer for each change of color. But you can double-click each Shape text layer and change the attributes for that shape. With Dynamic text, you have other options to color the type, such as filling it with a gradient, pattern, or weave, but only on a layer-by-layer basis.

Illustrator and Photoshop can color every single letter differently in a text block or on a text path, as you type or after input. To change letters before typing, change the foreground or fill color when you want the color of the type to change. After input, simply highlight the letters and recolor.

The color swatches on Photoshop's Options bar and Character palette always match; these have priority over the Toolbox swatch, they maintain the color of the last edited text, and any new text you input (even on a new layer) will have that color... *unless* you change the foreground color from the Toolbox as you type, which changes the palette and Options bar swatches.

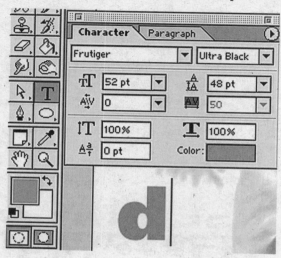

A question mark in the Options bar swatch means you have clicked a Type layer in the Layers palette that has multiple colors, or you've highlighted letters that are differently colored. If you click the icon and choose a new color, all text on that layer (or in your selection) will be recolored with the new color.

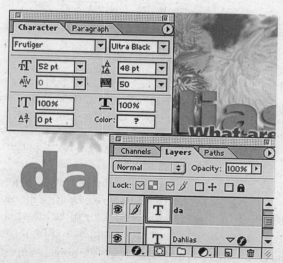

In Illustrator, you can also stroke the text with a different color. You can fill or stroke text with a pattern here too, but not a gradient. Styles used on the type objects may also affect the color.

Horizontal and Vertical Scale

Scaling text is generally used to achieve a certain effect and not as a substitute for, say, a condensed typeface. In Painter you scale the entire layer, as a function of the Dynamic Text dialog box. If you are relying on the visual rather than the numeric to decide on type width and height, you can use the Stretch tool (the top-right icon in the Adjustment tab of the dialog box). Click in the image and drag with the tool to stretch the text. Text shapes can be scaled individually or as a group with Effects ➤ Orientation ➤ Scale. Uncheck Constrain Aspect Ratio to separate vertical and horizontal scaling.

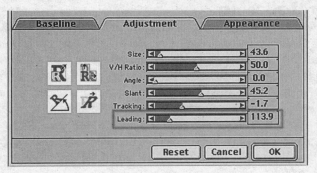

Illustrator and Photoshop let you distort all the text, part, or only one letter. Highlight text and use the Vertical or Horizontal Scale sections of the Character palette. If you don't see icons for these in Illustrator, choose Character ➤ Show Options. In both applications, you can choose the bounding box for the type with a selection tool and drag to scale the type: top or bottom handles scale vertically, side handles scale horizontally, and corner handles scale both at once.

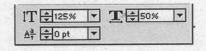

Baseline Shift

There is no baseline shift of individual characters in Painter; use arrow keys to move the whole text layer pixel-by-pixel. In Illustrator and Photoshop, the Baseline Shift area is the last item on the Character palette (use Character ➤ Show Options to see this in Illustrator). Enter a positive number to move text up, negative to move text down. Keyboard shortcuts for changing baseline shift are exactly the same as for leading, except you add the Shift keyshift+Alt/Option+up or down arrow and again, add the Ctrl/Command key for bigger changes. In both applications, you highlight the text you want to shift, all or part of it. Baseline shift is especially important in Illustrator path text, where setting the baseline to the midpoint of the letters can give you a better flow over a curve.

Anti-aliasing

The anti-alias setting is only meaningful when type will be rasterized, primarily for online usage. The typeface you use will help you determine which setting is appropriate. Some typefaces look good with Strong antialias; some look too beefy. Some curves or crossbars may be lost with the Smooth setting, and Crisp looks best for some faces. You may find it best at small point sizes not to alias the text at all or to turn off the Fractional Widths option in the Character palette menu. It's best to test! In this image, the top row is Cronos 637, middle is ITC Tiepolo Book, and bottom is Bodoni Regular. This is 24 pt text on 28 leading with a tracking value of 20.

Text characters for television	**Text characters for television**	**Text characters for television**
Text characters for television	Text characters for television	Text characters for television
Text characters for television	**Text characters for television**	Text characters for television
Crisp	**Strong**	Smooth

Type Styles

Photoshop gives you two Faux styles, Bold and Italic, to add something extra to your type arsenal. Photoshop 6 also added a whole bunch of other styling items, such as strikethrough text and ligatures. You can find them all in the Character palette pop-up. You cannot warp text that has the Faux Bold style applied, and these styles may not print correctly from PostScript printers.

Illustrator abhors applied styles, so you're not allowed to bold or italicize there. However, you can Shear the type to slant it or increase the Horizontal Scale to fatten it up a bit. You could also use a stroke on the type if that gives more of the look you're after. It's surprising that there's not an auto setting for superscript and subscript in Illustrator as there is in Photoshop; you have to use baseline shift and resize the type. However, this does give you a lot more control over exactly how your characters will look. In this example, I set the point of origin to the left and below the type, then skewed it to the right

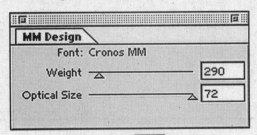

And a big Illustrator plus for type-heads is the ability to work with multiple master fonts to get just the right look for your project.

Part ii

Painter lets you pick from Plain, Italic, Bold, and Bold Italic for some fonts in the font list in Dynamic Text. There is also a Slant option in the Adjustment tab of the Dynamic Text dialog box, and you can set horizontal scale to greater than 50 for stretched type. If you use the Text tool, you can add a stroke for extra weight, and use Effects ➢ Orientation ➢ Distort to slant the type.

Copying Type Specifications

In Photoshop, you can duplicate a Type layer and change the text. In Painter, you can copy and paste a Dynamic Text layer, then go in and edit the text. In neither program can you take just a couple of options and apply them to another block of text.

Illustrator gives you great flexibility in copying type specs with the Eyedropper and Paint Bucket tools; the Eyedropper picks up text attributes, and the Paint Bucket applies attributes. I've opened the Character tab for the Eyedropper and the Paragraph tab for the Paint Bucket tools. The attributes are the same for both tools.

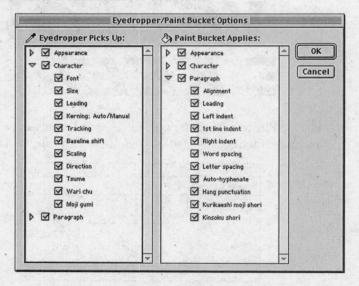

To use the Eyedropper, first highlight the text you want to change using one of the text or selection tools. Then switch to the Eyedropper and click the text that has the attributes you want to copy.

This. is. ¶
Illu**s**trator¶
Text∞

Lobsters

That's it; the type specs will be applied to the highlighted text, as shown here:

This. is. ¶

Illu**St**rator
Text∞
Lobsters

Once you have picked up some type specs with the Eyedropper, you can pour them with the Paint Bucket. Text need not be selected first. Simply drag with the Paint Bucket over the text you want to change or, if you want to change the whole block of type, click the baseline. The attributes that you can transfer are in the tool options; select either tool and press Enter or Return to choose.

Editing Text

Nobody's perfect. You'll often find you need to fix a typo, change a word, or even recast entire sentences. Fortunately, the tools you need to edit text are there.

Selecting Text

In Painter, highlighting text in the text-entry area of Dynamic Text is strictly for the purpose of editing the text; you cannot apply any attributes or effects to selected text. Copy the layer in place (Alt/Option-click with the Layer Adjuster tool) when you want to change attributes for some of the text. In all three applications, you can click with the Text or Type tool to set the insertion point at the beginning of the highlight, then shift-click to highlight to the second click point. In all three, Ctrl/Command+A selects all; clicking with Illustrator's Selection tool also chooses the entire block of type, whether one word or many paragraphs.

In Illustrator and Photoshop, use Ctrl/Command+right or left arrow keys to move the insertion point to the next or previous word. In Illustrator, you can also use Ctrl/Command+up or down arrow to move to the beginning or end of a paragraph. Adding the Shift key to any of these shortcuts highlights the text as you go. Home and End go to the beginning and end of the line or text block. In all three apps, double-click to select a word. For Photoshop, triple-click to select a line, click four times to select a paragraph, and five times to select all the text in a text block. For Illustrator, triple-clicking highlights a line of point text or a paragraph of area text.

Advanced Illustrator Features

As I mentioned before, Illustrator rivals a page layout program in its ability to handle text. You wouldn't want to set a book with it, but you might choose it for a brochure or poster that requires large blocks of nicely set type. Choose Type ➢ Check Spelling to spell-check the entire document. You can add special words to your user dictionary, and Illustrator 9 ships with quite a few foreign-language dictionaries. Use File ➢ Open or File ➢ Place to import text into your document. Type ➢ Find Fonts lets you replace fonts selectively. The top pane shows the fonts currently in your document. Click a font to replace it; Illustrator will find each occurrence of the typeface and allow you to choose an alternative or skip that occurrence. It even shows which type of font you'll be choosing, in case you want to not mix TrueType with Type 1. Very sophisticated.

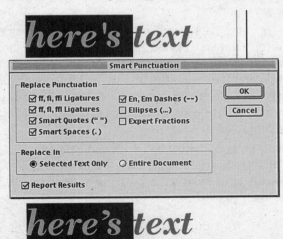

Type ➢ Show Hidden Characters is useful when you want to check the formatting of text, and Type ➢ Smart Punctuation changes all those nontypographical characters that get input when the average citizen types. In this image, the top is text has a straight apostrophe. After running the Smart Punctuation filter, the apostrophe is curled, as it should be.

Part ii

Paragraph Specs

Painter knows nothing about paragraph specifications. Type is type, and a layer of type is treated as the same paragraph whether you've input carriage returns or not. So you can set type flush left, centered, or flush right. That's it.

Illustrator knows what a return is all about. Because you've input paragraph returns if you set more than one line of point text in a block of type, you can change the alignment on a line-by-line basis. Illustrator will align from the insertion point. If you are using area text, each paragraph can be set separately.

You can also justify area text in Illustrator, and you can align vertical type as top, centered, bottom, or justified. In Photoshop, point text is aligned at the layer level; all text on a layer is aligned the same. Paragraph text is different: each paragraph can have its own alignment. Point text can only be flush left, flush right, or centered, but paragraph text can be those plus justified with the last line flush left, flush right, centered, or completely justified.

Illustrator and Photoshop both handle margins and indents, but again, not exactly the same. Because Illustrator has a history of being a specialized type tool, it has a few more options in setting margins.

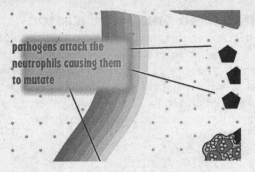

You can set a negative number for any of the indent settings, causing the text to actually hang outside the bounding box. This makes it easy to set up hanging indents for bullet points or numbered text. As with Alignment, when you set point text in Illustrator you can set margins and indents on a line-by-line basis; in Photoshop when you apply any of the paragraph specifications to point text, all the text on the layer takes on those specifications. In Illustrator, set hanging punctuation via the a check box at the bottom of the expanded Paragraph palette, in Photoshop set hanging punctuation using Paragraph ➤ Roman Hanging Punctuation.

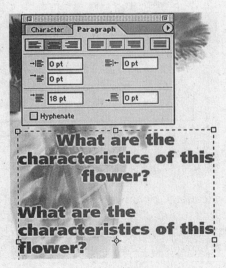

Part ii

Hyphenation and Justification

Those of you coming from page layout applications will be so grateful for Adobe's robust abilities to deal with hyphenation and justification. And surprisingly, the stronger of the two applications is Photoshop; look at the dialog boxes here to compare its extensive controls with Illustrator's puny ones. Illustrator does let you set hyphenation exceptions from Preferences, and you can enter a discretionary hyphen by typing Ctrl/Command+Shift+(hyphen).

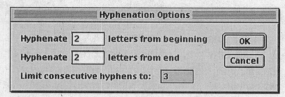

Justification options are on the Paragraph palette in Illustrator (choose Paragraph ➤ Show Options) and on the Paragraph palette menu in Photoshop.

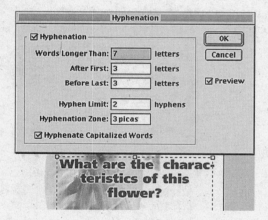

Both applications let you choose Desired word and character spacing for nonjustified text and Desired, Minimum, and Maximum spacing for justified text. Photoshop also lets you scale the characters themselves if that will give you better justification. I've known a few people who weren't above scaling type by up to five percent to make a paragraph hang as they wanted. This feature's for them. If you use really large margins for Glyph Scaling, you can get some great effects for display text.

Application-Specific Commands

To set tabs in Illustrator, use Type ➤ Tab Ruler. You can set left, right, center, or decimal tabs for horizontal text and bottom tabs for vertical text. Check the Snap box if you want your tabs to set exactly at the ruler units. Type ➤ Fit Headline adds tracking to a non-multiple master headline to make it fit within its bounding box. For multiple master fonts, the command should adjust both the weight of the font and the tracking, but I've had some buggy results with weights changing unevenly. To use Type ➤ Wrap ➤ Make, the graphic that you want text to wrap around must be in front of the text itself. You can only use area text to do this. There's no quick way to set the offset of the text from the graphic, and you may not like the look that Illustrator gives you automatically.

You can move the graphic by using the Group Selection tool, clicking only enough times to take the graphic and not the text, or you can create an unpainted boundary area for the graphic that you can tweak to move text only from certain areas.

If you need columns of text, create a text block in Illustrator, then use the Type ➤ Rows And Columns command to input the number of equal-width columns (and/or rows) that you need. If, however, you need unequal columns or unusually shaped text blocks, you can link the blocks using Type ➤ Blocks ➤ Link. In either method, you can manually adjust the size and shape of a text block using the Direct Selection tool.

Photoshop doesn't have the same advanced features that Illustrator has, but it does have multiline composition for paragraph text, which works within your hyphenation and justification settings to give you better-looking text with fewer hyphens without a lot of manual tweaking.

Part ii

Type on a Path

Not only does Painter set Dynamic text type on a path, it does some rather nifty things that Illustrator cannot do. First, you can choose how the type adheres to the curve. It's inexplicable that Illustrator has never implemented this; some third-party extensions give you the ability to warp type more elegantly, but it seems a small thing to ask. Second, you can add a return to your text and Painter will set the next line of text to the same curve at a baseline determined by the leading you have set. Painter uses only open paths, and it builds the basic path for you from within the Dynamic Text dialog box. You can edit the path from there also. Once you enter the text, you can choose the Curve Style and use the editing tools to change the shape of the curve.

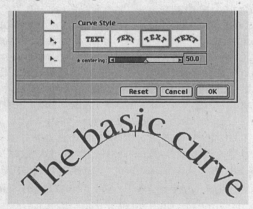

The four styles are Straight, Vertical, Baseline (the most like Illustrator), and Transform. Vertical adjusts the letters to keep them upright. How the curve rotates and bends affects whether the Vertical type is forward or backward.

Baseline maintains the shape of the letters as they adhere to the baseline. If you want to maintain the shape of the letters, choose Baseline style.

Transform distorts the letters to spread across gaps caused by the curve, as shown here:

Use these styles as a starting point, then grab the curve handles, add points, or use the adjustments to make changes. Although Photoshop does not use the same terminology or the type-on-a-path metaphor, you can distort the type easily by changing the basic Warp style, then using the sliders to add perspective. And remember, Painter's type will print as bitmaps, whereas Illustrator's and Photoshop's will print as vector artwork unless you rasterize it.

In Illustrator, you draw a curve with the Pen tool, then use the Path Type tool to place the type on the path. It can be either an open or closed path, but if you use a closed path, make sure you use the Path Type tool or Alt/Option-click the path with the regular Type tool, or else Illustrator will assume you want to set area text. As soon as you get close to an open path with the Type tool, you'll see it change to the Path Type tool. Where you click the path is the insertion point, and type flows in the direction of the path as you input. This may shock and amaze you if you happen to build a path from right to left and then place text; it shows up upside down. No matter, you can flip it later.

If your path is too short for all the text to fit, switch to Artwork mode and you'll see a tiny box with a + sign to let you know that there is text overflow out there in the ozone somewhere.

Use the regular path-editing tools to extend the path until all the text fits.

Photoshop doesn't exactly set type on a path; it uses the "envelope" technology to warp type. When you click the next to last button on the Options bar (the "T" with the curve underneath), you are presented with a dialog with a drop-down list and controls that let you choose a basic envelope style. Then choose how much of the effect you apply with the Bend slider or how you distort the perspective with Horizontal and Vertical Distortion. You can apply text warp to both point and paragraph text.

Changing Path Shape

Don't expect the same finesse with Painter's Dynamic Text path-editing tools that you would have with Illustrator. Still, for the added ability to manipulate the way type sits on the curve, I'll deal. Use Painter's Reshape tool to grab control handles and bend the curve. You need not add a point just to lengthen the curve; you can drag the endpoint with the Reshape tool.

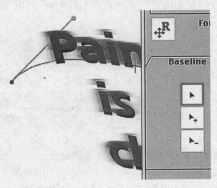

Illustrator gives you the full array of tools for editing the shape of your path, with the exclusion of the Scissors if you are using an open path and the Knife. You cannot split a single path that contains type, although you can use the Scissors to cut open a closed one. This is true for both path and area text.

Moving Type on a Path

Moving text on a path is one of those funny little nonintuitive things that you get used to doing in Illustrator. Instead of using a Type tool, you use a selection tool. If you are in a Type tool, you can click the Direct Selection arrow in the Toolbox, otherwise click the text baseline with the Selection tool (in Illustrator 9 it's called the Move tool) and you get a tall I-beam. It looks different than the flashing cursor; it's blue and looks like a capital I. Drag this (still with the selection tool) in the direction you want the text to go.

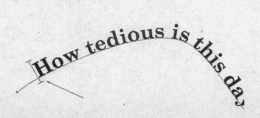

In Painter's Dynamic Text dialog, you can use the alignment icons for left, center, or right on the Straight baseline curve style. The ±centering slider in the dialog's Baseline tab moves you among those options for the other curve styles, but what the numbers mean depends on which alignment icon you have chosen. Moving the slider toward the left moves the text to the left. Zero is flush left, 50 is centered, and 100 is flush right. If moving text via the slider doesn't give you the result you expect, check to see which alignment icon is active.

Though Photoshop does not allow you to actually move type on a path, if you have set paragraph text, you can change the left and right indents to shift text within the warped area. Here, changing the left indent of the paragraph moved it further into the bounding box and gave me more of the letter shape that I wanted.

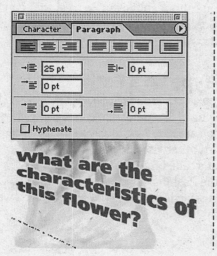

Flipping Type Across the Path

You can flip an entire layer of text in Photoshop, but you cannot flip type on a path (because you can't set type on a path). In Painter, use the Angle Adjustment slider to rotate or flip the text around the path if you are using the Straight or Vertical curve style. Flipping using the Angle Adjustment has different results depending on the baseline curve style. This is Vertical style with Angle set to 180°.

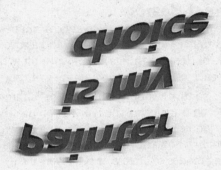

This allows you to create effects that would require a lot more work in Illustrator. You can flip a Dynamic Text layer, using Effects ➢ Orientation, but it turns into an Image layer.

You can flip type on a path in Illustrator, but it's not the easiest thing to do (or rather to manage; sometimes it happens all too easily).

If you are editing the text and still in the Type tool, you can click the Direct Selection arrow in the Toolbox; otherwise click the text baseline with the Selection arrow to get the I-beam. Then either drag the I-beam up or down across the path (sometimes it's easier to drag to the end of the path and over) or double-click the I-beam with the Selection arrow. Your type flips and can still be edited. You still may need to drag the text along the path to align it properly or even see all of it. Here, I've dragged the I-beam across the path and into the new position.

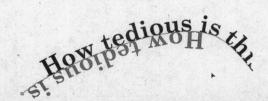

Text Effects

It's hard to choose a favorite application for adding cool effects to type. All three can do amazing things. You have a bit more flexibility with Photoshop and Illustrator in terms of adding effects and keeping the text editable, but the type of effect you need may be your only true deciding factor.

Text Effect Basics

Any Photoshop effects (now called styles) can be added to a Type layer. You can customize your own effects or add a saved style from the Styles palette. One of the nice things about working with Photoshop is the ability to tailor each effect to the text you're working with.

You can also turn visibility on or off for different effects to quickly check how each transforms the type. If you use the type as a clipping group mask, you can move Fill or Adjustment layers up or down in the palette to change how they affect the type. You can change the opacities and blending modes of effects or Fill layers easily, but if you use layer effects you'll be able to save settings you like as a style. Here everything but the warp has been saved to the Styles palette.

Though Photoshop cannot blur a Type layer with a filter, you can get a blurred effect by adding an Outer Glow in the same color as the text itself. Experiment with blending modes and opacity for the exact look you want.

Painter works with both text and its shadow as part of the Dynamic text. You can apply fills and blurs to both, and with Painter's vast array of Art Materials, you have a lot of choices for how to color your text. If you make the Art Materials palette visible before opening the Dynamic Text dialog, the palette is then available to try different fills while you are in the dialog. You can reposition the shadow in the image by clicking the Shadow button, then using the Move icon to reposition the shadow in the image.

Painter can change the opacity for either the text or the shadow (if you've applied one), independently in the Opacity field for Dynamic Text, or together via the Opacity slider on the Layers palette. Once type is set, you can add other dynamic effects such as Burn, Bevel, or Tear. However, once you apply other Dynamic layers or use effects, your text is no longer editable.

Illustrator has my vote for craziest possible effects, because you can add live vector effects to the type object but also to any additional fills or strokes that you add to the type object. Using the Appearance palette in conjunction with the Transparency palette, you can target each stroke or fill (or the text itself) to add the effect or change the blending mode or transparency. You can blur text with Effects ➤ Blur and either Gaussian or Radial. The text remains editable, but this is an effect that will cause type to rasterize when printed, so make sure that's what you intend.

Here, I've applied live effects to both the fill and stroke of this type object. The text itself is colored light blue but the fill of the type object is orange.

Part ii

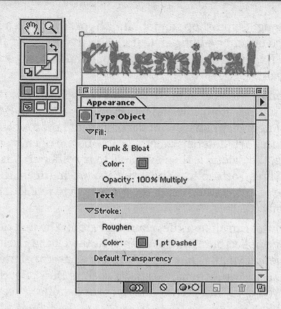

Here, the text is stroked with a 1-point dashed line, and I've colored each stroke separately. The type object is stroked and filled. To make the dashed line show up, I've moved the Text above the Type Object's stroke and fill in the Appearance palette.

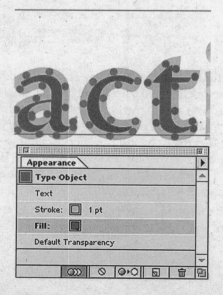

Filling Text

Suddenly, in the last year or two, you can do all these incredible things with text. I'll start with Illustrator. You can now add multiple fills and strokes to objects, including type objects. You still make the original fill and stroke the same old way, choosing the color before or after you type. And you still change individual letters by highlighting the ones you want to change with the Type tool and changing them with the fill and stroke squares. But if you want to get wild, open the Appearance palette. If you select the type with a selection tool, the Appearance palette tells you that you are now working with the type object.

Use the palette menu to add a new fill or stroke or both. Target any fill or stroke in the Appearance palette and change its blending mode or opacity in the Transparency palette. Or use the Effects menu to add an effect to that single fill or stroke rather than the entire type object. Here, the text itself is blue with a magenta stroke, but there are two additional strokes above it with wider widths and blending modes.

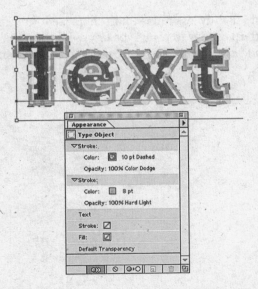

The order of the effects, fills, and strokes can be rearranged in the Appearance palette allowing you to quickly change the effect. It's way too much fun.

Only slightly less fun is Photoshop. Here you can add a color, gradient, or pattern overlay to your Type layer (or all three if you like), but you can only add one of each and you cannot change the stacking order of layer effects.

However, you can add a Pattern, Gradient, or Color Fill layer above the Type layer, then Alt/Option-click the line between the layers to make the Fill layer clip to the type. If you use this method, you can add multiple patterns, colors, gradients, and other types of adjustments. Plus you can add a layer mask to the layer to selectively change the effects. Here, I've kept those effects and added two Fill layers that are clipped to the text. I've manipulated their blending modes and painted out the layer mask over the o on the Pattern Fill layer.

If you use Dynamic Text in Painter, you can color both the text itself and its shadow with either color, pattern, gradient, or weaves. You have all of Painter's art materials at your fingertips, and that's a lot. However, you can't stack multiple effects on top of each other unless you make a copy of the layer itself and change the parameters.

Painter's Art Materials palette remains active while you're in the dialog so you can experiment with different looks. You can even choose a pattern fill with a gradient shadow or some other unusual combination.

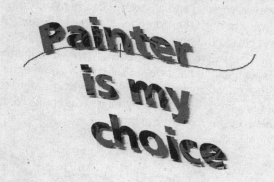

Transforming Text

Painter does not allow you to use the regular transformation tools with Dynamic Text. As soon as you try to use Effects ➤ Orientation, the layer becomes an Image layer. Even if you cancel out of the transformation, you must remember to Undo Commit Plug-In Layer to keep the layer dynamic. In Photoshop, you can use most of the Transform tools on a Type layer. In Illustrator, you can use all the Transform tools, although Twirl affects the path that type is on, not the type itself. But hey, check out that Free Transform tool with type. In both Photoshop and Illustrator, you can transform the type by transforming its bounding box with the Move tool.

Rendering Text

The next sections cover those techniques you'll need to know for rendering your text.

Rasterizing Text

You want to keep your type layers "dynamic" or "editable" as long as possible, because editing text as text is so much easier. However, there will probably come a time when you want to apply some surface effect or paint, and you'll have to rasterize. Any time you rasterize type, I recommend duplicating the type layer before rendering, to keep the type specs available. Though you are less likely to rasterize your type in Illustrator, use Object ➤ Rasterize if you need bitmap information. In Painter, though Dynamic text is rasterized, you are not able to paint it with brushes because it resides on a special layer. Click the layer in the Layers palette and use Dynamic Layers ➤ Commit to commit the layer to an Image layer, or just start to paint it and you will be prompted to commit. In Photoshop use the Type or Layer options from the Layer ➤ Rasterize submenu to make the type into a regular Image layer; this will preserve any layer effects or styles you have applied. Here is an image that was painted in Painter with a variety of brushes, including F/X Fairy Dust, then saved as a Photoshop file and had Layer ➤ Styles ➤ Emboss applied.

Outlining Text

This is a "must know" area of Illustrator. At the end of the creation process, you create outlines of your type so often that there's a keyboard shortcut to speed it up: Ctrl/Command+Shift+O. Outlines enable you to move type into other applications, to edit the type shapes themselves, and to pass your work on to others who may not have the fonts you've used. Reasons not to Create Outlines include no longer being able to edit the text of your document; also, outlines of small type may not be true to the shape of the original. Still, this is a most useful command. If you work with type, especially designing logos, it's a must.

In Photoshop, two commands can be used to create outlines of your text. Layer ➤ Type ➤ Convert To Shape makes the text shapes editable with the path-editing tools by creating a Shape layer with a clipping mask in the shape of the text.

If there were different colors in your text before converting, Photoshop will take the color of the first letter as the color for the layer, as you are only allowed a single color for Shape layers. Your second possibility for outline text is to create a work path. This path will appear in the Paths palette and can be loaded as a selection on any layer or saved with the document as a clipping path for the entire file.

Painter's text shapes are vector-based outlines; they can be edited with shape-editing tools and exported to Illustrator format. Dynamic Text layers can be converted to outlines with a bit of work. First, choose Dynamic Layers ➢ Commit. You now have an Image layer with mask. On the Masks palette, select the layer mask and choose Masks ➢ Copy Mask. Select the new mask and click Load Selection. Once you have a selection outline, use Selections ➢ Convert To Shape.

Transferring Type between Applications:

Due of the variety of strengths and weaknesses of each of the programs that we've covered here, you may find yourself wanting to transfer type images between the applications.

Transferring from Photoshop

If you plan to bring a text layer from Photoshop to Painter, use Layer ➢ Rasterize ➢ Layer before you save. If you've applied any layer effects to the text, make sure you rasterize those also; Painter will not read any layer with effects applied. You can then open your Photoshop file into Painter and paint away. When Illustrator opens a Photoshop file, it rasterizes the Type layers but keeps the layer itself intact unless you had applied layer effects before saving (in which case, it flattens the layer to the Background). If you used Fill layers clipped to the text layer, those fills are flattened into the layer. There should be an update of Photoshop soon to deal with some of the incompatibility issues.

Transferring from Painter

I've had much better luck going back and forth between Painter and Photoshop than Painter and Illustrator (although Illustrator to Painter works quite well). You can save your Painter file as a Photoshop file and the Dynamic Text layer will remain a layer, but no longer be a text layer. Shape text (like all other Painter shapes) is rasterized when saved as a Photoshop file. To go from Painter to Illustrator, you can export text shapes created with the Text tool as an Adobe Illustrator file, but type shapes don't always transfer accurately. Plus, my beautiful type sometimes loses curves or edges and is no longer recognizable as Frutiger Black or whatever. For example, this text was set in Painter as Shape text, then exported to Illustrator format. It's supposed to be Stone Serif, but when I opened it in Illustrator, the shapes were no longer accurate.

Text

On the other hand, you can save the file as a TIFF or EPS and place them into Illustrator. Of course, they're rasterized. If this is what you have to do, choose TIFF if on-screen type readability is an issue.

Transferring from Illustrator

Photoshop can read text exported from Illustrator 9.02 but only if the text is on a layer all by itself. It doesn't matter what level of the hierarchy you are on, but if your text is not on the top level, make sure you check the Write Nested Layers box. Use File ➤ Export and choose Photoshop 5 as the file type. Choose the color mode and correct resolution for the file and check Write Layers and Editable Text. If you do not check all the correct boxes, your type will probably still appear in the document but be rasterized.

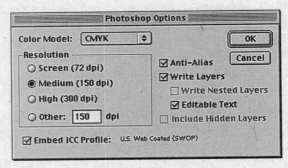

If you try to edit the text from Illustrator in Photoshop, you get this alert. Actually, sometimes the text changes but sometimes it looks exactly the same.

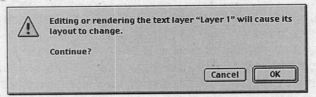

You can copy and paste converted type from Illustrator to Photoshop as either pixels or paths.

From Illustrator to Painter, you will be sending paths. So create outlines from your type first, then save your file in Illustrator 8 format. In Painter, use File ≻ Acquire. If it's easier, you can simply copy and paste the outlines from Illustrator. If you don't see what you were expecting, open and close the eye icon for that layer; you should get all the paths that you pasted. And, by the way, if outlines are what you want in Photoshop, you can copy and paste there, too.

WHAT'S NEXT

While this part of the book was probably fun (or, at least, I hope so), you'll find that the next part will be even more of a kick. You'll learn how to transform images, create 3D effects, and perform other magic. First up, a few clever projects you can use to master some special Photoshop effects.

Part ii

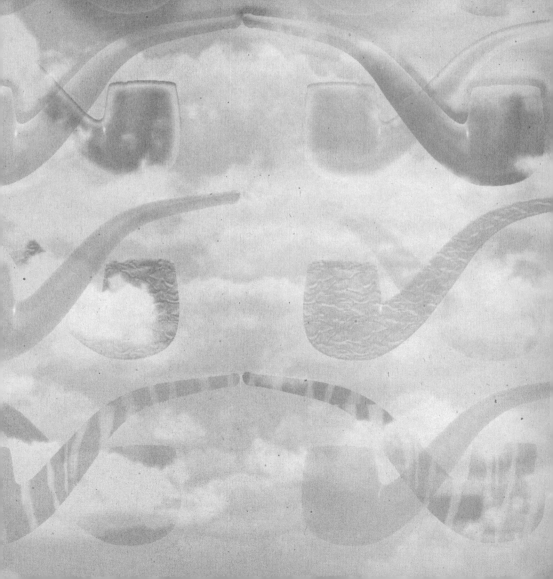

PART iii
FUN WITH PHOTOSHOP 6

Chapter 14

TRANSFORM IMAGES WITH FILTERS

What you see isn't necessarily what you have to get in the digital realm. Photoshop lets you do a lot more than combine and retouch images or correct the color balance. You can transform images completely by changing the shape and size of portions of an image, adding a texture of brush strokes, or giving a harsh image a soft romantic glow. Many of these effects can be accomplished using Photoshop's built-in plug-ins or third-party tools like Eye Candy 4000, Xenofex, and Kai's Power Tools. This chapter will serve as your introduction to these filters. You'll find more examples of filter techniques in the Reference Guide at the end of this book.

Adapted from *Photoshop 6! I Didn' t Know You Could Do That...* by David D. Busch

ISBN 0-7821-2918-8   288 pages $24.99

Using filters found in the Artistic, Brush Strokes, Pixelate, and Stylize submenus of the Filter menu, Photoshop makes it easy to generate effects that are strongly reminiscent of the styles of "real" artists. These kinds of filters have one thing in common: They reduce the amount of information in an image by combining or moving pixels. At first glance, the effect seems to be that of having turned a photograph into a painting. Instead of the harsh reality of the original image, we have a more organic, often softer picture that appears to have been created rather than captured.

However, in deference to true artists, including the art teacher at my children's school (who also happens to be their mother), I need to point out that just blindly applying filters helter-skelter won't produce true art. In a real painting, a brush stroke is applied in exactly the right size, shape, hue, and direction to provide a particular bit of detail from the artist's vision. Computers can't reproduce that insight. To get the best effects, a human—you—needs to remain in control of the creative process.

MIMIC CUBISM WITHOUT THE CUBES

For this one, I looked high and low for images—literally—combining a sea-level photograph of the Atlantic North Coast of Spain with a shot of a trio of storks (actually, one stork cloned twice) captured in the highest provincial capital in Spain, Avila. Here's how I merged the two pictures and transformed them into a reasonable facsimile of a painting. If you want to follow along, you can find the original photos on the Sybex Web site. I used Alien Skin's Xenofex filters, but Photoshop's native plug-ins can be used as well.

NOTE
To download practice files mentioned in this book, navigate to the Sybex Web site (www.sybex.com) and enter **2991** into the search box. When you get to the page for *Photoshop 6 Complete*, follow the links to download the file.

1. First, select the sky around the storks. The easy way to do this is to select the sky with the Magic wand (holding down the Shift key to select more and more parts of it), and then use Select ➤ Similar to grab the remainder of the sky.

NOTE

Precision isn't critical because the stork background is a shade of blue similar to that of the sky in the seashore picture. Any stray bits will blend in well, especially after the pixel-pushing that follows.

2. Use Select ➢ Inverse (or press Shift+Ctrl/Command+I) to reverse the selection so it includes only the storks.

3. Press Ctrl/Command+C to copy the storks, move to the seashore image, and press Ctrl/Command+V to paste the storks down into the image.

4. Choose Edit ➢ Transform ➢ Resize, and make the storks any size you want within the composition. Drag them to a location you like, either heading out to sea or back toward shore after a long session of whatever it is storks would do if they were sea-going birds.

5. Flatten the image to merge the storks and the seashore, and then make a copy of the layer using Layer ➢ Duplicate Layer.

6. On the upper layer, apply a filter to fracture the image into a lot of little pieces. I used Alien Skin's Xenofex filter, as shown in this figure.

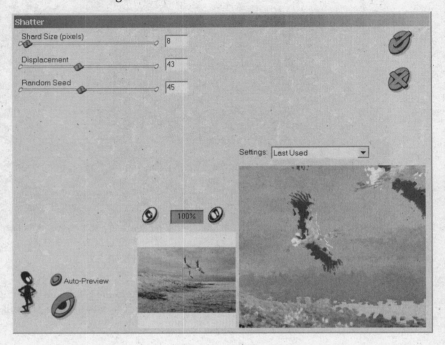

The most important parameter is the Shard Size slider. I used a small value to make the little pieces very small. The Displacement slider determines how far the pieces are moved from their original location. I used a value of 43. The Random Seed slider determines the random pattern; you only need to change this if you apply the filter to the same image multiple times and want different looks each time.

NOTE

Photoshop's Stylize ➢ Tile filter can also be used to get a somewhat different effect. Experiment with the number of tiles to be used (80 to 99 are good starter values) and the kind of background between the tiles. I've used the Inverse Image setting with success.

7. Here's a step many forget to follow: Use Filter ≻ Sharpen ≻ Unsharp Mask, and accentuate the effect. Move the Amount slider until you get a pronounced brush-stroke effect. Usually 100 to 150 percent will do it.

8. OK, we've managed to fracture the stork/seagulls all to heck. You can restore them so they are recognizable. To do so, use a soft-brushed eraser to remove the shattered storks on the upper layer and reveal, at least in part, their unaltered cousins underneath. When you're done, the image should look something like this one.

Part iii

CREATE MASTERPIECES WITH MASTER STROKES

Brush-stroke and painting-oriented plug-ins are by far the majority among Photoshop's native filters. However, you can't just blindly apply them, point to the results, and crow, "Hey, I meant to do that!" I can't count the number of times I've seen published examples of "computer manipulated images" in photography publications that were nothing more than straight photos with an ordinary Photoshop filter applied using the default settings. With a little creativity, you can go way beyond the ordinary. I'll show you all the things I was able to do with a single photograph.

This castle in Spain is perfect fodder for a digital painting.

Try these transmogrifications. Here are four variations on a theme:

1. The first thing to do is select the sky and save the selection. The sky and the castle in this photo need to be worked with separately because their tonal values are so different. Click the Add button in the toolbar (a sensational new Photoshop 6 feature) and then use the Magic Wand to select multiple areas, and Select ➢ Similar to make sure you grab every last pixel. If necessary, use Quick Mask mode (press **Q** to activate) and paint with a brush to grab any stray pixels. Then save the selection with Select ➢ Save Selection.

NOTE

Learn to use the New, Add, Subtract, and Intersect buttons in the toolbar. They're a dramatic improvement over earlier versions of Photoshop, in which it was all too easy to lose a selection when your finger slipped off a key or you clicked somewhere outside the selection.

2. To get the effect shown in the figure below, apply Filter ≻ Brush Strokes ≻ Angled Strokes. Use a very short stroke length, such as 3 to 5, to provide a lot of detail from the original image. Increase the sharpness to 6 or 8 so the strokes will be very clear. I used the Unsharp Mask filter to accentuate the effect even more.

NOTE

When using Photoshop's various brush stroke filters, you should use small stroke or brush sizes to preserve as much detail as possible. For greater control, fade the filter after application by pressing Shift+Ctrl/Command+F. You can also apply the filter to a duplicate layer and adjust the opacity until you obtain the exact effect you want.

3. For the look in the following figure, use Filter ≻ Brush Strokes ≻ Ink Outlines. A brush stroke length of 1 looks good, but you'll want a lower Dark Intensity (around 9) and higher Light Intensity (I used 25) to keep the picture from being too dark and dismal.

Before applying the filter, I loaded the sky selection and copied the sky to a new layer, and then I processed the castle and sky separately so they both would end up with about the same degree of brightness, but with the castle having quite a bit more contrast. Sharpen both with Unsharp Mask to get the amount of detail you like.

4. The image shown in the next figure is one of my favorite Photoshop painting techniques. It uses the Brush Strokes ➢ Accented Edges filter.

Besides supplying a glow to the important edges of the image, setting the Edge Brightness slider to a high level (from 30 to 50) always generates some interesting pastel colors. The orange hue produced in this case really reproduces the sun-baked tone of Spanish structures of this sort. Use a small edge width to preserve detail.

5. The Dry Brush filter, found in the Artistic submenu, is an easy one to use effectively. You can play with the brush size, amount of detail rendered by the filter, and texture. I set the Brush Detail slider to the maximum (10) and the other two to the minimum (1) and added some sharpening to get the effect shown here.

CREATE NIGHT FROM DAY

This version looks great in black and white (it is a night scene, after all), but it really comes alive in full color, with a deep, rich blue night sky and eerie colors in the castle walls and along the horizon. Here are the steps I took to produce this image:

1. Starting with the original image, I applied the Stylize ➢ Find Edges filter. There are no settings for this filter. Just apply it,

and check out the results, which are shown in the following figure. As is, this effect is interesting enough to stand on its own. You could increase the contrast and brightness to create an image that looks like it was sketched.

2. Press Ctrl/Command+I to invert the image and reveal the night scene hidden within. If you like, you can load the sky selection you saved earlier and ramp up the contrast dramatically to produce the look shown next.

3. Press Ctrl/Command+U to produce the Hue/Saturation dialog box, and move the Saturation slider to between 80 and 100 percent to create a rich, eerie effect.

4. Load the sky selection, and make a copy of the sky area. Paste it down in a new layer.

5. Choose a very dark blue and a medium blue from the Swatches palette as the foreground and background colors.

6. Lock the transparency for the sky layer by clicking the Transparency box in the Layers palette (it's the left-most box just above the layers themselves).

7. Use the Gradient tool to apply a foreground-to-background linear gradient to the sky layer. Make sure the darkest blue is at the top, with the lightest blue at the bottom, near the horizon (simulating a "sky glow" effect).

8. Create a duplicate of this layer.

9. In the upper, duplicate layer, use Filter ➤ Noise ➤ Add Noise to add Gaussian monochromatic specks to the sky layer. Increase the noise value until the sky has the number of stars you'd like.

10. With the sky layer still active, choose Layer ➤ Add Layer Mask ➤ Reveal All to activate a layer mask.

NOTE

When a layer mask is used, click in the Mask Layer thumbnail (at right in the layer) to work with the mask itself. Click the image thumbnail (at left) to work with the image.

Part iii

11. Using the Gradient tool again, choose the Black-White gradient from the drop-down list in the Option bar, and apply the gradient to the layer mask, with the white at the top and black at the bottom. This creates a mask that reveals all of the starry sky at the top, but fades away to let the deep blue, starless sky of the layer beneath to show through at the bottom.

12. As a finishing touch, load the sky selection again, and press Shift+Ctrl/Command+I to invert it. On the bottom layer (which contains the castle image), make a copy of the castle. Click the top layer, and paste it down.

13. Apply the Outer Glow layer style, using the settings shown in the following figure. I set the size of the glow to 40 pixels, used a soft yellow as the background color, and added 42 percent noise to blend the glow in with the "noisy" sky. I set Opacity to 24 percent to further blend the glow and the sky. The result was a subtle amount of separation between the castle and the stars.

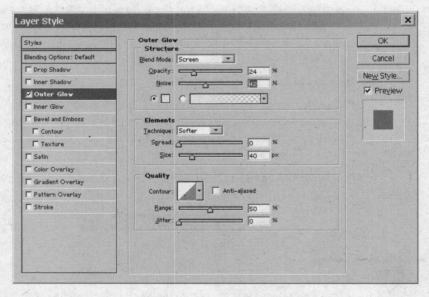

The resulting image, shown in this figure, looks pretty good in black and white, but it verges on the startling in full color. Check it out on the Web site for this book.

CREATE A ROMANTIC GLOW

Photographers have long known that a soft, diffuse glow adds a romantic look to portraits of women. Before digital magic became common, camera wielders resorted to placing bits of nylon stockings in front of their lenses, smearing petroleum jelly on filters, and using special lens attachments designed to hide or obscure facial flaws. Today, we can do the same thing, but with much greater control, using Photoshop. Consider this photograph.

Part iii

The picture is nice enough as it is, even though there are slight hints of darkening under the eyes, a few stray wrinkles here and there, and a crease or two around the mouth. All of these defects may not survive the printing process—but trust me, they are there. Luckily, they can be banished in short order, using the following steps:

1. Use the Artistic ➢ Film Grain filter to add a kind of random noise to the image that resembles photographic film grain. The dialog box, shown in the next figure, has controls to let you adjust the amount of grain, the highlight area (in effect, increasing or decreasing contrast), and intensity (how strongly the grain overpowers the original image).

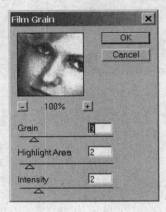

NOTE

Grainy pictures became an artistic outlet in the mid-1960s. Photographers utilized the ultra-grainy, high-contrast look of pictures taken in dim available light by using fast films and extended ("push") processing. It was a case of "as long as the pictures are going to be very grainy anyway, let's pretend that's what we wanted all along."

2. A better choice is usually the Distort ➢ Diffuse Glow filter (don't ask me why it's located in the Distort submenu). It produces a soft, glowing effect while adding a grainy texture.

The dialog box has a Graininess slider, along with two more that can be a little confusing:

- ▶ The Glow Amount slider controls the size and intensity of the highlight glow. Adjust this too far, and you can completely wipe out your image.

- ▶ The Clear Amount slider controls the fuzziness of the entire image.

WARNING

Diffuse Glow always applies pixels of the background color to the image. For the best results, your background should be the default white. If you happen to have another color, especially a dark hue, the effects will be strange—to say the least.

The finished images will look something like these.

The effect of Film Grain is seen on the left, and the effect of the Diffuse Glow is seen on the right.

Part iii

3. Apply Diffuse Glow to other kinds of images, rather than strictly to portraits. The next figure shows a woodland scene that has been brightened and given a romantic look thanks to a judicious application of this filter.

ADD SPECIAL EFFECTS WITH LIGHTING

With lots of controls for you to play with and achieve many different creative effects, Photoshop's Lighting Effects filter, found in the Render submenu, is a mini-program in its own right. It can be used to apply both lighting (as if the image were being illuminated by a light source) and texture. Textures can range from subtle to outrageous and from matte to shiny and metallic. I decided to see what Lighting Effects could do to this mundane photo of a fledgling rock star in action.

Add Illumination

First, try out the illumination features of the filter:

1. Choose Filter ➤ Render ➤ Lighting Effects to produce the following dialog box.

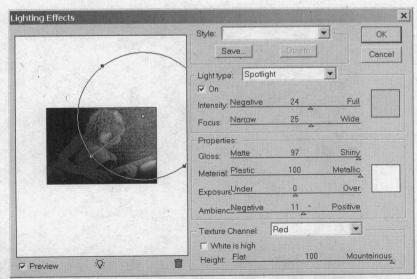

2. Select Spotlight from the drop-down Light Type list. Also available are Directional (less tightly focused than Spotlight) and Omni (which appears to be coming from all directions).

3. Adjust the intensity of the light and its other properties.

4. The ellipse in the Preview window shows the coverage area of the light and its point source (the handle in the center of the ellipse). You can drag the source to any point in the preview (even well outside the picture area, as if the light were located some distance from the subject) and drag the four side handles of the ellipse to change the shape of the coverage.

5. Click the Light Bulb icon at the bottom of the Preview, and drag into the preview area to create a second light source. You can specify light type, intensity, location, and other properties as with the first.

NOTE

To turn on or turn off a light, select the light by clicking one of its handles, and then check or uncheck the On box.

6. Click OK to apply the lighting effect, and then boost contrast, if necessary, to end up with an image something like the one shown next.

Add Texture

Lighting Effects can also be used to add a texture to images. Follow these steps to see some of the great things you can do:

1. Choose Render ➤ Lighting Effects from the Filter menu. Set up your lighting as before, using a spotlight and fairly dramatic lighting.

2. Set the Gloss slider to maximum Shiny. Set the Material slider to maximum Metallic. You can use the Exposure sliders to control brightness and the Ambience slider to adjust contrast, if you like.

3. Because this image is predominantly red, choose Red as the Texture Channel from the drop-down list at the bottom of the dialog box.

4. Click the White Is High box. This will make the lighter areas of the image "higher" in terms of the 3D texture you're applying, while the darker areas are "lower."

5. For maximum texture, move the Height slider all the way to the right to the Mountainous setting.

6. Click OK.

7. Adjust brightness/contrast, and sharpen to taste.

8. I added some flames using Eye Candy 4000's Fire filter to get the flaming fingers of fate shown in this figure.

Add a Spotlight

I used several different effects for the image shown in this figure. Lens flare adds an interesting effect, as if a spotlight were visible.

These are the steps:

1. Apply Lighting Effects, using a small amount of texture.

2. Add a lens flare with the Render ➤ Lens Flare filter, using the 105mm Prime, with brightness set to 100 percent. Drag the crosshair point on the preview window to position the light anywhere you like.

3. Select the background to the left of the guitarist, invert, and apply Eye Candy 4000's Corona filter behind him. I used a purple glow.

NOTE

The Lens Flare settings are named after the effects you get with common wide-angle to telephoto lenses mounted on a 35mm camera when pointed toward a bright light source. A 50mm to 300mm zoom lens is a complex optic with lots of lens elements that let the light bounce around inside, producing a broad, fuzzy flare. A 35mm "prime" lens generates another sort of glare because it takes in so much light from such a wide angle. A 105mm "prime" lens creates a third type with its narrower angle of view and (generally) fewer optics inside the lens barrel.

FIX FAULTY PERSPECTIVE

Sometimes, twisting an image isn't done to create distortion, but to correct it. A good example of this is the need to fix pictures of tall buildings in which the structure seems to be falling backward. The problem in the following figure was caused by tilting the camera to take in the upper portion of the building. As a result, the bottom portion of the film plane is closer to the base of the edifice, while the top of the film is farther away. The only way to correct what photographers call *perspective distortion* in the camera is to use a special lens or a tilting camera back that will allow the film and subject to remain parallel even while the lens tilts.

However, Photoshop can do the same job easily if you know a few tricks. Here they are—applied to the image, a photo of a massive Roman arch at the top of a hill in Medinaceli, Spain. Because the arch is perched on a hill, the photographer couldn't simply back up and take the picture from a distance that didn't require tilting the camera. You may find yourself in a similar situation when doing architectural photography when your back is up against a wall (literally) and you can't move farther away or use a lens with a wider angle.

To correct the problem, follow these steps:

1. The first step is to increase the size of the canvas (this will give you a little room to stretch the archway in some new and interesting directions). Use Image ➢ Canvas Size, and increase the size by 125 percent in both horizontal and vertical directions. The exact amount doesn't matter because you're going to crop the image later anyway.

2. Choose View ➢ New Guides to create a horizontal Photoshop guideline. Drag it down near the base of the arch. Repeat, creating a horizontal guide that you drag down to just above the top of the arch. Type in a value other than the default 0-pixel position to place the guide's initial position away from the side of the canvas. That makes it easier to grab and drag.

3. Repeat Step 2, creating a pair of vertical guidelines. Your image will now look something this one.

4. Select the area to be corrected, and choose Edit ➢ Transform ➢ Distort. Using this mode instead of Transform ➢ Perspective gives you the flexibility to transform each of the four edges of the arch independently.

5. Drag the top handles of the selection until the top edge of the arch is parallel with the upper horizontal guide. Repeat with the lower handles and the lower horizontal guide.

6. Drag each of the sets of side handles to align the sides of the arch with the side guides. Your image should look something like the next one.

7. Crop the image into a rectangle. Use the Rubber Stamp tool to clone portions of the image to fill in any blank spots. You'll end up with something like the image shown in the top figure on the next page. But we don't have to stop there.

8. I selected the sky area with the Magic Wand (just as we did in the previous exercises) and applied Alien Skin's Xenofex Little Fluffy Clouds plug-in. The most important parameters for this filter are the Puff Size (in pixels) and Coverage (in percentage—the lower the percentage, the more your background sky will show through). The percentage I used doesn't matter;

select an amount that pleases you as you view the preview. This filter is far superior to Photoshop's own Clouds filter, which doesn't have controls and produces less realistic clouds.

9. Inverting my selection, I adjusted the brightness and contrast of the arch a bit, and added some sharpening.

Some clouds make the finishing touch.

FILL THE SKY WITH BUBBLES, RAIN, OR SNOW

Here's a quickie that shows you how a fantasy image can be created quickly if you have the right plug-ins at your disposal. This one uses Ulead's Particle filter, a remarkably flexible plug-in that has lots of weather effects, such as Rain and Snow, as well as Firefly, Smoke, a decent Clouds filter, Fire particles, and a Star effect. I'm going to use several of these to get a couple different effects. The unmodified image of an ordinary, sunny day is shown here.

Let It Rain

To add rain to the picture, follow these steps:

1. First, select the sky area with the Magic Wand. It may take a few tries because the clouds make the process a little trickier. If necessary, use Quick Mask mode to paint or erase areas. Save the selection.

2. For a rainy effect, darken the sky and reduce the contrast using Photoshop's Brightness/Contrast controls. You can select a combination that varies anywhere between dismal (dark and low contrast) and forboding (dark, but with high contrast).

3. Apply the Ulead Particle Rain filter, using the dialog box shown in this figure.

You can adjust the length and density of the rain, from a light drizzle to drenching sheets. Use the Opacity and Blur controls to adjust how much of the background image appears behind the rain.

4. Click OK to apply the rain effect. Your finished effect can be seen at the left in the following figure.

As you can see, rain and snow don't fall mainly on the plain in Segovia, Spain.

Let It Snow

You can always have a white Christmas with the following steps:

1. Work with a copy of the previously used image. Save the sky selection for reuse.

2. Select the sidewalk area in front of the castle, and apply a cloud filter to give it the look of being covered with freshly fallen snow. Fade the cloud filter so the paving underneath shows through.

3. Press **Q** to enter Quick Mask mode, and use a soft brush to select the tops of the towers, roofs, walls, and the bench. Press **Q** again to exit Quick Mask mode.

4. Use Ulead's Particle Effects Snow filter to dust snow on the selections. You may want to repeat the process two or three times to add enough snow. Just remember to click the Random button each time you visit the dialog box so the snow will be dusted in a different place each time.

5. Press Ctrl+A to select the entire image, and apply the snow filter to the overall scene once or twice. Your finished image will look like the one on the right in the previous figure.

Add Tiny Bubbles—or Huge Ones

Here are the polka steps that would make Lawrence Welk happy:

1. If you'd rather have bubbles instead of rain or snow, activate the sky selection you saved.

2. Apply Ulead Particle Effects' Bubble filter. Adjust the Density (number of bubbles overall), Size (the maximum size a bubble can be), Variance (the percentage difference between the largest and smallest bubbles), and other parameters.

3. You can apply the filter several times. Press Random between applications to place the bubbles in a new location.

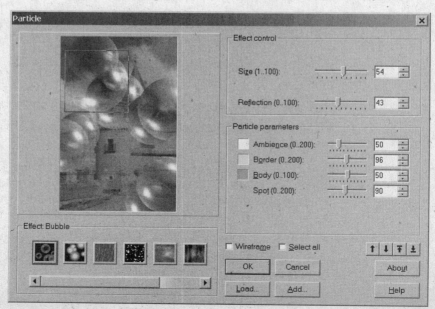

NOTE

The filter displays the bubbles in a preview window, as seen in the following figure. Amazingly, you can select each bubble individually and move it around the window. Do this when you find that a bubble obscures some portion of the image you don't want covered. You could, for example, apply the bubbles to the entire image and move the ones that blocked important parts of the castle.

4. Apply the filter several times if you want. The next figure shows the final image with the bubbles applied only to the sky (on the left) and overlapping the castle with custom-arranged bubbles (on the right).

CREATE AN OTHERWORLDLY LANDSCAPE

I'm going to show you how to put a whole raft of tools to work to create an otherworldly landscape. You don't even need to begin with a sensational picture. I'm going to work with an ordinary sunset scenic picture, like the one shown next. You can use your own, if you like. You'll need Kai's Power Tools, version 3.0 or later, to perform this magic trick.

The Planar Tiling filter used here is also furnished with some later versions of KPT, but the program may not install it for you automatically.

1. Start with the basic image, and create a duplicate layer.

2. Apply the Planar Tiling filter, choosing Perspective Tiling from the dialog box. KPT will create multiple copies of the image and squeeze them all down into the lower half of the picture, arranged in a perspective layout with a horizon halfway up from the bottom of the image, as shown here.

3. Arrange the original, unmodified layer so it extends above the horizon, as you can see in the next figure. The image is already starting to look otherworldly.

4. Create a circular selection on the unmodified background layer, and copy it to a new layer of its own.

5. Apply the KPT Glass Lens filter, using the Bright mode. Adjust the Opacity so the original image still shows underneath.

6. Use Photoshop's Burn toning tool with a large soft brush, and darken the lower left side of the sphere, adding some shading.

7. I duplicated the sphere layer, filled it with black, applied a vigorous Gaussian blur, and then used Edit ➤ Transform ➤ Scale to flatten the layer into a shadow. I made the shadow's opacity around 20 percent and moved it to the left and beneath the sphere to enhance the hovering effect.

8. Finally, I applied an Outer Glow layer style, using a soft yellow hue to provide separation between the sphere and its

background. The image, which radiates a science fiction tone, looked like the one shown next.

9. If you want a really eerie effect, add the Eye Candy 4000 Electrify filter to the sphere, using short electrical tendrils to give the object a "plasma sphere" look. You can see that variation in this figure, which has a spacey, "plasma" look.

WHAT'S NEXT

Your graphics don't have to just sit there on the page or screen. You can make a great leap forward by simulating 3D effects using the tools built right into Photoshop. The next chapter shows you some easy ways to create a three-dimensional look.

Part iii

Chapter 15

Amazing 3D Effects

Many of the best features of Photoshop 6 are designed to help you move your flat, uninteresting images into the third dimension. Without some 3D effects, many images just lay there like ancient Egyptian tomb drawings. Fortunately, you can easily make your images jump off the page or screen by using Photoshop's built-in effects, techniques you can learn, third-party 3D tools such as Corel Bryce, or even your scanner.

This chapter will introduce you to some killer 3D effects techniques, while the chapter that follows shows you how to create even more three-dimensional looks "the hard way."

Adapted from *Photoshop 6! I Didn't Know You Could Do That...* by David D. Busch

ISBN 0-7821-2918-8   288 pages $24.99

CREATE 3D EFFECTS WITH YOUR SCANNER

You can create great-looking 3D effects with your scanner by grabbing scans of 3D objects and then manipulating them in Photoshop to make them appear to jump off your image. Here are a couple of projects that will show you how 3D scanning works and will give you some ideas of what to do once you've changed the image.

Things you scan don't have to be flat! I grab images of three-dimensional objects all the time for eBay auctions, and you can use your scanner to get 3D images for any Photoshop project. The advantages of scanning 3D objects are that you don't have to use a conventional or digital camera and a scanner is quite a bit faster for grabbing an image than either alternative. I can scan an image into Photoshop in 30 seconds or less. It takes a lot longer than that to set up lighting and then transfer an image from my digital camera to Photoshop.

NOTE

The maximum thickness of a 3D object that can be scanned successfully varies by the scanner. Most scanners have sufficient *depth-of-focus* (the distance that an object can be from the scanner glass and still appear sharp) to successfully scan half an inch or more. More inexpensive scanners using a newer type of sensor may have very limited depth-of-focus. These sensors are called *contact-image sensors* (CIS) because the sensor moves at a much smaller distance to the glass than conventional scanners, and the original must be, more or less, in contact with the glass to be captured sharply.

Here are some tips for scanning 3D objects:

▶ Make sure your scanner glass is clean.

▶ Lay the object on the glass carefully to avoid scratching the glass.

▶ If you want a white or light-colored background, drape a piece of paper over the object. That will provide smooth shadows that conform to the shape of your object, as shown in this figure.

Don't rely on the white cover of your scanner; it is probably dirty and will create uneven shadows because some parts of the object will be much farther from the background than others.

▶ For a dark background, just leave your scanner cover all the way up, as you can see in the next figure.

▶ Parts of the object that are farther away from the glass will receive less illumination and will appear darker. This effect is referred to as *light-falloff*. This is most apparent with objects that are relatively "deep" or "thick" compared to their width, as you can see in the left-hand bunny candy dispenser in the next figure.

Use Photoshop's Quick Mask feature to paint a soft mask onto the darker portions. Then use Image ➢ Adjust ➢ Levels, or you can use Image ➢ Adjust ➢ Brightness/Contrast to even the tone, as you can see in the right-hand bunny in the next figure.

(Check out the original on the downloadable from the Web site to see how dramatic the difference can be.)

NOTE

To download practice files mentioned in this book, navigate to the Sybex Web site (www.sybex.com) and enter **2991** into the search box. When you get to the page for *Photoshop 6 Complete*, follow the links to download the file.

CREATE ROUGH, REALISTIC 3D HOLES

Here's a clever way to put a scan of an object with some holes onto your page.

1. Grab some pieces of corrugated cardboard, and tear a few artistic-looking holes in them. I used cardboard with a white upper surface and a brown underside, for contrast. Brown-on-brown cardboard doesn't create a look that is quite as dramatic.

2. Scan the pieces. Place some black paper behind the hole to make it easier to select the aperture later in Photoshop. I used 300 dpi resolution, which is plenty to work with, but it doesn't produce an extra-large file size.

3. In Photoshop, use a soft, white paintbrush to paint around the edges of the hole to fade it out to pure white. Set the Opacity of the brush to 25% to simplify producing a fade-out effect. One result of this technique is to make it easy to place this graphic on a Web page with a white background; it will seamlessly blend in.

4. Use the Magic Wand or your favorite selection technique to select the hole itself. The Magic Wand plus Select ➢ Similar will usually grab all the pixels in the hole, while leaving the rest of the image alone (this is the reason you used black paper instead of white).

5. Create a new layer, and fill the hole selection with white.

6. Use Layer ➢ Layer Style ➢ Inner Shadow to create a shadow "under" the hole that makes it look as if it were cut out. (You can also use Eye Candy's Cut Out filter, if you like.) In the dialog box shown below, work with these controls:

   ▶ Manipulate the Opacity slider to make the inner shadow more or less dramatic. I used a value of 89 percent.

   ▶ Use the Distance slider to adjust how far the shadow casts into the hole from the edge. I used 10 pixels for my setting.

   ▶ The Size slider controls how blurry the shadow is, and, therefore, how large it is. I used a 16-pixel setting to produce a soft, but still distinct shadow.

Part iii

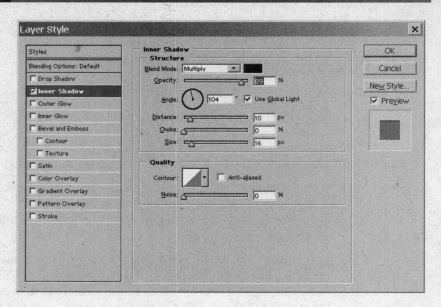

7. If you like, you can add a little random noise to the shadowed hole to give it a little texture. I used Filter ➢ Noise ➢ Add Noise, and then I specified 4 percent monochrome Gaussian noise in the dialog box.

8. Flatten the image and use it the way it is, or add some text to create a logo, Web page button, or other distinctive artwork, as shown in the following two figures.

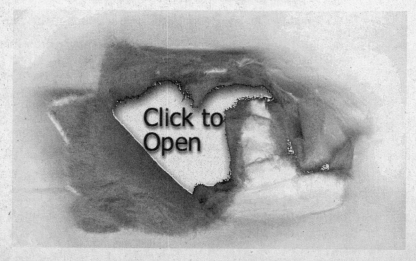

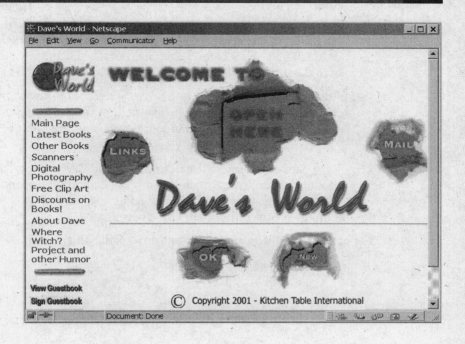

MAKE REALISTIC BUTTONS AND SCREW HEADS

Photoshop and its plug-ins have plenty of button and bevel tools you can use to create decent-looking raised 3D objects from scratch. Add a few drop shadows (and Photoshop 6's Drop Shadow layer style makes that easy), and you have a good-looking object. Use these techniques to achieve a look that goes beyond the cookie-cutter button look everyone else is using.

Screw Heads

To make realistic screw heads, just follow these directions:

1. In an empty layer, hold down the Shift key while you drag with the Elliptical Marquee tool to create a perfect circle.

2. Use the Gradient tool to fill the circle with the radial gradient of your choice. I used the Copper gradient style to provide a metallic effect.

3. For a more realistic 3D effect, use Photoshop's Spherize filter, KPT 3's Glass Lens, or Eye Candy 4000's Glass plug-in. I used KPT 3's Glass Lens in this case because I like the kind of highlight it provides.

4. Add texture using Photoshop's Texturizer tool (Canvas or Sandstone, with very low Relief values, on the order of 2 or 3) or, as I did, simply add random noise using the Filter ➤ Noise ➤ Add Noise plug-in.

5. For a hard-edged screw, leave the screw head the way it is. To produce a rounded-edge screw, apply Photoshop's Bevel and Emboss layer style. Set the Soften slider to 5 pixels to make a rounded edge rather than a true bevel.

Your basic screw heads, *sans* grooves, will look like this.

You can use either one to get in the groove, so to speak, using these steps:

1. Make a thin rectangular selection across the center of the screw head, copy it, and paste it down into a new layer. Paste it down twice more.

2. Use Photoshop's Brightness/Contrast control separately on each of the three layers.

   ▶ Use the Brightness slider to make the top layer of the three layers about 25 percent darker.

   ▶ Use the Brightness slider to make the next layer down 85 percent darker.

   ▶ Use the Brightness layer to make the bottom layer of the three layers 75 percent brighter.

3. Select the middle and bottom layers separately, and use the cursor arrow keys to nudge them up 5 or 6 pixels and down 5 or 6 pixels, respectively. This creates a carved 3D effect, as if the layers were a groove. The farther up or down you move the "light" and "dark" layers, the deeper the groove will appear to be. Your screw head will look like the one at left in this figure.

4. You can flatten the image to finish the slot-head screw, or you can continue with the next steps to produce a Philips-type screw head.

A Philips screw head is not much harder to create. Just follow these steps:

1. Merge the three groove layers down to a single layer by making all three visible, selecting the top layer of the three layers, and then pressing Ctrl/Command+E twice to merge them.

2. In the groove layer, click with the Magic Wand outside the groove, and then press Shift+Ctrl/Command+I to invert the selection to the groove itself.

3. Choose Select ➤ Modify ➤ Smooth and a pixel value that will round off the edges of the rectangular groove. This amount will vary depending on how large your groove is, but a value of about half the width of the groove is a good start. For my 10-pixel high groove, I used a value of 10.

4. Use Shift+Ctrl/Command+I to invert the selection again, and then press the Delete key. That will remove everything outside the selection, giving you a rounded-end groove.

5. Duplicate the groove layer and then rotate it 90 degrees counterclockwise. Place the vertical groove on top of the horizontal groove.

6. Select the area where the two overlap, and press Delete to remove it. Your Philips-head screw will look like the right-hand image in the previous figure.

Create a Real Button

Working on a sewing-oriented Web site? How about some buttons that look like buttons? Even if you're not building a Web site you might want to achieve a realistic button look. Although you could do it with earlier versions of Photoshop, the new layer styles make this a no-brainer, if you know what to do.

1. In an empty transparent layer, create a circular selection by holding down the Shift key as you drag with the Elliptical Marquee tool.

2. Fill the circle with a dark-to-light linear gradient, using either black and white, or your choice of colors as the foreground and background shades.

3. Apply the Bevel and Emboss layer style, as shown here.

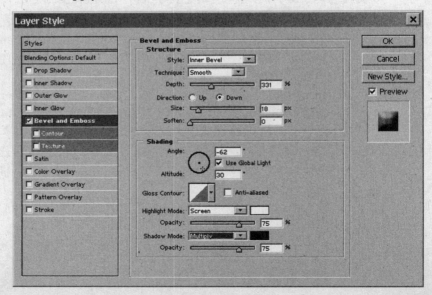

- ► Choose Inner Bevel to produce an edge for the button.

- ► Select Smooth Technique to create a rounded edge.

- ► Click the Down button to make the disk concave.

- ► Move the Depth slider to adjust the amount of concavity. I used 331 percent to assure a pronounced concave effect.

- ► Adjust the Size slider to control the width of the edge of the button. I used 18 pixels.

4. Use the Elliptical Marquee tool to select a buttonhole, and press Delete. Repeat for the second buttonhole. (Do this four times if you want a four-hole button—just be sure to make each hole smaller.)

Notice that the layer style applies to each of the holes you create, so they have the same concave shape as the button itself. This really cool effect is the result of Photoshop's Layer Styles capability!

You'll end up with buttons like the ones in the array shown in the following figure.

Part iii

CREATE A 3D TURNTABLE AND OTHER OBJECTS FROM SCRATCH!

Although most of the projects in this book are small but eye-opening explorations into Photoshop's often unexplored capabilities, in the real world you'll most often have to put together a lot of different techniques. The next exercise puts a whole raft of tools to work to create the phonograph record turntable shown in this figure.

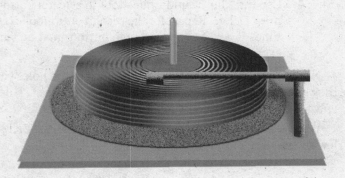

Although the final image may look remarkably lifelike, it was created entirely from scratch in Photoshop. I'll show you how to reproduce this object, of course, but you'll probably find the tricks more useful in building realistic objects of other types. Because the entire project is more complex than most in this book, I'll break it down into easy-to-handle pieces.

Create a Record

The first step is to create a phonograph record (aka "LP") and then learn how to give it a 3D appearance through the use of perspective.

1. In an empty transparent layer, create a perfect circle by holding down the Shift key as you drag with the Elliptical Marquee tool.

2. Fill the selection with a radial gradient, using the Copper preset from the drop-down list in the Option bar.

3. Choose Filter ➤ Distort ➤ ZigZag, and select Pond Ripples from the drop-down list in the ZigZag dialog box.

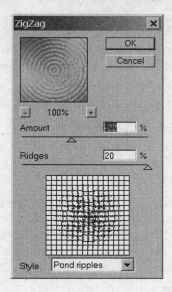

4. Set the Amount slider to −22 percent to produce a concentric groove effect, and set the Ridges slider to 20 percent in order to generate a whole bunch of them.

NOTE

In real life, a record doesn't have multiple concentric grooves: it has one groove that spirals from the outer edge to the center. However, it's easier to get an even-looking appearance doing it this way. You can't get the right kind of spiral with Photoshop's built-in tools.

5. Using the Rectangular Marquee tool, select the upper half of the disc, using the center point as a guide. Copy the top half and paste it down.

6. Use Edit ≻ Transform ≻ Flip Vertical to flip the top half, and then move it down to cover the bottom half of the disk.

7. With the upper layer active, press Ctrl/Command+E to merge the two halves of the disc.

8. Choose Image ≻ Adjust ≻ Invert to reverse the tones of the disc. Use the Brightness/Contrast control to your taste to make the disc look more shiny and record-like.

Part iii

9. Create a new transparent layer above the disc. Using the Elliptical Marquee tool, click in the exact center of the disc. Hold down the Alt/Option and Shift keys while dragging to create a circle around the center of the disc. Make it large enough to resemble a record label.

10. Fill the selection with a color (I used Red). If you want a more realistic label, add some text.

11. In the Layers palette, change the opacity of the label's layer to about 85 percent. You should be able to see through the label to the disc underneath.

12. Use the Brush tool with a small, hard-edged brush (the size will vary depending on how large you've made the record; the brush should be big enough to resemble the hole in the center of a long-playing record). Using white as your foreground color, click in the exact center to make a hole in the record.

13. Merge the visible layers by pressing Shift+Ctrl/Command+E. Your completed record should look something like this one.

Make a Stack O' Tracks

The next step is to create a pile of LP records, as if they were stacked on a turntable. This is where we learn how to create a 3D effect using Photoshop's perspective tools.

1. Select the disc, and then choose Edit ➢ Transform ➢ Perspective.

2. Drag the handles at the corners to warp the disc into a perspective view, with the handles closer to each other at the top than at the bottom. The disc looks like the one shown next.

Press Enter to apply the transformation.

3. With the disc still selected, choose Layer ➢ Layer Style ➢ Outer Glow. Use the values shown in this figure to create a faint glow around the edges that will help separate each disk from the ones below it.

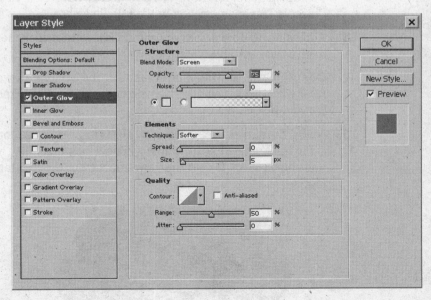

4. Duplicate the layer six or seven times to create a set of records. Nudge each layer a few pixels above the layer below it to arrange them into a stack, like the one shown here.

Construct a Turntable Platter

Records don't spin by themselves. They need a turntable platter.

1. Create one more duplicate layer of the discs, and then use Edit ➤ Transform ➤ Scale to enlarge it slightly to produce a turntable under the whole stack.

2. Use Edit ➤ Fill, and fill the larger turntable disc with 50 percent gray from the drop-down list in the Fill dialog box. Lock the transparency for the layer before you do this, or check the Preserve Transparency box in the Fill dialog box.

3. Add some random noise (you should know the drill by now) to give the turntable a texture.

4. Duplicate the turntable layer, and fill the original (lower) layer with black, using Edit ➤ Fill with the Preserve Transparency box marked.

5. Nudge the darker layer down a few pixels to give the turntable some thickness. Your turntable will now look much like the one shown next. Delete the glow effect from the turntable layers.

Combine Layers into a Manageable Set

You're in the home stretch now. You've learned enough to coast through creating the other components of a record player turntable. This is the perfect opportunity to learn about Photoshop 6's new Layer Sets capability, too.

1. With the Rectangular Marquee tool, create a rectangle large enough to serve as the base for the turntable. Fill it with 50 percent gray using Edit ➤ Fill.

2. Duplicate the layer, and use the Brightness/Contrast control to darken it.

3. Nudge the lower layer a few pixels down to finish the turntable base.

4. If you like, you could merge all the visible layers by making the top layer active and pressing Shift+Ctrl/Command+E. However, Photoshop's new Layer Sets capability provides an easier way to reduce the number of layers you have to manage at one time, while preserving their "editability." Choose New Layer Set from the Layers palette's flyout menu, and type in a name, such as **Stack of Tracks.**

5. A folder named "Stack of Tracks" appears in the Layers palette. Click each layer you want to add to the set in turn, and drag it into the folder. You'll see the layer text indented slightly, indicating that it is part of the layer above, as shown in the left side of this figure.

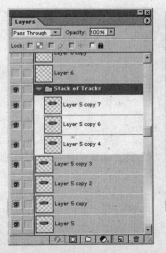

Note that the layer order needs to be the same inside the folder. You may have to reorder the layers after dragging into the set.

6. Click the down-pointing triangle (▼) in the layer set's layer to collapse the layers into a "closed" folder, effectively hiding them from view, as shown at right in the previous figure. Even so, you can open the layer set at any time, and edit the layers.

Add the Finishing Touches

Just follow these easy steps:

1. On a new transparent layer, create a thin vertical selection with the Rectangular Marquee. Make the selection about the size of a spindle that would fit through the holes of the record stack.

2. Choose Select ➤ Modify ➤ Smooth, and specify a value of about five pixels to round off the ends of the spindle.

3. Fill the spindle with a linear gradient, or do as I did and use Eye Candy 4000's Chrome plug-in.

4. Nip off the end of the spindle, and move it above the record stack, positioned as if it were going into the hole in the records.

5. Repeat Steps 1 through 3 to create a tone arm in four tubular segments, as shown here.

Then merge the layers to create a single layer holding the tone arm.

6. For the ultimate in realism, create shadows for the spindle and tone arm. Duplicate the spindle and tone arm layers. Fill the lower versions with black, and apply a Gaussian blur. Rotate the spindle's shadow counterclockwise by 90 degrees, and use Edit ➤ Transform ➤ Skew to stretch the tone arm's shadow to a realistic angle.

7. Flatten the image, and you're done.

Wrap an Image Around a 3D Object

Wouldn't it be great if you could "wrap" an image you created around a 3D object in Photoshop? You could, for example, create a globe by taking a map and wrapping it around a sphere, as shown in this example.

Or, you could mock up a new package for a product by creating the package front and then wrapping it around a 3D rectangular shape. It really would be great, but Photoshop doesn't quite have the tools—yet! The biggest drawback is that Photoshop's 3D Transform plug-in lacks lighting controls. So, once you've wrapped an image around a shape, it doesn't look all that much different from before—just twisted out of shape a bit.

Because of its limited capabilities and confusing controls, some Photoshop guides have only a paragraph or two covering 3D Transform—usually lumped in with the other Rendering filters. But don't panic! I'll show you how to do some actually useful things with this capability, relying on Photoshop's other capabilities to make up for some of the missing features.

The globe in the previous figure was fairly easy to create. I took a flat, 3D map of Australia, and placed it on a sphere using the 3D Transform dialog box.

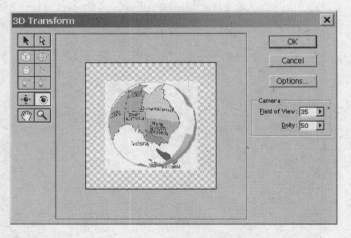

I'll show you how to use its options in the project that follows. After I created the basic globe, I used Photoshop's Lighting Effects plug-in to provide the lighting the 3D Transform tool lacks. Then I applied a halo around the globe (the Outer Glow layer style) and some clouds.

While globes are a ball, let's try something a little more challenging: creating a package mock-up for an advertising campaign.

1. The first step is to create the packaging itself in 2D form, as shown in the next example.

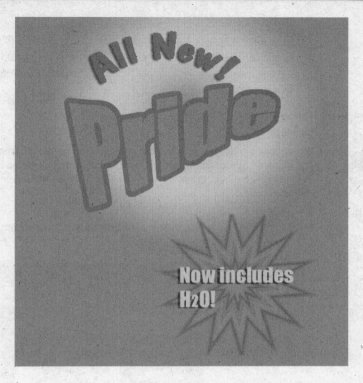

► Fill an empty layer with a radial gradient using the Orange-Yellow-Orange Photoshop preset (available from the drop-down list in the Option bar).

► Create the **All New** text, warped into an arc with the Text Warp feature. Then apply a drop-shadow layer style.

► Create the **Pride** text with the Rise Text Warp feature, fill it with random noise, and then stroke the edges with dark green paint 10-pixels wide.

► Add **Now Includes H₂O** text, with a drop-shadow added, and a background star created with Eye Candy 4000's Star plug-in.

The fonts, colors, settings, and actual text aren't important. You can vary the effects all you like to create your own packaging, or use the Pride file from the CD-ROM.

Part iii

2. Crop the packaging artwork into a tall box shape, and paste into a new empty layer. Make sure there is enough room in the layer to move the artwork around as you rotate it. If necessary, use Image ➢ Canvas Size to increase the area you can work within.

WARNING

When working with the 3D Transform filter, it's always best to create a new layer. The filter can render on the current layer, but the transmogrified image will tend to blend into the background. Place it on its own layer where you can work with it further.

3. Choose Filter ➢ Render ➢ 3D Transform to produce this dialog box.

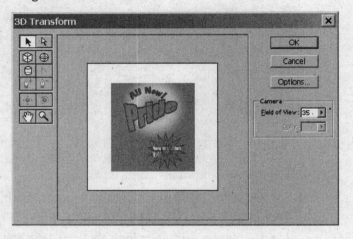

Your artwork will appear in the preview window of the 3D Transform dialog box.

4. Click on the Cube icon at the left side of the dialog box. You can also choose from sphere and cylinder shapes.

5. Drag in the preview area to create a cube-shaped framework, known as a *wireframe*.

6. To make the wireframe conform to the shape of the artwork, you'll need to drag three of the handles to three corners of the

artwork's rectangular shape. I've put arrows in the following figure to show you which handles go where. Use the white arrow (at the top right of the dialog box's tool palette) to move the handles.

7. The fourth handle controls the "thickness" of the cube. Move it so it makes the shape relatively thin, as shown next.

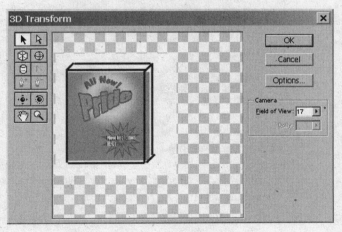

(I've exaggerated the wireframe lines in the illustration so it will show up on the printed page; in real life, the wireframe is a set of thin green lines.)

8. Click the Options button in the dialog box, and unmark the Display Background box. That will allow you to view your artwork wrapped around the shape, without any of the background that might remain showing.

9. Four controls at the bottom left of the dialog box let you pan the viewpoint of the shape (as with a camera) from side to side and up and down, rotate it in 3D space as you would with a trackball, move the shape around, and zoom in and out. Use the trackball control to rotate the shape, as shown in the next figure.

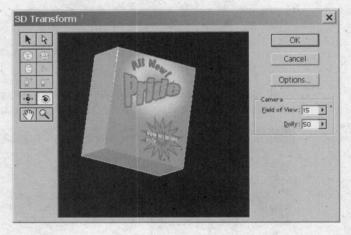

10. Click the Options button again, and choose rendering and anti-aliasing quality from the drop-down lists. If you're just experimenting, leave them both set at Low for the fastest rendering speed. When you're ready to lock in your effect, set them both at High for maximum quality.

11. I finished my mock-up by adding a drop-shadow layer style and a multicolored background to get the final image. Your final image will look like this.

IMPORT 3D GRAPHICS FROM OTHER PROGRAMS

If you want the most flexibility in working with 3D objects in Photoshop, consider importing your three-dimensional graphics from another program, such as Corel Bryce, Caligari trueSpace, and SoftImage 3D. However, these programs can be prohibitively expensive (some of them, such as Alias Wavefront's Maya, are priced in four-digit territory) because they include animation tools that you probably don't need.

However, you can still buy some 3D applications for under $50, including Ulead's Cool3D. The key to making the most of any 3D program you have access to is to do all the lighting, shading, texturizing in the original application. Make sure you choose the viewing angle in the original application, too. Then, save a copy in the application's native format, and export an image in a form Photoshop can read. That way, you'll be able to

Part iii

return to the 3D file and make modifications if there are some changes you need to make that can't be done in Photoshop.

Cool3D is a perfect tool for learning how to work with Photoshop in conjunction with 3D applications. It's relatively easy to learn (even though it does boast a mind-numbing set of features), and it creates high-resolution BMP files (in addition to compressed GIF and JPEG format files) that Photoshop can read with no trouble.

Although doing justice to Cool3D would take an entire chapter, at minimum, and a full book of this size for more complete coverage, this project will get you started. The goal here is to demonstrate how you can quickly create 3D text and objects and export them to Photoshop. Install Cool3D (you can download a trial version from the Ulead Web site at http://www.ulead.com), and we're ready to get to work.

1. Launch Cool3D. You'll be faced with this daunting workspace.

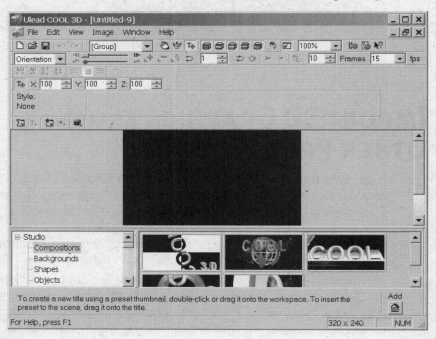

2. Cool 3D offers several ways to put objects in your working window. Insert text, graphics, or a geometric shape by clicking the buttons immediately above and to the left of the working window. From left to right, they are:

Insert Text   A window pops up for you to enter and format text.

Edit Text   Active only when text has already been entered.

Insert Graphics   Produces a pop-up mini-drawing program with tools you can use to create shapes of your own fiendish design, including polygons, ellipses, and complex shapes.

Edit Graphics   Active only when there are graphics to be edited using the drawing module.

Insert Geometric Shape   You can choose Sphere, Cube, Cone, Cylinder, or Pyramid from a drop-down list.

3. Alternatively, you can choose objects from Cool3D's libraries, available from a scrolling collapsing/expanding list in the lower-left corner of the workspace. The options appear in a preview window to the right of the libraries; just double-click a selection or drag it into the working window.

4. You can insert multiple objects and work with them individually, giving each its own texture, orientation, color, or other attributes.

5. Freely change the position, rotation, and size of each object using the tools on the Standard (top) toolbar.

6. Finally, apply any of the special effects, bevels, textures, back-grounds, and other options available from the scrolling Libraries window. The next figure shows a typical example of what you can do.

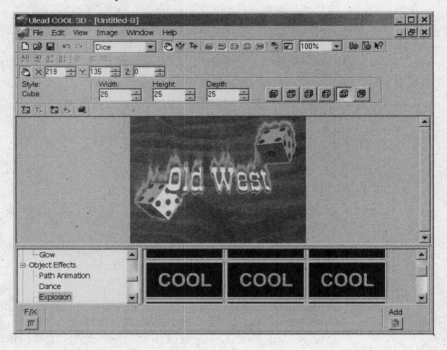

7. Save the file in BMP format by choosing File ➤ Create Image Files ➤ BMP File. You can load this file into Photoshop and work with it further.

8. Save a version in Cool3D format, too, for later work.

NOTE

Don't apply a background within Cool3D if you think you might want to create your own in Photoshop. You'll avoid tediously separating your text or objects from its Cool3D background manually.

If you decide you want different effects or need to reorient your objects, just reload the Cool3D version and make your modifications. This figure shows some alternative versions of the original artwork.

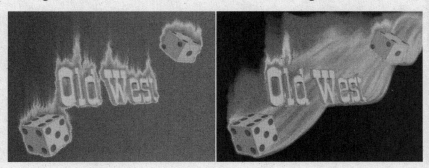

WHAT'S NEXT

The next chapter shows you some additional ways of creating 3D looks, using digital photography as a basis for the original images.

Chapter 16

CREATING 3D IMAGES THE HARD WAY

With your computer, you can postprocess your digital images to look at them in novel ways. By using special software, you can create panoramic views, murals, 3D models, and entire 3D scenes. You can even blow up your digital images to poster size or larger. Let your computer's processing power calculate new viewpoints for your digital snapshots.

This chapter will show you how to go beyond Photoshop to create 3D images using third-party tools such as PhotoDeluxe and PhotoVista.

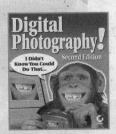

Adapted from *Digital Photography! I Didn't Know You Could Do That...* by Erica Sadun

ISBN 0-7821-2965-X   384 pages $24.99

WHAT A VISTA! CREATE PANORAMAS

Does your vision exceed your viewfinder? Does your resolution fall short of your landscape? Sometimes, we come across scenes so big, detailed, or geometrically complex, we cannot hope to photograph them in their entirety—or at least, not with just one picture.

Panoramas can capture a greater whole. With panoramas, you can stitch together a series of images to produce a composite image of arbitrary size. Panoramas create a wider reality than any single image can hope to show. For example, a panorama can present the entire arc of a rainbow, as shown below.

You may run across two basic varieties of panoramas:

▶ The more common row-type is generally referred to as a *vista*. To produce a simple vista, you stitch together a linear series of pictures.

▶ A two-dimensional version is called a *quilt*. Quilts are made up of photos snapped in two dimensions, both rows and columns. Stitched together, side by side and up and down, these form a full mosaic.

When you create a panorama, you can either work by hand or with a special-purpose program that stitches your image for you. Each has its advantages. Working by hand is essentially free. It can be done quickly in almost any image-processing program. It also allows you to stitch quilts, a capability that many stitching programs lack.

In contrast, a stitching program creates much better results without the obvious edges you'll find in homemade panoramas. It automatically handles image rotation and warping caused by camera angle, unsteady hands, and varying lens properties. Stitching programs range from free-ware to quite costly commercial products. They generally produce superb results, but you may need to wait a while for your panorama to process.

Create Panoramas with PhotoDeluxe

You can create your own panorama using Adobe PhotoDeluxe. Take out your digital camera and snap a few pictures along some natural line.

After you've taken your panoramic shots, follow these steps:

1. Fire up PhotoDeluxe (you can download a trial copy at http://www.adobe.com) and set up PhotoDeluxe in power mode (to display the advanced menus, Layers palette, and Selections palette).

2. Create a new, large, blank image in PhotoDeluxe. Select an image size larger than you think you'll ever need space for. You can always crop it down later.

3. One by one, copy your images into separate layers. Open each image, copy it, and paste it into the panorama image. PhotoDeluxe will create a layer for each pasted copy.

4. Use PhotoDeluxe's move and rotate features to arrange your images. Make sure that common features align correctly. If you need to see both layers at once, double-click the upper layer and reduce the layer transparency to 50%. Align the layer and then make it opaque again.

5. Merge the image layers. Click the right-pointing arrow below the Close button on the Layers palette (to the right of the Text layer) and select Merge Layers. This will collapse your image into a single layer.

6. Click the Get & Fix Photo tab of the activity bar and select Rotate & Size ➤ Trim & Size.

7. Click 1 - Trim ➤ Trim. Outline the final image, omitting the uneven edges. Then click OK.

8. Click 2 - Done to complete the task.

This method provides a simple way to create a panorama. However, it almost always produces natural flaws. Take a look at the image shown below. The rectangles highlight the obvious stitching errors: the clouds that moved between the shots, slight rotation errors where the tree does not line up with itself, and the lighting gradient between the right and left edges of each image.

Creating Panoramas with PhotoVista

Compare the results of creating a panorama in PhotoDeluxe (the rainbow photo) with the panorama shown below, which was created with MGI's PhotoVista software. This software produces an almost flawless image, displaying none of the imaging errors inherent in a hand-stitching attempt.

MGI PhotoVista Virtual Tour provides excellent panoramic vista creation and interaction software. You can download a trial copy of the software at MGI'sc Web site (www.mgisoft.com). This software allows you to stitch panoramas into immersible views. If you like, you can then upload a special interactive version to your favorite Internet hosting site. On-site, you and your online friends can dive into your vistas. A special-purpose Java applet lets you zoom around your panorama. With just a few steps, you can create a "virtual reality" of your own.

PhotoVista stitches your photos together automatically. To create and then upload your panorama, install the PhotoVista software from the trial copy available at the MGI Web site, and then follow these instructions:

1. Select File ➢ Open Source Images.

2. Select the images you wish to add and drag them to the Source Files box on the right side of the window. Then click OK.

3. If you snapped your pictures in portrait mode, click the rotation icon (the bent arrow) until your photos return to their upright and locked position.

4. If needed, drag each image into its correct position.

5. Click the camera icon, select your camera, and click OK. Your pictures are ready to stitch, as in the example below.

6. Click the stitch panorama icon, found at the bottom right of the screen. This icon looks like a series of upright rectangles. Doing so brings up the Stitch Options dialogue box. If you're stitching a circular panorama, make sure to check the Full 360 Degree Panorama option. You can either preview the stitch or simply click Full Stitch to create your vista.

NOTE

Other stitching options allow you to disable the warping and blending functions and to crop non-image areas from your results.

7. Wait for the stitching to finish. In the case of a full stitch, this may take several minutes.

8. Enjoy and explore your new panorama. You can move between the stitched image and the panoramic viewer by selecting from the Panorama menu. You can also print your panorama by choosing File ➢ Print View.

9. When you're satisfied with your creation, you can save it as a picture file. Choose File ➢ Save As, choose JPEG or Bitmap, navigate to any location on the disk, name the file and click Save.

10. Having saved your picture as a flat image, you may now want to explore PhotoVista's 3D fly-around capabilities. To continue, you must keep the Stitched_Result window open. Select Panorama ➢ Save As and choose the Flashpix file type. Select "For Java" for Export to HTML, navigate to where you wish to save your file, name it, and click Save.

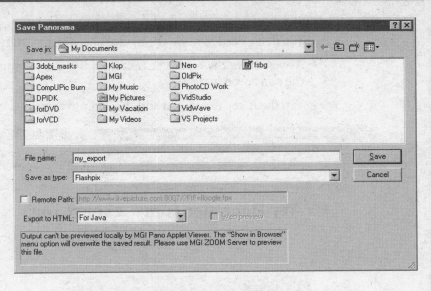

11. Choose an image quality level and click OK. The better the quality, the bigger the file size.

12. In the directory you specified, you will find four files. In the example I used in the previous picture, PhotoVista created `my_export.jpg`, `my_export.ivr`, `my_export.htm`, and `panoapplet.jar`. The first three depend on the filename you specified. The last is always named "`panoapplet.jar`".

13. Upload these four files to your favorite Web hosting site or open the `my_export.htm` file locally in your Web browser. The interactive applet will appear. You can explore the panoramic view by panning through it and zooming in and out, as follows:

    ▶ Drag your mouse along the image, and the panorama will move in that direction. (It's a little counterintuitive, but it works.)

- ▶ Keep the mouse button depressed to continue panning. You don't need to move the mouse once the pan starts.

- ▶ As you move the mouse farther from the image center, the pan speed increases.

- ▶ Tap the A key to zoom in and the Z key to zoom out.

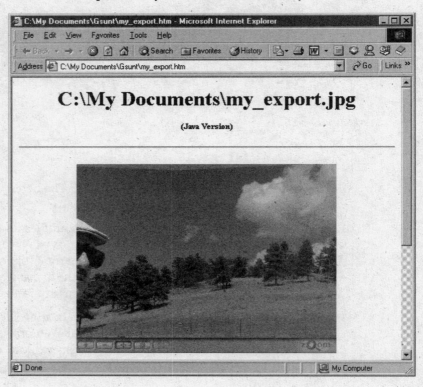

Comparing Panorama Software

MGI PhotoVista's flyaround applet does not provide the only draw for the program. Output, 3D-object creation, and virtual tours all add to its value.

PhotoVista's excellent rendering and superior output offer the most important reason to use this software. Compare the following image output, from PhotoVista, Ulead Cool 360, and Adobe Photoshop Elements, respectively. Notice the difference in quality along the blends and, particularly, among the buffalo towards the right of the picture. Only PhotoVista gets each buffalo right, without a telltale stitching shadow.

In addition, the MGI package offers 3D object creation and virtual tours. By photographing an object from multiple angles, you can create a "fly-around" that allows people to see the object from all sides. This can prove especially useful for those who want to buy or sell on an auction site, such as eBay. Potential buyers can see an object from many angles. The virtual tours add hotspots to your interactive panoramas so your viewers can "click through" to associated Web pages. For example, clicking on a restaurant in an image of a city street might link you to its menu. This feature takes panoramas into a whole new dimension, adding meaning and function to mere fly-around capabilities.

Part iii

Low-Tech Panoramas

Are you looking for the truly low-tech approach to creating a composite image? Try this one: Snap a whole bunch of overlapping pictures that cover a small area, print them, and tape them together by hand. You can't get any more primitive than that. This method allows you to create life-size or near-life-size collages. Tons of detail result with minimal computer work.

Take a look at the baby (Sofia) next to her mural in the photo below. Of course, the fine details in this image might have worked better had she stayed asleep during the photo session. (Sometimes, it's hard to combine good lighting and no flash with a sleeping baby.) To assure uniform image distance, I laid a yardstick over the rails of her crib and used it to steady my digital camera. It's important that you don't vary the distance. When elements scale differently between photos, they cannot be matched.

I printed each image on large-sized, stiff paper, and then reassembled her on the wall. With some scotch tape, a little scissors work, and patience, I was able to create a special and unique montage.

Panorama Tips

Digital cameras easily capture panoramas. Just fit pictures together with your favorite image program or stitch them in a special-purpose application. Shoot as many images as you can—the more, the better—and overlap, overlap, overlap! Here are some tips for creating panoramas:

▶ With digital cameras, you never know which picture will turn out to be the best. Image quality varies, as does color, contrast, and focus. Take many pictures to maximize your keepers.

▶ Don't try to be efficient when snapping your pictures. Trying to match image edges is a surefire way to lose important pieces of your picture. Instead, overlap and take extra shots where possible. You'll be surprised as many unimportant details become fascinating or merely helpful when you compile the collage. Remember that there's no film to waste in digital cameras.

▶ Tripods hold your digital camera steady. Admittedly, they are cumbersome and cannot be carried in your pocket the way you carry a digital camera. If you don't have a traditional tripod with you, use a makeshift object to level your camera—a flat fence-top, a friend's shoulder, or even an upright stick.

▶ Scaling occurs when pictures are taken at different distances from a relatively close object (a building, say, rather than distant mountains). Try to maintain a uniform distance from your subject when you get close up.

▶ For far-away panoramas, rotate your camera to take pictures of rainbows, mountains, or city skylines. Because they are far away, the scenery does not change significantly when you move left and right. Instead, swing your camera around a fixed point to capture a distant panorama.

▶ For nearby panoramas of murals, houses, family groups, and so forth, be careful how you move your camera. Odd angles may distort nearby objects, so you should set up your tripod parallel to the desired scene and move your camera strictly left and right, up and down, to shoot your pictures.

Cool Panorama Ideas

Panoramic vistas give us a view of the world that we normally wouldn't see. Panoramas can take place outside or inside, with multiple subjects or just a few, and very close in or very far away.

You'll be surprised at the varying ways you can use panoramas in your everyday life. Here are some ideas:

▶ If you're selling your house, use a panorama to let people "walk" around your rooms and get a better feel for the property. Create a 360-degree panorama to allow people to visualize space from any angle. Since panoramas work both inside and outside, you can just as easily create a panorama of your living room as your backyard.

▶ When you're visiting a garden, panoramas let you get very close to a bed of flowers or a vine-laced trellis. Stitch together the small "detail" pictures, and you'll get to see all the little facets and textures that make up the planting. Detail panoramas also allow you to photograph a favorite painting or tapestry.

▶ Perhaps you need to take a picture of a large group of people, such as a graduating class or the crowd at a football game. Stitch together your images, and you've created a complete picture that offers greater image detail and a wider scope than you could possibly capture in a single snapshot.

▶ Head up to the mountains to create a panorama. Panoramas easily capture the magnificence of nature. Photograph the wide vistas as they completely surround you. Nothing works better for feeling immersed into a scene than a photo that extends beyond your natural limits of view. Whether you're on a plateau or in a valley, a panorama can capture that special feeling of "being there."

▶ If you're decorating a room, you can use a your panoramas to create a wall border or a special art piece. Let your imagination go wild!

CREATE 3D IMAGES

Let's put aside the camera and the software for a moment and work with our hands. Hold your thumb out at arm's length and look at it first with one eye and then the other. Notice how it seems to move a little? Now move your thumb about 6 inches away from your eye and repeat. Your thumb will seem to jump even more as you switch eyes. Put down your arm and look at some object far across the room. When you switch between your left and right eyes, it will hardly appear to move at all. This magical property is called *parallax* or *stereopsis*, and it's how we humans see three dimensions. When our eyes record slightly different positions for objects in our view, our brains go to work and figure out how far away each object lies.

"How quaint," you might be thinking as you glance surreptitiously at your watch. Don't be so blasé! This wonderful expression of optical science allows you to create your own 3D photos. With just your digital camera and a little careful alignment, you can tame parallax.

The 3D Key

The key to creating 3D photos is to begin with two photos that approximate the location of our eyes. You need a left image and a right image taken at exactly the same height and orientation, but offset horizontally by about 2.5 inches. You can do this the easy way or the precise way.

Here's the easy way: Hold your camera's viewfinder up to your left eye and snap, and then transfer the viewfinder to your right eye and snap again. You need to stay very still between the two images, and you must keep the camera absolutely level. This cheap and fast method gives decent results for very little effort. It's the one that I use most of the time, particularly when I'm on vacation. For reasons that I don't even begin to understand, this technique is called the "Cha Cha" or "Rock and Roll" method.

NOTE

By changing the spacing between the images, you will change the way we see 3D. Use a larger spacing, such as 6 or 8 inches, to make your subjects appear smaller, as if seen from a "giant's eye" viewpoint. A smaller spacing enlarges your subjects, as viewed from an "ant's eye" viewpoint.

The precise way for creating 3D pictures requires only a tripod and a yardstick. Tape the yardstick to the ground perpendicular to your subject. Set up your tripod with two legs facing forward, each touching the yardstick. After snapping your first image, slide your tripod along the yardstick to ensure that you maintain absolute horizontal integrity. The yardstick will also help you measure the absolute change of 2.5 inches.

Whichever way you decide to snap your pictures, make sure to remember which image is right and which image is left. You'll need this information when you return to your computer and prepare your 3D stereo pair.

NOTE

If you have the time, the money, and the will, you can purchase a special-purpose dual-CCD digital camera that takes stereo images with a single click. These cameras tend to be bought by 3D hobbyists with a lot of money. You can see one at www.stereoscopy.com/3d-images/camera.html.

Side by Side

It's easy to create a stereo pair, like the sample shown here. You just print the left image next to the right one. However, getting them both on the same page, aligned, and the right sizes may take a few steps. You can use PhotoDeluxe's sizing tools to match up your images.

You'll want to end up with a small, sharp print. The following steps set a final print width of 6 inches, a stereo-image standard. You can choose other widths as desired. You may also opt for resolutions other than 300 pixels per inch, although this resolution provides high pixel density while shrinking the print size.

1. Start PhotoDeluxe and open your "right" image. Select Size ➤ Photo Size. Change the resolution to 300 pixels per inch and the width to 3 inches. Notice that the height resizes automatically. Click OK. Minimize the window.

2. Repeat Step 1 for the "left" image. This time, leave the window open and displayed.

3. Select Size ➤ Canvas Size. Change the width to 6 inches and click OK.

4. Drag the left image all the way to the left of the canvas.

5. Open the right image and drag a copy of it onto the right side of the canvas. Adjust the alignment as needed.

6. Save your image and print it.

Congratulations! You've just created your first stereo image pair.

Stereo Viewing

When I was in school, we learned to cross our eyes to see stereo pairs. The cross-eye method works by teaching you to focus your eyes at infinity rather than on a particular object. Do you see the two circles below? If you can relax your eyes until you see three circles rather than two, you can learn to view stereograms without a special viewer.

On the other hand, if this headache-inducing method is not for you, I offer two alternatives: You can use a commercial viewing product, or you can create your own stereo-viewing box.

Use a Lorgnette

Lorgnettes are a type of glasses that have a short handle. You hold the handle and look through the lenses.

Berezin Stereo Photography Products offers a 3D-viewing lorgnette for just a few dollars. The Berezin lorgnette, shown in the next image, allows you to view stereo pairs without effort. The special optics do all of the work for you. Just hold the lorgnette in front of your eyes (or eyeglasses) and move your stereo picture until it "pops" into 3D. The effect is spectacular.

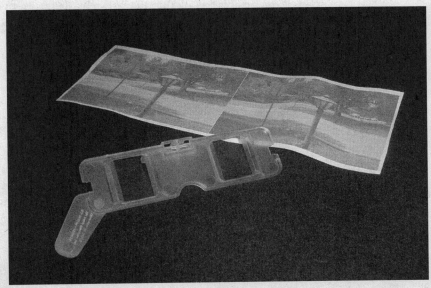

NOTE

To order or get more information about the Berezin lorgnette, visit the Berezin Web site at www.berezin.com/3d.

The lorgnette arrives flat in a standard envelope. Remove it and fold down the spacer bar at the top of the unit. Hold the lorgnette by the handle and place the spacer bar at the top of your nose. With your other hand, hold the stereo image pair at arm's distance. Slowly move it back and forth until the two pictures merge into a single 3D view. And that's all there is to it. With a lorgnette, viewing stereo pairs is a snap!

Build Your Own Viewer

Are you ready to build your own stereo viewer? All you need is a shoebox, a manila file folder, tape, and scissors. This box approximates the stereo-optiscopes that were all the rage in the nineteenth century. You can still find 3D stereo pictures at most antique stores and auctions. In fact, there are entire books devoted to stereo images from the U.S. Civil War.

Here are step-by-step instructions for this project:

1. Cut two holes on one of the short sides of the shoe box, as illustrated below. You will look through these holes to see the pictures. Make them about three-quarters of an inch across and spaced comfortably to look through. You may also add a space to accommodate your nose so it will not press against the box.

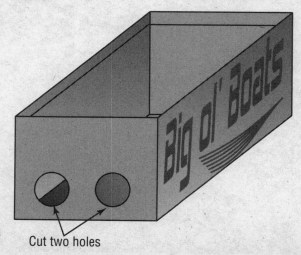

Cut two holes

2. Place the folder, with the bent side down, along the side of the box. Fold the folder top over the side, as shown here.

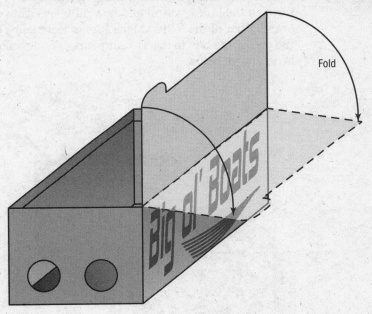

Fold

Big ol' Boats

3. Staple or tape the bottom of the folder to keep it together. Open the top to make a T-shape along the crease you just made, as in the following illustration.

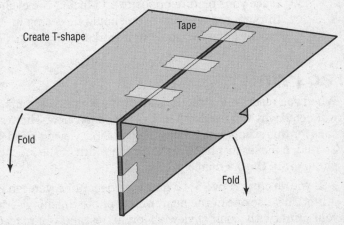

Create T-shape

Tape

Fold

Fold

4. Tape the folder to the exact center of the box with the top of the T-shape resting on the top of the shoebox. When you look through the holes, you should now only see either one side or the other of the folder. Make sure to leave some space at the end of the box to insert your pictures and to allow light in, as shown below.

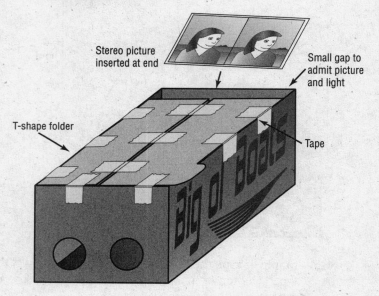

Stereo picture inserted at end

Small gap to admit picture and light

T-shape folder

Tape

5. Place your picture opposite and facing the eyeholes. Look through the eyeholes—you should be seeing in 3D. It's not exactly a ViewMaster, but it works.

Stereo Prints

When you read the instructions for sizing your image pairs, you may have wondered why you needed 3 inches per stereo view. There are two reasons for this sizing. First, many historical 3D viewers used 3-inch prints. Second, 6 inches just happens to be the width of the most common photo print, the 4 × 6 inch print.

If you've created two 3 × 3 inch stereo pictures, you can easily order prints. Just use one of the many online photo-finishing services. Combine your prints with a pair of viewing lorgnettes, and you're ready to roll out an entire stereo world of your own.

WARNING

Make sure to avoid the Zoom to Fit or Zoom and Crop options when ordering your prints. You may want to fit your pictures in a black-filled 4 × 6 inch frame before uploading them.

Are you looking for a larger solution? Several online finishing sites, most notably Wolf Camera (www.wolfcamera.com), provide "panorama-sized" finishes, which are approximately 4 × 10 inches. These prints cost under a dollar and allow you to print larger-format stereo pairs.

WHAT'S NEXT

The next chapter focuses on a very special non-Photoshop product, Genuine Fractals PrintPro, which allows you to enlarge and scale images to create poster-sized enlargements from small images.

Chapter 17

BLOWING UP YOUR IMAGES USING GENUINE FRACTALS

Y ou can always recognize 35mm snobs. They pin you to a wall at parties, talk about how wonderful traditional optics are, and lecture on how digital photography will never catch up. In particular, they mention how they can enlarge their photos "to the limits of the silver-halide molecules," a feat that you can never hope to accomplish with your new-fangled (and doomed-to-obscurity) digital camera. This may have been true once, but it isn't any more.

With Genuine Fractals, an Altamira PrintPro product, your digital images can decorate the side of a barn. You can snicker at the poor 35mm camera snobs holding tight to their miserable and costly poster-sized enlargements. With Genuine Fractals, the power is digital, and it is only going to get better.

Here's how it works: The Genuine Fractals PrintPro product converts your image into a mathematical representation. The

Adapted from *Digital Photography! I Didn' t Know You Could Do That...* by Erica Sadun
ISBN 0-7821-2965-X   384 pages $24.99

best part is that this representation is resolution-independent. With fractals, you don't deal with pixels; you deal with scalable textures. And you can scale these textures arbitrarily. The mathematical model allows you to open your pictures at any virtual resolution. You can create images ten times as large as the original or bigger. This product works so well with image editors like Photoshop that we're going to provide a short introduction to it in this chapter.

NOTE

Genuine Fractals uses a special technology called *wavelets* to encode your image. Unlike other wavelet products, Genuine Fractals places emphasis on image scaling rather than file compression, although a certain degree of image compression occurs as a side effect.

Fractalize It

You can download a demo version of Genuine Fractals PrintPro at www.genuinefractals.com. You'll need to install the demo so that you can try it out. Place it in your PhotoDeluxe Plug-Ins folder to complete the installation. Once you've installed the Genuine Fractals demo, you can try it out. First, fire up PhotoDeluxe, load a picture, and save it in the Genuine Fractals format. Then you can reopen your picture and scale it.

Here are the steps for putting a picture in Genuine Fractals format:

1. Open your image in PhotoDeluxe and select File ➤ Export ➤ File Format.

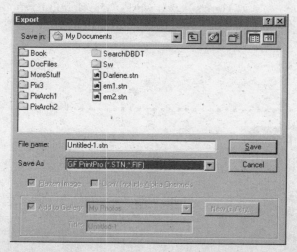

2. Choose GF PrintPro from the Save As drop-down list.

3. Name your image with the .stn extension and click Save to save it to disk.

4. The Altamira demo screen appears, as shown below. This screen tells you how many demo uses you have left before your demo license expires. In all, the demo allows you to open or save files 20 times. Click this screen to continue.

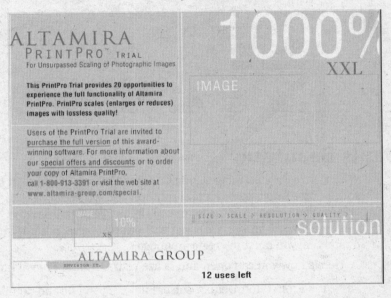

5. Choose an encoding scheme. As shown below, your choices are Lossless or Visually Lossless. Lossless takes more space but preserves image quality exactly. Visually Lossless provides more disk-efficient encoding at the price of small changes in your image. Click Save to save your file in Genuine Fractals format.

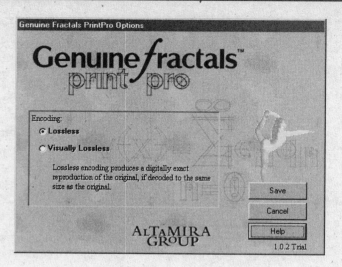

Big Is Beautiful

When you save your image using Genuine Fractals PrintPro, it converts your photos into a fractal representation and writes it out to disk. To enlarge your photo, you need to read the image back from disk. Because Genuine Fractal images are saved without pixels, each time you open a fractal file, you must re-create an image.

Here's how you can open and resize your Genuine Fractal file:

1. From PhotoDeluxe, select File ➤ Open File and double-click the Genuine Fractals file (with an .stn extension) that you wish to open.

2. The Altamira demo screen appears. Click this screen to continue.

3. The Genuine Fractals PrintPro Options window opens, as shown below. This window allows you to specify the size of the window you wish to open. For this example, in the Scale To section of the window, set the Width option to 400 percent. The Height scale will automatically update.

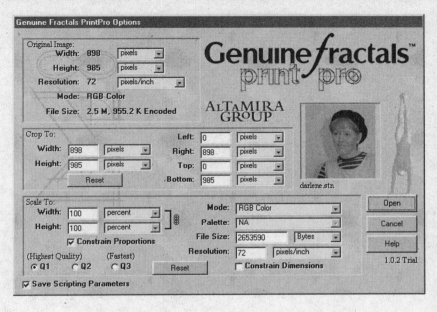

4. Click Open. Your image will open in PhotoDeluxe. The new photo will be 16 times larger than your original (both the height and width scale by a factor of four).

5. As with other PhotoDeluxe operations, a progress bar will appear at the bottom of the window. Watch this bar to estimate the amount of time left to reconstruct your photo. The larger the original photo and the larger the magnification, the more time it will take your computer to create the new image.

6. Save, print, and enjoy your enlarged image.

As an example of the results, the graphic below shows an original photo superimposed on the enlargement. Compare the sizes of the images and the excellent quality of the blown-up image. Keep in mind that the original is 1600 × 1200 pixels.

Part iii

WARNING

Enlarging images to excess can adversely affect your computer. Always keep your PC's memory limitations in mind. Ideally, when working with digital images, you should have as much RAM, speed, and hard disk space as you can afford. What makes up the ideal computer darkroom? It's hard to say. However, working with the image shown above regularly crashed my 96-megabyte, 366-megahertz PC.

The graphic below shows detail from the left eyes of both images above. The original image, zoomed, is on the left. The Genuine Fractal version sits to its right. I've used PhotoDeluxe's built-in resizing to expand the original to the same dimensions as the Genuine Fractals image.

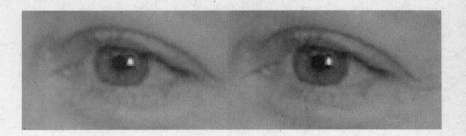

NOTE

PhotoDeluxe, like many other image-editing programs, uses bicubic interpolation to guess intermediate values between pixels. The fractal results don't need to guess. They build texture from underlying patterns and lack that blocky, zoomed-in look you usually get when enlarging photos.

When using Genuine Fractals, keep in mind that it needs a fairly large picture to start with. When it creates fractals, more data means better enlargements. I've gotten terrific results with my Nikon CoolPix 800, a 1200 × 1600 pixel camera. However, I've also gotten decent enlargements from my Ricoh-2e, with only 768 × 512 pixels. Most people use Genuine Fractals with scanned pictures and negatives, but it works extremely well with digital camera shots, too.

WHAT'S NEXT

In the next section of this book, you'll learn how to apply Photoshop to Web graphics. First up is a chapter that explains some of the finer details of graphics file formats and how to optimize them.

Part iii

PART iv
PHOTOSHOP 6 AND THE WEB

Chapter 18

UNDERSTANDING WEB GRAPHICS

Confounding to some, challenging to others, Web graphics demand a precise and knowing hand. Plenty of myths surround the issue, and poor practices keep the Web looking less than slick.

Whether you come from a design background or are just learning how to create Web graphics with Photoshop, there is no reason not to demand the best from your Web site's look.

The goal is to create aesthetically pleasing, content-rich sites that load with speed. But how do you deliver this given the diversity of *bandwidth* that exists? Bandwidth refers to the amount of literal space available to transmit data. Connections can range in speed from the slower 14.4 modems to T1 lines common on many corporate desktops, to the broadband cable modems that are cropping up around the world for relatively affordable prices.

Adapted from *Web by Design*: *The Complete Guide*
by Molly E. Holzchlag
ISBN 0-7821-2201-9   928 pages $49.99

The reason speed influences Web graphics is because the browser must have a short conversation, known as a *query*, with the Web server where the graphics reside. This query is essentially your HTML page saying "Yo, server! I need a graphic called `molly.jpg` from the images, and I need you to send it now." The server looks for the file, delivers it, and your HTML code determines where and how to place it within your layout.

Web designers are typically forced to conserve bandwidth for those on a slower Net connection by keeping file sizes to a minimum. Unfortunately, many designers are not aware that there are techniques that can spare the loss of quality resulting from their efforts to meet low bandwidth demands. This sacrifice is due more to a lack of careful selection, optimization, and proper sizing and layout than the true limitations of Web graphic technology.

This chapter will leave you with a wealth of skills that can help you become a better producer of Web graphics with Photoshop—and capable of either applying those skills immediately or overseeing the project management of those who can.

MYTH SHMYTH

Before we get started with the nitty-gritty, let's address a variety of Web graphic myths that exist. It's important to help eradicate misunderstandings about Web graphics from the start.

1. A good-looking site cannot be a fast-loading site.

    This is totally false. You can have a good-looking site that loads fast, too. Just look at the Weekly Wire XTRA page. It looks great and loads quickly (see Figure 18.1).

2. A graphic has to be tiny both dimensionally and in terms of kilobytes in order to be good.

    Wrong again. A graphic should be visually appropriate in terms of dimension. It's what you do with the graphic that makes the difference in kilobytes, not how big or small it visually appears.

3. It's okay to have unclear and messy-looking graphics. Everyone knows that this is a limitation of the Web.

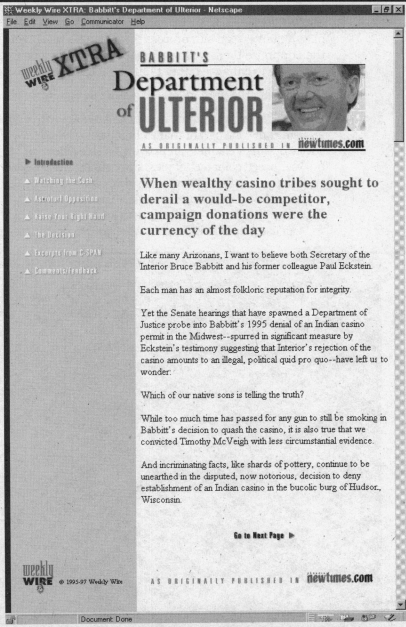

FIGURE 18.1: This Weekly Wire XTRA page looks great and loads fast.

Bad-looking graphics come from limitations on the part of the Web designer. If you carefully plan what graphics a page requires, scan and process those images wisely, and then optimize them well, you'll have good looking images that serve to enhance rather than detract from your site.

4. Graphics are the primary way of getting design into a site.

Web site design is a combination of techniques, with graphics being only one part of that technique. By taking the advice of earlier chapters and relying on safe palettes, browser-based color techniques, and defined and consistent custom palettes for a site, you can have plenty of color and splash without *ever* using a graphic. Figure 18.2 shows a page from the Core Wave site. It then stands to reason that you can use graphics to enhance what you've already created.

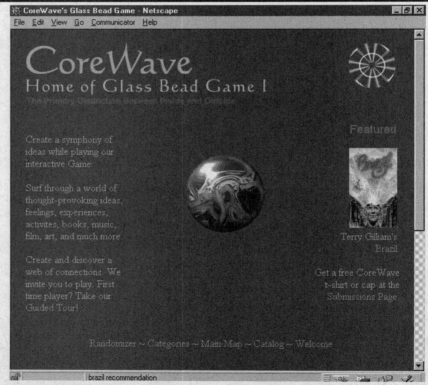

FIGURE 18.2: Core Wave demonstrates extraordinary use of browser-based color with precision graphics to create an unusual look and feel.

Myth shmyth! By following good Web graphic practices, you'll actually end up with a greater facility to choose graphics for your pages. When properly chosen, scanned, and optimized, these graphics will allow you to meet the needs of those with limited bandwidth, giving you clean, crisp images that load quickly and look terrific.

GRAPHIC SKILLS EVALUATION

There are typically two groups of individuals who are attempting to work with Web graphics. The first group is made up of professional graphic designers who have skills in print and computer-based design, but aren't particularly familiar with designing for the Web environment. The other group is made up of individuals who have little or no formal design background but come to the Web with an enthusiasm and desire to learn how to manage or work as members of Web graphic design projects.

Both groups approach the task with a set of skills and challenges. This evaluation will describe those and help you position yourself to be ready for getting the most out of this chapter by providing tips, tricks, and words of wisdom from professionals in the field.

The Graphic Designer

Those of you with a graphic design background obviously have the edge in that you have practical as well as aesthetic skills, such as knowing how to use Photoshop or using graphics to enhance the look of a printed page. You are also more likely to keep up with available materials and resources, and understand how to use other software programs that are applicable for Web graphic design.

The challenge for a traditional graphic artist is to readjust your thinking to the Web's low-resolution environment. No high-resolution work here, you're working at 72 DPI and only hundreds of pixels rather than thousands. If you can manage to reorganize your approach, you're almost guaranteed success. The expertise, judgement, and personal touch you've worked long and hard to develop can be expressed in this medium.

If you don't learn to shift your thinking you run the risk of ending up in a situation where you mimic what you've done in the print arena. Your graphics will be too large in dimension and kilobyte size. Your design might not fit the constraints of the small realm of the computer screen. Worst of all, your personal frustration could persuade you to abandon

Web graphics, which could result in the Web—which needs every great graphic designer it can get—losing the benefit of your unique talents.

Graphic designers new to this environment need to remember these things:

- ▶ Keep an open mind.
- ▶ Read as much as you can.
- ▶ Practice the techniques.
- ▶ Study the work of other talented Web graphic artists.

Yes, you will have to face some unhappy truths. You'll sacrifice high-resolution design, broad-spectrum palettes, reasonable control of colors, and any vertical design worthy of mention. On the other hand, you'll end up challenging your design skills.

Limitations are very often the catalyst that forces innovative solutions to problems. Use those limitations to grow. There will always be a need for good print designers, and there's nothing that says you can't do both. Get Web-savvy and you not only improve the aesthetics of the Web, but your marketability as well.

The Graphic Design Novice

It's possible that you are interested in the field of Web design and are exploring what skills you'll need to enter into the profession. Perhaps you are already working in Web design as a technologist, but don't have a graphic design background. For you, the formidable task is learning the methods and simultaneously gaining art skills—no easy quest! Fortunately, many excellent resources exist for you, and with a good dose of motivation and an open mind, you will definitely be able to live up to the challenge.

There will be some individuals who are totally frustrated or simply not interested in the graphic elements of Web design. If you're one of these individuals and are responsible for the implementation of Web sites, you can hire graphic designers, photographers, and illustrators by the hour or in a permanent position to assist you in your goals.

While I obviously want to encourage you to learn the concepts and methods involved with Web graphic design, I also am very concerned that the quality of work you do is the best it can be. If you're one of those people who believes firmly that you don't have an artistic bone in your body and you are unwilling to challenge that belief, that's okay. Web graphic designers can be hired to assist you. That's still no reason to not approach this chapter with enthusiasm, learning what you can to empower you in your goals.

WEB GRAPHIC TOOLS

Once you've evaluated where you stand in the realm of Web graphic design you should look at the tools you'll need. Whether you'll use them or simply have them for others on your team does not matter—there are some very specific tools you *must* have if you wish to address Web graphic concerns.

NOTE

I'll be writing under the assumption that you have a decent computer (Mac, PowerPC, or PC—it doesn't matter the type just as long as it has plenty of disk space, RAM, and a 24-bit color card and monitor) and a flatbed scanner. These are the minimum of hardware requirements necessary to perform Web graphic technology tasks.

You'll need tools to sketch ideas, create designs, work with typography, enhance photos and art, scan images, and optimize graphics. This section will give you an overview of what these tools are, where to find more information about them, and give you an idea of their cost.

Photoshop: It's All That

In order to create and manage your graphics, several important tools will be necessary to have. The most important one, hands-down, is Photoshop.

There are many designers working out there who like using other paint and photographic programs, and there are certainly a number of those programs that you'll use *in addition* to Photoshop. But make no mistake—the industry standard is Photoshop, and Photoshop is the standard to which you should hold yourself as a Web graphics professional.

Photoshop is a powerful, sophisticated tool that enables you to take a Web graphic from concept to optimization without ever having to engage another piece of software. The strongest argument of them all is that if you want to be *marketable* as a Web designer, Photoshop skills are going to be an essential. This doesn't mean you're not going to want other software.

Chapters 12 and 13 discussed some of the advantages of programs like Adobe Illustrator and Corel procreate Painter. Professional graphic designers know that having additional tools such as an illustration program, 3-D graphics program, plug-in tools, and multimedia packages such as Director are going to further enhance their ability to create a variety of graphic and multimedia designs. But for now, Photoshop is your most important graphic design purchase.

Graphic Support Software

Other types of graphic software that you'll want to know about and consider for purchase include:

An animated GIF program   Animated GIFs are an easy and popular way to get animations onto your page without resorting to alternatives that will cost more money and not be as cross-platform and cross-browser compatible. More on animated GIFs and related software can be found in Chapter 23.

Debabelizer Pro   You can take tedious guesswork out of optimization with this powerful program that processes and optimizes graphics. Optimization is the process by which you gain control of as much data in a given graphic as you can during the compression process. While you can do everything that Debabelizer does to a graphic by hand in Photoshop, Debabelizer has the added advantage of batch processing files as well as offering up file type and size comparisons. Be wary however—Debabelizer Pro is a considerable expense. I've only used it when working for design companies requiring large quantities of graphic production. For smaller clients and specific applications I prefer to use Photoshop and do my optimization by hand. You'll need to evaluate your circumstances to come up with the most sensible approach.

Drawing programs and miscellaneous paint programs   In addition to Photoshop, many designers use the full spectrum of Adobe products, particularly Illustrator, which offers a variety of drawing and typesetting options worthy of note. Adobe has been involved with desktop publishing and design software for so long their products have become the industry standard. There are also a number of other programs that designers find useful, including Paint Shop Pro, which comes in handy when looking for an inexpensive route before jumping in to the more serious commitment of Photoshop, and Ulead Technologies has a wide range of graphic programs.

Graphic enhancement programs and plug-ins   The way you present a graphic is as important as the graphic's quality itself. Look at the difference between the photograph in Figure 18.3 and the one in Figure 18.4. While either is acceptable, Figure 18.4 has the added intrigue of a photo treatment. This kind of enhancement adds a level of sophistication to your work. In this example, Photographic Edges from a company called Auto F/X have been used. Another very popular plug-in is Kai's Power Tools. Ulead also makes impressive, inexpensive, and popular graphics utilities, the company Web site is located at www.ulead.com.

FIGURE 18.3: An unadorned photograph

FIGURE 18.4: The photograph with an edge effect applied

Graphic source material   You'll want to have sources for icons, patterns, stock photos, and fonts. These can be acquired on CD-ROM and used royalty-free.

NOTE

I have students and readers who complain about the high price and formidable learning curves of Web graphic tools. If you're just starting out, several thousand dollars for software does seem somewhat daunting, as does the expense and time spent learning the software, but the dollars and precious time you're going to shell out for software and education is very low compared to the high-quality results you're going to need in order to be competitive in the Web design industry.

TIP

Stock art can get costly, too. But the results are worth it. Think smart. If you're doing a specific project, write the cost of the specialty goods you need for that project into the specs. This way you get the materials paid for *and* have them available for future work.

Another issue to consider is original source material. Many designers advocate using professional illustrators and photographers to provide the source material for your graphics. This is an ideal situation, but it's not realistic in every case. When you can afford professional, original work, by all means go for it. It supports other design professionals and brings a fresh, original look to the sites in question. When you can't choose this option, the software resources in this section should help you find a range of options from semi-professional to very high-quality stock materials.

The Five S's of Image Production

You've evaluated yourself, and assessed the tool situation. Now you're ready to move into the nitty-gritty of Web graphic production. I'm going to start you out with my five-fold philosophy.

Many of you will be familiar with the acronym GIGO. It stands for "garbage in, garbage out." The idea is that if you start with poor quality stock or resources, there's very little chance you will improve that quality without having to use every trick in the book and then some.

With that as a foundation, you can then move on to scan, size, select attractive treatments, and save your files in the appropriate format. The final step is perhaps the most complicated of all. As a result, it demands its own study, which we'll address later in the "File Formats" section.

Here's my five-fold philosophy, aptly termed the Five S's of Image Production.

1. Start with quality.

2. Scan the image.

3. Size images appropriately.

4. Select attractive treatments such as matting, filters, borders, and edge effects.

5. Save files in the proper format for the type of graphic image you're working with.

Now let's take an in-depth look at the steps in this process.

Starting with Quality

Whether you are using stock images or hiring an illustrator or photographer to provide them for you, it is vitally important that you use quality material. I say this only to fully impress upon you that if you take only one lesson away from this chapter, it's that *quality counts*. If you begin with good materials, you have the advantage of ending up with better results in less time. Remember, in order to get file sizes down, quality is often lost. Start with quality, and you can be much more confident that aggressively optimizing your graphics for speed won't result in terrible images.

Figure 18.5 is an example of good photographic material. Note how the image is clean and crisp. On the other hand, a messy source (Figure 18.6) will require much more time and effort to work with, and who knows what kind of results you'll achieve in that time.

FIGURE 18.5: A clean, crisp photo

FIGURE 18.6: A crumpled photocopy will not suffice as source material.

Scanning Techniques

There are two principal issues that must be dealt with when scanning graphics for use on the Web:

1. Source material

2. Scanning resolution

How you deal with each of these issues can make a difference in the quality of the scan.

Source Material

Source material refers to *what* it is you're attempting to scan. Photos should be clear, clean, and of the highest quality possible. Hand-drawn or printed materials should also be very clean—look carefully for speckles or dust. Use a professional quality dusting gas to clean your source materials, and follow your scanner manufacturer's recommendations for cleaning your scanner's surface. Anything that you can clean up *before* you scan will greatly improve the quality of the scan.

Many graphic artists like to scan real objects. This is part of *organic design*—utilizing literal artifacts from the real-time world and using them to inspire computer-based graphics.

For Figure 18.7, I took a few things off of my desk and scanned them. Be creative with this technique. Again, the main concern is that the object and your scanning surface are both clear of dust and debris.

FIGURE 18.7: Organic art objects from my desk

Scanning Resolution

While your scanner might offer a range of scanning resolutions, the end result of any image scanned for the Web is going to be 72 DPI. While some designers find that scanning at a higher resolution such as 300 DPI and *then* reducing to 72 DPI renders better results, the verdict is still out on whether that is true.

Whether you choose to scan at 72 DPI or scan at a higher resolution (like 300 DPI and reduce), is really a personal call. It's sometimes possible to get better end results by scanning at 300 DPI and then reducing to 72 DPI later on. On other occasions, that doesn't hold true. The difference in quality is often very slight—the type of difference that normally won't be seen when a figure is optimized for the Web. Find out what works best for your type of scanner and appeals to your sensibilities. Either way, the end result is going to be 72 DPI.

Yes, I hear the cries of print graphic artists as I write about 72 DPI. It's the lowest resolution on the totem pole. I have to remind you, though, that these images aren't going to be printed. In this environment, you don't *need* high resolution in order to make an image appear clear and attractive in the computer graphic environment.

Part iv

Sizing Images

The issue of sizing images is proportion. I'm not referring to the kilobyte size of the image, but, the width and height of the image. You'll want to be sure that the literal dimensions of your graphics are proportionately appropriate for the Web environment. This does not include background graphics, which we'll cover in detail later in this chapter. The concern here is spot graphics and detail pieces such as buttons and rules.

After having thoroughly bombarded you with the resolution and constrained space issues involved in Web design, you needn't be reminded that you are working for standard computer screens, with a common resolution of 640 × 480 pixels. This means that in order to keep your designs within the dimensions of that resolution, the actual parts have to be smaller—particularly where width is concerned. Remember that there is actually *less visible space* than the 640 × 480 resolution because your Web browser's interface takes up some of that space as well.

Horizontal designs are rarely considered wise, unless you are really thoughtful about the design or have a significant reason to design that way. Figure 18.8 shows the home page of Circle of Friends, a group dedicated to raising awareness about spinal chord injuries. The horizontal design is appropriate as it communicates how many victims of such injuries view the world. Unless you have such a provocative reason to design horizontally, it's usually wise to avoid it.

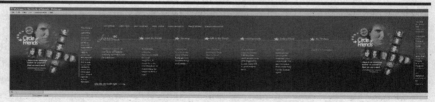

FIGURE 18.8: Horizontal design is a Web rarity.

Images should always be less than an *absolute* maximum of 600 pixels in width, with 595 pixels being the recommended maximum.

The length of graphics will be determined by the overall layout of your individual page. It's wise to keep the length of your images approximate to each individual screen length. In other words, you should be able to see the entirety of an image without having to scroll down to see it. Yale's HTML style guide recommends a screen length to run *no longer* than 295 pixels per screen.

Of paramount importance is the proportion of one element to other elements on the page. If you've done your layout preparation, you've got a jumpstart on this. Even so, keeping proportion and proximity (how close objects are to one another) in between the text, other images or media, and the image in question. Certainly there's room for variation in size, just be sure that the ultimate look isn't out of balance. Compare Figure 18.9, which shows a graphic photo that is out of balance with other elements on the page, to Figure 18.10. In that figure, the proportion is logical and therefore easy to look at.

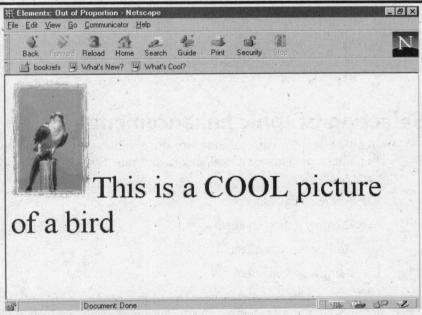

FIGURE 18.9: This page is out of balance.

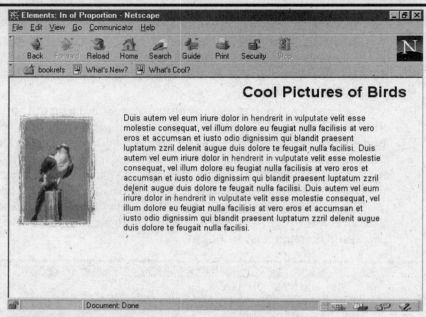

FIGURE 18.10: The elements on this page are logically proportioned.

Selecting Graphic Enhancements

Graphic enhancements are added to your graphics using native Photoshop filters, plug-ins, or miscellaneous software. Some examples of enhancements include:

- ▶ Adding a light source
- ▶ Creating a drop shadow
- ▶ Adding an edge effect
- ▶ Using a special effect

These, and other enhancement techniques can bring life and dimension to your graphics. Adding effects helps make your site look more interesting, and therefore more professional.

Figure 18.11 is a photograph before a light source has been added. In Figure 18.12, a light source has been applied along with a drop shadow to add dimension to the photograph. Figure 18.13 shows the same photograph with an edge effect applied. Finally, Figure 18.14 shows the original photograph with a special ripple effect added to it.

FIGURE 18.11: A source photo

FIGURE 18.12: A drop shadow is added

FIGURE 18.13: An edge effect is applied

FIGURE 18.14: The source photo with a ripple effect

These techniques are truly the tip of the iceberg when it comes to Web graphic design. This book is full of advanced Photoshop techniques that can be used to maximize your images for use on the Web.

Saving Files in Proper Format

You've heard me use the word *optimization* but may not know exactly to what it refers. In a nutshell, optimization is achieved by selecting a file format for the appropriate file of an image you are working on, and then using that format's native options to reduce the file's size in kilobytes while maintaining the highest quality image available.

So, saving files in proper format is not just the fifth step of good image production, it's the first step in optimization.

FILE FORMATS

There are two dominant and useful file formats used on the Web, the GIF and the JPEG (also known as JPG). Understanding the difference in how these file formats compress data is key to ensuring that the end product is speedy *and* attractive. You'll learn more about these formats in the next chapter.

There are special considerations regarding each format. For example, GIFs can be transparent, interlaced, or used to create animations. JPEGs can be progressively rendered, and enjoy the distinction of using a compression method that does not reduce the number of colors in an image.

How and when to use each of these types of files is critical to optimization, as you will soon see.

GIF

You'll hear this one pronounced with a hard "G." It makes sense to say it that way because the acronym stands for *Graphic Interchange Format*. However, the proper pronunciation is "jiff."

GIFs hold the distinction of being the longest supported graphic file format in Web design.

Technology

CompuServe created the GIF. Bear in mind that compression for any file type is based on mathematical algorithms that make little sense to most of us. We don't really need to understand that information in order to use graphics well, although the math-heads among you might enjoy researching the compression algorithms for the file formats discussed here. You have my blessing, and an express command to go forth and have fun.

Me? I'll stick to what I can understand (a math genius I am not). The type of compression used by GIFs is called *lossless*. In simple terms, this means that the information is saved by figuring out how much of an image uses the same information, and saving those sections with a specific numeric pattern. Therefore, flat images with little color stand to compress well—because they will have lots of sections of the same patterns.

A GIF palette is limited to 256 colors total. So, if you have 10 shades of yellow, that's 10 different numeric patterns. If you end up with too many patterns, the compression method has to figure out how to fit into the palette limitations. Often, what we see as one color is really many—yellow is made up of various pigments, or in the case of digitized colors pixels of individual color.

GIF compression will throw out some of the repetitive information and select from the information it has. This means the pale yellow in your image might suddenly become a neon yellow.

Technique

In order to work well with GIFs, you need to know what kind of files are best served by lossless compression methods. GIFs tend to do very well with any image that has few colors, such as simple line art or images with flat color. This suggests that any images with many different colors, variations of color, light sources, gradients, and the like are *not* good candidates for GIF compression as they contain too much information!

Remember this equation: A good candidate for GIF compression equals an image that is simple and has few colors.

Figure 18.15 and Figure 18.16 are both good examples of GIF candidates. They are flat color line-drawings with no color gradations or complicated information.

FIGURE 18.15: This image is a good candidate for GIF optimization.

FIGURE 18.16: Another example of a good GIF candidate

JPEG

Pronounce this one "jay-peg." You'll also see it spelled as JPG. The acronym stands for *Joint Photographic Experts Group*. A group of photographic experts got together to create the JPEG standard.

Technology

The math behind the JPEG is a bit more complex than the GIF. To describe the technology in understandable terms, consider JPEG a *lossy* compression method. Instead of hanging on to areas of important data, JPEG technology tosses out data that is deemed unimportant. Of course, it has to do this with some kind of logic, so the JPEG compression divides the image into square sections before it begins to apply the really advanced math.

This translates into JPEG compression offering you the decision as to how much compression you want. You can choose to keep lots of data intact, or lose a lot of data, depending upon the ratio you wish to employ. The result of losing too much data, however, might be the appearance of *artifacts*. These are weird ghost shapes or blocks of illogical color, which you can see in the photograph in Figure 18.17.

FIGURE 18.17: If JPEGs are compressed too much, artifacts appear.

Technique

Because lossy compression allows the designer to keep a lot of visual information, this means that unlike the GIF format, anything with a lot of color or gradients will translate well into the JPEG file format.

Good candidates for JPEGs include photographs—especially where there's lots of color resulting from light such as in skies, sunsets, and the like—and graphics using gradient fills.

Figure 18.18 shows a photograph saved as a JPEG. The gradation in the sky appears smooth and natural. There are subtle light changes in the image, which remain intact in the JPEG format but would most certainly be lost if a GIF were to be used.

FIGURE 18.18: The sky looks natural in this JPEG.

OPTIMIZATION

As mentioned earlier, optimization is the process by which an image is reduced to its smallest file size while retaining its best quality.

Part iv

The first step in optimization is to determine which file format is appropriate for the file. The general rule, as we've determined in our previous discussion, is as follows:

▶ The GIF file format is best used for line art and images with few colors.

▶ The JPEG file format is the best format for photographs and art with lots of colors and gradations of color.

There is sometimes a gray area between the use of GIFs versus JPEGs. One example is a black and white photograph with little gradation. In this particular instance, a GIF might be a better choice. It's difficult to tell unless you put the image through optimization with both. This is where Debabelizer Pro comes in handy, as it can make these comparisons for you. Another program that achieves this at a fraction of the cost is Photo Impact from Ulead Systems (www.ulead.com). On a few occasions, a graphic designer will *want* to exploit the dithering that occurs with GIFs in order to induce a specific effect. In this case, the designer will have to work with the graphic in a trial-and-error fashion until the desired look is achieved.

After determining the file type, the next step is to work with that file type's innate technology in order to get the lowest file size while retaining the best quality. The next sections will explain how this is done, and take you through a step-by-step example for optimizing both a GIF and a JPEG.

You'll learn more about graphics formats and optimizing graphics in Chapter 19.

Working with GIFs

There are several terms you'll need to know. They are:

Indexing   A software program such as Photoshop will take an image file and count its colors. If there are more than 256 colors in an image, indexing will reduce the palette to 256 colors. At that point, you have the freedom to determine if further reduction in colors is appropriate.

Palette type   There are several types of indexed color palettes. The one that is most important to you is going to be the *adaptive* color palette. This palette allows you to determine the various aspects of the palette, such as color depth and dithering. Another important palette is the *exact* palette. You'll see this appear when an image already has less than 256 colors.

Color depth   This is also referred to as *bit* depth. This is basically the amount of data that will be saved with your image. Optimization of GIFs largely depends upon your ability to reduce bit depth.

Number of colors   This is the total number of colors in the image, which can be as low as 8 and as high as 256. Limiting colors is helpful in terms of reducing total file size. Typically, you'll only need to worry about managing your color depth, and the number of colors will reduce appropriately.

Dithering   Dithering is the process of allowing the computer to make decisions as to what colors to put into an image. For example, if you have three yellows next to one another, the computer may select the yellow that is in its own palette. This means that your pastel could end up as a neon. You can control how much your colors dither in Photoshop, but ideally, you will not want any dithering at all.

Optimizing JPEGs

JPEG compression in Photoshop has the following settings:

Maximum   This is the highest setting, and maintains as much of the file's integrity as possible.

High   Still a good choice, some lossy compression occurs at this level.

Medium   Lossy compression really goes to work here, reducing the file size even more—but often at a noticeable degradation to the image's integrity.

Low   At this level, most JPEGs are unacceptable, as the appearance of artifacts becomes very noticeable. This setting should be avoided unless you are able to maintain the image's strength without encountering serious problems with clarity.

ADDITIONAL GRAPHIC TECHNIQUES

Three additional graphic techniques you'll want to be familiar with include:

- ▶ Progressive rendering
- ▶ Transparency
- ▶ GIF animation

Progressive rendering is the progressive appearance of graphics—a very handy technique that helps keep people's visual attention while graphics are loading. A site visitor will see the entire graphic appear in a fuzzy fashion, and then become progressively more clear.

This can be done in two ways on the Web. The most popular and effective is the use of *interlaced GIFs*. Figure 18.19 shows an interlaced GIF in the midst of rendering; Figure 18.20 shows the final form. This technique can be applied to any GIF. Photoshop supports interlacing, as do many plug-in tools.

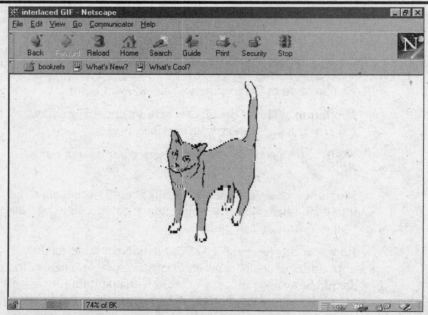

FIGURE 18.19: An interlaced GIF in the process of rendering

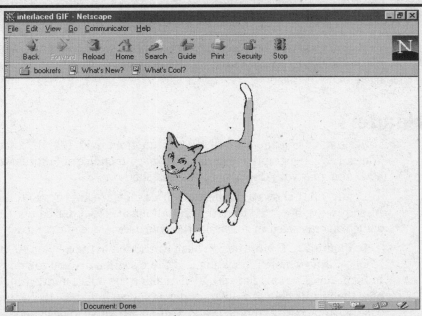

FIGURE 18.20: The GIF in its fully rendered form

Progressive JPEGs are the JPEG answer to interlacing. You cannot interlace a JPEG, but there are programs, including Photoshop, that create what is known as a progressive JPEG. I'm personally not too fond of them, as I believe the technology is somewhat preliminary, not well-supported by browsers, and the quality is fairly inconsistent.

Without progressive rendering, JPEGs will scroll rather than render progressively, but if you've done your optimization, layout, and coding in a sensible fashion, it's not an obvious problem—particularly because the results are so attractive.

Transparency is the technique that allows you to create textured or multi-colored backgrounds and "tape" a graphic over them without disrupting the background design. It involves making certain colors transparent in the graphic, and having those transparent colors disappear when placed on a textured page. This technique takes a little bit of patience and time to learn, but can be done successfully in Photoshop.

Finally, *animated GIFs* take advantage of a looping element in the GIF format. They are an extremely popular way to add active media to your pages.

Part iv

GRAPHIC APPLICATIONS

Now that you know how to work with graphics we're going to look at the methods Web designers employ to come up with a variety of graphics used on a Web page.

Headers

Using graphical headers is a nice departure from rigid, HTML-based text. You can add logographic material, control your choice of fonts as well as add color, play with dimension, and add shadows.

Figure 18.21 shows a flat header with a typeface known as Whimsy. Already we've departed from the limitations of HTML-based text, and while you only see it in grayscale, the type uses a nice maroon color.

In Figure 18.22, more design has been added to the header. As a result, it is now more interesting, but there's still more you can do with it. In Figure 18.23 a lens flare is added, making the image a little fun. Compare the results here to a plain header as shown in Figure 18.24, and you can quickly see why graphic headers are so attractive to designers.

FIGURE 18.21: Flat header with Whimsy typeface

FIGURE 18.22: A design adds personality to the look

FIGURE 18.23: A lens flare adds some fun

Fun With Fonts

FIGURE 18.24: A plain text header—Can you say "boring?"

Background Graphics

Using graphics to create backgrounds is a great way to add style to your pages. However, be careful how you use them. The Web is filled with graphic backgrounds that are cliché, or that clash with the design. Background graphics should serve the design, not detract from it.

Backgrounds can be either GIF or JPEG formats. This will depend upon what kind of image you're using for your background. Be sure to try out your optimization skills when designing background images. With careful optimization, you can create very complex background designs that take up little memory.

Tiles

By using small tiles with a pattern, you can create a wallpaper effect. Essentially, the tiles are repeated both on the horizontal and vertical axis until they fill the available background.

Some of the issues you should be aware of when working with background tiles include:

File size   A background tile should be appropriate in both dimensional size and kilobytes. Remember that the larger the file, the longer the load time—and the fewer available kilobytes for other graphics.

Seamed tiles   If you have a visible border around your tile (Figure 18.25), you will end up showing the world the fact that background tiles are repeated (Figure 18.26). This effect may be desirous to your design, but be aware that the seams show.

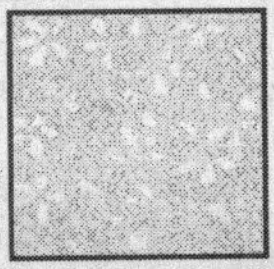

FIGURE 18.25: Tile with seams

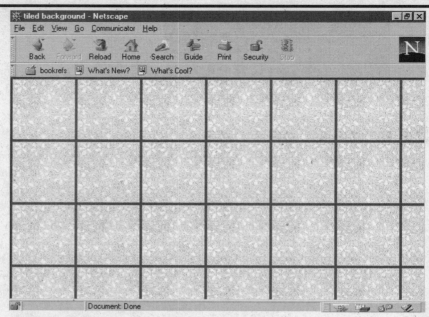

FIGURE 18.26: Seamed tiles show the repeat pattern

Seamless tiles   These are harder to create and involve a fine hand. The objective is to make the tiles appear without any seam at all. You must anticipate how the tiles will fit together, and use advanced drawing techniques to ensure that a tile appears seamless. Figure 18.27 shows a seamless background tile, and Figure 18.28 shows the wallpaper-style results.

Another important concern is readability. Your background design should *never* interfere with a visitor's ability to read the text that will be placed on top of it. Be sure to fully test your design with the chosen text and link colors in order to ensure that both the aesthetic look of the tile and the clarity of any text remain intact.

FIGURE 18.27: A seamless tile

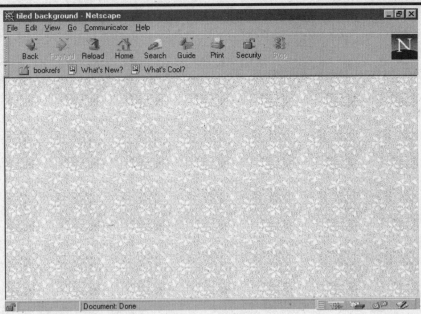

FIGURE 18.28: Seamless tile creates a true wallpaper effect.

Margin Backgrounds

This is an extremely popular way of designing backgrounds for the Web. You can create a right, left, or top margin to use with tables. Some designers like to employ both a left and right margin, which can be a welcome departure from the standard left or right.

Margin backgrounds can be made up of flat color (Figure 18.29) or with a texture or design (Figure 18.30) in the margin field. The text field can be a flat color (Figure 18.31) or a texture (Figure 18.32). These combinations add a lot of visual interest to a site. Again, be careful that the backgrounds do not interfere with readability.

The major concern with margin backgrounds is size. Because all backgrounds are a repeated pattern, you'll have to understand how this pattern affects the design you're creating. The vertical repetition works to our advantage because we can keep the tile thin and use the vertical repeat to create our pattern. If a margin background's width is too short, however, it will repeat at inconvenient points along the horizontal axis in your design. Furthermore, this repetition causes problems at a variety of resolutions.

Part iv

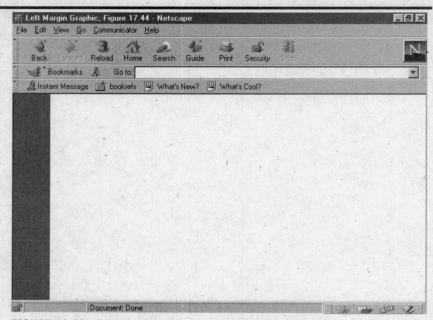

FIGURE 18.29: Flat color for a left-margin background graphic

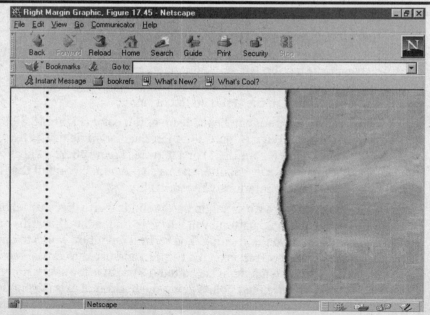

FIGURE 18.30: This background graphic has a design in the right margin.

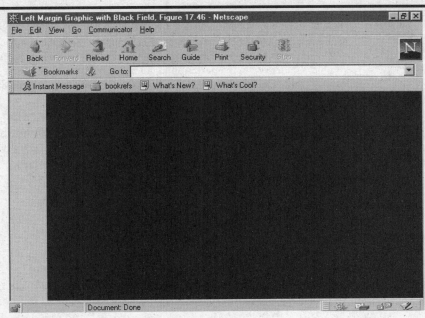

FIGURE 18.31: Note the flat color text field

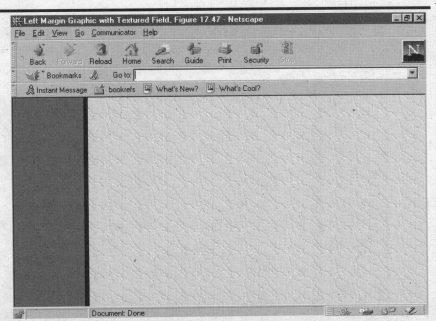

FIGURE 18.32: In this case, the text field is a texture.

NOTE

Background graphics tile into the browser's available space. They do not affect width and height concerns. This means that you can have a very long background graphic. When used in the background, no horizontal scroll bar will be forced. However, the same graphic placed in the foreground will force a scroll bar.

If you create a tile that is 640 pixels in width, and you're viewing on a screen that has a 640 × 480 resolution, you'll see the background that you created without running the risk of repeating on the horizontal axis. But what happens when you view the same page at 800 × 600 resolution or higher? The tile repeats (Figure 18.33).

Designers remedy this by designing vertical tiles at an average of 1024 pixels in width. This covers a range of resolutions without running into a problem.

Top margin designs work in a similar fashion, but the repeat axis problem occurs in reverse. If you don't make the tile long enough to fit the page, the top margin will repeat (Figure 18.34) on the horizon. Therefore, top margin backgrounds should be long—as long as you need for a given page. The width can be kept short, however, as the tiling mechanism will fill the page appropriately (Figure 18.35).

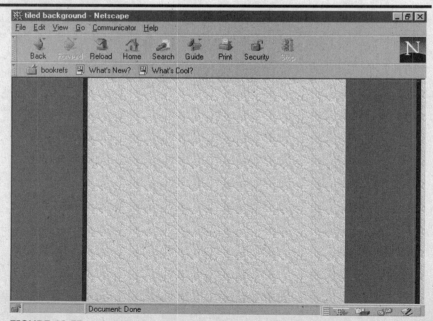

FIGURE 18.33: A background that's too short risks repeating at higher resolution.

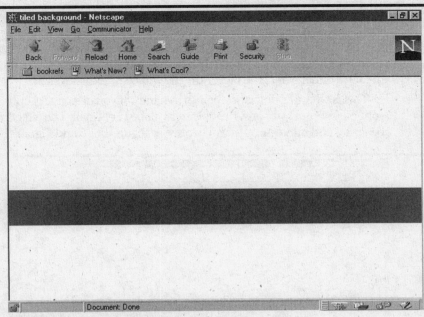

FIGURE 18.34: Vertical tile repeating on the horizontal axis

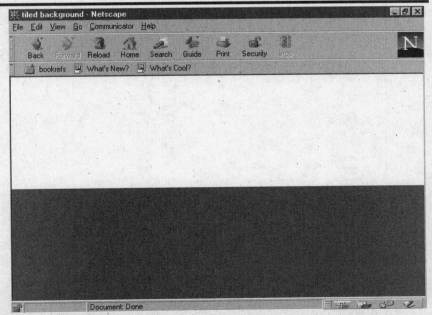

FIGURE 18.35: The full effect of a top-margin tile

Full Background Design

There will be occasions where you'll want to use full images as a background. In these instances, you'll have to determine how to handle repetition. Another concern with full backgrounds is file size. Logically, the larger the file's dimensions, the bigger the file will be in terms of size.

This is where optimization comes in handy. If you design and optimize your background properly, the file sizes will be very small. The effects can be beautiful and interesting, as you can see in Figure 18.36 and Figure 18.37.

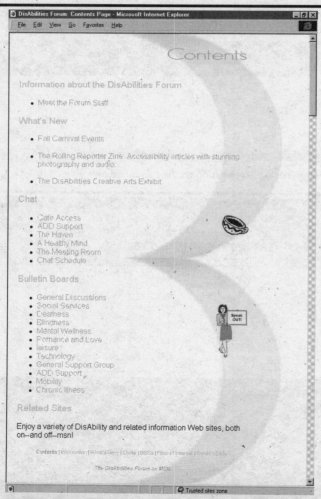

FIGURE 18.36: This full-page background repeats, but does so in an interesting fashion.

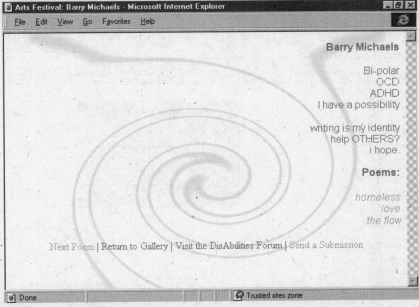

FIGURE 18.37: This full-page background is highly artistic and the repeat factor doesn't negatively affect the design.

Photos and Illustrations

Photos and illustrations can help illustrate a Web page. The trick with these kinds of images is to enhance the overall design rather than detract from it.

In Figure 18.38, you can see a photograph that is integrated with and relevant to the text on the page. Figure 18.39 shows a piece of clip art that performs a similar role.

Processing photos and illustrations should be done with precise optimization techniques in place. You already know that you don't want to have excessive amounts of graphics on a page. When you add up backgrounds, headers, and any image maps, you start running into higher numbers in the memory department.

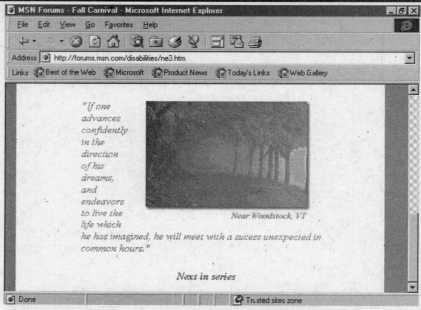

FIGURE 18.38: The photograph is complimentary to the text and vice-versa.

FIGURE 18.39: This illustration is integrated well with the contents that surround it.

WHAT'S NEXT

In the next chapter, you're going to learn more about Web graphics formats, including more on JPGs, GIFs, and a newer format called Portable Network Graphics (PNG).

Chapter 19

MORE ON WEB GRAPHIC FORMATS

I f you were designing Web sites five or six ago, making graphics was pretty simple. Back then, Web browsers supported only one internal graphic file format—GIF—and the biggest decision was how to pronounce it. There were no animations, no streaming videos, and certainly no possibility of anything resembling interactive multimedia.

Today, the situation is totally different. Designers now have hundreds of tools and an endless list of emerging technologies. If they were to research even a fraction of these technologies, they would run the risk of wasting lots of time on something that may never have a practical application. It's enough to make Web designers wish they were working in print.

Adapted from *Mastering Photoshop 5.5 for the Web*
by Matt Straznitskas
ISBN 0-7821-2605-7   672 pages $39.99

Fortunately, one of Photoshop's great strengths is that it has consistently adopted only the features that Web designers truly need. The program has been around so long that Adobe isn't about to add some new file format simply because it's a buzzword. And once Adobe does add a new tool, chances are good that it will be a solid, well-considered enhancement to the program.

This chapter provides instruction on how to save images in the popular Web graphic file formats, as well as details on the unique features of each format. You'll learn more about GIF and JPEG, dithering, interlacing, and transparency.

INTERNALLY SUPPORTED GRAPHICS

Unlike HTML, which must be supported by Web browsers, there is no standard graphic format for the Web. In fact, the World Wide Web was intentionally designed as an open multimedia space, capable of handling an unlimited number of graphic standards. But in practice, the Web isn't as open as it seems.

While it is possible to attach any graphic file to a Web page, few of the possible formats are supported internally in the browser. This means that while you can attach a PostScript file to a Web page and view it with another program, no browser will be able to display the file on the Web page itself.

Today's Web browsers also support a wide array of plug-in–based media. Plug-in technology was developed by Netscape as a way of adding additional capability to a Web browser. Software firms, such as Macromedia and Progressive Networks, have developed plug-ins that offer interactive games, real-time audio broadcasts, and other cutting edge media.

The problem with plug-in technology is that users must have the appropriate software installed to experience the media. While all of the popular plug-ins are available for download, not everyone is willing to get the software. If a Web site visitor isn't willing to download and install the Shockwave plug-in, there's no way they're going to be able to experience the snazzy Macromedia Director movie you've created.

Fortunately, the manufacturers of Web browsers have settled on a few internally supported graphic formats. Graphics Interchange Format (GIF), Joint Photographic Experts Group (JPEG), and Portable Network Graphics (PNG) are file formats that have been adopted to varying degrees by Netscape and Microsoft. If you create a GIF file and link it into a Web page's HTML code, people will be able to see it without downloading additional software.

With each new version of Photoshop, Adobe has added and upgraded tools for encoding Web graphic formats as they have emerged. The program currently supports GIF, JPEG, and PNG file formats, and provides a number of tools for creating such files. While these file formats lack some of the visual punch of other cutting-edge Web technologies, they continue to serve as workhorses and form the backbone of most of the Web page designs created today.

GRAPHICS INTERCHANGE FORMAT (GIF)

As noted in the last chapter, GIF is the most popular graphic format on the Web. You'll recall that the GIF format was originally invented for use on CompuServe, one of the first commercial online networks. Since it was designed for use on a computer network with low-bandwidth users, GIF proved to be an ideal choice as the first internally supported graphic format for the Web. To this day, the majority of graphics seen on Web pages are GIFs.

Compression

GIF became so popular because of its ability to compress graphic data efficiently. GIF relies on the Lempel-Ziv Welch (LZW) algorithm (named after the three developers of the technique), a mathematical formula that can transform large files into smaller files that are more suited for the Web. The LZW algorithm works its magic by compressing a series of symbols into a single symbol multiplied by its number of appearances. For example, if 10 black pixels were grouped together in a graphic, file formats without compression would represent the 10 black pixels as 10 symbols. However, GIF notes this repetition by using only two symbols: the number of times the color repeats and the color itself. Instead of 10 elements of data, there are only two (see Figure 19.1).

NOTE

LZW compression is called a "lossless" data format because, although the data is being compacted, the decompressed graphic looks exactly the same as the original file.

Part iv

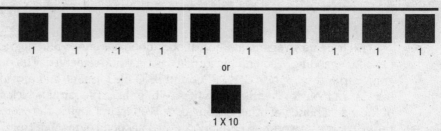

1   1   1   1   1   1   1   1   1   1

or

1 X 10

FIGURE 19.1: The GIF LZW compression method notes a series of pixels with the same color rather than noting each individual pixel.

Indexed Color Mode

The GIF format is limited to a 256-color palette. This means that no matter how many colors a file contains, it will need to slim down to 256 colors or fewer if it wants to become a GIF. This limitation goes back to the fact that the GIF standard was designed for low-bandwidth network situations. Since every color that is included in a graphic is additional data, fewer colors mean smaller file sizes and shorter downloads. Photoshop has provided Indexed Color mode as a way of automatically removing colors from a graphic.

Converting to Indexed Color Mode

To convert an image from RGB mode to Indexed Color mode, do the following:

1. Select Image ➢ Mode ➢ Indexed Color from the Menu Bar to view the Indexed Color dialog box.

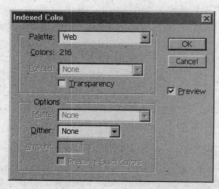

2. Select Web from the Palette drop-down menu.

3. Click OK.

Dithering

When two or more colors are placed closely together in certain patterns, the human eye tends to blend the colors naturally into a single hue. Photoshop takes advantage of this process by using its Dithering feature to simulate colors that may not be available in a limited color palette. Since GIF can save no more than 256 colors, dithering can be useful for simulating color in graphics that contain a wide range of hues.

Whether you want to use the Dither option depends on the type of graphic you are converting. If the graphic has been designed with only a few colors, there is usually no need to apply the Dither option. However, if your graphic contains subtle shading or a wide variety of color variations, dithering is a must.

Figure 19.2 demonstrates the advantages of using dithering on a graphic that is composed of many values. While both graphics have been converted to 256 colors, the file on the left has not implemented dithering and is very coarse. The file on the right has been processed with Photoshop's Dithering feature and is more natural.

FIGURE 19.2: Non-dithered versus dithered

WARNING

Graphics with a wide tonal range that don't have dithering applied can develop harsh transitions called *banding*.

Part iv

Dithering an Image

To apply Photoshop's Dithering effect to an image, open an image and do the following:

1. From the Menu Bar, select Image ➤ Mode ➤ Indexed Color. The Indexed Color dialog box appears.

2. Choose Web from the Palette drop-down menu.

3. Select Diffusion from the Dither drop-down menu.

4. In Amount, input the degree to which you would like the image dithered (between 1% and 100%)

5. Select Preserve Exact Colors.

6. Click OK.

The image will now be mapped to the 216 browser-safe color palette. Any colors in the original image that weren't in the 216-color palette will be simulated with a pattern of browser-safe colors.

Interlacing

When a graphic is downloaded from the Web, it usually loads from top to bottom. Interlacing is an alternate effect whereby different parts of a graphic will unveil simultaneously.

As shown in Figure 19.3, an interlaced GIF is saved line by line in a series of steps. Starting from the top of the image and first line of pixels, an interlaced GIF saves every eighth line. Then, starting from the fourth line, every eighth line down is saved. Ultimately, all of the lines of pixels in the image are saved in this fashion.

When the image is downloaded to a Web browser, it will unveil in a similar manner. As different portions of the image load simultaneously, our eyes can piece together what the file represents well before the whole image has downloaded (see Figure 19.4).

Interlacing serves two purposes. First, if a person can recognize an image before the entire graphic has downloaded, the viewer can move on to reading other information on the page. This is particularly important for people who are operating with very little bandwidth. Second, the interlacing effect can serve as limited entertainment that helps engage the viewer as the rest of the graphic downloads.

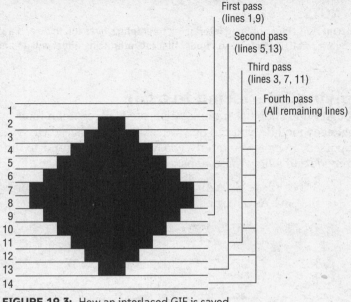

First pass
(lines 1,9)

Second pass
(lines 5,13)

Third pass
(lines 3, 7, 11)

Fourth pass
(All remaining lines)

FIGURE 19.3: How an interlaced GIF is saved

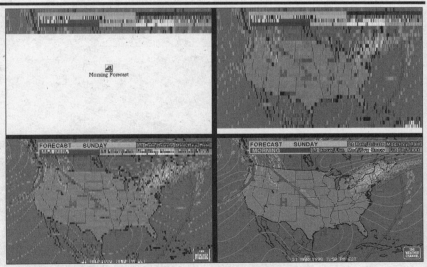

FIGURE 19.4: An interlaced GIF downloading from the Web

NOTE

Only consider applying interlacing to graphics over 10K in size. If a graphic is very small, it will load so rapidly that the interlacing effect will go unnoticed.

Applying Interlacing to a GIF

Although Photoshop has more sophisticated GIF creation tools in its ImageReady module, you can quickly create an interlaced GIF with Photoshop itself. To create an interlaced GIF, convert a graphic to Indexed Color mode and follow these steps:

1. Select File ➤ Save As from the Menu Bar. This will bring up the Save As dialog box.

2. From the Save As drop-down menu, select the CompuServe GIF file format and click Save. This will bring up the GIF Options dialog box.

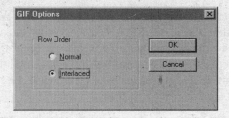

3. From the Row Order options, select the Interlaced radio button.

4. Click OK.

The GIF will now gradually render itself as it is downloaded in a modern Web browser.

Transparency

The Transparency effect is how you make one or more colors in a graphic "invisible," allowing other underlying graphics to show through. Why would you need to create a graphic with transparent colors? The most common reason is that all Web graphics are confined to a rectilinear shape. It is not possible to save a circle or irregularly shaped object without also including the space around it.

GIF's Transparency effect is a way to solve that problem. For example, in Figure 19.5 we have a sphere placed above a patterned background image. The graphic has no transparency effect, and the area surrounding the sphere is black. Clearly, the sphere is not integrated into the overall design.

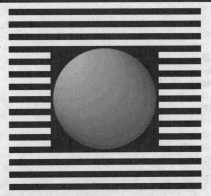

FIGURE 19.5: An opaque graphic on a patterned background

Another problem with the Web is that most Web browsers still do not support absolute positioning. If a Web page has a dramatic background image and a designer places a graphic on top of that image, there is no way to predict exactly where that top image will end up. The end result is a background and graphic combination that doesn't line up properly (see Figure 19.6).

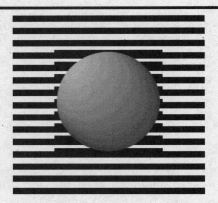

FIGURE 19.6: A misaligned Web graphic and background

Instead of including some of the background image in the graphic, a better approach is to put the sphere on a solid color and make the color transparent. The final effect looks much more integrated (see Figure 19.7).

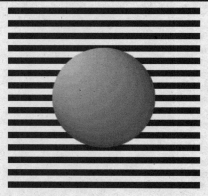

FIGURE 19.7: A transparent graphic on a graphic background

Applying the Transparency Effect

Once you have designed a Web graphic and converted it to Indexed Color mode, you're ready to apply a Transparency effect, and learn about Photoshop's Save for Web facility at the same time.

1. Choose Save for Web from the File menu, to open your image in ImageReady's Save For Web dialog box.

2. ImageReady has three preview windows, marked with tabs in the document labeled Optimized, 2-Up, and 4-Up. Click the 2-Up tab for the view shown in this figure.

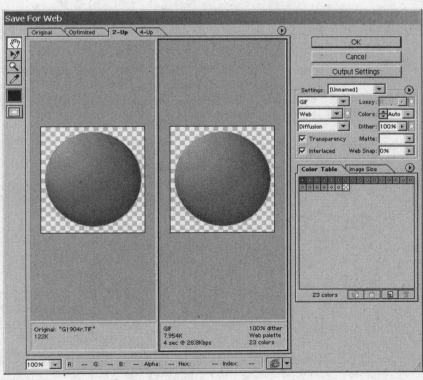

NOTE

The Optimized view shows what your image will look like with ImageReady's default optimization; the 2-Up tab displays your original image at the left or top, with the optimized version at the right or underneath (the layout depends on the orientation of your original image). The 4-Up tab displays your original image and three possible optimization schemes.

3. Choose the Optimized tab. Choose the file format in which you want to save the image. Here, I've selected GIF, the Web palette, diffusion, and both transparency and interlacing from the settings at the right side of the dialog box.

NOTE

If you've created a custom set of parameters for a particular file format, you can save those settings for re-use by selecting Save Settings from the Optimize palette's flyout menu.

4. Click the 4-Up button to view several possible optimization scenarios, as shown in the next image. Click in the preview showing the option that looks best to you.

5. Click the Eyedropper tool at the left side of the dialog box, and then use it to choose a color that will be transparent in the final GIF. In this case, you'd want to click the transparent area outside the circle.

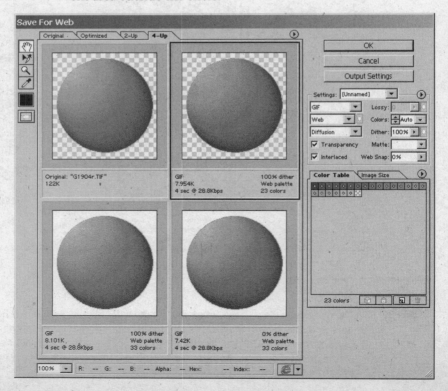

5. Click OK to produce the Save Optimized As dialog box to save your fine-tuned image.

Halos

One of the pitfalls of using the Transparency tool is that it can create an effect called *halos*. Photoshop applies anti-aliasing to smooth the edges of objects as they are drawn. For example, if a dark blue circle is drawn on a white background, Photoshop will create intermediate colors—in this case lighter blues—between the edges of the circle and the background (see Figure 19.8).

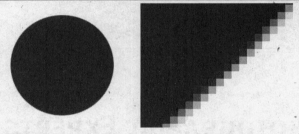

FIGURE 19.8: Photoshop's anti-aliasing technique

While this smoothing effect makes Photoshop graphics looks great, it can play havoc with graphics that have transparent backgrounds. When such images are put on the Web and placed on top of patterns or other colors, the anti-aliasing "fringe" becomes apparent. Figure 19.9 shows a black circle on a black background. Ideally, the result should be a completely black screen. But in this case, the halo creates an outline of the circle.

While halos can never be totally eliminated, there are a couple of preventative steps you can take. First, choose a transparency color that is as close as possible in hue and value to the color or pattern that the graphic will be sitting on. If a Web background image is a brick wall, select a dark red for the transparency color. Photoshop will create intermediate steps from the edge of the object to the dark red color that will be much harder to see once the object is placed on the brick wall background.

The second step is to pick background patterns that have as little contrast as possible. Patterns like black and white checkerboard are especially hard to deal with. In general, most Web designers stay away from full-screen, patterned background images to avoid problems with halos.

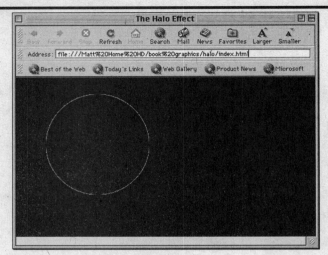

FIGURE 19.9: The halo effect

Joint Photographic Experts Group (JPEG)

The Joint Photographic Experts Group (JPEG—pronounced "jay-peg") is a compression standard that was developed for shrinking the file size of continuous tone images. It is best applied to photographs or graphics with complicated shading and lighting effects. Common uses of the JPEG format on the Web include product shots, 3D-rendered environments, and subtly shaded graphics.

Compression

JPEG compresses an image by saving a complete black-and-white version of it and most of its color information. Since not all of the color information is retained, JPEG is called a *lossy* format. This lossy nature of JPEG is usually seen, especially in highly compressed files, as a fuzzy or noisy patchwork of pixels (see Figure 19.10).

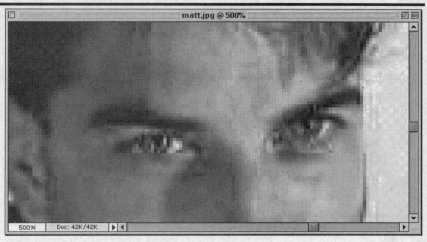

FIGURE 19.10: Detail of JPEG's noisy compression

Unlike the GIF compression algorithm that analyzes files line by line, JPEG breaks the image into zones of similar color. Thus, using the JPEG format for stark graphics that have large areas of the same color usually offers poor results. In such situations, GIF is a better alternative and compresses files much better than JPEG (see Figure 19.11).

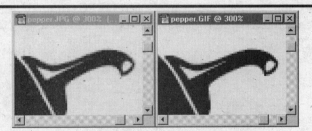

FIGURE 19.11: JPEG versus GIF in a line art scenario

However, JPEG shines as a compression method from both a file size and a quality standpoint when it is applied to graphics that contain a wide range of tonal values. Figure 19.12 demonstrates how subtle values are retained much better with the JPEG format.

FIGURE 19.12: JPEG versus GIF in a wide tonal range scenario

WARNING

Always edit work in the original native Photoshop file and not from subsequent JPEGs. Even the highest quality setting in Photoshop's JPEG encoder creates a lossy image that is unsuitable for additional editing.

The Photoshop JPEG Encoder

You can use ImageReady to optimize JPEGs just as you did with a GIF in the previous section. However, you can also save JPEGs from Photoshop's File menu. JPEG Options dialog box pops up automatically to let you make the required settings.

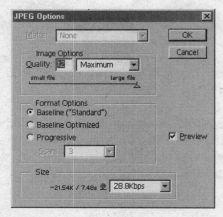

The upper portion of the dialog box is dedicated to adjusting the Image Options via the Quality setting. Zero is the lowest quality, and 12

is the highest quality. As indicated on the controls, a lower quality setting results in a smaller file and faster download time, and a higher quality setting results in a larger file and slower download time. Figure 19.13 demonstrates the relative difference in file size based on the two settings.

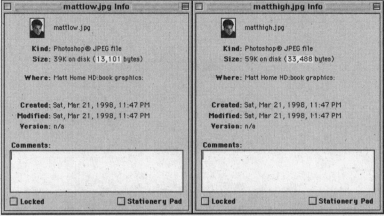

FIGURE 19.13: A low-quality versus a high-quality JPEG

TIP

To check a file size in Windows, right-click the file and select Properties. On the Mac, click the file once and select File ➤ Get Info. In both dialog boxes, be sure to refer to the figure in parentheses—this is the exact file size.

The middle portion of the JPEG Options dialog box provides formatting options. The Baseline Optimized feature provides enhanced color quality and offers slightly smaller file size compared to the Baseline ("Standard") option. The Progressive option creates an effect similar to interlacing, which is discussed earlier in the chapter. The bottom portion of the JPEG Options dialog box provides insight into the size of the file and how long it will take to download at various modem speeds.

TIP

Unlike GIFs, JPEGs cannot be saved in Indexed Color mode. Instead, save JPEGs in RGB color mode.

Creating a JPEG

To create a JPEG using Photoshop, follow these steps:

1. Open a document in RGB mode and select File ➤ Save A Copy from the Menu Bar. The Save As dialog box appears.

2. In the Save As dialog box, select the JPEG format from the Save As drop-down menu and click Save. The JPEG Options dialog box appears.

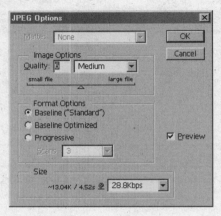

TIP

The Matte drop-down is active in the JPEG Options dialog box if you have transparent pixels in the image you are saving. Unlike the GIF format, JPEG does not support transparency. The Matte feature simply allows you to convert transparent areas to a selected color.

3. In the Image Options area, adjust the quality to a setting that is appropriate for your image. Quality settings from 3 to 6 often strike a good balance between quality and file size.

4. Select Baseline Optimized from the Format Options area.

5. Toggle the Size drop-down menu to see how long the graphic will take to download at different modem speeds.

6. Click OK.

NOTE

It is best to experiment with different levels of compression for each JPEG and arrive at a setting that balances quality and file size.

Progressive JPEGs

One of the features of Photoshop's JPEG Encoder is the ability to create progressive files. Progressive JPEGs are similar to interlaced GIFs in that they affect the way a JPEG appears as it is downloaded. Rather than load from top to bottom, progressive JPEGs download different areas of the graphic at the same time. This provides the viewer with an overall sense of what is contained in the image before the entire JPEG is completely downloaded.

Photoshop's JPEG Options dialog box offers a Progressive option in the Format Options area. The Progressive option provides a Scans setting that can be set from 3 to 5. The selection reflects the successive number of steps the file will render as it is downloaded. For example, Scans set to 3 will create a JPEG that downloads in three steps, while the 5 setting will download in five steps.

WARNING

While saving a JPEG with Photoshop's Progressive setting sometimes results in the smallest file size compared to Baseline and Baseline Optimized, the progressive JPEG standard is only supported by recent Web browsers.

Creating a Progressive JPEG

To create a progressive JPEG, follow these steps:

1. Open a document in RGB mode and select File ➢ Save A Copy from the Menu Bar.

2. In the Save As dialog box, select the JPEG format from the Save As drop-down menu and click Save.

3. Select Progressive from the Format Options area and indicate the number of Scans.

4. Click OK.

Portable Network Graphics(PNG)

In 1994, Unisys, the inventor of the GIF compression method, announced that they would be demanding licensing fees from developers of software that supported the GIF format. The potential cost associated with using GIF, combined with JPEG's lossy nature, led to a grassroots effort to develop a new graphic format. The proposed format would be patent free and would also improve upon the GIF and JPEG formats.

The result of this effort is called Portable Network Graphics (PNG—pronounced "ping"). Despite the fact that implementation of PNG on the Web still remains limited, Photoshop has provided the basic tools for encoding files to PNG format.

However, the PNG specification includes some truly spectacular capabilities, such as automatic cross-platform color adjustment and variable transparency effects, which have yet to be included in Photoshop's PNG Encoder. Adobe is expected to add these capabilities over time if the popularity of the format grows.

What's Next

One of the basic skills you'll need for working with color for the Web is an understanding of basic color theory. We'll delve into that in the next chapter, in which you'll learn about how color works for both printed and screen display applications.

Chapter 20

COLOR AND THE WEB

O ur very lives depend on light—it nourishes the fruits and vegetables that we eat, our physical bodies, and more. Light goes far beyond human sensory perception. But it is our own sensory perception that takes light and interprets it as color; color is dependent upon light.

This cycle is important because while color in and of itself is not a necessity for survival, it is an important part of our biological, social, and aesthetic worlds. Color is so integrated into our lives that its power goes unnoticed yet is tapped into every day.

Visual artists have to understand the subtle power of color in order to harness it and create art with impact. Web designers are no exception, and should take special care to study the lessons that color has to teach us.

Adapted from *Web by Design: The Complete Guide*
by Molly E. Holzchlag
ISBN 0-7821-2201-9   928 pages $49.99

This chapter covers a number of color issues that will help Web designers tap into that power using Photoshop, combine it with Web technologies, and use color to design successful Web sites with impact. Some of the topics featured include subtractive and additive color.

COLOR THEORY

Color has been studied for centuries, and there are many fine resources describing this evolution. Some of those resources can be found in the objects that make up fine art. Artists must relate to light and color to express their art, and so must you.

Color theory begins with the color wheel and proceeds into a breakdown of how variations of primary colors come into being. The computer environment is somewhat limited in its ability to properly exhibit color, but that is a limitation of technology and not of your ability to work within that technology once you have a good understanding of color theory.

Subtractive Color: Red, Yellow, Blue

The information in this section is based on the study of *Subtractive Color Synthesis*. Subtractive color absorbs, reflects, and transmits light. The synthesis is the process of this color in the natural world. Subtractive color begins with primary colors: red, yellow, and blue. The *subtractive color wheel* is made up of a sampling of colors, including the three primary colors, as well as secondary, intermediate, and tertiary colors.

Primaries   All colors are the result of some combination of three colors: red, yellow, and blue. These colors are referred to as *primary*, because they are the first colors to technically exist. Without them, no other color is possible.

Secondaries   The next step is to mix pairs of the primaries together. For example, if you mix red and yellow, you come up with orange. Blue and yellow create green, and purple is created by mixing red with blue. Orange, green, and purple are the *secondary* colors found on the color wheel.

Intermediates   When two primaries are mixed together in a ratio of 2:1, the results are referred to as *intermediate color*. These colors are gradations that lie between the primary and secondary colors.

> **Tertiaries**   Tertiary colors are combinations of primary colors in any other ratio than previously described.

Remember that this color wheel is based on the tactile world rather than the digital—it's the kind of color wheel you might be familiar with from childhood. It's important for you to gain a sense of how color is created and perceived off of the computer screen before you are introduced to the way it is created on the screen.

From your basic subtractive color wheel, a range of color components can emerge. The following relate directly to the color wheel.

> **Tints and shades**   Along with primary, secondary, tertiary, and intermediate colors, you can get *tints* by mixing colors with white to lighten, and *shades*, by adding black to a given color to darken it.

> **Similarity, complementary, and contrasts**   Colors that are adjacent to one another on the wheel, such as blue and purple, are considered to be *similar. Complementary* colors are those that are opposite on the wheel, such as orange and blue. Finally, *contrast* results from colors that are at least three (depending upon the color wheel you're looking at) colors removed from one another, such as red and green.

Other color components include properties, relationships, and effects.

Properties of Color

I'll admit it—I'm a shopaholic! I love clothing and shoes, and I especially love the color and textures of fabric. I often unwind by going on a shopping spree. I also enjoy looking through fashion catalogs, and one of my most relaxing times (until the credit card comes due, of course) is to sit back with a good catalog and a cup of hot Darjeeling tea.

Wine, chocolate, and peacock are only some of the colors that are in fashion this season. Where do these colors fit into the spectrum? What determines the difference between a navy blue and a peacock blue? What defines cinnamon versus cocoa?

Colors have properties, including hue, value, and saturation (also referred to as *intensity*). These properties are derived from the amount of color and how much light is used in that color.

> **Hue**   Hue is simply the visible difference of one color from another. For example, red is different than green, and purple is

different than brown. Whether a color is primary, secondary, intermediate, or tertiary isn't important with regard to hue. Hues can be described as warm or cool.

Warmth   Hues found in the yellow-to-red range are considered to be *warm*. They emit a sense of heat.

Coolness   *Cool* colors are those ranging from green to blue. Think of ice blue, or the cool sense of a forest a deep green can inspire.

Value   Chocolate brown is darker than tan, and sky blue is lighter than navy. A color's *value* is defined by the amount of light or dark in that color.

Saturation   Also referred to as *intensity*, you can think of *saturation* as being the brightness of a color. Peacock blue is very bright, whereas navy is rather dull. Similarly, those popular neon lime greens reminiscent of the 1960s are much more intense than a forest green.

NOTE

And what about black and white? As many people have heard described, black is all colors combined, and white is lack of color. Similarly, black can be described as absence of light, and white as *being* light. A more technical way to think about black and white is to refer to the properties of hue and saturation—which neither black nor white possess! Why then, are there "shades" of gray? The reason is found in *value*. The amount of light or dark in white or black determines the resulting value of gray (Figure 20.1).

FIGURE 20.1: Black, white, and gray values

Each hue can contain a different value and saturation. When you think of all the variations that are potentially held within each of these properties, you can begin to see that color is much more than meets the eye.

Color Relationships

I'm in a red rage! I'm green with envy over my ex-boyfriend's purple passion for that peaches n' cream blonde beauty he started dating. I'm so blue, in fact, that I've thought about whiting out his name from all of my little black books.

Colors, like people, have relationships with one another. Some, like a good marriage, are harmonious. Others, like the unhappy example in the former paragraph, are discordant. *Harmonious* colors are those that, when combined, foster a sense of peace and relaxation—a light shade of peach, a shade of light green, and a shade of dark green create a harmonious mix. *Discordant* colors are those that cause you to do a double-take—bright yellow and black can be considered discordant.

Color Effects

Beyond properties and relationships, there are special color effects. Silk and satin shine, the inside of a seashell has a multicolored radiance, and religious imagery seems to be of an almost unworldly light. These effects can be created by artists and designers and can quickly add appeal to a given design.

Color effects include the following:

Luster Silk and satin are *lustrous*; they have a shining quality about them. This quality is the visual perception of small areas of light combined with black contrast. While this is achieved naturally with a given fabric's relationship to light, artists can create it by relying on black contrast between the lustrous areas and the background, as in the picture below.

Iridescence I have a clamshell sitting on my desk. I found it on a New Jersey beach when I was a child. I was undoubtedly fascinated by the many colors inside that changed like a sparkling rainbow as I held it to the light. This is *iridescence* or *opalescence*. A designer can achieve an iridescent effect by using gray in the same areas of luster's black contrast.

Luminosity   This effect is an interesting one—it relies on contrast just like its companions, luster and iridescence. However, *luminosity* is more about delicate light differences. Objects appear luminous when the contrast is very subtle.

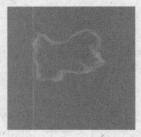

Transparency   Plastic wrap is *transparent*—it is clear. Transparent effects cause the eye to perceive the image as being see-through.

Chroma   What happens when colored light hits a colored object? When the winter's white and streaming sun comes through my window and lands on the Saltillo tile on my sun porch, the areas where patches of sun land are lighter than the patches that are shaded. This effect is *chromatic* (chroma means color).

Today's sophisticated graphic programs, such as Photoshop, offer digital methods to achieve a wide range of effects. Web designers can use Photoshop to create graphics and can apply these effects as appropriate their work.

WHAT COLORS MEAN

Fast food restaurants often use yellow, red, and orange for their design motifs. Hotel rooms frequently use colors such as brown, tan, or shades of blue or green. A judge's chamber might have rich mahogany wood, green marble, deep maroon leather. Clothing, as I've already noted, can be any color.

The way we use color in our everyday lives—whether we are consciously aware of it or not—is very specific. It's no accident that a person who wishes to remain inconspicuous will choose neutral colors rather than shocking pink, or that a magazine's cover is bright.

Colors have potent psychological impact. This has been proven in many studies. That impact may also be different depending upon an individual's social upbringing. Purple, in the English-speaking western world, is associated with royalty, but in the Islamic world, it is associated with prostitutes! Similarly, black is the color of mourning for most people in the Western world, whereas white denotes mourning in many Eastern cultures.

Designers need to be familiar with the general meanings of color, and would do well to check with a client if that client has a specific audience. For example, if you were creating an Islamic online newspaper, knowing about that culture's color associations might keep you out of an unfortunate or embarrassing situation.

The following chart defines the meanings of prominently used colors—bearing in mind that most readers of this book are from Western, Judeo-Christian cultures.

Color	Significance
Red	Love, passion, heat, flame, feminine power
Green	Fertility, peace, nature, earth
Blue	Truth, clarity, dignity, power
Yellow	Energy, joy, lightness of being

Color	Significance
Purple	Royalty, wealth, sophistication
Brown	Masculinity, stability, weight
Black	Death, rebellion, darkness, elegance
White	Light, purity, cleanliness, emptiness

WEB COLOR TECHNOLOGY

Digital delivery of color information is rather different from the way the eye delivers color to the brain, and the way the brain deals with the perception of that color. Computers, in a sense, are finite in their ability to deliver color to the screen, because technology simply cannot achieve the more powerful abilities of tangible nature.

Computer Color: Additive Synthesis

Computers can do a pretty darn good job of dealing with color, but they must approach it from a different mathematical method than in the "real" world. The essence of color technology as defined by the computer is reliant upon three elements: the quality of the computer, the computer card, and the computer monitor. If one is substandard, computer color will be substandard.

It's also important to note that computer platforms handle color differently, as you will soon see. Also, what you are looking at color *through* is going to determine the quality of that color. In the case of Web design, it is the browser that limits color significantly; the designer must be well aware of this, in order to deftly move through the digital world with strength and consistency.

Additive Color: Red, Green, Blue

But wait, I just taught you that red, blue, and *yellow* are necessary to create other colors. While this is true in the tactile world, in the digital world, the three primary colors are red, green, and blue referred to as RGB for short.

How did this happen? Computer monitors and televisions cannot take paint, like you can, and mix it together to get other colors. They must *add* color based on the RGB system. Additive color is unlike the tangible world's subtractive color. In the RGB world, adding red to green creates yellow! If you did this with paint, pigment, or dye, you'd end up with a dark brown.

RGB values are derived from a method that numerically determines how much red, green, and blue make up the color in question. Each color contains a percentage of red, green, and blue. In Photoshop, you can use the color picker tool and get RGB values immediately (see Figure 20.2).

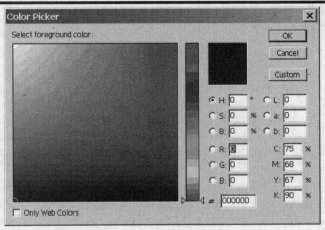

FIGURE 20.2: RGB options in Photoshop

NOTE

What about other color methods, like CMY color? Cyan-magenta-yellow color is used in print, which has specific requirements not immediately necessary for this Web design discussion. Print designers must be familiar with this color method in order to work with computer-to-print color.

Gamma

Of great significance to digital color, and specifically to Web color, is *Gamma*. Gamma is a complex mathematical system that, very simply described, influences the way the information on the computer screen is displayed. In order to display that information with the most accurate color, Gamma must often be corrected to the appropriate numerical value.

Different computer platforms offer different methods of dealing with Gamma correction. Macintosh and SGI machines come with the necessary equipment to perform Gamma correction—so unless your monitor is very old, or there is some malfunction with the system, Macs and SGI machines present color as accurately as possible. This is one reason why designers have preferred Macs, and why SGI machines are frequently used in video and animation production.

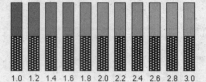

FIGURE 20.3: Gamma Measurement Image

When a computer offers little or no Gamma correction, images will appear darker—so much so that a lot of the color that the viewer *should* see goes by misperceived, or completely unseen. This, in turn, means that your beautiful color schemes may not appear beautiful to a significant portion of your audience.

What can you do about this? Some experts claim that you should always work in higher contrasts in order to allow for the best chance of having your color seen. This isn't always realistic, so my recommendation is that you maintain a strong awareness of the problem, and design with high contrast *when you know the audience will require it.*

To return to the very first chapter's lessons on accessibility—determine the importance of your viewing audience's need to see the information. If many of your visitors are older, or have known visual problems, a higher-contrast design might be in your best interest. Also, for information-rich sites, you may always offer a downloadable or online text version of the site, being sure to use white and black (strong contrast) as the delivery mechanism for that information.

RGB to Hexadecimal

In order to translate RGB color values into a system that HTML understands, you will have to convert the RGB value to *hexadecimal.*

Hexadecimal is the base 16 number system, which consists of the numerals 0–15 and the letters A–F. A byte (8 bits) can be represented using two hexadecimal characters, which make any combination of binary information less cumbersome to understand. In relation to Web color, hexadecimal values *always* appear with six characters. For example, a hexadecimal value will look like this: "FFCCFF."

You can find the hexadecimal value of any color on your own with Photoshop's Color Picker, or by setting one of the two Color Readouts in the Info Palette to Web Color. Choose Palette Options from the Info Palette's flyout menu, and select Web Color from the readout's drop-down list. Thereafter, the color of any pixels under the cursor will be displayed in hexadecimal values in that readout in the Info Palette.

Safe Palettes

A safe palette is a palette containing 216 RGB colors that are going to remain as stable from one browser to another, between platforms, and at different monitor color capacities and resolutions as possible—taking into consideration the effects that problems with Gamma might create.

If colors outside the safe palette are used, many potential Web site visitors will experience *dithering*. This is the process by which the computer puts the color it has available into the color you've called for. Yes, that's right, if you've asked for a soft, pale yellow outside the safe palette, you might end up having visitors who see that color as bright neon!

So why only 216 colors, when many computers can display 256 colors, and most sold today display *millions* of colors?

The first answer is "blame it on Microsoft."

When developing the Windows 3.1 Operating System for the PC, Microsoft reserved 40 colors from the original 256 to use as system colors. Since so many visitors to the Web use PCs, the problems stemming from this limitation have been far-reaching.

The second answer is "blame it on Netscape."

Once you're done blaming the problem on Microsoft, you can extend the blame to include Netscape—who developed a 216-color palette *into* the browser!

After you're done enjoying a few minutes sputtering mean words to software developers who have further complicated your life as a Web designer, you can thank several people for figuring out ways of providing solutions to the color problem. The *safe palette* is the result—a color palette that provides the 216 non-dithering colors. You can select from this palette to create your graphics and browser-based color.

WHAT'S NEXT

Adobe Photoshop includes a powerful image-editing tool that's optimized for Web graphics, called ImageReady. Your introduction to this weapon is slated for the next chapter.

Chapter 21

CREATING WEB GRAPHICS

As you probably know, a Web page is not one large, single graphic. Instead, it is a mosaic of smaller, individual graphics and computer-generated type held together with HTML.

This chapter covers all of the types of graphics that comprise a typical Web page. Keep in mind that not all of the graphics mentioned need to be included on every Web page you design. If you make your graphic choices based on a design's underlying theme or concept, you'll be in good shape. You'll learn the nuts and bolts of inserting graphics into a Web page in the chapter that follows this one.

Adapted from *Mastering Photoshop 5.5 for the Web*
by Matt Staznitskas
0-7821-2605-7   672 pages $39.99

IMAGEREADY

For years, Web designers were second-class citizens when it came to Photoshop. Adobe had invested tremendous resources in making Photoshop the premier image-editing tool for print, so when the Web came along, much of the program was not of use to Web designers. Since version 5.5 of the program, Adobe has beefed up its Web graphic formatting tools, and the program can be used to create some great site layouts and images.

However, Photoshop can't perform highly specific Web chores like conveniently creating Web background tiles, animation, and JavaScript mouseovers. And that's precisely the point of ImageReady, a separate application that ships with Photoshop 5.5 and later versions. ImageReady makes creating specific types of Web graphics a breeze. The program also seamlessly works with Photoshop files.

Since ImageReady is used to create many of the effects and graphics depicted in this chapter, we will now take a look at this very special application.

The ImageReady Interface

At first glance, ImageReady and Photoshop look so similar that you may think that you're in the same application (see Figure 21.1). Many of the features are similar, including support for layers, history, and color. The main toolbar also contains many of the same Photoshop tools, including the Marquee, Move, and Type tools.

By far the biggest physical difference between the two interfaces is the presence of an Animation palette that provides a way to create animated GIFs from layered Photoshop files.

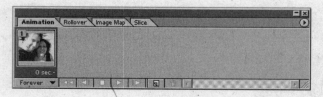

NOTE

See Chapter 23 for more about using ImageReady's animation features.

FIGURE 21.1: The ImageReady interface

Launching ImageReady

ImageReady can be launched like any other application. However, Image-Ready is now tightly integrated into Photoshop. To launch ImageReady within the Photoshop environment, do the following:

1. Launch Photoshop and create an image.

2. Save the image.

3. At the bottom of the main Photoshop toolbar, click the Jump To icon (see Figure 21.2). This will launch the ImageReady application with your Photoshop graphic in the main window.

FIGURE 21.2: Activating the Jump To feature at the bottom of the Photoshop toolbar

Part iv

Working between Applications

The great thing about working between Photoshop and ImageReady is that you can make changes to an image in one application and the edits will be automatically made to the image in the other application. Check it out:

1. Following Steps 1–3 above, create an image in Photoshop and use the Jump To button to launch ImageReady.

2. Next, jump back to Photoshop and make an edit to the image.

3. Select File ➢ Save (or press Ctrl+S) to save the edits to the image.

4. Click Photoshop's Jump To button to go back over to ImageReady.

5. ImageReady will appear, and the image will be automatically updated with the changes you made in Photoshop.

You will now see that the graphic in ImageReady has been updated to reflect the changes you made in Photoshop. This can be a very powerful tool when you are working on a graphic in ImageReady and want to utilize a particular Photoshop tool.

BACKGROUND GRAPHICS

As shown in Figure 21.3, the best way to think about creating Web graphics is to envision a Web page as having two planes. The top plane is where all of the assorted Web graphics sit—headers, menu buttons, photos, and so on. The bottom plane is where the background sits. Backgrounds can be either a solid color specified in HTML or actual graphics.

Background Specifics

Using graphics to create backgrounds is a great way to add style to your pages. However, if you're going to use them, use them well. The Web is filled with graphic backgrounds that are clichéd, or that clash with the design. Background graphics should serve the overall design, not detract from it.

Backgrounds can be in either GIF or JPEG format, depending on what kind of image you use. With careful optimization, you can create very complex background designs that download quickly. Generally speaking, your backgrounds should be less than 20KB. On the Web, smaller is definitely better.

Plane 1:
Individual Web graphics and text

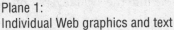

Plane 2:
Web background color/image

FIGURE 21.3: The two layers in a Web page: Web graphics (top) and the background area (bottom)

WARNING

Background graphics should never be transparent. It's also a good idea to avoid interlaced GIFs or progressive JPEGs. Stick to standard, noninterlaced GIFs or JPEGs for maximum background stability.

There are two main background styles: square tile and margin-style tile strip. Each style has subsets, and you will learn to work with a variety of functional as well as decorative graphic types.

Square Tiles

Strictly speaking, all backgrounds are tiles. Whether they take the form of a square or a rectangle, they literally *tile* into the available background space.

Using square tiles, you can create a pattern or wallpaper effect. Tiles should typically be 100 pixels by 100 pixels, although you will find occasion to make them larger, or perhaps smaller. The 100×100 guideline, however, is a good one to follow in most instances of square tiling.

If you have a visible border around your tile, or a single image centered on the tile, you will end up showing the world that your background tiles are repeated (see Figure 21.4). While this effect may be desirable for your design, be aware that it is usually considered amateurish.

For professional results, you'll want to create a tile that is *seamless*. Seamless tiles create a visual effect much like wallpaper on a wall. The design is consistent and smooth.

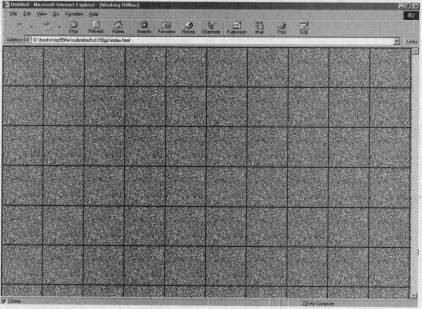

FIGURE 21.4: Repeated tile with visible borders

Seamless Tiles

Figure 21.5 shows an image that would normally be very difficult to translate into a seamless background tile. Thanks to ImageReady, creating seamless tiles is a snap.

WARNING

A background tile should be appropriate in both dimensional size and kilobytes. Remember that the larger the file, the longer the load time.

FIGURE 21.5: An image to be used as a background graphic in a Web page

To create a seamless tile with ImageReady, follow these steps:

1. Create an image in Photoshop to be used as a background tile.

2. Select the Jump To option at the bottom of the Photoshop toolbar to launch ImageReady.

3. In ImageReady, select Filter ➤ Other ➤ Tile Maker. This will launch the Tile Maker dialog box.

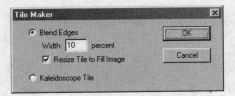

4. You can use either Blend Edges or Kaleidoscope Tile. In Figure 21.6, the Blend Edges option was used for a more typical background image.

Part iv

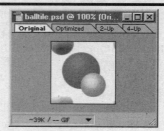

FIGURE 21.6: The image with the Tile Maker filter applied

The edges of the graphic are now blended and can be used as a background in a Web page (see Figure 21.7).

An important concern regarding background design is readability. Your background shouldn't interfere with a visitor's ability to read the text that will be placed on top of the background. Be sure to fully test your design with the chosen text and link colors to ensure that both the aesthetic look of the tile and the clarity of any text remain intact.

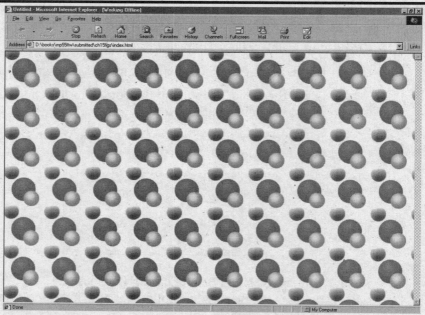

FIGURE 21.7: The tiled background in a Web page

Margin Backgrounds

The problem with using HTML to specify background color is that it can be only one solid color. For example, you cannot use HTML to create a page that is half black and half white. For this reason, margin background graphics are extremely popular on the Web. The margin field can be made up of a flat color (see Figure 21.8) or a texture or design (see Figure 21.9). For the sake of readability, in most cases you will want to stick with flat color margins.

Margin backgrounds can be either decorative or functional. Decorative margins are used to create color and texture splashes, fills, or bleeds. Functional margins use the margin area for both decorative and practical purposes, such as the implementation of links, text information, buttons, or a combination thereof.

The major concern with margin backgrounds is size. Because all backgrounds are loaded in a repeat pattern, you must understand how this pattern affects the design you're creating. Vertical repetition can work to your advantage because you can keep the tile thin and use the vertical repeat to create the pattern. If a margin background is not wide enough, however, it will repeat at inconvenient points along the horizontal axis in your design. Furthermore, this repetition causes problems at a variety of resolutions.

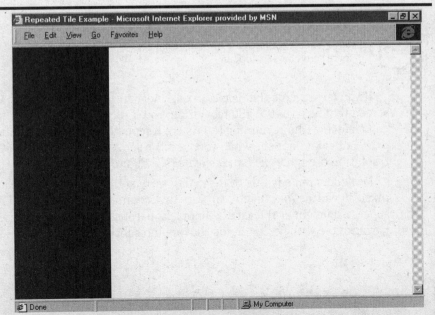

FIGURE 21.8: A margin background with flat color

Part IV

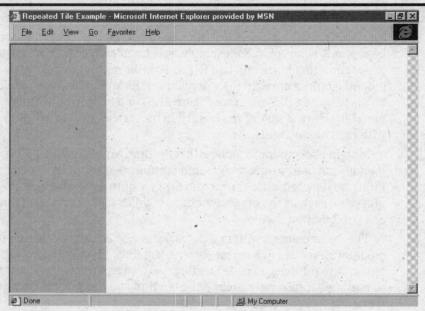

FIGURE 21.9: A margin background with a textured margin field

NOTE

Background graphics tile into all of the browser's available space but do not force scroll bars to appear.

If you create a tile that is 640 pixels wide, and you're viewing on a screen that has a 640 × 480 resolution, you'll see the background that you created without running the risk of it repeating on the horizontal axis. But what happens when you view the same page at an 800 × 600 resolution or higher? The tile repeats (see Figure 21.10).

Designers remedy this by designing vertical tiles at an average of 1,200 pixels in width. Your height can vary to accommodate the design. The suggested height is at least 20–30 pixels, because some older browsers have trouble with backgrounds that are too short.

FIGURE 21.10: A background that isn't wide enough risks being repeated at a higher resolution.

Top margin designs work in a similar fashion, but the repeat axis problem occurs in reverse. If you don't make the tile long enough to fit the page, the top margin will repeat (see Figure 21.11). Therefore, top margin backgrounds should be long—as long as you need for a given page. The width can be kept short, however, as the tiling mechanism will fill the page appropriately (see Figure 21.12).

WARNING

Test your Web page backgrounds on as many computers and browsers as possible. You'll be surprised how often text and graphics move around in different environments and ruin your background effect.

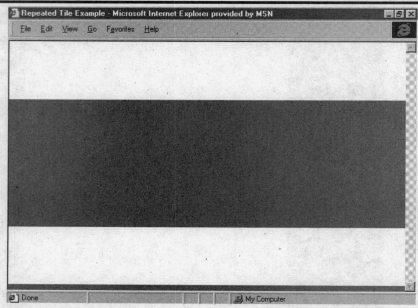

FIGURE 21.11: A vertical tile repeating on the horizontal axis

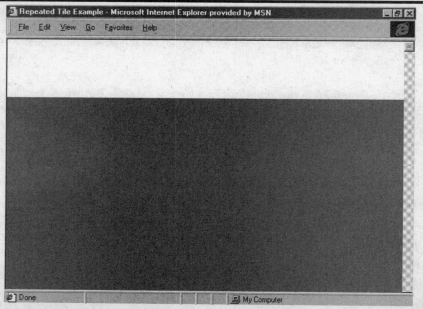

FIGURE 21.12: The desired effect of a top margin tile

Making a Decorative Margin

Decorative margins use a pattern within the margin (see Figure 21.13).

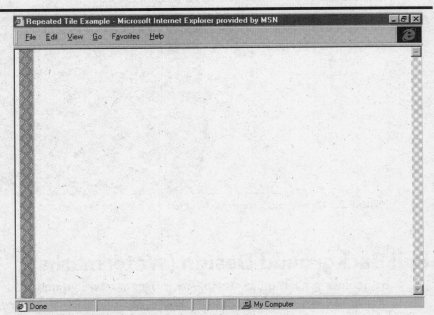

FIGURE 21.13: A decorative margin pattern

To create a decorative margin, open Photoshop and follow these steps:

1. Create a new file, with dimensions 1,200 pixels wide by 50 pixels high.

2. Fill the file with the color or pattern you want.

3. Make a new layer and add the decorative pattern to the section desired. In the example, a decorative strip was added to the left.

4. Choose File ➤ Save For Web to optimize the image as a GIF.

Functional Margins

Essentially, a functional margin is similar to a decorative margin, except that you must have enough room for content, as well as ensure that any pattern you use does not interfere with the text or graphics that will go on top of it.

To build a functional margin, follow the same steps for creating a decorative margin in the previous section. Remember, however, that a functional margin will typically be wider (see Figure 21.14).

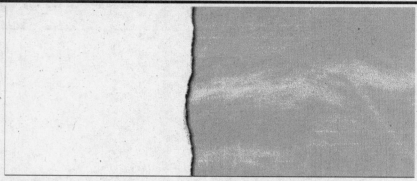

FIGURE 21.14: Functional margins tend to be wider than decorative ones.

Full Background Design (Watermarks)

Sometimes you'll want to use full-size images as a background, also known as a *watermark*. In these instances, you'll have to determine how to handle repetition—people with very large monitors might see the image repeat down the page depending on how large you make it. Unless it's at least 800 pixels deep by 1,200 pixels wide, many people will be able to see it repeat.

Another concern with full backgrounds is file size. Logically, the larger the file's dimensions, the bigger the file will be in terms of kilobytes. However, if the file is designed and optimized properly, the size can remain within acceptable limits, and the effects can be quite interesting (see Figure 21.15).

Making a Watermark

To make a watermark, open Photoshop and follow these steps:

1. Create a new file with appropriate dimensions, preparing for an 800 × 600 average, but keeping in mind that visitors will be viewing the site at resolutions of 640 × 480 and higher.

2. Fill the file with your Web-safe background color.

3. Make a new layer.

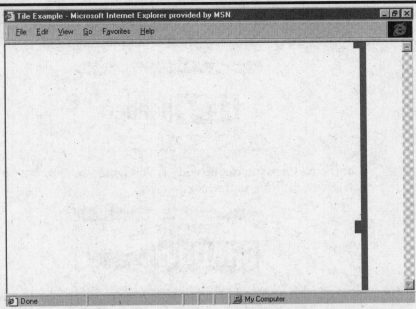

FIGURE 21.15: This full-page background is highly artistic, and any possible repeat factor won't negatively affect the design.

4. Add your watermark to the new layer.

5. Use the Opacity slider to adjust the image for the best visual advantage.

6. Save the image in an appropriate Web file format (GIF or JPEG).

WARNING
Older Web browsers do not support JPEG files as a background image format.

HEADERS

Using graphical headers is a nice departure from tired HTML-based text headers. You can add logo-graphic material, control your choice of fonts. for more information on graphic type), and use colors, patterns, and light sources as you so desire.

Part iv

Shown below is a flat header using graphic type. Already we've departed from the limitations of HTML-based text. While you see it only in grayscale, the type uses several colors and variations.

But there's more you can do with it. Now a drop shadow can be added, which gives a little fun to the look.

If you compare these headers to the plain HTML header shown below, you can easily see why graphic headers are so attractive to designers.

Plain HTML Header

TIP

Headers for most Web sites measure approximately 350 × 50 pixels, although this will vary greatly depending upon your look and feel.

BUTTONS

As depicted in Figure 21.16, buttons help add color, style, and interest to your Web pages. Buttons can be a combination of images, logographic material, and type. In the following exercises, we'll work with type, but you should feel free to experiment with a variety of graphic materials.

FIGURE 21.16: Different types of Web page buttons all developed by creating simple shapes, applying the Bevel And Emboss layer effect, and adding a text element or symbol

Creating a Button

Creating buttons is very similar to creating graphic headers, except that their size is obviously going to be different. In this example, we'll develop a circular button that is 50 × 50 pixels in dimension. Follow these steps:

1. Select File ➢ New.

2. Create a file 50 × 50 pixels in size.

3. Add a layer to the file by selecting Layer ➢ New ➢ Layer.

4. Use the circular Marquee tool to draw a circle.

5. Fill the circle with a color by selecting a Web-safe color and pressing Alt+Backspace (Windows) or Option+Backspace (Mac).

6. Give the image dimension by selecting Layer Style ➢ Bevel And Emboss and using the Inner Bevel style. The button will now have dimension.

7. Add type with the Type tool.

8. Save the graphic as a GIF by choosing File ➤ Save For Web.

As shown here, the final effect is a button with dimension and interest.

PHOTOS AND ILLUSTRATIONS

Photos and illustrations add visual information to a Web page, and used in combination, they can be quite striking. One problem with combining photos and illustrations is that the two types of images usually are best saved in different formats. Flat illustrations are best saved as GIFs, while photos are better saved as JPEGs.

Slicing Complex Artwork

The key to saving graphics like the one in Figure 21.17 is to slice up an image in order to separate out the photo and graphic elements.

Fortunately, ImageReady has an automated feature for slicing different parts of a graphic and creating the HTML that will allow the image to be reassembled.

FIGURE 21.17: An image that combines photos and illustrations

To generate the elements of an HTML table-based mosaic, follow these steps:

1. Open an image in ImageReady and place guides along areas of the image where you would like it sliced up.

2. Select Slices ➤ Create Slices From Guides. As depicted below, the image now has indicators showing how the image will be chopped up.

3. Choose File ➤ Save Optimized As, and select Save HTML and Save Images in the Save Optimized As dialog box.

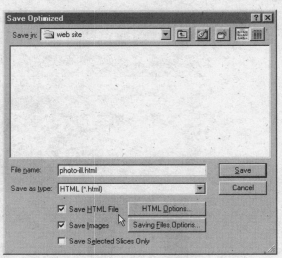

4. Now take a look at the directory in which you saved your file. You will notice that multiple images with a unique numbering system have been saved in an Images directory.

The best part is that ImageReady also creates the source code for the HTML that will display the image. Clicking the HTML file that ImageReady created will not only launch a Web browser with the mosaic intact, but by selecting View ➤ Source from a standard browser, you will see the actual HTML that ImageReady has created (see Figure 21.18).

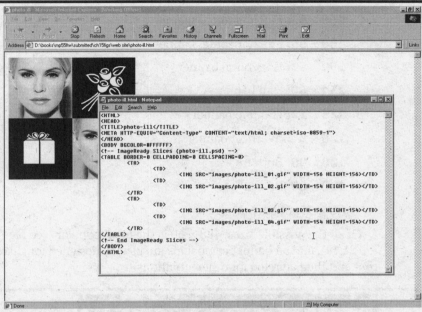

FIGURE 21.18: The resulting HTML generated by ImageReady

NOTE
See Chapter 22 for more about using HTML to build Web pages.

ADVERTISING BANNERS

Search engines and other content-driven Web sites tend to rely on ad banners to support themselves. Thus, designers are often asked by clients to create ad banners that will grab attention and drive visitors to a particular Web site. Ad banners are also used as *house ads* to promote other areas or happenings within a Web site.

Advertising banners can come in all shapes and sizes, with over 200 different ad dimensions in use. This poses significant problems and costs for advertisers, as well as for designers who often need to re-create a banner for a variety of different applications. However, there has been some standardization over the past few years. The following sizes are the most common (in pixels):

468 × 60: Full horizontal banner

460 × 55: Full horizontal banner

392 × 72: Horizontal banner

234 × 60: Half banner

125 × 125: Square banner

120 × 240: Vertical banner

120 × 90: Button

120 × 60: Button

88 × 31: Micro button

Of all the possible sizes, 468 × 60 is the most popular (see Figure 21.19), and ad banner campaigns are usually designed for this size first and then adapted for other situations.

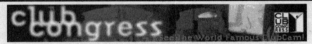

FIGURE 21.19: A standard-size ad banner, 468 × 60

Banners should also follow these guidelines:

▶ Banners are typically GIFs, often animated. Some content providers allow the use of other technologies as well, such as Java or Shockwave, but this is not common.

▶ Banners must be fairly small in file size. Eight kilobytes or less is usually the size required by content providers.

▶ Animated banners are usually not allowed to *loop* more than three times.

Again, individual content providers may have their own requirements. Be sure to contact your provider's sales rep for a list of exact specifications.

Creating a Standard Advertising Banner

To create a standard advertising banner, be sure to follow the guidelines in the prior section. Then follow these steps:

1. In Photoshop, select File ➢ New.

2. Create a file that is 468 × 60 pixels.

3. Select Edit ➢ Fill, and fill with the Web-safe color of your choice.

4. Add type or images as appropriate.

5. Select File ➢ Save For Web, and use the dialog box to create an optimized GIF that adheres to the file-size requirements of the site in which the banner will be placed.

Your banner is ready for prime time!

WHAT'S NEXT

Now that you know how to create many different kinds of images that can be used on the Web, you may want to pick up some tips on writing the HTML code that will place them on your Web page. That's scheduled for the next chapter.

Chapter 22

ADDING IMAGES TO YOUR WEB PAGES

Your next step toward becoming a Web graphics pro is including images, which can add pizzazz to your Web pages, help provide information, or just add a splash of color. The key to including images is to do so wisely—that is, choose graphics that have a purpose, use appropriate file formats, and employ graphics that help you design your pages effectively. By taking the time to use images wisely, you can maximize their effectiveness for your visitors.

In this chapter, we'll show you how to choose appropriate images, choose file formats, use images for different purposes, and develop image maps (those clickable images with multiple links). We'll cover general image map principles, so you'll be prepared to use all the different types of image maps, then describe the special image map tools built into ImageReady.

Adapted from *Mastering HTML 4 Premium Edition*
by Deborah S. Ray and Eric J. Ray
ISBN 0-7821-2524-7   1,216 pages $49.99

DEVELOPING IMAGES

Although images add life to your Web pages, they can become a liability if not developed properly. For example, images can take F-O-R-E-V-E-R to load, becoming an obstacle for your visitors. Likewise, images can unnecessarily hog page space (or disk space), perhaps obscuring important content. So, your goal in using images is to develop them properly by considering three things:

▶ File size

▶ Physical dimensions

▶ File type

Determining File Size

Think of image files as being three-dimensional, having height and width as well as a number of colors. For example, a 16-color image not only has height and width, which you can see on the screen, but it also has 16 *layers*, one for each color. Therefore, the image's basic file size equals width × height × color depth.

You can reduce file size and, therefore, make your images as efficient as possible with the following techniques:

▶ Reduce the number of colors. For example, you can reduce the color depth of an image that has millions of colors to only 256 colors with surprisingly little degradation in quality.

▶ Reduce the physical image size. For example, you can reduce an image from 600 × 400 pixels to 300 × 200 pixels. The resulting smaller image includes the details and clarity of the larger size, yet it occupies significantly less disk space. (You'll find guidelines for sizing images in the following section, "Dealing with Physical Size.")

▶ Use a format that *compresses* the file to cram more data into less space.

Dealing with Physical Size

The physical size of an image is its height and width, and affects not only how it appears in a browser, but also how quickly it loads. Just how big should images be? Well, that depends. Many sites use itty-bitty images, such as buttons and icons, that effectively add color or dimension to a Web page. Other sites use larger graphics for logos or button bars, which are also effective. There's no "right" size for images; instead, the key is to consider the following:

- ▶ The image's purpose
- ▶ The overall page design
- ▶ Your visitors' computer settings

Consider Image Purpose

Every time you add an image to a page, you need a good reason for doing so—to illustrate a point, to show a person or a location, to outline a process, or simply to add some color and zest to an otherwise humdrum document. Be sure that every image enhances content, design, or both.

When determining the size of an image, consider its importance. For example, if your visitors need an image to understand a concept, the image should be larger. On the other hand, an image that merely adds a splash of color should probably be a bit smaller. If you're not sure how important an image is, lean toward smaller. Remember, images add to loading time and can affect how easily a visitor can access your pages.

Consider Page Design

Images are visually "weighty" objects—that is, they attract attention faster than other page elements. Images that are too large often overwhelm page contents and obscure the message. When determining image size, in particular, consider how the image will appear relative to other page elements. Here are some questions to ask yourself:

- ▶ Will the page include multiple graphics?
- ▶ Will the page incorporate borders and shading, which are also weightier than text?
- ▶ Will the page contain a substantive amount of text or only a few words? Text can make up in volume what it lacks in visual weight. A lot of text balances a graphic more effectively than a small amount of text.

Consider Visitors' Computer Settings

Your visitors' computer settings will also affect how images appear on-screen. An image that's 600 × 400 pixels will take up practically the entire screen at a resolution of 640×480. But that same image will take up much less screen space on a computer set to $1{,}280 \times 1{,}040$. A good rule of thumb is to limit image size to no more than 600×400 pixels. An image of this size will fit completely within the browser window on Windows computers using the lowest (and, unfortunately, still quite common) screen resolution of 640×480 pixels. And, of course, if you can make images smaller, do so to help speed loading time.

TIP

To convey content adequately, few images need to be larger than 600×400 pixels. Something in the 300×200 pixels range is usually a good size for photographs, and buttons are generally 50×50 pixels or smaller.

ADDING IMAGES

In this section, we're going to create some Web pages for ASR Outfitters, a mountaineering and hiking supply company that is a mythical, miniversion of REI, the recreation equipment retailer. In the process, you'll learn how to include images in an HTML document. Although this may seem like putting the cart before the horse, knowing how to include images makes learning to develop them easier.

Table 22.1 shows the main image tags and attributes used to insert images in Web pages.

TABLE 22.1:   Image Tags and Attributes

Tag	Use
`<IMG>`	Marks an image within an HTML document
`ALT="..."`	Specifies alternative text to display if an image is not displayed
`SRC="..."`	Points to an image file (URL) to include
`HEIGHT=n`	Specifies the final height of an image in pixels
`WIDTH=n`	Specifies the final width of an image in pixels
`BORDER=n`	Specifies the width of a border around an image in pixels
`ALIGN="..."`	Specifies image alignment as TOP, MIDDLE, BOTTOM, LEFT, or RIGHT

Adding an Image

Adding an image is similar to adding the tags and attributes you've already used. You use the <IMG> tag, which specifies an image, plus the SRC= attribute to specify the image filename or URL. For example, if you're including an image that's located within the same folder as your document, your code might look like this:

```
<IMG SRC="logo.gif">
```

Or, if you're including an image located on the Web, you would include an absolute URL, like this:

```
<IMG SRC="http://www.asroutfitters.com/gifs/asrlogo.gif">
```

A URL used in the SRC= attribute is called a *remote reference*. Referencing logos and images remotely has certain advantages and some significant drawbacks. One advantage is that remote references to images ensure that you're always using the current logo. For example, if ASR Outfitters hires a graphic design company to change its corporate image, a franchisee's site that uses remote references to the main site will reflect the changes as soon as the main site changes. Additionally, remote references lighten the load on your server and reduce the number of files you must manage and manipulate.

On the downside, changes that are out of your control can easily break links from your site. If the ASR Outfitters Webmaster decides to move the images from a GIFs subdirectory into an images subdirectory, the franchisee's images will no longer work, because the SRC= attribute points to the subdirectory that no longer contains the image files. From the visitor's perspective, the franchisee simply has a nonfunctional site—the visitor really doesn't know or care about the reason.

COPYRIGHT LAWS APPLY TO IMAGES

Be careful about linking to remote images, as you may be using copyrighted material. For example, if Bad Karma Hiking Equipment decided that the ASR Outfitters images were cool and incorporated those cool images in a site design by using remote links without permission, they would be infringing on ASR Outfitters' copyrighted material. This also applies to background images (covered later in this chapter) and any other content in any document. Be careful!

Additionally, network glitches or server problems can also render your images inoperative if you link to them remotely. If the load on your own site is significant and you use remote images, the other site may be swamped with the demand and not even know why. Overall, you're probably better off copying the images to your local folder or at least to a different folder on your server, rather than relying on remote servers.

To add images to your document, start with a basic HTML document that, along with content, includes the following tags:

```
!DOCTYPE
<HTML>
<HEAD>
<BODY>
```

We used this basic document for ASR Outfitters:

```
<!DOCTYPE HTML PUBLIC "-//W3C//DTD HTML 4.0//EN">
<HTML>
<HEAD>
<TITLE>ASR Outfitters</TITLE>
</HEAD>
<BODY>
<H1 ALIGN=CENTER>ASR Outfitters</H1>
<P>We provide mountaineering and hiking equipment nationwide
via mail order as well as through our stores in the Rocky
Mountains.</P>
<HR WIDTH=70% SIZE=8 NOSHADE>
<P>Please select from the following links:</P>
<UL>
<LI><A HREF="camping.html">Camping News</A>
<LI><A HREF="catalog.html">Catalog</A>
<LI><A HREF="clubs.html">Clubs</A>
<LI><A HREF="contact.html">Contact Us</A>
<LI><A HREF="weather.html">Check Weather</A>
</UL>
<HR WIDTH=70% SIZE=8 NOSHADE>
<CENTER>
<ADDRESS ALIGN=CENTER>ASR Outfitters<BR>
```

```
<A HREF="mailto:info@asroutfitters.com">info@asroutfitters.
com</A><BR>

4700 N. Center<BR>

South Logan, UT 87654<BR>

801-555-3422<BR>

</ADDRESS>

</CENTER>

</BODY>

</HTML>
```

To add an image to this basic document, follow these steps:

1. Insert an <IMG> tag where you want the image to appear.

   ```
   <H1 ALIGN=CENTER>ASR Outfitters</H1>
   <IMG>
   <P>We provide mountaineering and hiking equipment
   nationwide via mail order as well as through our stores
   in the Rocky Mountains.</P>
   ```

2. Add an SRC="..." attribute pointing to the image filename. In this example, the filename is asrlogo.gif, and it's in the same folder as the document; so that's all that's required.

   ```
   <IMG SRC="asrlogo.gif">
   ```

3. In this case, add a line break tag <BR> after the <IMG> tag so that the next text starts on the following line (and not in any available space behind the image).

   ```
   <IMG SRC="asrlogo.gif"><BR>
   ```

4. Because the image duplicates the content of the first-level heading, consider removing the first-level heading.

5. The first-level heading was centered, so consider adding a <CENTER> tag around the logo to center it.

   ```
   <CENTER><IMG SRC="asrlogo.gif"><BR></CENTER>
   ```

NOTE

The <IMG> tag supports ALIGN= attributes with values of TOP, MIDDLE, BOTTOM, LEFT, and RIGHT, but does not support horizontal centering. If you want to use horizontal centering, use the <CENTER> tag. See the "Aligning the Image" section, later in this chapter, for more information.

You can see the resulting image in the ASR Web page shown in Figure 22.1.

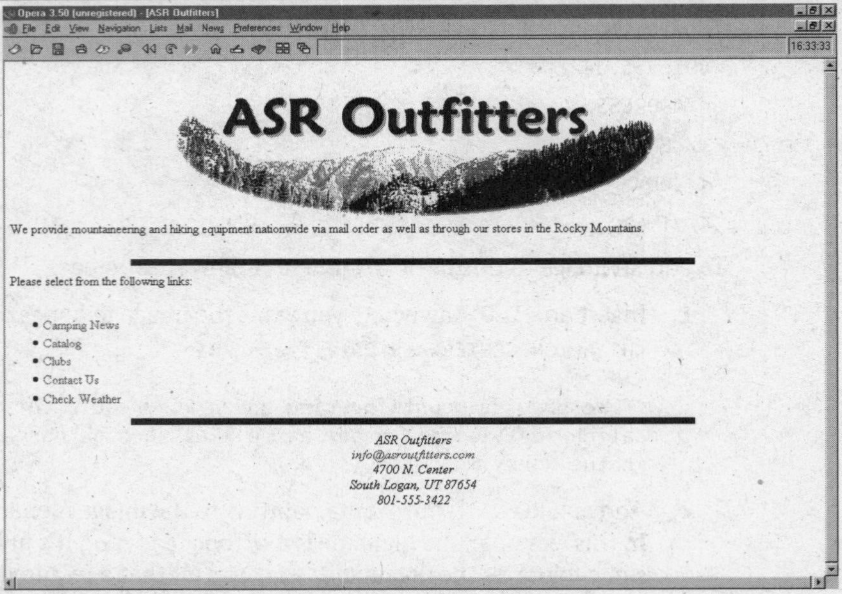

FIGURE 22.1: An image in the ASR Web page

Including Alternative Text

Alternative text describes an image that you have inserted. You include alternative text for the following reasons:

▶ Some of your visitors may be using text-only browsers.

▶ A visitor may have turned off images so that a file will load faster.

▶ Sometimes browsers don't display images correctly.

▶ Sometimes images don't display because the links aren't working properly.

▶ Sometimes browsers display alternative text while images load.

Alternative text should be clear and concise. Provide your visitors with enough information so that they can understand the image content without viewing it. For example, alternative text for a logo can be as simple as the company name and the word *logo*. Even text as simple as "ASR Sample Photograph" or "ASR Content-Free Image" is helpful to visitors. If they see only the word *Image* (as they would if you omit the ALT= attribute), they'll have to load the images to see the content.

To add alternative text to your images, simply add the ALT= attribute to the <IMG> tag, like this:

```
<IMG SRC="asrlogo.gif" ALT="ASR Outfitters Logo">
```

The resulting alternative text is shown in Figure 22.2.

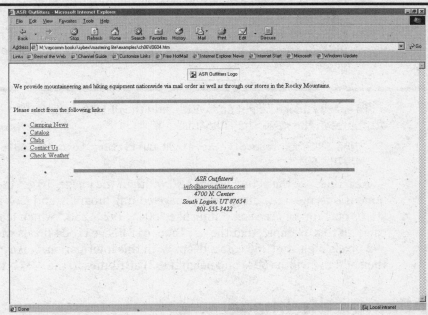

FIGURE 22.2: Alternative text provides information about the image.

Specifying Height and Width

You can speed the loading time of images by specifying an image's height and width. As the browser loads the page, it notes the height and width attributes and leaves that much space for the image. Next, it lays out the remaining text, and then it goes back and fills in the image. If you do not include these attributes, the browser has to load enough of the image to get the dimensions before it can lay out the rest of the text, thereby slowing the display of other page elements.

SPEEDING PERCEIVED IMAGE-LOADING TIME WITH NETSCAPE

A Netscape-specific tag, LOWSRC=, works in conjunction with the SRC= attribute; it tells the browser to load a smaller version of the image first and then load the full image.

The idea is to use a small image (in terms of file size) for the LOWSRC= image. For example, use a JPG image that is compressed as much as possible but that retains the dimensions of the original image. This image appears quickly, and, if the visitor stays on the page long enough, the full image then loads.

This attribute, although not universally recognized, causes no adverse effects in browsers that don't support it—they simply ignore it.

To specify image height and width, add the HEIGHT= and WIDTH= attributes in the <IMG> tag, like this:

```
<IMG SRC="asrlogo.gif" ALT="ASR Outfitters Logo" HEIGHT="192"
WIDTH="604">
```

As a rule, use the actual height and width of the image. To get the dimensions, open the image in an image-editing program, and look at the status bar. You will see something like "604 × 192 × 256," which indicates, in this example, that the asrlogo.gif image is 604 pixels wide, 192 pixels high, and 256 colors deep. With this information, you can then add the width (604) and height (192) attributes to the <IMG> tag.

Aligning the Image

HTML provides several image alignment options:

▶ Three vertical options align the image with respect to a line of text.

▶ Two options align the image to the left or to the right of the window (with corresponding text wrap).

The alignment options within the <IMG> tag override other alignment settings within the HTML document (for example, the <CENTER> tags surrounding the <IMG> tag).

FORMATTING USING THE TRANSPARENT GIF TRICK

You can use transparent images to help force specific spacing in your documents. Suppose you want a blank space between two paragraphs. Because you can't insert a carriage return like you would in a word processor, you have to put in the blank space some other way—inserting a transparent GIF works really well in this case. A transparent GIF could also ensure that text appears a specific distance from the left margin.

To add spacing in a document with a transparent GIF, simply create a 1×1 pixel transparent GIF in your image-editing software and then insert that GIF into your HTML document.

Does the space have to be 1 pixel wide or 1 pixel high? Not necessarily. You can insert the itty-bitty (and thus very fast to download) image in the document and specify the size in which it will appear in a Web browser by adding the HEIGHT= and WIDTH= attributes. For example, your code might look like this:

```
<IMG SRC="trans.gif" HEIGHT="10" WIDTH="1">
```

This example results in a blank space that's 10 pixels high and 1 pixel wide—ideal for ensuring spacing between paragraphs! Or set the height to 1 and the width to 10 to indent text.

We present this option to you because, well, lots of people use it, and if you have really specific formatting needs, it works. Keep in mind, though, that it's not standard and that we don't recommend it. HTML doesn't pretend to provide exact layout control, and attempting to get it is likely to prove frustrating.

By default, images align on the left, with a single line of accompanying text appearing on the same line; however, long text wraps to the following line. To ensure that accompanying text appears beside the image, specify ALIGN="LEFT" in the <IMG> tag, like this:

```
<IMG SRC="asrlogo.gif" ALT="ASR Outfitters Logo" WIDTH="604"
HEIGHT="192" ALIGN="LEFT">
```

The text appears to the right of the left-aligned image, as shown in Figure 22.3.

You can create attractive effects by combining image alignment and text alignment. For example, setting an image to ALIGN="RIGHT" and then setting the accompanying text to ALIGN="RIGHT" forces the text to be flush against the image with a ragged left margin, as shown in Figure 22.4.

Part iv

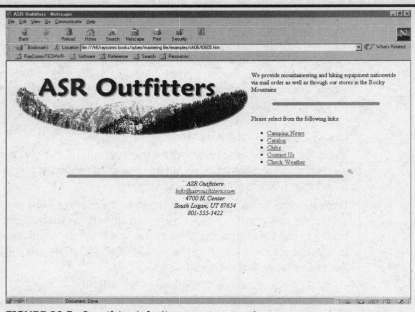

FIGURE 22.3: Specifying left alignment ensures that accompanying text appears to the right of the image.

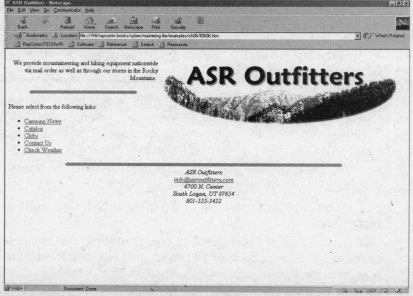

FIGURE 22.4: Specifying right alignment for the image and text produces appealing results.

The remaining alignment options—TOP, MIDDLE, and BOTTOM—offer more in the context of small images. You use them to align the image within the text. For example, using ALIGN="TOP" aligns the top of the image with the top of the surrounding text, and the remainder of the image hangs below the text line. Using ALIGN="MIDDLE" places the middle of an image at the baseline of surrounding text. Similarly, using ALIGN="BOTTOM" places the bottom of an image on the same line as the text, and the remainder of the image extends considerably higher than the surrounding text. The effect of these options is shown in Figure 22.5.

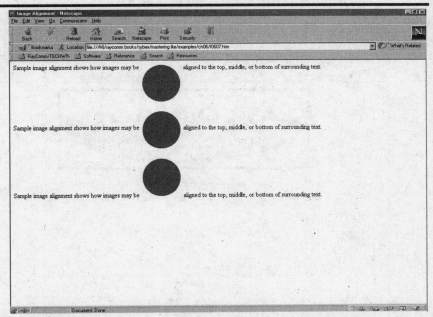

FIGURE 22.5: Top, middle, and bottom alignment float the image differently in relationship to the surrounding text.

Controlling the Border

You control the border around an image with the BORDER= attribute. In most browsers, by default, the border is visible only on images that are used as links. To turn the border off for all images, add the BORDER="0" attribute to the <IMG> tag, resulting in a complete image tag:

```
<IMG SRC="asrlogo.gif" ALT="ASR Outfitters Logo" WIDTH="604"
HEIGHT="192" BORDER="0">
```

TIP

Remember, placing quotes around numeric values, such as 0, 192, or 604, is optional in attributes.

Likewise, you can increase the border width around an image by increasing the value in the BORDER= attribute, like this:

```
<IMG SRC="asrlogo.gif" ALT="ASR Outfitters Logo" WIDTH="604"
HEIGHT="192" BORDER="7">
```

The resulting border looks like that in Figure 22.6.

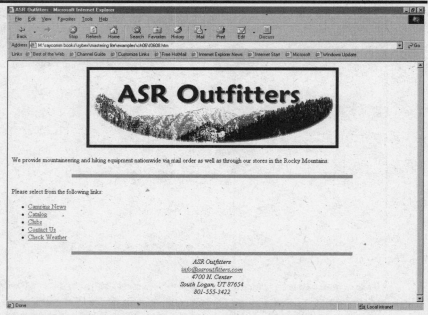

FIGURE 22.6: Setting a large border width frames your images.

Choosing Suitable Colors

When creating your own images—or choosing colors for Web page or table backgrounds—you want to choose colors that look good in most browsers, most of the time. If you're selecting colors for text or for small swatches, choose anything that appeals to you. However, if you're selecting a background color or a color that will appear in broad expanses of your HTML documents, be careful.

If you choose a color that is not available on a viewer's system, the browser will dither the color to approximate its appearance. *Dithering* is the technical term for substituting other colors, partially or wholly, to minimize the impact of not having the correct color. Dithering in photographs or small images is rarely noticeable, but dithering in large single-color areas results in blotchy or mottled appearances.

Now, consider that a large number of your visitors—or, at least, a large number of Web users in general—have computers set to display 256 colors. Sounds like the solution is to choose one of those 256 colors, doesn't it? Not quite. Macintosh, Unix, and Windows each use a different set of colors for system functions, and those colors—up to 40—are taken from the available 256, leaving only 216 colors for general use. If you choose one of these 216 colors, however, you can be fairly certain that the colors will look as good as they can in all browsers on all platforms. These remaining 216 colors are evenly distributed over the color spectrum, giving you a wide range from which to choose.

In computer-ese, colors are represented as proportions of red, green, and blue (RGB) and are specified by an RGB number. These RGB numbers combine to produce all available colors.

To specify a color, you provide numeric values to represent the proportions of red, green, and blue. In most image-editing programs, you can provide values in decimal numbers. However, when you're specifying colors in some image-editing programs and for colors within a Web page, you use hexadecimal numbers.

What are these numbers? They are the decimal values 0, 51, 102, 153, 204, 255 for each color. That is, a good (preferred) color might be 51, 51, 51 for the red, green, and blue values. In hexadecimal, the good values are 00, 33, 66, 99, CC, FF, so the corresponding sample color would be #333333. Where do these good values come from?

Table 22.2 lists the preferred (good) RGB values using hexadecimal numbers; Table 22.3 lists the values using decimal numbers. To create a safe (nondithering) color, choose one value from each column. For example, choose 66 from the first column, 33 from the second, and 00 from the third to create an RGB color of 663300.

Part iv

TABLE 22.2: Preferred RGB Values in Hexadecimal

RED	GREEN	BLUE
00	00	00
33	33	33
66	66	66
99	99	99
CC	CC	CC
FF	FF	FF

TABLE 22.3: Preferred RGB Values in Decimal

RED	GREEN	BLUE
0	0	0
51	51	51
102	102	102
153	153	153
204	204	204
255	255	255

As a rule, colors close to these colors will also not dither, but there's no hard and fast rule on how "close" is close enough. For example, we tried 000001 and found that it didn't visibly dither on our computers... this time.

USING IMAGES AS LINKS

Using images as links offers two distinct advantages to both you and your visitors. First, images really can be as good as a thousand words. Often, including an image link can replace several words or lines of text, leaving valuable space for other page elements.

Second, you can also use *thumbnails*, which are smaller images that link to a larger one. By doing so, you can let visitors get the gist of an image and choose whether they want to load the larger version. (You'll find details about thumbnails in a later section, "Creating Thumbnails.")

Creating Image Links

To add an image as a link, start by adding an image tag. In this example, we are adding a fancy button to the ASR Outfitters page to replace the more prosaic Camping News bulleted list item. The name of the image is `camping.gif`, and the file it should link to is `camping.html`.

NOTE

When you use images as links, alternative text is critical. If clicking the image is the only way visitors can connect to the other page, the alternative text is their only clue if the image is not displayed (because of technical difficulties, because they've turned off images, because they have a text-only browser, because they use a screen-reading program for the visually impaired, and so on).

Here are the steps for adding an image link:

1. Add an image tag and an SRC= attribute to the document.
   ```
   <IMG SRC="camping.gif">
   ```

2. Include alternative text using the ALT= attribute.
   ```
   <IMG SRC="camping.gif" ALT="Camping News">
   ```

3. Add the remaining attributes you want to include, like the HEIGHT= and WIDTH= and BORDER= attributes. If you choose to use BORDER="0" and turn off the border completely, be sure that the image is visually identified as a link. Otherwise, your visitors might not know it's a link unless they pass their mouse over it and see the pointing-hand cursor.
   ```
   <IMG SRC="camping.gif" WIDTH="300" HEIGHT="82"
   BORDER="0"  ALT="Camping News">
   ```

4. Add the link anchor tag, <A>, before and after the image.
   ```
   <A><IMG SRC="camping.gif" WIDTH="300" HEIGHT="82"
   BORDER="0" ALT="Camping News"></A>
   ```

5. Add the HREF= attribute to the opening anchor tag to specify the image filename.
   ```
   <A HREF="camping.html"><IMG SRC="camping.gif"
   WIDTH="300" HEIGHT="82" BORDER="0" ALT="Camping
   News"></A>
   ```

Part iv

Now you have an image that acts as a link to the `camping.html` file. After adding a couple more images and surrounding them all with the `<CENTER>` tags, the ASR Outfitters page is similar to Figure 22.7.

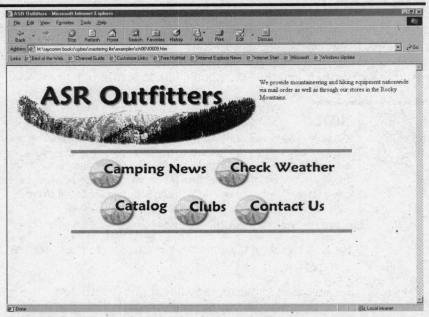

FIGURE 22.7: Image links can make a page much more attractive (and slower to load).

Creating Thumbnails

As we mentioned earlier, a thumbnail is a smaller version of an image, but it is also a link to the larger version. Thumbnails can also link to multimedia applets or to other content that is time-consuming to download or not universally accessible.

For example, ASR Outfitters included a thumbnail of the original photograph that inspired its logo. This thumbnail links to the original photograph, a larger image.

To add a thumbnail image, start by having both images—the thumbnail and the larger version—available. Make a thumbnail by starting with the full-size version (scanned from your private collection or from any other source). Then, use your image-editing software to resize or resample the image to a much smaller size—as small as possible while still retaining the gist of the image. Save this second image under a different name. Then follow these steps:

1. Include the thumbnail image in your document as you'd include any other image. For example, the code might look like this:

   ```
   <IMG SRC="photo-thumbnail.jpg" HEIGHT="78" WIDTH="193"
   ALIGN="RIGHT" BORDER="1" ALT="Thumbnail of Original
   Photo">
   ```

2. Add a link from the thumbnail to the larger image.

   ```
   <A HREF="photo.jpg"><IMG SRC="photo-thumbnail.jpg"
   HEIGHT="78" WIDTH="193" ALIGN="RIGHT" BORDER="1"
   ALT="Thumbnail of Original Photo"></A>
   ```

If you set the border to 0, be sure that the supporting text or other cues in the HTML document make it clear that the image is, in fact, a link to a larger photograph. Alternatively, do as we did and simply set BORDER="1" to make clear that an image is a link. Here's the result from the bottom corner of the ASR Outfitters home page:

Although you can achieve the same visual effect in your document by using the original image and setting a smaller display size with the HEIGHT= and WIDTH= attributes, this technique defeats the purpose of thumbnails. Even if you reset the display size with HEIGHT= and WIDTH=, the entire (full-size) image will have to be downloaded to your computer. The trick to effective thumbnails is to reduce both the dimensions and the actual file size to the smallest possible value so the page will load quickly.

CREATING IMAGE MAPS

An image map, also called a *clickable image*, is a single image that contains multiple links. In your Web travels, you may have used image maps without knowing it. Clicking on a portion of an image map takes you to

Part iv

the link connected with that part of the visual presentation. For example, a physician might present an image map of the human body to a patient, with instructions for the patient to "click where it hurts." Another good use replaces individual images (that browsers could realign depending on the window width) with a single *graphical menu*. Figure 22.8 shows a sample image map from the ASR Outfitters Web site. (Visitors can click on each area for weather conditions—weather at the high peaks and lower elevations—and even the ultraviolet index.)

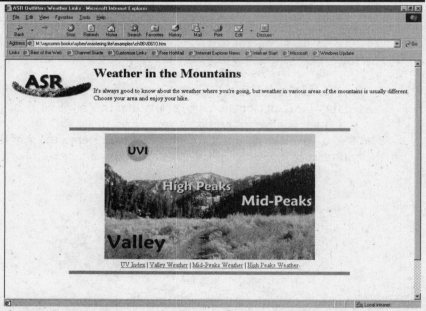

FIGURE 22.8: Image maps are single images with multiple links to other information or graphics.

Understanding Image Map Types

The two types of image maps are the following:

- ▶ Server-side
- ▶ Client-side

The feature distinguishing the two types is where the processing takes place (where a visitor's mouse-click is translated into a link to another document). The processing can occur either on the server (hence, server-side image map) or on the visitor's computer (hence, client-side image map).

Server-Side Image Maps

In a server-side image map, the coordinates of the click are transmitted to the server computer, which determines the instructions that apply to that click. The server then sends that information back to the client, which then sends a request for the appropriate document. The server computer does the calculating and tells the client what to do.

The advantages to using server-side image maps are that they have been around longer than client-side maps and that they are widely supported. The disadvantages to using server-side image maps include the following:

▶ Because a server-side image map requires input from the server, it generally responds slower than a client-side image map, depending on network traffic.

▶ The server may need supplemental software to process the image map.

▶ The server administrator may have to specify how the image map is processed.

Client-Side Image Maps

Generally, you'll want to use client-side image maps for several reasons. To start with, they're faster (because there's no need for back-and-forth communication between client and server to process the map) and more reliable, for those browsers that support client-side maps (and most do). For example, if a document with a client-side image map comes from Server A and points to a document on Server B, the client can do the calculations and request the document directly from Server B.

Client-side image maps are more user-friendly than server-side image maps. When a visitor moves the cursor over an image map link within a document, the status bar generally displays the URL of the link. Newer browsers, including the latest versions of Netscape Navigator and Internet Explorer, also show information about the link in a small pop-up window. In contrast, when a visitor places the cursor over a server-side image map link, the status bar displays only the coordinates of the cursor.

Finally, client-side image maps are better for you, the Web author, because you can use and test them before you put the image map on the server. In contrast, server-side maps do not work until they have been installed on the server, making testing much more difficult.

TIP

If your visitors might be using particularly old browsers, consider using both client-side and server-side image maps. If browsers see a client-side map, they'll use it. If they don't recognize the client-side image map, they'll revert to the server-side map. The only disadvantage to this approach is that you have to do twice as much work.

Making Appropriate Image Maps

Poorly constructed or carelessly selected image maps can be much worse than no image map at all. The inherent disadvantages of images (for example, their download time and their inaccessibility for text-only browsers) apply in spades to image maps. When determining whether an image map is appropriate for your needs, ask the following questions.

Is the Image Map Linking to a Stable Navigational Structure?   If the links will be changing or if the overall site navigation structure isn't completely worked out, it's not time for an image map. Revising image maps is possible, but generally a real hassle. Often it's easier to completely redo an image map than to update it.

Is the Image Final?   If the image hasn't passed all levels of review and isn't polished, you're not ready to make an image map. Changes as trivial as cropping the image slightly or rescaling the image by a few percentage points can completely break your map.

Is the Image Function Appropriate to an Image Map?   Flashy images on a home page are good candidates for image maps, particularly if the design reflects the corporate image. In many cases, an intricate design must be a single image—browsers cannot always accurately assemble individual images into the arrangement the designer intends. However, pages buried within an intranet site or that have a technical and practical focus are less likely to benefit from an image map.

Is the Image Content Appropriate to an Image Map?   Artificial or gratuitous use of image maps can be a real drawback to otherwise fine Web pages. Is clicking certain spots in an image really the best way for your visitors to link to the information they need? For example, in a Web site about automobile repair and diagnosis for the layperson, an image map with a picture of a car and the instructions to click where the funny sound seems to originate is completely appropriate. In a site directed at experienced mechanics, however, a list of parts (hood, trunk, dashboard, tire) would be much faster and more appropriate.

Does the Function or Content Merit an Image Map?   If both do, that's great. If one does, you can probably proceed with an image map. If, however, the links on a page don't need to be flashy and the content is not substantially clarified with an image map, omit the image map entirely.

Can the Image Map Be Completely Reused?   If you are planning to use an image map on several pages (you will use exactly the same image and code), its value increases. In this case, it's more likely to be worth the download time than if it's for one-time use.

If you answered no to one or more of these questions, consider using traditional, individual images or navigation aids. For example, if you can easily break the content or image into multiple smaller images with no significant problems, strongly consider doing so. Remember that image maps are time-consuming to develop and may not be available to all your visitors, so be sure an image map is right for your needs before developing one.

Selecting an Image

When you select a suitable image to use as an image map, follow the same guidelines as you would for choosing other images:

▶ Be sure that the image supports the content.

▶ Be sure that the physical size is as small as possible, but large enough to convey the content.

▶ Be sure that the file size is as small as possible.

For example, if you are creating an auto-repair image map for laypersons, use a simple drawing or schematic. At the other extreme, however, is the ASR Outfitters image map, which is primarily a visual attraction with only a tangential function. The image map shown in Figure 22.8, earlier in this

Part iv

chapter, is part of a localized weather page. Visitors can click an area to get the weather for that region.

Setting Alternate Navigation

Unless you know beyond a doubt that *all* your visitors have graphical browsers and will choose to view images, you must provide alternate navigation options. Those who don't see the images—for whatever reason— won't be able to link to the information via your image, so provide text-based alternatives. An easy solution is to create a list of links. For example, alternate navigation for the image shown in Figure 22.8, earlier in this chapter, might look like the following code:

```
<BR>
<A HREF="uvi.html">UV Index</A> |
<A HREF="valley.html">Valley Weather</A> |
<A HREF="midpeaks.html">Mid-Peaks Weather</A> |
<A HREF="highpeaks.html">High Peaks Weather</A>
```

In this code, the vertical line (|) separates the links and creates the menu effect, as shown at the bottom of Figure 22.8.

TIP

Creating the alternate navigation before you develop the image map helps remind you of the links to include.

Creating Client-Side Image Maps

Creating a client-side image map involves three steps:

1. Defining the image area
2. Creating the image map
3. Activating the image map

Defining Image Areas

All image maps are simply a combination of three shapes:

▶ Circles

▶ Rectangles

▶ Polygons (any shapes other than circles and rectangles)

You can create almost any image by combining these shapes. Figure 22.9 shows the ASR Outfitters image map from within a map-editing program. The UVI link is a circle, the valley temperatures link is a rectangle, and the mid- and high-peak links are triangles.

NOTE

You don't have to be precise with most map definitions. You can assume that most visitors will click somewhere in the middle of the link area; if not, they're likely to try again.

The next three sections show you how to define these three shapes. Before you get started, open an image in an image-editing or -mapping program.

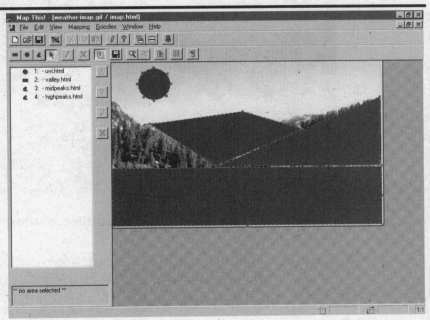

FIGURE 22.9: This image map includes a circle, a rectangle, and two polygons.

TIP

If you'll be developing several image maps, we recommend installing and using image-mapping software available on the Internet. If you're creating simple maps or if you're only doing a few, however, creating them manually is almost as easy.

Defining Circles   To define a circle, follow these steps:

1. Identify the center and the radius. Use the pointer tool to
    point at the center of the circle, and note the coordinates in
    the status bar of your paint program. For example, in Paint
    Shop Pro, the pointer tool looks like a magnifying glass, and
    the xy coordinates are at the bottom of the window. The x
    is the number of pixels from the edge of the image, and the
    y is the number of pixels from the top.

2. Move the cursor horizontally to the edge of the circle and note
    the coordinates.

3. Subtract the first x coordinate from the second x coordinate
    to get the radius of the circle.

4. Make a note of these coordinates.

Defining Rectangles   To define a rectangle, follow these steps:

1. Identify the upper-left corner and the lower-right corner.
    Point your mouse at the upper-left corner of the rectangle
    and record the coordinates; then point at the lower-right cor-
    ner and record the coordinates.

2. Make a note of these coordinates.

Defining Polygons   To define a polygon, follow these steps:

1. Identify each point on the shape, moving in order around the shape. You can start at any point on the perimeter and proceed clockwise or counterclockwise, as long as you don't skip points. For example, in the ASR Outfitters map, the Mid-Peaks area can be defined with three points—making a right triangle with the long side running between the Mid-Peaks and High Peaks areas. The High Peaks area might include several points across the top of the mountains, or it might be as simple as another triangle.

2. Make a note of these coordinates.

Creating the Image Map

When you create an image map, you include tags and attributes that tell a browser what to do when a visitor clicks the defined map areas. You can include this information within the HTML document that contains the image map, or you can include it in a separate document. The first case is more common, but if you'll be using the image map (say, as a navigation aid) in several documents, consider storing it in a separate file and referencing it from each of the documents.

You can place the map definition block anywhere within the body of your HTML document, but it is easier to update and maintain if you place it either immediately after the opening <BODY> tag or immediately before the closing </BODY> tag. Table 22.4 explains image map tags and attributes.

TABLE 22.4: Image Map Tags and Attributes

Tag/Attribute	Use
USEMAP="..."	Names the client-side map definition to use. Attribute of <IMG> tag.
ISMAP	Specifies that the image uses a server-side image map. Attribute of <IMG> tag.
<MAP>	Marks the map definition block within the HTML document.
NAME="..."	Provides a name for the map definition block.
<AREA>	Defines an area within the map.

Continued on next page

Part iv

TABLE 22.4:   Image Map Tags and Attributes *(continued)*

TAG/ATTRIBUTE	USE
SHAPE="..."	Identifies the shape of an area as RECT, CIRCLE, or POLY.
HREF="..."	Specifies a target for area. A click in the area links to this URL.
NOHREF	Specifies that a click in this area will not link anywhere.
COORDS="x,y, x1,y1,x2,y2"	Identifies the shape of an area.
ALT="..."	Provides alternate text (or pop-up text) describing each link.

To include a client-side image map, follow these steps (we'll use the ASR Outfitters page in this example):

1. Within your HTML document, add opening and closing <MAP> tags.

   <MAP>
   </MAP>
   </BODY>

2. Give the map a clear, descriptive name with a NAME= attribute. This name is comparable to the NAME= attribute of the <A> tag. It provides an internal anchor of sorts that you can link to from either the same document or other documents.

   <MAP **NAME="weather_zones">**

3. Add an <AREA> tag for one of the shapes.

   <MAP NAME="weather_zones">
   <AREA>

4. Add a SHAPE= attribute to the <AREA> tag. In this example, CIRCLE represents the UVI area in the ASR example map.

   <AREA **SHAPE=CIRCLE>**

5. Add the COORDS= attribute with the xy coordinates of the center of the circle and with the radius of the circle.

   <AREA SHAPE=CIRCLE **COORDS="82,43,30">**

6. Add an HREF= attribute pointing to the target file. You can use relative or absolute URLs in client-side image maps, but,

as with other links, using relative URLs is a good idea. In this case, the area links to a file called `uvi.html` in the same folder.

```
<AREA SHAPE=CIRCLE COORDS="82,43,30" HREF="uvi.html">
```

7. Add the ALT= attribute describing the link for use in pop-ups.

```
<AREA SHAPE=CIRCLE COORDS="82,43,30" HREF="uvi.html"
ALT="UV Index">
```

NOTE

As you add areas, some may overlap others. The first area defined overrides overlapping areas.

8. Add additional <AREA> tags, one at a time. In this example, the next <AREA> tag is for the Valley area, so it is a RECT (or RECTANGLE). The coordinates for the top left and lower right are required to link to `valley.html`.

```
<AREA SHAPE=CIRCLE COORDS="82,43,30" HREF="uvi.html"
ALT="UV Index">
<AREA SHAPE=RECT COORDS="1,209,516,320"
HREF="valley.html" ALT="Valley Weather">
```

9. For the Mid-Peaks area, a triangle will suffice to define the area; so the shape is a POLYGON with three pairs of coordinates. This links to `midpeaks.html`.

```
<AREA SHAPE=CIRCLE COORDS="82,43,30" HREF="uvi.html"
ALT="UV Index">
<AREA SHAPE=RECT COORDS="1,209,516,320"
HREF="valley.html" ALT="Valley Weather">
<AREA SHAPE=POLY COORDS="199,207,513,205,514,71"
HREF="midpeaks.html" ALT="Mid-Peaks Weather">
```

10. The High Peaks area is easily defined with a figure containing four corners—vaguely diamond shaped, as in the following example.

```
<AREA SHAPE=CIRCLE COORDS="82,43,30" HREF="uvi.html"
ALT="UV Index">
<AREA SHAPE=RECT COORDS="1,209,516,320"
HREF="valley.html" ALT="Valley Weather">
<AREA SHAPE=POLY COORDS="199,207,513,205,514,71"
HREF="midpeaks.html" ALT="Mid-Peaks Weather">
<AREA SHAPE=POLY COORDS="63,123,251,98,365,134,198,204,
73,121" HREF="highpeaks.html" ALT="High Peaks Weather">
```

Part iv

Refer to Figure 22.9 for a reminder of what this shape looks like.

11. Set the HREF= attribute for the remaining areas. You could set the remaining area so that nothing at all will happen when a visitor clicks there.

```
<AREA SHAPE=default NOHREF>
```

That's all there is to it. The final map looks something like the following code:

```
<MAP NAME="weather_zones">

<AREA SHAPE=CIRCLE COORDS="82,43,30" HREF="uvi.html" ALT="UV
Index">

<AREA SHAPE=RECT COORDS="1,209,516,320" HREF="valley.html"
ALT="Valley Weather">

<AREA SHAPE=POLY COORDS="199,207,513,205,514,71" HREF=
"midpeaks.html" ALT="Mid-Peaks Weather">

<AREA SHAPE=POLY
COORDS="63,123,251,98,365,134,198,204,73,121" HREF=
"highpeaks.html" ALT="High Peaks Weather">

<AREA SHAPE=default NOHREF>
</MAP>
```

Activating the Image Map

Before you can activate the map, you must place the map image in your document. The image tag (in a new document from the ASR site) looks like this:

```
<CENTER>

<IMG SRC="weather-imap.gif" ALIGN="" WIDTH="516" HEIGHT="320"
BORDER="0" ALT="Weather Zones in the Mountains">

</CENTER>
```

To connect the image to the map definition created in the previous section, simply add the USEMAP= attribute, as in the following example.

```
<IMG SRC="weather-imap.gif" ALIGN="" WIDTH="516" HEIGHT="320"
BORDER="0" ALT="Weather Zones in the Mountains" USEMAP=
"#weather_zones">
```

NOTE

The USEMAP= attribute requires a pound sign (#) in the value to indicate that the link goes to a place within a document.

If you want to link to a map definition in another document, add an absolute URL to the USEMAP= attribute. If you do this, test thoroughly because not all browsers support this feature. The final map looks like that shown in Figure 22.10.

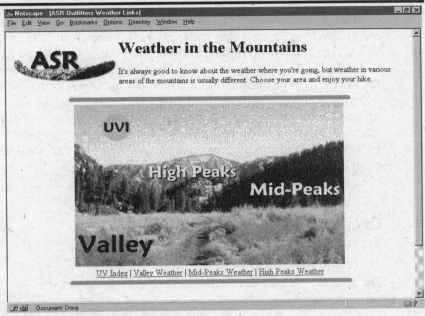

FIGURE 22.10: The ASR Outfitters image map

Creating Server-Side Image Maps

The process for making server-side maps is virtually identical to that of making client-side image maps. The only real differences are in map file format. Each type of server can have a different type of image map configuration.

In practice, however, only two main server-side map formats exist: NCSA (National Center for Supercomputing Applications) and CERN (Centre Européen pour la Recherche Nucléaire). They function in similar ways, but each requires a slightly different format for map definitions. Each format represents an implementation of server-side image maps from the earliest server software these organizations produced.

NOTE

Ask your server administrator which image map format you'll need to use for a server-side image map. Additionally, check on what the URL is for using a server-side image map.

The only real issue with converting your client-side image map to a server-side image map is that you must know more about (be sure of) the URLs. For example, everything in the ASR example was located initially in one folder. To properly set up a server-side map, we need to determine the full path to the information. Because of limitations in the NCSA image map implementation, the map should be contained in a subdirectory, not in the server root. ASR will put the image map document, the map file, and the associated (linked) files together in the weather subdirectory on www.asroutfitters.com. Therefore, the complete URL to the main file is as follows:

```
http://www.asroutfitters.com/weather/asrweather-imap.html
```

Creating an NCSA Image Map

In general, the NCSA image map format is as follows:

```
method URL coordinates
```

The code for the sample client-side image map looks like this:

```
<MAP NAME="weather_zones">
<AREA SHAPE=CIRCLE COORDS="82,43,30" HREF="uvi.html" ALT="UV
Index">
<AREA SHAPE=RECT COORDS="1,209,516,320" HREF="valley.html"
ALT="Valley Weather">
<AREA SHAPE=POLY COORDS="199,207,513,205,514,71" HREF="mid-
peaks.html" ALT="Mid-Peaks Weather">
<AREA SHAPE=POLY
COORDS="63,123,251,98,365,134,198,204,73,121" HREF="high-
peaks.html" ALT="High Peaks Weather">
<AREA SHAPE=default NOHREF>
</MAP>
```

You use an NCSA server-side map file like this:

```
default /weather/asrweather-imap.html
circle /weather/uvi.html 82,43,30
rect /weather/valley.html 1,209,516,320
```

```
poly /weather/midpeaks.html 199,207,513,205,514,71
poly /weather/highpeaks.html 63,123,251,98,365,134,198,
204,73,121
```

The `default` item points explicitly back to the file containing the map; so clicks outside active areas will not link to other pages. The remaining lines include the shape, URL, and coordinates, just as the client-side map definition file did, but using a slightly different format.

NOTE

The NCSA server-side format also supports a point shape (in addition to the circle, rectangle, and polygon) with a single pair of coordinates. A click near the point takes a visitor to that URL. If you provide multiple points, the server chooses the closest one to your click. Because other image map formats do not support the point, we recommend using only the existing shapes.

After you create this map file, save it with a map extension. ASR places the map file in the same folder as the rest of the files—that is, in the `/weather` folder, just below the server root.

Activating NCSA-Style Server-Side Image Maps

Activating the server-side image map makes much more sense if you think of it as making the image a link (though one with an added level of complexity). Follow these steps:

1. Start with the map in your document (the client-side map, if you choose).

   ```
   <IMG SRC="weather-imap.gif" ALIGN="" WIDTH="516"
   HEIGHT="320" BORDER="0" ALT="Weather Zones in the
   Mountains" USEMAP="#weather_zones">
   ```

2. Add the ISMAP attribute to the <IMG> tag, as shown here:

   ```
   <IMG SRC="weather-imap.gif" ALIGN="" WIDTH="516"
   HEIGHT="320" BORDER="0" ALT="Weather Zones in the
   Mountains" USEMAP="#weather_zones" ISMAP>
   ```

3. Add a link around the image.

   ```
   <A>
   <IMG SRC="weather-imap.gif" ALIGN="" WIDTH="516"
   HEIGHT="320" BORDER="0" ALT="Weather Zones in the
   Mountains" USEMAP="#weather_zones" ISMAP>
   </A>
   ```

Part iv

4. Add the HREF= attribute specified by the network administrator. In all probability, it will look something like this:

```
<A HREF="http://www.asroutfitters.com/cgi-bin/imagemap/
weather/weather-imap.map">
<IMG SRC="weather-imap.gif" ALIGN="" WIDTH="516"
HEIGHT="320" BORDER="0" ALT="Weather Zones in the
Mountains" USEMAP="#weather_zones" ISMAP>
</A>
```

If the client recognizes a client-side image map, it disregards the server-side map. If the client cannot recognize the client-side map, it uses the server-side map.

TIP

When you've finished creating the map, be sure to upload the map file at the same time you upload the rest of your files. That's an easy one to forget.

Implementing CERN-Style Image Maps

CERN-style maps are considerably less common than NCSA-style maps. Again, the same basic information is included, but slightly reshuffled. The original client-side map format is as follows:

```
<MAP NAME="weather_zones">

<AREA SHAPE=CIRCLE COORDS="82,43,30" HREF="uvi.html" ALT="UV
Index">

<AREA SHAPE=RECT COORDS="1,209,516,320" HREF="valley.html"
ALT="Valley Weather">

<AREA SHAPE=POLY COORDS="199,207,513,205,514,71" HREF=
"midpeaks.html" ALT="Mid-Peaks Weather">

<AREA SHAPE=POLY COORDS="63,123,251,98,365,134,198,204,
73,121" HREF="highpeaks.html" ALT="High Peaks Weather">

<AREA SHAPE=default NOHREF>

</MAP>
```

After converting it, you end up with a CERN map file of the following:

```
default /weather/asrweather-imap.html

circle (82,43) 30 /weather/uvi.html
rect (1,209) (516,320) /weather/valley.html
poly (199,207) (513,205) (514,71) /weather/midpeaks.html
poly (63,123) (251,98) (365,134) (198,204) (73,121)
/weather/highpeaks.html
```

The major differences are that the coordinate pairs are enclosed in parentheses, the coordinates go before the URLs, and the rectangle can use any two opposite coordinates, rather than the top left and lower right. The URLs can be either absolute or server-relative.

TIP

Other types of servers exist, and administrators configure their servers differently. Asking up-front how to implement a server-side image map will reduce frustration.

IMAGE MAPS IN IMAGEREADY

ImageReady gives you two ways to create an image map: by using the special image map tool, or by converting a layer into an image map. When you use the image map tool, you simply drag in the image area to define a map area. In contrast, when you create a layer-based image map, each layer's content defines the shape of the image map area.

To create an image map area using an image map tool:

1. Select either the rectangle image map tool, the circle image map tool, or the polygon image map tool in the toolbox. Hold down the Alt/Option key and click the tool's icon until the version you want is displayed.

2. Drag in the image to outline the image map area desired with the rectangular or circular tools, as shown in Figure 22.11. Hold down the Alt/Option key as you drag to define an area from its center. You can also use the polygon image map tool to click the points that define the image map area.

3. If you're using the rectangle or circle image map tool, you can also select the Fixed Size check box in the Image Map Options bar to specify set values for the image map area's dimensions in pixels.

4. Enter the URL, alternate text, and other parameters in the Image Map palette.

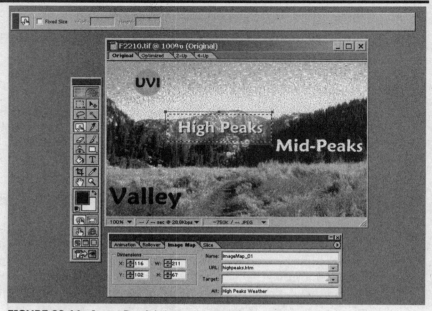

FIGURE 22.11: ImageReady's image map tools

To create an image map area from a layer:

1. In the Layers palette, choose a layer from which to create an image map area.

2. Choose Layer ➤ New Layer Based Image Map Area to define the layer as an image map area.

USING BACKGROUND IMAGES

Most browsers support background images, the patterns or images behind the text in HTML documents. As a rule, background images are *tiled* throughout the available space, meaning that they are multiple copies of one image placed side by side to fill the screen.

Tiling offers two main advantages. First, you can produce a *seamless background*, meaning that the casual viewer cannot see where individual images start and stop. Figure 22.12 shows a seamless background.

FIGURE 22.12: In seamless backgrounds, the tiled images blend together.

Second, you can develop more visually interesting backgrounds by ensuring that background images tile either horizontally or vertically. For example, an image that is only 10 pixels high and 1,280 pixels wide is as wide or wider than any browser window is likely to be. Therefore, the image will repeat vertically, but not horizontally. This can produce a vertical band, as shown in Figure 22.13.

TIP

The magic number 1,280 ensures that no browser can be wider than the image. If you use a narrower image, you might have an attractive image when viewed at 800 × 600 resolution, but with two vertical bands (on the left and near the right) at 1,024 × 768 resolution, for example.

Similarly, you can use a tall image to produce a tiled horizontal band, as shown in Figure 22.14. Pay careful attention to making the image taller than your page could possibly be; otherwise, the background will repeat. A good technique is also to make the image fade into the background color of the document.

Part iv

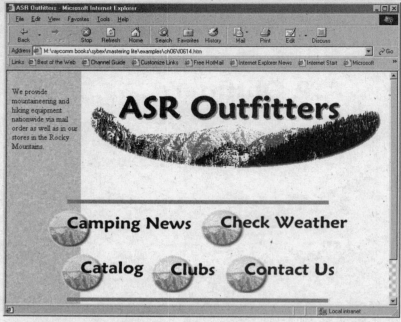

FIGURE 22.13: Wide images tile only vertically.

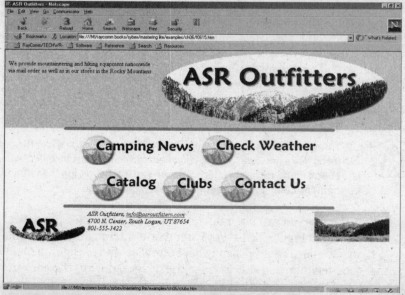

FIGURE 22.14: A horizontal band looks like this in a browser.

If you use background images in your document and the color of the image does not adequately contrast with the text color, reset your document colors. You might also want to set the colors to complement your background image.

To add a background image, use the attributes in Table 22.5 in the opening <BODY> tag.

TABLE 22.5: Background Attributes

Tag	Use
BACKGROUND="..."	Uses URL to identify an image for the background of an HTML document
BGPROPERTIES=FIXED	Sets the background image as nontiled, nonscrolling for use with Internet Explorer

To specify a background image, add the BACKGROUND= attribute to your opening <BODY> tag.

```
<BODY BACKGROUND="asrback.jpg">
```

TIP

You can use Style Sheets to include background images behind individual page elements, rather than placing a background image behind the entire page.

When you develop background images, you will find that creating a seamless image is difficult. Although some programs, such as Paint Shop Pro, offer a menu option to create a seamless image, you still often see a vague repeating pattern.

If you have a background image that you want to use as a watermark of sorts for your pages—and if your visitors will use Internet Explorer—add the BGPROPERTIES=FIXED attribute. This attribute prevents the image from tiling throughout the background. The full code for the <BODY> tag is as follows:

```
<BODY BACKGROUND="asrbackfull.jpg" BGPROPERTIES=FIXED>
```

This produces the effect shown in Figure 22.15.

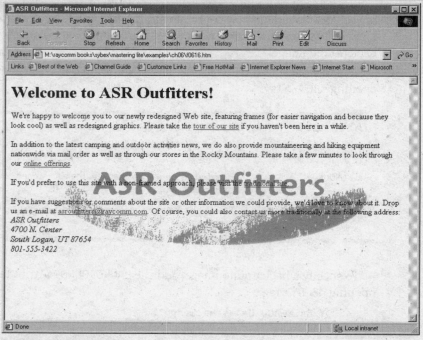

FIGURE 22.15: A fixed background acts as a watermark.

WHAT'S NEXT

Images can add more than static interest to your Web page. You can make your pages jump to life with movement by including tasteful animations. The next chapter will show you how to use ImageReady to create mini-movies with animated GIFs.

Chapter 23

CREATING WEB ANIMATIONS WITH PHOTOSHOP AND IMAGEREADY

I f you've spent more than five minutes on the Web, you've surely seen some form of animation. Annoying advertising banners, spinning globes, silly cartoons—they're all examples of simple and sometimes crass use of Web animation technology. However, in the hands of talented designers, Web animation can also be a powerful way to attract the attention of a Web site visitor and communicate messages far more effectively than simple text and graphics.

This chapter details how to create effective Web animations using Photoshop and ImageReady. Included are critical animation techniques such as creating animations from layers, tweening, and optimizing animations for use on the Web.

Adapted from *Mastering Photoshop 5.5 for the Web*
by Matt Straznitskas
ISBN 0-7821-2605-7   672 pages $39.99

ANIMATED GIFs

When the GIF file format was created by CompuServe, it included a little-known feature that allowed designers to store multiple images in a single GIF. These images play in sequence, much like an animated cartoon. Additionally, one can specify the length of time that passes between the loading of each image. If the time is short, the animation will speed up, and if it is long, the animation will slow down.

GIF animations can be made to play once, to loop forever, or to play any number of times. However, there are some things that you can't do with animated GIFs, including:

Sound   The GIF format does not allow for the inclusion of any kind of audio.

Interactivity   While an animated GIF can be hyperlinked to another Web page or element, it is not possible to make individual elements of an animation interactive.

To create animations that include audio and greater levels of interactivity, alternate file formats and applications must be used.

TIP
Macromedia's Flash application supports rich audio formats such as MP3 as well as highly refined interactivity.

PLANNING A GIF ANIMATION

The starting point in creating a GIF animation is to conceive of an idea for an animated effect. Some ideas might be a bouncing ball, a bird flapping its wings, or a logo fading in and out. When conceiving of an animated GIF effect, keep in mind the following:

▶ The number of frames in a GIF animation has a significant effect on the final file size of the animated GIF. Try to be as concise as possible in communicating the idea without ruining the illusion of motion.

▶ If you are planning to integrate your animation into a Web page, be cognizant of background color. If the animation is on a black background and your Web page background is also black, the animation won't have discernable edges. Elements coming in or going out from the edges of the animation will appear to be cut off when the animation is situated on a Web page.

▶ If you would like the elements in an animation to appear integrated with an overall Web page, be sure to match up the page's background color with the animation's background color.

Creating Animation Layers in Photoshop

While Photoshop cannot itself compile an animation, the application can be used to generate the individual frames that make up a Web movie. Figure 23.1 shows a logo designed in Photoshop. The animation concept was that the black logo would emerge from darkness, be illuminated by a white light, and then fade back into darkness.

BrainBug™

FIGURE 23.1: A logo to be animated

First, the logo was placed on a black background and had a white glow applied around the logo via the Layer ➤ Layer Style ➤ Outer Glow command (see Figure 23.2).

FIGURE 23.2: The logo on a black background with an Outer Glow layer effect applied

Then the backlighting effect was adjusted to create two intermediate steps between pure darkness and full brightness (see Figure 23.3).

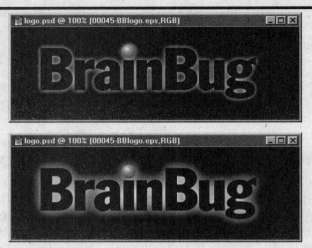

FIGURE 23.3: Two intermediate steps between darkness and full brightness

In Figure 23.4, the three layers are displayed in the Layers palette.

FIGURE 23.4: The three layers in the Layers palette

At this point, Photoshop hits a brick wall as an animation tool. Fortunately, the ImageReady application can take the Photoshop file's layers and turn them into a finished animated GIF.

PRODUCING ANIMATIONS WITH IMAGEREADY

The ImageReady feature that gets all of the headlines is Animation, and not without reason. ImageReady's GIF animation tools are located within the program's Animation palette. Saving animated GIFs is done through the program's standard saving options under the File menu.

The Animation Palette

At the heart of ImageReady's animation capabilities is the Animation palette, a control that provides a wide range of motion-based tools (see Figure 23.5).

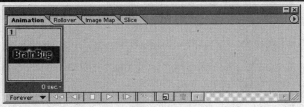

FIGURE 23.5: ImageReady's Animation palette

The Animation palette includes the following features:

Frame Number   Each frame in an animation is numbered in the upper-left corner.

Delay Menu   Under each frame is an interframe delay time—the amount of time until the next frame loads. Clicking the time will launch interframe delay options.

Looping Options   The lower-left corner of the Animation palette offers possible looping options. You can specify the number of times the animation will loop (Forever, Once, or any number of times) on a Web page.

Play Options   The bottom middle of the Animation palette is dedicated to various animation display options, including Rewind, Stop, Play, and Forward.

The remainder of the Animation palette includes New Frame and Trash commands along the bottom right of the palette.

Also included on the Animation palette is a menu that offers the following options:

New Frame   Use this command to create a new frame. Alternatively, you can click the New Frame icon at the bottom right of the Animation palette.

Delete Frame   Remove the currently selected frame or frames by using this command. Alternatively, you can use the Delete Frame icon at the bottom right of the Animation palette.

Delete Animation   Deletes all frames in the animation.

Copy Frame   Copies the currently selected frame.

Paste Frame   Pastes the most recently copied frame into the animation.

Select All Frames   Selects all the frames in the animation.

Tween   Launches a dialog box that allows you to create in-between frames (between two currently selected frames).

Reverse Frames   Reverses the order of two or more currently selected frames in an animation.

Optimize Animation   Uses up to two techniques (Bounding Box and Redundant Pixel elimination) to dramatically shrink the size of an animation.

Match Layer Across Frames   Takes the elements from the currently selected layer and inserts them into all frames in the animation.

Make Frames From Layers   Allows you to take a Photoshop document with layers and automatically create an animation.

Flatten Frames Into Layers   Merges the frames in an animation into one layer.

Palette Options   Provides you with three possible size settings for the display of frames in the Animation palette.

Creating an Animation from a Photoshop File

Setting up an animation in ImageReady based on a layered Photoshop file is a straightforward process. Simply follow these steps:

1. In Photoshop, open the file you wish to animate and click the Jump To button at the bottom of the main toolbar. This will launch the ImageReady application, loading the file you wish to animate.

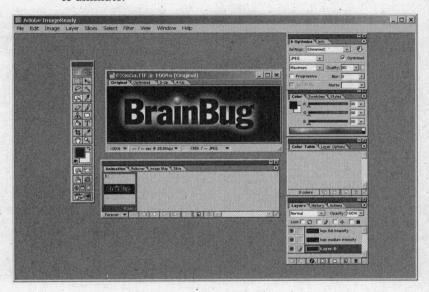

2. From the Animation palette, select Make Frames From Layers.

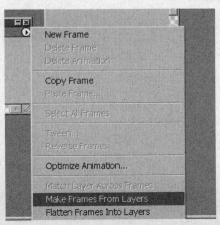

The frames have now been loaded into the Animation palette.

3. To preview the animation, click the Play button at the bottom of the Animation palette.

4. To preview the animation in a Web browser, select File ➢ Preview In ➢ *Your Web browser of choice*. The following graphic shows the animation in a Web browser, complete with the HTML code responsible for displaying the animation.

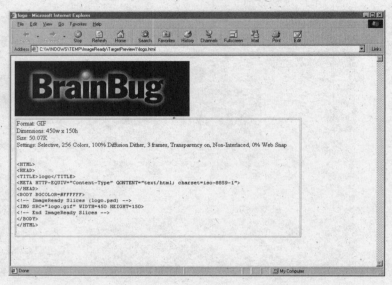

5. To save the file as an animated GIF, select File ➢ Save Optimized As.

If the animation is moving too fast or too slow, you can set a new value by clicking under each frame, altering the interframe delay time (as shown below), and resaving the animation.

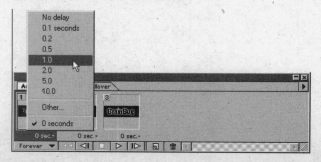

Tweening

ImageReady's tweening feature is a powerful way to automatically create intermediate frames in an animation. Tweening is an incredibly useful technique, and one that can be applied to all sorts of graphics and text.

To use the tweening feature, do the following:

1. Launch ImageReady and create a new file, 300 × 300 pixels.

2. Create a new layer by selecting Layer ➤ New ➤Layer.

3. Draw a circle in the upper-left corner with the Elliptical Marquee tool and fill with a color.

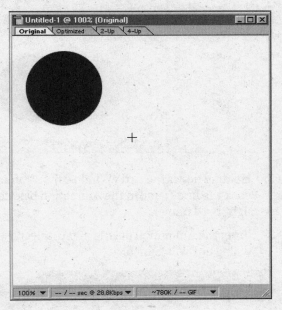

TIP

ImageReady includes a selection tool not found in Photoshop—the Rounded Rectangle Marquee tool.

4. Deselect the circle.

5. From the Animation palette menu, select New Frame.

6. With the Move tool, click and drag the circle to the lower-right corner of the file (as shown below). In the Animation palette, you will notice that the second frame reflects this new location.

7. Holding down the Ctrl (Windows) or Command (Mac) key, click the first frame in the Animation palette. This will highlight both frames.

8. From the Animation palette menu, select Tween. The Tween dialog box will launch.

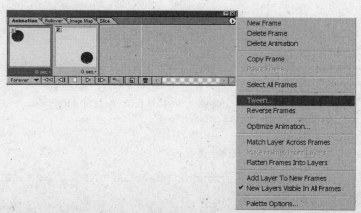

9. In the Tween dialog box, select 5 in the Frames To Add box and make sure that the Opacity check box is deselected.

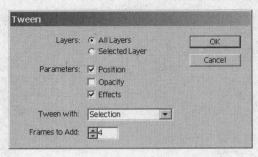

10. Click OK. As shown in Figure 23.6, the Animation palette now contains seven frames—the two originals and the five new "tweened" frames.

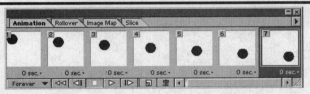

FIGURE 23.6: The resulting frames in the Animation palette

By playing the animation, you'll see that all of the in-between steps have been added to the animation.

Creating Complex Animations

The past two animations have demonstrated powerful techniques for creating rather straightforward movies. In this exercise, we will walk through the development of a more involved animation, one that includes text, graphics, and photography in an interesting way. Let's get started:

1. Launch ImageReady and create an image that is 500×300 pixels.

2. Create a new layer and set some text in the upper portion of the graphic with the Type tool, as shown below.

3. Deselect the text.

4. As in the previous example, create a new frame and tween the text to the lower portion of the image with three intermediate frames.

5. Create a new layer, draw a rectangle with the Marquee tool, and fill the rectangle under the text.

6. Create a new layer and put a photograph in the space above the text.

7. Set the opacity of the photo layer to 10% using the slider in the Layer palette.

8. Add a new frame to the animation by selecting New Frame from the Animation palette menu.

9. As shown below, move the rectangle right up under the text.

10. On the photo layer, adjust the opacity to 100%.

11. Tween the last two frames of the animation, adding two intermediate frames. Be sure the Opacity option is selected.

12. Save the animation by selecting File ➢ Save Optimized.

The frames from the resulting animation are displayed in Figure 23.7. This dramatic animation includes a text element, a graphic, and a photograph.

FIGURE 23.7: The resulting frames from the animation

FIGURE 23.7: continued

FIGURE 23.7: continued

FIGURE 23.7: continued

FIGURE 23.7: continued

FIGURE 23.7: continued

FIGURE 23.7: continued

FIGURE 23.7: continued

FIGURE 23.7: continued

WHAT'S NEXT

Although ImageReady does a great job of creating animations, if you have another Adobe tool, LiveMotion, you can generate even more realistic effects. The next chapter will show you how to go beyond the basic Photoshop toolkit to use the important movie-making capabilities of LiveMotion.

Chapter 24

CREATING WEB ANIMATIONS
WITH ADOBE LIVEMOTION

It's now time to expand beyond the boundaries of Photoshop and ImageReady to learn some of the fun and exciting aspects of LiveMotion—those of creating animations. Animating your work with this tool brings life to your site or to your presentations and, if done correctly, can give you or your clients a strong recognition base that will make people want to come back for more. Within this chapter, you'll be exploring the ways to animate various objects that you create and import, and you'll learn how to make text literally jump for joy. You'll also learn a few interesting tricks to help you create some special effects that will make your viewers ask, "How'd they do that?"

Adapted from *LiveMotion Visual JumpStart*
by Richard Schrand
ISBN 0-7821-2848-3   304 pages $19.99

BUILDING VECTOR OBJECTS

Vector objects are at the heart of most Shockwave animations you see on the Web. They are usually seen as animated rings, rotating circles, lines, and boxes flying across the screen. Being resolution-independent, these objects can be scaled down to nothingness or enlarged to fill the screen of a movie theater, and they won't show any degradation in quality. So they're the perfect objects to use for many designs.

The Pen Tool

The Pen tool is, quite literally, just that. You can draw any object you want with it; all you need is a little practice. In fact, the spaceship that is Live-Motion's logo was created using the Pen tool. Using the Pen tool is fairly simple, although it does take a bit of practice to get used to it. You lay down points by clicking on the workspace, and these points are automatically connected. You can make straight and curved lines with this tool. So how exactly does it work? Time to find out right now.

Practicing with the Pen Tool

First, create a document that is 640 × 480 pixels. Select a Web-safe color scheme, and then select the Pen tool.

1. Click once in the document. This creates the first point on your workspace.

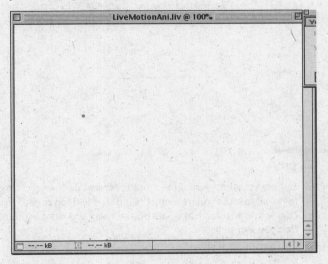

2. Hold down the Shift key and create another point. The two points are now connected.

NOTE

By holding down the Shift key when using the Pen tool, your points are constrained to straight lines. This works at 45-degree angles.

Part iv

3. While holding down the Shift key again, create a point above and to the center of the line you just created.

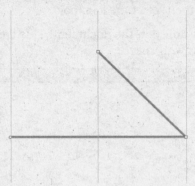

TIP

To help you align your work more precisely, do the following: Press Ctrl/Command+R to reveal rulers along the left side and top of your workspace. Move the cursor into the vertical or horizontal ruler and drag a guideline into the position you want.

4. Move the Pen tool back to the first point (which is represented by a red circle) you created and click again to close the triangle.

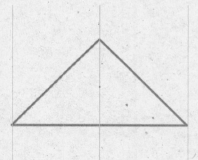

5. Making a curved line uses these same principles. Before you start, choose the Selection tool and click anywhere on the screen outside of the triangle to deselect the triangle you just made. Now, lay down a new point using the leftmost guide-line (if you placed one) as the starting point.

6. Create a second point. This time it doesn't matter if you hold the Shift key or not. But do not release the mouse button.

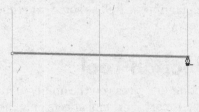

7. With this second point still selected, move your mouse around while continuing to hold the mouse button down. You'll notice handles coming out from the point you just made, and the line begins to curve in relationship to your movements.

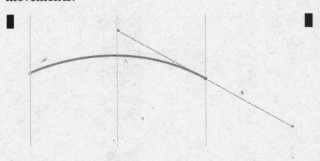

8. Without switching from the Pen tool, place your cursor over either endpoint of the control handle. This allows you to fine-tune your curve by moving the control handle around the screen.

With some planning as well as some experimentation, you can create nearly any object you want.

The Pen Selection Tool

The Pen Selection tool gives you the ability to make additional modifications to your vector art. This tool affects only the chosen point along your *vector path*, effectively changing the shape of an object you've made.

1. Select the Pen Selection tool from the toolbar.

2. Place it over either endpoint of the curved path you just made and drag that point to another location on the screen.

3. Now place the Pen Selection tool along the top point of the triangle you drew at the beginning of this chapter. Click once to select this point.

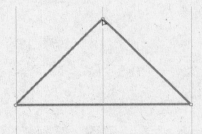

4. Drag this point around to see how it affects the triangle's look.

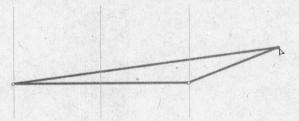

The Transform Tool

Unlike the Pen Selection tool, the Transform tool affects the entire graphic you created. It can give you some very interesting skewed effects, depending on the type of vector art you're modifying. It can also make the object look as if it were drawn using calligraphy. Before you start on this portion, undo the change you made to the triangle by pressing Ctrl/Command+Z.

1. Choose the Ellipse tool from the toolbar and create a circle on the workspace.

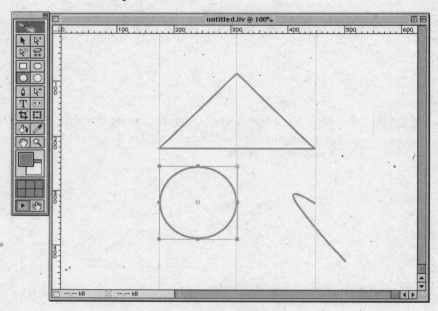

2. Select the Transform tool from the toolbar.

3. Place your cursor on any of the modification points (in the graphic, it's placed at the top center point) and begin moving it to screen right.

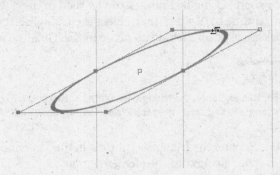

4. Now select any other point on the manipulator box and move it until you come up with something that looks interesting to you.

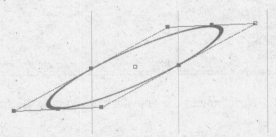

ANIMATING SHAPES

For the purposes of this section, delete all the shapes you just created except for the triangle, and open the Timeline window. Our work from here on is going to use this window extensively, so take a few moments to set up your screen so that the Timeline window is unobscured.

Zoom

You need to set some parameters in the Timeline before you begin creating your zoom. Using techniques you learned in previous chapters, set the animation time to 05s and then select the triangle either by clicking it in the workspace or by clicking its name in the Timeline window itself.

NOTE

For this example, the triangle was filled with a color. To do this, make sure the triangle is selected, open the Properties window, and click the Fill button.

1. Expand the triangle's controls in the Timeline by clicking the triangle next to the element's name.

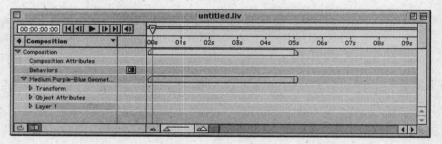

2. Now expand the Transform options in the list.

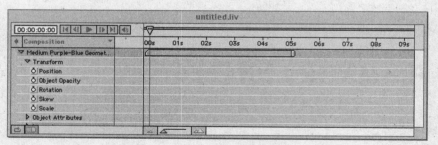

3. The first thing you'll do is change the starting size of the triangle. Make sure the Timeline marker is at 00s. Then change the triangle size in one of two ways: by selecting a corner

point on the triangle in the workspace and dragging it down to the size you want, or by changing the parameters in the Transform window.

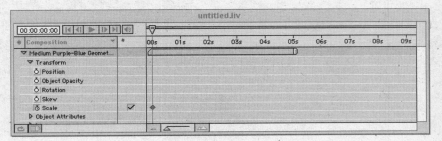

4. Move the Timeline marker to 02s.

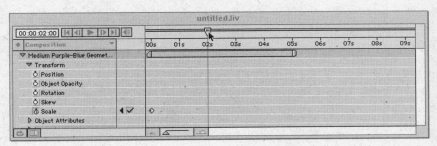

5. Click the Scale check box to set a new keyframe. This tells the program that a new basic frame should be set.

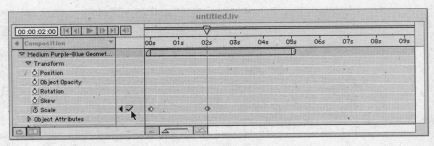

6. Resize the triangle close to its original size, using the guide-lines to help you.

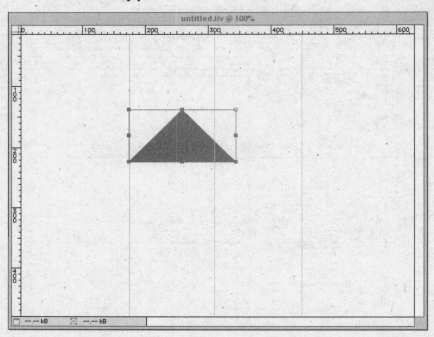

7. Move the Timeline marker back and forth between the two keyframes to see your zoom in action.

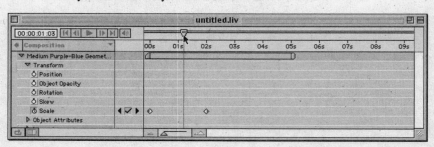

Spin

The zoom has now been created, but you still have three seconds to play with. Plus, during the zoom you just created you want to see the triangle spin. Let's create that portion of the animation now.

1. Move the Timeline marker to 01s and set a keyframe by clicking the Rotation check box. This is where the spin will begin.

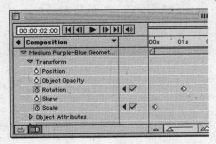

2. Place the Timeline marker at 02s and click the Rotation check box to set a keyframe. Open the Transform window (if it isn't already) and in the Rotation control box type **-360**. The spin is now completed.

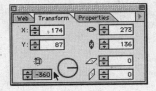

3. The spin's timing needs to be changed. Select the first keyframe marker in the Rotation area of the Timeline.

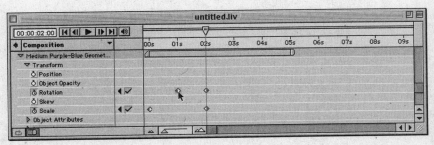

Part iv

4. Drag this marker just to the right of 00s. This changes the starting point of the rotation you just created.

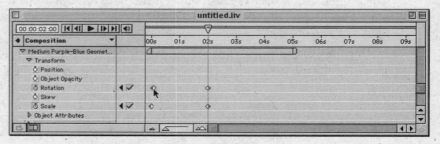

5. Drag the 02s keyframe marker to approximately 03.5s to change the end of rotation.

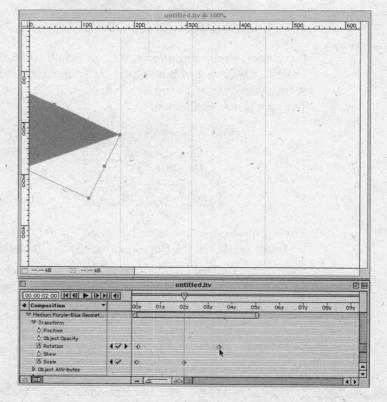

Notice that as you move the end of the Rotation keyframe marker, your triangle moves. This graphic is showing its position at the point in time where the Timeline marker is placed.

Creating a Motion Path

As you created the zoom and spin, you probably noticed the edges of the triangle moving off the workspace. If you saved your file at this point, that's exactly what would happen in the resulting Shockwave file. But you can fix that by creating a motion path.

1. Select Position in the Timeline and move the Timeline marker back to 00s.

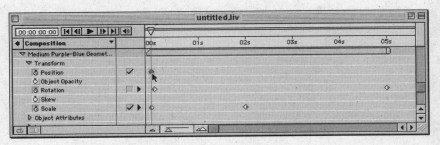

2. In the workspace, move the triangle to the upper-left corner of the screen. You have now created a new starting point.

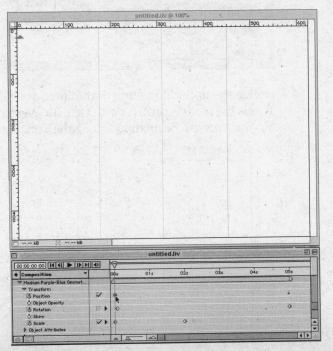

3. Now move the Timeline marker to 05s and then move the triangle from the upper-left corner to the lower-right corner of the workspace until it's totally off the screen.

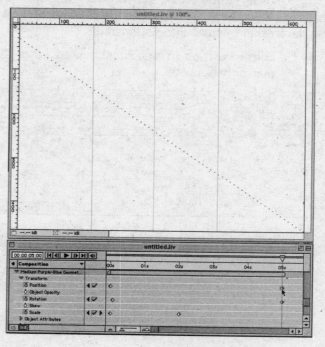

4. Notice the dotted blue line that follows your movements. This is the motion path. As with virtually everything in Live-Motion, this can be modified along the Timeline as well.

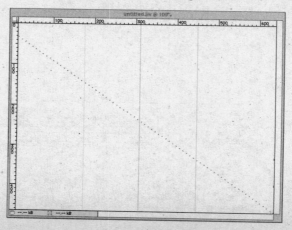

5. Play your animation now. You'll see your triangle zoom, spin, and move across the screen.

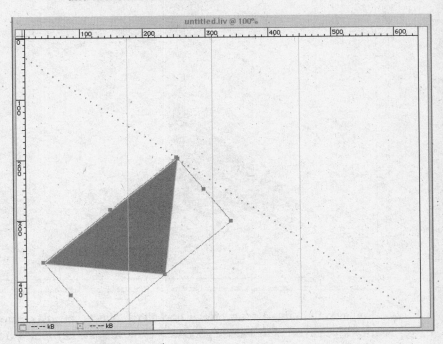

6. Again, notice that the edge of the triangle moves off screen during the rotation. Fix this by moving the Timeline marker to 02s and creating a new keyframe in the Position area.

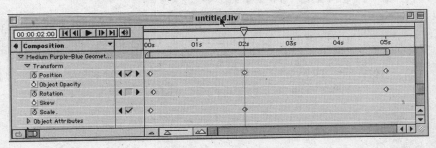

7. Move the triangle to a new place on the workspace. The path changes to reflect your movement.

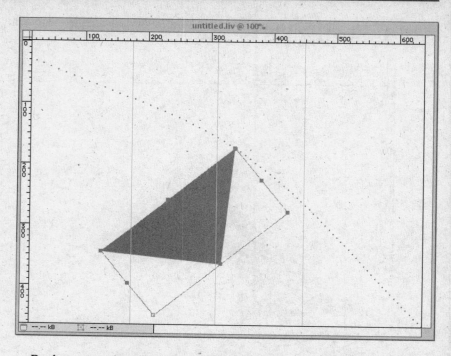

Replay your animation now to see how all the effects you just created work with each other. It's also a good idea to move some keyframes around on the Timeline to see how that would affect the overall animation.

WORKING WITH TEXT

While there isn't a lot of difference between working with text and what you just did, there are a lot of differences in how you can modify your text. For this section, create a new document or use the file LiveMotionAni.liv from the Sybex Web site. The latter file has all the elements already placed so you can focus on building some interesting animations.

NOTE

To download practice files mentioned in this book, navigate to the Sybex Web site (www.sybex.com) and enter 2991 into the search box. When you get to the page for Photoshop Complete, follow the links to download the file.

Building a Dissolve

Here you'll use a block of text. If you're not using the above-mentioned file from the Sybex Web site, go ahead and compose your own using the Type tool. The block of text we'll use for the demonstration is the body text that starts with "is the easiest way..."

1. Activate the block of text by selecting it either in the workspace or on the appropriate layer in the Timeline.

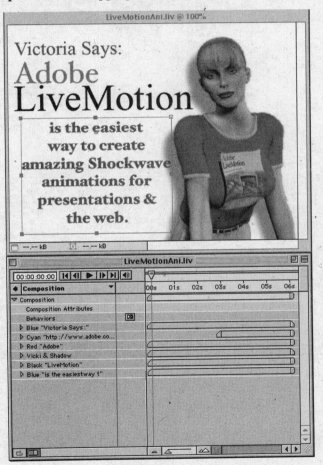

2. Expand the layer's options, and then expand the Transform area.

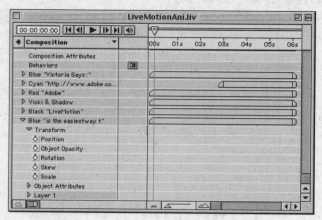

3. Select Object Opacity. Open the Opacity window, and at 00s, set the text's opacity to 0.

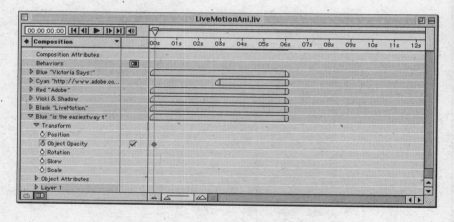

4. Move the Timeline marker to 03s and create a new Opacity keyframe, keeping it set to 0.

NOTE

You want to keep the Opacity setting at 0 so the dissolve won't start happening from the beginning of the animation. We want this text to remain hidden until the last two seconds of the animation.

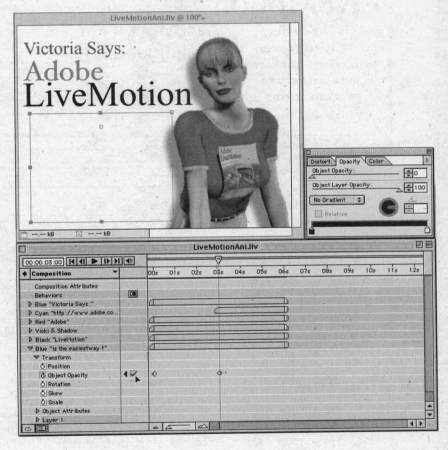

5. Move the Timeline marker to 04s and set another keyframe. Change the Opacity setting to 100. And that's it. You've now created a dissolve in LiveMotion.

Rotating Text

Save the file you just worked on, but don't close it. For this portion, you'll be bringing in both the "Victoria Says:" and "Adobe" text lines at the beginning of your animation. Before you start, make sure that the Timeline marker is set at 00s.

1.   Begin by opening the Transform window. Select the "Victoria Says:" text, expand the Timeline options for this layer, select Rotation, and then rotate the text 24 degrees.

2. Choose Position and move the "Victoria Says:" text off screen in the upper-left corner.

3. Now select the "Adobe" text, choose Position in its Timeline layer options, and move the text off the left side of the screen. Use the Left arrow key on your keyboard to position the text totally off the workspace.

TIP

Hold down the Shift key to constrain the horizontal position of the text as you move it.

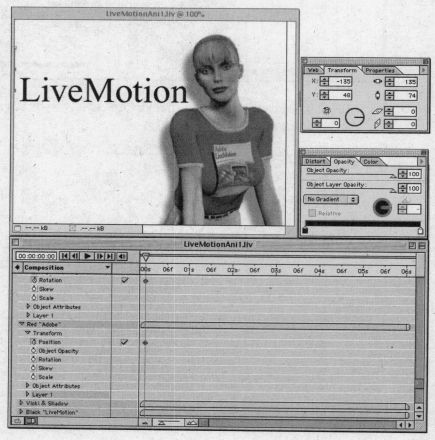

4. Move the Timeline marker to 01s 06f. Select the "Victoria Says:" text and move it back to its original position on the workspace. Then set its Rotation to 0.

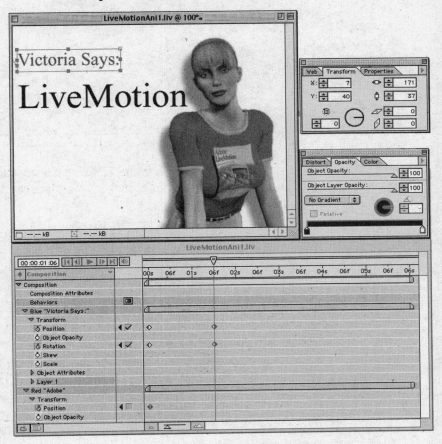

5. Select the "Adobe" text, select Position to add a keyframe, then move the Timeline marker to 02s. Move "Adobe" back into place.

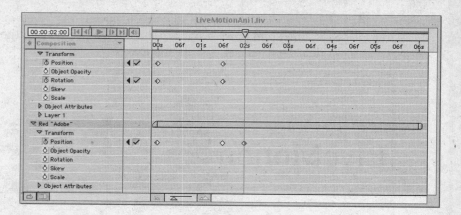

6. To add some more interest, slide the Timeline marker back until the upright portion of the "b" in Adobe just touches the "V" in Victoria.

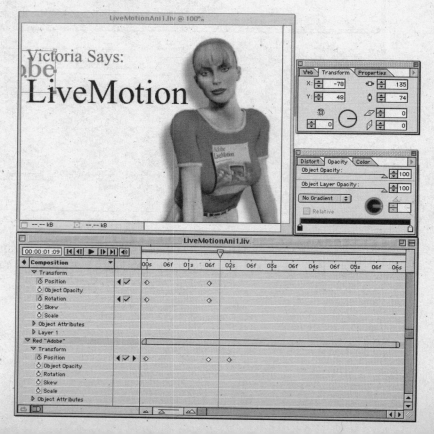

7. Select "Victoria Says:" and change the Rotation to 10.

8. Move the Timeline marker slightly to the right. Move "Victoria Says:" up until it's comfortably above "Adobe."

9. Again, move the Timeline marker to the point just after "Adobe" slides into place and change the "Victoria Says:" Rotation back to 0.

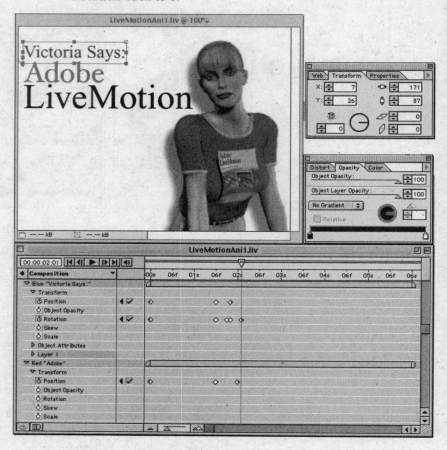

You've now created text that moves in, interacts with other text, rotates, and locks into position.

Working with Individual Letters

Now it's time to work with the text "LiveMotion." You can separate a block of text into individual letters, which is exactly what you'll do now. In this section, because of space considerations, we'll describe how to work with only two of the letters, the "L" and the "M." But you'll want to modify each of the letters in the text for the completed animation.

1. With "LiveMotion" selected in the Timeline, select Object ➤ Break Apart Text from the pull-down menu.

2. Notice that each letter now has its own layer in the Timeline.

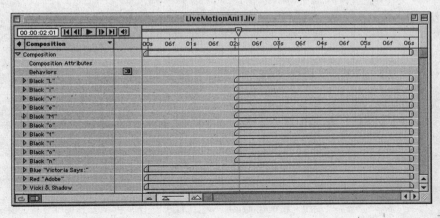

3. Click anywhere outside the "LiveMotion" text in the work-space to deselect the text, then choose the "L" layer in the Timeline window and expand it to reveal the options.

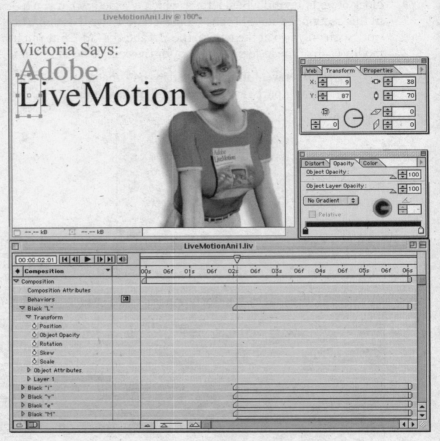

4. Set keyframes at various positions between 00s and 01s, and at each keyframe, change the Rotation so that the letter "L" rocks back and forth.

5. Here's a cool trick: With the Shift key held down, select all the Rotation keyframes except for the first one. Hold down the Alt/Option key on the keyboard and drag the selected keyframes to the right. Duplicate keyframes are made.

6. Repeat this process until the keyframes extend just past the 02s mark in the Timeline.

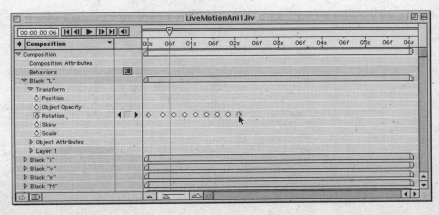

7. Return the Timeline marker to 00s and select the "M" layer. Expand it to reveal the options and choose Skew.

8. Repeat step 4, changing the Skew angle at each of the newly created keyframes.

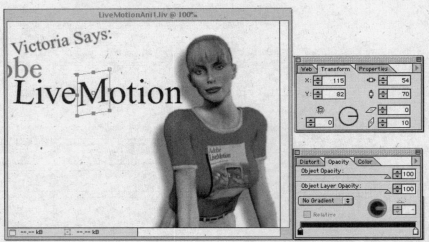

9. Repeat step 5 to duplicate all the keyframes except the first one.

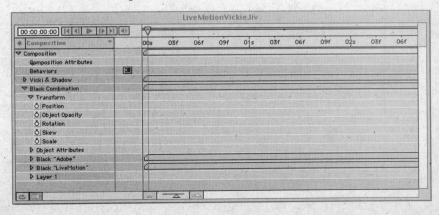

Now take some time and modify each of the other letters, giving them different animated looks. The final animation, titled `LiveMotionAni1.liv`, can be found on the Sybex Web site.

INTERACTING WITH IMAGES

You probably noticed our model, Vicki, in the various pictures throughout this chapter. She's a 3D model from Zygote (`www.zygote.com`) that was posed and saved as a layered Photoshop document. The shadow is one layer; Vicki is the other. In this section, we'll get the Adobe LiveMotion title to move around her using various tricks before locking into place.

1. Select the Black Combination layer in the `LiveMotion-Vicki.liv` file from the Sybex Web site, and expand it to show the options.

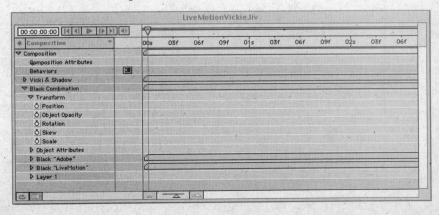

2. Open Transform, and select Position and Scale to set keyframes at 00s. Set the Width of this layer to 5, and place the layer behind Vicki's head. You will still see the bounding box as long as the text is selected.

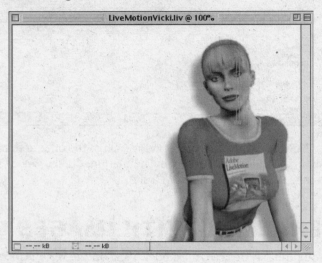

3. Move the Timeline marker to 02s, change the layer's width back to 283, and then change the layer's position so it's coming out from behind Vicki.

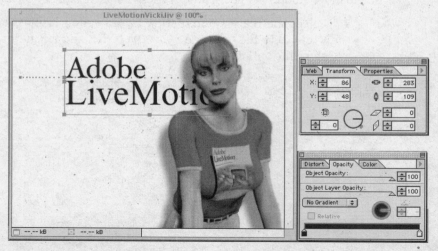

4. Finish out the movement at 03s so the layer is fully revealed.

5. Move to the end of the Timeline, place the cursor over the end of the layer's indicator, and move the end to 03s.

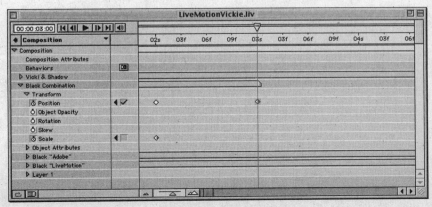

6. Choose Edit ➢ Duplicate to copy the Black Combination layer. It is automatically positioned as the top layer, which is where you want it. Select this duplicated layer in the Timeline.

7. Expand this layer's options, and delete all the keyframes except the last one. Move this to the beginning of the new layer, which should be at the 03s mark.

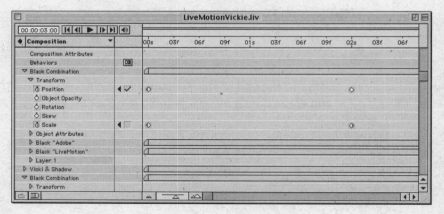

8. If need be, select Scale and change it to 283.

9. Shorten this layer in the Timeline to the 06s mark, activate a keyframe in the Position layer, and move the layer off the bottom of the workspace.

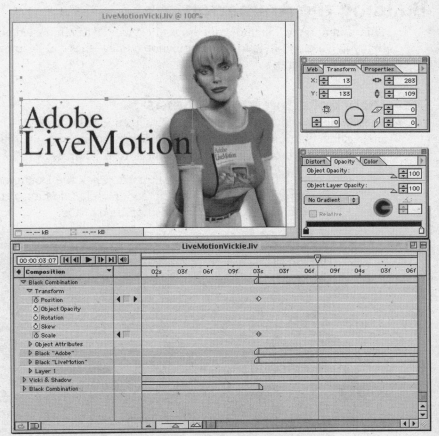

OPTIMIZING AND VIEWING FILES IN A BROWSER

As your LiveMotion prowess expands and your animations become more complicated, it will become extremely important to know how to optimize your work so it runs smoothly in browsers such as Internet Explorer and Netscape Communicator. So in this section, you will create a more complex animation in LiveMotion and optimize the file.

Building the Animation

This animation will include numerous effects and a few imported images that you'll assign filters to. The Photoshop 6 image files can be found on the Sybex Web site.

Incorporating the Elements

The file you're about to create is a splash screen for a home page. The site, again a fictitious one, deals with 3D design, so the photographic images that will be shown all feature some sort of 3D artwork.

1. Create a file that is 640 × 480 pixels. Click the Document Background Color chip in the Tool panel and change the color to Black. Set the Composition time to 10s.

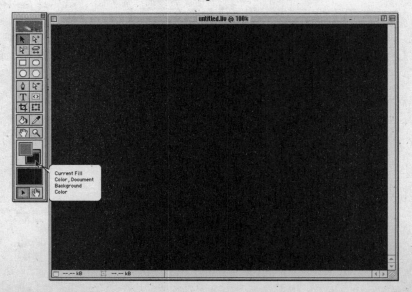

2. Place the following files onto the Timeline:

BabySketch.jpg

BigJohn.jpg

Mummy.jpg

Nutsy.jpg

Squash.jpg (You will need to resize this image using the Transform options.)

TheLastCookie.jpg.

▶ Notice that when one of the JPEG files is selected, you can access the filters under Object ➤ Filters.

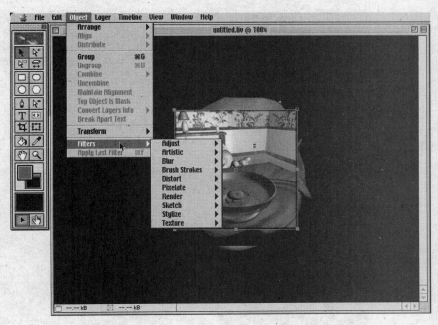

3. If any image layers are selected, deselect them and activate the Pen tool. Draw a series of straight lines in different areas of the workspace. Make each of these lines a different color, and make sure the width is 24 pixels or less.

NOTE

You will need to deselect each line after you've created it before drawing the next one.

Part iv

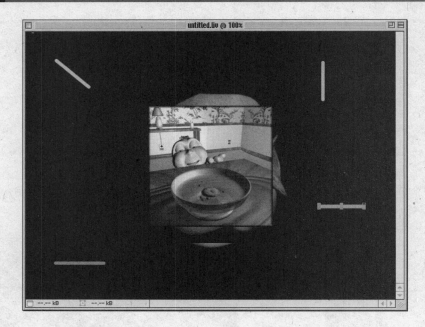

4. Change the Softness of each of the lines to 10 in the Layer window.

NOTE

Switch to the Select tool after creating a line in order to change its color.

5. Now that these base elements are set, it's time to position them. Move each of the elements off the edge of the workspace so all you're left with is the main screen.

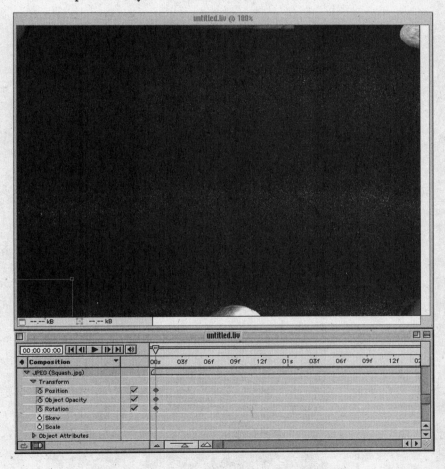

6. Set the Opacity for all the JPEG images to 0. Select the JPEG (Squash.jpg) layer. Expand the layer's Timeline controls, and set Rotation in the Transform window to 63.

Part iv

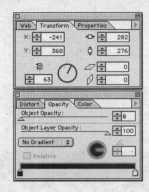

7. Set the Squash layer's end time to 03s.

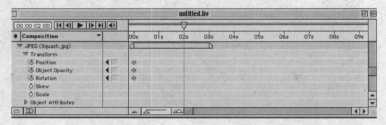

8. Set the Timeline marker to 02s. Change the Opacity to 100. Move Squash.jpg in a diagonal path close to the upper-right corner of the workspace, and then select Position in the Timeline by clicking the Position button. Finally, change Rotation to 45.

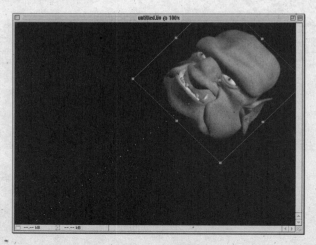

9. Add a Filter effect to the image. This will affect the image throughout its animation, so select something that you can live with. Here the Grain filter has been used, found under Texture in the Filters menu.

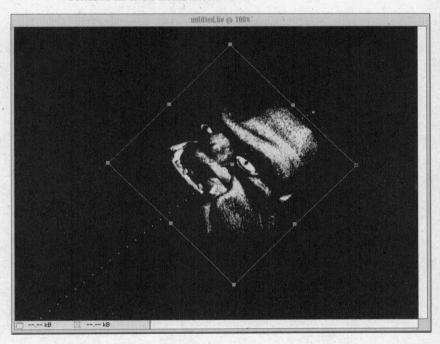

Repeat these steps to make the other images fly across the screen, fading out at the end. Also apply different filters to the images, and change the starting points for each so they don't cross over each other.

Assigning an Active Matte

One area not covered yet is the use of *mattes* on an image or element. Mattes act as areas that mask out parts of the image, making them clear. In the case of the images you are using, the edges are square and can block out other pictures. Here's how to assign mattes to an image or object.

1. Select the Mummy.jpg layer. Open the Properties window and, in the Alpha Channel pop-up, select Active Matte.

2. Open the Library window. There are a number of premade mattes for you to use. The black areas indicate the area that will be seen.

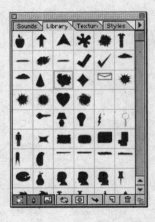

3. Drag an image onto the Active Matte panel in the Properties window.

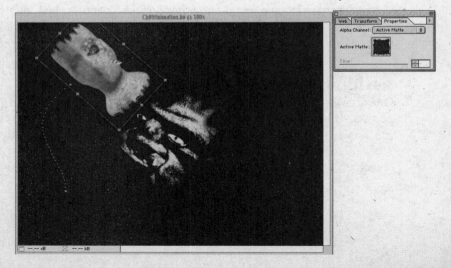

TIP

You can create your own mattes in a program like Adobe Photoshop, and import and save them in the Library window for later use.

Now animate the lines so they fly through the scene at various points in time. Add some text letting people know what site they are visiting, and save your file.

NOTE

The file we created is available for download in the Chapter09Files folder on the Sybex Web site. You can use this to practice on as you work through the next section of the chapter.

Optimizing

As you'll see, with so much going on in the animation, the playback can bog down in LiveMotion. You need to make sure it won't do that on the Web, so you need to optimize the file for smooth, unencumbered playback.

Optimization Setup

Follow these steps to set up optimization:

1. Select View ➤ Active Export Preview. This activates an information box at the bottom left of the workspace.

Part iv

2. The file that is being used as demonstration is 13.9KB. The smaller the file size, the faster the file will load over the Web.

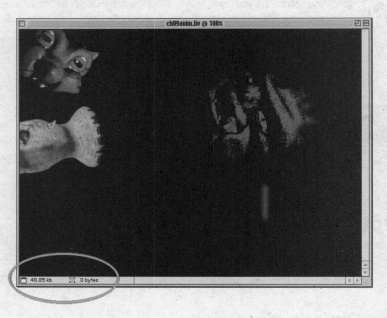

TIP

Try to keep your files at 50KB or less. This makes for a fairly small file size, guaranteeing fast loading over slower modems. If you have a file that is over 100KB, you might need to see what could be dropped from the animation (without affecting the overall design) so that it will load faster.

NOTE

File size information is automatically updated when you use the Export Settings window prior to saving your file.

3. Choose File ➢ Export Settings to open the Export window.

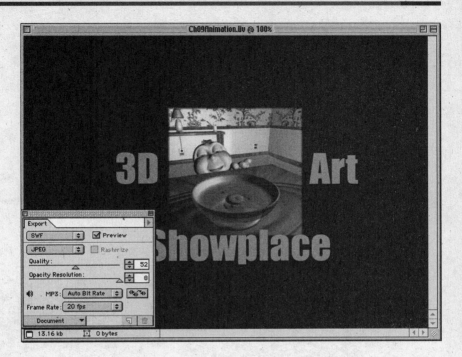

NOTE

The Export window has been placed immediately over the Active Export Pre-view information screen for easier viewing.

4. You have various options when saving your LiveMotion file. The first pop-up menu determines the file format. Your choices are as follows:

Photoshop Saves the file as a single image in Photoshop format.

GIF Saves the file as a GIF animation. This selection generates the GIF file and an HTML document. Expect colors to be different and playback to be slow if you're saving a complicated animation.

JPEG Saves your work as a static JPEG file and an HTML document. The color quality of playback is much better than with GIF when using photographic or non–vector graphic images, although the quality can vary dramatically depending on the settings you choose.

PNG-Indexed   PNG is a file format that creates high-quality images that are small in size. This format converts the file's colors to Web-safe colors.

PNG-Truecolor   Uses the Windows color chart when saving a file.

NOTE

If you are using a Mac, this setting will use the system color palette instead of the Windows color palette.

SWF-Shockwave   This is the format you will save in more times than not.

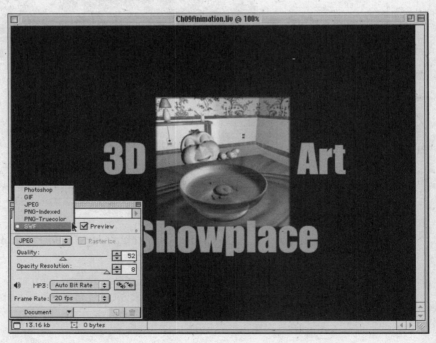

TIP

Make sure the Preview check box is selected so you can see your changes on the workspace screen. This helps you determine how your saved file will look.

5. As you make changes in the Export window, the file size is automatically updated so you can choose the most efficient method in which to save your file.

6. Once you have chosen the format for your file, select File Export or File Export As, and you're ready to put your work on the Web.

Part iv

Viewing Your File in Your Browser

In LiveMotion, you have the ability to assign one or more browsers so you can view your work on them prior to saving the file. To preview your work, do the following.

1. Select File Preview In. If this is your first time using this feature, you will be asked to pick out the browser you want to use. Once you have assigned one or more browsers to use, the browsers will be listed in the Preview In sublist.

TIP

You will definitely want to have more than one browser assigned to the Preview In feature so you can see how your work will look on the different browsers visitors might use.

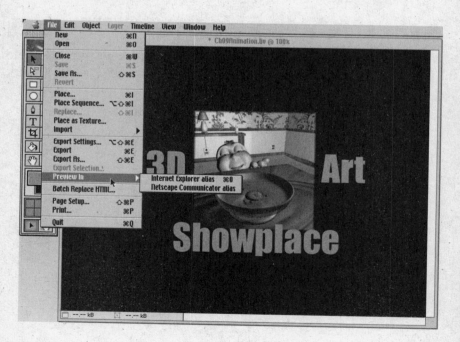

2. When you choose the browser, it will automatically be launched, and the animation will play. Click Refresh to see it again.

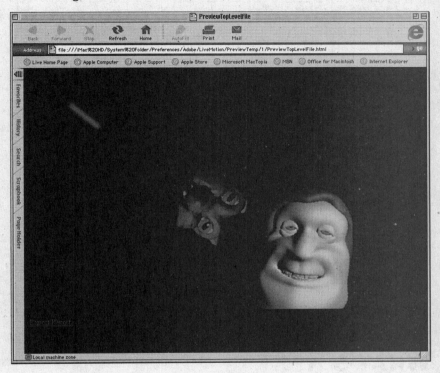

3. A report is also generated that shows you approximately how long it will take for your animation to be downloaded at different modem speeds. This is generated as an HTML document stored in the same location as the animation.

TIP

To view this HTML report, double-click the file, and your browser will automatically open. This is where you will view the report.

Part iv

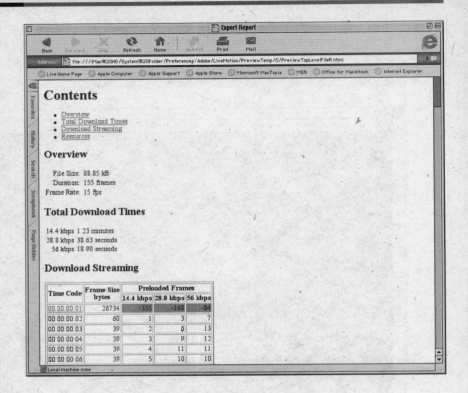

WHAT'S NEXT

This chapter has concentrated on preparing images and animations that exist only in cyberspace on Web pages. The next chapter deals with important concerns when making hard copies for the real world, including printing your Photoshop documents, managing color, and troubleshooting an ink-jet printer.

PART V
PRINTING YOUR IMAGES

Chapter 25

SOME DAY MY PRINTS WILL COME

Your mother was right. You should share. Your digital camera captures great memories. Shouldn't you share them with friends and family? Sure, you could e-mail the digital versions, but a print is something tangible that doesn't require a computer to access. You can turn your digital photos into prints, either at home on your own printer or by using a finishing service. With only a few steps, you can make memories that really will last a lifetime or beyond.

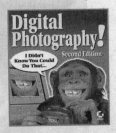

Adapted from *Digital Photography! I Didn't Know You Could Do That...* by Erica Sadun
ISBN 0-7821-2965-X   384 pages $24.99

Know Your Printer

These days, you can create terrific prints using your home printer. A home-based printer excels when you want to print just a few pictures at a time and you need rapid turnaround. The prints may not match the fineness and longevity of those from a photo finisher, but often you don't need those qualities. You may want to produce a birthday card, a poster, a business proposal, or a school assignment. For these projects, you can save time and energy simply by using your printer.

Ink-jet printers are the most common for home use, but there are several other types that can handle photo printing as well. Here's a quick summary of the top printer styles.

Ink-Jet Printers

Ink-jet printers are today's belles of the ball. These printers provide affordable and convenient printing solutions. You can pick up a high-quality ink-jet system for a very reasonable price. Many stores even bundle an ink-jet printer in with a computer. These printers produce good resolution and high-quality colors, and they are easy to use. Over the past few years, ink-jet quality has continued to climb higher. If you were put off by ink-jet quality in the past, look again. Today's printers are much improved.

Ink-jet printers work by squirting colored dyes onto paper. The paper absorbs these quick-drying inks to create your output. Ink-jets work well with both black and colored inks. This allows you to mix pictures and text on a single page. You can buy special-quality ink-jet photo paper, which works with your printer's dyes to produce professional-looking, glossy images. By picking the right paper (see "Know Your Paper," later in this chapter), you can create masterpieces without ever leaving your home.

On the downside, ink-jet printers have some disadvantages:

- ▶ They can be fussy. You must regularly clean their ink nozzles.

- ▶ If you print a lot of color pictures, you will need to refill your ink, and refills can be expensive.

- ▶ Ink-jets are notoriously slow, although more recent models can zip along nicely.

- ▶ Sometimes the paper-advance mechanism creates white lines within your picture.

▶ When you print a goof, you're stuck with it. You've lost the ink, paper, and the time it took to create that goof.

You may not want to use an ink-jet printer to create special keepsakes. For all other print jobs, it may be just the thing.

NOTE

Sometimes, after running your ink cartridges through a self-clean cycle, they may still seem clogged. You can use cotton swabs to clean the nozzles. Dip the swabs in rubbing alcohol and dab lightly at the nozzles to loosen and clear the ink. Avoid dripping the alcohol, and use care when dabbing.

Dye-Sublimation Printers

Dye-sublimation (*dye-sub* for short) printers are just starting to infiltrate the consumer market. Although expensive, these printers produce outstanding quality prints. Looking at a photo printed on a dye-sub printer, you might compare it favorably to a picture you see in a magazine.

Dye-sub printers work by heating ribbons of colored inks. The melted inks bond with the paper. The higher the heat, the more ink transferred and the more intense the color produced.

Dye-sub printers may produce great quality, but they do have their drawbacks:

▶ Along with the high cost for the printer itself comes the high cost for its supplies. Keeping your printer in ink can strain the wallet.

▶ They do not fare well at printing text. You can't replace your general-function printer with a dye-sub unit. At best, you can use it as a special-purpose second printer.

▶ Only the most expensive models can create full-size (8 × 10 inch) output. Many dye-sub printers can create only small images.

NOTE

I own a dye-sublimation printer that is a few years old. It creates 0.75 × 1.5 *inch* prints! Of course, today's dye-sub printers work with more standard output sizes, creating 3.5 × 5 inch or 4 × 6 inch prints.

Laser Printers

You can produce decent black-and-white prints using a laser printer. You probably won't want to frame these prints, but they work very well in school reports and business proposals when you don't need true color.

Laser printers approximate tone by using a technique called *dithering*. Darker areas print using more dots. Lighter areas use fewer dots.

Of course, if you really have the bucks to spend, you can pick up a color laser printer. These cost only a few thousand dollars.

KNOW YOUR PAPER

Many people think, "Paper is paper." They are wrong, at least when it comes to the paper for photo prints. Paper quality affects print quality. Often, the paper you print on can enhance or detract from your images. Today, you can purchase a vast range of paper types.

Plain Paper

Printing on "plain paper" offers both advantages and drawbacks. Paper cost is low; you can pick up a ream for a few dollars. On the other hand, the fibrous nature of the paper means that ink will spread to some degree before drying. The fibers wick the dyes as they are applied. Because of this, you can expect pictures printed on untreated paper to look a little fuzzier than those printed on special, photo-quality paper.

You can improve your plain-paper prints by purchasing bright, heavy stock. When shopping, look for key advertising phrases: Bright White, Brighter White, Heavy Weight, and Premium Grade. Brighter paper improves color quality and trueness. Heavier paper produces stiffer, more durable prints, with fewer curling problems. Avoid cheap, low-weight paper, because eventually the loose fibers can clog your printer.

There's one more tip for plain-paper printing: Purchase high-quality ink-jet paper from the same manufacturer that made your ink-jet printer. Each manufacturer fine-tunes its printer in different ways. You can be sure that each printer is tuned to produce the best results on its companion product.

Glossy Photo Paper

You can pick up ink-jet photographic-quality paper at almost any office supply store. This paper is very stiff (photo weight) and very bright. It is designed to avoid spreading ink and to produce a glossy finish after printing. Although prices are dropping, expect to spend up to a dollar a sheet for this product.

Here are a few tips to keep in mind when using photo paper with your ink-jet:

▶ Print on the slightly rough/slightly glossy side. Although the way that you load paper varies by printer, you can always determine which side receives the ink. Orient the paper so that the photo will be printed on the rougher, glossier side.

▶ Avoid handling the paper. Keep fingerprints off the page, both before and after printing.

▶ Keep your paper dry and cool. Moisture and high temperatures can destroy both your prints and your paper.

▶ Don't mix paper types. In fact, it is recommended that you insert only one sheet of photo paper in your printer at a time. This avoids some jamming issues and ensures that you print your picture on the correct stock.

▶ Carefully adjust your printing dialog box settings. Make sure to specify a photo-grade paper and the best print quality before printing.

▶ Let your prints air dry, image side up, for an hour after printing. During that time, avoid touching or breathing on your paper. This allows your colors to set true. (Ambient humidity and ink quality will affect drying time.)

▶ You may stack your dried prints, but insert plain paper between each print. If any ink bleeds, it will affect the inserts rather than the next print.

▶ As with plain paper, you should try to match your photo-paper brand to your printer. You can be sure each manufacturer has fine-tuned its printer to work best with its own brand of photo paper.

▶ Photo paper is sensitive to ultraviolet (UV) light. When displaying your pictures, be sure to keep your photo out of direct sunlight and, if possible, use UV-blocking glass for the picture frame.

Part v

Special-Purpose Paper

Today, you can purchase an almost unlimited variety of specialty papers. These range from heavy-bond sheets to glossy print-to-the-edge cards. Check the paper section in your local office supply store or craft shop to get an idea of the range of product offerings.

Each package of specialty paper should contain instructions. Read these directions and follow them. They will help you to produce the best results with each paper type.

NOTE

If you're printing greeting cards, you can save a lot of money by buying bulk card stock rather than the prefolded variety. Recently, I visited Wal-Mart and purchased a pack of 10 half-fold card stock (with envelopes) for about $8. At the same visit, I bought a pack of 150 (yes, that's right, 150, but without envelopes) unfolded card stock for $4. I consider 15 times the stock at half the cost to be a nice deal.

PRINT 'EM UP

If you want to print some pictures on your new, expensive specialty paper (or even your cheap, plain paper), but find it's a pain to get the prints to look just right, you can let someone else do the hard work for you. Adobe PhotoDeluxe provides a variety of print styles and layouts. These help you conserve paper while printing one or more images at a time.

Before you begin, here's a tip to help you minimize your risk and conserve your specialty paper: Test print on plain paper before committing to your specialty stock. Sure, this consumes extra ink, but glossy or photo-weight stock usually costs a lot more per print than the ink.

Print One

Okay, we're not talking rocket science here. We're just going to print one copy of a picture on one page, using PhotoDeluxe's special features. Can it get any simpler?

1. Launch PhotoDeluxe and open your picture.

2. Click the Get & Fix Photo tab of the Activity bar. Then choose Print ➤ Print Preview. This step allows you to preview how

your picture will print before committing it to your printer. You will print everything within the large rectangle. When you finish examining the preview, click OK. You are now ready to print.

3. Choose Print ➤ Print. The Print dialog box will appear, as shown below. Carefully set the options for your print job. Make sure to specify the proper resolution, print quality, and paper type. Also check that you've selected between black-and-white and color output.

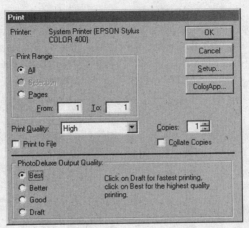

4. Select an output quality for your PhotoDeluxe image. Choose between Draft, Good, Better, and Best. When using specialty print stock, always select Best.

5. Use the Print dialog box to select the paper type and orientation.

6. After setting your print options and output quality, click OK to begin printing.

WARNING

Always set the correct orientation. Both PhotoDeluxe and your system's Print dialog box will let you choose between landscape or portrait prints. In the Print dialog box, simply click the appropriate icon. In PhotoDeluxe, choose File ➤ Page Setup or Get & Fix Photo ➤ Print ➤ Page Setup. Don't waste paper by forgetting this step.

Print Many

PhotoDeluxe allows you to print several copies of a photo on a single page. This both increases your printing efficiency (less wasted paper) and allows you to print on special-purpose stock. Your stock options (okay, forgive me, but it was an obvious pun) include such choices as sheets of labels, business cards, or stickers.

Here's how to print multiple copies on a single page:

1. Launch PhotoDeluxe and open your picture.

2. Click the Get & Fix Photo tab of the Activity bar. Then choose Print ➤ Print Multiple On A Page. The Print Multiple dialog box will appear. As shown below, this dialog box presents a preview of your print job, showing the maximum number of images that will fit on your page.

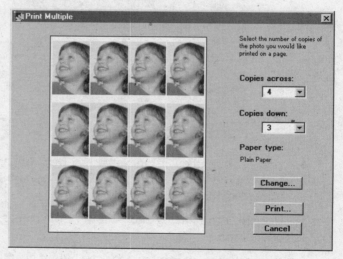

NOTE

PhotoDeluxe does not resize your images. You will not be able to fit any more items on your page than shown in the Print Multiple dialog box without shrinking your picture.

3. If you want to print fewer copies than the maximum, reduce the number of copies in either the Copies Across or the Copies Down box.

4. PhotoDeluxe assumes you will print on plain 8.5 × 11-inch paper. To print on another stock size, click the Change button, select your correct paper brand and type, and then click OK.

5. Click the Print button to continue. The Print dialog box will appear. As when you're printing a single copy (described in the previous section), set the options for your print job. Then click OK to begin printing.

After you've printed multiple photo copies on a page, you'll want to cut out the separate prints. See the "Cut It Out" section for some cutting tips.

Print Standard Sizes

When you print pictures using standard sizes, you can fit them into standard picture frames and photo album pockets. Unlike when you use the Print Multiple On A Page option, PhotoDeluxe's Print Standard Sizes option does not try to use every inch of the page. Instead, you select from a variety of print sheet layouts. These include two 4 × 6- inch prints or a 5 × 7-inch photo surrounded by a bunch of wallet-sized photos. If you've ever ordered pictures from a photo studio, these sheets will look familiar. You also have the option of printing different photos on the same page.

Here's how to print standard sizes:

1. Launch PhotoDeluxe. Click the Get & Fix Photo tab of the Activity bar and select Print ➢ Print Standard Sizes. The Activity bar will display the steps in the Print Standard Sizes guided activity.

2. Click 1 – Style ➢ Different Photos. (Choose this option even if you decide to use only one photo.)

3. Click 2 – Layout ➢ Choose Layout. Double-click one of the page templates.

4. Click 3 – Add ➢ Open File. Select your first image using the file browser. Click Open to confirm your selection. PhotoDeluxe will add your photo to the first standard print, automatically sizing it. Continue to find and open the file for each print on the page. Your page will look something like the one shown below.

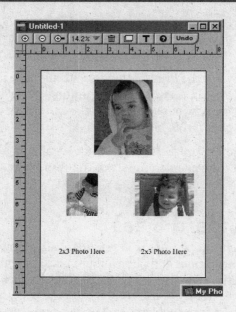

5. Click 4 - Print ➣ Print. The Print dialog box will appear. As when you're printing one or multiple copies, set the options for your print job. Then click OK.

6. Click 5 - Done.

Now you can cut out your standard prints, as described in the next section.

Cut It Out

Some paper stock arrives perforated, but most doesn't. When you print multiple images on an unperforated page, you'll need to cut it to detach the individual prints. Here are some tips to keep in mind for the best results:

▶ Avoid using scissors. Most people can't cut clean lines using hand-held scissors. (And if you do use scissors, don't run with them!)

▶ When possible, use a rotary paper cutter. This style of paper cutter creates more uniform and controlled cuts. The other, guillotine-style, paper cutter may rotate a page during cutting and unintentionally cut into your photos.

▶ Use scrapbook tools (such as circular cutters, crimping shears, and so forth) *after* separating the photos. This protects your other pictures from any tool-based errors such as slips and overcuts.

▶ Make full-page cuts first. Determine which cut lines completely bisect your page and perform these cuts before any others. Do not attempt a "halfway" cut. This usually results in overcutting into a picture or torn areas where cuts do not intersect.

RACE TO THE FINISH LINE

Did you know that you can make real photos from your digital pictures? Over the past year, many photo finishers have added digital imaging to their product lines. These photos will last as long as "normal" photos, with the same durability, feel, and archival quality. In fact, they really are normal photos.

The photo finishers print your photos on real photo paper (traditional photo-quality silver-halide) and produce pictures that look nearly as good as 35mm prints. The difference is that instead of printing from negatives, they print using digital projection. Typically, a set of three high-resolution colored lasers draw on photo paper using complementary colors. Then the finisher develops the photo paper using a standard "wet" process.

Choose Your Finisher

You can find any number of digital photo finishers on the Internet. These sites offer many of the most exciting and innovative digital-imaging solutions around. They allow you to upload your pictures and order prints in a wide variety of styles and sizes, but that's not all. Most allow you to arrange your photos, annotate them, store them in albums, and share them with friends as well. Some sites support guest books; others offer slide shows.

Choosing between finishers can be hard. So many offer such wonderful deals and services that you may end up creating accounts on a dozen or more. Don't be put off by that. With a few exceptions, these sites provide free membership, generous storage allocations, and almost unlimited storage time. Recently, large megastores like Wal-Mart have entered the photo-finishing arena. The advantage here is that since these megastores are so ubiquitous, you can just drive over and pick up your order at their store, saving you a bundle on shipping-and-handling fees.

Expect to pay somewhere between a quarter and 75 cents for most 3 × 5 inch and 4 × 6 inch prints. On top of that, add a dollar or two or three for shipping and handling. Always check for specials before submitting your order. Some processors offer bulk discounts, especially when you order multiple prints of the same photo.

Make the Cut

When you plan to use a photo-finishing service, you must keep two key things in mind: resolution and aspect ratio. The greater your camera's resolution, the better your prints will look and the bigger the prints you can order. The aspect ratio determines how your pictures work with standard print sizes. Before you order your prints, take the time to learn more about both.

Resolution

You've probably heard the phrase "megapixel camera." This phrase refers to a camera's resolution—in this case, a camera that can capture more than a million picture elements, or *pixels*, at once. As the pixel count increases, so does the quality of your images and (not coincidentally) the camera price. Inexpensive cameras may capture images as small as 320 × 240 pixels. Other, very expensive, models might take pictures containing multiple millions of pixels. This is important because your camera's resolution determines how you can choose a proper print size.

Often, people order large prints from small images. This is a big mistake. These pictures will look rotten. Small images simply do not contain enough information to create a large print. The print will look blocky and fuzzy. Instead, use the following chart to determine the minimum print size for your images.

Print Size (in Inches)	Minimum Size (in Pixels)	Good Size (in Pixels)
3.5 × 5	640 × 480	800 × 600
4 × 6	800 × 600	1,024 × 768
5 × 7	1,024 × 768	1,280 × 960
8 × 10	1,280 × 960	1,600 × 1,200
11 × 14	1,600 × 1,200	1,712 × 1,368
12 × 18	1,712 × 1,368	2,400 × 3,600

Print Size (in Inches)	Minimum Size (in Pixels)	Good Size (in Pixels)
16 × 24	1,600 × 2,400	3,200 × 4,800
24 × 36	2,400 × 3,600	4,800 × 7,200

This means that if you own a 640 × 480 camera, you should try to stick to 3.5 × 5 inch prints. If you own a 1,280 × 960 camera, you might order prints in any size up to 8 × 10 inches. The 8 × 10-inch print may not look spectacular, but it should hold up to reasonable scrutiny.

In general, you can always select a smaller print size than your image resolution might suggest. In fact, print quality improves as you print smaller, because image density increases. You can see this phenomenon in a 35mm print. Use a magnifying glass to look closely at the print. The closer you look, the more details you see, because 35mm prints have very high image density. It works the same way with digital prints—the higher the image density, the finer the detail and sharpness in your print.

I've recently developed what I like to call Erica's Photo Print Rule of 100s. (Catchy title, eh?) It works like this: When ordering prints, include at least 100 pixels per linear inch of height and width. When printing a 5 × 7, aim for at least 500 × 700 pixels. For an 8 × 10 print, nothing smaller than 800 × 1,000 pixels will print particularly well. Of course, 200 or more pixels per linear inch will produce even better results. Most finishers consider 300ppi to produce "best" quality prints. Keep in mind that this rule applies primarily to digital photography rather than scanned images. Always use higher resolutions for scanned sources because of quality loss introduced by the scanning process.

Aspect Ratios

An aspect ratio is defined by the ratio between your image's width and height. The following chart shows print sizes and their aspect ratios.

Print Size (in Inches)	Aspect Ratio	Image Size (in Pixels)	Aspect Ratio
3.5 × 5	1 : 1.43	320 × 240	1 : 1.33
4 × 6	1 : 1.50	640 × 480	1 : 1.33
5 × 7	1 : 1.40	768 × 512	1 : 1.50
8 × 10	1 : 1.25	1,024 × 768	1 : 1.33
11 × 14	1 : 1.27	1,600 × 1200	1 : 1.33

Sometimes, the aspect ratio of a digital image does not exactly match the aspect ratio of a print. When this happens, your picture's proportions will not precisely match those of the printed version. In this case, the photo finisher must choose between two approaches, which are illustrated below.

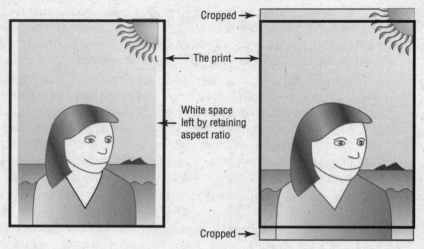

Choice 1: Leaving extra white space   Choice 2: Cropping to match aspect ratio

First, the finisher can retain the image's aspect ratio by leaving white space on one or both sides of the print. This allows you to cut off the excess paper and return your print to your original aspect ratio. Unfortunately, if you do so, your image may not fit in a standard-size frame or photo album insert. Also, be aware that although the excess white space usually appears as a white color, some finishers digitally fill your picture with a black background, so the excess space may appear black. Results will vary by finisher.

Second, the finisher can adjust the image's aspect ratio by cropping the top, bottom, or both. This usually works great and produces a pleasing, standard-size picture. Unfortunately, sometimes things can go wrong—photos may arrive with missing heads or feet (or missing ears, when the "top" of a photo in portrait orientation is cropped). Also, by taking this chop-to-fit approach, the finisher changes the underlying composition. Although this method generally produces the most successful prints, sometimes it can create the biggest goofs.

So what can you do? Many photo finishers now allow *you* to choose which method you want to use for your images. By allowing the decision to rest with the customer, they increase satisfaction while limiting unpleasant surprises. If your finisher does not allow you to choose, make sure to determine in advance which method will be used. If you don't like their method, find another finisher.

Another thing you can do is to adjust your pictures in advance. Photo-Deluxe allows you to trim your photos to a standard size. With this feature, you control exactly how your pictures will turn out. Say you want to create a 5×7-inch print. You can create an image with a 1:1.4 aspect ratio before submitting it to the photo finisher. In this way, you can ensure that the print you order will visually match the image you upload. To size your images, follow the instructions in the "Print Standard Sizes" section earlier in the chapter.

Just Do It!

When you're ready to order your high-quality prints from a photo finisher, just follow these steps:

1. Prepare your photos in Photoshop or PhotoDeluxe.

2. Select an online finisher. Determine that the finisher's pricing and delivery methods are satisfactory.

3. Upload your images to the finishing site. Several finishers now offer a variety of finish styles, including matte, glossy, and satin. Before you order, you may want to check if you can request a particular finish.

4. Place your order and wait. Your photos should be delivered within a week.

That's all you need to do. And you'll be amazed and delighted by the results. The ease and convenience of today's online photo finishing cannot be matched.

Upload Solutions

Each photo-finishing site provides one or more upload solutions, which vary by finisher. Make sure to determine which works best for you and with your computer. These include the following solutions:

Web Page Uploads   Nearly every site offers a Web page that allows you to upload one or more images at once. Although this provides the most universal solution, this method has many drawbacks. Uploads proceed slowly and without any feedback. You must individually select each image for upload. You can't use drag and drop. Often, you can't upload more than five or ten images at once. Sometimes, you can't determine if your computer is merely busy uploading or has crashed.

Stand-alone Applications   Most sites now provide Windows-compatible (and, occasionally, Macintosh-compatible) programs that allow you to upload many pictures at once. These programs can run unattended, allowing you to send a large number of pictures without human intervention. Also, many of them allow you to select an upload folder so you don't need to add each photo individually.

Plug-ins   Some sites offer Netscape or Microsoft Internet Explorer plug-ins. These expand the capabilities of your Web browser, allowing you to upload one or more images using drag and drop. The jury is still out on this upload method. Sometimes, the plug-ins can crash your browser or computer. Time will tell if this method proves popular or drops out of use.

E-mail Upload   A few finishing sites allow you to attach your images to e-mail. Just write a letter to the site, attach an image, and send the message. This method is tremendously convenient and avoids problems associated with software compatibility and browser types. In fact, this method opens up photo finishing to WebTV users who might not own a personal computer.

FTP Sites   Some sites have started to provide upload access through the File Transfer Protocol (FTP). This standard allows you to perform batch uploads using very common and standard FTP software. While this procedure targets more computer-proficient customers, it offers a number of advantages. You probably do not need to install yet another piece of software on your machine. An FTP program is already built into many operating systems and works with any site that supports FTP transfer. You can use FTP to transfer a large number of pictures at once, with a minimum of interaction. Most FTP programs work happily in the background as you turn your attention to other tasks. Finally, this procedure allows Linux users (and users of other nonstandard operating systems) to access sites and purchase prints from finishers who might otherwise not be able to accept their business.

Disks by Mail and Walk-in   Some finishers allow you to stop by a storefront and drop off a disk or send a CD-R (recordable CD) or floppy disk by regular mail. Floppy disk acceptance, however, is dropping by the wayside. Some finishers that used to accept floppy disks (containing a Zip or Stuff-it archive of your images) now reject them because better cameras now produce larger pictures that, even when zipped, don't fit well or at all on a floppy disk. In contrast, CD acceptance continues to grow. To submit a CD, simply create a CD-R containing your images. Unless instructed to do otherwise, don't put your pictures into folders or subdirectories. Check ahead and see what image formats are supported by your finisher. Do not submit any pictures or files that your finisher cannot print. Keep things simple. Remember, the person receiving and processing your CD is, more likely than not, a part-time high-school student earning minimum wage.

Don't Look a Gift Horse...

Did you know you could order your pictures as gift items as well as prints? Most finishers offer photo gift items or have partnered with sites that do. You can order photos on items as diverse as mouse pads, tote bags, T-shirts, license plates, boxer briefs, and ceramic tiles. Be sure to check out the offerings on each finishing site to get some great gift ideas.

WHAT'S NEXT

The next chapter covers some techniques for managing color and printing with Photoshop 6. You'll learn how to use color settings, previews, and more about printing from ink-jet printers.

Chapter 26

MANAGING COLOR AND PRINTING WITH PHOTOSHOP 6

You labored long and hard to get the color exactly right. You used all the tricks—Levels, Curves, Selective Color, Color Balance, Adjustment layers, the Unsharp Mask filter—and the image looked perfect on the monitor. Unfortunately, what your printer spit out looks quite different. Those beautiful sky blues and brilliant magentas turned to gloomy grays and muddy maroons. Furthermore, the image looks quite different from monitor to monitor.

If you're a digital artist or graphic designer using Photoshop to print color images, you probably frequently ask yourself two very important questions: How can I be confident that the color on my monitor will be matched by the color of the printer? And how can I trust that the color on *my* monitor will look like the color on *your* monitor? These questions are about how you *manage* color from one device to another, and that's what this

Adapted from *Mastering Photoshop 6*
by Steve Romaniello
ISBN 0-7821-2841-6   896 pages $49.99

chapter is about. In this chapter, you'll read about why you need to manage color, how to manage color between monitors, converting colors, and printing images.

WHY MANAGE COLOR?

In the years before the desktop publishing revolution, professional color systems were used in the creation and modification of high-quality printing and publishing. These methods of color management relied on what is called "closed-loop" color, the idea being that nothing ever escapes the system. No outside files were accepted, and no files were ever allowed to leave the system except in the form of separated film, ready for printing. Looking back, those were the "good ol' days" when the reliability of color was—mostly—under control. The systems were expensive, and compared to today's computers, very slow. But they worked.

Desktop technologies created a *distributed* model for color production. Some of the work was done on a computer not connected to a prepress color system. It was the differences between systems—different monitors, different viewing conditions, and different software applications—that created the need for color management.

Scientists went to work on the problem in the late 1980s, developing a model for color management that would eventually provide software tools to ensure that color would match, location to location and device to device. The first practical color management system, Apple ColorSync, arrived in 1991, and has undergone improvements since. Over the years, the idea of color management has migrated to most professional software applications—including Adobe Photoshop. Today most computers and operating systems have a facility for color management, and most applications have built-in support for color management. The challenge is getting it to work.

THE COLOR WORKING SPACE

In the fall of 1998, the Photoshop development team rocked the design and printing community with a completely new outlook on color. The release of Photoshop 5.0 got the attention of all color practitioners in the digital imaging world by introducing the concept of the *color working space*. Prior to Photoshop 5, "color" was only the color available on the computer monitor. The curious thing about that philosophy is, there are so many different types of monitors that the color of a document on one computer may very well appear dissimilar to the same document on another monitor. It was impossible to maintain color accuracy, or to display an image correctly on any other machine.

The color working space changed all that by creating an environment for handling the color that was separate from the monitor. Under this model, it is possible to scan, save, work and store an image with a color space other than that of the monitor. The image is embedded with an ICC (International Color Consortium) profile that describes the color working space (sometimes called simply *color space* or *working space*). The image can then move from one computer to another with its profile and can appear the same on two different monitors.

The color working space concept created the opportunity for Photoshop to accommodate images from scanners and other sources whose color gamuts exceed the available colors on monitor. The color working space allows for color to be captured, modified, stored, and output without harming the color gamut of the original.

A WINDOW INTO A WINDOW

To grasp the concept of color working space, imagine that the image you see on your monitor exists on a separate, parallel plane, just behind your monitor, and that your monitor acts like a window into the image. The image you see may be the entire image, but it might not be. It might be distorted by the window's characteristics or size. Perhaps the window is not perfectly transparent, perhaps it is slightly tinted, or perhaps light is reflecting off of its surface causing the image to appear different than the image that exists in the color working space.

In fact, computer monitors really behave like windows into our images, modifying the "reality" of the actual image and displaying something that is appropriate to the monitor's abilities, but not always appropriate to the qualities of the image itself.

For professional graphic artists, the monitor is an excellent window into the image. This is true because we spend considerable sums of money on quality monitors that have good color gamuts and a range of brightness that will allow us to see *almost* all the qualities of the image in Photoshop. But lesser monitors don't provide such an undistorted view.

Monitor Quality

To better understand this, consider the monitor. Monitors are light emitters: they create light from electrical energy. A cathode ray tube monitor like the one on your computer is a television-like picture tube. As illustrated in Figure 26.1, it uses electrons beamed at the monitor's face from the back of the picture tube to stimulate mineral phosphors that are coated on the inside of the face of the tube, creating light of a single color on the face. The electrons are invisible to the human eye, but when they strike the coating, the phosphors react, emitting visible light in a spectrum that is within the color gamut of human vision. Activating those phosphors in combination with others causes "color" to be created on the face of the picture tube.

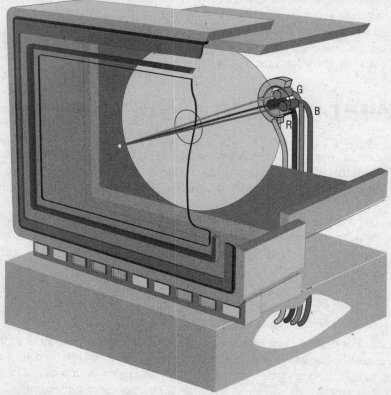

FIGURE 26.1: A cross-section of a cathode-ray tube showing the separate high-voltage amplifiers for the red, green, and blue signals.

As with many electromechanical devices, there is considerable variability in the manufacture of picture tubes and in the quality of minerals used to coat the inside of the tube. Some computer monitors sell for less than $100, while others sell for more than $1,500. In addition to the size of the monitor, there are quality issues to take into account when evaluating a monitor's color. Is the color quality of a sub-$100 monitor likely to be very good? How will it compare to the color quality of a graphic arts–quality monitor designed for critical color decisions? Cost-cutting measures taken by the makers of low-cost monitors include coating the monitor with phosphors of inconsistent quality or low purity. It might be possible to reduce manufacturing costs by reducing the quality control checks that are made in manufacture to ensure that each monitor meets the company's standards. By contrast, a graphic arts–quality monitor will be made from components that cost more to make, more to test, and more to deliver to the end user.

The Photoshop team's challenge with version 5, then, was to make it possible to create an image on a computer with a $1,500 monitor that could be viewed on a monitor of lesser quality, and continue in production—without damaging the color of the image in the process.

Monitor Profiles

A monitor's characteristics are described by its ability to display pure red, green, and blue colors as bright, clear components of an image. In the visual arts we use such colors, and the millions of color permutations possible when mixing them together, to make our photos and illustrations. In order for Photoshop to display an image correctly, it must know the characteristics of the monitor you are using. To do this, we provide Photoshop with a piece of software called a *monitor profile*.

The monitor profile is made by one of several means. The easiest method is to make a visual calibration of your monitor using version 5 or later version of Adobe Gamma to test and adjust the appearance of the monitor, and then save the resulting information as a *color profile*.

Adobe Gamma is a software monitor calibrator that allows the artist to build and save a monitor profile without having to spend money on more costly measurement instruments and software that serve this purpose. Gamma is installed when Photoshop is installed. To use it, follow the on-screen instructions.

Part V

The Viewing Environment

Professionals in the printing and publishing industries have known for years that good color on a computer monitor is accomplished partly by putting the monitor into a "proper" viewing environment. The International Organization for Standardization (ISO) and its partner national organizations recently adopted a new color standard for viewing color for the photographic and graphic arts industries worldwide. Called ISO 3664, the standard dictates, among other things, that a proper viewing environment is a workspace without windows or skylights—no natural light at all. They also specify that the color of the walls should be neutral gray (the ISO committee specifies the color Munsell N5 through N7 for the walls). The walls should be absent of colorful artwork, and the artist in front of the computer should be wearing neutral clothing, preferably gray or black. Room lighting recommendations in the ISO standard are for very low, preferably diffuse lighting of the proper 5000° K temperature.

Is this a happy place to work? It's pretty dull, but it's a workplace where color can be viewed most accurately. Some design studios and professional prepress operations have such a workplace, but reserve it for "soft proofing" visits, which provide an opportunity for workers to go into the "cave" only long enough to approve color on-screen.

Determining a Monitor Profile

Just having the monitor profile and a proper viewing environment are not enough. You must first tell your operating system about the profile, setting it as the system profile, and then, when you launch Photoshop, it will use your monitor profile for some of its color display calculations.

There are two ways to tell your system about the monitor profile you have created on a Macintosh. Under the Apple menu, choose Control Panels ➤ Monitors and click the Color icon; from the ColorSync menu, choose a profile. Or choose Control Panels ➤ ColorSync directly from the Apple menu to display the dialog box. Click the Set Profile button and choose a profile from the list.

On Windows 98 or 2000, choose Start ➤ Settings ➤ Control Panel ➤ Display ➤ Color Management. (Windows 95 and NT do not support color management.) With Windows XP, choose Start ➤ Control Panel ➤ Display ➤ Color Management.

NOTE

The Windows path will depend on the video board you have installed. For some boards, you may have to choose Control Panel ➤ Display ➤ Settings ➤ Advanced ➤ Color Management.

Choose the system profile or the profile you created with Adobe Gamma or another monitor-profiling application. The computer will know how to correct the color displayed on your monitor through the profile, making adjustments on the fly to all images displayed on screen.

Photoshop automatically looks to the operating system to get the name of the current monitor profile, and you cannot change that setting from within the latest version of Photoshop. But it is possible to "turn color management off" in the Color Settings control panel. This has the effect of returning Photoshop 6 approximately to the functionality of Photoshop 4, limiting the color gamut to that of the monitor and disabling all color-space conversions.

THE YIN/YANG OF COLOR

When we discuss the *gamuts* of color working spaces, we must understand that the gamut of a monitor is a triangular space with its corners in the red, green, and blue areas of an industry-standard color chart. The gamut chart in Figure 26.2 plots the available colors of a device (a monitor, for example) compared to the gamut of colors humans can see—and the differences are extreme.

All of the color spaces of the world of graphic arts and photography converge inside a large triangle that falls well within the colors of human vision. With Photoshop's support for the color working space, we want to choose a space that is adequate to accommodate most if not all the colors of our output device, while providing a reasonable view of that color on our monitor.

Unfortunately, the color system used for printing color on paper is the physical opposite of the color system used to emit light on the face of a monitor. With light-emitting devices, the unit creates, and mixes, colors from the three additive color primaries—red, green, and blue. When you add approximately equal parts of red, green, and blue light on a monitor at full intensity, you get "white."

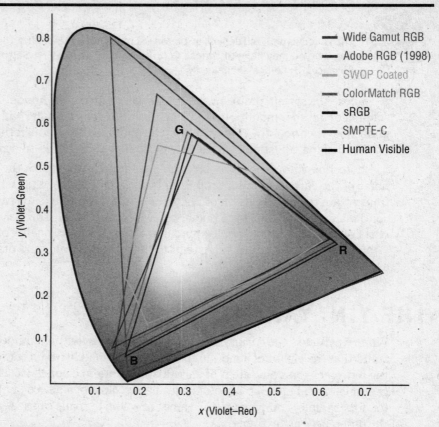

FIGURE 26.2: The color gamuts of various colors working spaces

The vibrancy and brightness of these primary colors on a picture tube are usually far greater in those primary colors than they can ever be on the printed page, because the printing process begins with the available "white" light in the viewing environment, and then filters out components of that light to simulate color. The processes are called *additive* (for light-emitting devices) and *subtractive* (for printed products).

When you put pigment on a sheet of paper, superimposing the primary colors of ink (cyan, yellow, magenta) on top of each other, in an ideal world you would get pure black, but in reality, because of impurities in the ink, you get something that approximates deep, yucky brown. (Technical term!) Because pigments subtract light components from the white light in the environment, they reduce its intensity, making it less bright than unfiltered light. Subtractive colorants always reduce the amount of light reflected back at the viewer, and thus it's very hard for the printed page to compete with the bright color on a nice computer monitor. And there we have the classic yin/yang of color—the conflict between the two scientific principles of color reproduction—and another reason we need color management in our lives. The strengths of emitted light on a monitor are the weaknesses of colors on the printed page.

It is common to hear people say that there is *less* color available on the printed page than on a monitor, but that is not necessarily true. If you calculate the *area* occupied by the plot of monitor colors, and compare it to the *area* of colors available on the printed page, the two areas will be approximately equal. But they are *very different.* Where the monitor is strongest in red, green, and blue, the printed page is strongest in yellow, cyan, and magenta, the color complements of monitor colors.

If we want to reproduce the best color possible on the printed page, while still displaying the color in the same images, we must acknowledge and accept the weakness of the monitor relative to the printed page, and vice versa. The compromises we must learn to accept are that there are colors—mostly in the range of cyan to pale green—that we can print, but cannot see on even the best monitor. Likewise, there are colors in the deep blue (you could call it purple) and vibrant green points that we can display on a monitor, but cannot print with the standard four-color ink sets used on ink-jet printers and printing machines.

Making a Colorful Match

Choosing a color working space that is appropriate to the printed page is critically important so that we don't force Photoshop to remap the colors in an image. We want to pick a working space that is not too big (so we don't add colors that are out of the printable range) and not too small (so we don't omit colors needed to accurately represent the image).

The gamut chart in Figure 26.2 and in the color section shows the comparative gamuts of several of Photoshop's color working spaces. Superimposed in yellow is the gamut of standard printing inks on glossy paper (called the SWOP Coated gamut).

Gamma

Gamma is a number, from 1.0 to about 2.5, that describes the curvature of a contrast curve control for a monitor. The Macintosh has traditionally used a gamma of 1.8, which is relatively flat compared to television. Windows PCs use a 2.2 gamma value, which is more contrasty and more saturated. The gamma of Windows is closer to the "natural" appearance of the world, while the 1.8 gamma adopted by the Macintosh is more like the contrast of printing on good paper. If you are working on images destined for television, the World Wide Web, or multimedia, it's better to use a gamma of 2.2. If your destination is the printed page, a gamma of 1.8 to 2.0 may be more appropriate.

Getting to Know RGB Color Working Space

The color working space is, as already mentioned, a plane for holding and handling images in Photoshop that is independent of the monitor. Color working spaces include a variety of oddly named spaces that usually confound the new visitor. But, we'll work on that....

The RGB color working spaces of Adobe Photoshop include five standard color spaces. Photoshop also has the ability to choose others that that are designed for other working environments or offer special qualities that assist in your work. Each has a combination of characteristics, including its color temperature, gamma, and white point (the phosphor settings for "white"). White is a variable thing in the world of computer-generated color, because the effective "whiteness" of the non-image areas is a key component in getting the color on the screen to match the color that is produced by a printer or a commercial printing press.

sRGB IEC61966-2.1

Of the color spaces available, sRGB (the *s* stands for *standardized*) is the smallest. This means that it puts serious limitations on the colors available in your color palette in Photoshop. The sRGB space, designed by Microsoft and Hewlett-Packard, is well-suited to corporate computer monitors and images destined for viewing on the World Wide Web. sRGB has taken a lot of flack for being destructive to images of large color gamut, and indeed it is. But, if you look at the purpose of sRGB—making images look good on corporate computers—the color space makes more sense and is useful for its intended purpose.

It is, unfortunately, set as the default color working space in Photoshop 6 (as it was in 5), and that is the root of the controversy surrounding it. Adobe allows you to change the setting—but most people don't realize that it is important to do so. Use sRGB as your color working space, or convert images to this space, when developing images strictly for display on the Web or in corporate environments. Otherwise use...

Adobe RGB (1998)

The Adobe RGB (1998) color working space is large enough to accommodate graphic arts images and most scanned images, and allows for good representation on most high-quality monitors. Adobe RGB (1998) has a white point of 6500 K, which is in line with the latest ISO standard (ISO 3664) for color viewing in critical color conditions. Its gamma, a measurement of contrast and saturation, is 2.2. Adobe RGB (1998) is also able to accommodate conversions to CMYK for printing with good results; very little of the CMYK color is clipped or remapped in the process.

TIP

Don't confuse the *K* that crops up in color discussions about white point with *K for* kilobytes or black (as in CMYK). Here it stands for degrees Kelvin; 6500 K is approximately the "temperature" of outdoor ambient light in the middle of a clear day.

Apple RGB

The original "graphic arts" monitor was the Apple 13-inch RGB monitor. It created an industry, providing color previews to millions of users from 1988 to about 1995, when it was replaced by better and larger monitors. Based on a Sony picture tube, the Apple monitor had good color saturation and a small but reasonable color gamut. The Apple RGB color working space is a good choice for converting images from unknown sources. Almost all the stock photos made between 1988 and 1995 were made with computers and scanners connected to an Apple 13-inch monitor, and though the quality of monitors has improved substantially since then, that monitor still represents the colors of the era. This Apple RGB working space uses 6500 K color temperature for white and a 1.8 gamma, which is relatively flat in appearance.

ColorMatch RGB

The Radius PressView monitor was, for years, the viewing standard of the graphic and visual arts. Almost all professional color work was created on monitors in this class. Now discontinued, the PressView will live on in the form of a color working space that matches its now-famous characteristics.

ColorMatch RGB represents a good gamut of colors, a 1.8 gamma, and a 5000 K white point, which causes some monitors to turn a sickly yellow color. Use this one if it causes the colors on your screen to look good while maintaining a pleasant white. If your monitor turns yellowish, switch to Adobe RGB (1998), as that will deliver a bluer white and a more attractive appearance on many monitors. If you have a PressView, this is an excellent working space for you.

Monitor RGB

This profile sets the color working space to the current monitor profile. Use this working space if other programs in your workflow where you will be viewing the image do not support color management.

Other Color Working Spaces

We are able to choose or load other RGB color working spaces that were the primary spaces in Photoshop 5.0 and 5.5. These appear, along with several dozen others, in the Edit ➢ Color Settings dialog box under Working Spaces RGB. They include:

CIE RGB   The International Commission on Illumination (CIE) is an organization of scientists who work with color. CIE standards determine how we measure and describe color in every field of human endeavor. This working space is based on the CIE standard RGB color space, a 2.2 gamma, and 6500 K white point. Its gamut of colors is slightly larger than that of the Apple monitor, and it works almost identically when opening or converting images from older files, those that were created and saved from early versions of Photoshop.

NTSC (1953)   The North American Television Standards Committee established a color gamut and a white point for television in the U.S. that is maintained to this day. Use this color space if you are working on images that will be displayed on television. The gamma is 2.2, and the white point is a very cool-blue Standard Illuminant C.

PAL/SECAM   PAL and SECAM are European and Asian standards for television color and contrast. As with the NTSC setting above, if your work is destined for television outside North America, this setting is appropriate. The gamma is 2.2, and the white point is 6500 K.

SMPTE-C   A movie industry standard, the SMPTE-C standard is compliant with the Society of Motion Picture and Television Engineers standards for motion picture illuminants. It has the same white point as the two television standards, above, and its color temperature is 6500 K.

Wide Gamut RGB   Adobe created this color working space to accommodate images created on the computer, where vibrant greens, bright reds, and cobalt blues are created and must be maintained. This color space is particularly well suited to work that is destined for an RGB film recorder. The gamma is 2.2, and the white point is a yellowish 5000 K, especially useful to those recording onto "electronic" color transparency films. Wide Gamut may sound attractive to those who believe that more is better, but in fact, too large a color gamut can be damaging to many images. Wide Gamut color remapping will result in strange color shifts in images. Know what you are doing before using this space.

There are numerous RGB spaces for profiles of specific monitors, laptop computers, printers, or working conditions. You can save and load specific profiles from other sources, or you can make your own using Adobe Gamma or a device called a colorimeter, which measures white point, black point, and gamma.

COLOR SETTINGS

This new version of the program is significantly different than its predecessor and has some new functions for handling color. Photoshop 6 uses ICC color management at all times (even when color management is technically "off"). The settings you select for color handling can make a huge difference in the appearance and reproduction of color.

Choose Edit ➢ Color Settings (Figure 26.3) to access the primary color control window. It has two modes: Standard and Advanced. (The Conversion Options and Advanced Controls areas shown in the figure are hidden if you uncheck Advanced.) Venture into this environment to take control over color in your world of Adobe Photoshop.

You should configure color settings prior to opening a document or creating a new document. The Color Settings dialog box controls your color working spaces, your color management policies, and your settings for what should happen when Photoshop opens an image that either has no embedded profile or has one that is different from the current color working space.

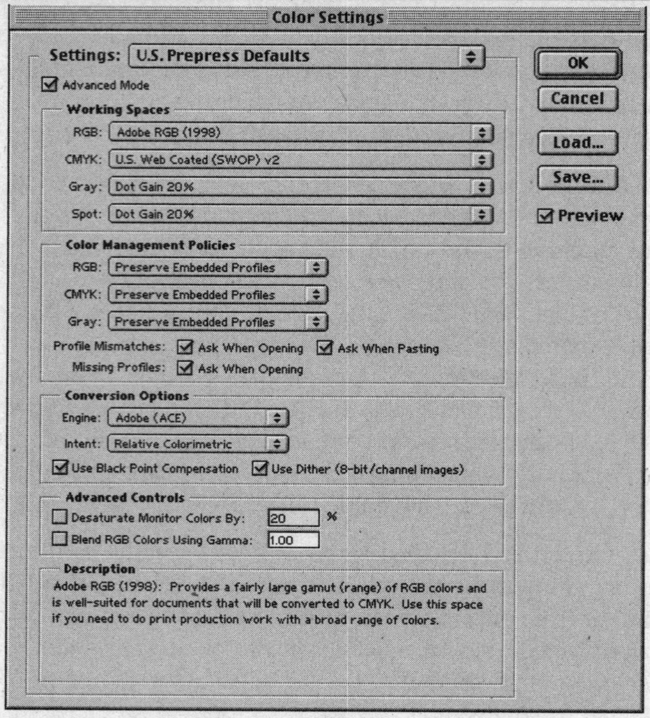

FIGURE 26.3: The Color Settings controls

First, set your color working space according to the kind of work you do. Choose a setting from the Settings pull-down menu. If you are in doubt, a good place to start is with U.S. Prepress Defaults, which includes the Adobe RGB (1998) color space and typical North American standards for printing color, U.S. Web Coated (SWOP) v2. As mentioned, this is a good space for both RGB and CMYK colors, and will cause little, if any, harm to images handled by the program.

CMYK Working Space

If you plan on converting your image from RGB mode to CMYK, you can choose a color working space for CMYK. If you have a four-color (CMYK) profile for a printer, for example, or a printing press that you normally use, you can set it if it's on the list. If you don't have a custom profile to use, there are several "generic" CMYK profiles you can load. For North America, you can use the SWOP (Specifications for Web Offset Publications) standard profiles. There should be at least two in your system, one for gloss papers and another for uncoated papers. If you are outside North America, choose either Eurostandard (coated or uncoated) or the Japan Standard profiles as appropriate to your location. These CMYK profiles will be used when you convert to CMYK with the Mode ➢ CMYK or Mode ➢ Convert To Profile functions, and the results will be acceptable.

Color Management Policies

Color management policies determine how Photoshop deals with color profiles when opening a document. You can determine how Photoshop deals with documents that have no profiles, or embedded profiles different from the profiles specified in the Color Settings dialog box.

If we simply reopen a file on the same machine, using the same color working space specified in the Color Settings dialog box, the file will open without interruption. But if we move the file to another machine running Photoshop, or we open an image that came from another machine, Photoshop puts on the brakes, asking, in effect, "Wait. This file is not from around these parts. What should I do with it?"

Putting the responsibility for controlling how files are opened on the user, Photoshop asks us to set one of the policies for each type of file we might be opening, RGB, CMYK, and Grayscale. Our choices for these policies are:

Off   When set to Off, files with unknown profiles will be opened with color management turned off. This causes Photoshop to behave more like Photoshop 4 (Adobe calls it "pre-color management"), where the monitor's color gamut limits the color available in any image.

Preserve Embedded Profiles   Opening images that already have a color working space profile embedded will retain that space. Any new documents will be created within the current color working space. This is a safe approach to opening files with embedded profiles, as it will allow these images to be opened without making any modification to the color working space of the image. And, after working on the file, it's possible to save the document and retain the embedded profile. When importing color to an RGB or grayscale document—cutting and pasting an image from another with a different profile document, for example—appearance takes priority over numeric values. When importing color to a CMYK document, numeric values takes priority over appearance.

Convert To Working RGB/CMYK/Grayscale   (This option changes according to the image type.) This will cause mathematic conversion, remapping all the color values in the image to the current color working space. This conversion can cause drastic changes in the color of an image from a color space much smaller or much larger than the current space. For example, if an image is from a stock photo source and shows normal skin tones, let's assume it has an embedded profile for the Apple 13-inch monitor. If we are working in Wide Gamut RGB, opening the image into the current working space will cause the skin tones to shift strongly toward red, making these skin tones appear unacceptably warm. It is preferable to leave the color in its embedded profile space, which will open this image as an Apple RGB color space. Though the gamut of colors is not as great as our current working space, the colors will look good and we will do no harm to the image.

Whenever Photoshop opens an image into a working space other than the default, it will mark the title bar with an asterisk to indicate that it is not using the default working space.

The Embedded Profile Mismatch Dialog Box

In the Color Settings dialog, there are three Ask When Opening or Pasting check boxes. These determine the behavior of Photoshop 6 when opening an image with no profile, a mismatched profile, or when pasting an image into a Photoshop document. It is a very good idea to check each of these boxes so that you can decide, on a case-by-case basis, how to deal with these variables as they arrive. When you open or paste from a mismatched image, the Embedded Profile Mismatch dialog box (Figure 26.4) will be displayed, displaying the name of the embedded profile. (If the file has no profile at all, the Missing Profile dialog comes up instead; that feature is described in its own section later in this chapter.)

You certainly do not want Photoshop to assume that importing an Apple RGB image into Wide Gamut RGB space is acceptable! Though it takes a few seconds to make these choices as they occur, the result is a conscious decision, and a skill that can be learned over time.

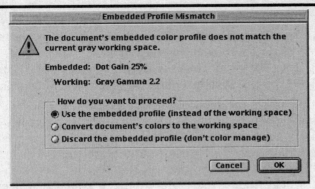

FIGURE 26.4: Photoshop can alert you that the image you're opening or pasting from doesn't use your current color profile.

Of course, there may be circumstances under which you would want all CMYK images with mismatched profiles to be mapped to your current CMYK working space. If this is the case, you can set that CMYK working space in the menu in the Color Settings dialog box, and then uncheck the Profile Mismatches check box to cause this to occur every time an image is opened.

WARNING

This will also cause RGB images to open into your RGB working space without notice.

ADVANCED COLOR SETTINGS

The Color Settings dialog also has an Advanced Mode check box at the top, which will cause the dialog box to grow to include some additional settings called Conversion Options and Advanced Controls. The Conversion Options allow us to set or change the color management "engine" that is used for color conversions. Depending on the options available on your computer, those options range from a selection of two to six or more.

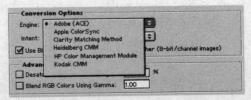

Engine

Adobe has its own color management engine (in the parlance of the industry this is called a CMM, or color management module): Adobe Color Engine (ACE). Other CMMs you might encounter include Apple Color-Sync, Apple, Heidelberg, Kodak, Imation, Agfa, X-Rite, and Microsoft.

Which engine you choose depends on your level of sophistication and your understanding of these various CMMs. Each of the companies whose names are reflected in the CMMs suggests that theirs is the superior method for converting color because of the method of polynomial witchcraft they perform on color. Adobe similarly claims that theirs is superior. A good suggestion is to use a CMM that is available in all of the applications you use to manage color. This will ensure that color is not being converted differently between applications. For example, if you use Adobe Photoshop to make some conversions and QuarkXPress (through Apple ColorSync) to make others, then it would be a good idea to set Photoshop to use Apple ColorSync, so that all your conversions are done with the same mathematical "engine."

In reality (and with apologies to the various authors of these CMMs), the net effect of a color management engine is essentially the same. Very, very subtle differences can be discerned by experts on this matter, so it's not worth a lot of worry. You are certainly welcome to try various combinations of engines and rendering intents, and decide for yourself.

Conversions through Rendering Intent

It is the *intent* of this chapter to clarify the settings for color management in Adobe Photoshop 6. Unfortunately, this is the point at which that become increasingly difficult.

The ICC has established a set of four "rendering intent" settings under which color conversions can be made. Each has a purpose, and each can be used to maximize the quality of your images for a particular task. Rendering intents cause the color of an image to be modified while it is being moved into a new color space. These modifications can appear as subtle changes or glow-in-the-dark shifts that make color images look very odd. Here we will examine them and identify their purposes.

Perceptual

Perceptual is a rendering intent designed to make photos of generalized subjects look "good" when converted to a new color space. The Perceptual rendering intent uses a method of remapping colors that preserves the relationships between colors to maintain a "pleasant" appearance. Though color accuracy will often suffer, the appearance of the image will generally follow the appearance of the original scene. Most photo applications default to Perceptual rendering, and Photoshop does this also. Most people find it pleasing, but read on before making a decision about your imaging policies.

Saturation

Saturation is for business graphics and illustrations made with solid colors. Of the four intents, it is the easiest to understand and the easiest to use. Saturation rendering will result in bright, fully saturated colors in solid areas, and fairly strong contrast applied to differences in color. Saturation rendering sacrifices color accuracy for sharp contrast and saturation. It simply lives up to its name.

If you convert images from EPS illustration programs like Adobe Illustrator, the Saturation rendering intent will result in a better-looking image after conversion than the other intents. Saturation is best used when converting graphs or financial presentations.

Relative Colorimetric

Relative Colorimetric rendering is a method where color precision is preferred over saturation, resulting in a more accurate conversion of colors into a new color space. Adobe recommends that Relative Colorimetric rendering be used for most color conversions. One of the key components of this rendering intent is its handling of white. Relative Colorimetric rendering moves the white of the image to the white point of the working space, which usually means that, as they say in the ad biz, "whiter whites and brighter brights" in the result than in the original.

For those who use QuarkXPress, this is the default and at present the only rendering intent supported by the program, so working with this setting in Photoshop will match the effect of using color management in QuarkXPress. Other applications, such as Adobe InDesign, are more enlightened when it comes to choices of rendering intent and allow us to make our own decisions when it comes to color modification.

Absolute Colorimetric

This rendering intent is very much like the Relative intent, except that it renders the whites differently. Whites in the source will remain the same in the resulting file. While this sounds obscure, it produces an image that can be used effectively for proofing files that will print on non-white or off-white papers (like newsprint). Absolute Colorimetric is a rendering intent that is designed for those who have a very specific reason for using it; otherwise, avoid it.

Black Point Compensation/Dither

There are two additional settings in the Color Settings dialog under Conversion Options: Use Black Point Compensation and Use Dither (8-Bit/Channel Images). Black Point Compensation is generally left checked, as it is used to maintain saturation of solid black in conversions where the normal behavior of a conversion will desaturate blacks.

An example of this can be seen when converting RGB images to CMYK for print. If we leave this box unchecked and make a conversion (Image ➢ Mode ➢ CMYK), the darkest blacks will often be remapped to the closest color that is within the gamut of the destination profile, which might include an adjustment for dot-gain error or what is called *total ink coverage*. This adjustment will desaturate the solids in order to keep their value below the total ink coverage number, but will result in some washed-out colors where a solid would be better. Use Black Point Compensation corrects this problem.

The Use Dither check box will cause 16-bit images to be *dithered* when converted to 8-bit images. Dithering is a method of alternating tonal value steps in tiny steps to smooth out tonal shifts. Checking this setting will result in smoother gradations in the converted file. Though the resulting files will likely be larger, the result is worth the price.

Advanced Controls

There are two controls in the color settings window that are new to Photoshop 6: Desaturate Monitor Colors By and Blend RGB Colors Using Gamma. Though recommended for "advanced users only," these settings can have a positive impact on the accuracy of the preview of images on our monitors.

Desaturating Monitor Colors

This option instructs Photoshop to desaturate colors by a specified amount when displayed on the monitor. This option can be helpful when attempting to view the full range of colors in images with color gamuts larger than that of

Part v

your monitor. An example of this might be viewing on any monitor an image whose color working space is Wide Gamut RGB. Since the gamut in Wide Gamut is larger than any production monitor, this function will simulate the tonality of the image—even though the monitor can't display the actual color beyond the range of its phosphors. Be careful, though—using this feature can cause errors between the displayed color and final output color.

Blending RGB Colors

The Blend RGB Colors Using Gamma setting controls the blending of RGB colors on screen. When the option is selected, RGB colors are blended using a selected curve. The range of values available here is between 1.0, which is linear (it has no effect), and 2.2, which creates a slightly more contrasty image.

When the option is not selected, RGB colors are blended in the document's color space, matching the color display behavior of other applications.

Opening Images with Missing Profiles

When you open an image with a mismatched profile or a file with no profile, you can choose from several options.

Missing Profile

A new twist on opening images is the Missing Profile warning in Photoshop 6; it shows itself when an image not containing an embedded profile is opened.

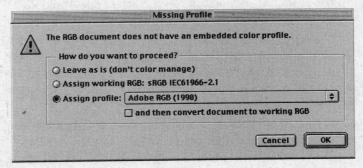

Leave As Is	The image will not be color-managed.
Assign Working RGB	The current RGB working space is assigned to the image.
Assign Profile	The image will be assigned a profile selected from the pop-up menu.

The Assign Profile setting has a secondary check box that will subsequently convert the document to the current working space. This will result in the image taking on the embedded profile of the current working space when it is saved. The net effect of this is to convert the colors to a working space that you think is the correct one for the original image, then assign it to the current working space so its embedded profile will be adequate for the reproduction plans you have.

Passing images through this dialog requires some thought. If you know (or can guess) the source of the image, it is best to assign a profile appropriate to that source. For example, if the image comes from an older stock photo disk, or from a source for which you have a profile, assign an appropriate profile. Converting to the working space after the assignment will cause the current working space profile to be embedded when the image is saved. It does not otherwise change the color in the image.

As an example, say an image is opened from a Digital Stock disc that was created prior to the common use of ICC profiles. Though Digital Stock scanned everything with a calibrated monitor, the images themselves were not embedded with a scanner profile. Later, when ICC profiles became more common, Digital Stock (later acquired by Corbis) posted their profile on the Web; applying that profile now results in the image being adjusted correctly for display.

But what if you don't have the right source profile? It's easy enough to try a few to find a workable solution to your problem. If you assume that the image was scanned and saved on a Macintosh computer using an Apple 13-inch RGB monitor, you can assign the Apple RGB working space to the image. This will usually work.

If you think that the image comes from a Windows PC with a "standard" monitor, try sRGB and the result will probably be good enough. There is not much difference between the color spaces of the Apple 13 and sRGB spaces, and images processed into those spaces will look almost identical.

If, by contrast, the processed image seems flat and lacking in color, it is likely that it came from a larger color space like Adobe RGB (1998); close the image without saving, then reopen it, assigning the Adobe RGB (1998) space. It will probably look much better. Remember that for this technique to work, your monitor must be calibrated and profiled. If not, the image you see on screen may not be the image you'll see in print.

PREVIEWING IN CMYK

The world of graphic arts reproduction is changing, and many printing firms are now using a fully color-managed workflow in preparation for printing. Those who do so want you to provide your images to them in RGB color, with embedded working space profiles.

Printers request these files because there is no "generic" CMYK separation that is correct for all different types of paper and ink sets. The separation made for sheet-fed offset on uncoated paper is drastically different than the separation made for Web-fed glossy paper. Printers want control over this conversion.

When an image is destined for the printed page, it is necessary to preview the image before sending the file to the printer. It's also necessary to be able to preview an image in CMYK without making the *conversion* to CMYK. Photoshop 6 has a new control, called Proof Colors, that allows the on-screen preview to simulate a variety of reproduction processes without converting the file to the final color space. This new feature takes the place of Preview In CMYK in earlier versions, and the new version is much more capable. It maintains the same keystroke command, however: Command+Y on MacOS and Ctrl+Y on Windows.

To prepare for and carry out an on-screen proof, first tell Photoshop what kind of proof you want to see. Choose View ➢ Proof Setup (Figure 26.5) to select the type of proof to preview. The top option is for Custom set-ups, which allow essentially any profile to be applied for the proof.

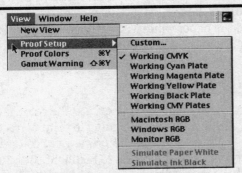

FIGURE 26.5: The Proof Setup allows you to assign any profile and rendering intent as the proof destination.

Once the set-up has been completed, the image on screen can be "proofed" by choosing View ➤ Proof Colors or hitting Cmd/Ctrl+Y. The image will change temporarily to preview in the color space chosen in the Setup window. Options include proofing CMYK, each channel individually, or the CMY colors without black. Three RGB monitor profiles are also available, one for a generic Macintosh monitor, one for a generic Windows monitor, and one for the monitor set as Monitor RGB. Where possible, Photoshop will look to the operating system to get the assigned profile for the monitor for this proofing simulation.

Simulate Paper White and Ink Black

One of the capabilities of Photoshop with regard to proofing is the ability to show the white point of the converted image as a *bright white*, using the monitor's white as the target, or the *paper white*, as measured and calculated in the ICC profile. When working with papers like newsprint and other non-white substrates, the proof can be a better simulation of the actual product if you check the box for Paper White at the bottom of the View ➤ Proof Setup menu. When this is invoked, the image will darken significantly and show a proof that more accurately represents the appearance of the image on the non-white substrate.

Simulating Ink Black in the proof setup will cause the proof to represent the actual measured black of the profile rather than a solid black as dark as the monitor might make it. When this happens, you will see the darkest black from the measured profile, and the image will usually shift away from deep, solid black to a slightly lighter charcoal image. On most images, the differences are very hard to see. Some profiles are able to represent the dark blacks and the paper white with tremendous range, and these will cause less of a shift on the screen during a proof event.

Show Out-of-Gamut Colors

Almost always, there are colors in an image that exceed the color gamut of the reproducing device. These colors are not going to print correctly when converted to CMYK and put on a press. To preview the colors that will not print accurately, you can ask Photoshop to highlight the out-of-gamut areas on screen with a special color by choosing View ➤ Gamut Warning. Usually these colors are very small amounts of relatively unimportant information in an image, but checking is a good idea because the out-of-gamut color might be *the most important* color in the image.

On the Sybex Web site, I've included a photo of Venice's gondolas from Photo Disk (`gamwarn1.tif`) that shows color and tonality very nicely on screen. But when Gamut Warning is turned on (`gamwarn2.tif`), the colors that exceed the currently selected CMYK profile are shown in medium gray. These areas, some of them crucial to this particular image, indicate that the colors on the printed sheet will not look as vibrant as the colors in the original. (This gamut-warning image is included on the Web site as `Venice.psd`.)

NOTE

To download sample files mentioned in this book, navigate to the Sybex Web site (`www.sybex.com`) and enter 2991 into the search box. When you get to the page for Photoshop Complete, follow the links to download the file.

TIP

If the image contains a great deal of gray so as to make the gamut warning less distinct, the warning color can be changed in the Transparency & Gamut preferences.

Converting Files

In spite of the color-managed workflow options, many Photoshop practitioners prefer to make their own CMYK conversions. Some printers insist that all files arriving for output be CMYK. To make such conversions, we must set the proper ICC color profile in the Color Settings window, and then make a change of Mode to CMYK. It couldn't be any simpler! But remember that the quality of a color separation made in Photoshop is dependent on the quality of the CMYK profile.

Converting Profiles

It's possible to convert your color mode and profile by using Image ➢ Mode ➢ Convert To Profile (which replaces the Profile-To-Profile control in Photoshop 5.5). This dialog box allows you to select from RGB, CMYK, and other profile types, and also select the rendering intent for the image you're making. If you choose a profile that requires a change in color mode, Photoshop makes the switch; if you're in an RGB file, for instance, and select a CMYK profile, your file ends up in CMYK mode, and vice versa.

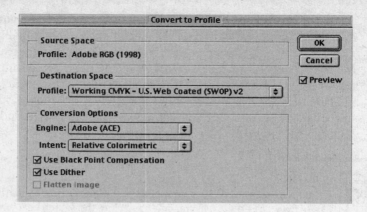

Assigning Profiles

To make the conversion from one profile to another *without changing color mode*, use Image ≻ Mode ≻ Assign Profile. This is helpful if an image was opened with color management turned off, and you want to assign a profile to the image so it can be processed in an ICC-compliant workflow. When working in RGB, only RGB profiles are available in this menu, and only CMYK profiles for those images.

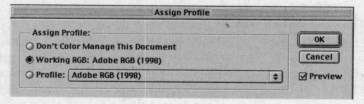

Grayscale Profiles

Converting from color to black-and-white (also called monochrome or grayscale) in previous versions of Photoshop was less than ideal. Photoshop's luminance-only conversion was seldom optimal. Converting with the Color Mixer made it better, but the ability to use proper grayscale ICC profiles for grayscale conversions makes a better looking image by far.

The image in Figure 26.6 was converted with the 25% Dot Gain Grayscale in Photoshop 6. Notice how nicely the image appears in one color. Conversions using Image ≻ Mode ≻ Grayscale have often been "too mechanical" to have much artistic value, and the methods using the Color Mixer and calculations were too tedious to be effective in production. Using a profile, the conversion not only is correct for the reproduction process, but results in a more pleasing image.

FIGURE 26.6: An image converted from color to Grayscale using the Mode ➤ Grayscale command

Spot Color Profiles

Spot color profiles are treated like grayscale profiles by Photoshop 6 and are applied in the same way. There are standard profiles loaded by the program, which follow the example of various dot-gain values. If you are inclined to make your own profiles, it's a process of printing a gray ramp scale (it is printed automatically by Photoshop if we choose Calibration Bars when printing), then measuring the resulting target patches with a reflection densitometer.

What you are measuring is *dot area*, which measures the ratio of ink to paper for a selected spot on the printed page. If you read the 50% patch, for example, you will get a value of 73 in typical gloss offset environments. To build a profile, you enter the actual measured values of dot area into a custom dot-gain table (Figure 26.7), accessible from the Color Settings dialog box by choosing Custom Dot Gain from either the Gray or Spot pop-up lists in the Working Spaces area. Saving the resulting curve creates an ICC profile.

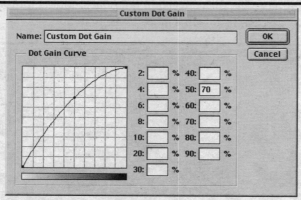

FIGURE 26.7: A custom dot gain table

A custom dot gain table allows you to enter actual grayscale performance curves, which are then used to compensate for the gain you experience. These curves are translated into grayscale and spot color profiles by Photoshop.

After being created in Photoshop, these profiles are available to any application that supports ICC profiles. Saving a custom profile is done in the Gray or Spot pop-up list in the Working Spaces area of Color Settings—choose Save Gray or Save Spot. The effect of using ICC grayscale profiles on images to be converted for monochrome printing is to create a file that is optimized for reproduction on the measured paper and ink that was used to make the dot area measurements. It is, in essence, a method for matching the image to the printing capabilities of the chosen process.

PRINTING FROM INK-JET PRINTERS

Once you've completed your image, assigned RGB profiles to it, and converted it or not converted it depending on the circumstances, you can print it. If you are printing to the majority of desktop ink-jet printers, you may not want to convert to CMYK because the printer uses the RGB information to convert the image to CMYK on the fly.

Ink-jet printing results can vary dramatically from model to model because of their different gamuts. If you have the printer's profile, the results will be more predictable. If you don't have the profile of a specific printer, you can improve the results on ink-jet printers by printing the image in RGB and letting the printer software do the conversion on the fly. You can then use the print as a proof to recalibrate your monitor (using Adobe Gamma) to display the image as close to the proof as possible. Save the Adobe Gamma settings to be used specifically for editing images printed on the target printer. Make your adjustments to the image based on the on-screen display and save the image as a separate file, identifying it for the specific printer. This is a funky, trial-and-error way to match the printed image to the monitor, but it works—providing you're willing to pull a number of prints and tweak adjustments to get as close a match as possible.

A more accurate and reliable method is to invest in a spectrophotometer and take a reading from the print, then plug the information into a profile-writing program and load the profile into the Color Settings dialog box. You'll find information on troubleshooting ink-jet printers in the next chapter.

THE PRINTING DIALOGS

Several dialog boxes offer similar functions for ultimately printing your image. They are Page Setup, Print Options, and Print.

Page Setup

Choose File ➢ Page Setup to determine the paper size, orientation, and scale of the image. The dialog box will include different options depending on your installed printer, sometimes including some of the same options found in the Print Options dialog box.

Print Options

Choose File ➢ Print Options to set up your printing specifications (Figure 26.8). There are several new features in the Photoshop 6 version of this dialog box. For example, the preview image on the left side of the screen displays the image's size in relation to the paper.

Position specifies the location of the printed image on the current paper size. Scaled Print Size lets you increase or decrease the image while maintaining the image's constrained proportions. Check the Scale To Fit Media box to size the image to fit the paper. Check Show Bounding Box to manually scale and reposition the image by dragging. If you have an active selection, you can then choose to print only that part of the image with the Print Selected Area option.

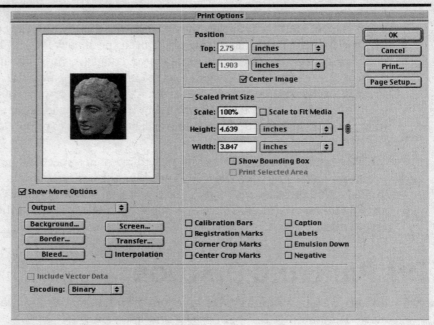

FIGURE 26.8: The Print Options dialog box

Check the Show More Options box to expand the dialog box. In the expanded area, a pop-up list offers two sets of settings, Output or Color Management.

Output Options

Some of the Output options are identical to the settings found under File ➤ Page Setup ➤ Adobe Photoshop 6. Some of these options are demonstrated in Figure 26.9.

Background   Choose a color from the Color Picker for the area surrounding the image.

Border   Enter a value form a 0.00 to 10.00 points in points, inches, or millimeters to produce a black border around the image.

Bleed   Enter a value from 0.00 to 0.125 inches to specify the width of the bleed. When printed, crop marks will appear inside rather than outside the image.

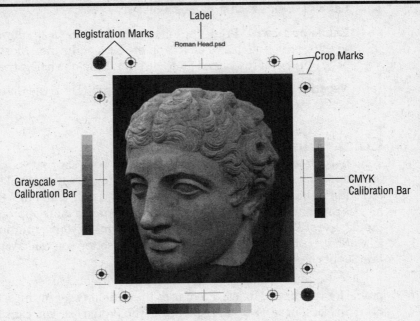

FIGURE 26.9: A printed image with various Print Options selected

Screen   Enter values for screen frequency, angle, and shape for the halftone screens or individual color separations.

Transfer   This function is designed to compensate for poorly calibrated printers. If a printer is printing too dark, for example, adjust the curve to lighten the image to achieve better results.

Interpolation   Check this box to automatically reduce the jagged edges of a low-resolution image by resampling up when printing.

Calibration Bars   Selecting this option produces an 11-step grayscale wedge for measuring dot densities with a densitometer. On CMYK images, a gradient tint bar is printed on each separation.

Registration Marks   These marks, including bull's-eyes and star targets, are used to register color separations.

Crop Marks   Prints crop marks where the page is to be trimmed.

Captions   Prints text entered in the File Info box.

Labels   Prints the file name on images.

Emulsion Down   Prints the emulsion side of the image down so the type is readable when it is on the back of the film. Most plate burners in the United States use emulsion-down negatives.

Negative   Prints a negative image. Most printers in the United States use negative film to burn plates.

Color Management Options

You can color-manage the image while printing. Let's say that your image is set up with profiles for prepress output to an imagesetter to make color separations, but you're going to print to an ink-jet printer to proof the image. You can temporarily convert the document to a more appropriate profile, like sRGB1e61966-2.1 just before you print. If you're printing to a PostScript printer like a laser printer or imagesetter, you can designate PostScript color management.

Choose a source space: Document uses the current *color* settings as a profile for the printed image, Proof uses the current *proof* settings. Under Print Space, choose a working space from the Profile list. You can also choose a rendering intent.

And of course, click the Print button to print the image.

Print

You can also select the Print dialog box to print the image with File ➤ Print (Figure 26.10). The Print dialog box will be configured differently depending on the printer you have selected. Some of the functions found in the Print Options dialog box may be redundant or irrelevant, like specifying multiple pages and collation. (Photoshop does not support multiple-page documents.)

PREFLIGHT CHECKLIST

As a final note, I've provided a very general checklist of operations you should perform to ensure accuracy at the printer. These operations are covered in this chapter.

1. Calibrate your monitor.

2. Scan the image at the proper resolution.

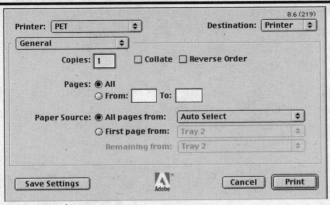

FIGURE 26.10: The Print dialog box

3. In the Color Settings dialog box, choose the appropriate color profiles for display and printing.

4. Open the image. Duplicate it, crop it, and adjust its color.

5. Edit the image using Photoshop's powerful tools and commands.

6. Duplicate the image again and flatten it.

7. Apply the Unsharp Mask filter.

8. Under File ➢ Page Setup, choose an orientation (portrait or landscape).

9. In the Print Options dialog box, set up the image for printing, choosing print size and position on the page, and attach crop marks, labels, etc.

10. Print the image. This will be a proof.

11. If necessary, recalibrate your monitor and print the image again.

WHAT'S NEXT

The final chapter of this book will help you get the best possible hard copies with an ink-jet printer by providing some valuable troubleshooting tips.

Chapter 27

TROUBLESHOOTING INK-JET PRINTERS

The ink-jet printer began as a "poor person's laser," producing near laser quality black-and-white output at a fraction of the cost of a real laser printer. As the technology continued to develop, affordable color ink-jet printers became available (while color laser printers were still way beyond the reach of ordinary people), and ink-jet printers exploded in popularity because they provided an affordable way for the average home or small-business user to get color printouts.

Today, most ink-jet printers still cost less than laser printers. Ink-jet output is not quite as crisp as output from a laser printer; you can tell the difference if you look closely with a magnifying glass. Ink-jet output can also sometimes smear if you touch it immediately after it exits the printer. However, the difference is minor, and ink-jet output looks professional enough for almost any home or business use. The drawbacks? Ink-jet printing speed has traditionally been slower than that of laser printers

Adapted from *The Complete PC Upgrade & Maintenance Guide* by Mark Minasi
ISBN 0-7821-2990-0   1488 pages $59.99

(8–12 pages per minute, as opposed to 12–24), and their per-page cost (of the ink versus laser toner) is slightly higher.

As with laser printers, most problems associated with ink-jet printers can be attributed to either human error or ignorance. You see, ink-jet printers aren't like television sets. You can't just plug them in, turn them on, and expect them to work flawlessly for their entire life without a little Tender Loving Care.

Getting the most out of your ink-jet printer means getting it to work right and then maintaining it in good working order. Once you learn the ropes of regular preventive maintenance and some emergency trouble-shooting, in this chapter, you'll be able to get quality printouts every time you hit Print.

PARTS OF AN INK-JET PRINTER

Ink-jet printers are fairly simple machines in concept. They all have several common pieces:

- ► An outer case to hold the inner parts.
- ► A paper-feed mechanism.
- ► Printer cartridges, which hold the ink and can be black or a combination of black and color.
- ► Ink-jets that control the distribution of ink on the page. These are often built into the ink cartridges, so you don't see them or work with them separately.
- ► A carrier that holds the printer cartridges and moves them back and forth over the paper.
- ► A paper-exit tray.

Some printers are multifunction devices that also include scanning, faxing, or copying capabilities. Such units will have additional parts; check the manual to learn more about them. Some of these devices are not ink-jets, however, but rather simple laser or optical black-and-white printers.

The Case

Ink-jet printer cases come in all shapes, sizes, and even a few colors. Ultimately, the type of case depends on the model of printer you have. Each manufacturer has designed its case to fit a variety of design and mechanical factors, so they aren't compatible with each other.

Most printer cases have some sort of lid or hatch that lifts up to give you access to the ink cartridges. You will not need to remove the entire outer case for routine operation. Should you need to perform more drastic operations on the printer, however, you can (on most models) remove a few screws and lift off the entire outer plastic shell.

You won't find any sort of manual for removing the printer's outer casing, as the manufacturer doesn't want you to do it. Instead, they want you to send your printer to an authorized repair center if there are problems that necessitate removing the case. However, I once took an ink-jet printer apart to clean the inner workings (it was all gunked up with ink) and was able to disassemble it and put it back together with no problems. The key is to work slowly and examine carefully how each piece fits with the others.

Did I mention that the case probably won't be just one piece? That's true. The printer I took apart had something like eight pieces to its outer case. Two pieces make up the supporting base, three or four parts fit together to form the outer front of the printer, and a few more hold the paper-feed and paper-exit trays.

Whatever you do, don't force anything. Carefully note where all the screws are and remove them one at a time, putting the screws in a safe place so you don't lose them. If the screws are different sizes, write this on a piece of paper. When you try to put the case back together, this information is invaluable. After you take off one piece of the case, set it aside and move on to the next. As you remove the pieces of the case, look closely to see how they all fit together. Sometimes it seems like a jigsaw puzzle, so write some notes if you need to, so you remember the details.

When you disassemble your printer, you can clean each piece of the outer case with an alcohol-based cleaning solution and a soft cloth or paper towel. This is a good idea if ink has sprayed on any inner surfaces or you happen to get inky fingerprints on any of the pieces (as I did).

The Paper-Feed Mechanism

The paper-feed mechanism usually holds approximately 100 sheets of paper or more (it really depends on your printer), and feeds the paper into the printer. On some printers, there is a separate, removable tray that holds the paper; on other printers you simply stack the paper up against the feed mechanism. Most ink-jet printers allow you to use different sizes of paper, including standard letter, envelope, and greeting card–sized paper. An adjustable feed guide helps you position various types of paper correctly for feeding.

Some printers have the capability of feeding paper in from either the front or the back. Typically, HP ink-jet printers are front loaders while just about every other major printer manufacturer uses a gravity feed from the rear. The advantage of the front loader is a smaller footprint on your desktop. The disadvantage is the limitation in the thickness of the media supported. Some printers have a manual feed feature, which you can use to manually insert a single page at a time of some nonstandard paper size, like envelopes, that the printer doesn't normally support using the standard paper feed bin.

One of the most common problems with either type of paper-feed mechanism is in the rubber wheels that grab the paper—called grabber wheels. Through use, the grabber wheels begin to lose their traction due to becoming clogged with paper dust, resulting in misfeeds. The solution is simple—take a cotton swab and clean the wheels with denatured alcohol.

If cleaning the grabber wheels doesn't resolve the problem, it may be that the gears on the paper-feed mechanism have become worn and are starting to fail to pull paper into the printer smoothly and evenly. With newer printers, this happens very rarely. On some printers, the gears start making an annoying squeaking sound too, and oiling them doesn't help much. In such cases, it's usually worth it (to me, anyway) to take the printer to an authorized service center and have the feed mechanism refurbished. It's not that you can't do it yourself, but the authorized service centers have better access to the needed parts. Of course, with good quality color ink-jet printers costing less than $100, it is probably a better use of your money to simply replace the printer.

Printer Cartridges

The printer cartridges hold the ink that your printer uses. Make sure you use printer cartridges that are compatible with your make and model of printer, as they come in different shapes and sizes. Most look like little boxes, and some have carefully designed nozzles and electronic contacts built in. Other, simpler styles of printer cartridges are simply ink reservoirs that feed into the printer cartridge carrier, which has the more complicated parts.

Almost all color ink-jet printers today have both color and black ink cartridges that you can replace separately. (On older, cheaper models, cyan, yellow, and magenta had to be combined to make what is called "composite" black, and it resulted in a somewhat muddy gray.)

Some color printers have the three primary colors in one cartridge, whereas other models allow you to purchase and install each of the three colors separately (magenta, yellow, and cyan). The primary disadvantage to the "three colors in one box" type is that you may not use the three colors at the same rate. If you run out of cyan, for example, you have no choice but to replace the entire cartridge to restore your color printing capability, or live with your inability to print blues and greens, as well as cyans. (That's because blue is made up of cyan and magenta inks, while green is produced by combining cyan and yellow ink; if you're missing cyan, your blues will come out magenta, and your greens will appear yellow.)

Printer cartridges are manufactured with a protective piece of plastic and transparent tape that covers the nozzles and contacts. Make sure to remove this prior to installing.

At the end of this chapter, I'll tell you more about cartridges, including how they can be refilled (and why you may *not* want to do so).

The Printer Cartridge Carrier

The printer cartridge carrier holds the printer cartridges and moves back and forth over the paper while ink is being sprayed onto the paper. To install printer cartridges, you may have to move a lever or press a button on the printer to put the carrier in a position to accept the cartridges, and then snap them into place. On some printers, the cartridge carriers come out of the printer completely, and then go back in with the new cartridge.

The Exit Tray

The exit tray holds the paper after it comes out of the printer. Many models of ink-jet printers have sliding pieces to the exit tray, enabling you to retract the tray in order to save space when you're not using it. When you print, extend the tray to its full length to catch the paper.

A few printers have a lever you can flip to make the output come out at the opposite end of the printer from normal. For example, if the output normally comes out the front, you could make it come out the back. Why would you want to do this? Primarily, to get a straight path through the printer. If you are printing on some stiff medium, such as cardboard, you can avoid the otherwise-inevitable curling by allowing the paper to exit the printer in a straight line from the spot where it entered, rather than curling around a roller on its way out. I am just joking about the cardboard—be careful about the thickness of paper you pass through your printer.

HOW AN INK-JET PRINTER WORKS

At the most basic level, ink-jet printers work by blowing jets of ink onto paper. The older generation of impact dot matrix printers use a mechanical print head that physically impacts a ribbon, thereby transferring ink to the paper. In contrast, ink-jet printer "heads" don't physically touch the paper at all. Instead, these printers force ink through nozzles and spray the ink right onto the paper. Depending on the printer and its technology, there can be between 21 and 128 nozzles for each of the four colors (cyan, yellow, magenta, and black). By mixing the colors, the printer can produce almost any color.

There are two types of ink-jet printers: thermal and piezo. These are two different technologies used to force the ink from the cartridge and through the nozzles.

Thermal ink-jets use the older of the two technologies. They heat the ink in the cartridge (to about 400 degrees Fahrenheit), causing vapor bubbles in the cartridge that rise to the top and force the ink out through the nozzle. The vacuum caused by the expelled ink draws more ink down into the nozzles, making a constant stream.

Piezo printing uses an electric charge instead of heat. It charges piezo-electric crystals in the nozzles, which change their shape as a result of the electric current, forcing the ink out through the nozzles.

The output of both technologies is essentially the same. The primary difference between the two is that, with the thermal ink-jets, every time you replace the ink cartridge, you replace the print head. Traditionally with piezo technology, only the ink cartridge is replaced and the print head is a permanent part of the printer.

COMMON PROBLEMS AND POSSIBLE SOLUTIONS

Just about all printer problems can be easily fixed if you know where to look. Although I attempt in this section to give you a good general sense of what problems might occur and how to prevent them, you should read the manuals that came with your printer carefully.

The list of things that can go wrong with printing is fairly large, but you can organize them into general categories to help you troubleshoot. The point is to try to remove problems that might not be affecting you and to point you in the right general direction. Try thinking along these lines to categorize your printer problem:

- ▶ Your printer seems to be working, but nothing is printing.

- ▶ There are color problems.

- ▶ The printer appears dead.

- ▶ Printing seems very slow, but is working.

- ▶ The quality of your printouts is smeared or generally poor.

- ▶ The output is garbled or formatted incorrectly.

- ▶ The paper is jammed or not feeding correctly.

I'll cover each of these symptoms in turn.

Printer Works but Nothing Prints

This problem may be as simple as running out of ink. Most printers come with software status controls built into their Windows driver. Right-click the printer's icon in Windows, choose Properties (it works basically the same in all Windows versions), and look for a status monitor in the Printer Properties dialog box that indicates the ink level. Replace any cartridges that indicate they are out of ink. Figure 27.1 shows the ink levels for an Epson printer. Be aware that most status programs, like the status monitor shown in Figure 27.1, are separate programs that may or may not be installed at the same time as your printer driver. Also note that all of these status programs require bidirectional IEEE-1294 printer cables to work.

If that doesn't work, try running the nozzle check and/or print head cleaning routine that is a part of your printer control program. Your nozzles might be clogged up. This is sometimes a problem if you haven't printed in a long time. A nozzle check prints a test pattern using all the jets, so you can see whether any are malfunctioning. Head cleaning self-cleans each jet. You will want to run these two utilities, first one and then the other, to check the current nozzle functioning and to improve it. Head cleaning uses up a small amount of ink, however, so if you do it a lot, you'll end up wasting ink. Still, you will find that if the problem is clogged jets, running the head cleaning routines—sometimes up to 10 times—may restore the printer. If you haven't used the printer in several months, there is a chance that the ink has dried up and you will need to replace the cartridge(s). Piezo technology print heads are a little more susceptible than thermal printers to this phenomenon. This is because with thermal print heads the print head and ink supply are integrated into a single unit. Each time you replace the ink cartridge, you get a new print head. If the ink in your piezo print head should dry up, replacing the ink cartridge won't necessarily solve the problem.

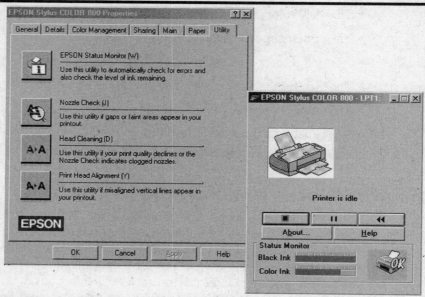

FIGURE 27.1: This status monitor for the Epson Stylus Color 800 shows the color and black ink levels.

True story: One time I was working with a printer that hadn't been used in over a year. Nearly all the nozzles were clogged, so I had to run the head cleaning routine 20 times in a row. The quality kept getting better and better, and I was feeling encouraged, but then the blue nozzles just quit. Kaput. Nothing. I panicked. Had I ruined the printer by repeated cleaning? Nope, I had just depleted all the blue ink. So I installed a new cartridge, and it worked perfectly. Incidentally, on many printer models, installing a new ink cartridge also takes care of any clogged nozzles, because the ink-jets are built into the cartridge. (This isn't the case for all models.)

If, after cleaning the print heads, you see intermittent output on the page, try cleaning them several more times; this can sometimes break loose the crud that's clogging up some of the jets. Most printers enable you to run the head cleaning routine by pressing certain buttons on the printer (check your documentation) or by choosing an option in the printer's Properties box (as shown in Figure 27.2).

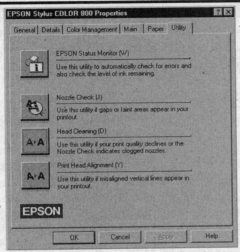

FIGURE 27.2: Most printers have utilities such as nozzle checking and head cleaning built into the driver.

If that fails, take your print cartridges out and check whether any obstructions might be blocking the ink. If you've recently replaced your printer cartridges, check them to make sure you removed all the protective coverings from the print nozzles and contacts.

WARNING

The documentation for some printer models claims that if you remove an ink cartridge after initially inserting it, it becomes useless and you can't reinsert it. I have reinserted a cartridge in one such printer successfully, despite the instructions, but if you have a printer that claims this, try all other troubleshooting first before you resort to removing the cartridge for examination and reinsertion.

Color Is Wrong

If the colors on your printout don't match what you see onscreen, the most likely problem is that one of the color jets is clogged. Check the printout—do all greens look yellow, and is the blue magenta instead? That means you're out of cyan. See the instructions in the preceding section for replacing an ink cartridge and/or cleaning the print heads.

If the color problem is more subtle (all colors appear, but they look too dark, too blue, or whatever), the problem might be with your monitor's color calibration. If your video card ships with a utility that allows you to calibrate your monitor's color, you should run it. There might also be a utility built into your printer driver or video card driver; try displaying the device's Properties to look for one.

Sometimes the problem lies with the color management scheme selected by the application from which you are printing. For example, if you are printing from CorelDRAW, its color management profile is active by default. So, when printing to an Epson printer (whose color management is also on by default), the result of these two color management programs trying to out-think one another can be less than desirable output. I recommend turning off all color management except the one that came with the printer—which you might not be able to turn off anyhow.

Printer Doesn't Print at All

Ah, the dead printer. Fear not, the problem is usually simple.

First, check that the printer is plugged in and the power is on. Then, check your printer cable connections. Try removing the printer cable and reseating it at both ends.

If these aren't causing the problem, make sure that the printer appears in your operating system and that it is online and currently selected as the default printer. In Windows, check the Printers list (Start ➢ Settings ➢ Printers); a checkmark next to the printer's icon indicates that it's the default. Right-click it and choose Set as Default if needed. Sometimes strange things happen and this gets messed up. I've seen cases of printers disappearing or suddenly going offline.

If your default printer is a network printer, make sure your network connection is up and running. If the printer appears "faded" or "grayed out" in the Printers window, it's because the printer is not available for some reason (usually due to a failure in the network connection to it).

Next, open the print queue for your printer (by double-clicking its icon in the Printers list) to see whether printing is currently paused. (The title bar will read "Paused" if it is.) Choose Printer ➢ Pause Printing to unpause it. You might have paused printing and forgotten to reset it.

If the printer's status is User Intervention, that means the printer is waiting on something. If it's a network printer, there could be a warning or error message on the host computer's screen, waiting to be answered. Or the printer could be out of paper or have a paper jam.

Printing Is Slow or Intermittent

Slow or intermittent printing could be caused by a couple of things. First, double-check your cable connection to the printer. If your printer is capable of bidirectional communications, make sure your printer cable is also. (Most printer cables bought today are bidirectional, but an old one you found in someone's junk drawer may not be. You can't tell by looking at them, but it will say on the packaging of a new one you buy.) Bidirectional communications enable the printer to communicate with the operating system (and vice versa), so that your printer control program can communicate with the printer and return error messages and ink levels. Bidirectional printing must also be enabled for the port that the printer is using (probably LPT1) in your PC's BIOS. You'll find several variations on the bidirectional theme in most newer computers: bidirectional, EPP (Enhanced Parallel Port, used primarily by non-printer peripherals, such as parallel-port hard drives, tape drives, and such), ECP (Extended Capability Port, used by the latest generation of printers and scanners), and EPP+ECP (both types active at once). (SPP, if available, means Standard Parallel Port.) Plain old bidirectional may work for you: check your printer's documentation to see if it requires one of the other bidirectional options.

Slow printing could also be caused by your printer driver settings. In most cases, you can choose to print in draft, normal, or high-resolution mode. The higher the quality, the more time the printing will take. If you're printing at 1200 dpi (dots per inch), your printout may take a very long time. If you want it to print faster and don't need the higher quality, lower your print quality settings through the printer's print settings. You can set these by displaying the printer's properties (right-click it and choose Properties), or, within some applications, with a PRINT SETUP command.

Finally, slow printing can be the result of using the wrong driver for your printer. If you let Windows autodetect your printer instead of running the setup software that came with the printer, you may not be using the best possible driver. Dig through the documentation that came with the printer and find its SETUP CD, and run that to install the specific driver for your printer. When given a choice between a driver provided by the

Windows operating system and one provided by the printer manufacturer, always choose the one from the printer manufacturer. The one provided by the Windows OS tends to be a no-frills version and often does not support many of the advanced features of the printer.

Next, never ever assume that the printer driver that came with the printer you just bought is the most current driver. It may have been manufactured, boxed, and sent to the distribution warehouse several driver revisions ago. Always go the manufacturer's Web page to download the most current driver for your operating system. If the newest driver isn't for your operating system, don't use it. Only use the driver for the operating system you are using with your printer. Sounds obvious, right? If I had a nickel for every time that someone had selected the newest driver without regard to the operating system, I'd have a lot of nickels.

Quality Is Poor

If the printer prints, but the output isn't as good as you think it should be, you've got some investigative work to do to find out why.

First, check to see what quality mode the printer is set to operate in. As I mentioned earlier, the higher the quality, the slower the printing. Sometimes people set their printers to draft quality (the fastest, lowest-quality setting) and forget that they've done so. Check the printer's Properties box to view and change the quality setting. Figure 27.3 shows an example.

FIGURE 27.3: Most printers enable you to choose from several quality settings.

While you're there looking at the quality setting, see also whether there is a Media Type or Paper Type setting. With ink-jet printers, plain old copy paper doesn't produce as good an image as special ink-jet paper with a shinier surface and less porous "holes." The less porous the paper, the higher the dpi setting you can use for the printout. Using a very high dpi (such as 2400) with plain paper can actually result in a printout that looks *worse* than a printout at a lower resolution (720, perhaps) because the paper can't handle the dots being that close together because of its porousness. For best results, buy paper made especially for ink-jet printers, because it enables you to print at higher dpi.

Next, clean your print heads through the printer control program, as described in the previous "Printer Works but Nothing Prints" section. A clogged nozzle can result in stripes on the page (*banding*), or "bald" patches where there is no printing.

Your print heads may also be out of alignment. Run the print head alignment routine from your printer (probably built into the printer driver, as with the other utilities you've seen so far in this chapter). This aligns the print heads and nozzles so that the black and color ink cartridges print at the same location on the page. This one does its stuff the first time, so you should not have to do it multiple times for best results (as with head cleaning).

Check your ink levels. Low ink results in banding or streaking. If you're low on color ink, your printout will appear washed out or oddly miscolored. You may be out of one of the three primary colors used in color printing.

If your HP printer appears to be smearing, remove your print cartridges and inspect them manually to see if there is a buildup of paper debris. If there is, take a cotton swab and clean the print head portion of the cartridge and replace it in the holder. Reinstall the cartridges and make sure they are properly seated in the carrier. Remember that not all printers allow you to reinsert the same cartridge after removing it (at least not according to the documentation; you might still be able to do so). On some HP printers you will be requested to run the alignment procedure again, because the program thinks you have installed a new cartridge.

If you have problems at the edge of the page, such as output being cut off at the edges, you may be trying to print material outside of the effective print area of your printer. No printer will let you print across the full width of a standard sheet of paper. This is because the edge of the paper is used to hold it in place while transporting the paper through the printer. Most modern applications that support a Print Preview function are aware of the printable area of the selected printer and media and will show you exactly what will and will not print.

An exception to this paper edge issue is the newest Epson photo printers, which offer true borderless printing. This should not be confused with earlier borderless printing, which was accomplished using a special paper with perforated edges that you removed after the printing was complete.

Output Is Garbled or Formatted Incorrectly

If you print a nicely formatted word processing document, but it comes out with the wrong fonts, skewed margins, or junk characters, the problem is possibly a corrupt printer driver but more than likely it is an interrupted print job.

If you interrupt a print job, many times the information header for the job is lost, so when the job is restarted, the printer begins receiving the control information about the print job but has no way of knowing that, so rather than using the information to set up the print job, it prints all of that gibberish—on many sheets of paper. The solution is to take the paper out of the printer until the printer and finally the computer figure it is out of paper. At that time you should receive an error message, which will give you the opportunity to cancel the print jobs.

If it is a busted driver, you can repair the driver problem by deleting the printer from the Printers list and reinstalling it using the disk that came with the printer. If you don't have such a disk, download the needed setup software from the manufacturer's Web site. Windows comes with drivers for many popular printers, and you can use the Windows-provided driver in a pinch, if one from the manufacturer is not available. (The Windows version may not have as many features, so I try to always use the manufacturer-supplied drivers whenever possible.)

The driver is not always to blame, however. One time I had a very frustrating service call, in which the printer was printing the output scrunched up on the left side of each page. The printout would appear perfectly in Print Preview onscreen, but without fail, each page came out distorted. I tried reinstalling the driver. I tried resetting the printer. I tried printing from DOS. Nothing worked. Finally I checked inside the printer and noticed that the ink cartridges were not completely seated in their holders. I gave them a firm push into place, and voilà! Problem solved. Weird but true.

Paper Is Stuck or Not Moving

If paper jams in your printer, stop what you are doing and carefully but firmly pull the paper out of the printer. Try not to rip the paper as you pull it out, because you don't want to have small pieces of paper caught inside the printer. When you've removed the jammed piece of paper, throw it away and resend your job to the printer.

If paper fails to feed at all, check that the paper is seated correctly in the paper tray. If any obstructions are blocking the paper, carefully remove them. If a piece of paper is bent, it may not feed correctly. You'll have to throw it away.

You should also check to ensure that you haven't overloaded the paper feed tray. Too many sheets in the tray can easily cause jams or feed problems. Sometimes using very thick or very thin paper can cause feed problems too. Try to use a standard paper weight (20 lb or so) whenever possible.

Most printers also have paper guides that snuggle up against your paper and keep it straight as it feeds into the printer. These guides can be set for different sizes of paper. Make sure the guide is properly set and isn't loose.

Other issues that cause misfeeds or no feeds are media related. For example, most printers that can print to envelopes print one at a time or have a limit of five or eight unless you have a dedicated envelope feeder. Transparency material can be difficult for some printers to pick up and may have to be fed one sheet at a time.

Finally, make sure your printer is on a flat, stable surface. If it is tilted at an angle or on a shaky table, that might cause feed problems—I doubt it, but all things are possible.

COMMON ERROR MESSAGES

Although each printer will have error messages that are unique to its particular make and model, here are a few error messages you might encounter.

Ink Low

This signifies that your printer cartridge is running out of ink. You should replace the printer cartridge soon. Some printer manufacturers recommend that you don't change an ink cartridge until the printer reports that the ink is completely out. You can make that call yourself, but it's nice to have the advance Ink Low warning so you can make sure you have a new cartridge available.

WARNING

Ink cartridges tend to dry out on the shelf. Don't stockpile ink cartridges; after six months or so they lose their freshness.

Out of Memory

Laser printers are page printers—they print entire pages at a time, so they must have a lot of memory in them to store a whole page. In contrast, ink-jet printers are line printers—they print line-by-line, so they don't typically need a great deal of memory. You seldom hear of memory upgrades available for ink-jet printers because it's simply not an issue.

Therefore, if you get an Out of Memory error message on-screen as you print to an ink-jet printer, it most likely refers to a lack of memory on your PC, rather than on your printer. Usually it does not really mean that you should add memory to your PC; rather, it means that memory-hogging programs you have run on your PC have allocated all the available memory, and there isn't enough left for the printer driver to spool its output to the printer. In such a case, it's best to restart your PC and resubmit your print job after doing so.

Out of Paper

You are either completely out of paper, or if your printer has multiple paper sources, you may have designated an empty tray. You'll have to load more paper in your printer or switch to another paper tray to continue.

Paper Jam

Paper has jammed somewhere in your printer, preventing it from continuing. Carefully but firmly pull the paper out of the printer, hopefully in one piece. Depending on where the paper jam occurs, you may have to pull it out of the top (or paper-feed area) or the bottom (the paper-exit tray). If you can't reach the paper easily, you might have to open the access panel to reach inside your printer.

Print Head Failure

If your printer cartridges are not working correctly, you might receive a Print Head Failure error message. Dirty, fouled, or clogged printer cartridges can cause this problem. Clean your printer head through your printer control program, and if necessary, remove the ink cartridges and clean them with a clean cloth.

PREVENTIVE MAINTENANCE

If you own a car, you're probably used to the concept of preventive maintenance. You change your oil every 3000 miles or every three months, check the air in the tires, check other fluid levels, and routinely put gas in it so it will run. Printers also require some regular maintenance, although it is far less troublesome than what you need to do for a car.

Clean the Print Heads

Although you don't want to overdo it, you should clean your print heads periodically by running the head cleaning utility (as discussed earlier in the chapter). This should remove any built up "gunk" or ink on the print heads and help ensure consistently high-quality printouts.

Align the Print Heads

Every time you install new printer cartridges, you should also align your print heads. This keeps the color and black ink cartridges aligned so there are no gaps between black and color portions of your printout. Your printer may do this automatically, but it doesn't hurt to do it manually by using the head alignment utility in your printer driver (again, covered earlier in the chapter).

Realigning print heads might also be necessary after moving your printer or bumping into it accidentally.

Complete Overhaul

It is rarely necessary to take your printer apart and clean the inner parts. You shouldn't take this step unless you are comfortable with it, but if you print a lot and find that your printouts aren't very good and you've run through the standard steps to fix quality problems, your printer may just be dirty inside.

Carefully remove the outer case and disassemble your printer, cleaning each part as you go along with an alcohol-based cleaner. This will remove any ink that has dried on the parts. You may have to soak some pieces to get the ink off them. A small glass jar works well for the smaller pieces. Just soak them for 15 to 30 minutes and wipe them off with a cloth or towel. When everything is clean, reassemble your printer and print out a test page (after you've realigned the print heads).

REFILLING INK CARTRIDGES

Due to the cost of today's ink-jet printer cartridges (often $20–$30 for black and upwards of $30 for color), the cottage industry of refillable ink-jet cartridges has emerged. It should be said that most manufacturers do not recommend this, but what they don't know won't hurt them. In fact, some manufacturers make their printer cartridges very hard to get into by yourself, thus making it hard for you to refill them without special tools or equipment.

You should be able to purchase kits made specifically for your brand of printer and model of printer cartridges if your printer is popular enough. This method gives you some assurance that your new cartridge will contain ink with the same characteristics as the retail printer cartridge. If not, you may be stuck with buying the officially designated replacement cartridges.

Refilling ink cartridges involves removing the lid of the existing printer cartridge and simply refilling it. Due to the wide variety of existing printer cartridges, you should carefully follow the instructions provided with the kit you buy.

You should not refill a cartridge more than once. That's because, on most printers, the print jets are built into the cartridges. When you replace the ink cartridge, you also give yourself a brand-new set of jets. If you continually refill and reuse the same cartridge, you're never getting new jets, and your print quality can start to suffer. You'll get clogged jets more and more often, resulting in more head cleaning, which in turn wastes ink, and before you know it, you're caught in a vicious circle. Yes, it's okay to be a little thrifty and refill occasionally, but don't be so cheap that you cheat yourself out of decent quality printouts.

While all of the above is possible, I do not recommend buying generic replacement cartridges or refilling them because the color inks never look as good as the manufacturer's ink—regardless of what the ads tell you. I have compared many brand name replacements and the results have always been noticeably inferior to the results with the manufacturer's cartridge.

TROUBLESHOOTING TIPS

Here's a summary of the troubleshooting procedures covered in the chapter:

▶ For print quality problems, check the utilities built into the printer's driver. (Right-click the printer and choose Properties to display the available tools and settings.)

▶ Use the nozzle checking utility to see whether any jets are clogged; then use the head cleaning utility to clean them. This uses ink, so balance the need for cleaning with your need not to waste ink.

▶ If the color is seriously off, one of the ink colors is probably out, or its nozzles are clogged. If the color problem is more uniform, check the color calibration for the video card and/or the printer. One or both may have a color correction utility.

▶ If the printer doesn't print at all, check all your connections, and make sure the printer is installed correctly in your operating system.

▶ Make sure the printer isn't offline, paused, or requiring user intervention (such as adding more paper).

▶ If the printer is accessed through a network, make sure your network connection is up and running.

▶ If the printer prints slowly, try decreasing the quality setting for a draft print. You can usually do this through the printer's Properties box. Slow printing may also be the result of using the wrong driver.

▶ Poor print quality can mean you are running out of one or more colors of ink, that the print heads are misaligned or clogged, or that you're using a draft quality setting.

▶ Garbled output indicates a problem with the printer driver. Remove the printer from Windows (or other operating system) and reinstall.

WHAT'S NEXT

This concludes the chapter-oriented portion of our very complete look at Photoshop and its features. You'll find that there's still a lot of meat to explore in the Reference section, including some juicy looks at various filter effects and a rich glossary with all the terms you need to know to use Photoshop successfully.

Reference Section

Adapted from *Photoshop at Your Fingertips* by David D. Busch

Coming in 2002   ISBN 0-7821-4092-0

Glossary adapted from *Mastering Photoshop 6* by Steve Romaniello

ISBN 0-7821-2841-6   896 pages $49.99 and *Photoshop at Your Fingertips*

PHOTOSHOP 6 KEYBOARD SHORTCUTS

These are the most frequently used keyboard shortcuts for Photoshop 6. When a command calls for "special" keys, such as the Ctrl/Command key, Shift key, or Alt/Option key, you should press the special key(s) first, and then the other key, holding down all the keys at once. For example, to use Shift+Ctrl/Command+M to jump to ImageReady, you should press and hold the Shift and Ctrl/Command keys (at the same time or in any order), then press the M key while continuing to hold down the Shift and Ctrl/Command keys. The Ctrl/Command notation means to hold down the Ctrl key if you're using a PC and the Command key if you're using a Macintosh. Similarly, Alt/Option means the Alt key on a PC and the Option key on a Macintosh. Note that the Macintosh's Control key is not the same as the PC's Ctrl key. On a Macintosh, you use the Control key with the mouse button to generate the PC's right-click.

Tools

This listing shows the shortcuts used to select tools from the Photoshop Tool palette. You don't need to press any special keys to use these shortcuts, just the normal keystroke will do. (Photoshop doesn't accept keyboard input except when you're using a dialog box, the text tools, and the like.)

Airbrush	J
Blur/Sharpen/Smudge	R (Hold Shift to cycle)
Crop	C
Default Colors	D
Direct/Path Selection Tool	A (Hold Shift to cycle)
Dodge/Burn/Sponge	O (Hold Shift to cycle)
Eraser/Background Eraser/ Magic Eraser	E (Hold Shift to cycle)
Eyedropper/Sampler/Measure	I (Hold Shift to cycle)
Gradient/Paint Bucket Tools	G (Hold Shift to cycle)
Hand Tool	H

History/Art History Brush	Y (Hold Shift to cycle)
Lasso Tools	L (Hold Shift to cycle)
Magic Wand	W
Marquee Tools	M (Hold Shift to cycle)
Line/Shape Tools	U (Hold Shift to cycle)
Move	V
Slice Tools	K (Hold Shift to cycle)
Paintbrush/Pencil Tools	B (Hold Shift to cycle)
Select Next Brush	+[
Select Previous Brush	+]
Pen Tools	P (Hold Shift to cycle)
Notes Tools	N (Hold Shift to cycle)
Quick Mask Mode	Q (Toggle)
Stamp/Clone Tools	S (Hold Shift to cycle)
Switch Colors	X
Type Tool	T
Zoom Tool	Z
Jump to ImageReady	Ctrl/Command+Shift+M
Full Screen Mode/Menu Bar/ Standard (Hold Shift to cycle)	F

Blending Modes

These keyboard shortcuts control the Blending mode used by painting tools, such as the Paintbrush or Paint Bucket.

Behind	Shift+Alt/Option+Q
Color	Shift+Alt/Option+C
Color Burn	Shift+Alt/Option+B
Color Dodge	Shift+Alt/Option+D
Darken	Shift+Alt/Option+K

Difference	Shift+Alt/Option+E
Dissolve	Shift+Alt/Option+I
Exclusion	Shift+Alt/Option+X
Hard Light	Shift+Alt/Option+H
Hue	Shift+Alt/Option+U
Lighten	Shift+Alt/Option+G
Luminosity	Shift+Alt/Option+Y
Multiply	Shift+Alt/Option+M
Normal	Shift+Alt/Option+N
Overlay	Shift+Alt/Option+O
Saturation	Shift+Alt/Option+T
Screen	Shift+Alt/Option+S
Soft Light	Shift+Alt/Option+F
Normal	Shift+Alt/Option+L
Cycle Blending Modes Up	Shift+Minus key (−)
Cycle Blending Modes Down	Shift+Plus key (+)

Liquify

Liquify is Photoshop's liquid-smudging tool.

Liquify	Ctrl/Command+Shift+X

Color/Contrast Adjustment

These shortcuts give you fast access to Photoshop's color and contrast adjustments.

Color Balance	Ctrl/Command+B
Auto Levels	Ctrl/Command+Shift+L
CMYK Preview	Ctrl/Command+Y
Color Balance with Last Settings	Ctrl/Command+Alt/Option B

Curves	Ctrl/Command+M
Curves with Last Settings	Ctrl/Command+Alt/ Option+M
Desaturate	Ctrl/Command+Shift+U
Gamut Warning	Ctrl/Command+Shift+Y
Hue/Saturation	Ctrl/Command+U
Hue/Saturation with Last Settings	Ctrl/Command+Alt/ Option+U
Invert	Ctrl/Command+I
Levels	Ctrl/Command+L
Levels with Last Settings	Ctrl/Command+Alt/ Option+L
Color Settings	Ctrl/Command+Shift+K

Selections

Use these shortcuts to manipulate your selections.

Deselect	Ctrl/Command+D
Feather Selection	Ctrl/Command+Alt/ Option+D
Invert Selection	Ctrl/Command+Shift+I
Reselect	Ctrl/Command+Shift+D
Select All	Ctrl/Command+A

Editing

Photoshop's copying, cutting, pasting, transformation, and other editing effects can be accessed using these shortcuts.

Copy	Ctrl/Command+C
Copy Merged	Ctrl/Command+Shift+C
Cut	Ctrl/Command+X
Fade Last Filter	Ctrl/Command+Shift+F

Last Filter	Ctrl/Command+F
Fill with Background Color	Ctrl/Command+DEL
Fill with Foreground Color	Alt/Option+DEL
Free Transform	Ctrl/Command+T
Transform Again	Ctrl/Command+Shift+Alt/Option+T
Paste	Ctrl/Command+V
Paste outside Selection	Ctrl/Command+Shift+Alt/Option+V
Paste into Selection	Ctrl/Command+Shift+V
Step Back in History	Ctrl/Command+Alt/Option+Z
Step Forward in History	Ctrl/Command+Shift+Z
Undo	Ctrl/Command+Z
Preferences	Ctrl/Command+K
Preferences (Last Used)	Ctrl/Command+Alt/Option+K

Type

Here are some shortcuts to speed your text operations.

Align Left	Ctrl/Command+Shift+L
Align Right	Ctrl/Command+Shift+R
Center Text	Ctrl/Command+Shift+C
Decrease Type Size by 10pt	Ctrl/Command+Shift+Alt/Option+<
Decrease Type Size by 2pt	Ctrl/Command+Shift+<
Increase Type Size by 10pt	Ctrl/Command+Shift+Alt/Option+>
Increase Type Size by 2pt	Ctrl/Command+Shift+>

File

Most File commands can be accessed using one of these keyboard shortcuts.

Close	Ctrl/Command+W
Close All	Shift+Ctrl/Command+W
New Document	Ctrl/Command+N
Open	Ctrl/Command+O
Page Setup	Ctrl/Command+Shift+P
Print	Ctrl/Command+P
Print Options	Ctrl/Command+Alt/ Option+P
Quit	Ctrl/Command+Q
Save	Ctrl/Command+S
Save a Copy	Ctrl/Command+Alt/ Option+S
Save for Web	Ctrl/Command+Alt/ Option+Shift+S
Save As...	Ctrl/Command+Shift+S

Palettes

Only a few of the Palettes can be shown or hidden with keyboard shortcuts. Here are the holdovers from earlier versions of Photoshop.

Show/Hide Color Palette	F6
Show/Hide Layers Palette	F7
Show/Hide Info Palette	F8
Show/Hide Actions Palette	F9

Layers and Channels

You can save many clicks in the Layers and Channels palettes by memorizing these handy shortcuts.

Ascend through Layers	Alt/Option+]
Bring Layer to Front	Ctrl/Command+Shift+]
Descend through Layers	Alt/Option+[
Group with Previous	Ctrl/Command+G
Ungroup Layers	Ctrl/Command+Shift+G
Layer Copy	Ctrl/Command+J
Layer Cut	Ctrl/Command+Shift+J
Merge Down	Ctrl/Command+E
Merge Visible	Ctrl/Command+Shift+E
Merge Visible to Active Layer	Ctrl/Command+Shift+Alt/Option+E
Move Layer Down	Ctrl/Command+[
Move Layer Up	Ctrl/Command+]
New Layer	Ctrl/Command+Shift+N
Lock Transparency	/
Select Bottom Layer	Shift+Alt/Option+[
Select Top Layer	Shift+Alt/Option+]
Send Layer to Back	Ctrl/Command+Shift+[
Select Channel 1+9	Ctrl/Command+1+9

View

These shortcuts are useful for toggling between common viewing modes.

Hide Selection Edges	Ctrl/Command+H
Lock/Unlock Guides	Ctrl/Command+Alt/Option+;
Show/Hide Menubar	Shift+F

Show/Hide Grid	Ctrl/Command+"
Show/Hide Guides	Ctrl/Command+;
Show/Hide Rulers	Ctrl/Command+R
Snap to Grid	Ctrl/Command+Shift+"
Snap to Guides	Ctrl/Command+Shift+;
View Actual Pixels	Ctrl/Command+Alt/ Option+0
Zoom In	Ctrl/Command+Alt/ Option++
Zoom Out	Ctrl/Command+Alt/ Option+−

THE TOP EIGHT PHOTOSHOP 6 QUESTIONS

You'll find the answers to all these questions within the pages of this book, but here is a quick reference to some of the most popular queries. If you don't know exactly how to carry out a particular step, just refer to the cross-referenced chapter for detailed instructions.

How Can I Add or Subtract from a Selection?

Photoshop 6 has a great new facility that simplifies adding and subtracting from selections. No longer do you need to remember to hold down the Shift or Alt/Option keys, or risk losing your selection entirely. When you choose any selection tool, a set of four icons appears in the Options bar. Click in any of these boxes to activate a new selection mode. From left to right, the icons are:

New Selection   Anything you select will become a new selection.

Add to Selection   Anything you select will be added to the existing selection.

Subtract from Selection   Anything you select will be
removed from the existing selection.

Intersect with Selection   Only the portions that are common
to the existing selection and your additional selection will be
selected.

For more information on adding or subtracting selections, see
Chapter 3.

How Much Memory Do I Need to Run Photoshop?

Add as much memory to your system as you can afford (and do it when
prices are low!) Photoshop may run on a system with 64MB of RAM, but
it won't be any fun. Your minimum for Mac OS 9, OS X, Windows 98, or
Windows ME should be 128MB of memory. More is even better, as long
as you avoid the problems you can encounter using more than 512 MB of
RAM with Windows 95/98 or Me with certain computer systems. Windows NT, 2000, and XP need more RAM just for the OS, so you'll want
256MB or more to run Photoshop under these operating systems.

To allocate memory to Photoshop under Windows, use the Memory &
Image Cache preferences dialog box within Photoshop, and in the Physical Memory Usage area, change the Used by Photoshop parameter from
50 to 80 percent.

Mac OS, in contrast, lets you specify how much memory each application
should use from the operating system itself. Make sure you've exited Photoshop, select the Photoshop application's icon, then choose the File ➤ Get
Info ➤ Memory dialog box Change the Preferred Size setting to reflect the
amount of RAM you want to devote to Photoshop.

For more information on Photoshop memory, see Chapter 2.

How Do I Correct Color?

Photoshop offers several ways to correct your colors. Choose the one
that's easiest for you.

▶ Choose Image ➤ Adjust ➤ Color Balance (or press Ctrl/
Command+B) to summon the Color Balance dialog box, and
adjust the three sliders labeled Cyan/Red, Magenta/Green, and

Yellow/Blue until the image looks good. You can modify the shadows, midtones, or highlights of an image by choosing the appropriate radio button in the Tone Balance area of the dialog box.

▶ You can also color correct an image using Photoshop's Hue/Saturation (and Lightness) control. The advantage of correcting color this way is that you can change the saturation of individual colors or of all the colors in an image, without modifying the hue or lightness/darkness of those colors. Choose Image ➢ Adjust ➢ Hue/Saturation (or press Ctrl/Command+U) to view the dialog box. Then, change the Saturation value until the picture gains, in Preview mode, the richness of color you are looking for. If the color is slightly off, experiment with the Hue control to find a setting that corrects any imbalance. Make adjustments to the brightness of the image by moving the Lightness slider. This varies only the relative darkness or lightness of all the colors in the image.

▶ Photoshop also offers a Variations mode that generates several versions of an image, arranged in an array so you can view a small copy of each one and compare them. Choose Image ➢ Adjust ➢ Variations, then click in the thumbnails that provide an improved view of your image.

For more information on correcting color, see Chapter 20.

How Do I Write a Macro?

While manually applying steps isn't exactly reinventing the wheel, it's work you won't have to do if you think ahead and create an action first. It's easy. The hardest part is to remember to make the recording options available by turning off Button mode in the Actions palette. Just uncheck Button Mode in the flyout menu at the right side of the Actions palette.

Then choose New Action from the Actions palette's flyout menu, and enter a name for the action that is easy to remember. If you want, you can associate the action to a shortcut key and/or button color. When you click Record, Photoshop will start memorizing any steps you carry out. Click the Stop Recording button at the bottom of the Actions palette to finish your macro.

For more information on using actions in Photoshop, see Chapter 11.

How Do I Create an Animation?

Photoshop and ImageReady have all the tools you need to create great-looking animated images, using the built-in capabilities of the versatile GIF format. Just create separate images for each frame of your animation on individual Photoshop layers. Then, jump to ImageReady and choose Make Frames from Layers from the Animation palette's flyout menu. Then, click the down-pointing arrow beneath each of your new frames, and choose a delay time of .2 seconds. This value determines how quickly the animation will run. Finally, select Forever from the Looping Options drop-down list. You can also specify that the animation will run one-time only or a specified number of times. Watch your animation by clicking the Play button, located just below the frames. Was that easy, or what?

You'll find more advanced animation techniques in Chapters 23 and 24.

How Can I Extract an Image from Its Background?

Photoshop offers some great tools for removing an object from its background (so you can, say, paste it down seamlessly in another image). You can use the Magnetic Lasso to grab an image with well-defined edges, delete unwanted areas with the Background Eraser, or easiest of all, grab an image with the Extract command.

Extract is your best choice for grabbing objects with wispy edges, such as hair or fur, but it also works with hard-edged shapes. This tool has a lot of options, but you don't need to use all of them to get good results. Activate the Extract dialog box by pressing Alt/Option+Ctrl/Command+X, or choosing Image ➤ Extract from the menu bar. Click the edge highlighter or marker tool at the top of the dialog box's toolbox. Choose a brush size that will let you "paint" the edges of the object. Paint the edges with the marker. Use the Eraser tool to remove markings you don't want. When you're finished completely enclosing the object, click the Paint Bucket tool in the dialog box's toolbox and fill the area you want to protect with the fill color.

Finally, click the Preview button to get a look at what your object will look like when extracted, then click the OK button to apply the extracted image.

You'll find more information on extracting images in Chapters 3 and 4.

How Do I Turn a Black-and-White Image into a Full-Color Image?

Sometimes you have only a black-and-white picture when you need a color one. Photoshop makes it easy to perform this transformation. Just take a grayscale image and convert it to RGB color using Image ➤ Mode ➤ RGB Color. Create a new transparent layer using Layer ➤ New Layer, and specify Overlay as the Blending mode for this layer. Add colors to the new layer to "paint" over your black-and-white image. Adjust the opacity of the layer so the color blends with the original. Create additional transparent layers and repeat this step until you've added all the colors you want. Then flatten the image and admire your work.

For more information on working with color images, see Chapter 20.

What Resolution Do I Need to Scan Images into Photoshop?

Scanner resolution isn't as critical as you think. There are various formulas floating around you can use to calculate "optimum" resolution, but most of the time you don't need them.

With line art, such as black-and-white or color drawings, you should scan at the same resolution used for final output. If an image is destined for a 600 dpi laser printer, then 600 spi is your best choice. This arrangement allows a one-to-one correlation between scanned pixels and printed dots, and reduces the likelihood of *jaggies*—the stairstepping effect.

For black-and-white or color photos, you should choose the resolution based upon two factors: what you plan to do with the photo, and whether you plan on enlarging it. For instance, if you are printing the image, you should scan at 150 to 200 pixels per printed inch. If you are scanning for a web page, you would want to used something like 72 or 75 dpi.

If you're going to be converting a page of text to an editable document using optical character recognition, (OCR), scanning at a setting as low as 300 spi will provide enough detail to allow the OCR software to reliably differentiate 10 point or larger typefaces. If you're scanning material with smaller type, 400 to 600 spi (up to the maximum optical resolution of the scanner) can be useful.

For more information on working with scanned images, see Chapter 5.

FILTERS REFERENCE

Photoshop's built-in filter set offers a bewildering variety of looks and a staggering number of different combinations of controls and settings. In this section, I've tried to make visualizing each filter's properties and selecting the one you want a little easier by compiling a series of more than 90 variations on the same image, each with a different Photoshop filter applied. You'll also find quick notes on some of the controls used by each filter, although there won't be a detailed description of how each and every slider affects an image. That's because the actual effects can vary widely, depending on the make-up of your original image. Most Adobe filters feature similar dialog boxes, with a reduced-size preview image and one or more sliders or drop-down lists you can use to select various effects options and the amount of each effect. A few filters, such as Texturizer, have additional dialog boxes with further controls.

Figure R.1 shows the unmodified image before any filters are applied.

FIGURE R.1: Our original image before any of Photoshop's filters have been applied.

Artistic Filters

Photoshop's Artistic filters are a hodge-podge of plug-ins that help you create an arty look using different media (Colored Pencils, Pastels, or Smudge Sticks), tools (such as the Palette Knife), and effects (including Plastic Wrap or Film Grain). Although, you'll find most of the filters that create painterly brush stroke effects in other filter groups, there are a few here, including Dry Brush and Watercolor.

Colored Pencil

Colored Pencil redraws your image, using the image's own colors, with a pencil-like effect. The strokes are applied in a crosshatch fashion to delineate the edges of your image, while the current background color is allowed to show through the less detailed portions of your image, as if it were the paper on which the drawing was made. You have three controls: a Pencil Width slider, which adjusts the broadness of the strokes; Stroke Pressure, which modifies their intensity; and Paper Brightness, which determines how strongly the background color shows through smooth details in your image. This is a tricky filter to use, but I've found that using the Brightness/Contrast controls to increase contrast once the filter has been applied can approve the appearance dramatically.

Cutout

The Cutout filter is an unusual "posterizing" technique in which the image shapes are seemingly built up from similarly colored cutouts of paper. You can combine this filter with Emboss, discussed later in the "Stylized Filters" section, to make the shapes look as if they were actually cut out of paper. The Number of Levels control specifies the number of tones used to posterize the image. Edge Simplicity governs the complexity of the cutout shapes, while Edge Fidelity adjusts how well the shapes match the actual outlines of the underlying image.

Dry Brush

The Dry Brush filter mimics a natural-media effect—stroking with a brush that's almost devoid of paint—in a fairly predictable way. It posterizes your image, so that the bands of colors themselves become the strokes, as all similar colors in a particular area are reduced to one average hue. You can adjust the size of the brush, with larger brushes applying broader strokes. The Brush Detail control allows you to change the amount of detail in each area by modifying the roughness of the edges. The Texture control applies light, medium, or heavy texture to the image.

Film Grain

Film grain is a uniquely photographic phenomenon, rather than a painterly effect, and as such it tends to lend more of a modern look to images, (as opposed to the "Old Masters" air of some of the other Photoshop filters). Grain is a bug-turned-feature that resulted when photographers found that enlarging small sections of photos, or attempting to push film's sensitivity to new heights in low-light photography, produced interesting effects. When images are abused in this way, the clumps of silver in the film (or the clumps of dye left behind when a color negative or transparency is processed) add a distinct texture to the picture.

You can adjust the amount of Grain, the size of the Highlight area, and the Intensity of the highlights. The Grain setting controls the density of what appear to be random little black grains that are sprinkled throughout your image. The higher the value, the more details of your image obscured by the grain overlay. Since the Film Grain filter applies more grain to the highlights than to the shadows and midtones, the Highlight Area slider determines how many tones are considered highlights; at higher values, virtually all of the image is given the full treatment. The Intensity slider controls how strongly the grain is applied to the highlight areas.

Fresco

Fresco is a technique in which watercolors are applied to wet plaster (*fresco* is Italian for fresh) and allowed to dry, forming a permanent image on the wall or other structure on which the plaster resides. If you're an artist-type, and can work fast, fresco is a great way to produce murals.

Because the plaster is sticky and dries quickly, fresco images are distinguished by their short, jabby strokes. Its controls are similar to the Dry Brush filter. Both filters add a posterization effect to your image, but Fresco lightens the highlights considerably, and is a little more "smeary" in appearance. But, like Dry Brush, you can vary the brush size, amount of brush detail, and degree of texture applied to your image.

Neon Glow

Neon Glow is similar to the Diffuse Glow filter, found inexplicably under the Distort filter group in Photoshop. Diffuse Glow's grainy diffusion is replaced here by a colored glowing effect. It makes the object appear as if it were radiating light of the color you select; the default is blue, but you can choose any color by double-clicking in the Glow Color patch. The effect doesn't work too well with humans, but looks great with text or other objects. The Glow Size slider has both positive and negative values (from 0 to +24 or –24) with the center as the zero point. Positive values set the glow to the outside of dark objects and the inside of light objects, while negative values do the reverse. The higher the number, the larger the glow.

The Glow Brightness control modifies the luminance of the glow. A preview box shows the current glow color. Click on it to pop up a color picker you can use to select another glow color. The current foreground and background color are also used: this filter gives you a two-color image with a third hue used for the glow.

Paint Daubs

Paint Daubs offers you six different brush types from a drop-down list, a selection of brush sizes, and some sharpness controls. You can choose from simple, light rough, dark rough, wide sharp, wide blurry, or sparkle brush types (used in this illustration). It's easy to obscure all the detail in your image with this filter, so use it carefully.

Palette Knife

Take the knife that artists use to apply paints to their palette, and paint with it instead—you'll end up with a highly abstract image composed of irregular globs of pigment. That's the effect you get with the Palette Knife filter. The Stroke Size slider adjusts the size of the "knife" you're using, while the Stroke Detail control can be used to specify how much of the detail in your original image is retained. The Softness control increases or decreases the roughness of the edges of the palette strokes.

Plastic Wrap

This filter provides an amazingly true representation of a subject image wrapped in bright plastic. If you ever need a shrink-wrapped subject, this is the filter that can provide it for you. The Highlight Strength control changes how the glowing plastic reflections at the edges of certain details are represented. The Detail slider controls how "clingy" the plastic wrap will be to the subject. The Smoothness slider determines how many wrinkles are in the plastic wrap.

Poster Edges

This converts full-color or gray-scale images into reduced color versions by combining similar colors into bands of a single hue, and outlining all the important edges in your image with black. In many cases, the finished photo looks as if it were an original drawing that was hand-colored in poster fashion. Poster Edges gives you three controls. You can adjust the relative Edge Thickness of the black lines used to outline the edges and specify their Edge Intensity with another control. A third slider lets you specify the degree of Posterization—that is, how many tones are used to produce the effect. Note that with this filter the value represents only a relative degree, not the actual number of tones used.

Rough Pastels

This filter transforms your image into a rough chalk drawing, using the default canvas texture or an alternate texture—such as brick, burlap, sandstone, or one from your own file (when you choose Load Texture from the drop-down Texture list)—as a background. The least amount of texture is applied to the brightest areas, while darker areas take on more of the underlying texture. You can picture how this filter works by imagining a canvas with chalk applied: the thicker the chalk, the less of the canvas texture shows through. You can specify Stroke length, the amount of Stroke Detail, and a specific Texture to be used, along with Scaling (relative size of the texture), Relief (how "high" the texture is above the background), and Light Direction.

Smudge Stick

This filter paints your image in strokes that blend dark areas into the lighter areas. You can control the Stroke Length, Highlight Area, and Highlight Intensity. Smudge Stick is another filter that must be used with caution if you want to preserve detail in your original image.

Sponge

The Sponge effect is highly textured, with contrasting splotches of color. You can adjust Brush Size, Definition, and Smoothness, using the appropriate sliders. A larger brush size produces a more abstract image, while increasing the definition and reducing the smoothness provides the roughest image.

Underpainting

The Underpainting filter produces the effect you might get if you texturized an image in one layer, then combined it with an unaltered version of the same image in a layer applied on top of the first. It's otherwise similar to the Texturizer filter, but with the addition of Brush Size and Texture Coverage controls.

Watercolor

Watercolors produce their distinctive pastel effect because the pigments that dissolve in water are typically not as strong or opaque as those that can be carried in oil or acrylic paints. In addition, watercolors tend to soak into the paper, carrying bits of color outside the original strokes as the water spreads. The Watercolor filter offers the same soft, diffused effect with a bit more control for the electronic artist. It's a good plug-in for landscapes, romantic portrait subjects, or any image that can be improved with a soft look.

You can specify the amount of Brush Detail, but you'll find that the blending effect of this filter doesn't work well with small, detailed strokes. Use higher values to get broad strokes that show off the pastels and blended colors. At the same time, you'll often want to use low Shadow Intensity settings to avoid an overly contrasty look. Any of three levels of Texture can also be applied.

Blur Filters

Photoshop neophytes are sometimes slow to learn the advantages of the various blur filters because, after all, who wants a blurry image? You'll quickly learn, however, that many images can be improved by some careful blurring of excess grain, unwanted details, or intrusive backgrounds. For example, if you blur everything but the most important object in your image, that object may actually appear to be sharper than it was.

Blur

This filter softens an image by reducing the amount of contrast between pixels. It's a single-step filter with no controls at all; select it from the Filter menu, and it does its stuff without further intervention from you.

Blur More

This filter is basically the same as the Blur filter, but it provides roughly two to three times as much blurring in one step. Both Blur and Blur More are quick-and-dirty solutions; in most cases you'll get better results using Gaussian Blur, described next.

Gaussian Blur

Gaussian Blur is applied more often than the other stock blurring options, because it provides you with a healthy degree of control. The blurring is applied not linearly over the entire image or selection, but according to a bell-shaped curve Photoshop calculates using a weighted average of the pixels in the selection. In addition, where Blur/Blur More simply diffuse the area they are applied to, Gaussian Blur has the added effect of putting a haze-like noise in the blurred area, which can be desirable when generating shadows. The only control you need to worry about with the Gaussian Blur filter is the radius setting, from .01 pixel to 250 pixels. The higher the radius setting, the more pronounced the blurring effect. You'll want to play with Gaussian Blur quite a bit, because it can be your best friend when you have noisy, scratchy images that badly need cleaning up.

Motion Blur

Motion Blur filter verges on being a special effect. It duplicates the blurring you get when a fast-moving subject races across the field of view when a photograph is taken with a shutter speed that is too slow to freeze the action. You have two controls to work with: an angle for the blurring effect, which represents the direction of motion of the subject, from −90 degrees to +90 degrees (type in a figure, or drag the dial of the "clock") and a blur amount, continuously variable from 1 to 999 pixels through the slider at the bottom of the dialog box.

Radial Blur

Radial Blur is an effect derived from traditional photography. When zoom lenses first became popular, some experimental souls discovered that by zooming in or out while a picture was being taken (long exposures of half-a-second or more are sometimes required), an image that contained blurry intermediate versions of the original subject was produced.

A related effect can be generated by spinning the image around a selected axis, producing blur in the direction of the spin. Either type of radial blur adds a feeling of motion to an otherwise static image. You can choose between the two types by clicking on the Spin or Zoom radio buttons. Move the axis around which the image will blur by sliding the center point in the "Preview" Window (which doesn't show a preview at all), and adjust the amount of blurring from 1 to 100 by using the slider control. Because both types of Radial Blur take a long time to calculate, Photoshop gives you a "quality" mode option. Use Draft to get a quick idea of what the effect will look like. Good may be good enough for some applications. If you check off Best mode, you'll get the smoothest blur, but sit back and be ready to wait while for your finished image.

Smart Blur

Smart Blur is a sophisticated blurring effect with some interesting controls. You can choose Radius (the size of the area the filter examines for dissimilar pixels), Threshold (the amount of difference between pixels for blurring to occur), Low, Medium, and High Quality levels, and whether the blur is applied to the entire selection (Normal), only to the transitions between colors (Edge Only), or to the Overlay Edge. You'll need to experiment with this filter to see exactly how it works.

Brush Stroke Filters

Photoshop's brush filters provide a quick way of simulating a painter's efforts by adding brush-like textures to the tones of your image. Keep in mind that there's a large difference between changing an existing image into brush strokes with a computer, and actually creating an image from scratch using brush strokes and a true artist's creative talents. Don't expect your brush simulations to have the same aesthetic qualities of a real piece of art, but the results can still be quite attractive.

Accented Edges

The Accented Edges filter works a little like the Find Edges filter, but you have extra control over the width, smoothness, and brightness of the edges located in your image. Edge Width adjusts the relative width of the edges, Edge Brightness controls whether the edges are stroked in a dark or light tone, while Smoothness determines how closely the edges follow the actual edges in the image. Higher settings produce more gradual transitions from one angle to the next.

Angled Strokes

This filter must be used with care, since it produces such strong effects. Angled Strokes paints your image using diagonal strokes in one direction for the dark tones, and diagonal strokes going in the other direction to represent the light tones in an image. The Direction Balance is a key control. Slide it to the right to shift the emphasis toward the right-angled strokes; move to the left to emphasize the left-angled strokes. If you want to watch this control at work in its most dramatic mode, change the Stroke Length slider to the maximum (50) and the Sharpness control to 10. Your entire image will be rendered in left and right strokes that you can see clearly. Adjust Direction Balance to see the different effects you can achieve.

Crosshatch

Crosshatch adds a cross pattern of pencil-like strokes to your image, adding texture without destroying all the original colors and detail of the original. It's a good arty effect with an unusual degree of control. Not only can you specify the Stroke Length and Sharpness but the number of times in succession the filter is applied, as well. The more repetitions, the stronger the effect.

Dark Strokes

The Dark Strokes filter has two effects on your image. First, it reduces the number of different tones in the image through a posterization-like effect that combines similar tones in an unusual way. Instead of grouping similar colors together, Dark Strokes makes dark tones darker and light tones lighter, increasing contrast. At the same time, each tone is rendered using diagonal brush strokes—short strokes for dark tones and longer strokes for light tones. Controls let you adjust balance between light and dark tones, as well as set their respective intensity.

Ink Outlines

Ink Outlines produces a "corroded" ink drawing: an image with the outlines and edges enhanced, but without losing the original colors. You can use it to create a cartoon-like appearance, or combine with other filters to generate a more painterly effect. You can adjust the length of the Strokes, Dark Intensity, and Light Intensity. Moving the Light Intensity control all the way to the right can produce an especially interesting effect.

Spatter

The Spatter filter is another easy-to-use painterly effect that reproduces a look that would be generated if an airbrush could spatter out different color hues. While you can use the effect to soften portrait or landscape subjects, it also makes a great tool for creating endless abstract backgrounds. The only controls you have to worry about are the Spray Radius slider, which adjusts the number of pixels covered by the sputtering spray emitted by your imaginary airbrush, and the Smoothness control, which modifies the evenness of the effect.

Sprayed Strokes

This filter uses angled, sprayed strokes of wet paint. You can adjust the Stroke Length, Direction, and Radius of the spray emitted. This is a good filter for creating painterly images, artsy backgrounds, or adding a painted effect to pictures that have been processed with other filters.

Sumi-e

Take a wet brush, load it with ink, and draw on a highly absorbent rice paper and what do you get? "Ink painting," or, in Japanese, *sumi-e*. This filter doesn't convert your image to monochrome, however, but it does add the effect of painting on blotter paper with ink. The controls are simple to master—just Stroke Width, Stroke Pressure, and Contrast. This filter works best with landscapes or abstracts, because it tends to blur portrait subjects into unrecognizability.

Distort Filters

Photoshop's distortion filters can twist and turn your images in dramatic ways, or add strong textures that almost totally mask the original image. Some of the most interesting filters of all are available in this group, including my personal favorite, described next.

Diffuse Glow

Diffuse Glow can produce a radiant luminescence in any image, which seems to suffuse from the subject and fill the picture with a wonderful luster. At the same time, this plug-in softens harsh details. It's great for romantic portraits or for lending a fantasy air to landscapes. Diffuse Glow works equally well with color or black-and-white images.

The Graininess slider adds or reduces the amount of grain applied to an image. A large amount obscures unwanted detail and adds to the dreamy look of the image. The Glow Amount control adjusts the strength of the glow, as if you were turning up the voltage on a light source. The higher the setting, the more glow spread throughout your picture. The Clear Amount slider controls the size of the area in the image that is not affected by the glow. You can use this control with the Glow Amount slider to simultaneously specify how strong a glow effect is produced and how much of the image is illuminated by it. The current background color becomes the color of the glow. That's an important point. Beginners sometimes forget this, and then wonder why their glow effect looks weird. If you want a glowing white effect, make sure the background color is white. Anything else will tint your image. You can use this feature to good advantage, by selecting background colors with a very slight tint of yellow, gold, or red, to add a sunny or warm glow to your image.

Displace

The Displace filter uses an image, called a displacement map, to determine how to distort a selection. Portions of the image are twisted in various directions, depending on the gray levels found in the displacement map. You'll want to experiment with different files to see exactly how this filter works.

Glass

This is a multipurpose filter you can use to produce glass-block effects, warping, watery ripples, and dozens of other looks. The flexibility comes from the multitude of combinations you can achieve using just five different controls. You can specify the amount of distortion (choose a high number for some wild effects) and smoothness of the glass. A separate Texture drop-down list allows you to choose from glass blocks, frosted glass, tiny glass lenses (to re-create a fly's-eye viewpoint) and even canvas. You can also apply a texture file of your choice to the image.

For images with individual features (e.g., tiny lens) you can select a scaling to control the relative size of the image and the underlying texture. The texture can be inverted, too.

Ocean Ripple

The Ocean Ripple filter gives you a wavy effect, supposedly something like the ripples on a pond, except we usually expect those to be concentric. You can choose Ripple Size and Ripple Magnitude (the distance between ripples).

Pinch

The Pinch filter squeezes an image toward its center, or pushes it out toward its outer edges. You can pinch the entire image, or just a selection. The only control you have available is an Amount slider, which can be varied from 0 to 100 percent (to pinch inward) or from 0 to −100 percent (to push outward).

The grid shown in the window next to the Preview Window gives you an idea of the amount and direction of distortion you're going to get. You can't change the center point though, except by reselecting a different portion of your image. The pinching effect is always applied around the center point of the selection.

If you're pinching a rectangular-shaped selection, the filter automatically blends the affected area into the surrounding image. There's a simple reason for this. When you administer Pinch to a rectangular image or selection, Photoshop applies the filter to an elliptical section of the selection—the largest ellipse that will fit inside the square or rectangle. The effect is feathered into the rest of the selection, providing a smooth transition.

If your selection is round, elliptical, or irregular in shape, or if it consists of discontinuous multiple selections, the Pinch effect will be applied to the largest ellipse that can fit inside, but there will be an abrupt boundary at the selection border. To avoid this, make your selection first, then choose Select ➤ Feather, and specify 5 pixels or more as your feather radius. The Pinching effect will be applied to the entire selection, gradually tapering off in the feathered portion.

Polar Coordinates

This filter takes quite awhile to get used to, because its function may be difficult to understand—unless you work with maps a lot. Those who create world maps have a real problem: the Earth is a sphere, more or less, but maps are most convenient when expressed in a flat, two-dimensional format that can be printed in a chart book.

Some maps cut the Earth into sections, like the peel of an orange, with the cuts concentrated in ocean areas that contain few land masses. Ocean navigators hate maps with the seas cut up like that. They'd rather have a version in which the oceans are intact and the land masses dissected. However, in either mode, with many sections, the distortions are minimized.

Other maps, like the infamous Mercator Projection, exaggerate the distance between the horizontal lines of latitude as you move from the equator, giving us a Greenland, Alaska, and Antarctica that are enormously out of proportion. Still other maps view the world from a polar perspective, giving a reasonably accurate view of what the Earth would look like from space, if viewed from above the North or South poles.

The Polar Coordinates filter can take a rectangular image (it doesn't have to be a map) and distort it as if it were viewed from space. You end up with a circle with the bottom portion of the original image wrapped along the outside of the circle, while the top portion of the original image is squeezed into the center of the circle.

The same filter can take a circular image (or even one of another shape) and change it back to rectangular format—cutting the peel off, so to speak, laying it flat, and filling in the missing sections. Polar Coordinates can perform some useful effects if you take the time to experiment with it. The dialog box for this filter has just two buttons—Rectangular to Polar and Polar to Rectangular—and an inadequate Preview Window.

Ripple

Ripple makes images look as if you were viewing them through a glass block that has been distorted or melted. With other settings, the effects start to resemble water flowing over pebbles in a stream. You'll find that the Ripple filter can give you quite different looks depending on how you adjust the controls. Happily, experimentation is fairly easy, since there are only two sliders to fiddle with. The Ripple Size drop-down list adjusts the size of the ripples themselves, and the Amount slider sets the amount of waviness in each ripple.

Shear

The Shear filter distorts the pixels in an image or selection based on a curve you specify in the dialog box. When you first activate the filter, the "curve" shown on the grid is a straight line with draggable endpoints at the top and bottom ends. Each time you click on the line, a new control handle appears. A total of 16 handles can be created on the curve (plus the two end points), and any of them can be dragged to produce complex curves. If you goof or just want to start over, click the Reset button to return to the basic straight line you first saw.

Click either the Wrap Around or Repeat Edge pixels radio buttons to specify how areas that are empty when the image has been dragged to fit your curve should be filled in. The former option uses pixels from the opposite edge of the image to fill in the blanks, while the latter just adds pixels of the same tone and color as those just outside the empty area boundary.

Spherize

This filter maps your image or selection onto a sphere, represented by the wireframe shown on the grid in the dialog box. You can specify an "outward" bulge from 0 to 100 percent, or an "inward" indentation of 0 to −100 percent. Negative values produce an effect that is quite similar to that of the Pinch filter.

However, the Sphere filter also lets you distort your image around a vertical or horizontal cylinder by clicking on the Horizontal only or Vertical only radio buttons.

If your selection area is not round, this filter will carve out a circular area in the middle of the selection, and warp that, instead. You can use feathering to blend the selection into the rest of your image.

The Spherize filter is one you'll probably use a lot, and not just for mapping images onto globes. You can use it to create spheres from scratch, too.

Twirl

The Twirl filter acts like one of those rotating paint swirlers that creates art by spinning a turntable full of wet paint. The pixels in the center of your image or selection move more drastically than those on the periphery, which lag behind. The effect is quite striking. Your only control is the slider that specifies degrees of twisting; you can use from −999 to +999 degrees. Yup, that's not a misprint. A setting of 180 degrees would cause the center to spin a half revolution more than the edges; at 361 degrees, the center actually "laps" the edges. The maximum 999 degrees is nearly three full spins, producing a whirlpool-like effect. Positive numbers give you a clockwise spin effect; negative numbers reverse the spin to counterclockwise. Use this filter to create whirlpools, paint swirls, or special textures.

Wave

The Wave filter's flexibility comes from the no less than 13 different controls you can use to specify how your image is stirred up. You can choose from three kinds of waves, specify the number, size, and frequency of the ripples, and even randomize things if you want a natural appearance. You can spend a lot of time figuring out how Wave works but, on the plus side, you can achieve effects that are unlikely to be duplicated. Think unique. The key controls you can work with are described here:

Number of generators   Sets the number of points where waves are created. Up to 999 different little wave generators can be entered.

Wavelength Minimum/Maximum   Sets the distance from one wave crest to the next, using numbers from 1 to 999.

Amplitude Minimum/Maximum   Sets the height of the waves, also settable from 1 to 999.

Horizontal/Vertical Scale   Lets you determine how much distortion you get per wave, with values from 1 to 100 percent.

How Undefined Areas Are Filled In   Lets you have pixels wrap around from one side to another or just stretched from the edge to fill the empty spaces.

Type of Wave   Lets you choose from smooth sine waves, pointy triangle waves, or chunky square waves.

Randomize   If you just want waves, and don't care what they look like, click on this button to supply random values.

Zigzag

The Zigzag filter should be your choice for producing ripples in an image, since you don't really get zigzags at all (unless you count the Around Center option, which does alternate the direction the ripples rotate). You can specify an amount of distortion from −100 to +100. The number of ridges (1 to 20) can also be specified.

You may select from:

Pond ripples that Adobe defines as ripples that progress from the upper left or lower right (depending on whether you've entered a positive or negative number).

Out from center ripples that are generated from the center of your image or selection.

Around center, whirlpool-like ripples that revolve around the center of the image or selection, first in one direction, then in the other.

Noise Filters

Noise filters actually blur images in their own way, by adding random pixels to an image or selection, thereby replacing details that are there with the noise. Adding noise blurs an image without reducing the contrast.

Standard blur filters obscure details in an image by smoothing everything out and reducing contrast. You may not want that effect if you end up with a smooth surface that looks fake because it should contain some texture.

Noise filters add texture to areas that have been made too smooth by other effects or filters or which have been painted in from scratch using a non-textured brush. Adding noise can actually help these smooth areas blend into other parts of the image that already do have texture. In other cases, a bit of noise can mask very fine scratches or dust spots in an image.

Because of the random nature of the noise, the added texture often won't be very apparent, especially when applied to monochrome/grayscale images.

Add Noise

The Add Noise filter has several controls:

Select an Amount from 1 to 999. The default is 32. This value is used to determine how much the random colors added to the selection will vary from the color that is already present (or from the gray tones, if you're working with a monochrome image).

Choose either Uniform or Gaussian distribution of the noise.   Uniform distribution uses random numbers in the range from 0 to the number you specified with the Amount slider. The random number is then added to the color value of the pixel to arrive at the noise amount for that pixel. Gaussian distribution uses a bell-shaped curve calculated from the values of the pixels in the selected area, producing a more pronounced speckling effect.

Check off the Monochromatic box.   This applies the noise only to the brightness/darkness elements of the image without modifying the colors themselves. This can reduce the "color specks" effect that often results from applying noise to an image.

Despeckle

Despeckle is similar in some ways to the Sharpen Edges filter. Instead of increasing the contrast in the edges and leaving the rest of the image or selection alone, Despeckle decreases the contrast in all of the selection except for the edges. In both cases the edges end up with relatively more detail than the rest of the image. Don't confuse this filter with Dust & Scratches. It can remedy dust spots in an image through its blurring effect, but that's a bonus—Despeckle is a much "dumber" filter that doesn't specifically search for spots.

You can tell which to use by following these guidelines:

▶ If your image has dust spots in random locations and you don't need edge enhancement, use Dust & Scratches.

▶ If your image is already relatively sharp, to the point where there is objectionable detail or noise in the image areas, use Despeckle to provide a blurring effect that doesn't mask edge detail.

▶ If your image doesn't contain excessive noise, use Sharpen Edges to sharpen it up a bit without introducing an undesirable texture.

Despeckle has no controls you need to adjust.

Dust & Scratches

The Dust & Scratches filter selectively blurs areas of your image that contain dots spots, scratches, and other defects. When the filter is applied, Photoshop examines each pixel in the image, moving outward radially to look for abrupt transitions in tone that might indicate a dust spot on the image. If a spot is found, the area is blurred to minimize the appearance of the defect. This filter has two controls.

The Radius slider adjusts the size of the area searched for the abrupt transition, measured in pixels. You can select from 1 to 16 pixels. If your image is inhabited by really humongous dust spots, you might find a value of about 4 pixels useful, but for most pictures either a one or 2-pixel radius should be sufficient. The larger the radius you select, the greater the blurring effect on your image. Always use the smallest radius you can get away with.

You'll note that some defects will still be visible, but these can be cleaned up using the Rubber Stamp tool by cloning parts of the image over the dust or scratches that remain. The filter did most of the job, saving hours of hand-retouching with the Rubber Stamp.

The Threshold slider tells the filter just how drastic a transition must be before it should be considered a defect. Your image may be infested with nasty white spots (or black spots if made from a transparency), or you may have some gray spots that crept in somehow. Once you've set the radius slider to the lowest setting that still eliminates the spots in the Preview Window, adjust the Threshold slider up from zero until defects begin to reappear.

Your goal in balancing these two controls is to eliminate as many defects as possible without blurring your image too drastically.

Median

The Median filter reduces noise by minimizing the difference between brightness values of adjacent pixels, blending them together when possible. The filter works by replacing the center pixel of a group with one having the median brightness value of those pixels. You can specify the radius of the search using the only control offered with this filter.

Pixelate Filters

In general, Photoshop's pixelation filters add dots or other regular shapes to your image in one way or another. You can use them to create artsy images or just for the special effects they generate.

Color Halftone

Most color halftone filters should be considered special effects, rather than ways to actually generate color separations required to print color on a printing press. That's because these plug-ins don't have the accuracy required to produce color separations; all they do is take each color layer of your image and change it into a pattern of dots. The size of the dots varies depending on the darkness or density of that portion of your image: highlight areas are represented by small dots; shadows and solids are represented by larger dots.

Crystallize

This filter converts your image or selection to random polygons, each with a maximum cell size that you specify, from 3 to 300 pixels. The value can be typed in or entered using a slider. That's the only parameter you can control; the color of each cell is determined by the average underlying tone of the image beneath the cell.

Facet

This filter changes blocks of pixels that are similar in color to one tone, producing a faceted effect like the face of a diamond (or maybe like the face of Bizarro Superman, if you remember him). This is a kind of posterization, but with the reduction in number of colors taking place in a seemingly randomized way over the entire image. Details are masked, so this is an excellent filter to use with grainy, dust-laden, or otherwise imperfect photographs.

The Facet filter has no dialog box or options; you apply it directly to any selection or an to entire image. The effect becomes more pronounced with repeated applications. Just use Ctrl/Command+F to apply the filter several times until you get the look you desire.

Fragment

If you want to duplicate the Fragment Filter without using your computer, peel an onion, then look at the world around you through tear-filled eyes. If you live in California, you can also get the same effect by taking a few snapshots during the next earthquake. This filter produces a shaky image that doesn't have a lot of application when applied to entire images. It can be used to add some random texture to backgrounds, or to apply a little motion blur to edges of an object. Like Facet, Fragment has no options or parameters. Just apply it until you're happy with the results, or fade it to reduce its effects.

Mezzotint

The Mezzotint filter is another technique borrowed from traditional printing, in which a special overlay is placed on top of a photograph to add a pattern during duplication. Digital filters offer much the same effect with a little less flexibility, since the range of mezzotints you can achieve with Photoshop is fairly limited. Only dots (fine, medium, grainy or coarse), lines, or strokes (in short, medium, and long varieties) can be applied. You can rotate your image, apply this filter, then rotate it back to the original orientation if you want to change the direction of the lines or strokes.

Mosaic

True mosaic is an artistic process of creating pictures by inlaying small pieces of colored stone or glass in mortar. However, this mosaic filter simply divides a photo into squares and averages the tones within those squares to produce a pixelated effect. Your only control is the size of the squares. The Mosaic filter divides your image into an array of blocks, using a cell size you specify. Then, it averages the color and brightness of all the pixels in each cell, and creates a new mega-pixel from the value that results. This can actually be a pretty cool filter to use when you want to create an abstract image of a subject that screams "computer-generated!" at the viewer, but one that can still be recognized if you squint or move back a little. Mosaic is a popular effect among graphic designers preparing illustrations for magazines. You can choose a cell size from 2 to 64 pixels.

Pointillize

This is one filter that will enrage artists and please everyone else. It purports to create a pointillistic image, but don't expect to generate anything that reminds you of Georges Seurat. What you end up with is more of a randomized image with lots of little dots on it (many in colors that you may not remember seeing in our original). Generally the pixelation reproduces the detail in your original photograph. You can select a cell size from 3 to 300 pixels.

The most difficult thing about using this filter is selecting a compatible background color. All the spaces between dots are filled in with your current background color. If you're using the defaults, that's white. Softer pastels that match the predominant tones of your image make a better choice, unless you want the image to look as if it were overlaid with a snowstorm.

Render Filters

Photoshop's rendering filters all create something from nothing—so to speak—generating clouds, light flares, and textures that didn't exist in your image originally. Some of them, such as the Cloud filter, pay no attention to the existing pixels at all; others use the underlying image to determine how new pixels are created.

Clouds

The Clouds filter is an incredibly useful plug-in that can be used to add realistic cloud textures to any picture that has a flat, uninteresting sky. You can also use this filter to create cloud-like mist or smog behind any object. There are no controls or dialog boxes to fool with, nor is there a need to have any texture at all in the area to be filled. Just select the sky or other area you want to fill with clouds and apply the filter. Opaque clouds are created using fractal algorithms, producing a highly realistic effect. Clouds uses the current foreground and background colors to generate its cloud effects. You can select a blue-and-white tone to produce realistic clouds. However, you can get some great science-fiction effects with yellow, orange, or magenta skies.

Difference Clouds

The Difference Clouds filter works much like the plain Clouds filter, but uses the current image information in the scene to calculate the difference in pixel values between the clouds and the underlying image. The end product is an image that is a combination of clouds and a weird, negative image. If you apply Difference Clouds to an image without existing texture, with few contrasting colors, or with a subtle gradient, you'll get a relatively mild cloud effect. This filter really needs some image information to produce dramatic results. Try applying Difference Clouds several times in succession to get increasingly interesting results. Each time you use the filter, colors are inverted and new combinations result.

Lens Flare

Lens Flare is a prime example of turning a bug into a feature—in this case, it's an optical bug found in every camera lens to one extent or another. The (usually) unwanted reflections of light inside the barrel of a photographic lens can produce flaring effects. While there are various remedies for this "problem," many photographers—and now digital image artists—have learned to incorporate this effect into their pictures. The Lens Flare filter can create this sort of distortion for you, making your image manipulation seem that much more "real" (photographic) while generating suns, stars, and light sources where there were none. You don't need to know anything about photography or optics to use Lens Flare. The filter's dialog box gives you enough feedback through the Preview window to let you play with various combinations of parameters until you get the amount and type of flare that you like.

The flare is generated inside your image or selection using a center point you can specify by dragging the crosshair in the Preview window. The amount of flare can be adjusted using the Brightness slider, from 10 percent to 300 percent. The lens-type radio buttons let you choose the particular type of photographic lens that will be simulated. Different optics generate different flare patterns. Increasing the Brightness value makes the flaring more pronounced, as if the source light were brighter. The flare spreads into the other areas of the image. The maximum of 300 percent will usually wash out your picture; you'll want to use much lower settings in most cases.

Lighting Effects

The Lighting Effects filter allows you to define up to 16 different light sources to "illuminate" your image from any angle you choose in the picture's original two-dimensional plane. That is, you can't move the light sources "behind" any portion of the image in 3D fashion. Even so, the effects you can create with this filter are very photographic in nature. If you know anything about photo lighting, you'll love this filter! And if you don't, you'll have a ball playing with it and learning about the various moods you can create through lighting alone.

Not only can you specify the direction and type of light source with Lighting Effects, but you can add textures and perform other magic. For photographic neophytes, the best way to learn about this filter is to simply play with it.

Texture Fill

Texture Fill automatically loads grayscale information from a file of your choice and uses it to create a texture in your image. For best results, then, you'll want to use textures that can be seamlessly tiled—that is, they have been designed so the patterns at the edges on all four sides align when tiled in this way. If the image the texture is being loaded into is smaller than the grayscale file, the texture file will be cropped.

Sharpen Filters

Sharpen filters all improve the apparent sharpness of an image by increasing the contrast between adjacent pixels. Photoshop's sharpen tools can be applied to your overall image, or just to the edges of objects in images.

Sharpen/Sharpen More

The Sharpen and Sharpen More filters bring blurry images into focus. When applied directly to an image, you have no control over how much sharpening is applied; Sharpen adds a little bit of crispness, while Sharpen More provides a lot.

Here are some tips for using each of these filters. You can always reapply either of them to keep sharpening an image, although after two applications Sharpen More begins to look like more like a special effect than an image-enhancer. These sharpen filters increase contrast. If your image is low in contrast, experiment with applying sharpening first, then adjusting brightness/contrast of your sharpened image. Reverse the order of the steps and you may end up with an image that is too contrasty for your taste.

Sharpen Edges

Think of Sharpen Edges as a "quickie" version of the Unsharp Masking filter described in the next section. Like the Sharpen/Sharpen More filters, you have no control over the amount of sharpening that is produced. For that reason, you may want to use Sharpen Edges only on images that don't require a lot of fine-tuning, reserving the more sophisticated Unsharp Masking technique for pictures that demand the extra control.

As I said earlier, Sharpen Edges differs from the Sharpen/Sharpen More filters by sharpening only the significant edges; it doesn't produce the grainy effect that results when the image or selection is made crisper in its entirety. Most of your image will remain as smooth, or blurry, as it was, but by sharpening the edges it may look quite a bit sharper.

As you gain practice using these filters, you'll learn which images can benefit from Sharpen Edges, and which need Sharpen/Unsharpen. These guidelines may help:

▸ Buildings and other heavily-textured objects that contain many fine details can benefit from overall sharpening. Use Sharpen or Sharpen More.

▸ People and faces often look better with only the edges enhanced. With most portraits, the outlines of eyes and other features should look sharp, but you don't want every flaw in the skin to be accentuated. Use Sharpen Edges.

Unsharp Mask

Unsharp masking, like many features of Photoshop, is derived from a photographic technique (you don't think they pulled the name "Photoshop" out of a hat, do you?) Despite the conclusion you might draw from the name, Unsharp Masking is used to make images sharper.

The technique was first applied to images made on sheet film, in sizes from around 4×5 to 8×10 inches or larger. To produce the effect conventionally, a film positive is made from the original film negative (a negative of the negative, so to speak). The positive is slightly blurred, which spreads the image slightly. When the positive and negative are sandwiched together and used to expose a new image, light areas of the positive correspond very closely to the dark areas of the negative, and vice versa, canceling each other out to a certain extent. However, at the edges of the image the blurring in the positive produces areas that don't cancel out, resulting in lighter and darker lines on either side of the edges. This extra emphasis on the edges of the image adds the appearance of sharpness.

It's fairly easy for a computer to simulate the blurry positive mask and then mate it with a negative image of the original picture—with an added advantage. We can have greater control over the amount of blur in the mask, the radius around the edges that are masked, and a threshold level (relative brightness) at which the effect begins to be applied. The Unsharp Mask filter is similar in many ways to the Sharpen Edges filter, but with this enhanced control.

This filter has the following controls:

Amount slider   controls the amount of edge enhancement used. You can vary the sharpening effect from 1 percent to 500 percent.

Radius slider   determines the width of the edge that will be operated on, measured in pixels, with valid values from .1 (very narrow) to 250 pixels (very wide). You should adjust the range to take into account the resolution of your image. Low-resolution images (under 100 dpi) can't benefit from much more than 1- to 3-pixels' worth of edge sharpening, while higher resolution images (300 dpi and up) can accommodate values of 10 or more. You'll know if your values are set too high—you'll get thick, poster-like edges that aren't realistic, accompanied by a high degree of contrast. You may, in fact, like the weird appearance, but you've left the realm of sharpening and ventured into special effects at this point.

Threshold slider   is used to set the amount of contrast that must exist between adjacent pixels before the edge is sharpened. Values from 0 to 255 can be used; a very low value means that edges with relatively small contrast differences will be accentuated. High values mean that the difference must be very great before any additional sharpening is applied. Normally, you'll need this control only when the default value produces an image with excessive noise or some other undesirable effect. To be honest, in my tests, changing the Threshold slider produced effects that were hard to predict, because they varied widely depending on how the other two controls were adjusted, and the nature of the image itself. Your best bet is to set the Amount and Radius sliders first, then experiment with Threshold to see if you like the results any better.

Sketch Filters

None of Photoshop's filter groups describes exactly all the filters found in that group, and the Sketch group is no exception. You'll find lots of useful filters that evoke images an artist might produce on a sketchpad with chalk, charcoal, or other media. But you'll also discover filters that produce sculpted effects, such as the one you get with Bas Relief or Chrome.

Bas Relief

This filter provides a quite different effect from the Emboss plug-in. Bas Relief makes the image appear to have been carved from stone, a look you can enhance by applying a sandstone texture to the selection using the Texturizer filter.

The colors in your image are lost, since the current foreground and background colors are used to create your carving. As a result, this is one filter that works just as well with grayscale images as it does with color. If you want to retain at least some of the hues, use the Emboss filter, instead. With Bas Relief, you can adjust the amount of detail retained from your original image, the position of the apparent light source used to illuminate the resulting 3D image, and the smoothness of the surface.

Chalk & Charcoal

This filter gives you the effects of a mixed-media drawing using rough chalk to express the midtones and highlights, and charcoal for the shadows. The diagonal lines used obliterate quite a bit of your image detail, so you should use this filter with pictures that have strong, bold areas. If Photoshop's default colors (black and white) are used, the charcoal will be black and the chalk white. However, you can choose any set of colors, even reversing their relationship (with the background darker than the foreground) to generate interesting effects. The relative amount of area devoted to the highlights and shadows can be adjusted using the Charcoal Area and Chalk Area sliders. The pressure of the strokes is also variable.

Charcoal

This filter turns your image into a charcoal drawing, using the current background color as the underlying canvas, with the charcoal strokes applied using the foreground color. You can adjust the thickness of the stick of charcoal, the amount of detail applied, and the balance between the light/dark areas of the image.

Chrome

If used correctly, Chrome can be a stunning and versatile filter, adding a slick metallic effect straight out of Terminator 2. When applied, it smoothes out the details of your image and adds a 3D effect, making the lightest areas the "highest" in the transformed image and the darkest areas the "lowest." There are only two controls, which adjust the amount of detail represented in the final image and the degree of smoothness.

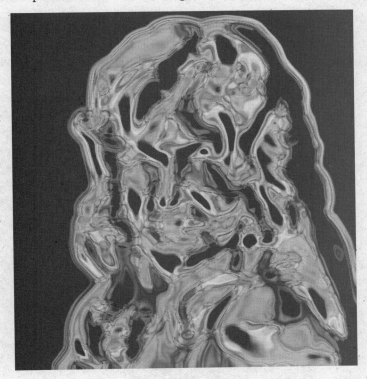

Conté Crayon

Georges Seurat supposedly developed the soft, smudgy, atmospheric effects that made Conté Crayon popular in the 19th Century. Photoshop's version gives you deeply rendered dark tones, textured midtones, and clean whites. These crayons are commonly available in different colors, from black to sepia, and you can use the foreground and background colors of your application to control the hues to simulate actual commercial crayons. The original colors of your image are lost. The Foreground and Background Level controls can be used to adjust the amount of the foreground and background colors, respectively. You may have to fiddle with these to find the right combination to represent your image without overpowering it.

Graphic Pen

The Graphic Pen filter obliterates the detail in your image with a series of monochrome strokes that can be applied in right or left diagonal directions as well as horizontally and vertically. It is tricky to use, because it's easy to obscure all the detail in an image with overly enthusiastic stroking, lengthy strokes, or an unfortunate selection of light and dark balance. The Stroke Length slider controls how much detail is preserved. Adjust the Light/Dark Balance slider to select the areas of the image to which the strokes are applied: lighter settings sketch in the highlights, while darker settings use the shadow areas for the strokes.

If you don't like the right diagonal strokes applied as the default (they are a good compromise with images that have an equal mixture of horizontal and vertical components), you can change to vertical or horizontal strokes, as shown in the lower left- and lower right-hand sections of the graphic, respectively. Vertical strokes break up and show predominant horizontal lines well (say, a landscape), while horizontal strokes do the same thing for images with strong vertical strokes (such as a stand of pine trees).

Halftone Screen

This is a versatile effect, changing your image into a black-and-white halftone screen, replacing all the original colors with shades of gray—or another set of colors, since Halftone Screen uses your application's current foreground and background colors. Only three controls are required. The Size slider controls the size of the halftone dots used. These are fake dots, composed as they are of gray-scale pixels rather than hard-edge single-tone pixels that you'd find in a digital image. You can select the type of screen, from Dot, Line, and Circle, and adjust the contrast of your image as the filter is applied.

Note Paper

This filter creates the look of embossed paper, but with a flatter image than you get with Emboss or Bas Relief. It really does look as if the image were created out of paper. There are three controls at your disposal: Image Balance, Graininess, and Relief. This plug-in changes your color or gray-scale image into a high-contrast black-and-white image (if you're using the default black/white colors) or into an image using another color pair. It's worthwhile to experiment with color combinations to get the best effect.

The key to using Note Paper is the Image Balance slider. Very small changes with this control make dramatic modifications to how much of your image appears embossed. You can also increase the amount of grain in the image. When Grain is set to zero, a useful carved-from-plastic look results.

Photocopy

Remember when photocopiers produced washed-out, high-contrast images of any photograph you deigned to submit to the xerographic process. Since low-tech has become chic again (witness all the broken "typewriter" fonts in the trendier magazines), even this high-tech way of achieving the photocopy look can be useful. Your desktop publications will take on a casual air when you make all your photographs appear as if you had to copy them on an old photocopier. All the black tones in your image will be outlined, while midtones will turn either black or white, depending on how you have the Darkness slider set. You can also adjust the amount of detail in the processed image.

Plaster

I'm not sure that the Plaster filter really gives you a plaster look, but it certainly does produce an outrageous and useful 3D effect. In some cases, your images will take on a molten plastic look, while in others you'll see more of a sunken effect.

Dark areas of the image are raised, while light areas are flattened or sunk into depressions. The foreground and background colors of the application are used to transform your image. You can work with three different controls, which operate much like their counterparts in the Bas Relief filter. The Image Balance filter is important, since you can use it to control how much of the important detail in your original image shows up. You'll find that even small adjustments can make a dramatic difference. Select a Light position and Smoothness value to fine-tune your image.

Reticulation

Reticulation is an old photographic effect caused by rapid changes in the temperature of the film during development, when the gelatin is soft, the image becomes "wrinkled," producing the effect duplicated by this filter. Reticulation was originally a bad thing, until photographers discovered that it added an interesting texture to their images. Even so, it was a drastic step, since the process abused original camera negatives in a way that couldn't be reversed, and it was unpredictable to boot. The first few times I tried it, I managed to boil the emulsion right off the film and ended up with a sticky mess rather than a cool picture. With this filter, you can adjust the density of the light grains and the amount of both black and white levels.

Stamp

This filter re-creates the effects you get with rubber or wooden stamps. Artists and artisans have often produced interesting, repeatable patterns by carving an image out of a block of wood or from a piece of rubber or linoleum glued to a block of wood. Since world supplies of linoleum dried up when all the linoleum mines in Macronesia were closed down, the electronic equivalent provided by the Stamp filter has been the closest we can get to the original effect. You can adjust light/dark balance, and you should do so carefully to insure that the important outlines of your image are represented in your finished stamp. The Smoothness control can adjust how rough the stamp's outlines appear. This filter uses the foreground and background colors you've selected, transforming your photo into a two-tone, stencil-like image.

Torn Edges

The Torn Edges filter gives your image (what else?) torn edges. It converts color images to two-color, using the current foreground and background hues. The Image Balance control is the most important, as it governs how much of your original image will be viewable in the final version.

You can also adjust smoothness and contrast, and you may need to experiment to get the best settings, since even small adjustments in any of these three controls can produce dramatically different images.

Water Paper

Water-based paints applied to wet paper will tend to migrate along the fibers, producing a blurry effect. The Water Paper filter lets you control the length of the fibers, the brightness, and the relative contrast of the image. The effects you can get with this filter vary considerably as you manipulate the controls.

Stylize Filters

Photoshop's Stylize filters are a diverse group that provides a variety of effects that add an arty look to your images. It's hard to find a common element among all of them, other than they each add a certain style that's unmistakable.

Diffuse

The Diffuse filter divides your image or selection up into 4-pixel elements (you can't control the size of the cell), then moves pixels towards the edges, or higher-contrast areas of your image. This tends to smudge the image in a pleasing way, producing a very nice artistic effect.

Emboss

Emboss raises the edges of your image above its imaginary "surface" much like an address embosser presses a 3D version of your name, address, or monogram into stationery or an envelope. This digital filter more or less discards most of the colors in your image, providing a stamped-metal effect. You can modify the angle for the imaginary light source that casts the shadow of the raised surface, in degrees; the Height of the embossing, from 1 to 10 pixels (the larger the number, the greater the 3D effect); and the Amount of embossing, from 1 to 500 percent. This control adjusts the contrast between the embossed edges and the rest of the image, so you can fine-tune the effect to a surprising degree.

Extrude

Combine the Mosaic filter with Emboss and you get something like the Extrude filter, which squeezes your image through an imaginary mesh, something like a child's clay "factory" for photographs.

There are lots of controls for this filter, but note that this filter does not have a Preview box; it's a processor-intensive effect that takes so long to produce that you couldn't realistically be presented with a preview in anything approaching real time. The parameters you can work with are:

Type   You can choose to have rectangular blocks or pointy pyramids "extrude" from your picture.

Size   This sets the dimensions of each cell in the square grid used to extrude your image, from 2 to 255 pixels.

Depth   This sets the maximum height of each block squeezed from your image, from 1 to 255 pixels. You can further select random depth (adjacent blocks may be any size up to the maximum you specified), or level-based (the lightest blocks are higher; darkest blocks are shorter).

Solid front faces   Check this box, and the faces of the blocks are the predominant color of the block. Unchecked, the faces retain the original image detail of the block.

Mask incomplete blocks   Check this box and hidden areas of blocks are not shown.

Find Edges

I love the Find Edges filter, because it's so easy to use and produces such dramatic effects, much like drawings created with colored pencils. There are no controls or dialog boxes to worry about. The filter works so quickly you can experiment on many different images, discovering those that are most suitable. After playing with it awhile, you'll discover that Find Edges emphasizes the transitions between one color to another, and changes solid colors to softer pastel versions of the complement (opposite color) of the tones in those areas. That is, blues are changed to yellow, cyans to reds, and so forth, much as if you were producing a negative of the original. You can get some great effects by inverting your image after applying Find Edges.

Glowing Edges

Glowing Edges adds wild colors to the edges of your image, producing a strange, abstract mask-like effect that you can enhance further by inverting the image, increasing the brightness and contrast, and using other tweaks. The controls at your command are the same as those of Accented Edges, (which operates in a similar manner, but without reversing the tones of your image): Edge Width adjusts the relative width of the edges; Edge Brightness controls whether the edges are stroked in a dark or light tone; and Smoothness determines how closely the edges follow the actual edges in the image.

Solarize

Photoshop's Solarize filter is not the best I've seen among image editors in general, since it has no controls. You can't specify the amount of solarization, although different effects can be produced by applying the filter to selections of an image or by inverting the effect.

Solarization was originally a photographic effect produced (at first by accident, until photographers noticed how cool the effect looked and started doing it on purpose) when a negative or transparency being developed was exposed to light partway through the development process. The denser sections of the image that had already been developed were affected differently than the parts of the image that had not been fully developed. What you got was a partial reversal of the image.

Tiles

The Tiles filter divides your image into individual squares but retains all
the detail in each section. You can specify the number of tiles, from 1 to
99, and the amount of space each will be offset, in percentages from 1 to
90. The "grout" between tiles can be filled with either the current foreground or background color, a negative version of the image that would
normally appear in the grout space, or an unaltered version of the image.
This is another filter that doesn't have a Preview window. You can tile a
smaller selection to see how it looks if you don't want to wait for the
entire image area to be tiled.

Trace Contour

The Trace Contours filter is often mentally grouped with the Find Edges plug-in, but they are very different in practice. For one thing, you can adjust the brightness level Trace Contours uses as the threshold to outline edges in your image; that is, you can change which edges of an image are limned with the Level slider. Higher values set the threshold so that lighter edges are outlined; lower values apply the effect to darker edges. Clicking the Lower or Upper radio buttons tells Photoshop to either outline values above the level set on the slider or below.

Trace Contours creates different outlines for each color channel, so you can sometimes get interesting effects by separating the color channels and working with them individually.

Wind

Wind can create a variety of wind-blown and streaky effects, in virtually any direction you please. It can simulate dripping paint or create an image reminiscent of superhero The Flash streaking by on his way to a crime scene. There are several secrets to using Wind effectively.

First, choose your images carefully. When you have a picture with an empty or dark area that the wind effect can smear your image into, the results are much more impressive. It also helps if your subject can be enhanced by the streaky effect. A house may look pretty blah when streaked, but adding a wind-effected baseball player sliding into second base raises the action level several notches.

You're not limited to left and right wind directions, regardless of what you may think from the dialog box. You can get some fabulous effects by rotating an image, applying Wind, then rotating it back to its original orientation. Instead of a gust of wind from the left or right, you end up with a dripping effect. You can even rotate the image in other than 90 degree increments to create interesting smearing. Or, streak your image from two different directions to create a wild wet-paint splotchy look that looks a lot more like something created by a real artist than most computer-generated images do.

Texture Filters

Texture filters all add a 3D effect while overlaying the original image with a texture of some kind. These filters can make your image jump right off the printed or Web page if used shrewdly.

Craquelure

If you want an ancient example of how a bug becomes a feature, look no farther than the Craquelure filter. In only a few short hundred years, the bane of ancient artists has become a quality that professional photographers, and now computer image workers, will actually get paid for. Paints applied to canvas or some other surface don't retain their pristine surface—broken only by carefully-applied brush strokes—for very long. The paints themselves aren't stable, composed as they are of exotic substances that can include egg whites, clay, and weird chemicals or plants used as pigment. Over time, the surface can crack, providing a texture associated with old paintings. You can achieve a similar effect, which adds a nice 3D look, using the Craquelure filter.

You can control the crack spacing, depth, and brightness. The default spacing of 15 gives you a good mixture of cracks and image area. Decreasing the spacing much below 10 makes the cracks so wide that the raised, embossed portion of the image may be just a few isolated bumps. Increasing the spacing to 50 or more produces an image that resembles your original, with a sparse distribution of cracks.

The depth and brightness settings change the appearance of the cracks themselves. You'll find that deeper or shallower cracks can dramatically change the effect. Changing brightness reduces or increases the amount of original image detail that shows in the cracks.

Grain

Where the Film Grain filter, discussed earlier in the "Artistic Filters" section, lets you adjust the amount of grain and how the granules are applied to highlights, the Grain plug-in works with contrast (the darkness of the grain in relation to the image area surrounding it) plus the shape of the granules. You can also control how much grain is added. The 10 available types of

grain cover several varieties often seen in photographs, plus some new ones that offer imaginative artistic effects. You can choose from regular, soft, sprinkles, clumped, contrasty, enlarged, stippled, horizontal, vertical, or speckle grain patterns. You may have to examine the results to see the difference between, say, clumped and speckle. The stippled effect uses foreground and background colors, while sprinkles uses just the foreground color.

Mosaic Tiles

Mosaic Tiles produces a more realistic mosaic effect than Photoshop's similarly (and deceptively) named Mosaic filter. This one produces a look reminiscent of Craquelure, but with each portion of the image isolated by a more regular series of cracks that do look like tiles set into a wall in traditional mosaic fashion. You can adjust Tile Size, Grout Width, and lightness/darkness of the grout.

Patchwork

Patchwork actually produces another mosaic effect, as if the artwork were produced using only square tiles that have been tightly set together. You can vary the relative square size from 0 to 10 (not in pixels) and the amount of relief from 0 to 25.

Stained Glass

If you dream of a filter that can convert any image into a beautiful stained-glass window or Tiffany lampshade, dream on. This filter does create some great effects, but the irregularly-shaped chips of "glass" created out of your image don't really mimic true stained or leaded glass very well. Instead, the effect is more of an image viewed *through* a stained glass window. The current foreground color is used for the leaded inserts between the glass pieces, but the other colors come from your image itself. You can control the size of the glass pieces (cells), the thickness of the leading, and the intensity of the light source behind the window that transilluminates your image.

Even the thinnest borders will intrude on the image too much for a realistic rendition. Large cell sizes produce abstract images that have no resemblance to your original subject. Small cell sizes generate images that, as I said, aren't especially stained-glass-like.

Texturizer

The Texturizer controls let you select from the type of texture to be applied, using a drop-down list. Brick, burlap, canvas, and sandstone are supplied, and these are suitable for a remarkable number of different images. However, you can also work with a texture file of your own. Custom textures can be created by scanning common household objects and surfaces. Don't worry too much about the size of the custom texture: if the image is too small to texturize your entire selection, it will be automatically tiled. Don't try to get away with too small of a texture file, however; tiny images tiled can add a repeating pattern to your image that you probably won't like.

Video Filters

Video filters are really only of use if you're working with images captured from video sources. Most Photoshop users never have the occasion to put them to work, but I'll describe their purpose, anyway.

De-Interlace

The De-Interlace filter reconstructs missing information in images captured from video. Each video frame consists of two alternating lines of pixels, each making up half the entire image, and painted in interlaced fashion on your television screen to provide one complete picture. Video frame grabs commonly consist of only one of these two fields, so your digital image is, in effect, missing every other line.

De-Interlace recreates the missing lines either by duplicating the ones already present, or by guessing—or interpolating—the value of the pixels using the lines on either side of the missing one. The De-Interlace dialog box allows you to choose which set of lines to use and your preferred method of synthesizing the new information.

NTSC Colors

This filter changes the colors of an image to match the gamut defined by the NTSC for reproduction on television. The NTSC (National Television Systems Committee, but known within the industry as Never Twice Same Color) is a standards-setting organization that provides specifications for many of the technical standards that must be met by broadcasters in the United States. The television system used in the Western Hemisphere and Japan is called NTSC after this body. (Great Britain and Germany use the PAL—phase alternation line—color system, while SECAM—after the French words for system electronic color with memory—is used in France and many countries of the former Soviet Union.)

However, it's enough to know that colors that can be reproduced by NTSC systems are fewer than can be handled by your computer, just as the color gamut of CMYK printing systems is different from what you see on-screen in RGB mode.

If you're creating an image that will be displayed on television, such as a digital presentation copied to tape or a title slide used for advertising or other purposes, and color fidelity is important to you, use the NTSC Colors filter. It will modify the colors in your image to match the NTSC gamut. You can then preview the final image to make sure it's what you want, then print to a film recorder (to generate a slide) or save to disk for display.

There are no dialog boxes or controls for this filter; just apply it to your image. The changes are rather subtle, and wouldn't show up in a black-and-white picture in any case, so an illustration won't do you a lot of good.

Other Filters

Everything that doesn't fit into the other categories has been lumped here into Photoshop's Other group. Despite the amorphous quality of this group, you'll find some useful filters here.

Custom

This is Photoshop's user-unfriendly facility for creating your own customized filters. The dialog box represents a matrix with the center representing a pixel and the surrounding boxes each of the pixels surrounding the target pixel. You can type values into the surrounding boxes to determine how Photoshop will change the brightness of the adjacent pixels, based on the value of the one in the center. Once you've entered values, Photoshop will apply them to each of the pixels in an image or selection in turn.

Needless to say, this filter is of most use to those who understand the mathematics of how images are formed, but you'll find that a little experimenting can pay serendipitous dividends in the form of unexpected effects.

Dither Box

This filter lets you create custom dither patterns for a particular RGB color. Advanced users can work with this filter to create more realistic images from limited color palettes. Again, practical experience is more illustrative for understanding the effects of this filter than an actual illustration would be.

High Pass

This filter is sometimes neglected because it's so hard to picture what it does in your mind. However, a simple way to think about the High Pass filter is as a color-blurring filter that works on the opposite elements of your image than those affected by the Gaussian Blur filter. The latter smoothes out high-frequency information—edges and sharp color transitions, for example. High Pass, on the other hand, keeps those areas sharp, and blurs the rest of your image area.

Adobe recommends using this filter to smooth out extraneous detail in a continuous tone image before converting to a one-bit (black-and-white) image. The edges (which will be converted to black lines) are retained, while other detail (which will be converted to white) is smoothed out and eliminated. The filter can also make one-bit images look better by removing dirt or other artifacts.

The High Pass dialog box has just one control: the radius of the pixels around the image pixels that you want retained. You can specify from .1 to 250 pixels. A low number produces the strongest effects; few pixels next to the edges are left alone. The higher the number, the more pixels ignored by the filter, and the less dramatic the changes. You can use this filter to create line art from continuous tone scans. The effects are almost always better than going directly from grayscale to bitmap using the Mode menu.

Maximum/Minimum

This pair of filters generates interesting abstract effects by adding spreads (widened areas) and chokes (narrowed areas) to your images. They are generally used to modify masks. Your only control is a slider to specify the number of pixels evaluated for brightness values. They spread out and contract white areas. While there are technical prepress applications for these facilities, you can also experiment to get interesting effects on your own.

Offset

The Offset filter is most often used to create images that can be tiled seamlessly. What it does is move a selection or portions of an image in precise increments, say, 5 pixels to the right, and 10 down. You can specify that the hole left by your selection's move can be filled with the current background color. You can also specify that edge pixels are repeated in the undefined area left behind.

This option stretches the pixels around the hole to fill in the empty area. That eliminates the gaping hole, but may or may not be pleasing, depending on how much detail was in the image area you moved. If you're moving a section that has an even texture, the transition may be smooth. Otherwise, it might not be much better than just filling in with background color. Finally, the image can be made to wrap around. That is, image area from the opposite side is used to fill in the empty areas. It lets you create seamless textures that can be used to tile any size area with Texture Fill or other tools, or on Web pages.

GLOSSARY

achromatic color   An unsaturated color, such as gray.

action   A Photoshop macro or script that automates a single operation or a sequence of operations. Photoshop comes with default Actions, and you can create and save custom Actions to a file. When you need a particular Action or Action sequence, you can play it and apply its operations to any image by pressing a function key.

Actions palette   The Photoshop palette that contains controls for recording and playing back Actions.

additive primary colors   Red, green, and blue, which are used to create all other colors when direct, or transmitted, light is used (for example, on a computer monitor). When pure red, green, and blue are superimposed on one another, they create white. Photoshop's primary image manipulation mode is RGB. Web graphics are usually prepared in an image editor's RGB mode.

adjustment layer   A layer that can be used to modify the contrast, brightness, color, and other factors of the layers below it, without changing the pixels themselves. Adjustment layers can be edited, turned on and off, and otherwise manipulated to provide flexible effects to the layers they are applied to.

Adobe Gamma calibration package   A package that includes Adobe Gamma software, the Gamma Wizard, and ICC (International Color Consortium) color profiles for some RGB devices. You can use the Gamma software to calibrate your monitor.

airbrush   An artist's tool that sprays a fine mist of paint. Photoshop's version has user-configurable brushes that can apply a spray of a selected tone to an area.

alpha channel   An 8-bit, grayscale representation of an image. Alpha channels are selections that have been stored for later use. The values of gray can represent tonality, color, opacity, or semitransparency. Image formats that support alpha channels include Photoshop (PSD), Photoshop 2.0, Photoshop PDF, PICT, Pict Resource, Pixar, Raw, Targa, TIFF, and Photoshop DCS 2.0.

ambient lighting   The overall nondirectional lighting that fills an area. When using lighting effects filters, you can place specific lights around your subject, and use ambient lighting to fill in the dark areas not illuminated by one of the main lights.

anamorphic An image that has been enlarged or reduced more in one direction than another. The image looks "squashed" or "stretched" in a given dimension.

animated GIF A GIF file that contains the multiple images of an animation; these images are displayed one after another by a Web browser to produce the illusion of movement.

animation Computer graphics used to prepare moving sequences of images. On the Web, you'll find animations in the form of animated GIFs, QuickTime movies, Flash images, and other formats.

anti-alias A process that adds a border around an edge that blends into the adjacent color to create a small transition zone. Without the anti-alias, an image would look stair-stepped, without smooth transitions between colors. The width of an anti-alias is determined by the resolution of the image; you have no control over its size.

applet A small application, especially one produced for Web use with the Java language supported by the latest browsers.

applications program interface (API) A common interface that allows software engineers to write programs that will operate with a broad range of computer configurations.

archive To store files that are no longer active, usually on a removable disk or tape.

artifact An unintentional image element produced in error by an imaging device or inaccurate software. Dirty optics are one common reason for artifacts.

ascender The portion of a lowercase letter that rises above the top of the main portion of the letter.

aspect ratio The proportions of an image; e.g., an 8×10–inch photo has a 4:5 aspect ratio.

attribute Characteristics of a page, character, or object, such as line width, fill, underlining, boldface, or font.

automatic document feeder (ADF) A device attached to a scanner that automatically feeds one page at a time, allowing the scanning of multiple pages.

autotrace   A feature found in many object-oriented image editing programs or standalone programs that allows you to trace a bit map image and convert it to an outline or vector format.

background   The color or pattern of a Web page on which text and images are displayed. Also, the bottom layer of a Photoshop image or the area behind layers. The contents of all layers float on top of the Background. Unlike a layer, the Background is opaque and cannot support transparency. If the document contains more than one layer, the Background is always at the bottom of the stack and cannot be moved and placed in a higher position. When new layers are added to the document, their content always appears in front of the Background. However, you can convert a Background into an ordinary, movable layer by giving it a name.

backlighting   A lighting effect produced when the main light source is located behind the subject. If no frontlighting, fill, or ambient lighting is used in conjunction with backlighting, the effect is a silhouette. You can simulate backlighting with filters.

bandwidth   The amount of information that a communications link can carry at one time.

baseline   An imaginary line on which type rests.

baseline shift   The movement of the baseline of a character horizontally or vertically from its default starting position. Unlike *leading*, which affects all of the characters in a paragraph, baseline shift affects individual characters.

batch Action   An Action that will be applied to all of the images in a folder automatically, also known as *batch processing*. You can batch-process a group of images within a folder or from a different source, such as a digital camera or scanner with a document feeder.

Bézier curve   An editable curved line like those produced by Photoshop's Paths tool.

bilevel   An image that stores only black-and-white information, with no gray tones; Photoshop calls such images *bitmaps*.

bit   A binary digit—either a 1 or a 0. Scanners typically use multiple bits to represent information about each pixel of an image. A 1-bit scan can store only black or white information about a pixel. A 2-bit scan can include four different gray levels or values—00, 01, 10, or 11. Other values include 15- and 16-bit images (with 32,767 and 65,535 colors, respectively); and 24-bit images (with 16.8 million colors). See also *bit depth*.

bit depth   Refers to the amount of information per color channel. Photoshop can read images with 16 bits of information per channel, such as a 48-bit RGB or a 64-bit CMYK color image. Even though images with higher bit depths contain more color information, they are displayed on the monitor at the bit-depth capability of the computer's video card, which is 24 bits in most cases.

bitmap   A description of an image that represents each pixel as a number in a row and column format. In Photoshop parlance, each bit in the map can be represented by a 1 or a 0 (black or white), but in the rest of the world, numbers as large as 32 can be used to describe the density, color, and transparency information in a pixel.

black   The color formed by the absence of reflected or transmitted light; e.g., the combination of 100 percent values of cyan, magenta, and yellow ink (in the subtractive color system), or 0 values of red, green, and blue light (in the additive color system).

black point   The darkest pixel in the shadow areas of an image. In Photoshop, you can set this point in the Levels and Curves dialog boxes.

black printer   A printing plate used to add black ink to a cyan-magenta-yellow image, emphasizing neutral tones and adding detail to shadows. A skeleton black printer adds black ink only to darker areas; a full-range black printer adds at least some black to all of an image.

bleed   A printed image that extends right up to the edge of a page, often accomplished by trimming a larger image down to a finished size.

blend   To create a more realistic transition between image areas. Image editing software like Photoshop allows you to merge overlapping sections of images to blend the boundary between them.

blending mode   A preprogrammed color formula that determines how the pixels in an image are combined or affected by painting, image-editing, or layer-merging operations. In Photoshop, the Mode menu on the Options bar and in the Layers palette offers a choice of 19 blending modes.

blur   To reduce the contrast between pixels that form edges in an image, softening it.

brightness   The amount of light and dark shades in an image. The relative lightness or darkness of the color, usually measured as a percentage from 0 percent (black) to 100 percent (white).

burn   In photography, to expose part of a print for a longer period, making it darker than it would be with a straight exposure. In lithography, to expose a printing plate. In Photoshop, to darken a portion of an image, using Burn mode of Photoshop's toning tool.

byte   Eight bits, which can represent any number from 0000000 to 11111111 binary (0 to 255 decimal).

cache   A fast memory buffer used to store information read from disk or from slower RAM to allow the operating system or Photoshop to access it more quickly.

calibrated monitor   The foundation from which all other color settings are determined. You can use a calibration device or the Adobe Gamma calibration package to calibrate your monitor.

calibration   A process used to correct for the variation in output of a device like a printer or monitor when compared to the original image and the data you get from the scanner.

calibration bars   The grayscale or color indicators that appear on printed output. When you print a CMYK color separation, the calibration bars appear only on the black plate. On a color image, the calibration bars are the color swatches printed at the sides of the image.

camera ready   Artwork in a form usable for producing negatives or plates for printing.

canvas   In Photoshop, the surface on which your image resides.

cast   A tinge of color in an image, usually an undesired color.

CCD   Charge-Coupled Device. A type of solid-state sensor used in scanners and video capture devices. Compared to older imaging devices, including video tubes, CCDs are more sensitive and less prone to memory problems that can cause blurring of images.

channel   One of the layers that make up an image. An RGB image has three channels: one each for the red, green, and blue information. A CMYK image has four channels, cyan, magenta, yellow, and black. A grayscale image contains just one channel. Additional masking channels, or *alpha channels*, can be added to any of these.

Channel Mixer   A Photoshop feature that allows you to adjust the color information of each channel. You can establish color values on a specific channel as a mixture of any or all of the color channels' brightness values.

Channels palette   The Photoshop palette that allows you to work with an image's color information, or channels, and create alpha channels.

Character palette   The Photoshop palette that contains settings for type, such as size, tracking, kerning, and leading.

chroma   Color or hue.

Chromalin   The DuPont trademark for a type of color proof used for representing how color halftones will appear on the printed page.

chromatic color   A color with at least one hue available, with a visible level of color saturation.

chrome   Photographer-talk for a color transparency such as Kodachrome, Ektachrome, or Fujichrome.

CIE (Commission Internationale de l'Eclairage)   An international organization of scientists who work with matters relating to color and lighting. The organization is also called the International Commission on Illumination.

clickable image   A graphic or image map in an HTML document that can be clicked on to retrieve associated URLs and their contents.

client-side image map   A clickable image map that includes the URLs available for access and their coordinates on a page, directly on the page itself, so a Web browser supporting this feature can follow the designated hyperlinks without intervention by the server.

clip art   Generic artwork available for scanning, desktop, or Web publishing, and other uses with few restrictions.

clipboard   An area of memory used to store images and text so they can be interchanged between layers, windows, or applications. Photoshop has its own internal Clipboard, and can export and import to and from the Mac or PC's system Clipboard.

clipping group   Layers grouped together to create effects. In order to join two layers into a clipping group, the image on the bottom layer must be surrounded by transparency. When a layer is clipped, it fills the shape of the image on the layer below it, so that it acts as a mask to clip the layer immediately above it.

clipping path A path designed to be used as a mask in other applications. In Photoshop, the Clipping Paths option in the Paths palette menu allows you to create a path that will knock out the area outside the path when it is opened in another program. The interior portion of the path will be displayed, and the area outside the path will be transparent.

clone To copy pixels from one part of an image to another with Photoshop's Rubber Stamp tool and Pattern Stamp tools.

CMYK color model A model that defines all possible colors in percentages of cyan, magenta, yellow, and black.

color channels Color information from an image. The number of color channels depends on the image's color mode. For example, Photoshop configures the information for an RGB image into three color channels, for the red, green, and blue components, plus a composite RGB channel, which displays the entire image in full color. The computer processes the information in each channel as an independent grayscale image. Each pixel is assigned a specific numeric gray value, where black equals 0 and white equals 255. Each color channel is actually an 8-bit grayscale image that supports 256 shades of gray.

color correction Changing the color balance of an image to produce a desired effect, usually a more accurate representation of the colors in an image. It is used to compensate for the deficiencies of process color inks, inaccuracies in a color separation, or an undesired color balance in the original image. Color correction is done using one of several available color models, including RGB and CMYK.

color depth The number of bits of information used to represent color values in an image; the higher the number of bits, the greater the number of colors (and shades) that can be represented. See also *bit depth*.

color key A set of four acetate overlays, each with a halftone representing one of the colors of a color separation and tinted in that color. When combined, color keys can be used for proofing color separations.

color management module (CMM) The color management engine used by software to convert colors. The Adobe engine is ACE (Adobe Color Engine). Others you might encounter include Agfa, Apple ColorSync, Apple, Heidelberg, Imation, Kodak, Microsoft, and X-Rite.

color management policies Rules that determine how Photoshop deals with color profiles when opening RGB, CMYK, or grayscale files.

color mapping   Operations that can radically alter existing colors in an image. Color mapping provides the means to alter the basic characteristics of color while maintaining the image's detail.

color mode or model   A system of displaying or printing color. Photoshop supports the HSB color model and RGB, CMYK, Lab, Indexed, Duotone, Grayscale, Multichannel, and Bitmap color modes.

color separation   An image that has been separated into the four process colors: cyan, magenta, yellow, and black (CMYK). The image is then printed on four separate plates, one for each of the process colors.

color space   The colors produced by a specific device, such as a printer or monitor. Photoshop 6 allows you to edit and store an image with a color space other than that of your monitor. The image is embedded with an ICC (International Color Consortium) profile that describes the working color space. The image can then move from one computer to another with its profile, and it can be displayed on two different monitors and appear the same regardless of the monitors' settings.

color wheel   A circle representing the spectrum of visible colors.

colorize   To convert gray pixels to colored pixels. Before a black-and-white image can be colorized in Photoshop, you must change its mode from Grayscale to a mode that supports color (RGB, CMYK, or Lab). By colorizing, you apply color to the image without affecting the lightness relationships of the individual pixels, thereby maintaining the image's detail.

comp   A layout that combines type, graphics, and photographic material, also called a composite or comprehensive.

complementary color   Generally, the opposite hue of a color on a color wheel, which is called the direct complement. For example, green is the direct complement of magenta.

compression   Reducing the size of a file by encoding using smaller sets of numbers that don't include redundant information. Some kinds of compression, such as JPEG, can degrade images, while others, including GIF and PNG, preserve all the detail in the original.

constrain   To limit a tool in some way, such as forcing a brush to paint in a straight line or an object being rotated to a fixed increment.

continuous tone   Images that contain tones from the darkest to the lightest, with an infinite range of variations in between.

contrast   The range between the lightest and darkest tones in an image. A high contrast image is one in which the shades fall at the extremes of the range between white and black. In a low contrast image, the tones are closer together.

contrast   The range of individual tones between the lightest and darkest shades in an image.

convolve   A process used by imaging filters, which takes the values of surrounding pixels to calculate new values for sharpening, blurring, or creating another effect.

copy dot   Photographic reproduction of a halftone image, in which the halftone dots of a previously screened image are carefully copied as if they were line art. The same technique can be used in scanning to capture a halftoned image. If the original dot sizes are maintained, the quality of the finished image can be good.

crop mark   A mark placed on a page larger than the desired finished page to show where the page should be trimmed to final size.

crop   To trim an image or page by adjusting the boundaries.

Curves   A Photoshop color-adjustment tool that allows you to lighten, darken, add contrast, and solarize images.

darken   The process of selectively changing pixel values to darker ones.

data compression   A method of reducing the size of files, such as image files, by representing the sets of binary numbers in the file with a shorter string that conveys the same information.

default   The value or parameter that is automatically used for a tool, action, or function, unless you specify otherwise using a dialog box or some other method.

defringe   To remove the outer edge pixels of a selection, often when merging a selection with an underlying image.

densitometer   An electronic device used to measure the density of an image.

density range The range from the smallest highlight dot a press can print to the largest shadow dot it can print.

density The ability of an object to stop or absorb light. The less the light is reflected or transmitted by an object, the higher its density.

desaturate To reduce the purity or vividness of a color, as with Photoshop's Sponge tool. Desaturated colors appear washed out and diluted.

descender The portion of a lowercase letter that extends below the *baseline*, such as the tail on the letter y.

diffusion The random distribution of gray tones in an area of an image, often used to produce a *mezzotint* effect.

digitize To convert information, usually analog information such as that found in continuous tone images, to a numeric format that can be accepted by a computer.

displacement map A Photoshop file used by the Displace filter to control the shifting of pixels in an image horizontally or vertically in order to produce a particular special effect.

distort To stretch a selection along either of its axes. Unlike skewing, distortion is not restricted to a single border at a time.

dither A method of distributing pixels to extend the visual range of color on screen, such as producing the effect of shades of gray on a black-and-white display or more colors on an 8-bit color display. By making adjacent pixels different colors, dithering gives the illusion of a third color.

dodging A photographic term for blocking part of an image as it is exposed, lightening its tones.

dot A unit used to represent a portion of an image. A dot can correspond to one of the pixels used to capture or show an image on the screen, or groups of pixels can be collected to produce larger printer dots of varying sizes to represent gray.

dot etching A technique in photographic halftoning in which the size of the halftone dots is changed to alter tone values.

dot gain The tendency of a printing dot to grow from the original size when halftoned to its final printed size on paper. This effect is most pronounced on offset presses using poor quality papers, which allow ink to absorb and spread.

dots per inch (dpi)   The resolution of an image, expressed in the number of pixels or printer dots in an inch. Scanner resolution is also commonly expressed in dpi, but, technically, scanners use an optical technique that makes *samples per inch* a more accurate term.

drop cap   The first letter of a paragraph, set in a larger point size than the rest of the text. It may rise above the first line or extend below, in which case the drop cap is inset into the text block.

Droplet   A mini-application that contains Actions. A Droplet can sit on the desktop or be saved to a disk file. You can apply an operation to a file or group of files by dragging the file or folder onto the Droplet's icon.

drum scanner   A type of scanner that uses a spinning drum. The image is taped to a drum that spins very rapidly while the scanner's sensors record its color and tonality information.

dummy   A rough approximation of a publication, used to gauge layout.

Duotone   An image that uses two inks. Duotone can add a wider tonal range in a grayscale image by using more than one shade of ink to fill in the gaps. Duotone curves let you control the density of each ink in the highlights, midtones, and shadows. Photoshop creates duotones by applying the various curves you've defined to a single image.

Duotone mode   A Photoshop mode that displays Duotones, which are images that have been separated into two spot colors. Duotone mode supports Tritones (images with three colors) and Quadtones (images with four colors). The Duotone color information is contained on one color channel. Photoshop displays a preview that is an RGB simulation of the ink combinations.

dye sublimation   A printing technique in which solid inks are heated directly into a gas, which then diffuses into a polyester substrate to form an image. Because dye sublimation printers can reproduce 256 different hues for each color, they can print in excess of 16.7 million different colors.

emboss   A Photoshop technique that makes an image appear to be raised above the surface, in a 3D effect.

emulsion side   The side of a piece of film that contains the image, usually with a matte, nonglossy finish. This side is placed in contact with the emulsion side of another piece of film (when making a duplicate) or the printing plate. That way, the image is sharper than it would be if it were diffused by the base material of the film. Image processing workers need to understand this concept when producing images oriented properly (either right-reading or wrong-reading) for production.

emulsion The light-sensitive coating on a piece of film, paper, or printing plate.

encapsulated PostScript (EPS) An image format for PostScript printers, which can include a bitmap description of an image file or an outline-oriented image of line graphics and text. Photoshop can import both bitmap and line-oriented EPS files, but can export only the bitmapped version.

equalization A technique for distributing image data across a greater range of pixel values. Typical equalization techniques include *gamma correction* and adaptive histogram equalization.

export To transfer text or images from a document to another format, using Photoshop's Save As or Export functions.

extrude To create a 3D effect by adding edges to an outline shape as if it were clay pushed through a mold.

eyedropper Photoshop's tool used to sample color from one part of an image, so it can be used to paint or draw elsewhere.

fade-out rate The rate at which the Photoshop Paintbrush and Airbrush tools fade out as you paint with them to simulate an actual brush stroke.

feather A process that creates a gradual transition between the inside and the outside of image borders. When you apply an effect to a feathered selection, it diminishes and becomes more transparent, producing a softening or blurring effect. Feathering gradually blends colored pixels into each other and eliminates hard edges. Feathering differs from anti-aliasing in that you can determine the size of the soft edge in pixels.

feather edge The area along the border of a selection that is partially affected by changes you make to the selection.

file format A set way in which a particular application stores information on a disk. This standardization makes it possible for different applications to load each others' files, since they know what to expect from a predictable file format.

fill To cover a selected area with a tone or pattern. Fills can be solid, transparent, or have a gradient transition from one color or tone to another.

Fill layer   A Photoshop 6 method for filling an area. Fill layers combine the action of the Fill command with the flexibility of layers. You can create Fill layers with colors, gradients, or patterns.

filter   A Photoshop feature that changes the pixels in an image to produce blurring, sharpening, and other special effects.

flat   A low contrast image. Also, the assembled and registered negatives or positives used to expose a printing plate.

flatbed scanner   A type of scanner that reads a line of an image at a time, recording it as a series of samples, or pixels, by bouncing light off the area it needs to digitize. The scanner directs the bounced light to a series of detectors that convert color and intensity into digital levels.

floating selection   In Photoshop, a selection that has been moved or pasted on an image or converted to a floating selection using the Float command in the Select menu. The selection floats above the pixels in the underlying image until it is deselected, and it can be moved without affecting the underlying image.

font   A group of letters, numbers, and symbols in one size and typeface. Garamond and Helvetica are typefaces; 11-point Helvetica Bold is a font.

four-color printing   Another term for process color, in which cyan, magenta, yellow, and black inks are used to reproduce all the hues of the spectrum.

FPO   For Position Only. Artwork deemed not good enough for reproduction, used to help gauge how a page layout looks.

fractal   A kind of image in which each component is made up of ever smaller versions of the component. Sets of fractal images can be calculated using formulas developed by mathematicians such as Mandelbrot and Julia and used as textures in images. More recently, fractal calculations have been used to highly compress image files.

frequency   The number of lines per inch in a halftone screen.

frisket   Another name for a mask, used to shield portions of an image from the effects of various tools that are applied to other areas of the image.

full-color image   An image that uses 24-bit color. A full-color image uses three 8-bit primary color channels—for red, green, and blue—each containing 256 colors. These three channels produce a potential of nearly 16.8 million colors (256^3 = 16,777,216). Photorealistic images that consist of smooth gradations and subtle tonal variations require full color to be properly displayed.

galley   A typeset copy of a publication used for proofreading and estimating length.

gamma   A numerical way of representing the contrast of an image, shown as the slope of a line showing tones from white to black. Gamma is a method of tonal correction that takes the human eye's perception of neighboring values into account. Gamma values range from 1.0 to about 2.5. The Macintosh has traditionally used a gamma of 1.8, which is relatively flat compared to television. Windows PCs use a 2.2 gamma value, which has more contrast and is more saturated.

gamma correction   A method for changing the brightness, contrast, or color balance of an image by assigning new values to the gray or color tones of an image. Gamma correction can be either linear or nonlinear. Linear correction applies the same amount of change to all the tones. Nonlinear correction varies the changes tone-by-tone, or in highlight, midtone, and shadow areas separately to produce a more accurate or improved appearance.

gamut   The range of viewable and printable colors for a particular color model, such as RGB (used for monitors) or CMYK (used for printing). When a color cannot be displayed or printed, Photoshop can warn you that the color is "out of gamut." In terms of color working spaces, the gamut of a monitor is a triangular space with its corners in the red, green, and blue areas of an industry-standard color gamut chart. The gamut chart plots the device's available colors compared to the gamut of colors humans can see.

gang scan   The process of scanning more than one picture at a time, used when images are of the same density and color balance range.

Gaussian blur   A method of diffusing an image by using a bell-shaped curve to calculate which pixels will be blurred, rather than blurring all pixels in the selected area uniformly.

GIF87a and GIF89a   The Graphics Interchange Formats, used for Web applications and for saving animations produced in ImageReady. GIF is a *lossless-compression* format that compresses the image through reduction of the available colors. GIF87a does not support transparency. GIF89a is used to omit the visibility of selected colors on a Web browser.

gradient   Variations of color that subtly blend into one another. Photoshop gradients blend multiple colors into each other or into transparency over a specified distance.

gradient fill   A fill that displays a gradual transition from the foreground color to the background color. In Photoshop, gradient fills are added with the Gradient tool.

graphics tablet   A pad on which you draw with a pen-like device called a stylus, used as an alternative to a mouse.

gray component removal   A process in which portions of an image that have a combination of cyan, magenta, and yellow are made purer by replacing equivalent amounts of all three with black. GCR is generally more extreme and uses more black than undercolor removal (UCR).

gray map   A graph that shows the relationship between the original brightness values of an image and the output values after image processing.

grayscale image   An image that use an 8-bit system, in which any pixel can be one of 256 shades of gray. Each pixel contains 8 bits of information. Each bit can either be on (black) or off (white), which produces 256 possible combinations.

Grayscale mode   A Photoshop color mode that displays black-and-white images. A grayscale image is composed of one channel consisting of up to 256 levels of gray, with 8 bits of color information per pixel. Each pixel has a brightness value between 0 (black) to 255 (white). Grayscale pixels may also be measured in percentages of black ink, from 0 percent (white) to 100 percent (black). When color images are converted to Grayscale mode, their hue and saturation information is discarded and their brightness (or luminosity) values remain.

grid   In Photoshop, a series of equally spaced horizontal and vertical lines that create a visual matrix. A grid helps you see the global relations between aligned elements on a page. Grids do not print.

guide   In Photoshop, a horizontal or vertical line that can be positioned anywhere on the image's surface. Guides do not print.

gutter   The inner margin of a page that must be included to allow for binding.

halftone   The reproduction of a continuous-tone image, which is made by using a screen that breaks the image into various size dots. The resolution, or number of lines per inch (lpi), of a halftone depends on the printer's capabilities. The tonal densities of an image are determined by the size of the dots. The larger the dot, the more ink deposited, and the darker the area appears. When you send an image to a printer, Photoshop, in tandem with the printer driver software, automatically converts the tonal information contained in pixels into dot-density information that the printer uses to construct the image.

halftone screen   Refers to the dot density of a printed image, measured in lines per inch (lpi). A halftone screen, also called screen frequency, is a grid of dots.

handles   Small squares that appear in the corners (and often at the sides) of a square used to define an area to be scanned or an object in an image editing program. The user can grab the handles with the mouse cursor and resize the area or object.

highlight   The lightest part of an image, represented on a digital image by pixels with high numeric values or on a halftone by the smallest dots or the absence of dots.

histogram   A graph of the brightness values of an image. The more lines the histogram has, the more tonal values are present in the image. The length of a line represents the relative quantity of pixels of a particular brightness. The taller the line, the more pixels of a particular tonal range the image will contain. Histograms are displayed in Photoshop's Levels and Threshold dialog boxes.

History palette   The Photoshop palette that records all of the changes that you make to an image during a session, as a series of individual states. You can use the History palette to revert to former versions of an image and to create special effects. The History palette also works in conjunction with the History Brush and Art History Brush tools.

hotspot   In an image map, an area that links to another Web page or URL.

HSB color model   A color model that uses hue, saturation, and brightness characteristics to define each color.

HTML (HyperText Markup Language)   The programming language used to create Web pages.

hue   The color of light that is reflected from an opaque object or transmitted through a transparent one. Hue in Photoshop is measured by its position on a color wheel, from 0 to 360 degrees.

ICC   See *International Color Consortium*.

image caching   A mechanism that accelerates screen redrawing during the editing process by storing image information in memory rather than on the hard disk.

image link   A link on a Web page activated by clicking an image.

image map   An image on a Web page that has multiple links to another Web page or URL. Each link is called a hotspot. Image maps let you define circular, polygonal, or rectangular areas as links.

image size   The physical size and resolution of an image. The size of an image specifies the exact number of pixels that compose a picture.

ImageReady   A companion program to Photoshop, used to create Web graphics.

ink-jet   A printing technology in which dots of ink are sprayed on paper.

indexed color image   A single-channel image, with 8 bits of color information per pixel. The index is a color lookup table containing up to 256 colors.

Indexed color mode   A color mode that uses a maximum of 256 colors to display full-color images. When you convert an image color to Indexed mode, Photoshop stores the color information as a color lookup table. You can then use a specific palette to display the image to match the colors as closely as possible to the original. Because it contains fewer colors, Indexed color mode creates smaller file sizes than the other color modes produce.

Info palette   The Photoshop palette that shows information about the current image. By default, the Info palette displays Actual Color and CMYK fields, the X and Y coordinates of the position of the cursor, and the height and width of the selection. This palette can display values in many different modes, including Web, HSB, Lab, Total Ink, and Opacity.

interlacing   A way of displaying an image (particularly interlaced GIF or JPEG images) in multiple fields, for example, odd-numbered lines first, then even-numbered lines, thereby updating or refreshing half the image on the screen at a time, allowing visitors to view a rough version of an image even before the entire file has been downloaded from a Web page.

International Color Consortium (ICC)   An organization that sets standards for color management systems and components.

interpolation   A technique used to calculate the value of the new pixels required whenever you resize or change the resolution of an image, based on the values of surrounding pixels.

inverse   In Photoshop, to reverse the selection; that is, to change the selected area to the portion that you did not select with a selection tool.

invert   To change an image into its negative; black becomes white, white becomes black, dark gray becomes light gray, and so forth. Colors are also changed to the complementary color; green becomes magenta, blue turns to yellow, and red is changed to cyan.

jaggies   Staircasing of lines that are not perfectly horizontal or vertical. Jaggies are produced when the pixels used to portray a slanted line aren't small enough to be invisible, because of the high contrast of the line and its surrounding pixels, like at the edges of letters. See also *anti-aliasing*.

JPEG (Joint Photographic Experts Group)   A *lossy-compression* file format that supports 24-bit color and is used to preserve the tonal variations in photographs. JPEG compresses file size by selectively discarding data. JPEG compression can degrade sharp detail in images and is not recommended for images with type or solid areas of color. JPEG does not support transparency. When you save an image as a JPEG, transparency is replaced by the matte color. See also *matting*.

justified   Text aligned at both right and left margins.

kern   To adjust the amount of space between two adjacent letters.

knockout   An area that prevents ink from printing on part of an image, so that the spot color can print directly on the paper. Knockouts keep a spot color from overprinting another spot color or a portion of the underlying image.

Lab color mode   A color mode that is device independent. Lab color consists of three channels: a luminance or lightness channel (L), a green–red component (a), and a blue–yellow component (b). Lab can be used to adjust an image's luminance and color independently of each other.

labels   A Photoshop printing option that prints the document and channel name on the image.

landscape   The orientation of a page in which the longest dimension is horizontal, also called wide orientation.

lasso   A tool used to select irregularly shaped areas in a bitmapped image.

layer   A software feature that allows you to isolate image elements so that you can work on each one individually. You can also rearrange the positions of layers, allowing parts of an image to appear in front of other parts. Earlier versions of Photoshop supported 99 layers; Photoshop 6 supports an unlimited number.

layer mask   A mask that conceals an area from view. When you apply a layer mask to an image, you control the transparency of a particular part of the layer.

Layers palette   The Photoshop palette that contains controls for working with layers, including creating and deleting layers, reordering layers, merging layers, and many other layer-related functions.

layer set   A Photoshop 6 layer-management tool. Layer sets let you consolidate contiguous layers into a folder on the Layers palette. By highlighting the folder, you can apply certain operations to the layers as a group. For example, the layers in a layer set can be can simultaneously hidden, displayed, moved, or repositioned.

layer styles   Predefined Photoshop 6 effects (called Layer Effects in Photoshop 5), such as drop shadows, neon glowing edges, and deep embossing. Layer styles apply their effects to the edges of the layer. Because they may be translucent or soft-edged, the colors of the underlying layer can be seen through the effects.

leading   The amount of vertical spacing between lines of text from baseline to baseline.

lens flare   In photography, an effect produced by the reflection of light internally among elements of an optical lens. Bright light sources within or just outside the field of view cause lens flare. It can be reduced by the use of coatings on the lens elements or with the use of lens hoods, but photographers (and now digital image workers) have learned to use it as a creative element.

Levels   A Photoshop tool that allows you to adjust an image's tonal range. When you perform a Levels adjustment, you are actually reassigning pixel values.

ligature   A set of two characters that is designed to replace certain character combinations, such as fl and fi, to avoid spacing conflicts.

lighten   An image editing function that is the equivalent to the photographic darkroom technique of *dodging*. Gray tones in a specific area of an image are gradually changed to lighter values.

line art   Usually, images that consist only of white pixels and one color.

line screen   The resolution or frequency of a halftone screen, expressed in lines per inch.

linear gradient   A gradient that is projected from one point to another in a straight line.

lines per inch (lpi)   A measurement of the resolution of a halftone screen.

Liquify   A Photoshop 6 feature that allows you to distort pixels and transform areas of an image using a special set of distortion and transformation tools.

lithography   Another name for offset printing, which is a reproduction process in which sheets or continuous webs of material are printed by impressing them with images from ink applied to a rubber blanket on a rotating cylinder from a metal or plastic plate attached to a another cylinder.

lossless compression   An image-compression scheme that preserves image detail. When the image is decompressed, it is identical to the original version.

lossy compression   An image-compression scheme that creates smaller files but can affect image quality. When decompressed, the image produced is not identical to the original. Usually, colors have been blended, averaged, or estimated in the decompressed version.

luminance   The brightness or intensity of an image. Determined by the amount of gray in a hue, luminance reflects the lightness or darkness of a color. See also *saturation*.

LZW compression   A method of compacting TIFF files using the Lempel-Ziv Welch compression algorithm. It produces an average compression ratio of 2:1, but larger savings are produced with line art and continuous tone images with large areas of similar tonal values.

Magic Wand   A Photoshop tool used to select contiguous pixels that have the same brightness value or that of a range you select.

map file   File on the server that includes pixel coordinates of hotspots on an image map.

mapping   Assigning colors or grays in an image.

Marquee   The Photoshop selection tool used to mark rectangular and elliptical areas.

mask   An element that isolates and protects portions of an image. A masked area is not affected by image editing such as color changes or applied filters. Masks are stored as 8-bit grayscale channels and can be edited with Photoshop tools.

matting   Filling or blending transparent pixels with a matte color. Matting can be used with GIF, PNG, and JPEG files. It is typically used to set transparent image areas to the background color of a Web page.

mechanical   Camera-ready copy with text and art already in position for photographing.

mezzotint   An engraving that is produced by scraping a roughened surface to produce the effect of gray tones. Image editing and processing software can produce this effect with a process called error diffusion.

midtones   Parts of an image with tones of an intermediate value, usually in the 25 to 75 percent range.

moiré   An objectionable pattern caused by the interference of halftone screens, frequently generated by rescanning an image that has already been halftoned.

monitor profile   A description of a monitor's characteristics used by Photoshop to display images correctly on that monitor. One way to create a monitor profile is to make a visual calibration of your monitor using Adobe Gamma and then save the resulting information as a color profile.

monitor resolution   The number of pixels that occupy a linear inch of your monitor screen. The resolution for most Macintosh RGB monitors is 72 ppi. Most Windows VGA monitors have a resolution of 96 ppi.

monochrome   Having a single color.

monospaced type   Typeface in which all of the characters are the same horizontal width.

montage   An image made up of a number of separate images.

Multichannel mode   A Photoshop mode that allows you to view the spot-color channels in color separations. The number of channels in a Multichannel document depends on the number of channels in the source image before it was converted. Each channel in a Multichannel document contains 256 levels of gray. Multichannel mode will convert RGB to cyan, magenta, and yellow spot color channels, and CMYK into CMYK spot color channels.

Navigator palette   The Photoshop palette that shows a map of the current image displayed as a thumbnail. It indicates the exact location of what appears in the image window relative to the entire image and provides features for scrolling and zooming.

noise   In an image, pixels with randomly distributed color values. Noise is primarily a result of digitizing technology. Noise in digital photographs tends to be the product of low-light conditions.

negative   A representation of an image in which the tones are reversed. That is, blacks are shown as white, and vice versa.

neutral color   In RGB mode, a color in which red, green, and blue are present in equal amounts, producing a gray.

noise   Random pixels added to an image to increase apparent graininess.

NTSC   National Television Standard Code, the standard for video in the United States.

object graphics   Vector-oriented graphics, in which mathematical descriptions, rather than bitmaps, are used to describe images.

offset printing   See *lithography*.

opacity   The opposite of *transparency*; the degree to which a layer obscures the view of the layer beneath. High opacity means low transparency. Both terms are used in Photoshop.

optimization   In Photoshop and ImageReady, features that put images in the best possible form for Web applications, such as the file format, color-reduction method, and matting settings. In Photoshop, optimization settings are available in the Save For Web dialog box. In ImageReady, these settings are on the Optimize palette.

Optimize palette   The ImageReady palette that contains controls for optimizing images for Web applications.

Options bar   In Photoshop, the area that contains settings for tools. When you select a tool in the Tool palette, the Options bar changes to reflect the options available for the selected tool.

overprint colors   Two or more unscreened inks that are printed one on top of the other.

palette   A set of tones or colors available to produce an image, or a row of icons representing tools that can be used.

Palette Well   The Options bar area that can be used to store palettes. Clicking the palette's title tab in the Palette Well causes the palette to drop down temporarily so you can use its features.

PAL (Phase Alternation Line) system   The video standard for television used in Western Europe, Australia, Japan, and other countries.

PANTONE   A brand name of spot color inks. The PANTONE Matching System is a group of inks used to print spot colors. PANTONE inks are solid colors used to print solid or tinted areas. The PANTONE system is recognized all over the world.

PANTONE Matching System   A registered trade name for a system of color matching. If you tell your printer the PMS number of the color you want, that color can be reproduced exactly by mixing printing inks to a preset formula.

Paragraph palette   The Photoshop palette that contains settings that apply to entire text paragraphs, such as alignment and hyphenation.

path   A vector object that mathematically defines a specific area on an image. Vector objects are composed of anchor points and line segments known as *Bézier curves*. Paths enable you to create straight lines and curves with precision. If a path's two end points are joined, it encloses a shape. A path can be filled with color, stroked with an outline, or stored in the Paths palette or the Shape library for later use. A path also can be converted into a selection.

Paths palette   The Photoshop palette that contains controls for working paths, including creating deleting paths, filling paths, stroking paths, and saving work paths.

perspective   In Photoshop, a transformation that squeezes or stretches one edge of a selection, slanting the two adjacent sides either in or out. This produces an image that mimics the way you perceive a picture slanted at a distance.

Photo CD   A special type of CD-ROM developed by Eastman Kodak Company that can store high quality photographic images in a special space-saving format, along with music and other data. Photo CDs can be accessed by CD-ROM XA-compatible drives, using Kodak-supplied software or compatible programs such as Photoshop.

pixel   A picture element of a screen image.

pixels per inch (ppi)   The number of pixels that can be displayed per inch, usually used to refer to pixel resolution from a scanned image or on a monitor.

plate   A thin, light-sensitive sheet, usually of metal or plastic, which is exposed and then processed to develop an image of the page, then placed on a printing press to transfer ink to paper.

plugging   A defect on the final printed page in which areas between dots become filled due to dot gain, producing an area of solid color. See also *dot gain*.

plug-In   A module that can be accessed from within a program like Photoshop to provide special functions. Many plug-ins are image-processing filters that offer special effects.

PNG-8   A *lossless-compression* file format that supports 256 colors and transparency. PNG-8 is not supported by older Web browsers.

PNG-24   A lossless file format that supports 24-bit color, transparency, and matting. PNG-24 combines the attributes of JPEG and GIF. PNG-24 is not supported by older Web browsers.

point   Approximately $1/72$ of an inch outside the Macintosh world, exactly $1/72$ of an inch within it.

Portable Network Graphics   An RGB file format supported by Photoshop that offers progressive, interleaved display, more sophisticated transparency capabilities than the GIF format, and is lossless.

portrait   The orientation of a page in which the longest dimension is vertical, also called tall orientation.

position stat   A copy of a halftone that can be placed on a mechanical to illustrate positioning and cropping of the image.

posterization   A Photoshop effect produced by reducing the number of tones in an image to a level at which the tones are shown as poster-like bands.

PostScript   A page description language developed by Adobe, which allows any printing device to output a page at its highest resolution.

preferences   In Photoshop, settings that affect the appearance and behavior of the program, which are stored in the Preferences file.

prepress   The stages of the reproduction process that precede printing, when halftones, color separations, and printing plates are created.

Preset Manager   A library of palettes that can be used by Photoshop. As you add or delete items from the palettes, the currently loaded palette in the Preset Manager displays the changes. You can save the new palette and load any of the palettes on the system.

printer resolution   The number of dots that can be printed per linear inch, measured in dots per inch (dpi). These dots compose larger halftone dots on a halftone screen or stochastic (random pattern) dots on an ink-jet printer.

process color   The four color pigments used in color printing: cyan, magenta, yellow, and black (CMYK).

Proof Colors   A Photoshop 6 control that allows the on-screen preview to simulate a variety of reproduction processes without converting the file to the final color space. This feature takes the place of the Preview in CMYK feature in earlier Photoshop versions.

process camera   A graphic arts camera used to make color separations, photograph original artwork to produce halftones and page negatives, and to perform other photographic enlarging/reducing/duplicating tasks.

process colors   Cyan, magenta, yellow, and black, the basic ink colors used to produce all the other colors in four-color printing.

progressive JPEG   A type of JPEG image in which increasingly detailed versions of an image are displayed, allowing a visitor to a Web site to view a graphic in rough form before it is completely downloaded.

proof   A test copy of a printed sheet, which is used as a final check before a long duplication run begins.

quadtone   An image printed using black ink and three other colored inks.

quantization   Another name for posterization.

Quick Mask mode   A Photoshop mode that allows you to edit a selection as a mask. This mode provides an efficient method of making a temporary mask using the paint tools. Quick Masks can be converted into selections or stored as alpha channels in the Channels palette for later use.

radial gradient   A gradient that is projected from a center point outward in all directions.

random access memory (RAM)   The part of the computer's memory that stores information temporarily while the computer is on.

raster image processor (RIP)   Software on a computer or a device inside an imagesetter or PostScript printer that interprets a vector curve by connecting a series of straight-line segments.

raster image   An image that consists of a grid of pixels. Raster images are also called *bitmaps*. The file sizes of raster images are usually quite large compared to other types of computer-generated documents, because information needs to be stored for every pixel in the entire document. See also *raster-based software*.

raster-based software   Photoshop and other programs that create raster images. Raster-based software is best suited for editing, manipulating, and compositing scanned images, images from digital cameras and Photo CDs, continuous-tone photographs, realistic illustrations, and other graphics that require subtle blends, soft edges, shadow effects, and artistic filter effects like impressionist or watercolor.

rasterize   To convert vector information into pixel-based information. For example, you can rasterize type so that you can apply filters and other effects that do not work on vector-based type. Rasterized type cannot be edited as individual characters and appears at the same resolution as the document.

ray tracing   A method for producing realistic highlights, shadows, and reflections on a three-dimensional rendering by projecting the path of an imaginary beam of light from a particular location back to the viewpoint of the observing.

red eye   An effect from flash photography that appears to make a person's eyes glow red.

reflection copy   Original artwork that is viewed by light reflected from its surface, rather than transmitted through it.

register   To align images, usually different versions of the same page or sheet. Color separation negatives must be precisely registered to one another to insure that colors overlap in the proper places.

registration mark   A mark that appears on a printed image, generally for color separations, to help in aligning the printing plates.

rendering intents   Settings established by the International Color Consortium (ICC) under which color conversions can be made. Rendering intents cause the color of an image to be modified while it is being moved into a new color space. The four rendering intents are Perceptual, Saturation, Relative Colorimetric, and Absolute Colorimetric.

resample   To change the size or resolution of an image. Resampling down discards pixel information in an image; resampling up adds pixel information through interpolation.

resolution   The number of units that occupy a linear inch of an image, measured in pixels per inch (ppi) on an image or monitor or dots per inch (dpi) on a printer. The resolution of an image determines how large it will appear and how the pixels are distributed over its length and width. Resolution also determines the amount of detail that an image contains. High resolutions produce better quality but larger image file sizes. Resolution can also refer to the number of bits per pixel.

resolution-independent image   An image that automatically conforms to the highest resolution of the output device on which it is printed.

retouch   To edit an image, most often to remove flaws or to create a new effect.

RGB color mode   A color mode that represents the three colors—red, green, and blue—used by devices such as scanners or monitors to display color. Each range of color is separated into three separate entities called *color channels*. Each color channel can produce 256 different values, for a total of 16,777,216 possible colors in the entire RGB gamut. RGB is referred to as an *additive* color model. Each pixel contains three brightness values for red, green, and blue that range from 0 (black) to 255. When all three values are at the maximum, the effect is complete white. Colors with low brightness values are dark; colors with high brightness values are light.

RGB image   A three-channel image that contains a red, green, and blue channel.

right-reading image   An image, such as a film used to produce a printing plate, that reads correctly, left to right, when viewed as it will be placed down for exposure.

RIP   Raster Image Processor. A device found in printers that converts page images to a format that can be printed by the marking engine of the printer.

rollover   A mini-animation that is activated by mouse behavior. Rollovers add interactivity to Web page. Rollovers depend on layers for their behavior. You designate a rollover on an image by changing the visibility of a layer's content.

rubber stamp   A Photoshop tool that copies or clones part of an image to another area or image.

saturation   The purity of color; the amount by which a pure color is diluted with white or gray.

scale   To change the size of a piece of an image.

scanner   A device that captures an image of a piece of artwork and converts it to a bit-mapped image that the computer can handle.

scratch disk   An area of memory that Photoshop uses as a source of virtual memory to process images when the program requires more memory than the allocated amount.

screen   The halftone dots used to convert a continuous tone image to a black-and-white pattern that printers and printing presses can handle. Even expanses of tone can also be reproduced by using tint screens that consist of dots that are all the same size (measured in percentages).

screen angles   The angles at which the halftone screens are placed in relation to one another.

screen frequency   The density of dots on the halftone screen, commonly measured in lines per inch (lpi). Also known as *screen ruling*.

SECAM (Sequential Color and Memory) system   A video standard for television used in some European and Asian countries.

secondary color   A color produced by mixing two primary colors. For example, mixing red and green primary colors of light produces the secondary color magenta. Mixing the yellow and cyan primary colors of pigment produces blue as a secondary color.

selection   An area of an image chosen for manipulation, usually surrounded by a moving series of dots called a selection border.

separations   Film transparencies, each representing one of the primary colors (cyan, magenta, and yellow) plus black, used to produce individual printing plates.

serif   Short strokes at the ends of letters. Thought to help lead the eye and make text easier to read. Sans serif type lacks these strokes.

server-side image map   A way of navigating a Web page using an image map that transfers the coordinates of the user's mouse on a Web page back to the server, where a CGI program determines which URL to direct you to.

shade   A color with black added.

shadow   The darkest part of an image, represented on a digital image by pixels with low numeric values or on a halftone by the smallest or absence of dots.

sharpening   Increasing the apparent sharpness of an image by boosting the contrast between adjacent pixels that form an edge.

skew   To slant a selection along one axis, either vertical or horizontal. The degree of slant affects how pitched the final image appears.

slice   To cut an image into pieces, saving the individual parts as image files and writing an HTML document that reassembles the slices on the screen. Slicing increases the efficiency of displaying images with a Web browser by decreasing the download time. Slices also allow you to define rectangular areas as links to other Web pages or URLs.

smoothing   To blur the boundaries between edges of an image, often to reduce a rough or jagged appearance.

SMPTE-C   A movie industry standard, compliant with the Society of Motion Picture and Television Engineers standards for motion picture illuminants.

smudge   A Photoshop tool that smears part of an image, mixing surrounding tones together.

snap   A Photoshop feature that causes lines or objects being drawn or moved to be attracted to a grid or guides.

snapshot In Photoshop, a saved image state. By default, when the image is opened, the History palette displays a snapshot of the image as it appeared when it was last saved. You can save the current image to a snapshot to preserve that state.

solarization In photography, an effect produced by exposing film to light partially through the developing process. Some of the tones are reversed, generating an interesting effect. In digital photography, the same effect is produced by combining some positive areas of the image with some negative areas.

sort proof An on-screen document that appears as close as possible to what the image will look like if printed to a specific device. Image formats that allows you to embed a sort proof profile in the saved document are Photoshop EPS, Photoshop PDF, and Photoshop DCS 1.0 and 2.0.

spot The dots that produce images on an imagesetter or other device.

spot color Ink used in a print job in addition to black or process colors. Each spot color requires a plate of its own. Spot colors are printed in the order in which they appear in the Channels palette. Spot color channels are independent of the color mode of the image, which means that they are not blended with the other channels in a grayscale, RGB, or CMYK image. Spot color channels are also independent of layers, which means that you cannot apply spot colors to individual layers. Image formats that support spot color are Photoshop (PSD), Photoshop PDF, TIFF, and Photoshop DCS 2.0.

spot color overlay A sheet that shows one of the colors to be used in a publication for a given page. A separate overlay is prepared for each color and all are combined to create the finished page.

sRGB color space A color space designed for corporate computer monitors and images intended for Web applications. sRGB is the default color working space in Photoshop 6, but other color spaces are available.

state In Photoshop's History palette, a stored version of an image. Each time you perform an operation, the History palette produces a state with the name of the operation or tool that was used. The higher the state appears in the stack, the earlier in the process the state was made.

strip   To assemble a finished page by taping or otherwise fastening pieces of film containing halftones, line art, and text together in a complete page negative or positive. The most common format is as a negative, because dirt and other artifacts show up as pinholes, which can be easily spotted or opaqued out before the printing plates are made.

stroking   Outlining a selection border with a color. In Photoshop, strokes can vary in width and relative position on the selection border.

substrate   A base substance that is coated with another. In printing, the substrate is generally paper or acetate, and the second substance is usually ink or dye.

subtractive primary colors   Cyan, magenta, and yellow, which are the printing inks that theoretically absorb all color and produce black. Because pigments subtract light components from the white light in the environment, they reduce its intensity, making it less bright than unfiltered light. Subtractive colorants reduce the amount of light reflected back at the viewer.

thermal wax transfer   A printing technology in which dots of wax from a ribbon are applied to paper when heated by thousands of tiny elements in a printhead.

threshold   A predefined level used by the scanner to determine whether a pixel will be represented as black or white.

thumbnail   A miniature copy of a page or image that provides a preview of the original.

TIFF (Tagged Image File Format)   A standard graphics file format that can be used to store grayscale and color images plus selection masks.

tint   A color with white added to it. In graphic arts, often refers to the percentage of one color added to another.

tolerance   The range of color or tonal values that will be selected, with a tool like the Magic Wand, or filled with paint, when using a tool like the Paint Bucket.

Tool palette   In Photoshop, the area that contains icons for tools, also called the Toolbox. Some of the tool icons expand to provide access to tools that are not visible, bringing the entire number of tools to 50 plus paint swatches, Quick

Mask icons, view modes, and the Jump To command. The Tool palette is a floating palette that you can move or hide.

tool tip   A GUI identifier that appears when you hover your cursor over a screen element and wait a few seconds. For example, Photoshop includes tool tips for the tools on the Tool palette, as well as for many of its operations accessible from other palettes, Options bar, dialog boxes, and windows.

tracking   The global space between selected groups of characters in text.

transparency scanner   A type of scanner that passes light through the emulsions on a piece of negative film or a color slide. A transparency scanner's dynamic range determines its ability to distinguish color variations.

trap   A technique used in preparing images for printing color separations. Misalignments or shifting during printing can result in gaps in images. A trap is an overlap that prevents such gaps from appearing along the edges of objects in an image.

trapping   Trapping has two common meanings. To a printer, trapping may mean the ability of an ink to transfer as well onto another layer of ink as it does to the bare paper. In halftoning, poor trapping will result in tonal changes in the final image. In desktop publishing, trapping has an additional meaning of printing some images of one color slightly larger so they overlap another color, avoiding unsightly white space if the two colors are printed slightly out of register. Printers call this technique *spreading* and *choking*. See also *trap*.

triad   Three colors located approximately equidistant from one another on the color wheel. Red, green, and blue make up a triad; cyan, magenta, and yellow make up another. However, any three colors arranged similarly around the wheel can make up a triad.

trim size   Final size of a printed publication.

tritone   An image that has been separated into three spot colors.

tweening   From "in betweening," a method for adding transitions between frames in animations.

undercolor removal (UCR)   A technique that reduces the amount of cyan, magenta, and yellow in black and neutral shadows by replacing them with an equivalent amount of black. See also *gray component removal*.

unsharp masking   The process for increasing the contrast between adjacent pixels in an image, increasing sharpness.

vector image   An image defined as a series of straight-line vectors and curves, such as those produced with Photoshop's Pen tool.

Web colors   Colors that are browser-safe, meaning that all Web browsers can display them uniformly. Photoshop's Web-Safe Colors feature lets you choose colors that will not radically change when viewed on other monitors of the same quality and calibration as the one on which you are working.

white point   The lightest pixel in the highlight area of an image. In Photoshop, you can set this point in the Levels and Curves dialog boxes.

wire frame   A rendering technique that presents only the edges of a 3D object, as if it were modeled from pieces of wire. This is much faster than modeling the entire object including all surfaces.

work path   In Photoshop, a temporary element that records changes as you draw new sections of a path.

wrong-reading image   An image that is backward relative to the original subject—that is, a mirror image.

x-height   The height of a lowercase letter, such as the letter x, excluding ascenders and descenders

zoom   To magnify an image or specific area of an image to better see fine details.

INDEX

Note to the reader: Throughout this index **boldfaced** page numbers indicate primary discussions of a topic. *Italicized* page numbers indicate illustrations.

H

N

ABOUT THE CONTRIBUTORS

Some of the best—and best-selling—Sybex authors have contributed chapters from their current books to *Photoshop 6 Complete*.

David D. Busch is a leading demystifier of computer and imaging technology through numerous books. He contributed chapters from *Photoshop 6! I Didn't Know You Could Do That* and his upcoming *Photoshop X Instant Reference*. Prior to his incarnation as a computer fanatic, he operated his own commercial photo studio.

Wendy Crumpler contributed chapters from *Photoshop, Painter and Illustrator Side By Side, Second Edition*. She has been in advertising and design since 1980. She has done production, illustration, design, and training for major advertising agencies using a wide variety of software programs. Wendy has worked in print, television, CD interactive, interactive television, and computer-based training. She is the author of *Photoshop, Painter, and Illustrator Side-by-Side, First Edition*, and co-author of *Photoshop 6 Artistry*. Wendy and her husband, photographer Barry Haynes, live and work in Corvallis, Oregon.

Stephen Romaniello contributed chapters from *Mastering Photoshop 6*, as well as *Mastering Adobe GoLive 4*. He is an artist, writer, and educator who has been involved in digital graphics for more than a decade. A professor at Pima College in Tucson, Arizona, Steve conducts seminars in digital and web graphics, both nationally and internationally. He is CEO of GlobalEye Systems, a software-training and consulting provider.

Molly E. Holzchlag contributed chapters from *Web by Design* and *Mastering Adobe GoLive 4*. She is the author of several best-selling web design books, including *Sizzling Web Site Design*. A widely recognized Web design consultant and content provider, Molly also develops and teaches design courses for the New School University, the University of Phoenix, Pima Community College and DigitalThink.

Richard "Rick" Schrand contributed chapters from *LiveMotion Visual JumpStart* and *Photoshop 6 Visual JumpStart*. Rick is the founder of GRFX By Design <www.grfxbydesign>, in Madison Tennessee, a web designer, and an instructor in 3D animation. He is the author of several graphics books, including *Canoma Visual Insight* and has an extensive broadcasting background. Rick is active in the Pixels 3D and ZBrush discussion forums, and is the creator of the ZBrush manual.

Matt Straznitskas contributed chapters *from Photoshop 5.5 for the Web*. He is the founder and president of BrainBug (www.brainbug.com), an award-winning online marketing agency located in Farmington, Connecticut. BrainBug clients include Fortune 1000 companies such as Aetna, American Express, and Bank of America. A highly respected designer and online marketing strategist, Matt writes regularly about the Web for a number of business publications. He is the author of the best-selling *Mastering Photoshop 5 for the Web*.

Erica Sadun contributed chapters from *Digital Photography! I Didn't Know You Could Do That, Second Edition*. She began working with image capture techniques in 1984 and bought her first digital camera in 1996. She holds a master's degree from the University of Pennsylvania in digital imaging and a Ph.D. from Georgia Tech's Graphics, Visualization & Usability Center. She wrote the first edition of the best-seller *Digital Photography! I Didn't Know You Could Do That* as well as *Digital Video! I Didn't Know You Could Do That...*

Deborah S. Ray and **Eric J. Ray** contributed chapters from *Mastering HTML 4, Premium Edition*. They are owners of RayComm, Inc., a technical communications consulting firm that specializes in cutting-edge Internet and computing technologies. Together they have co-authored more than 10 computer books, including the first and second editions of *Mastering HTML 4* from Sybex. They also write a syndicated computer column, which is available in newspapers across North America, and serve as Technology Review Editors for Technical Communication, the Journal of the Society for Technical Communication.

Mark Minasi is a noted educator and author in the fields of PC computing, data communications, and operating systems. He contributed chapters from *The Complete PC Upgrade and Maintenance Guide*. His best-selling books include *Mastering Windows 2000 Server*, *Mastering Windows 2000 Professional*, *Mastering TCP/IP for NT*, *The Hard Disk Survival Kit*, and *Troubleshooting Windows*, all from Sybex. Mark also serves as CNN's resident computer expert.

THE COMPLETE PC UPGRADE & MAINTENANCE GUIDE, 12TH EDITION

MARK MINASI

ISBN: 0-7821-2990-0
1488 pp; 7 1/2" x 9"
$59.99

▶ This extensively revised and updated 12th edition of the best-selling guide to PC upgrading and maintenance includes updated information on memory, modems, sound boards, disk drives, printing problems, operating system upgrades, video capture, digital audio, networking, combo printers, vendor guides, memory, and more.

▶ Written in a friendly, easy-to-follow style, the book provides essential background and conceptual information that teaches readers how computers work.

▶ Loaded with more than 1,600 pages of hardcore information, this is the one book no professional, student, or serious home user can afford to be without!

MASTERING HTML 4, PREMIUM EDITION
DEBORAH S. RAY AND ERIC J. RAY

ISBN: 0-7821-2524-7
1216 pp; 7 1/2" x 9"
$49.99

Here's an unbeatable value—everything in Mastering HTML 4, plus 200 entirely new pages and a CD packed with code, a searchable HTML reference, and powerful Web utilities—all for $49.99! Special topics only available in the Premium Edition include; XML and DOM, expanded DHTML coverage, update on HTML development tools, and productivity enhancement tips throughout. Enjoy both print and electronic versions of the popular Master's Reference to HTML tags, style sheets, JavaScript, HTML special characters, and HTML color codes. This is as comprehensive as it gets!

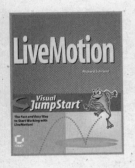

LIVEMOTION SIMPLY VISUAL
RICHARD SCHRAND

ISBN: 0-7821-2848-3
435 pp; 8" x 10"
$19.99

What's the best way to learn a graphics program? Visually, of course! Based on Sybex's best-selling JumpStart books for technical professionals, LiveMotion Visual JumpStart is the perfect way to rapidly master the essentials of Adobe's new cutting-edge vector-based Web graphics and animation tool. Thousands of first-time users will be looking for a book to learn the essentials of this highly anticipated new program. In painless, clear language—and with abundant illustrations—this book describes the user interface, important features and tools, and provides step-by-step instructions for creating professional-quality web graphics. And, it's packed with time saving tips on how to perform common tasks and use LiveMotion's features to improve productivity.

PHOTOSHOP 5.5 FOR THE WEB
MATT STRAZNITSKAS
ISBN: 0-7821-2605-7
670 pp; 7 1/2" x 9"
$39.99 US

Photoshop 5.5 incorporates Adobe's ImageReady graphics software, extending Photoshop's capabilities beyond print and making it a comprehensive web tool with animation and batch processing capabilities. Everyone working on the Web, from professionals to hobbyists putting up their first personal web pages, needs to learn Photoshop. This book takes an in-depth look at the unique issues faced by designers when manipulating files for the Web. It also highlights the work of 10 web gurus and provides real-world tips on working as a web designer. The full-color insert features work from top web designers, a web color-safe palette, and examples showcasing Photoshop's Web features.

MASTERING ADOBE GOLIVE 4
MOLLY E. HOLZSCHLAG AND STEPHEN ROMANIELLO
ISBN: 0-7821-2604-9
640 pp; 7 1/2" x 9"
$34.99 US

GoLive is Adobe's professional web development tool for web designers and publishers. Mastering Adobe GoLive 4 covers both the Windows and the Macintosh versions, with emphasis on features such as a movie editor for QuickTime 3, support for XML, and Actions Plus—12 of the most commonly requested JavaScript actions. This book contains hands-on tutorial projects and Web design advice from two pros—a nationally known web designer and a certified Adobe products trainer. A full-color insert is also included, showcasing the results achieved with GoLive and examples of the visual impact of well-designed web pages.